Special Edition
Using

MICROSOFT®
SQL Server™ 7.0

que®

Special Edition Using

MICROSOFT®
SQL Server™ 7.0

Stephen Wynkoop,
Administrator of the SQL Server FAQ
and Webmaster of SWYNK.COM

201 West 103rd Street, Indianapolis, Indiana 46290

Special Edition Using Microsoft® SQL Server™ 7.0

Copyright © 1999 by Que

International Standard Book Number: 0-7897-1523-6

Library of Congress Catalog Card Number: 98-85910

Printed in the United States of America

First Printing: January 1999

01 00 99   4   3

Trademarks

Warning and Disclaimer

EXECUTIVE EDITOR
Rosemarie Graham

ACQUISITIONS EDITOR
Rosemarie Graham

DEVELOPMENT EDITOR
Marla Reece-Hall

MANAGING EDITOR
Jodi Jensen

PROJECT EDITORS
Maureen McDaniel
Linda Morris

COPY EDITORS
Mike Henry
Linda Morris

INDEXER
Joy Dean Lee

PROOFREADER
Cynthia Fields

TECHNICAL EDITORS
Diane Gallagher
Sakhr Youness

SOFTWARE DEVELOPMENT SPECIALIST
Michael Hunter

TEAM COORDINATOR
Carol Ackerman

INTERIOR DESIGN
Ruth Lewis

COVER DESIGN
Dan Armstrong

LAYOUT TECHNICIANS
Brandon Allen
Tim Osborn
Staci Somers
Mark Walchle

Contents at a Glance

Table of Contents

About the Author

Stephen Wynkoop is the founder and Webmaster of SWYNK.COM, where he maintains comprehensive resources for Microsoft's technologies. He is also General Manager of IKON Office Solution's Emerging Technologies Division. At IKON, Stephen is responsible for building Internet and intranet service offerings, and for integrating training and technology advancement programs. Stephen is also a trainer, the author and co-author of several books, and speaks regularly at technical conferences around the United States.

Dedication

This book is dedicated to my wife and best friend, Julie.

Acknowledgments

Books on new or newly updated software are always a challenge. Long test cycles and last-minute changes make it exciting to work on these types of projects! It should come as a surprise to no one that this book about SQL Server 7.0 has been no exception to the rule. The last series of betas and testing have been, well, extended.

Mike Hotek (mhotek@swynk.com) has been a saving grace. Mike's contributions to this book include sanity checks, editing, suggestions, content, screaming, shouting, and his own blood, sweat, and tears. Mike deserves a major thank-you for his efforts in this book; without his help, it would be a very different animal indeed.

Diane Gallagher, the technical editor on this project, has been great! She's been meticulous like no other, and you can thank her for the accuracy of the examples. (Of course, if there are any errors, blame me!) She's been a great resource, and I appreciate all of her input.

The cast and crew at Macmillan Computer Publishing have spent numerous hours working through the chapters, examples, screen shots—all the time editing the book to be the best it can be. Of course, they're under the same deadlines—very short. My hat's off to all those folks, Rosemarie Graham, Marla Reece-Hall, and those behind the scenes, who have helped bring this book into being!

Many thanks to David Rogelberg of Studio B. David's been an excellent listener and is always ready with good, solid advice and ideas. Thanks!

Tell Us What You Think!

As the reader of this book, *you* are our most important critic and commentator. We value your opinion and want to know what we're doing right, what we could do better, what areas you'd like to see us publish in, and any other words of wisdom you're willing to pass our way.

As the Executive Editor for the Database team at Macmillan Computer Publishing, I welcome your comments. You can fax, email, or write me directly to let me know what you did or didn't like about this book—as well as what we can do to make our books stronger.

Please note that I cannot help you with technical problems related to the topic of this book, and that due to the high volume of mail I receive, I might not be able to reply to every message.

When you write, please be sure to include this book's title and author, as well as your name and phone or fax number. I will carefully review your comments and share them with the author and editors who worked on the book.

Fax: 317-817-7070

Email: databases@mcp.com

Mail: Rosemarie Graham
          Executive Editor
          Database Team
          Macmillan Computer Publishing
          201 West 103rd Street
          Indianapolis, IN 46290 USA

Introduction

In this chapter

SQL Server 7.0 is a massive step forward in the database server arena for both Microsoft and those who use its product. This book is an administrator's guide to using the product and its new features, and making sure your servers are as useful as possible to you and the users.

Microsoft SQL Server uses features similar to those found in other databases and some features that are unique. Most of these additional features are made possible by SQL Server's tight integration with the Windows NT operating system. SQL Server contains the data storage options and the capability to store and process the same volume of data as a mainframe or minicomputer.

Like most mainframe or minicomputer databases, SQL Server is a database that has seen an evolution from its introduction in the mid-1980s until today. Microsoft's SQL Server is founded in the mature and powerful relational model, currently the preferred model for data storage and retrieval.

Unlike mainframe and minicomputer databases, a server database is accessed by users, or clients, from other computer systems, rather than from input/output devices, such as terminals. Mechanisms must be in place for SQL Server to solve problems that arise from the access of data from perhaps hundreds of computer systems, each of which can process portions of the database independently from the data on the server.

Within the framework of a client/server database, a server database also must provide connectivity to client systems. This comes in the form of integration with communications elements and by working closely with the hosting operating system. Microsoft SQL Server's client/server connectivity uses the built-in network components of Windows NT on the various supported platforms.

Unlike a standalone PC database, a traditional mainframe, or a minicomputer database, a server database, such as Microsoft SQL Server, adds service-specific components such as OLE-DB and open database connectivity (ODBC) on top of the network components. These components enable the interconnection of different client applications without requiring changes to the server database or other existing client applications.

SQL Server also contains many of the front-end tools of PC databases that traditionally haven't been available as part of either mainframe or minicomputer databases. In addition to using a dialect of Structured Query Language (SQL), graphical user interface (GUI) applications can be used for the storage, retrieval, and administration of the database. With SQL 7, the capabilities of these GUI applications has increased many times. Designing databases, tables, and the relationships between them has literally never been easier.

With the use of database-aware components, you can also use SQL Server with your Internet-based applications. Tools such as Active Server Pages, the Internet Database Connector, ActiveX Data Objects, or ADO are available to help you integrate SQL Server database information into your Web pages.

Depending on the tool or approach you select, you have access that ranges from static Web pages to dynamic, scripting language–enhanced Web pages to Component Object Model–based solutions. These exciting tools are making Web-based applications a reality.

Who Should Use This Book

This book is written for all users of Microsoft SQL Server, from database users and developers to database administrators. It can be used by new users to learn about any feature of Microsoft SQL Server. It also serves as a reference for experienced users who need to learn about a feature of the product that they haven't yet used.

There are two different CD-ROMs provided with this book. The first CD-ROM provides sample Transact-SQL statements and demonstration applications. These are provided by several third-party vendors to give you a feeling for many of the products and services available in the market, as well as ideas for using SQL Server in your organization. You'll also find additional links to tools, articles and other resources on the Web at the following locations:

http://www.swynk.com	The author's site
http://www.mcp.com	The Macmillan site
http://www.microsoft.com	The Microsoft site

On the second CD-ROM provided with this book, you'll find the 120-day evaluation version of SQL Server 7.0. This will help you get started immediately with the product, and you'll be able to start working with this powerful software right away.

How to Use This Book

This book is divided into six sections. The sections are intended to present the use of SQL Server as a logical series of steps in the order in which the reader would most likely use the product. Ideally, you will go through the sections and their chapters in sequence.

Part I: Understanding The Basics

In Part I, the basic features of Microsoft SQL Server are discussed, and an overview of its capabilities is presented. In this section, you'll learn about necessary information that is related to Microsoft SQL Server. This background information about SQL Server is recommended for all new and current users of SQL Server who might be unfamiliar with it.

In Chapter 1, "Understanding Microsoft SQL Server 7.0 Fundamentals," you'll learn the origin and evolution of SQL Server and its implementation as a relational database. You'll also learn about the components of SQL Server, including the installation and configuration of the database and its client components.

Chapter 2, "Understanding the Underlying Operating System, Windows NT," explains the features of the operating system that SQL Server uses to obtain optimal performance. The SQL Server database components are designed solely for implementation on the Windows NT system.

Chapter 3, "Installing and Setting Up the Server and Client Software," covers the physical installation and configuration of the server engine and the tools you'll use with it. This covers both the server installation and the setup of the tools from the client system.

In Chapter 4, "Data Modeling and Database Design," you'll learn how to design a database. Moreover, you'll become familiar with the terminology that's associated with a relational database such as SQL Server.

Chapter 5, "Creating Databases and Transaction Logs," explains how to create the storage areas on a disk for your database and its backups.

Chapter 6, "Creating Database Tables and Using Datatypes," provides you with instructions on how to create database tables and choose the datatypes of the table columns. You can also read about the considerations involved in your choice of table and table column characteristics.

Part II: Up and Running with SQL Server

In Part II, you'll learn how to start working with SQL Server and extracting the information in your tables to make the best use of it. You'll also learn to manipulate the stored data, including combining data from multiple sources. If you are already familiar with SQL or the previous version of SQL Server, you'll still want to read the chapters in this section to learn how this version differs from the earlier version. You'll also want to learn about the additions that support the ANSI SQL standard.

Chapter 7, "Retrieving Data with Transact-SQL," provides instruction in the use of the SELECT statement and its new clauses designed to control the retrieval of targeted data.

Chapter 8, "Adding, Changing, and Deleting Information in Tables," continues the instruction on retrieving data begun in Chapter 7. Included is instruction on how to combine data from multiple tables.

Chapter 9, "Using Functions," provides a comprehensive treatment of the functions that you can use in Transact-SQL. The examples presented in the chapter are simple and direct, and facilitate the understanding of the use of the functions.

In Chapter 10, "Managing and Using Views," you will learn the definition and use of stored SELECT statements that will subsequently be used like an actual table. You'll also learn of the problem of disappearing rows, a phenomenon that occurs with the storage of rows through a view.

In Chapter 11, "Managing and Using Indexes and Keys," you learn how to define the database objects that are used to ensure fast retrieval of the rows of database tables. In addition, you'll learn to use the database object that is a basis for ensuring referential integrity in a database.

Chapter 12, "Understanding Transactions and Locking," provides an understanding of the synchronization mechanism used by SQL Server to ensure the integrity of database tables and operations.

Part III: Server-Side Logic and Capabilities

The n-tier and client/server models require that you have intelligence on the part of both the client-side computer and the server-side system. SQL Server provides several different tools in this arena, including the most prominent, stored procedures. In Part III, you'll learn about these and other capabilities that are managed and executed by the server-side of the client/server equation.

Chapter 13, "Managing and Using Rules, Constraints, and Defaults," contains information on how to restrict the values that might be inserted into database tables and other database structures.

Chapter 14, "Managing Stored Procedures and Using Flow-Control Statements," and Chapter 15, "Creating and Managing Triggers," discuss the capability of creating a set of Transact-SQL statements that can be stored and subsequently executed as a group. You can use flow-control statements, including conditional statements, to effectively write a SQL program that manipulates your database. In addition, you'll learn to create a set of SQL statements that are automatically activated when SELECT, INSERT, UPDATE, or DELETE statements are executed on a database.

In addition, Chapter 15 examines the role of triggers in the maintenance of database integrity and consistency. When action is taken on a parent table, the child tables can be adjusted appropriately using triggers. You will learn about the three types of triggers and how to control triggers with conditional logic.

Chapter 16, "Understanding Server, Database, and Query Options," provides you with the information necessary to configure your server and database for various uses and situations. In addition, you'll also learn to configure your queries against the database.

Chapter 17, "Setting Up and Managing Replication," discusses how you implement the automatic creation and maintenance of multiple copies of a database to enhance performance in the access of data.

Chapter 18, "Using the Distributed Transaction Coordinator," tells you how to extend the capabilities included in transactions across servers. This chapter explains the setup, use, and troubleshooting associated with these extended transaction capabilities.

Part IV: SQL Server Administration Topics

When your server is up and running, and during the formation of your ongoing maintenance plans, you'll find that several topics will come up. The chapters in this section will include management of security and backup approaches, as well as the art of optimizing your server.

Chapter 19, "SQL Server Administration," provides you with information about how to keep data consistently available to the users of client systems. Availability of data from a database is ensured by a combination of fault-tolerant mechanisms and the duplication of data before it's lost.

Chapter 20, "SQL Server Security," continues the discussion of maintaining data availability by explaining the implementation of proper security for SQL Server and its databases.

Chapter 21, "Optimizing Performance," explains how you can enhance a database and the retrieval of information from it using important calculations based on different storage factors. Moreover, you'll learn to use the built-in monitoring tool of the Windows NT system to monitor the performance of SQL Server components and applications.

Part V: Developing Applications and Solutions

This section of the book focuses entirely on development issues. These range from the use of the no-longer to be improved DB-LIB to how to access SQL Server with the now-mature Advanced Data Object technologies. These chapters will give you a great look at the different ways you can go about working with some of the more popular tools available for client-side applications development.

Chapter 22, "Backward Compatability Options for Developers," provides you with information about the client and server components used for the interconnection of systems. SQL Server and client applications depend on the network components and protocols for communication.

Chapter 23, "Understanding SQL Server and the Internet," provides full coverage of how to work with the Internet Database Connector (IDC) and a look at Advanced Data Objects that let you create more dynamic Web pages for your site.

Chapter 24, "Creating and Using Cursors," instructs you on the use of a feature of SQL Server that enables you to perform selection operations on individual rows of a database table. You can also randomly access an individual row and manipulate it without affecting other rows.

Chapter 25, "Using the SQL Agent," covers the new Agent capabilities of SQL Server. From automated notifications to scheduled tasks, the improvements in the Agent's capabilities will go a long way toward the minimal administrative intervention goals of SQL 7.

Chapter 26, "Integrating Microsoft Office Applications and SQL Server," details how you can migrate your application from Access 97 to SQL Server. This includes setting up views from queries, working with tables, and working through the details associated with the upsizing effort.

Chapter 27, "Using Advanced Data Objects with SQL Server 7.0," discusses the approach with the most comprehensive database integration capabilities, ADO.

Appendixes

The appendixes provide additional information on related topics that you'll want to know for your installation. From RAID configurations to working with the software included on the CD-ROM, the information is all here.

Also, it's important to check the author's Web site at `http://www.swynk.com` for late-breaking updates, new utilities and support from the vendors of the software included on the CD-ROM.

Conventions Used in This Book

The following font conventions are used in this book to help make reading it easier.

- *Italic type* is used to introduce new terms.
- Screen messages, code listings, and command samples appear in `monospace type`. For more details about syntax, see the following section, "Syntax Guidelines."
- Code that you are instructed to type appears in **`monospace bold type`**.

TIP Tips present short advice on a quick or often overlooked procedure, including shortcuts.

N O T E Notes present interesting or useful information that isn't necessarily essential to the discussion. A note provides additional information that might help you avoid problems or offers advice that relates to the topic. ▤

CAUTION

Cautions look like this and warn you about potential problems that a procedure might cause, unexpected results, or mistakes to avoid.

 This icon indicates you can also find the related information on the enclosed CD-ROM.

Syntax Guidelines

It's important to have a clearly defined way of describing Transact-SQL commands. In this book, the following rules apply:

- Anything in *italics* means that you have to substitute the italicized text with your own text.
- Anything placed inside square brackets "[…]" means that it can be optionally left out of the command.
- Anything placed inside curly braces "{ … }" means that one of the values must be chosen to complete the syntax.
- The available values are separated by the bar (or pipe) character ¦ (meaning "OR"). Consider the following example:

  ```
  {DISK ¦ TAPE ¦ DISKETTE}
  ```

  It would be translated as DISK or TAPE or DISKETTE.

- Finally, if you see "…" after any bracketed block in a Transact-SQL statement, it means that section can be repeated as many items as is appropriate.

Understanding the Basics

Understanding Microsoft SQL Server 7.0 Fundamentals

In this chapter

As the computer industry moves to more distributed environments and moves its data from mainframe- to microcomputer-based servers, you must understand the concepts behind a client/server database environment.

In several respects, server databases such as Microsoft SQL Server are identical to mainframe databases. The overwhelming majority of databases used on computer systems are relational databases. Also, server databases, such as relational databases on mainframe or minicomputer systems, support the use of Structured Query Language (SQL) as well as proprietary tools to access data.

Where you start to see differences in a PC-based client/server solution is in the architecture and physical implementation of the system. With a SQL Server solution, your users will be using intelligent client systems, such as personal computers. In a mainframe or minicomputer environment, users likely use a terminal or a PC using terminal-emulation software.

With more intelligent client systems, users can retrieve information from the server and manipulate it locally. This type of implementation optimizes the processing of the information, allowing each component to work on the information independently in the manner best suited for that component. The server focuses on the database processes, while the client focuses on the presentation of the information.

Why the Move to SQL Server and Why Upgrade Your 6.5 Installation to 7.0?

SQL Server is a significant tool in many regards. From data warehousing to applications that require not only large amounts of information, but many different simultaneous users, SQL Server is a key component in answering data management requirements.

This section highlights two different concepts, the first of which is why you should make the move to SQL Server in a general sense. This includes whether you're coming from no database or from one that your application simply is outgrowing.

Migration to SQL Server

Two key features of a server database become important because of the client access to data. The first feature is providing a single point of access to the data in the database. The second feature is the division of processing and manipulation between the client and server systems.

SQL Server enables client applications to control the information retrieved from the server using several specialized tools and techniques. These include options such as stored procedures, server-enforced rules, and triggers that permit processing to be done on the server automatically. You don't have to move all processing to the server, of course. You still can do appropriate information processing as needed on the client workstation.

Because mainframe or minicomputer systems traditionally do all processing on the host side, implementing systems in this environment initially can be simpler than in a true client/server implementation. This is because users work at terminals that are directly connected to the mainframe or minicomputer and work directly with the database using the processing power of the mainframe or minicomputer.

Although organizations routinely use SQL Server to manipulate millions of records, it provides several tools that help manage the system and its databases and tables. The Windows- and command-line–based tools that come with SQL Server let you work with the many different aspects of SQL Server. These tools can be used to

- Perform the administration of the databases
- Control access to data within the databases
- Control the manipulation of data within the databases

You can also use a command-line interface to perform all operations with SQL Server.

A dialect of the SQL language is used with SQL Server for interactive and application program access to data. SQL is the *de facto* standard for database operations, and every vendor's database product should include a version of it.

N O T E   The *Microsoft Open Database Connectivity* (ODBC) model uses SQL to connect to databases even in cases in which the underlying database doesn't natively support SQL. In those cases, SQL is translated into a set of commands to accomplish the requested call for the given database. After you master SQL, you can work with any ODBC data source you need to access, and you can use ODBC to make the translations needed for the underlying database engine.

As you'll see with SQL Server 7.0, OLE DB is also a major component of the data access picture. You'll use OLE DB when you work against the database and in those cases in which you must query external sources as well. ■

Although this book includes coverage of how to use the command-line tool to issue interactive SQL commands, remember that you can perform most operations through the application tools that use the Windows Graphical User Interface (GUI). You can use either interface or both interfaces, depending on your interest. If you're already familiar with another SQL dialect, you may initially find that issuing direct SQL commands for all operations is simpler.

Moving from SQL Server 6.5 to SQL Server 7.0

Microsoft has made significant enhancements to SQL Server with the version 7.0 release. Although Microsoft virtually redesigned SQL Server, it maintained compatibility with SQL Server 6.x in most cases from an administrative standpoint.

On the downside, when you upgrade you must update your database files, for two reasons. First, the database files that you're using with version 6.5 are not compatible with the 7.0 engine. This update was necessary to support the new capabilities of 7.0 and to make sure that future development and enhancement of the product were both supported and possible.

▶ For additional information about creating databases, **see** Chapter 5, "Creating Databases and Transaction Logs," **p. 93**

Second, the files that currently represent your device files have been dropped. Databases now have their own associated files on disk. As you'll soon see, this has significant advantage when it comes to managing the server.

In addition, the SQL dialect supported by SQL Server continues to include a superset of the ANSI standard SQL language elements. The following are some of these additions and enhancements:

- *On-demand memory.* Providing a key administrative advantage over previous versions, the dynamic memory management features tune your server on the fly and offer the best possible performance based on available memory and other application demands.

- *On-demand disk space allocation.* As with dynamic memory management, the new disk space allocation strategy offers you as the administrator more control and at the same time more automated response to the daily management of the server. As your database size needs grow, SQL Server can allocate a percentage of new disk space, fixed MB sizing, or nothing. These options are implemented to address the previous need to manually build new devices and extend databases to the new devices.

- *Full row-level locking.* Developers have asked for row-level locking since the inception of SQL Server. It's now possible, and is used in the lock escalation procedure within the server engine.

- *Recursive triggers (triggers calling triggers).* This new feature lets you manage more than one update to a given column. You can use recursive triggers when an update trigger would make a change that would in turn fire another trigger. With this recursive capability, you'll be able to address this type of situation.

- *New SQL security that supports NT groups and SQL Server roles.* User roles let you define groups and the security associated with them. This update lets you more closely manage the user rights, and it broadens the capability of the security system by adding new security permissions and methods of applying them to your user base. With SQL Server 7.0, "standard" security—that type based solely on SQL Server users—has been removed. Instead, you'll use integrated security to manage your accounts and access rights.

- *ADO, ODBC, OLE DB and SQL-DMO programming interfaces.* These all are supported, continuing to hold open the door for multiple third-party tools to manage and work with your databases.

- *Unicode support.* Unicode support is an industry standard manner of representing the information in your database. With Unicode support comes new datatypes and slightly different datatype sizing restrictions.

- *Windows 9x support.* With the introduction of Windows 9x support, you can now run SQL Server 7.0 on your laptop or desktop system. The desktop implementation is identical to the server version; the only difference is those items that are directly impacted by the operating system capabilities. An example of this type of difference is the management of user security, not available in the Windows 9x environment.

■ *Microsoft Management Console (MMC)*. Entirely new to SQL Server 7.0, the MMC is the replacement for the Enterprise Manager. MMC gives you the administrative access you need for your server. The MMC is also the new standard interface for all Microsoft server applications. The Enterprise Manager is now a snap-in to the MMC, which can also allow you to administer your NT, IIS, and MTS applications as well.

■ *Enhanced Query Analyzer and optimizer*. This is the replacement for what used to be ISQL/W. This new query tool adds color-coded queries and more analysis tools.

■ *Data Transformation Services*. Leverage OLE DB and provide a level of functionality never before present in SQL Server. This allows you to extract data from multiple data sources, scrub it, and perform operations on the data as it is moved from its source into SQL Server 7.0.

■ *Microsoft English Query*. One of the new features is the capability to query a known database with English-like sentences and questions. After you've taught the engine about the database table structure, you can use this tool to ask questions and have them translated into appropriate SQL.

■ *Wizards*. Microsoft has added several wizard-type interfaces to SQL Server 7.0, automating many of the functions required of the DBA. The wizards are evidence of an attempted move away from the need to have full-time, dedicated staff to run critical SQL Servers. It remains to be seen however, whether this will combine with the other features introduced to truly ease the administrative burden for SQL Server.

■ *OLAP*. Arguably one of the biggest features added to SQL Server 7.0 is an OLAP server. OLAP, Online Analytical Processing, has always been relegated to third party add-ons that extract data, package it, and allow users to analyze it for trends. In basic terms OLAP can be equated to "drill down" capabilities or pivot tables. With the inclusion of basic OLAP capabilities in SQL Server, it paves the way for widespread use of this very powerful analysis technique.

Understanding Relational Features of SQL Server

A key characteristic of SQL Server is that it's a relational database. You must understand the features of a relational database to effectively understand and access data with SQL Server. You can't construct successful queries to return data from a relational database unless you understand the basic features of a relational database.

▶ For more information about relational databases and establishing database structures, see Chapter 4, "Data Modeling and Database Design."

In a relational database, data is referenced as the rows and columns of a table. You can easily visualize data stored as a table because you often encounter data stored in tables in everyday life. For example, you reference train or plane schedules as a table (see Figure 1.1) and you also create typical worksheets as a table.

FIGURE 1.1

An example of a common table showing flights out of the Tucson area.

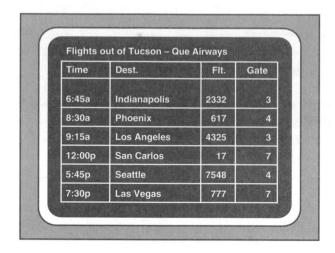

In the relational model implemented in Microsoft SQL Server, the rows of a database table are also unordered unless a clustered index is created for the table. After you create a clustered index for a table, the rows are stored in ascending order by the one or more columns that you use to create the index. Clustered indexes are covered in a later chapter.

▷ For more information about clustered indexes and the other types of indexes supported by SQL Server, see Chapter 11, "Managing and Using Indexes and Keys."

It's important, however, that the statements you use in the retrieval language to access table rows are independent of the order of the rows. If you require that the rows of a table be retrieved and displayed in an order, the statement that you issue to retrieve the rows must specify the row order. The rows are sorted as they're retrieved for your query.

The original relational model required each row to be uniquely defined by at least one column of a table, the unique key. The unique row requirement ensures that each row is accessed or changed independently and uniquely from other rows of the table. The query language used to access table rows can use only data stored within each row to separate one row from another.

SQL Server, however, doesn't require you to define unique table rows. You can create two or more rows of a table that can't be referenced separately from one another. Although you might not find a use for duplicate rows, some users feel such rows are desirable in some applications.

In Chapter 4, "Data Modeling and Database Design," you'll learn more about relational design concepts and techniques, but for now it's important to understand what's possible, if not practical. If you want to prevent duplicates, you can add a constraint to tables to prevent duplicate rows.

CAUTION

As you'll see in Chapter 4, unless you're absolutely certain you must allow the storage of duplicate rows (a very, very rare case indeed), you should ensure that table rows are unique. In the absence of enforced uniqueness, accidentally adding one or more duplicates to the table is too easy. After you add the duplicate rows, removing or updating them is difficult.

In the relational database model, data that's stored across tables in one or more databases is combined during the access of the rows during an inquiry. For example, if the Employees table contains columns such as Name, Department, and Badge, a second table named Pays can contain the columns Hours_Worked, PayRate, and Badge.

You can define the Badge column in both tables. This way, you can subsequently retrieve column values from both tables in a single query. You combine columns from multiple tables by using statements that call out the columns you need and specify the information common to both tables in the Where clause. You'll read more about the syntax of this operation, but for now, it's important to understand only that this pulling together of information based on common values is known as a *join*.

▶ For more information on using Where clauses, **see** Chapter 7, "Retrieving Data with Transact-SQL," **p. 155**

The example in the Employees and Pays tables uses the relational capabilities of SQL Server to retrieve information from each table using the corresponding badge numbers. The following is a sample Select statement:

```
Select * from Employees, Pays where Employees.Badge = Pays.Badge
```

Not surprisingly, if you modify or delete a badge number in the Employees table, the corresponding badge number in the Pays table must also be updated or deleted. This process of ensuring that corresponding values of related tables are maintained to keep table relationships intact is called *referential integrity*. This process can even include deleting related information in other tables if you remove a master record, as would be the case if a record in the Employees table were deleted and any corresponding records in the Pays table were also deleted.

Maintaining referential integrity is easiest if table rows are unique. This ensures that there will be only a single row in a second table. Make sure you maintain the badge number if it is modified or deleted in the first table. In the relational database model, the column, or set of columns, that uniquely defines the rows of a table is referred to as a *key*.

N O T E A key that uniquely defines the rows of a table is called a *primary key*. If you add to a second table the column that is a primary key in one table, the column added to the second table is called the *foreign key*. It's a foreign key because the new column referencing the first table is used only to allow the matching of corresponding rows between the tables. For more information see Chapter 11, "Managing and Using Indexes and Keys." ■

In earlier database systems, internal pointers were created and maintained within the database to link the corresponding rows stored in the tables. The pointer mechanism created a problem, however, because when the database was created, you had to define the data that was later combined during retrieval.

N O T E Some hierarchical and network databases don't use terms such as *table* or *row*. One example of these is Microsoft's Access database product.

Hierarchical and network databases use their own terminology to describe data. For example, the equivalent of a row of a relational database is called a *record*. The equivalent of a column of a relational database is called a *data item* or *field*. ▪

If you neglected to identify data that had to be combined later during retrieval, you couldn't do it after the database structure was created. You had to re-create the logical and physical structure of the database. The main problem involved with using hierarchical and network databases was that changes in data-retrieval combinations were impossible to make without redesigning the database.

In relational databases, such as SQL Server, you can add a new column to a table at any time. This enables you to create relationships with other tables. Unlike typical hierarchical or network databases, if you add a new column to a table, the database doesn't need to be redefined. Only a single table must be redefined. You don't need to unload the rows of the table and later reload the table to add a new column. You can use SQL's ALTER TABLE statement to modify existing tables. In addition, you can use the graphical tools that are part of Enterprise Manager to work with the information in your system.

▶ For more information about the ALTER TABLE statement, see Chapter 8, "Adding, Changing, and Deleting Information in Tables."

Exploring Client/Server, or N-Tier, Features of SQL Server

Client/server computing, now often called 3-tier or n-tier computing, is a type of distributed model for data storage, access, and processing. In a distributed processing system, multiple computers collectively perform a set of operations. An n-tier system uses at least two computers, one of which is nearly always a personal computer.

N O T E Distributed processing was introduced by minicomputer systems to provide the capabilities of large mainframe computers. The data storage, access, and processing capabilities of several minicomputers could match the processing capabilities of a mainframe computer for some operations by working together. ▪

Each system in this type of model performs one or more of the data storage, access, or processing operations. N-tier computing can't be done with a system that uses terminals or PCs running terminal emulators connected to another computer. In this arrangement, the terminal or the PC that's used as a terminal is simply too passive. It only sends and displays sets of characters.

When PCs and servers are connected, the overall processing should be divided between the server, mainframe, or minicomputer system and the client system. The client and the server each process work within its own capabilities, which is a form of teamwork that contributes to the efficiency and speed of the overall operation.

N-tier, and client/server as the name implies, also involves an unequal division of processing. The inequality results from the processing disparity between the server and the client. The larger and faster server computer transfers data faster, stores greater quantities of data, and typically performs more extensive processing than does the client system.

N O T E N-tier computing is quickly becoming the foundation of application development for the Internet, for good reason. N-tier optimizes the processing at the side of the transaction that makes the most sense, whether it be displaying information to the end user or sorting through information that should be returned for display.

By using n-tier technology on the Internet, many mainstream applications are coming online. At the same time, these applications are not causing the same level of bandwidth utilization that you would see in a completely client-side, or 1-tier, application environment.

You can find out more about this application of the n-tier approach in Chapter 23, "Understanding SQL Server and the Internet." ▪

Smaller PC systems are used as the client in these types of systems because the PCs perform proportionally less of the overall work, relying primarily on the server and its related, optimized components for heavy-duty data manipulation. Also, the PC's keyboard and monitor allow it to work as an input device by generating commands and data and as an output device by displaying data to the user.

N O T E A client and a server also are defined by the direction of the data flow and operational responsibilities. A large and powerful PC system can function as a server if it receives commands and data from one or more PC systems, processes the data, and returns information to other PC systems. The server is the computer system that receives requests for processing or information from other computer systems.

You can use large, powerful PCs as servers with less powerful PCs as clients and still qualify as using n-tier technology. In this environment, the PC servers are usually more powerful than an average PC. This helps them perform processing requests from many clients. ▪

Microsoft SQL Server is a perfect example of an n-tier system. The SQL Server database is installed on the Windows NT or Windows 9x platform. The Windows NT operating system provides an extremely broad range of processor systems to use as your server. Windows NT is supported on Intel x86 processor-based systems, Power PC, MIPS, and Alpha AXP RISC-processor–based systems.

SQL Server is provided with the server software that's installed on the server system and some client software that's installed on the client PC systems. Windows GUI application tools allow the database and all objects to be created, maintained, and accessed from the client.

The network software components required for the interconnection of clients and the server computer are built into the Windows NT system. Windows NT also provides a choice of network protocols for communication between the client and server systems. A client can run Windows 9x, which also contains built-in network software for connection with the Windows NT server system. The Windows 9x client and Windows NT or Windows 9x server systems support a wide range of network cards.

In a system in which the server application is a database such as SQL Server, the server is responsible for the creation and maintenance of database objects such as the table and indexes. The server maintains referential integrity and security and ensures that operations can be recovered in the event of numerous types of failures.

The client performs all user interaction, including information display and allowing manipulation of the application with the graphical user interface. After rows of data are retrieved from the server, the application can create copies to be held locally, and the data can be manipulated. You also can control the type of access to the information. Read-only access is often an excellent option, insulating the user from the master copies of the information that they work with on the server.

If you work with local copies of the information, you can work with the information locally without communicating with the server. After you complete your work, you can send changes back to the server or, if the information was for review only, simply discard the working databases. Of course, you also can manipulate the data directly in the SQL Server database from the client, if needed and allowed by your application. You must be sure to update the server with all changes so that other users can access the most recent data in the database.

You can also access SQL Server directly from the server. Direct server access is convenient, especially for administrative operations, but it isn't an n-tier, or client/server, approach because the operations occur locally rather than across the network. Although you can have client applications validate new or updated data, the validation should optimally be done at the server. For example, a column such as Badge can be checked to ensure that each new or updated badge number is unique and within a specified range. It's safer for the data to be validated at the server as a part of a SQL Server-defined mechanism. If the validation is defined at the server, it will always be in force whether or not the connected client performs a validation.

N O T E   A big benefit of using server-side validation is that you'll protect the database from access by applications that might access the database in "nonstandard" ways. This includes applications, such as Excel, Access, and Word, which can connect to the database using ODBC. In each case, rules and integrity checks that you implement on the server will still be enforced, even though the client application might be unknown.

If you rely on client applications to validate data before it's sent to the server, you must ensure that all the client applications do it consistently. You must also ensure that changes aren't made directly at the server, where no validation mechanism has been defined. Implementing server validation is simpler and more reliable, especially with the current industry-wide push to standardize interfaces and allow third-party applications to gain access to company information systems for additional analysis.

TIP You also can perform validation in client applications in addition to validation on the server. Client validation can be specific to the client application that isn't enforced by server validation mechanisms. When the updates are sent to the server, it will still enforce its own validation.

Examining SQL Server Features and Components

The core component of SQL Server is the relational database and its structure. SQL Server is a powerful, comprehensive database environment. There are certain parameters to using SQL Server, and they're pointed out here.

SQL Server enables you to define up to 32,767 databases. If you realize that the definition of a database is a centralized repository for the storage of information, it is difficult to be overly constrained by the 32,767-database limit. It's unlikely you'll encounter any situation in which you must define more than this very liberal limit. If you do, you'll certainly want to be looking at adding additional servers to your network to help balance the load. In a typical production installation, you'll often find that less than five, and often only one, application-oriented databases will be in service on any given server.

You can also define up to two billion tables within each of your 32,767 databases. It's not likely that you'll need anywhere near two billion tables in a database. With most typical systems, you'll have only several hundred tables in a database.

You can define up to 1,024 columns for each table. In Chapter 4 you'll see that when you normalize your database tables, you largely overcome this limitation. As you'll see, SQL Server allows columns from as many as 32 tables to be combined in a single query.

The number of rows in a table is effectively unlimited for SQL Server. You're limited in practice by the capacity of the storage medium on which tables are stored, and databases and their tables can be stored across multiple physical disks. SQL Server allows databases to expand to include up to 32,767 physical disks.

NOTE The maximum database size is 1,048,516TB. Each file (which would be the limit of the size for a physical disk) is limited to 32TB. These logical capacities make SQL Server databases virtually unlimited in size.

You can define up to 250 indexes for each table, only one of which can be defined as a clustered index. An *index* is a structure that allows the table rows to be retrieved more quickly than they could without using an index. In a *clustered index*, the table rows are sorted and maintained in storage in a physically ordered state. That is, rows that are sorted before and after one another are also stored in that sorted order. An index is often defined for the columns that are referenced in retrieval statements. Two hundred fifty indexes should provide fast retrieval of table rows.

Indexes require additional storage space in the database for the index structure that must be created and stored. One performance recommendation is to define as few indexes as possible because of the space they take up. You still must define enough indexes to allow the rapid retrieval of rows, but define the minimum number of indexes that you require. It would be unusual for you to need more than 250 for a single table.

> **N O T E**   A general rule of thumb for transactional databases is to create no more than 5 indexes per table. For decision support or query only databases, no more than 10 indexes should be created per table. ▇

Databases

You store databases and all the objects within them in disk files. SQL Server names your database files .MDF for the database and LDF For the log files. You can create up to 32,767 databases.

Each database is created with a set of system tables in which SQL Server records data about the database objects such as tables or indexes that you subsequently create. Like a relational database product, SQL Server keeps the control information about your database objects in a relational database, which is the set of system tables.

Transact-SQL

Structured Query Language (SQL) is the query language developed by IBM in the 1970s; it has become the *de facto* standard database query language for relational databases. The dialect of SQL that you use with SQL Server is Transact-SQL, which Microsoft implements as a core component of SQL Server.

Transact-SQL adds additional keywords to those of the original SQL for the formation of data retrieval, storage, and manipulation. When SQL Server's implementation of SQL was put into place, like other database vendors, Microsoft added features and extensions to the language.

> **N O T E**   Remember that some SQL dialect is used with all relational databases. If you work with more than one relational database, or if you must convert from one to another, using the most generic SQL syntax is best. If stored sets of SQL statements use generic syntax they can easily be converted or used across relational databases. ▇

Transact-SQL is best characterized as lean and mean. You have just enough enhancements to basic SQL to write functional queries. Transact-SQL contains statements to create logical storage units, the files on which databases reside. You can also use Transact-SQL statements to create the objects, such as tables, that are stored within the databases.

Not surprisingly, you can use Transact-SQL statements to add and manipulate data and other database objects. Four keywords are used to form statements that perform all basic data storage, retrieval, and manipulation.

- ▇ INSERT adds new rows to a database table.
- ▇ DELETE deletes rows from a table.

- UPDATE changes rows of a table.
- SELECT forms various statements for the retrieval of data from one or multiple tables.

The INSERT, DELETE, UPDATE, and SELECT statements, as well as other statements, use a generic form of SQL for data manipulation. The extensions to Transact-SQL are principally for flow control to direct the execution order of statements. Use flow-control statements in organized sets of SQL statements that are stored as objects within your database.

Stored sets of Transact-SQL statements contained within the SQL Server database are called *stored procedures*, which are compiled so that they rapidly execute SQL statements. You can use stored procedures in addition to programs for database access and manipulation because they can use variables and parameters, return errors and status, and use flow control to control the execution order of SQL statements.

▶ For more information on stored procedures and how to implement them, **see** Chapter 14, "Managing Stored Procedures and Using Flow-Control Statements," **p. 355**

A *trigger* is a special type of stored procedure used to maintain referential integrity in a SQL Server database. You can create insert, delete, and update triggers to control the addition, deletion, or updates to corresponding rows of related tables for which the trigger is defined. Triggers are an excellent way to maintain referential integrity because you have complete control over the operations that they perform, and they're server-based.

You also use several additional objects, such as rules, defaults, and constraints, to help control or apply values automatically to table columns. You use a *default* to supply a value to the column of a database table when the insertion of a new row doesn't specify a value for the column. A *rule* constrains the values that can be entered into the column of a table. A *constraint* is used to define a characteristic of a table column, such as requiring only unique values.

Command-Line Applications

You can issue SQL statements through the Interactive Structured Query Language (ISQL) utility. *Query Analyzer* is the Windows tool that allows you to use Transact-SQL with SQL Server from a graphical interface. For more information, see the section "Query Analyzer/ Optimizer and Profiler," later in this chapter. If you become familiar with Transact-SQL syntax, or if you prefer to work at the DOS command line, you can perform all operations on your databases through ISQL command lines.

From a command-line session, you invoke ISQL with the command ISQL. You can use several parameters on the ISQL command line. For example, you can enter the user name and password following ISQL to bring you directly into an ISQL command session.

The following example shows the initiation of a command session. The command prompt is successively numbered until the execution GO command is entered.

```
ISQL /Usa /P<password> /S<server>
1>
```

You can use the -? or /? switch to display a list of the syntax for the use of the ISQL command, as shown in the following example:

```
usage: ISQL [-U login id] [-e echo input]
      [-p print statistics] [-n remove numbering]
      [-c cmdend] [-h headers] [-w columnwidth] [-s colseparator]
      [-m errorlevel] [-t query timeout] [-l login timeout]
      [-L list servers] [-a packetsize]
      [-H hostname] [-P password]
      [-q "cmdline query"] [-Q "cmdline query" and exit]
      [-S server] [-d use database name]
      [-r msgs to stderr] [-E trusted connection]
      [-i inputfile] [-o outputfile]
       [-b On error batch abort]
       [-O use Old ISQL behavior disables the following]
            <EOF> batch processing
            Auto console width scaling
            Wide messages
            default errorlevel is -1 vs 1
      [-? show syntax summary (this screen)]
```

N O T E ISQL command-line parameters are case-sensitive. Be sure to observe the upper- and lowercase indications provided by the help from ISQL. ▪

Table 1.1 summarizes the function of each parameter. Each parameter, also called a *switch* in the Microsoft SQL Server documentation, is preceded with a forward slash (/) or a hyphen (-). The command ISQL /? displays the hyphens (-), although the hyphen or forward slash can be used. The use of the hyphen in command-line ISQL is inherited from the Sybase version of SQL Server.

Table 1.1 ISQL Command-Line Parameters

Parameter	Function
a *packet_size*	The packet size for data transfer 512 through 65535; the NT default is 8192
b	On error batch abort
c *cmdend*	Specifies the command terminator; the default is GO
d *dbname*	Issues a USE dbname command on entry into ISQL
E	Use trusted connection
e	Echo input
H *wksta_name*	Specifies the workstation name
h *headers*	The number of rows to print between column headings
i *inputfile*	Specifies an input batch file for execution
L	Lists the local and remote servers
l *timeout*	The login timeout
m *errorlevel*	Sets error-level displays to this level or higher

Parameter	Function
n	Omit prompt line numbers
O	Use old behavior
o *outputfile*	Specifies the file where statement output is directed
P *password*	Specifies password; prompted for if not specified
p	Display performance statistics
Q *"query"*	Executes a .SQL batch file and exits the ISQL session
q *"query"*	Executes a .SQL batch file
r [0¦1]	Controls redirection of error-level messages
S *servername*	Specifies the server name; default is local
s *colseparator*	Set column separator; default is blank
t *timeout*	Command timeout in seconds; default is no timeout
U *login_id*	Case-sensitive SQL Server user account name
w *columnwidth*	Set column width; default is 80
?	Shows syntax

Table 1.2 lists the set of commands used after you enter ISQL. These commands must be used at the beginning of a command line, which is a 1> prompt.

Table 1.2   ISQL Commands

Command	Purpose
GO	Default command terminator; executes a statement
RESET	Clears statements before execution
ED	Invokes the default system editor
!! *command*	Executes an NT command
QUIT or EXIT()	Exits ISQL
Ctrl+C	Terminates a query without exiting ISQL
SHUTDOWN	Stops the SQL Server and exits ISQL

TIP You can use the command-line recall feature of Windows NT, the up-arrow key, to recall previous commands that you've entered within ISQL. Your ISQL commands are limited to a maximum of 1,000 characters per line.

Applications

Six GUI applications are available to access and manage SQL Server installations.

The first of the applications enables you to enter Transact-SQL statements. The second, the SQL Client Configuration Utility, enables you to define the set of database and network library routines for database operations performed from a client system. The third, SQL Server Books Online, provides a complete set of SQL Server manuals organized for retrieval and searching.

Next is the SQL Service Manager, which is used to stop and start the SQL Server services. You can use the traffic light interface to control the SQL Server process and the SQL agent process.

Also available is the Microsoft Management Console, which provides access to the core administrative functions for SQL Server. The SQL Performance Monitor will help you tune your installation for best performance.

Query Analyzer/Optimizer and Profiler   A Windows version of the command-line ISQL called Query Analyzer issues Transact-SQL statements. You enter Transact-SQL commands in a separate query window within the Query Analyzer main window. You can cut, copy, paste, print, save, and edit previous queries more easily in Query Analyzer than you can through an ISQL command line.

After you start the Query Analyzer application, you sign in to SQL Server by indicating your user name, password (if necessary), and the server you want to use. SQL Server maintains its own list of users who can connect to a server from a client system by using a valid login ID and user name.

▶ For more information on implementing and managing SQL Server security, **see** Chapter 20, "SQL Server Security," **p. 519**

Figure 1.2 shows a select statement used to retrieve all rows from the system table sysdatabases, which contains a list of all defined databases. The tabular list of columns of information kept for the databases is displayed on the Results screen.

FIGURE 1.2

SQL statements are entered on the Query frame of Query Analyzer. Ctrl+E shows results in a simple listing, Ctrl+R uses a grid.

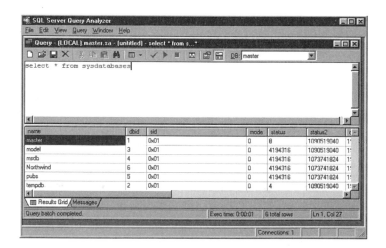

TIP If you have several different statements on the Query page, you can highlight the statement or statements you want to execute and then press Ctrl+E or Ctrl+R to execute them. Only the highlighted statements will be submitted to SQL Server.

Your query output is displayed in a separate Results screen, which is displayed in the lower frame. You can use the scrollbars to view the entire query output. For example, Figure 1.3 shows the files that are automatically created when SQL Server is installed.

FIGURE 1.3

You can use Query Analyzer from both the client and server systems and can use it to submit configuration commands and query statements.

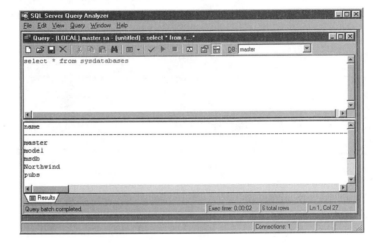

You can also use the Analyzer's profiler and optimizer features, which will help you diagnose and tune up your SQL statement's performance against your database. You can use these tools to watch exactly how the database engine will process your query, including the path it will take through the database tables.

The SQL Client Configuration Utility The SQL Client Configuration Utility defines the Net-Library and DB-Library used for communication between the client and server. Figure 1.4 shows the SQL Client Configuration Utility dialog box. You must consult the documentation of your client product to confirm that the correct version of the DB-Library is chosen.

NOTE Use the latest version of the network and database libraries on your system. If you have a mixed-version environment, you must consider either upgrading all servers to the most recent server software or attempting to use previous version drivers with the newer servers. This will work in most cases, but you might experience some problems using new features. ■

The Net-Library default is set to Named Pipes when you install the SQL Server client application tools on a client system. *Named pipes* is the default communication mechanism used for communication between the client application and the SQL Server system. You can choose a different network library to use an alternative communication mechanism from named pipes. For example, as Figure 1.5 shows, you can choose alternative mechanisms for the TCP/IP, IPX/SPX, and Banyan VINES transport protocols.

FIGURE 1.4

Establish the client configuration by selecting the appropriate tab on the setup dialog.

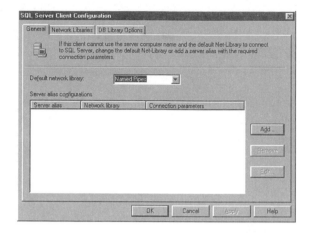

FIGURE 1.5

You can choose from the most popular network protocols when you set up the software.

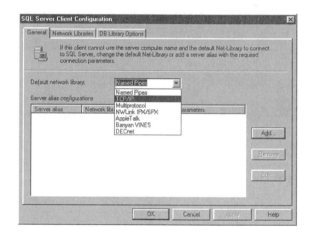

NOTE The SQL Client Configuration Utility is helpful because a client might need to connect to more than one server. By installing all different protocols needed, the client workstation will have access to the routines located in network and database libraries. ■

Using SQL Server Books Online   The SQL Server Books Online help facility contains the contents of 13 books, shown in Figure 1.6, and a glossary on SQL Server. Like Query Analyzer and the SQL Client Configuration Utility, the SQL Server Books Online application can be installed automatically on a client or server system. You'll find it extremely convenient to have quick access to such extensive documentation without leaving your computer system. These books include the entire text of the SQL server documentation as provided by Microsoft.

FIGURE 1.6
You can print or copy pages or complete sections of the Books Online information.

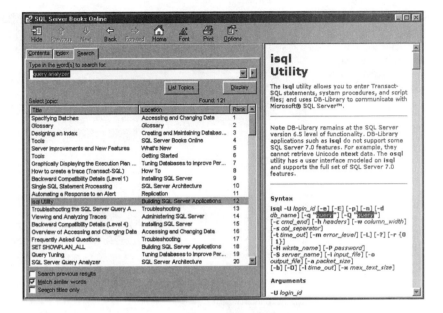

Part

I

Ch

1

SQL Service Manager   The SQL Service Manager is one of the only utilities available when you are physically working on the server. The SQL Service Manager application starts, stops, or pauses the SQL Server processes. You must start SQL Server before you can perform any operations with the databases. The SQL Service Manager is the easiest way to start either a local or remote server. Figure 1.7 shows the SQL Service Manager dialog box after the MSSQLServer service is started.

> **N O T E**   A service on Windows NT such as the MSSQLServer and SQLServerAgent of SQL Server are system processes that run in the background within NT. These background processes are used by SQL Server and client systems that require their functions. ■

The traffic light metaphor simplifies the starting, stopping, and pausing of SQL Server. Double-click Stop or the red light to stop SQL Server. Double-click Pause or the yellow light symbol to temporarily pause SQL Server if the server has been started.

T I P   You can minimize the SQL Service Manager and still observe the traffic lights to determine whether server service is stopped (red light) or started (green light). The icon that represents the service manager will still show the traffic light.

FIGURE 1.7

If you pause the
MSSQLServer service,
no additional client or
server connections are
permitted.

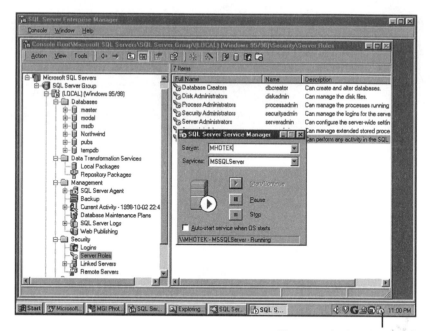

The status is also shown here

Microsoft Management Console/SQL Enterprise Manager   SQL Enterprise Manager is a
snap-in application for the Microsoft Management Console (MMC). It is the server application
that you use to perform nearly all administrative operations with local or remote servers. You
can even use SQL Enterprise Manager to start and stop both SQL Server services rather than
use the SQL Service Manager. SQL Enterprise Manager is also used to do the following:

- Manage user-account and server logins
- Back up and restore databases and transaction logs
- Start, stop, and configure servers
- Check database consistency
- Display server statistics
- Set up and manage database replication
- Create and manage database objects and tasks
- Create and control user accounts and groups
- Control the access control lists

You also might find that performing queries by using Transact-SQL commands from SQL
Enterprise Manager is convenient. Choose Tools, SQL Server Query Analyzer on the MMC
main window, shown in Figure 1.8, to bring up a window through which you can issue ISQL
statements.

FIGURE 1.8

In Enterprise Manager, you can issue SQL statements directly by using the Query Analyzer.

SQL Query Analyzer

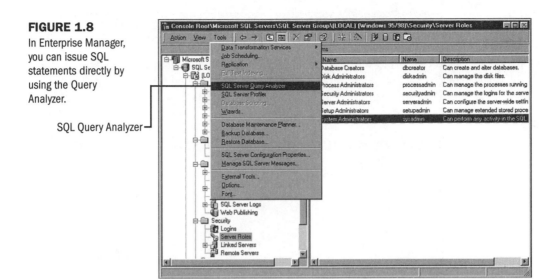

Although you also can perform all the administrative operations for SQL Server through ISQL, SQL Enterprise Manager enables you to perform the operations with pull-down menus and dialog boxes rather than on a command line. In Figure 1.9, the grouping of server objects under folders has been expanded to display several different types of server entities.

FIGURE 1.9

Server objects are displayed in a hierarchical fashion in the Server Manager window.

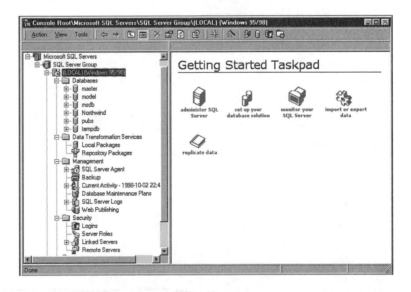

SQL Performance Monitor   The SQL Performance Monitor is a standard administrative application of the Windows NT operating system. SQL Server was written to allow SQL Server objects and counters to be displayed within the Performance Monitor with Windows NT object counters. For convenience, an additional icon is added that has a predefined set of objects and counters used to monitor SQL Server.

Figure 1.10 shows a chart view of several important SQL counters that you can use to monitor the performance of SQL Server on your system. The integration of the SQL Server objects; counters, such as the cache hit ratio; and user connections enables you to select and display SQL Server statistics with NT objects and counters.

FIGURE 1.10

The Performance Monitor is used to display statistics on the performance of both the system and SQL Server.

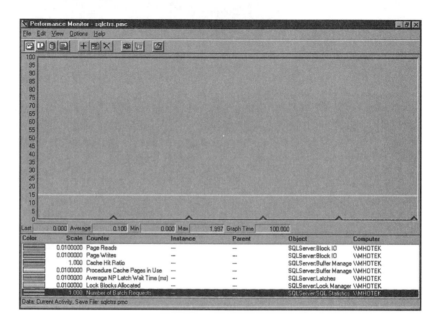

In addition to the chart display in Figure 1.10, you also can dynamically switch to display the counter information as a vertical bar graph rather than as a chart. You can also record object counters in a log for later display, or you can display the information as a tabular report.

The Performance Monitor enables you to set threshold values for SQL Server counter values. When the threshold value is reached, an alert is displayed within an Alert view of the Performance Monitor. A message can be sent to you about the alert even if you're working on a client workstation.

▶ For more information on performance monitoring techniques, **see** Chapter 21, "Optimizing Performance," **p. 539**

Managing SQL Server Security   In SQL Server 7.0 there is no longer a separate application for the management of security. Security is managed from the SQL Enterprise Manager through the definition of server roles as shown in Figure 1.11. Choose one of the following three security types you want to implement on your system during the installation of SQL Server:

■ *Standard security*. Standard security requires you to log in to SQL Server using a user name and ID.

■ *Integrated security*. Integrated security requires you to log in only to Windows NT. You don't need to log in a second time when you access SQL Server. You'll still be prompted to sign in, but your user name in SQL Server will be taken from your network login ID.

■ *Mixed security*. Mixed security enables you to log in to SQL Server or use the integrated login of Windows NT. Integrated logins can be used only with connections to the server from clients using named pipes.

FIGURE 1.11

Integrated security provides the simplest account management in SQL Server, but also requires the most comprehensive user setup.

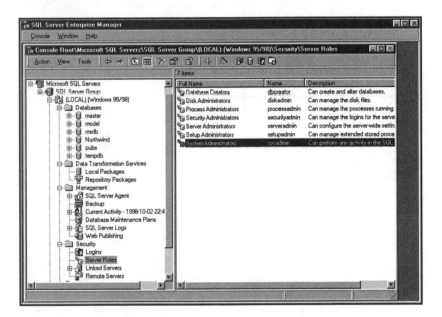

The Server Role object graphically maps Windows NT groups and users to SQL Server accounts and passwords. You can also use the Server Role object to find SQL Server access permissions for mapped accounts.

Distributed Transaction Coordinator   The distributed transaction coordinator (DTC) provides the capability to break up transactions across servers, allowing you to implement truly distributed applications and database integration. Although transactions are a standard part of a SQL Server-based application, using transactions across more than one physical server traditionally has been a problem.

With the DTC, you can now control these types of transactions, and you have the tools available to diagnose performance and bottleneck situations that arise. In addition, you have the ability to roll back failed transactions that include different servers.

▶ **See** Chapter 18, "Using the Distributed Transaction Coordinator," **p. 481**, to find out more about the Distributed Transaction Coordinator.

Other Utilities   You'll find that many other utilities are helpful with your SQL Server installation. For example, with Microsoft Office products, you can use the Microsoft Query, or MSQUERY, application to execute queries against tables managed by SQL Server. This utility is much like the query functionality found in Microsoft Access, allowing you to visually build and see the results of your SQL statements. It's also a key tool in learning how to use the SQL language because you can visually build the query that produces the results you need, then have the application show you the SQL statements that are used to create those results.

Microsoft Excel, Microsoft Access, and Visual Basic also all work very closely with Microsoft SQL Server, as do other third-party languages. Borland's Delphi development environment provides close-knit connectivity with SQL Server, and each of these can be used as a foundation for developing client/server applications for your users.

▶ For more information on using other applications to access SQL Server, including different development environments, **see** Chapter 22, "Backward Compatibility Options for Developers."

From Here...

Now that you've learned the basics of how SQL Server will be implemented in your organization, you'll begin working with the topics that will really make SQL Server get to work for you.

Be sure to also review Chapter 3, "Installing and Setting Up the Server and Client Software," so you understand what will be installed and where it will be located on your system.

For more information about selected topics, see the following chapters:

- Chapter 11, "Managing and Using Indexes and Keys," shows you how to create and use keys and indexes.
- Chapter 13, "Managing and Using Rules, Constraints, and Defaults," shows how to create and use rules and defaults.
- Chapter 15, "Creating and Managing Triggers," shows how to create and use triggers to maintain referential integrity in the database.
- Chapter 24,"Creating and Using Cursors," shows you how to use cursors in a programming language to manipulate rows of a database table one at a time.

Understanding the Underlying Operating System, Windows NT

In this chapter

Windows NT, the operating system that SQL Server runs under, has several mechanisms you should understand to help you use SQL Server more effectively. *Operating system components,* or *processes,* are sections of computer code that control how the computer's hardware and other software is used.

For example, some NT components control how one or more central processors are used by applications. The MSSQLServer and MSQLExecutive processes of SQL Server use Windows NT processes to service client systems.

Windows NT is also responsible for managing the security of the network and its associated resources. You create system users for the server and can control their access to resources, including SQL Server, on that system. Although it's outside the scope of this book to review the entire Windows NT security model, it's important that you have a comprehensive understanding of how your network is set up. This includes how users are defined and whether you plan to use this same security model in your SQL Server implementation.

N O T E　SQL Server also has a desktop version that runs on Windows 9x. This chapter focuses on the interaction between Windows NT and SQL Server, but keep in mind that it can be run in the lower-end operating system environments as well.

Throughout this book, youíll see references to small differences between the desktop and standard editions. Be sure to take note of these if you are using the desktop edition. ▪

In addition to processes of Windows NT that control the use of resources such as the CPUs, several system applications control aspects of the operating system that affect SQL Server. You can monitor the use of Windows NT and SQL Server processes through the Performance Monitor and change usage based on the statistics collected. You can display errors and other events returned as the results of SQL Server's activity through the Event Viewer, and by using the information returned, interpret and correct them.

It's also helpful to understand the different configurations of interconnections among the Windows NT servers that SQL Server is on. The interconnection of server and client is accomplished primarily through network software, which you must have a basic understanding of to communicate between client and server or server and server.

Later in this chapter, in the NT Domain Section, you'll see how to work with users on your system, and how to set up new users and assign rights.

▶ For information about how to establish SQL Server security, **see** Chapter 20, "SQL Server Security," **p. 519**

Understanding the Desktop Version of SQL Server 7

With SQL Server 7, you now have the option of running on Windows 9x. With this option come several changes to the operation of some features in SQL Server. Specifically, the integration of security with the operating system, multiprocessor capabilities, and large memory model management are not supported.

While the core SQL Server engine is identical to that installed on an NT Server system, these other capabilities are not possible in the Windows 9*x* environment—the operating system support is simply not there.

The balance of this chapter focuses on the integration of SQL Server with the operating system, domains, and how the operating system works. For other specific differences on the various platforms, keep an eye out for Notes throughout this book.

Part

I

Ch

2

Understanding Multiprocessing, Multitasking, and Multithreading

Working with and understanding the difference between the terms *multiprocessing*, *multitasking*, and *multithreading* often can be confusing. They are important in your use of SQL Server, however, because they affect the performance and scalability of the system. This section will briefly review each of them.

Multitasking and multiprocessing are two mechanisms of an operating system, such as Windows NT, that are used to enhance the processing capabilities of the server. Multitasking refers to the capability of the operating system to perform a bit of a time-share between processes. This means that each process in the system will receive a time-slice of attention from the CPU. Although it slows down the overall activity of the system, it also ensures that more than one process will get the attention of the CPU. This is why you will notice a difference in performance on the server when you have a number of processes running. The system will appear to be running slowly or be "bogged down," but in fact it's simply fulfilling more than one request in this time-slice mode.

Multiprocessing, on the other hand, happens when the server has more than one CPU installed. By taking advantage of the increased processing power of the system, NT can greatly improve performance on the system. Because the throughput is 100% more for each processor installed, the operating system's application of multitasking is much more effective, and the system will perform better overall.

> **N O T E** Even with the multiprocessing and multitasking capabilities of the operating system, memory continues to play a key role in the overall performance of your SQL Server. Unless your memory is in the neighborhood of 256MB or better, you should consider upgrading your memory if it's performance you're seeking. ▪

The simplest form of multitasking occurs when an operating system switches use of a computer system's CPU among multiple applications. The operating system must keep track of where each program has left off so the program can be started back up again when the program receives use of the central processor again. This is *round-robin scheduling*. Round-robin scheduling permits each process to use a CPU for a period of time, rather than allowing a CPU to be used exclusively by a process.

Each application must receive use of a CPU long enough to get some reasonable amount of work done. Also, the switching of the CPU must be accomplished quickly. If an operating system provides each application with enough time to use a CPU, and the switch among applications is done quickly enough, a user interacting with one application might work as if a CPU is dedicated to their exclusive use. Of course, as mentioned earlier, this performance can also be influenced by having too many applications waiting to use the CPU(s).

N O T E   The interval of time at which Windows NT exchanges use of the central processor is several hundred milliseconds. Windows NT maintains an elaborate technique to determine what program receives the use of the central processor next. Programs are assigned a priority from 0 to 31. NT grants use of the central processor to the program that has the highest priority, the one that has been waiting to use the central processor the longest, and works down the list of priorities in order. ■

Operating systems such as Windows NT perform a more sophisticated sharing of the use of a central processor than the simple round-robin approach mentioned earlier. A program on Windows NT can be written in several functional sections, and each section can receive use of a central processor independently. One definition of the term *multitasking* refers to the sharing of the use of a central processor by multiple sections of a program simultaneously.

A complete application program that can use the resources of a system is called a *process* in the Windows NT system. Each program section that can receive use of a Windows NT central processor is called a *thread.* A thread must have its own priority as well as other characteristics for Windows NT to schedule use of system resources separately for each thread. The term *multitasking* on Windows NT also refers to the use of the central processor of an NT system by multiple threads of the same or different processes.

A feature such as multitasking with multiple threads is most advantageous when more than a single processor is available to be shared. An application written in several threads can have each thread execute simultaneously on Windows NT. This is referred to as a *multiprocessor environment.*

You can use a powerful single-processor system for SQL Server such as a Digital Alpha AXP, MIPS R4000, PowerPC, or Intel Pentium system. Multiple CPU systems can be used by Windows NT because of its symmetric multiprocessing capability. *Symmetric multiprocessing* allows several threads to execute simultaneously, regardless of whether they're running application or operating system code.

N O T E   There are two types of multiprocessing capabilities: symmetric and asymmetric. Windows NT uses symmetric multiprocessing, which is most commonly implemented. *Symmetric multiprocessing* spreads the processes for both the operating system and applications among all available system CPUs. *Asymmetric multiprocessing* allows the operating system to be placed on a single CPU and applications to be spread among others. ■

N O T E   Multi-CPU systems are particularly advantageous for use as servers for a SQL Server database because I/O requests from client systems can be handled while other operations, such as account validation, are done in a second processor of the system. Multiple server requests can be done at a rate that greatly increases the number of workstation clients that can be served by the server. ■

Understanding Multiarchitecture

An important characteristic of Windows NT is its multiarchitecture feature. The term *architecture* refers to different types of hardware components that can be used on a computer system, especially different central processors. Windows NT runs on computer systems that use different microprocessors for their central processing units.

For example, Windows NT can run on a system that uses Intel 386, 486, or Pentium processors. NT can also run on x86 clones produced by such vendors as Cyrix and AMD. Windows NT will also run on Digital's Alpha AXP, MIPS R4000 series processors, and the PowerPC. The Windows NT distribution CD contains separate versions of the installation software for all four systems, with more compatible systems planned.

One great advantage of SQL Server using Windows NT as the operating system platform is the choice of many computer systems to use as a server for a SQL Server database. Windows NT and SQL Server are scalable from a desktop PC to a large Alpha AXP or MIPS system. It will even scale to systems with one or more processors that have enough power to replace a minicomputer or even a large mainframe system.

Understanding the Multiuser Environment of SQL Server on Windows NT

Traditional mainframe and minicomputer system databases were accessed by users sitting in front of input/output devices. Windows NT is unlike minicomputer or mainframe systems in that users don't use dumb terminals as the input or output devices. Instead, each user gains access to an NT system running SQL Server by using a computer system with its own operating system. As discussed in Chapter 1, "Understanding Microsoft SQL Server 7.0 Fundamentals," this is referred to as the client system. The multiple users of a Windows NT server access an application such as SQL Server from their own client computer system.

N O T E   *Dumb terminals* got their nickname because they simply transfer characters to and from the CPU, using the CPU to perform the work with the information. Dumb terminals, unlike PCs or other workstations, can't do any processing. Dumb terminals replaced the card readers and printers that were used as input and output devices on early computer systems. A dumb terminal combines separate input and output devices in a simple device for input and output. ■

Each user typically runs Windows for Workgroups, Windows 95, DOS, OS/2, or Windows NT Workstation on a client workstation system. Each operating system allows a user to run applications independently of a central server system. A user at a workstation employs connectivity software, usually the network operating system, to establish a connection to a central server computer running Windows NT Server.

Understanding the Windows NT Network Components

Windows NT provides the capability to establish networks and to connect to other computer systems. The connectivity feature of Windows NT is used for several purposes. A network connection can be made for the purpose of sharing the resources of different systems. You might create the connection to access information on a remote disk of another Windows NT or a non-Windows NT system. You might also need to transfer data between two systems. When you access the SQL Server database on the server system from a client system, you're wholly dependent on the communication connections that are established by the NT system.

You can also perform administrative operations through network connections to Windows NT. You use commands to learn the connection status of systems, monitor the flow of control and user data between connections, and alter the characteristics that affect the connections. You can also change the size of network and disk buffers, the temporary storage space in RAM used to store the data that comes from one system and is received into a second system.

The connectivity components of Windows NT are also used to connect an application on a client workstation to the SQL Server database on the NT server. All the previously specified uses for client/server connectivity, such as remote administration, monitoring, and data transfer, are necessary in a system using SQL Server.

▶ **See** Chapter 21, "Optimizing Performance," **p. 539**, for a more detailed discussion of using NT performance monitoring.

▶ For more information on administration of SQL Server, **see** Chapter 19 "SQL Server Administration," **p. 495**

Sharing Resources

Windows NT networks are set up as domains. Each domain can have a number of workgroups. A *domain* is one form of a Windows NT network. Before a computer can be added to a domain, an account must be set up. Rights for this account are controlled by the administrator.

Workgroups are logical groupings (made by department, task, or some other method) of systems on a network. Users are placed into workgroups to make it easier to locate and use shared resources.

Both methods for sharing resources could work for sharing a SQL Server resource. Workgroups are geared towards users and therefore don't offer sophisticated or versatile security measures. Windows NT offers excellent built-in security through its use of domains for implementation and administration. SQL Server can take full advantage of this security.

Installing Network Software

Use the Network Properties dialog box to add additional network protocols to enable access to and from different network types (see Figure 2.1). To access this dialog box, choose Settings, Control Panel from the Start menu and double-click the Network icon. Alternatively, you can right-click the Network Neighborhood icon on the desktop and choose Properties. Components can be added, removed, configured, or updated in this dialog box.

Part
I
Ch
2

FIGURE 2.1

You can manipulate several network software properties together.

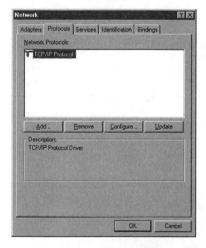

After entering new configuration information for a network component, you'll be prompted to either reboot the system or leave the system up and running (see Figure 2.2). Your network components won't be available until you reboot.

FIGURE 2.2

After the installation is complete, you'll need to reboot the system for the changes to take effect.

If you're adding the additional network software that comes with Windows NT, you need to confirm or change the path for the NT distribution. If you're installing optional network software, enter the path for its distribution.

Configuring Adapter Cards

If your NT workstation has a built-in network hardware interface or an installed network interface card (NIC), its associated network software is installed during the Windows NT Workstation or Server installation. You might add or change network interface cards on PC workstations that don't have network interfaces on their motherboards.

The manufacturers of network interface cards (NIC) use software, referred to as *drivers,* for their NIC. If you change from one NIC to another, you have to change the driver software. The need to change network adapters can arise for a number of reasons. For example, you might want to upgrade as faster cards become available, replace a faulty card, or add a new, special-function card to the system.

As mentioned, one of the reasons you might want to update your card is to improve network performance. You can change from a slower 8-bit NIC to a faster 16- or 32-bit NIC. The 16- or 32-bit NICs perform some network operations more quickly than 8-bit NICs. Other NIC characteristics, such as the buffer sizes and types of media supported, can also affect performance.

You might need to change the NIC on the server system to get adequate performance for queries made against your SQL Server database. You might also change the NIC on selected client systems that require faster access to the server database.

Choose the Add button from the Adapters page in the Network properties dialog box to bring up the Select Network Adapter dialog box. Select the name of the network adapter card from the Network Adapter Card list. The selected adapter card in Figure 2.3 is the 3Com Etherlink II Adapter.

FIGURE 2.3

You'll need to add adapter card software if you add a second or different NIC to your system.

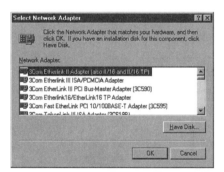

Network adapter cards typically require that an IRQ level and an I/O base address be specified when the adapter software is added. The IRQ level and I/O base address should match the one specified by the manufacturer. Windows NT can automatically detect and configure a number of adapter cards.

Before buying a NIC, consult with a reputable dealer, who can tell you whether the card can be set up automatically by Windows NT. You can also check with Microsoft to learn of NICs that can be automatically configured. Some of the major manufacturers provide NICs that also enable the IRQ and addresses to be set through software rather than jumpers on the card.

Cards that can be automatically set up can be advantageous to use, especially if you have a large number of other interface cards installed in your PC workstation.

Having lots of cards installed in your system makes it easier to have conflicts. Two cards that have identical IRQ and/or address settings by default will, if unchanged, cause problems for one another. Some interface cards allow few changes to be made to their IRQ or address settings. If some of your interface cards can be set to a large number of values through software, you can more easily prevent card-setting conflicts.

Ideally, you should check the specification of all cards that you want to use in your PC workstation to determine whether all IRQ and address conflicts can be eliminated. If you don't do this, you might have to later change one or more cards to eliminate conflicts and allow all cards to work, including your network card.

You should also check that the interface cards, including the network interface cards that you buy for NT, are supported. Microsoft provides a list of the supported interface cards, including network NICs, which can be used with Windows NT.

You should know the factory default settings for your network adapter card and the current settings, if you've changed them from the factory defaults. You should also run a diagnostic program to learn quickly if the network adapter cards function properly.

Select the adapter card from the Installed Adapter Card list and click OK to install the network adapter with the default NT driver. (You can also click Have Disk to use a manufacturer's driver.) Involvement of the user in the installation of adapter cards depends on the abilities of the card and the sophistication of the driver software. All the settings might be automatically determined or might need to be supplied in order to properly install an adapter card.

N O T E Many manufacturers repackage network adapter cards that are manufactured by other companies for PC workstations. If your network adapter card doesn't appear in the list, it might be shown under a different name. Check with the vendor from whom you bought the card, the documentation that came with the card, a diagnostic display of the card characteristics, or the labeling on the adapter board itself to find its designation. ■

 T I P Consider buying identical network adapter cards for PC workstations. Several adapter manufacturers provide additional software to diagnose and monitor network interface card operation, but only if you have matching NICs among PCs.

Understanding Workgroups

The capability to form workgroups is part of the built-in network features of Windows NT. Windows NT allows the interconnection of Windows NT systems into groups that can share each other's resources. A *workgroup* is a logical set of workstations that shares resources among one another. This is the basis for designating workstations as the members of the same workgroup.

The members of a workgroup can typically share the resources of one another equally. An example of a resource that can be shared among workgroup members equally is a disk drive and the directories and files on it.

This capability to share between workstations without a designated server system is called *peer-to-peer networking.* Each system can share access to another's resources after they become shared. In such an arrangement, the systems function as both clients and servers to one another. In this case, a *server* is a workstation that makes a resource such as a disk available to another workstation. A *client* is a workstation that accesses the resources of another workstation.

Workstations in a network that share each other's resources should be placed in a logical organization, which is the NT workgroup. You must designate which NT workstations become members of the same group. After you form workgroups, the resources for sharing can be set up. The underlying capability of peer-to-peer networking of workgroups permits workgroup client access to a SQL Server database. The peer-to-peer features of a workgroup can also be used to share related information about SQL Server, such as the documentation, which could reside on any shared disk in a workgroup.

After the disk-sharing feature is enabled on each system, for example, you can access another workgroup member's disks. You can execute applications, read or write databases, create documents and spreadsheets, and delete or rename files on the shared disk of another workstation in the workgroup.

A disk drive that's part of the hardware components of a workstation is called a *local drive.* Local disk drives are directly connected to a workstation.

A remote drive is a disk drive that's accessible to a workstation but isn't physically one of its hardware components. The remote drive is the local drive of another workstation. The physical connection to a remote drive is through the LAN.

Workstations that are part of the same network can be made members of the same workgroup. Workstations that need to access each other's resources should be made members of the same workgroup. This is the basic criteria for the formation of workgroups.

You can, however, define a workgroup based on your own criteria. The placement of two or more workstations into a workgroup is arbitrary, which means that an administrator has full control over who's made a member of the workgroup. You can have groups of only two members each if you have a need for such a configuration. You can even place workstations into the same workgroup that share no resources, although this would be unlikely.

You'll find that there's a practical limit on the number of systems that can be members of the same workgroup. A constraint results from the speed of the workstation's hardware, including its disk drives, amount of memory, processor, and system bus. The individual hardware components of a workstation that's used as a server in a workgroup might not be fast enough to enable it to serve many workgroup members.

Members of a workgroup might access a SQL Server database in a different workgroup as well as their own. However, it's more likely that the SQL Server database will be installed on a Windows NT server system in a domain. Members of one or more workgroups can still access the SQL Server database although it's placed into different types of logical organizations of client and server systems.

In a server-based, domain model network system, you can buy a large, powerful, and fast single system that's the only server in a group of workstations. If your server system is a Pentium, MIPS R4000, Alpha AXP processor, or multiple i486 processors, it can function as a server for a much larger number of workstations.

Traditional networking definitions have typically been that a network configuration is either a workstation/server network or a peer-to-peer network, not usually both. The fact is, with the introduction of Windows for Workgroups and continuing with Windows 95 and Windows NT Workstation, systems are more typically a mixture of server-based and peer-to-peer based networks. The appeal of the peer-to-peer type of network often is cost. You don't have to implement a huge system to act as a server to other workstations on the network in this environment. The disadvantage is that you won't typically be running hard-core server applications, such as SQL Server, on the workstations of these environments.

Also, as you implement your workgroups, you'll find logical groupings of your users emerging, even beyond the groups you've established. You should consider Windows NT domains if you find it difficult to administer workgroup networks. Domains enable you to group users into logical cross-sections and then use these groupings to manage security, access to the network, usernames, and more.

This latter type of centralized organization provides some of the features of a client/server-based network. If you require more of a client/server configuration for your workstations, including the capability to serve dozens or hundreds of clients, you'll want to use the additional features provided by the Windows NT Server.

A simple rule of thumb for peer-to-peer configured workgroups is to limit their members to no more than 20 or so. Microsoft suggests that you define fewer than 20, but how many members interact with one another simultaneously determines the actual limit. You'll find that you can deviate from the suggested limit of 20 workstations, but you should certainly keep the recommended values in mind as you configure your workgroups.

You might want to limit the numbers of members of a workgroup to fewer than 20 to allow for the occasional load put on your system by connections to your resources from outside your workgroup. Unlike the domain model mentioned earlier, a workgroup isn't a security mechanism and doesn't serve to restrict access to the resources of member workstations. Other members of the network can access the resources of workstations outside their own workgroups after they know the share name and optional password.

It might help you to understand workgroups by thinking of them as a loosely organized confederation rather than as an integrated republic. The members of a workgroup log on to their workstation, establishing their username for the network. Their username and password are checked in an account database that resides on a local disk. You administer each workstation separately, including the definition of separate accounts for each workstation.

You designate a workstation as a member of a workgroup or domain when you install Windows NT. You can later use the Network Control Panel to change your membership in a workgroup. You can designate a workstation as a member of only one workgroup at a time.

A new workgroup is created the first time you use its name. This occurs either during the installation of a Windows NT system or later when you change the name of your workgroup. Members of the same workgroup are displayed together when you examine the workstations of your network.

Members of a workgroup are together to simplify the sharing of resources. There's no restriction on the workstations that might become a member of a workgroup that's provided by Windows NT. You define the criteria for workstation membership.

You can use workstations with faster processors or multiple processors, and large fast disks in your workgroup to extend the 20-workstation limit of the workgroup network. Faster processors and faster disks help extend the limit by performing server tasks more quickly. This allows more workstations to interact as clients and servers with each other and still have acceptable performance.

You won't, however, be able to extend your network to a configuration in which your servers support 10,000 or more NT workstations. Although you can have several tens of thousands of interconnected NT systems, the realistic maximum number is far fewer and is limited by the number of systems that can perform well while interconnected. Real-life tests indicate that approximately 250 workstations, used in a busy network, are probably a realistic goal for sizing your network.

In a workgroup, you create and administer user accounts on each workstation. You log on to each workstation, and your username and password are validated at the local workstation. If you have the responsibility for the administration of more than one workstation, you must log on to each one to maintain its account database. This is particularly inconvenient if a user has accounts on several workstations and changes must be made to each one.

Specifying a domain for your computer rather than a workgroup is another option. As mentioned previously, a domain is a tightly administered group of workstations. You can read about domains in the next section, "Understanding Windows NT Domains."

TIP   If you cannot locate a workgroup or domain system that you want to connect to, you're probably experiencing a conflict with the network drivers on your system. Check to make sure you have the correct drivers installed and that you have matched your network configuration with the settings on your network card.

Also, if you find that you can see other workstations on your network, but cannot gain access to the server, check your username and password. It's likely that that password you used to log on to your workstation is not the same as the password established for your NT Domain account.

Understanding Windows NT Domains

If your client systems are either part of your local area network or on the Internet, *domains* are the fundamental architecture that controls how they access the resources on the network. Domains provide a means of logically grouping systems and users to facilitate administering the systems, accessing your server, and interacting with each other.

Windows for Workgroups introduced peer-to-peer networking for Microsoft platforms. Peer-level networking means that workstations share information stored on their local hard disks with other users on the network. Although this is a great way to share small-to-medium amounts of information on a few workstations, a serious bottleneck arises as the number of workstations and the traffic they generate grows.

Part

I

Ch

2

The bottleneck is the result of the need to balance access to the information over the network and performance on a given user's system. In systems where the number of workstations and the amount of shared information becomes a burden on the network, you should consider implementing a more powerful solution. That's where Windows NT comes in. With NT, domains become part of the network picture.

Figure 2.4 shows a sample domain configuration with a two-server domain and a single-server domain.

FIGURE 2.4

Servers belong to only a single domain, whereas users and systems can use more than one domain.

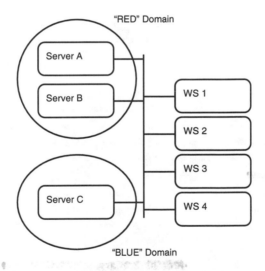

"RED" Domain

Server A

Server B

WS 1

WS 2

WS 3

Server C

WS 4

"BLUE" Domain

Initially system administrators might disagree with the drawing in Figure 2.4 because workstations belong in one domain or another. The point of the figure is that servers belong to one domain and one domain only. Workstations and users can sign into and out of different domains as needed, as long as they are authorized in another domain. The important thing is that when you enter, or log onto, a given domain, you must abide by the domain's accompanying rules and security parameters.

Set up and administer User Rights from the User Manager for Domains, located on the Administrative Tools menu in NT. The User Manager enables you to work with both users and groups. In addition, it enables you to assign all rights recognized by the system to those users. After you create the necessary users and groups, apply rights to your system and control access to the files and directories on it. Figure 2.5 shows the User Manager for Domains.

FIGURE 2.5
Users belong to groups. You control access to resources either by these group assignments or the individual users.

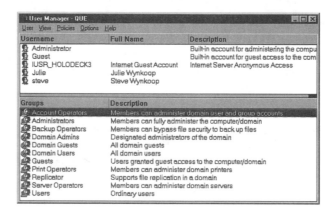

TIP

You can work with more than one user at a time. If you manage existing users and want to set up the group associations, logon times, and many other attributes, first select the users from the list by shift- and control-clicking the names on the list. Next select User, Properties.

CAUTION

Be very wary of one particular user. Consider strongly whether to disable the account altogether. The GUEST account is dangerous, because any user that logs on to your system without a valid username and assigned password is assigned to this account. Therefore, any privileges given that account are automatically provided to any user signing on to the system without otherwise defined access.

The built-in group EVERYONE is also in the system. Every user and group belongs to this group. In addition, its settings provide the default privileges to all resources when they are created, unless user access is explicitly revoked or modified. This means you can assign rights to limit access to your users, but unless you remove the rights for the group EVERYONE on the resource you set up, all users still have access to it.

In almost all cases, your best option is granting group rights to resources rather than granting these rights to users. This is true even in those cases where you grant access to a resource to only a single user. You'll save time and effort later when the user is either replaced or gains an assistant that needs to have the same level of access. When that happens, you need only to modify the members of the group. You won't need to change access privileges on resources on your system. Consider the following steps in planning to implement your system's user database:

- Decide whether you allow access to your system via the GUEST account. If not, disable the account. If you are concerned about security, it is highly recommended that you NEVER leave the GUEST account enabled.

- Define the users required on your system.

- Create the individual user accounts.

- Define the security rights profiles you will apply to the system.

- Create groups containing the users granted the rights you defined.

- Apply the security to the resources. Use the groups as the means of indicating access, or lack of access, to the resource.

- Apply the security to the resources based on individual users in those rare cases where it is warranted or required.

Part

I

Ch

2

> **CAUTION**
>
> Windows NT assigns user rights based on a Least Restrictive model. This means that if you belong to two different profiles, and one profile indicates you have no access to a resource but the other indicates that you do have access, you can gain access to the resource. This is because the least restrictive of the two profiles indicates that you are allowed access.
>
> Put simply, any user that you assign to the NOACCESS group, but that is not removed from other groups, can have more access rights than you planned. The effect of the NOACCESS group can be weakened because the other groups allow overriding user rights, granting user rights to certain resources. When you revoke access to an individual, be sure to review the associated account and ensure that it does not belong to other groups that can also influence effective rights.

Working with NT Users

The User Manager for Domains enables you to create new users a number of different ways. One of the most time-effective ways is the Copy command on the User menu. This copies the rights of an existing user. As you can see in Figure 2.6, there are a number of items you can set up for those users who access your system.

FIGURE 2.6

When you copy an existing user, the copy inherits the groups and privileges of the original.

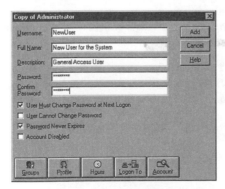

N O T E   If you select the Must Change Password option, there is an additional step the first time a user logs onto the system. Each person must change her password. This might seem like a good idea at first, but be wary of the user's particular system.

In some environments, specifically Windows 3.x systems, the system might not allow users to change their passwords. In these cases, you effectively lock the user out of the system, because NT bars them from the system until the password has been changed.

If you have a user blocked from signing onto the system, review the account and make sure this option is not checked. Also, make sure the Account Disabled option is not selected. This also prevents access to your system. ■

The next sections briefly cover the different aspects of the user account.

Assigning Groups

The Group Button enables you to set up the groups to which the user belongs. Figure 2.7 shows the Group Assignment dialog box.

FIGURE 2.7
Work with users in groups to simplify management tasks.

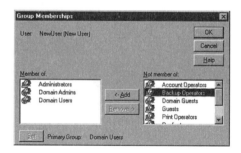

When you assign a user to a group, he gains the rights and privileges associated with that group. By double-clicking groups listed in the Member Of: and Not a Member Of: list boxes, you add and remove membership in groups. After the user is assigned to the appropriate groups, select OK to save the changes and return to the new user's Properties dialog box.

Controlling Access to Resources

After you create your users and groups, you must assign permissions. Assigning permissions is the final step toward securing your system at a general level. This section shows the basics of applying permissions to system resources.

The Windows Explorer is the key to applying security to various resources on your system. Select and right-click the directory resource you want to share. The shortcut menu that appears, shown in Figure 2.8, has an option to establish the sharing for the resource.

Selecting sharing not only sets up the share name and the number of users accessing the resource, but also offers the option to set permissions on the resource by selecting the Permissions button (see Figure 2.9).

FIGURE 2.8

Select Sharing from the menu to set up or maintain sharing options for the highlighted resource.

Part

I

Ch

2

FIGURE 2.9

Setting up the initial share information is straightforward.

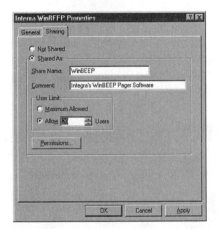

N O T E   The information presented here on creating share-level security on your system pertains to establishing shares on the server. Remember that share-based security is different from NTFS-based security. If you establish rights based on a share, they are not enforced unless the share is accessed.

If you use the directory that the share relates to, without using the share, the rights will have no effect.

If you need to protect content on the server, you must use NTFS for the file system. You must set rights based on the permissions for the directory, not the share. ■

N O T E   If you select a share name of more than the DOS-standard 8.3 format, some DOS workstations might not be able to access the resource. If you do select such a name, you are warned about this possibility as you apply the share information for the source. ■

If you select OK or Apply without setting Permissions, all users who have access to the resource via a share, a parent directory, and so on, will have Open, Full Control access to the resource. Be sure to select the Permissions button. In this dialog box you indicate the different permissions, users, and groups to apply to the resource. You should review the permissions assigned to a resource even if you intend to leave them unmodified from their defaults.

The underlying file system dictates how permissions change. If the NTFS (the NT File System) is installed, you gain additional options. These enable you to apply specific permission subsets, rather than just generic permission categories. The following list shows the general access permission categories you can assign:

- No Access—Users are unable to access, read from, or write to it.
- Read—Read users and groups read the directory, load and execute files located in the directory, and so on. They cannot delete objects, nor can they add new objects to the resource.
- Change—Change users can read, modify, and execute existing objects, but cannot insert new objects nor delete objects.
- Full Control—Full Control users have all rights to the resource.

When you select Add, you have two options. First, you can select single or multiple users and groups. Second, as a set, you can assign rights applying to the set of users. When you select OK, the users are listed in the Permissions text box. This verifies that the permissions are properly applied. Selecting OK once again saves and applies the changes. Now the resource is available with your declared permissions.

Understanding the NT Performance Monitor

You must be able to monitor the use of system resources by applications such as SQL Server's components to properly control the system. An extensive performance monitoring capability is provided as part of the Windows NT system. The Performance Monitor administrative tool controls the monitoring and display of system resources use.

The Performance Monitor tool graphically displays the performance of one or more computers of a network. Resources or entities that can be monitored are called *objects* and can include processes, threads, processors, and memory. Counters are used with objects to record usage statistics. You can record and later review performance information graphically displayed in a chart.

You can closely monitor the characteristics of the main resources of the computer system, the CPU(s), RAM, and disks in Windows NT by using the Performance Monitor. For example, you can collect and display the percentage of time both system code and user code, such as the SQL Server and SQL Monitor processes, use the CPU.

▶ **See** Chapter 21, "Optimizing Performance," **p. 539**, for a discussion on how to use the information returned by the Performance Monitor.

The Chart window, one of four displays called *views*, is brought up in an initialized state. Open the Performance Monitor from the Windows NT Administrative Tools group. Figure 2.10 shows the main window of the Performance Monitor.

FIGURE 2.10

The statistics are automatically collected from the system running currently after you select them.

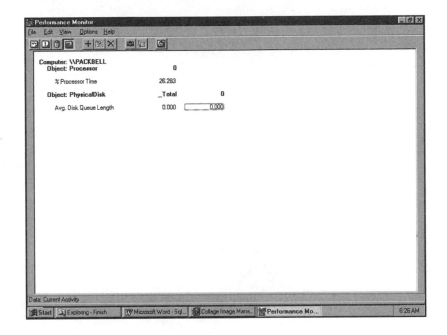

Part

I

Ch

2

N O T E   You need to manually start the logging process after you select the components you want to monitor. By default, when the monitor is loaded, the logging isn't yet active. ■

Logging isn't enabled when the Performance Monitor is started, so no information is displayed. The three additional views you can display are Alert, Log, and Report. To select objects to be monitored, displayed, or recorded in a log file, choose Add to Chart from the Edit menu. The Add to Chart dialog box appears, allowing you to select the objects for monitoring (see Figure 2.11).

FIGURE 2.11

If you have a multiple processor server, you can monitor each processor using the Instance field, which will show more than one instance if you have more than one processor.

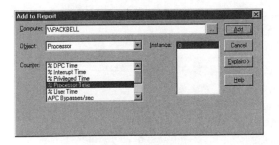

Selecting Objects and Counters in a Chart View

Select objects for monitoring in the Object drop-down list box. Use the Counter list box to select a counter for an object. Each object has a different default counter. The default object is Processor with a default counter of % Processor Time.

In the example shown in Figure 2.11, the percentage of processor time for the CPU of the system PACKBELL is selected for monitoring and display.

You can use the Explain button to bring up an explanation of the selected counter. For example, the counter % Processor Time is defined as the percentage of time a processor is executing an executable thread of code at the bottom of the Add to Chart dialog box.

After you select an object counter, use the Add button to add the counter line to the display. After you select all object counters, use the Done button to display the chart view. The Cancel button changes to Done when you select a counter for display. In the chart view shown in Figure 2.12, the percentage of time the processor was busy executing code is displayed graphically.

FIGURE 2.12

The display of each counter is automatically assigned a different color.

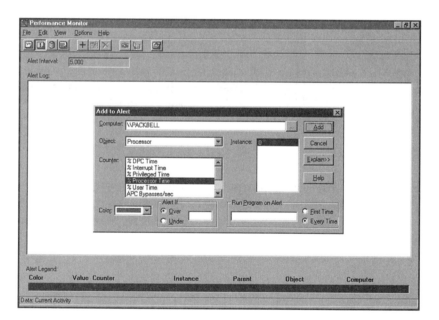

Displaying Information in a Report View

You can display the information collected by the Performance Monitor for object counters as a report rather than in a graphical representation. A report view presents the information in a tabular format rather than graphical. You might find a report format preferable for viewing statistics because the numeric representation of all counters is displayed. You can create a report by choosing the Report view from the View menu.

A new report is blank because you haven't selected any object counter information. You select the object counters for a report by opening the Edit menu and choosing Add to Report. Only object counter values will be displayed in the report. In the Add to Report dialog box, the counter % Processor Time for the object Processor on the system PACKBELL is added to the report (see Figure 2.13).

FIGURE 2.13

Multiple counters are available for monitoring most objects in the Performance Monitor.

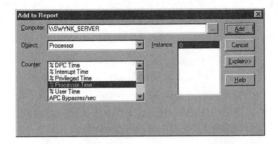

After you select the object counters, click the Done button to bring up the report view. The report is organized by objects, with all counters for the same object group together under a column header. Instances of the same object are displayed across the page, rather than in a single column.

The report view can be set up to show that the counters for each of the three objects should be included in the report. For the Processor and PhysicalDisk, the second column shows the instance. PhysicalDrive 0 denotes the first hard drive of the system. Instance 0 of the Processor denotes the first and only CPU of the computer system NT486.

Selecting Objects and Counters in an Alert View

An *alert* is a line of information displayed in the alert view of the Performance Monitor, when the value of an object counter is above or below a value that you define. The entry in the log includes a date and time stamp, the actual object counter value, the criteria for returning it, the object value counter, and the system.

Choose Alert from the View menu to bring up an alert view. The alert view is initialized by default. Choose Add to Alert from the Edit menu to bring up the Add to Alert dialog box (see Figure 2.14).

FIGURE 2.14

A program can be automatically started when the alert value is reached.

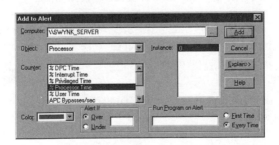

You select the computer, object counter, color, and instance if appropriate, similar to the way you did for chart views. Alerts are different in that they result in the display of information only if the object counter value is greater than or less than a value you define.

Selecting Objects in a Log View

The Log view allows the selection of objects and their counters to be logged for subsequent display and analysis. You bring up the log view by choosing Log from the View menu. Like the other views, it's initialized by default. No object counters are defined for it.

Choose Add to Log from the Edit menu to open the Add To Log dialog box (see Figure 2.15). You can select objects from this dialog box. Click the Done button to bring up the log view with your selected objects.

FIGURE 2.15

You can log the performance statistics from another Windows NT system running SQL Server by entering its name in the Computer text box.

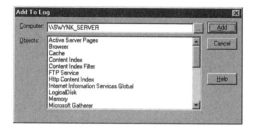

The selected objects appear in the view with all counters collected for each object. Choosing Log from the Options menu brings up the Log Option dialog box. Use this to specify the name to be given to the log file, its location, and the interval at which counters will be written to the log file. You can pause the log with the Pause button or stop it with the Stop button. Counters for the objects included in the log file are available for subsequent viewing.

Displaying and Interpreting SQL Server Events

An integrated logging tool is used on Windows NT to log information about application, system, and security operations called *events*. The Event Viewer controls the logging and subsequent display of information about all events.

The Event Viewer records the date and time of occurrence, source, type, category, ID number, username, and computer system for Windows NT and application-defined operations. You can then display these events by various categories, order, and amount of detail. Information about operations related to the use of Microsoft SQL Server is recorded primarily in the application log. It's also possible that information recorded in the system section is related to the use of SQL Server's system processes.

Events are occurrences you should know about that happen during the execution of user or system code. The events are logged in the event log file, which is enabled automatically at system startup. You can keep event logs and examine them later as printed reports. The Control Panel's Services item disables event logging.

N O T E You shouldn't disable event logging when using SQL Server. If you do, you'll lose the information recorded about database operations, which might help you correct problems later. ■

The first time you use the Event Viewer, its window displays events from the system log. As an example, the window is large enough to display one-line listings of 21 system events. The most recent event is listed first and is selected. If you've chosen Save Settings on Exit from the Options menu, the last log viewed will come up in the Event Viewer window when it's run again.

The Log menu allows you to choose from the System, Security, or Application logs to view events. For more information, see Figure 2.16.

FIGURE 2.16

Information about SQL Server events is recorded in the application log.

Date	Time	Source	Category	Event	User	Co
11/19/98	9:27:40 PM	Perflib	None	1011	N/A	
11/19/98	7:27:16 PM	MSSQLServer	Server	17055	Administrator	
11/19/98	7:27:15 PM	MSSQLServer	Server	17055	Administrator	
11/19/98	7:27:04 PM	MSSQLServer	Server	17055	Administrator	
11/19/98	7:27:02 PM	CI	CI Service	4137	N/A	
11/19/98	7:26:57 PM	SQLServerAgent	Service Control	101	N/A	
11/19/98	7:26:36 PM	MSSQLServer	Server	17055	N/A	
11/19/98	7:26:35 PM	MSSQLServer	Server	17055	N/A	
11/19/98	7:26:35 PM	MSSQLServer	Server	17055	N/A	
11/19/98	7:26:34 PM	MSSQLServer	Server	17055	N/A	
11/19/98	7:26:34 PM	MSSQLServer	Server	17055	N/A	
11/19/98	7:26:34 PM	MSSQLServer	Server	17055	N/A	
11/19/98	7:26:34 PM	MSSQLServer	Server	17055	N/A	
11/19/98	7:26:34 PM	MSSQLServer	Server	17055	N/A	
11/19/98	7:26:33 PM	MSSQLServer	Server	17055	N/A	
11/19/98	7:26:21 PM	MSSQLServer	NETLIB	19020	N/A	
11/19/98	7:26:21 PM	MSSQLServer	NETLIB	19020	N/A	
11/19/98	7:26:21 PM	MSSQLServer	NETLIB	19020	N/A	
11/19/98	7:26:20 PM	MSSQLServer	ODS	17052	N/A	
11/19/98	7:26:20 PM	MSSQLServer	ODS	17052	N/A	
11/19/98	7:26:20 PM	MSSQLServer	ODS	17052	N/A	

Configuring the Application Event Log

You should configure the application log of the Event Viewer after you install SQL Server. Choose Log Settings from the Log menu to bring up the Event Log Settings dialog box. You can set the maximum size for the log file in kilobytes, the length of time events are kept, and whether to overwrite events if the log file is full. Separate settings are kept for each of the three logs—system, security, and application. In Figure 2.17, the system log file is set to a maximum size of 512KB and events are set to be overwritten in a week.

FIGURE 2.17

Select Overwrite Events as Needed to ensure that no new events are lost at the expense of losing the oldest recorded events.

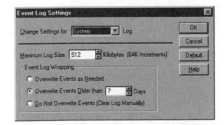

Displaying Event Details

Detail about an event can be viewed by double-clicking a selected event, or by choosing Detail from the View menu in the main windows of the Event Viewer. You must examine the detail of an event to learn the meaning of the event numbers.

The information at the top of the detail display is similar to an event line in the initial display of events. The description section of the Event Detail dialog box provides additional information about the event. Figure 2.18 shows the detail for an event from the application log.

FIGURE 2.18

If the Type field displays Information or Success, the event isn't an error but just the record of an event that occurred on the system.

For each logged event, several items of information are displayed. The items of information recorded for each event are the date, time, user, computer, event ID, source, type, and category.

You can use the information shown in Table 2.1 to help you interpret the information that's displayed in the Event Detail dialog box for events in all application logs.

Table 2.1   Item Descriptions for Logged Events

Item	Description
Event	Windows NT-assigned event number
Category	Event source; security source can be Login, Logoff, Shutdown, Use of User Rights, File, Print, Security Changes, or None
Computer	Name of computer on which error occurred
Date	Date of event
Event ID	Unique number for each source to identify event
Source	Program that was logged—for example, an application or a system component, including a driver

Item	Description
Time	Time of event
Type	Severity of error, such as Error, Warning, Information, Success, Audit, or Failure Audit displayed as an icon
User	Username when error occurred; can be blank (N/A)

Part

1

Ch

2

The Event Detail dialog box shows information about a normal stop of the SQL Server process, probably issued through the SQL Service Manager. The Type field shows an entry of Information, specifying that the event isn't an error. You can use the Description list box's scroll bar to display additional information, if any, for an event. The SQL Service Manager is discussed in Chapter 1, "Understanding Microsoft SQL Server 7.0 Fundamentals."

The last section of information in the Event Detail dialog box displays a byte dump in hexadecimal. Not all events display a dump—only those with relevant information. The information within the dump can be interpreted by someone with knowledge of the application code or the Windows NT system that caused the event. You can select the Words radio button to display the dump in words rather than bytes.

Use the Previous and Next buttons to display other events in the current log.

Using the View Menu

You can use the View menu to control other characteristics of the display of events in the main window of the Event Viewer (see Figure 2.19). For example, by default, the newest events are listed first in the window. Optionally, you can display events beginning with the oldest, rather than the most recent, listed first.

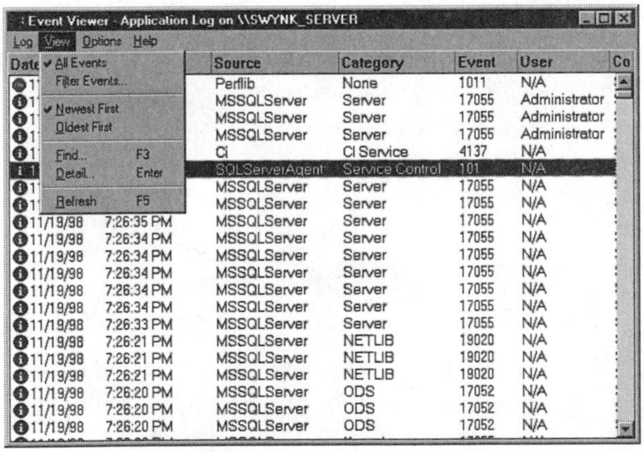

FIGURE 2.19

Choose Oldest First to reverse the order of displayed events.

Choose Find from the View menu to bring up the Find dialog box, shown in Figure 2.20. Use Find to locate events by criteria that you specify in the Find dialog box. You can enter various items for an event in the Find dialog box, including the source, category, event ID, computer, user, and any part of the description. If the event is found, the main Event Viewer window appears with the specified error selected. If the event isn't found, you see a `Search failed` error message.

FIGURE 2.20

Use the Direction radio buttons to define the direction of the search through the log.

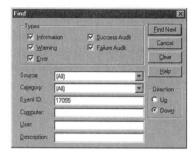

You can bring up the Filter dialog box to allow the selection of events using criteria based on one or more items of an event. You can select the events based on the date and time of all events or the first and last events of a range of dates and times. Also, you can enter the source, category, user, computer, and event ID to filter the events displayed.

By default, Information, Warning, Error, Success Audit, and Failure Audit are selected but can be deselected to restrict the events returned. Success Audit and Failure Audit are valid only for the security log.

Clearing the Event Log

Choose Clear All Events from the Log menu to empty a log file of all recorded events. If you choose Clear All Events, a precautionary dialog box appears. You can select the Cancel button to cancel the emptying of the event log.

N O T E If you look through the event log and notice transactions that are being completed when SQL Server is started, these are events that are being rolled back or rolled forward to synchronize with the point in time when the server was shut down.

This is how SQL Server maintains a consistent database in times of unexpected shutdowns. It will examine where it left off and will ensure that the databases are at the last possible point of consistency. ▧

Reality Check

During the implementation of Windows NT and the users on your system, it's easy to forget to remove or control the members in the EVERYONE group. In many implementations, this has led to unwanted access to resources on the server. Be sure to carefully review what groups your users are assigned to.

As a precaution, in my implementations, I've created a user that is representative of the rights I want to assign on a general basis. Later, when I add users to the system, I copy that original user, update the username and password, and I am assured that the user rights are appropriate. Of course in some cases you'll want to grant specific additional or lesser rights to a given user, but starting off with the copied user provides a good basis for new additions.

In addition, if you're using Remote Access Services (RAS) on your server, be sure you remove the GUEST account. If you don't, you might be opening your system to an additional means of logging in and searching through your systems. If a person calls in and logs in with an unknown username and password, that person is assigned to the GUEST account and given the corresponding rights.

From Here...

In this chapter you've learned about the characteristics of Windows NT relevant to the installation of Microsoft SQL Server. Windows NT's multithreaded design and support for multiple processors is ideally suited for an application such as SQL Server. In addition, the built-in network support of the Windows NT system makes possible a simple and straightforward connection from clients to SQL Server. Lastly, you learned that information returned by SQL Server is returned to the built-in reporting facilities of Windows NT, the Performance Monitor, and Event Viewer.

For further information on selected aspects of the topics mentioned in this chapter, you can review the following chapters:

- Chapter 21, "Optimizing Performance," teaches you how to optimize the performance of SQL Server, including the use of SQL Server–specific information returned by the Performance Monitor.
- Chapter 22, "Backward Comatibility Options for Developers," teaches you how to use client-workstation–based applications to access the server database.

CHAPTER 3

Installing and Setting Up the Server and Client Software

In this chapter

The installation of SQL Server is relatively simple and similar to the installation of other Microsoft products. In this chapter, you'll learn about the different steps and considerations to keep in mind as you set up your server system and the clients that will access it. You'll also learn the following:

- Installing the SQL Server software at the server
- Starting and stopping the server
- Installing SQL Server client utilities
- Obtaining help for SQL Server commands

Understanding Server Hardware and Software Requirements

The computer system for your SQL Server installation should be on the list of supported systems. If your system is an Intel Pentium processor or Alpha AXP, it should be 133 MHz or faster, according to Microsoft documentation. In practice, it's not recommended that you implement SQL Server in a production environment on anything less than a Pentium 200 with 32MB of RAM. Of course the faster the processor speed and more memory you have, the better the performance will be.

N O T E SQL Server 7.0 is a major advance for Microsoft and reflects the company's stance of "SQL Server everywhere." Previous versions of SQL Server would only run on Windows NT under either an Intel or Alpha processor. SQL Server 7.0 can now be run under Windows 95/98, NT Workstation, and NT Server.

The engine is exactly the same on all platforms and operates the same in all environments. The only differences in running SQL Server on different platforms are restrictions of the OS such as multiple processor support.

Also according to the documentation, you must have a minimum of 32MB of RAM for x86-based systems, although additional memory is recommended. A minimum of 32MB is suggested for a Windows NT Server system, but 64MB is more appropriate. Most RISC-based systems are usually configured with a minimum of 64MB and often are configured with 128MB of memory.

N O T E These stated minimums are just that: minimums. As you bring up systems, there are a number of factors that will impact these numbers. Be sure to pay special attention to any replication tasks you might wish to run and to the number of client systems that you'll be allowing to access the server during peak periods.

One of the biggest performance boosts you can offer in the SQL Server world is the addition of memory. This simple enhancement can improve performance by twofold or more in many cases.

These recommendations aren't unreasonable for a server system. Memory has become very inexpensive in recent years. In 1977, a quarter of a megabyte of memory for at least one manufacturer's system was priced at $17,000. Nowadays, you can buy 1MB of memory for much less than $50.

Although you might be using an Intel Pentium processor in your server system, its processing power and speed far exceed the large minicomputer systems of 10 to 15 years ago. Physically, your server might be only as large as a client system, but don't be deceived by that. ■

In addition to the processor and memory requirements, you must have SP3 and the mini service pack installed for NT systems, and be running Windows 98 or Windows 95 OSR2. You also need to have Internet Explorer 4.0 installed. Internet Explorer 4.0 is used as a plug in to the Microsoft Management Console to display information and Setup will not run unless Internet Explorer 4.0 is found on your system.

You must have at least 74MB of disk space to complete the installation. If you have only 74MB, however, you don't have any space to create additional databases. The typical install takes 163MB and a full installation requires 190MB. You should count on a minimal SQL Server installation requiring approximately 150MB to start.

You also need a CD-ROM drive to read the installation media unless you'll be installing from a network share, in which case you'll need the share name and sufficient rights to the directory containing SQL Server 7.

You don't need any additional network software because the Windows NT system contains built-in network software. You need a network interface card (NIC) that's supported by Windows NT. If you will access SQL Server directly only from the server system, without using a network for access, you don't need a NIC.

You can install SQL Server on a partition that uses either the FAT or NTFS file system. You'll probably want to take advantage of the recovery and security features of an NTFS disk partition rather than the older and simpler FAT disk system, although your installation might have considerations for other installed software that dictate this installation parameter.

N O T E If you will be installing SQL Server on an NT machine for local access, you will need to install the MS Loopback Adapter to access some of the functionality. On Windows 95/98 systems, you do not need any additional network software. ■

▶ For more information on the installation of NT Server, **see** Que's *Special Edition Using Microsoft Windows NT Server* by Roger Jennings.

Running Setup

Installing SQL Server is simple. The installation is similar to the installation of nearly all Microsoft Windows products, and it will appear familiar to you if you have installed a Windows application. If you are installing SQL Server under Windows NT, you must run the Setup program using an NT account that has Administrative privileges, such as the NT Administrator account.

Part

I

Ch

3

N O T E SQL Server 7.0 installation files for Intel systems are located under the x86 directory. The install files for Alpha systems are located under the Alpha directory. ■

To perform the installation, follow these steps:

1. Insert the CD.

2. If you do not have autorun enabled, you will need to perform this step. Type the drive letter of your CD drive, followed by **autorun** in the Run combo list box.

   The Setup program displays one or more message boxes after checking whether you are working from an Administrative account and whether SQL Server already is installed. Figure 3.1 shows the Welcome dialog box that appears when the SQL Server setup program is invoked.

FIGURE 3.1

The Microsoft SQL Server 7.0 installation screen.

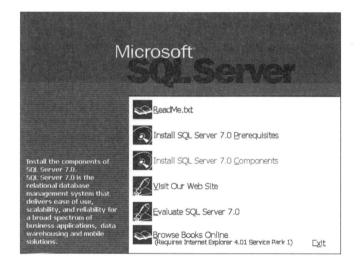

3. When you select Install SQL Server Components, you are presented with a dialog to install the Server, Decision Support Services, or English Query.

N O T E SQL Server 7.0 is looked at as an upgrade. Once you have installed and begun to explore the functionality outlined in this book, you will quickly understand that 7.0 is really an entirely new product that has many similarities to previous versions of SQL Server.

SQL Server 7.0 now includes services for decision support tools. These services are targeted at the OLAP (Online Analytical Processing) and data mining markets. These services promise to bring OLAP into the mainstream with their tight integration into Excel's Pivot Table technology. Installing the Decision Support Services requires a minimum of 64MB of RAM and 80MB of disk space. If you are installing them on a Windows 95 machine, you will also need to have DCOM95 installed.

English Query provides the user with the capability to construct and submit queries to SQL Server using plain English. English Query requires an additional 12MB of hard disk space. ■

4. When you select the Database Server option, you will have the option to select the appropriate SQL Server installation for your OS.

N O T E The Desktop edition is for Windows NT Workstation and Windows 95/98. The Standard edition is for Windows NT Server. The Enterprise edition is for Windows NT Enterprise Edition. ■

5. The actual installation program will be launched at this point. If you have ever installed a Microsoft product before, this will be very familiar. You will enter your name, company name, serial number, and agree to the license. You will then be presented with the familiar Typical, Minimum, and Custom options.

N O T E If you want to utilize the Full-Text Search capability, you must select a Custom install. ■

Part
I

Ch
3

Figure 3.2 shows the selection screen where you choose the components and sub-components that you want to include on the custom installation.

FIGURE 3.2
Specifying installation components from a custom setup.

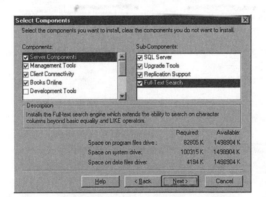

6. When you select Next, setup will copy the installation files to your system. When the files have been copied, you will be prompted to select the character set, sort order, and unicode collation as shown in Figure 3.3. If you're upgrading a previous installation of SQL Server, this information will be retained from the prior installation and you'll not be prompted for it here.

CAUTION

If you later must change your character set or sort order, you will have to rebuild the master database, so be sure you select carefully. Unless you have a compelling reason to do otherwise, you will typically select the Case-Insensitive option.

FIGURE 3.3

Selecting the character set, sort order, and unicode collation sequence.

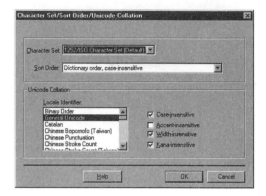

 TIP If you do need to reset the sort order, character set or unicode collation for your database, you'll need to rebuild your database and indicate the new options. When you do, the database will be reloaded with the new settings.

To rebuild the database, run `rebuildm.exe` from the `mssql7\binn` directory. Select the Settings button and you'll be presented with the same dialog box as above, letting you change the settings accordingly.

This should be a last-resort—select your options carefully on installation and avoid this process if at all possible.

7. Clicking the Next button displays the Network Libraries dialog box, shown in Figure 3.4, enabling you to define additional network support.

FIGURE 3.4

Selecting network library support

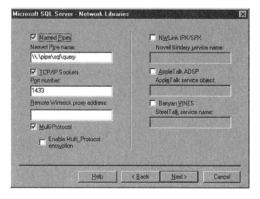

8. Click the Next button to go to the Services dialog box. You can run all Services under one account or specify an NT account for each service as shown in Figure 3.5.

FIGURE 3.5

If you are using an account other than LocalSystem, you should enter a password for the SQL Executive Service account that contains at least eight characters.

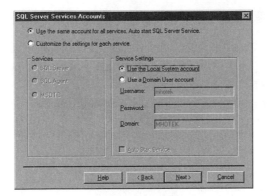

N O T E If you are running SQL Server under Windows 95/98, you will not see this Services dialog because services are not available under these two OSes. For NT systems, you must select the Customize the Settings for Each Service option if you want to specify each service to start automatically. If you do not, the Microsoft Distributed Transaction Coordinator (DTC) and SQL Agent services will be added as a manual startup. ■

T I P It's a good idea to use a separate NT account for this service rather than share the NT Administrator account. If you later change the NT Administrator account, or change the password associated with the account without realizing it's being used by the SQL Executive Service, the Executive Service will be unable to start.

9. Click Next. A File Copy in Progress dialog box appears, showing the progress of server files as they're copied from the distribution. As the installation proceeds, additional feedback is displayed on your monitor telling you that SQL Server is installing SQL Server.

After you have indicated the different setup options, the process will complete without further intervention. When the installation is completed successfully, click Reboot if you want to begin using SQL Server, otherwise SQL Server will start the next time your system is restarted.

N O T E Remember to manually start the SQL Server services after you reboot if you haven't defined automatic SQL Server startup, otherwise the service won't be started and you won't be able to log in to start working with it.

If you are running SQL Server under Windows 95/98, you must manually start SQL Server. For more information, see "Starting SQL Server with SQL Service Manager" later in this chapter. ■

Starting the Server

You have several options available for starting SQL Server on the system. You can configure the SQL Server services system to start automatically each time the Windows NT system is

Part

I

Ch

3

booted. You also can use the SQL Service Manager to start the SQL Server services. Several Windows application tools can optionally start SQL Server when the applications try to connect to the server. Finally, the server can be started using a command line.

Using Automatic Service Startup

You can enable the automatic startup of SQL Server each time the Windows NT system is started. To start up SQL Server each time the server is booted, select the Auto Start SQL Server at Boot Time check box in the Installation Options dialog box. This is shown above in Figure 3.5. You also can define an automatic startup for SQL Server after installation.

If you don't define SQL Server processes to automatically start up, you can later change it to automatic by using the Control Panel's Services option.

1. Open the Control Panel.
2. Double-click Services.
3. In the Services dialog box, scroll down the Service list box to find MSSQLServer.
4. Select MSSQLServer. The Startup should be Manual. A manual service isn't automatically started.
5. Click Startup to open the Service dialog box. See Figure 3.6.

FIGURE 3.6

You can change the Windows NT account that a service uses through the Service dialog box.

6. In the Startup Type section, select Automatic.

   You can also specify that the MSSQLServer process created by the automatic startup of the service uses an account other than the Administrator system account. If you use another account, you must specify the Password Never Expires characteristic in the NT Server's User Manager utility. You don't have to specify a different account from the system account for SQL Server.

> **CAUTION**
>
> It's very important that you consider your future uses for SQL Server as you install it with regard to user identities for the SQL processes.

If you're using, or will be using in the future, the email capabilities of SQL Server and the post office resides on a Novell server, you won't be able to access the mail system unless you establish a separate account for SQL Server.

SQL Server is also required to run under an account with Administrator privileges.

7. Click OK in the Service dialog box. The MSSQLServer Startup column should have changed from Manual to Automatic.

8. If you want to immediately start SQL Server, click Start. A message box appears, telling you that SQL Server is starting. If the SQL Server service is successfully started, Started is added in the Status column of the Services dialog box for the SQL Server service.

9. Click Close.

Starting SQL Server with SQL Service Manager

You can use the SQL Service Manager to start MSSQLServer. To start MSSQLServer by using the SQL Service Manager, follow these steps:

1. Click the Service Manager icon in the SQL Server 7.0 program group.

2. Click Start/Continue or double-click the green light.

   The status message at the bottom of the SQL Service Manager dialog box should change from Stopped to Starting. After SQL Server is started, the message changes to Running.

3. Either Close the Service Manager or minimize it to an icon. Note that, even if you close the Service Manager, SQL Server will continue running.

If you leave the Server Service Manager minimized, you can easily Stop or Pause SQL Server as needed.

Starting SQL Server Through Windows Applications

You can optionally start up SQL Server when you connect to the server locally from the server or remotely from a client system. For example, a client-side version of the Service Manager can be invoked from the toolbar of the SQL Enterprise Manager, allowing you to start and stop the server engine.

Starting SQL Server Through a Command Line

To start up SQL Server using a command line, follow these steps:

1. Open a command prompt and change to the Binn directory under your SQL Server directory structure (typically MSSQL7).

2. At the command prompt, enter this command line:

```
sqlservr -d drive:\directory\data\master.mdf
```

Part

I

Ch

3

Use -d to specify the name of the SQL Server master database.

drive is the drive letter you entered in the Drive text box of the SQL Server Installation Path dialog box. *directory* is the directory you entered in the Directory text box of the same dialog box. The default for the directory is mssql7 and the default for the drive is C.

Master.mdf is the name of the data file that's the SQL Server master database.

N O T E The sqlservr command line actually starts two system processes, both of which can have multiple threads. ▪

Installing the Client Software

Many of the SQL Server utilities that you use to manage the server, issue queries against it, and develop and debug your applications are available not only as server-based applications, but also client-side applications. The utilities installed will vary depending on the client environment you are installing into. All of the SQL Server tools that are available with 7.0 are 32-bit. If you're using a 16-bit client, such as Windows for Workgroups, you will only be able to configure the client connection and install any connectivity software.

N O T E If you are still running 16-bit clients, it is highly recommended that you upgrade to a 32-bit OS. ▪

Steps to Installing the SQL Server Client Utilities

To start Setup, select the processor subdirectory that corresponds to your system on the CD. It's most likely that you will be installing using the i386 subdirectory. This corresponds to the 32-bit installation of the utilities.

N O T E To avoid conflicts with system files, you should exit all other software applications prior to running the Setup program. If you don't, you might receive an error message as the files are copied to your system. This error message will prevent you from completing the installation successfully. Pay special attention to less-obvious applications such as the Office toolbar or other applications that run in the background. When in doubt, use the Windows Task Manager to verify the processes that are active on your system. ▪

Here are the steps to installing the software:

- ▪ Start SETUP.EXE to begin.
- ▪ Follow the steps outlined above, but only select the management utilities from the custom setup.

T I P   SQL Server 6.5 utilities can peacefully coexist with the 7.0 utilities as long as they are installed in separate directories. It is recommended that you uninstall these utilities because the 7.0 tools can connect to and manage previous versions of SQL Server.

■ You will be prompted to specify the utilities you want to install. Your control over the installation is complete, allowing you to fine-tune your requirements based on disk space constraints or your need for a specific utility.

■ The final phases of installation are automatic. The setup program will copy the routines to your system and update your system files.

■ At the end of the routine, you will be prompted to reboot the system, which will complete the process.

Once completed, you will be able to use the client workstation to administer, inquire into, and manage the different aspects of your SQL Server system.

From Here...

In this chapter you learned about the different options you have for installing the software on your systems, from both the client and server points of view. For more information about these and other related topics, please see the following chapters:

■ Chapter 2, "Understanding the Underlying Operating System, Windows NT," contains information about how to set up the operating system portion of your server. This will integrate into your selections for where and how to install SQL Server on your system.

■ Chapter 19, "SQL Server Administration," covers the different tasks you need to consider as you work with your server. These include backing up the system and more.

■ Chapter 20, "SQL Server Security," goes into the details of securing your server and controlling access to the objects in your databases.

Data Modeling and Database Design

Chances are good that when you started learning about development in the programming world, you began with flowcharting. Flowcharts are a great tool for diagramming programmatic flow and for laying out the different components of your system. The purpose is to discover flaws in logic and missing functionality before coding, rather than later during the cycle.

The reality is that flowcharts are rarely done. How many times have you been in a crunch to pull one together for a project, but waited until after the project was done to do the flowchart? This happens more often than any of us would like to admit. It's easy to pull it together after the fact because you already know what you've designed into the program, and you're not going to flowchart something you opted not to include in the application. It's a pretty safe way to approach things, provided you've reviewed the program along the way to ensure that the functionality meets the needs of your customer.

Database design isn't as open to modification along the way. Because changing a database table after the fact alters the foundation for all other parts of the system, even in subtle ways, it often requires major overhaul work in the balance of the system. A simple change to a table can mean that entire portions of the application will stop functioning.

The most important thing you can probably do when you bring up a database-oriented system is to diagram and design the database structure that will support the application. If you don't do this, you'll end up making some subtle—and often not-so-subtle—changes to the structure later, probably at a time when the changes are far more expensive in the development cycle.

N O T E The terminology surrounding computers must always be changing, it's a rule of the road. To that end, n-tier architecture is now referred to as either 3-tier or n-tier architecture. You'll see the terms used interchangeably, but in reality the n-tier is much more descriptive.

With the development of smarter client software, and the use of middle-ware, it's possible to have more than just two computing partners in a given solution, as is typically the case with n-tier. With the term "n-tier," you can more directly state that you're looking for a 3-tier system, 4-tier system, and so on. It's simply more descriptive. ▪

When you decide to develop a system based on Microsoft SQL Server, you've taken the first step toward implementing two separate architectures in your software. These are n-tier and relational database tables. Both are powerful if used correctly, and present a real-life advantage to your system, if you take time to pay attention to the rules along the way.

This chapter introduces you to those rules. The theory and practice that make up a n-tier system, including how you can determine the best location for a given piece of functionality to be implemented, guidelines for breaking apart procedural flow, and much more will be included.

Because the decision to move to n-tier depends heavily on the flow of the application and where things are physically being completed, SQL Server provides an ideal component to provide server-side functionality to bring n-tier to your applications. It's important to understand what pieces of the database design will dovetail into your desires to move to the n-tier world.

Understanding the Basics: Normalization

When you start working with relational databases, you inevitably end up hearing about data normalization and bringing things into third normal form. *Normalization* refers to how you implement the relationships and storage of data in your database tables. When you normalize a table, you try to limit the redundant data in the table. Many different levels, or types, of normalization exist, and a brief overview here will help you start.

Your overall goal is likely a 3NF, or *third normal form,* database. In most cases, this will be the best compromise between extremes when it comes to normalization versus functionality and ease of implementation. There are levels beyond 3NF but, in practice, they can begin to cloud the database design with more design issues than functional issues.

When you delve into the world of normalized databases, you are, by definition, starting down the road of relational databases. Before normalized databases, structures used a series of pointers to retain relationships between different tables and values. You might recall implementing linked lists, where each row in a database table contains a pointer to both the next and previous rows. To traverse the database, you simply walked up and down this list of links between records.

In the relational world, you define columns that relate to each other among tables. These columns are keys to other values. *Keys* are used to uniquely define a relationship to another instance or set of information. This chapter will get into more about keys as you work with the definitions of the different normalization levels.

What's in a Name?

A key difference between SQL Server-type database implementations and other more traditional PC-based databases is the terminology used to describe the databases and their information.
Databases contain one or more tables, and tables contain one or more columns of information.
For each table of columns, one or more rows may exist.

In more traditional terms, there was no concept of a database as in SQL Server. Instead, you had a file that contained records of fields. The following table shows a basic comparison of terms between a SQL Server implementation and a more traditional database, such as Btrieve or dBASE.

New Term	Old Term
Database	File
Table	N/A
Column	Field
Row	Record

You'll need to keep these terms in mind and, if you use the newer terms in describing the tables you're designing, you can avoid problems with ambiguity between developers and designers.

With relational databases, you don't use ordered, or sorted, rows. You use real-time statements, those that are evaluated when they are called or issued, to control the presentation of the information. You also use joins and views to control how information is retrieved, rather than trying to store the information in the most advantageous format possible at the outset. This enables more dynamic access to the information in the database tables. It also lets you simply store the information, and then retrieve it in any manner you like.

The next few sections look at the different types of normalization through the third normal form.

First Normal Form

In first normal form, or 1NF, the foundation for the relational system is put into place. In 1NF, you don't have multiple values represented in any single column. In database terms, this means that each value in the database table is *atomic*, or represented only once.

In the past you may have implemented a database schema that, for example, stored the item code for each item ordered with the order record, such as in a point of sale system. Later, when your program queried the order, it retrieved and parsed this field and could determine what was ordered with that order record. Figure 4.1 shows an example of this. You had the opportunity to store one or more item numbers with the order record.

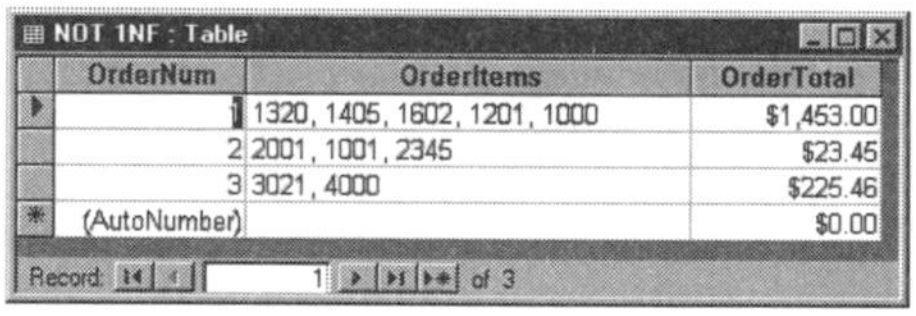

FIGURE 4.1

Without 1NF, you could store more than one logical item in a physical record. This isn't valid when you normalize your database.

OrderNum	OrderItems	OrderTotal
1	1320, 1405, 1602, 1201, 1000	$1,453.00
2	2001, 1001, 2345	$23.45
3	3021, 4000	$225.46
(AutoNumber)		$0.00

N O T E   These examples were created using Microsoft Access working with SQL Server because it's a good tool for creating tables quickly and easily. The tool you use is entirely up to you. The SQL Enterprise Manager, although a bit less visual, will still serve your purposes well. You'll also want to take a look at the end of this chapter and consider one or more of the database tools to help the process of creating tables and relationships. ■

With 1NF, duplicates aren't allowed. You need to create a schema that only records one item for each order record on file. To implement the point-of-sale solution mentioned earlier, you must have an order represented by one to *n* records containing the item code information that made up the order. This provides a slightly different challenge to retrieve the information for the record. You must have a means of retrieving each record associated with the order and making sure that you've retrieved each record, but no more or less. Of course, this will lead to order numbers, called out in each record. Later in this chapter, database design and entity relationship models will be covered. Figure 4.2 shows the results of this first pass at normalizing a database table.

FIGURE 4.2
With a 1NF table, each row is a single, atomic record. It must be able to stand alone.

1NF : Table

OrderNum	OrderItem	Description
1	1320	Milk
1	1405	Cookies
1	1602	Bread - French
1	1201	Bread - Italian
1	1000	Bread - American
2	2001	Cheese
2	1001	Bread - Swedish
2	2345	Bologna
3	3021	Paper Towels
3	4000	Eggs
0		

Record: 1 of 10

For now, simply remember that with 1NF, you must have each row contain only one instance of the information, and all column values must be atomic.

Second Normal Form

The first requirement for second normal form, or 2NF, is that it fulfills the requirements of 1NF. The second requirement is that each instance or row in the database table must be uniquely identifiable. To do this, you must often add a unique ID to each row. In the preceding example, when you broke apart the orders table, it first looks as though the structure fits this rule. You have, after all, instituted an order ID, and if you combine the order ID and the item code, you'd have a unique handle on the row, right? Wrong.

You could conceivably have a single order with more than one instance of an item. Consider when you go grocery shopping and buy your milk for the week. It's easy to see that you'd be buying multiple half-gallons of milk on the same order.

You'll need to add an OrderItemID column to the table to fulfill the requirements for 2NF (see Figure 4.3). You'll keep the OrderNum, but the OrderItemID will be the primary unique identifier for the item in a given row.

FIGURE 4.3
When you add a unique row ID for each line item, this table now fits the 2NF model.

2NF : Table

OrderItemID	OrderNum	OrderItem	Description
1	1	1320	Milk
2	1	1405	Cookies
3	1	1602	Bread - French
4	1	1201	Bread - Italian
5	1	1000	Bread - American
11	1	1320	Milk
6	2	2001	Cheese
7	2	1001	Bread - Swedish
8	2	2345	Bologna
9	3	3021	Paper Towels
10	3	4000	Eggs
(AutoNumber)	0		

Record: 1 of 11

NOTE Notice that, although a new item has been added as item 11, it can still be related back to the order based on the order number. A new way to uniquely identify the row within the table is the only thing that has been changed. ■

Third Normal Form

Third normal form, or 3NF, is really a lifesaver for the developer. All the work to normalize your database tables really pays off when you move to the 3NF model. As with 2NF reliance on first being compliant with 1NF, 3NF requires that you also be compliant with the 2NF model. In short, when you have a table that's in 3NF, you won't have redundant non-key information in your table that relies on non-key information in another table.

That's a strange definition until you understand what's really happening here. The whole goal of normalizing your tables is to remove redundant, non-key information in your tables. Reviewing Figure 4.3, you'll quickly see that this model is broken quite nicely. Because you're storing descriptions in the table, and because these descriptions are probably used elsewhere in the database, storing them individually in the table is a problem.

Here's where you start to see the real advantages of moving to 3NF. Remember, the simple examples that 'I'm using here relate to a grocery store. Imagine if you were storing your information as shown in Figure 4.3, and that you needed to change the description of ""Milk" to "Milk 2%" because your vendor has maliciously introduced "Milk 1%" to the mix. You'd need to write a utility to update the sales database tables and any other table that ever referenced "Milk" to show the correct percentage. Inconsistent information in the database is a real nightmare that will often lead to problems. Forgetting about just one table that needed to be updated can completely invalidate your use of the item "Milk" for sales history.

Normalization is the key to taking care of this problem. In Figure 4.4, it is corrected quite simply by removing the description from the table altogether.

FIGURE 4.4

To fit the 3NF model, the description column is removed from the Order Items table.

OrderItemID	OrderNum	OrderItem
1	1	1320
2	1	1405
3	1	1602
4	1	1201
5	1	1000
6	2	2001
7	2	1001
8	2	2345
9	3	3021
10	3	4000
11	1	1320
(AutoNumber)	0	0

Record: 1 of 11

Because an item code is already assigned to Milk, you have the information you need to set up the Inventory table shown in Figure 4.5.

Of course, after you've begun normalizing your table, it brings to mind the question of how to get a complete picture of the item sold. How can you find out all the information about the line item, what its description is, the sale price, and so forth? This is where relational databases and their use of Views come into play. In the example, you can create a query that returns the information you need quickly and easily. Figure 4.6 shows what a sample view returns to your application for the sample table.

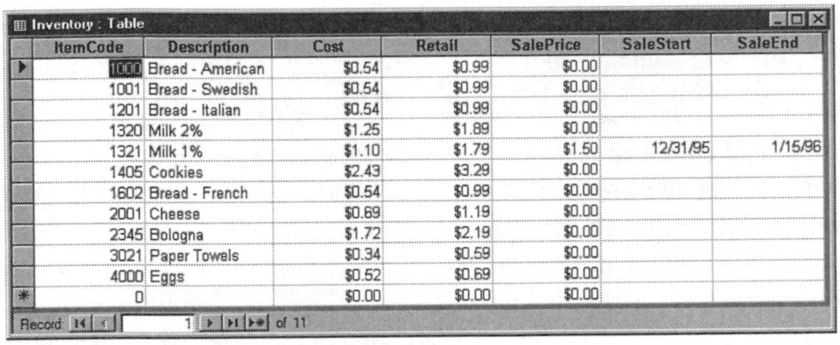

FIGURE 4.5

By creating an Inventory table, you create a "home base" to refer to and use any time you reference inventory items.

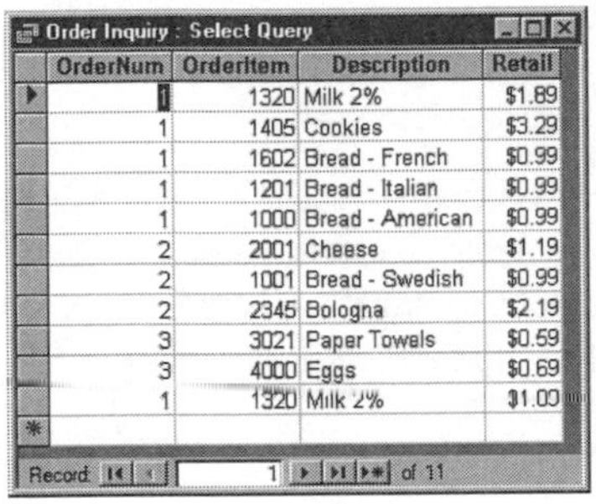

ItemCode	Description	Cost	Retail	SalePrice	SaleStart	SaleEnd
1000	Bread - American	$0.54	$0.99	$0.00		
1001	Bread - Swedish	$0.54	$0.99	$0.00		
1201	Bread - Italian	$0.54	$0.99	$0.00		
1320	Milk 2%	$1.25	$1.89	$0.00		
1321	Milk 1%	$1.10	$1.79	$1.50	12/31/95	1/15/96
1405	Cookies	$2.43	$3.29	$0.00		
1602	Bread - French	$0.54	$0.99	$0.00		
2001	Cheese	$0.69	$1.19	$0.00		
2345	Bologna	$1.72	$2.19	$0.00		
3021	Paper Towels	$0.34	$0.59	$0.00		
4000	Eggs	$0.52	$0.69	$0.00		
0		$0.00	$0.00	$0.00		

Record [◄][◄] 1 [►][►►][►*] of 11

FIGURE 4.6

When you create a relational view of the database tables, you can retrieve and work with a complete picture of the information even if it is dispersed across several tables.

OrderNum	OrderItem	Description	Retail
1	1320	Milk 2%	$1.89
1	1405	Cookies	$3.29
1	1602	Bread - French	$0.99
1	1201	Bread - Italian	$0.99
1	1000	Bread - American	$0.99
2	2001	Cheese	$1.19
2	1001	Bread - Swedish	$0.99
2	2345	Bologna	$2.19
3	3021	Paper Towels	$0.59
3	4000	Eggs	$0.69
1	1320	Milk 2%	$1.00

Record [◄][◄] 1 [►][►►][►*] of 11

▶ See Chapter 7, "Retrieving Data with Transact-SQL," **p. 155**, for more information

▶ See Chapter 10, "Managing and Using Views," **p. 257**, for more information.

You can see that by using the combined information between the tables, you still have the same full data set to work with, but, at the same time, are limiting the sources of information. You'll find quite often that the way you end up working with the information might not change. Only the methods used behind the scenes to retrieve that information change. This is the case with the 3NF table in this example. You're still storing the same information base. You're just retrieving the information using a different means, which, in this case, is a logical view of the two related tables.

Understanding the N-tier Model

Before you start designing your database, you'll need to understand where the functional components of your system will reside. It's important to understand where data manipulation is done, and what should be stored in the database versus what should be calculated or determined on the fly.

With SQL Server, you can implement true n-tier systems. This means that these systems can adhere to the concepts of n-tier, allowing you to divide functional components into cooperative operations that accomplish your application's goal. This sounds strange, but what it amounts to is dividing processing between the client and server in a way that makes sense to the application. With database-oriented systems, especially those with a database subsystem open and

Part
I

Ch
4

accessible from many different points, it makes sense to implement an intelligent database layer that will manage the data. This layer is responsible only for storage and inquiries as they relate to the information. It has no responsibility for the presentation of information.

In the next couple of sections, you'll review what types of functions and operations reside in the client/server sides of the n-tier model. Although these concepts aren't exhaustive, you need to understand them. For many people, n-tier is just a fancy term for a PC database that resides in a common location and is accessed by many different workstations. After reading this chapter, you should understand that n-tier is much more than a common storage location. You can't create an n-tier system by using Microsoft Access database tables, for example, regardless of whether the tables are stored on a file server or a local system because no intelligent engine can process the database independently of your application. The logic controlling the data is still driven by your client-side application.

N O T E   You can create Access-based n-tier systems by creating linked or attached tables to an Access system. These tables can be based in a server-based intelligent database system and will help you create an n-tier system in Access. By saying that Access database tables aren't n-tier, I refer only to the native Access database tables, typically contained in physical files with an .MDB extension. ∎

Typical Roles: The Client Side

Client-side applications are responsible for displaying information to users, manipulating information in the database and on the user display, reports, and user-interruptible operations. This means that any operation you submit to the server component of your system should never require intervention by users in order to complete the operation.

The client application will typically be written in a host language. These languages are often Delphi, PowerBuilder, Visual Basic, C, or C++. These applications allow users to perform add, change, and delete operations against the database, where applicable.

The client application should avoid, at nearly any cost, having to work with the entire database table's contents. When a set of information is worked with, you should always think of it as a *results set*, not the entire data set available to you. Results sets indicate that you should ask the server application to filter and limit the information that will be presented to you so that the operations you carry out are completed against as small a set of information as possible.

One of the best comparisons of an older system to n-tier is that of a file cabinet versus a folder. In older systems, you'd typically be doing the equivalent of asking for a file cabinet full of information and taking the time to sift through the all the contents to find the file you want. In this scenario, your client-side application is the piece doing the sifting. All information from the database table is passed through the client, and the client does the filtering to find the information you want to work with.

In the n-tier world, you simply request the file folder you want, and it is returned. You don't filter through the file cabinet, the server process does. This limits network traffic because only the results set is passed back over the network. The other very significant benefit of this is that it also increases performance for your application. Typically, server systems are powerful computing platforms. Because this optimized server platform can work with all information locally, it can do so at top speed. It will be processing the information at the highest rate possible.

In short, your client-side application should be optimized to work with the results sets. This works hand in hand with database structure and design because you need to make sure that you create the database in such a way that it can support this requirement. You'll have to define the joins, queries, stored procedures, and table structures to support this optimized query into the contents of the database.

In summary, here are some guidelines for the client side of your application:

- It should gather all needed information before making a request of the server.
- The client is responsible for all data display to the user.
- The client should work with results sets rather than tables.
- The client should do all data-manipulation operations.
- The client provides for all formatting of data and information presentation in reports.

Typical Roles: The Server Side

The server side of the n-tier equation is typically task-oriented. This means that operations are broken into logical components. This is now taking place with Microsoft's BackOffice offerings. There are now server-side components that control mainframe connectivity with the SNA, or Systems Network Architecture, Server, database access with SQL Server, electronic mail with the Exchange Server, Internet and intranet access with Internet Information Server, and more products on the horizon that will continue in this vein.

With SQL Server, your goal is to create the results sets required by the client-side applications. The database engine will be responsible for carrying out the information storage, update, and retrieval in the system. When you first start working with SQL Server, you'll notice that it has no user interface (UI) at all. Utilities are available to help you manage it, but SQL Server in and of itself has no UI. This is by design. SQL Server exists to fulfill requests made of it by returning the results from those requests. Unlike Access, dBASE, FoxPro, and others like them, SQL Server has no involvement in showing users the results of these queries.

When you're designing your database structures, you need to keep a very close eye on how you implement informational control in your system. For example, it might be that different people will need different access levels to the information. Security should be a major issue in querying of the database. Your table structures and joins need to reflect this requirement.

▶ **See** Chapter 20, "SQL Server Security," **p. 519**, for additional information about security considerations for your system.

You'll also need to keep in mind how users are going to be accessing your information. Remember that in today's world of open systems, new challenges exist in presenting and controlling

Part

I

Ch

4

information. As you create your database tables and the rules that govern them, you should assume absolutely nothing about the client side of the application. A good question to ask yourself is, "When I receive this information, what needs to happen with it?" You can answer it by saying, "It needs to be stored for later retrieval."

If you're storing sales information, you should validate the item code being sold. Does it exist in the inventory database? Is sufficient stock on hand to sell this item? Do you force sufficient stock levels, or do you allow a "negative stock" situation to occur and simply log the discrepancy in a suspected transactions table?

Each issue requires work on the database side through rules and triggers which let you define functionality that is carried out automatically by the server based on database values. It's true that you could expect the client application to complete these tasks, but what if someone is accessing your database from Excel or Word? Can you really assume that they've made sure that these checks are taking place? These important issues should be carried out by the server to make sure that they happen, regardless of the point of entry.

▶ For additional information about rules and triggers, **see** Chapter 15, "Creating and Managing Triggers," **p. 395** and Chapter 13, "Managing and Using Rules, Constraints, and Defaults," **p. 333**

Exceptions to the Rules and Roles

There are exceptions to any rule, and the n-tier model is certainly subject to this fact. There might be times when you need to do more processing on the client, or cases on the server when you want to blindly store information received. You'll need to address these on a case-by-case basis, but keep in mind that the n-tier model is there to help and guide your efforts. Always be very cautious when developing systems that fall outside the model because more often than not, you'll be asking for trouble.

It might seem like the right thing to do when you're implementing that really intricate trigger or rule, but a caution is in order: it can become a nightmare trying to move too much functionality into the wrong side of the client/server model. Think long and hard about other ways you can implement something if you find yourself putting into place an operation that breaks the n-tier model. You'll be glad you did.

Establishing a Roadmap to Your Database

Earlier it was mentioned that one way you could best go about designing your database is to diagram it and work out the relationships between tables on paper first. This helps point out any flaws in the different points of information that you might need to be able to extract from the system.

Database flowcharts consist of *entity relationship diagrams*, or ERDs. ERDs show exactly how a database is structured, what the relationships are between the tables, what rules and triggers are involved in maintaining referential integrity, and so forth. One big benefit of the ERD is that you can sit down with the client and take a logical walk through the database, making sure that the system serves the client's needs.

N O T E It's beyond the scope of this book to provide an all-encompassing view of the intricacies of entity relationship diagramming. The information and approach provided here is meant to fit 90 percent of the cases you will encounter. In some cases, you'll need to implement slightly different or less frequently used facets of the ERD systems. In those cases, you'll be best served by consulting the capabilities of your design software and database back end, the resources available on the Internet, and other sources of information on ERD. ■

Entity Relationship Diagramming: The Flowcharts of the Database World

Drawings of entity relationships include several different objects, such as entities, attributes, and relationships. There are specific ways to depict each aspect of your system. In Figure 4.7, you can see what a basic diagram for the point-of-sale system that you've been working with in the examples would look like.

FIGURE 4.7
This figure shows a relational diagram for the grocery sales system.

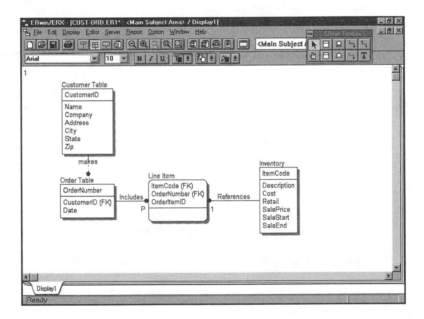

The customer table was added to be able to track an order for a customer, but apart from this addition, the table structure reflects the earlier tables and relationships. Take a look at how these basic objects (the entities, attributes, and relationships) apply to the simple model.

Using and Referencing Entities There are four boxes in Figure 4.8. Each box represents a table, or entity. These entities will become the tables in the database, and each box includes the columns that will be created for the table. Each entity's object has two sections, with a portion shown above the dividing line and a portion below it.

Part

I

Ch

4

Pg 302

FIGURE 4.8

The basic entity is represented by a box that typically contains two sections.

Attributes (Column Elements)
- NON-KEY
- KEY
  - non-primary
  - Primary

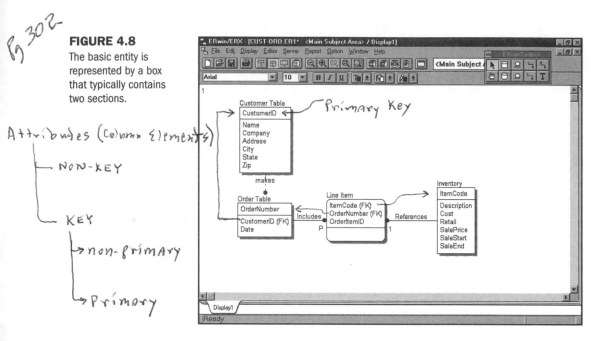

 TIP When you name entities, you should always make the name singular. It will help reinforce the fact that they contain only one instance of the object they represent.

The portion above the dividing line represents the identifying portion of the row. Remember, to have a normalized database in 3NF, you need to be able to uniquely identify each row instance in the database table. By placing the identifying characteristics above the line, it's easy to read and determine how the record will be retrieved in most cases.

In Figure 4.8, you can see that, by the definition for the customer table, you'll most likely be retrieving records from it by using the CustomerID.

N O T E Although this identifier might usually retrieve a record, it's not an exclusive handle to the row. In most systems you'll need to provide other avenues to retrieve rows. On the customer table, for example, it's likely that you'll need to implement some name searches. These searches wouldn't include the CustomerID, but after you found the customer the user wanted to work with, you'd likely retrieve the CustomerID for the selection and then retrieve the entire customer record that was selected. ■

Using and Referencing Attributes   Attributes go hand in hand with the entity object. *Attribute* is the term for the different column elements that make up the entity object, the table in the database. Attributes for the Customer table include the CustomerID, Name, Company, and so forth. Attributes are described as *key* or *non-key.*

As the name implies, non-key attributes are those items that make up the entity that don't depend on any other entity. In other words, they don't make up, nor are they a part of, a key that's used in the entity.

Key attributes come in two different types: primary and non-primary. Primary keys are always shown above the line, indicating that they're identifying attributes for this entity. If the attribute is a key to the entity but not a part of the identifying structure for the entity, it's placed below the line.

If an item refers to a key value in another table, it's known as a *foreign key*. Again, if you reference the basic model, shown in Figure 4.9, you can see that the Customer table doesn't have any foreign-key segments, but the Order table does, as indicated by the "(FK)." The foreign keys in the Order table are non-identifying, but help designate what customer the order refers to.

FIGURE 4.9

The basic ERD shows foreign keys as primary (identifying) and non-primary (non-identifying) columns in the sample tables.

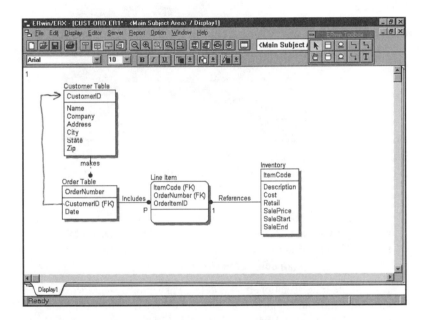

Moving from the Order table to the Line Item table, you'll see that the OrderNumber is listed as an identifying component of the Line Item table. This means that to find a specific instance of an order line item, you need to know the OrderItemID, the ItemCode, and the OrderNumber. In this implementation, the Line Item table is an associative table between the Inventory table and the Order table.

Using and Referencing Relationships If a "proof-is-in-the-pudding" segment to database design ever existed, it's in the relationships that you define between the different entities. It's easiest and most descriptive to look to your database ERDs to tell a story, in plain English, about what's happening in the database. Referring to Figure 4.9, you can see verbs between the entities. These verbs describe the relationships between the two entities and are also indicated by the relationship line between them.

A customer makes orders in the Order table, and an order includes line items that reference inventory items. You can also read the diagram in the other direction. For example, you could also say that inventory items are referenced by line items. In any event, you should be able to show concise paths for information to follow when trying to reach an end result.

In the examples, I'm using ER*win* by Logic Works. This tool enables you to define the different objects and then place the relationships between the objects appropriately. In the relationship between the Customer and Order tables, Figure 4.10 shows that the relationship is non-identifying and that the relationship is a zero, one, or more relationship.

FIGURE 4.10

ERwin enables you to easily define the relationship between the Customer and Order tables.

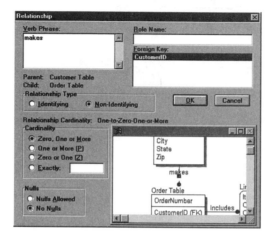

You can also see that the key in the Order table that will be used to retrieve the customer information is CustomerID. It's automatically added to the Order table, to the non-key portion of the record. If you define an identifying relationship, CustomerID will be moved to the top portion, or identifying key portion, of the Order table entity.

Each of the other relationships is defined in a similar manner. You can walk down the table structure and determine exactly how the different entities will interact. The next couple of sections look at a methodology that will guide you through the design process with the customer.

System Architecture Definition

There are several steps to creating a solid definition for a database structure. In many cases it's possible to point to flaws in the database design, only to realize that if the customer were more involved in the process, the problem could have been avoided.

When bringing a customer up to speed, terminology, methodology, and approach aren't the goal of client reviews. The goal of any system you'll endeavor to write is making sure that the database structure will support the functionality of the system. This is where the old maxim of "Determine the output first, the input will follow" comes to bear on a project. It's certainly true that the test of any system is the output. If you've created the best system ever devised to enable input of information, it's a sure bet that if you don't have a way to get meaningful information out of the system, your time has been all but wasted.

Review the User's Goals for the System

The first thing you need to do is decide what you'll be providing for the customer. It's probably safe to say that reports and output are nearly always a developer's least favorite part of a system to develop and implement. Often, one of the first statements made to the customer is, "We'll give you reporting tools to create your own reports. All we need to do now is figure out what needs to happen in the program." This is a formula for problems.

If you didn't know that the users needed to have an aging report from their point-of-sale system's accounts receivable subsystem, would you automatically store the date that the original invoice went out?

N O T E It might seem that involving the user only prolongs the development process. Many studies, and my personal experience, have shown that it's not the case. Spending the time now pays off many times over later in the project in terms of more reasonable deadlines, better designs, and more. ■

The only way you can truly ensure that you're not coding in vain is to make sure that you can fulfill the output needs of the system.

Here's a general set of guidelines that not only will enable you to ensure that you've hit at least the high points of your target audience, but will also map nicely to the database design topics I've' covered here:

■ Meet with your users and get a good overview of what they need from the system. Get as specific as possible with your discussion. Get copies of current forms, reports, screen shots of what they might have on their current systems, and so on.

■ Create a functional overview of the system. An overall system flowchart will be a good component of the overview, enabling the customers to review the system and make sure that you understand what's happening at different steps in the flow of work through the system.

■ Present the functional overview to the users. Walk through the system carefully to make sure that it's correct.

■ Create a set of tables using a good ERD tool. Don't worry initially about foreign keys and the like. It's more important at this point to simply make sure that you're gathering the right informational items for the users.

■ Present the database tables to the users, but not from the perspective that they should understand how and why you've laid out the tables the way you have. Have the customer ask you questions about where some bit of information will be stored. You want to make sure that you can show the customer all the information he needs. Of course, the first thing you should do, even before meeting with the customer, is to review the reports and samples that you obtained early on and make sure that you're addressing them appropriately.

■ Next, put into place the relationships between the tables as needed. Make sure that you can walk down all the logical paths that you expect the users will need, based on your needs analysis. There will be more information about resolving many-to-many joins later in this chapter.

■ Present this new schema to the users with a challenge. Ask them to present you with a query for information from the system. Can you satisfy it with identifying or non-identifying relationships? Can you get there from here? This is the test of your database design. You should be able to address each and every one of the stated intentions for the system.

N O T E   Systems get very complex very quickly. The importance of reviewing systems with users can't be overemphasized. In one such case, working with the users prevented a substantial design rewrite. It was found that, although the information was available to determine a specific-case customer, the database tables hadn't correctly provided for the relationships. By discovering this oversight early on, you'll save many, many hours of development time in the long run. ■

Avoid Many-to-Many Joins

In some cases, you'll be faced with a join situation that won't resolve to a single instance on either side of the database table equation. When this is the case, you'll want to consider implementing an associative table that provides a link between the tables. You can see a simple example of this technique in the sample system, because you really could just add ItemCode to the Order table.   ⌐ re pg 8?

N O T E   A *join* is a way of creating a logical view of your data. You specify how the information is retrieved, whether it's related to other tables, and what information you'd like to see. From there, SQL Server will return the results set to your client application in the form of a view on the table as you've defined it. ■

If you didn't have the associative table between the Order Table and the Inventory table, you would end up with a many-to-many relationship between the two. This isn't a good way to accomplish this, as you wouldn't have a singular path for identifying an instance of an order record. Figure 4.11 shows the associative table.   You would lose the OrderItem Id

When to Break the Mold

Sometimes, having the database tables fully normalized just won't work with the model you're putting into place. This is most likely to be encountered in terms of performance. You might end up with a join to return information that simply takes too long to complete.

For example, if you're working with static tables in your application, as might be the case with the Inventory table in the example, you might want to load that table to a local Access table for access by your application. If you were to do this once a day, you'd be reasonably assured of having correct and up-to-date information at the workstations.

FIGURE 4.11
An associative table has been implemented to remove the many-to-many relationship problem imposed by the Order and Inventory tables.

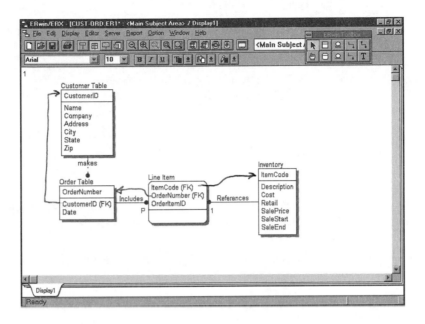

It might be that you're loading down tables that, when taken alone, don't provide a complete picture. For example, if you have a Customer table, an Account Balance table, and a Sales Representative table all related based on customer number, you'll end up with a three-way join to return a complete picture of the information.

You might want to consider denormalizing this set of tables at the client. In this case, you could create a single table that would hold the information from all three tables as a single row of information. That way, when you request information on customer X, you'll receive all the information you need, and a further join won't be required.

> **N O T E** Of course, in reality you wouldn't want to be manipulating something as potentially dynamic as the customer account balance in a remote mode. As a rule, you'll want to consider this method of denormalization only for static tables, or at least those that change only infrequently. ■

From Here...

In this chapter, you've reviewed a lot of information that can pay off in the long run for your applications. Be sure to normalize your database tables to the highest degree possible. If you find exceptions to the normalization goals, you should make sure that you're not overlooking some other method of getting the same task accomplished.

Review things carefully with your customers, such as whether the customer is an internal or external client. This will provide substantial leverage in your projects and will help you toward coming in on time and on budget.

Part
I

Ch
4

The following chapters provide additional information that you'll find useful in your database design efforts:

- Chapter 7, "Retrieving Data with Transact-SQL," shows how you create the joins that this chapter covers. It also shows how you can create the SQL statements that you'll need to retrieve the information in the format, order, and filtered results sets that you can most optimally work with.

- Chapter 10, "Managing and Using Views," shows how you can create the logical data sets that you'll be working with in SQL Server's relational environment.

- Chapter 13, "Managing and Using Rules, Constraints, and Defaults," shows how to implement business rules and data integrity in your database tables.

- Chapter 15, "Creating and Managing Triggers," will help you add referential integrity to your applications by enabling server-side processes when certain data-driven events occur.

- Chapter 20, "SQL Server Security," will help determine the best approach for securing your database and the objects contained within it.

CHAPTER 5

Creating Databases and Transaction Logs

With SQL Server 7, perhaps the most evident change from version 6.5 is the absence of devices. In the earlier version, devices were used to contain one or more databases and their associated logs and data elements. With 7.0, the database is actually a file on disk; devices are no longer used.

In general, it's very important to understand the following terms and the distinctions between them:

Databases are files that SQL Server uses to store objects such as tables and indexes. Only one database can be contained in a single file.

Transaction logs, covered in Chapter 12 "Understanding Transactions and Locking," are the work areas that SQL Server uses to manage a sort of picture of the information on your system in a "before and after" state. This before-and-after information is used to control transaction rollbacks should the need arise, and it is also used to recover a database, should it need to be restored or restarted unexpectedly. In version 7.0, the transaction logs are now in a separate file instead of contained in a table as they were in previous versions.

The lack of devices makes SQL Server much easier to administer. It provides the option to remove one of the most common problems with SQL Server 6.5, that of running out of space on the system even while disk space remained. You no longer need worry about running out of pre-defined disk space for your databases as they grow.

In the balance of this chapter, you'll see how to create databases and logs, how to back them up, and what types of media options you have available for storing your databases and backup files.

Defining Databases and Transaction Logs

Databases are logical entities in which SQL Server places tables and indexes. A database exists on one or more operating system files. However, a single operating system file can not contain multiple databases.

N O T E Prior versions of SQL Server defined a database device, which was a logical name for a physical operating system file. Multiple databases could then be placed in a single device. Database devices have been eliminated in version 7.0 and databases are now placed directly on the operating system files, which enables SQL Server to be used in a variety of systems from laptop and desktop platforms to SMP systems with 8 to 16 processors. ■

Every database has a transaction log associated with it. The transaction log is the place that SQL Server writes all the database transactions before writing them to the database.

There are two types of operations that are written to the transaction log. The first, as you might guess, is the process of working with transactions in the programming sense. These "open" transactions let your application ensure database consistency based on the process that is going on in your application. In other words, it's a form of checkpoint in your application that lets you make sure you get everything done that you expect for a specific operation.

The other type of information written to the transaction log is the before-and-after picture of information in your database when you perform operations on it. That is, when you update a row, the before-and-after values of the row are stored in the transaction log.

In either event, the transaction log is used to recover the database should an error occur that requires a roll-back or roll-forward of information. It is what SQL Server uses to ensure database consistency relative to both the rules managed by the server and the processing completed by your applications.

> **N O T E** Prior versions of SQL Server maintained the transaction log in a table called syslogs. This table no longer exists in version 7.0. The transaction log is now a separate file that is automatically created when a database is created. ∎

Logs are a sequential type of operation, typically logging new information to the end of the log. Because this is true, by placing the log on a different drive, you allow it to be fairly optimized, always ready for the next item to log. It won't have to re-seek the end of the log prior to writing the information to disk.

SQL Server can logically maintain up to 32,767 databases on a single server. However, it's likely that the server will run out of disk, memory, and CPU resources before this limit is ever reached. A database can be up to 1,048,516 TB (terabyte) in size. Given that physical disk sizes don't typically support this size of hard drive, it seems impossible to get a database much bigger than 320GB, 10GB/drive approximate current maximum disk size, by using SQL Server. However, a database file actually can be mapped to multiple physical devices, provided some form of software- or hardware-based striping is in use.

Striping is highly recommended because it provides substantial performance gains due to multiple physical disk drives being used for a single database device. When used with RAID, striping also provides an extra level of data integrity in case of a media failure.

> ▶ **See** Appendix B, "Redundant Arrays of Inexpensive Disks," for more information, **p. 715**

Part I Ch 5

SQL Server 7.0 introduces several new enhancements to databases that greatly improve their manageability. In previous versions of SQL Server, it was necessary for the DBA to physically allocate space to a database and transaction log. The DBA then had to monitor the size of the database and log to ensure they did not fill up. This could consume quite a bit of time in large enterprises and required a significant investment to manage.

The need to expand databases has been eliminated in 7.0. Databases and transaction logs can now grow automatically as data is added. You have the option to specify whether they will grow in increments of megabytes or by a given percentage. You can also constrain the maximum size of a database or transaction log if you are concerned about space. Without any constraints, the database and transaction log will grow to consume the entire drive they have been allocated to.

> **N O T E** You can still utilize the same behavior as in previous versions by disabling automatic file growth. However, this is not recommended because the automatic growth option allows you optimum use of your existing disk drives and relieves a large administrative burden for the system administrator. ∎

Creating a Database and Transaction Log

Creating the database is the last step that you have to complete prior to creating the tables and other structures on which your system will be based. When you create a new database, SQL Server uses a template database, the *model* database, as the starting point for the database. You can think of the model database as having the default objects that are implemented on your system's databases.

The model database consists of the standard SQL Server objects:

- Database Users—The only user created in a completely default system is the dbo, or Database Owner, user.

- Database Roles—Ten default roles are defined.

- Tables—Seventeen tables are included in the default model, which define the system tables your new database will be based upon.

- Views—Twenty views are provided that aid in retrieving information from the system tables.

- Stored Procedures—No stored procedures are included in the model database.

- Rules—Rules are not provided as part of the model database.

- Defaults—If you have defaults you want to impose on all new databases, you will need to manually add them; there are no defaults provided in the model database.

- User-Defined Datatypes.

- Database Diagrams—No diagrams are included in the default model database.

If you have certain attributes you want installed in any database you create, you can implement them in the model database. Then, when new databases are created, the custom attributes are inherited into the new database. One example of this is the case in which you have a series of database administrators that you want to have access to all databases created on the system. By including them in the user list, you can make sure they're included in each database, with appropriate rights, as the databases are created.

 T I P   To see the system tables in the MMC, you need to turn on the System Tables option. If you don't, you will only see the general system files. Select the Server and edit the registration properties to turn on this option.

You manage the model database as you do any other, and there are no limitations on the objects you can place within it. You can use SQL Enterprise Manager to work with the different objects in the database.

You can take one of two approaches to create a database and transaction log. You can use either SQL Enterprise Manager or the CREATE DATABASE command. Both of these are described in the following sections.

N O T E You must either be the System Administrator, or SA, for the SQL Server, or have been added
to the `sysadmin` or `dbcreator` role. If you do not have rights, SQL Server will not allow
you to create the new database. ■

Using SQL Enterprise Manager to Create Database and Transaction Logs

To create a database using SQL Enterprise Manager, follow these steps:

1. Launch SQL Enterprise Manager from the Microsoft SQL Server 7.0 group. Select the
   server that's going to be managed and highlight the Databases folder. The Databases
   window appears in the right pane. See Figure 5.1.

FIGURE 5.1

Each existing database
is represented as a
cylinder.

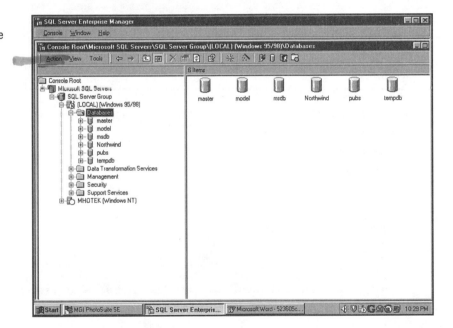

2. Select Action, New Database.
3. Enter the details about the database being added, including the name, the location of the
   files, initial size, whether you want the database to grow automatically, and whether you
   wish to restrict the size. This is shown in Figure 5.2.
4. Click OK.

Part

I

Ch

5

FIGURE 5.2
SQL Enterprise
Manager's New
Database dialog box.

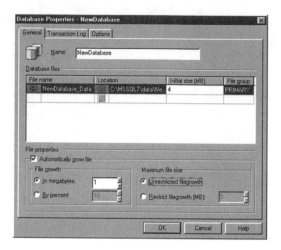

Using the CREATE DATABASE Command to Create Database and Transaction Logs

The CREATE DATABASE command is the Transact-SQL method to creating a database. The syntax for CREATE DATABASE is as follows:

```
CREATE DATABASE database_name
[ON { [PRIMARY] <filespec> } [,...n] ]
[LOG ON { <filespec> } [,...n] ]
[FOR RESTORE]
<filespec> ::=
  (NAME = logical_file_name,
   FILENAME = 'os_file_name'
  [, SIZE = size]
  [, MAXSIZE = { max_size ¦ UNLIMITED } ]
  [, FILEGROWTH = growth_increment] )
```

The options for the Transact-SQL command CREATE DATABASE are as shown in Table 5.1:

Table 5.1 CREATE DATABASE Parameters

Parameter	Description
database_name	This is the name of the database to be created. The database name must comply with the standard rules for naming objects.
ON	Specifies the list of disk files the data portion of the database is to be stored on.
PRIMARY	Specifies the file containing the logical start of the data and system tables. A database can only have one primary file. If this is omitted, the first file listed is the primary.

Parameter	Description
LOG ON	Specifies the list of disk files the transaction log is to be stored on. If this is not specified, the transaction log is created with a size of 25% of the total size of the data files.
logical_file_name	Specifies the name SQL Server will use to reference the file.
FILE NAME	Specifies the name of the operating system file.
os_file_name	Specifies the name of the operating system file, which must reside on the server on which SQL Server is installed.
SIZE	Specifies the initial size of the database.
MAX SIZE	Specifies the maximum size to which the database can grow. If UNLIMITED is specified, the database can grow as large as the free space on the disk drive.
FILE GROWTH	Specifies the amount a database will grow by. The default value is 256KB. The minimum is 64KB and any increment specification is rounded to the nearest 64KB. A setting of 0 specifies no database growth.
FOR RESTORE	This parameter disallows user access until a RESTORE operation has been completed on the database.

The following example creates the same database that was created in the preceding section by using Query Analyzer:

```
CREATE DATABASE NewDatabase
ON
( NAME = NewDatabase_dat,
  FILENAME = 'c:\mssql7\data\NewDatabase_data.mdf',
  SIZE = 4,
FILEGROWTH = 1MB )
LOG ON
( NAME = 'NewDatabase_log',
  FILENAME = 'c:\mssql7\data\NewDatabase_log.ldf',
  SIZE = 2MB,
FILEGROWTH = 1MB )
```

Displaying Database Information

When you're working with an existing database—for example, in those times where you want to reference other attributes of the database—it's helpful to determine exactly how the database is set up. As you might imagine by now, you can do this with both the SQL Enterprise Manager and ISQL.

The Database Properties window in SQL Enterprise Manager provides a graphical display of all the information about a database. You can also right-click on the database name in the Tree view, then select Properties from the resulting menu. Figure 5.3 shows the resulting dialog box that allows you to edit the different facets of the database configuration.

Part
I

Ch
5

FIGURE 5.3
You can add additional
file groups on the
General and Transaction
Log tabs.

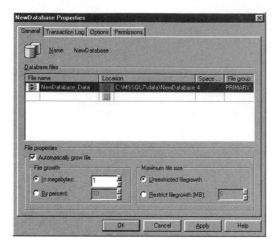

To view this information in ISQL, use the system-stored procedure sp_helpdb. The syntax for sp_helpdb is

    sp_helpdb database_name

If a database_name is supplied, sp_helpdb reports information about that database. If not, it reports information about all the databases on the server.

Sizing Databases and Transaction Logs

In previous versions of SQL Server, databases and transaction logs had to be manually expanded before they ran out of space. In 7.0, databases and transaction logs dynamically grow as data is added. You are only limited by the amount of physical hard disk space on your server.

> **N O T E** SQL Enterprise Manager also provides an option to shrink a database. This is done by internally calling DBCC SHRINKDB. In version 6.5, the database had to be in single-user mode; this operation can now be performed while other users are working in the database. For safety reasons, it is generally advisable to perform this operation when either no users are using the database or the usage is at a minimum.

> ▶ For additional information about using DBCC, please **see** the section "Using the DBCC Options," **p. 498**, in Chapter 19, "SQL Server Administration." ■

To manage the space, right-click your database in Enterprise Manager and select Properties. The resulting dialog, shown in Figure 5.4, will let you establish sizing parameters for both the database, shown as "General," and the transaction log.

FIGURE 5.4
Setting up sizing options is a matter of setting the appropriate options on the Properties for a given database.

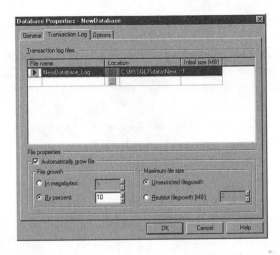

You will notice that you can control the amount by which the database will grow. You can indicate the percentage or you can show the size in megabytes by which the database file should be increased each time it grows.

You can improve the performance of your system if you're doing a lot of insert operations by increasing the incremental size in this dialog box. By making the database grow by a larger number, you can help keep the system from constantly having to extend the database.

You have the same options with the transaction log: increasing by a specific number of megabytes or increasing by a percentage.

You will also notice that you can add new file groups to the database and transaction log allocations. You can use this to spread the database or log across physical devices on your system, a technique that can help performance in some cases.

Dropping Databases

Dropping a database frees up any space that it consumed on the operating system and removes any objects that it contained.

Dropping a database isn't something you can easily undo, so be careful. If you do find you need to recover a database that has been dropped, you will be forced to restore the database and its associated transaction logs.

> **CAUTION**
>
> Except in cases in which you're absolutely certain that you don't need the database information any more, you should always first backup the database to disk and back up the resulting file prior to dropping the database.
>
> Having the resulting database backup file available will certainly save you your share of headaches in those cases in which a user needs "just one more thing" before you delete the database.

User accounts that had their default database as the database that's being dropped will have their default database changed to *master*. Only the SA or a user with the dbcreator or sysadmin roles can drop a database. The master, model, and tempDB databases can't be dropped by any user account. Also, any databases that are participating in replication or have active users can't be dropped until the replication is suspended or until the users have disconnected from the database.

Using SQL Enterprise Manager to Drop a Database   To use SQL Enterprise Manager to drop a database, follow these steps:

1. Run SQL Enterprise Manager, select the server that the database resides on, and select the Databases folder. The list of databases appears in the right pane. See Figure 5.5.

FIGURE 5.5

SQL Enterprise Manager's Manage Databases window lists all the active databases on the currently managed server.

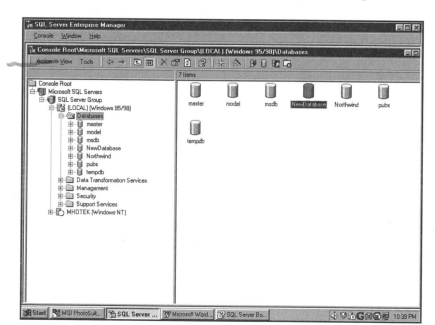

2. Click the database that you want to drop.
3. Select Action, Delete. You can also right-click the database and select the Delete option from the menu. A message box appears, asking for confirmation to drop the database as shown in Figure 5.6.
4. Click Yes and the database is dropped.

FIGURE 5.6

This message box is the last chance that you have to abort a database being dropped before SQL Enterprise Manager performs the drop.

Using the DROP DATABASE Command to Drop a Database The syntax for the DROP DATABASE command in Transact-SQL is as follows:

```
DROP DATABASE database_name, [database_name...]
```

database_name is the name of the database to be dropped.

Databases in all normal "states," including Active, Damaged, Suspect, Offline, and Not Recovered, can be dropped by using the DROP DATABASE command. A database that's still in Recovery status must be dropped using the system stored procedure sp_dbremove. If you have a database in this mode, it will be indicated by an error message when you use the DROP command

 If you have a database that you cannot access in order to drop it, you can use the DBCC command DBREPAIR to remove the database:

```
dbcc dbrepair(database_name, dropdb)
```

This will correct the problem with the database and immediately drop the database. You don't need this command as much with 7.0 because the DROP command will drop the database in most cases.

You can also use a stored procedure approach to dropping databases. The sp_dbremove command allows you to indicate the database to remove. When executed, it also removes the physical file on disk.

```
sp_dbremove database, [dropdev]
```

One other benefit of the stored procedure approach is that sp_dbremove will remove databases in *all* states, whether they are in recovery mode, suspect, or "normal" at the time the command is issued.

Using the TempDB Database

TempDB is a special database that's used by SQL Server to handle any "dynamic" SQL requests from users. TempDB is a workspace for SQL Server to use when it needs a temporary place for calculations, aggregations, and sorting operations. The sorts of things that TempDB is used for include the following:

- Creating temporary tables for sorting data.
- Holding temporary tables created by users and stored procedures.

■ Storing the data that matches any server cursors that are opened by a user process.

■ Holding values for temporary user-created global variables.

One key advantage to using TempDB is that its activity isn't logged. This means that any data manipulation activity done on TempDB temporary tables is much faster than normal disk devices.

This is a double-edged sword, however, because if SQL Server is brought down at any time, all the information in TempDB is lost. Take care not to rely on TempDB without having application code that can restart itself in the event of a server shutdown.

> **CAUTION**
>
> TempDB is a temporary storage area. If the server needs to be restarted, TempDB is re-created. This means that any information that was contained in TempDB is lost. Do not rely on the existence of any information in TempDB.

Creating Backup Devices

Backup devices are special devices that SQL Server uses to perform backups and to clear out the transaction logs on databases. By default, SQL Server creates backup devices for the use of backups and log clearing. Several types of backup devices can be created, based on the medium to which the data is being written.

■ *Disk.* A disk device can be a local disk device or a network disk device that's used for dumping data from the database as a backup. If the device is on the network, make sure that the NT server that's running SQL Server can access the network share where the device is placed.

■ *Tape.* A tape dump device is used to back up a database directly to a tape device attached to the local computer. It isn't possible to dump to a tape attached to a remote computer.

■ *Diskette.* A diskette dump device is provided for backward compatibility with earlier versions of SQL Server.

■ *Named pipe.* SQL Server has a named pipe interface to perform backups that allows third parties to hook in custom backup software and utilities. Named pipe devices aren't managed by SQL Enterprise Manager and must be explicitly referenced in a manual DUMP or LOAD command issued through ISQL or ISQL/W.

▶ **See** the section in Chapter 1, "Understanding Microsoft SQL Server 7.0 Fundamentals," titled "Command-Line Applications," **p. 23**

You can add a dump device to the system through SQL Enterprise Manager or by using the system stored procedure sp_adddumpdevice. The following two sections show you how to use both methods.

TIP You'll find it easier, and faster, if you first dump a database or transaction log to a disk-based dump device, then use a backup utility to move the resulting dump file to a tape or other backup media. Having SQL Server place database or log dumps directly on a backup device can be substantially slower as it's not optimized for that type of access.

N O T E In environments that require a high degree of recoverability and data protection, you might want to consider using simultaneous dumps to both disk and tape as this can protect you from failure of a single media type. ■

Using SQL Enterprise Manager to Add a Dump Device

Using SQL Enterprise Manager to add a dump device removes the burden on the DBA to remember the syntax required for the system stored procedures that must be executed to perform the task.

To add a dump device by using SQL Enterprise Manager, follow these steps:

1. Launch SQL Enterprise Manager from the Microsoft SQL Server 7.0 group. Select the server that's going to be managed. Select the Management folder and click the Backup item and you should see a screen similar to Figure 5.7

FIGURE 5.7
The current backup devices are shown in the right pane.

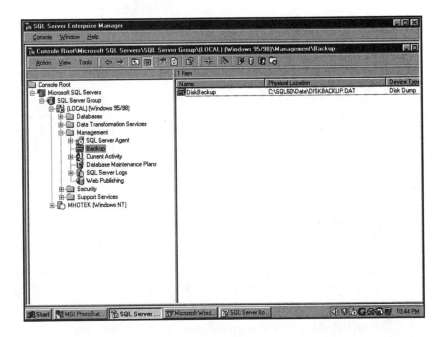

2. Select Action, New Backup Device. The New Backup Device dialog box appears. See Figure 5.8.

FIGURE 5.8

SQL Server places all disk-based dump devices in the BACKUP subdirectory by default.

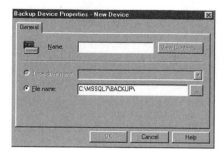

3. Enter a Name and specify a location for the device.

TIP   Click the ... button to find a particular directory on the server or network.

4. Specify whether the device is Tape or Disk, and then click the Create button. The device is added to SQL Server and to the list of available devices.

Using `sp_addumpdevice`

SQL Server's system stored procedure `sp_addumpdevice` is used to add dump devices to the system. `sp_addumpdevice` is the only way that you can add a diskette-based device for dumping to the SQL Server. The syntax for `sp_addumpdevice`, entered using Query Analyzer, is as follows:

```
sp_addumpdevice {'disk' | 'pipe' | 'tape'},
        'logical_name',
        'physical_name'
```

N O T E   Prior versions of SQL Server had some other parameters for `sp_addumpdevice` that were used to define the characteristics of the media being added. Those parameters are no longer necessary because SQL Server now inspects the device to determine its characteristics automatically. ▓

The options for the system stored procedure `sp_addumpdevice` are as follows:

▓ *logical_name*—This is the logical name of the device that's going to be used for backups or dumps.

▓ *physical_name*—This is the physical name of the device that's going to be used for the dump. For a `'disk'` or `'diskette'` dump device, specify the full path of the output file that should be created. For a `'tape'` device, reference the locally attached tape device by using Windows NT's Universal Naming Convention (UNC), such as `"\\.\tape0"`.

The following example adds a disk-based dump device to SQL Server:

```
sp_addumpdevice 'disk',
        'DiskBackup',
        'C:\SQL60\Data\DISKBACKUP.DAT'
```

The following example adds a remote disk-based dump device on the network workstation/ server MainFileServer:

```
sp_addumpdevice 'disk',
     'NetworkBackup',
     '\\MainFileServer\Data\NETBACKUP.DAT'
```

The following example adds a tape dump device to SQL Server:

```
sp_addumpdevice 'tape',
     'TapeBackup',
     '\\.\Tape0'
```

Dropping Devices

There are two ways to drop a device: by using SQL Enterprise Manager or by using the system stored procedure `sp_dropdevice`.

Using Enterprise Manager to Remove Dump Devices

SQL Enterprise Manager provides a simple interface to dropping dump devices so that the DBA does not have to remember the syntax of the `sp_dropdevice` system stored procedure.

To use Enterprise Manager to remove a dump device, follow these steps:

1. In the SQL Enterprise Manager select the Backup item in the Management folder.

   Select the backup device that you want to remove and select Action, Delete. See Figure 5.9. You can also highlight the backup device and press Delete. You will be prompted to confirm the action prior to continuing.

FIGURE 5.9
Confirming deletion of backup device.

> **N O T E** Prior versions of SQL Server required the DBA to specify deletion of the file created for a disk dump device or to use the Windows Explorer to remove this file. This is no longer necessary in version 7.0. ■

Using `sp_dropdevice` to Remove Dump Devices

The system stored procedure `sp_dropdevice` is provided for dropping dump devices from SQL Server. The syntax of `sp_dropdevice` is as follows:

```
sp_dropdevice logical_name [, DELFILE]
```

Part

I

Ch

5

The options for the system stored procedure `sp_dropdevice` are as follows:

- *logical_name*—This is the logical name of the device that's going to be used for backups or dumps.
- *DELFILE*—If DELFILE is included, the physical file that was created to hold the database dumps is also removed from the operating system.

Using Removable Media for Databases

A new feature introduced in SQL Server 6.0 enables databases to be placed on removable media such as CD-ROMs and magneto-optical (MO) drives. This feature permits the mass distribution of databases in a more friendly form than a backup tape, which the client must restore before using. Also, a CD-ROM-based database is truly read-only and is a great way of securing data integrity.

N O T E SQL Enterprise Manager doesn't have a user interface to allow the creation of removable media, so all the work has to be done with ISQL. It's possible to create a device and database on a removable drive attached to the Windows NT system. This won't, however, be the same as a removable-media-capable database and shouldn't be done. ▪

Creating a Removable Database

A removable database has to be created in such a way that three files are used: one for the system catalog, one for the user data, and one for the transaction log. Only the SA can create removable databases.

SQL Server has a special system stored procedure, `sp_create_removable`, that will create a database that will be acceptable for use when creating a database for removable media purposes. It's important that you use this stored procedure because it will guarantee that the database created is usable on a removable device. The syntax for `sp_create_removable` is as follows:

```
sp_create_removable database_name, sysdevice_name_,
     'sysdevice_physical', sysdevice_size,
     logdevice_name, 'logdevice_physical', logdevice_size,
     datadevice1_name, 'datadevice1_physical',
     datadevice1_size [... , datadevice16_name,
     'datadevice16_physical', datadevice16_size]
```

The options for the system stored procedure `sp_create_removable` are as follows:

Table 5.2 SP_CREATE REMOVABLE **Parameters**

Parameter	Description
database_name	The name of the database to be created.
sysdevice_name	The logical name to use for the device that will hold the system catalog tables.
sysdevice_physical	The physical device path and filename that will be used to store the data for the system catalog device.
Syssize	The size in megabytes of the device.
logdevice_name	The logical name to use for the device that will hold the transaction log.
logdevice_physical	The physical device path and filename that will be used to store the data for the log device.
Logsize	The size in megabytes of the device.
datadeviceN_name	The logical name to use for the device that will hold the user data. There can be up to 16 data devices.
datadeviceN_physical	The physical device path and filename that will be used to store the data for datadevice.
Datasize	The size in megabytes of the device.

The following example creates a 1MB data, log, and system catalog database and appropriate devices called MyRemovable:

```
/*----------------------------
sp_create_removable MyRemovable, MySys, 'C:\SQL60\DATA\REMOVABLE\MYSYS.DAT', 1,
     MyLog, 'C:\SQL60\DATA\REMOVABLE\MYLOG.DAT', 1,
     MyData, 'C:\SQL60\DATA\REMOVABLE\MYDATA.DAT', 1
----------------------------*/
CREATE DATABASE: allocating 512 pages on disk 'MySys'
Extending database by 512 pages on disk MyData
DBCC execution completed. If DBCC printed error messages, see your System
    Administrator.
Extending database by 512 pages on disk MyLog
DBCC execution completed. If DBCC printed error messages, see your System
    Administrator.
DBCC execution completed. If DBCC printed error messages, see your System
    Administrator.
```

Part

I

Ch

5

Using the Removable Database

While the database is in development, the following rules should be observed to ensure that the database is usable on removable media:

- Keep the SA as the Database Owner (DBO) of the database.
- Don't create any views or any stored procedures that reference objects that can't be found in the database.
- Don't add any users to the database or change any of the user permissions on the database. You can, however, add groups, and permissions may be assigned to those groups.
- Don't alter any of the database devices created by sp_create_removable.

After database development is completed and you want to test that the database is acceptable for removable media, you should run the system stored procedure sp_certify_removable. This procedure checks all the conditions required for a removable database and can automatically fix anything that it finds unacceptable. The syntax for sp_certify_removable is as follows:

```
sp_certify_removable database_name[, AUTO]
```

The options for the system stored procedure sp_certify_removable are as follows:

- *database_name*—This is the name of the database to be certified.
- AUTO—If AUTO is specified, the stored procedure will correct any problems that it encounters. If you don't specify AUTO, you should correct any problems found using normal SQL Server tools.

> **CAUTION**
>
> If sp_certify_removable reports that it corrected anything when the AUTO flag was specified, it's highly recommended that you retest your application program to make sure it's still compatible with the database. If no testing occurs, SQL Server could have rendered your application useless without your knowledge.

As part of its execution, sp_certify_removable also takes off-line all the files that have been created for use in the removable database and makes them available for copying to the actual physical device. The output from sp_certify_removable is very important because it indicates the database characteristics to use when installing the removable database into a SQL Server.

The following example shows the MyRemovable database being certified and brought off-line:

```
/*---------------------------
sp_certify_removable MyRemovable, AUTO
--------------------------*/
DBCC execution completed. If DBCC printed error messages, see your System
    Administrator.
DBCC execution completed. If DBCC printed error messages, see your System
    Administrator.
```

Using Removable Media for Databases

Using Removable Media for Databases | **111**

```
DBCC execution completed. If DBCC printed error messages, see your System
    Administrator.
File: 'C:\SQL60\DATA\REMOVABLE\MYLOG.DAT' closed.
Device dropped.
The following devices are ready for removal.  Please note this info. for
    use when installing on a remote system:

Device name  Device type  Sequence    Device frag. used by database
Physical file name
-----------------------------------------------------------------
-------------------
MySys         System + Log 1           1 MB
C:\SQL60\DATA\REMOVABLE\MYSYS.DAT
MyData        Data         2           1 MB
C:\SQL60\DATA\REMOVABLE\MYDATA.DAT

Database is now offline
Closing device 'MyData' and marking it 'deferred'.
Device option set.
Closing device 'MySys' and marking it 'deferred'.
Device option set.
```

Installing the Removable Database

After a distribution media/device is made, you must install it on the target SQL Server. Installation is achieved by using the information supplied in the output from sp_certify_removable. This information should be distributed with each CD-ROM or device that the removable media is placed on.

The system stored procedure sp_attach_db is used to install a database from removable media. The syntax for sp_attach_db is as follows:

```
sp_attach_db [@dbname =] 'dbname',[@filename1 =] 'filename_n' [,Ö16]
```

The options for the system-stored procedure sp_attach_db are as follows:

Table 5.3	sp_attach_db **Parameters**
dbname	The name of the database to be installed. This can be any name that's valid for database and doesn't need to be the same as the original device.
filename	The physical name, including path, of a database file.

The database is installed but left on the CD-ROM:

```
sp_attach_db MyRemovable, 'e:\MyData.dat'
```

After all the data files are installed, you need to place the database online so users can access it. This is achieved by using sp_dboption. The following example shows you how to bring MyRemovable online:

```
sp_dboption MyRemovable, OFFLINE, FALSE
```

▶ **See** the Chapter 16 section titled "Displaying and Setting Database Options," **p. 430**

Part

I

Ch

5

Uninstalling a Removable Media Database

If a removable media database is no longer required, you can remove it by using the system stored procedure sp_dbremove. This procedure removes any entries from the system catalog relating to the database that was installed. The syntax for sp_dbremove is as follows:

```
sp_dbremove database_name[, dropdev]
```

The options for the system stored procedure sp_dbremove are as follows:

■ *database_name*—This is the name of the database to be removed or dropped.

■ dropdev—If the keyword dropdev is supplied, sp_dbremove also removes any references in the system catalog to devices that were created as a result of the removable media database being created.

sp_dbremove doesn't remove the physical data files that were used to store the database devices. This needs to be done manually. See the Caution in the previous section for more information about removing device files manually.

From Here...

In this chapter, you learned all about databases and file groups. This chapter provided you with information on how to create all the fundamentals for your server. From here you should consider looking at the following chapters to further develop your SQL Server and application programming knowledge:

■ Chapter 6, "Creating Database Tables and Using Datatypes," shows how you can create tables in the databases and segments created in this chapter.

■ Chapter 11, "Managing and Using Indexes and Keys," explains how to place the new indexes you create on the new index segments that you created in this chapter.

■ Chapter 16, "Understanding Server, Database, and Query Options," explains how to further configure your SQL Server and databases for better performance.

■ Chapter 19, "SQL Server Administration," tells you how to use the backup devices for backups and restores.

CHAPTER 6

Creating Database Tables and Using Datatypes

In this chapter

Data-processing systems involve the storage, processing, and retrieval of information. You must define where data will be stored before it can be processed and retrieved. All units of information, from characters to the logical definition of the entire database, can be defined through SQL Server components.

You may recall from prior chapters that the structure of a SQL Server system is as follows:

- Databases are stored in physical files on your hard disk. These files typically have an extension of .MDF.

- Databases are created on one or more files. Databases are the storage mechanism for the information associated with your application, and the databases give you a means of setting up logical boundaries between this application and others. The database is also the starting point for most security relative to your application.

- Transaction logs are also created in one or more log files. These files have an extension of .LDF.

- Tables are sets of related information stored within the database. In older systems that do not use this approach to storage, tables are the equivalent of the physical files on disk, one table per file. In dBASE for example, the equivalent is a single database file on disk relates to one table within a database.

- Columns are individual pieces of information, traditionally referred to as fields. If you think of a table as a spreadsheet, you will have a good idea of how it is laid out.

- Rows are sets of columns and there is one row per record in more traditional, non-SQL terms. Again, if you think of a spreadsheet metaphor, this makes a good deal of sense.

In this chapter you will find out how to create the tables and the components of the table, the row and column. As with other database systems, each column can have a specific datatype associated with it, and each datatype has certain characteristics.

Creating Tables

Data in a relational database such as SQL Server is stored in tables that are two-dimensional arrays. You will recall from Chapter 1, "Understanding Microsoft SQL Server 7.0 Fundamentals," that you have had experience working with tables from everyday life, such as train or bus schedules.

The columns and rows of a table are already familiar to database users. Tables were chosen as the logical structure for storing data because of their familiarity to users and ease of use for retrieving, displaying, and manipulating data.

You can create SQL Server database tables with the `CREATE TABLE` Transact-SQL statement or with SQL Enterprise Manager. In the next two sections, you will see how to create tables using these two approaches.

You can create up to two billion tables in each database. The major part of the creation of a table is the definition of the datatypes for columns, which is explained in the balance of this chapter.

Using Transact-SQL to Create Tables

In Transact-SQL, you can create tables using the CREATE TABLE statement. CREATE TABLE lets you set up several different options to the table, including where it's located, how the columns are defined, and so on. The syntax for CREATE TABLE is as follows:

```
CREATE TABLE [[database.]owner.]table_name
(column_name datatype [not null ¦ null] IDENTITY[(seed, increment)]][constraint]
[, column_name datatype [not null ¦ null IDENTITY[(seed, increment)]]].
[constraint]...)
  [ON file group]
```

> **N O T E** For more information on identity columns, see the "identity Property" section later in this chapter. ■

Enter the name of the table (table_name) following the keywords CREATE TABLE. You can use up to 128 characters to name a database object, such as a table. The column names are entered within parentheses. You define the name and type of the column by entering a column name up to 128 characters long, followed by a Transact-SQL datatype.

> **N O T E** Everything stored in a database is stored as an object. A database object, such as a table, has information kept about it in system tables. For example, a table created by you has the name of the table, the type of data that is stored in its columns, and other characteristics stored in the system table sysobjects. ■

Optionally, you can enter the database in which the table is created, as well as an owner of the table. You will find it more convenient to define the current database in which you're working first with a USE database-name command. After you define your current database with the USE command, all subsequent commands are performed within the database specified with the USE command.

> **N O T E** Your SQL Server account is defined with a current database. The default database you're directed to should be the one in which you work exclusively or most often. ■

If you don't enter the name of the owner of an object, such as a table, when you create a table, you will be its owner. Often, tables are created from the SA account to restrict subsequent access to the tables.

The owner of the database in which the table is defined is automatically granted the CREATE TABLE permission, which allows the creation of tables. The database owner and the SA can grant CREATE TABLE permission to other users so that they can create tables in the database. You don't have to grant permission to create temporary tables in a database.

Using SQL Enterprise Manager to Create Tables

Using SQL Enterprise Manager to create tables gives you the advantage of the graphical interface to specifying the different attributes to the table. This includes things such as datatypes,

Part

I

Ch

6

column lengths, and so on. To create tables with Enterprise Manager, you will still need to know the same information as when you create the tables with ISQL or OSQL. The difference is in how the interface takes care of some of the details for you.

To begin working with tables, start Enterprise Manager and select the server you want to work with. Next, open the Databases tree and open the database you want to add the new table to. When you do, you will see the various object types that make up a database. You are presented with the following list:

- Database Users
- Database Roles
- Tables
- SQL Server Views
- Stored Procedures
- Rules
- Defaults
- User Defined Datatypes
- Database Diagrams

Right-click on the Tables option and select the New Table option. When you do, you will be presented with a new dialog box, allowing you to define a table for your system. See Figure 6.1 for an example with some of the values already entered.

FIGURE 6.1

SQL Enterprise Manager will walk you through the options necessary to create a table.

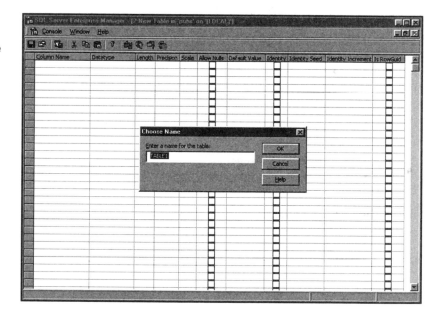

When you create a new column, you're prompted for the different datatypes, including any custom datatypes you have created, with a drop-down list box in the Datatype column in the dialog box. This ensures that you select valid datatypes, and in some cases, the Size attribute will be determined for you based on the datatype selection. See Figure 6.2.

FIGURE 6.2
You will be prompted for the datatype, and Enterprise Manager might try to indicate pre-set sizes for you based on your selection.

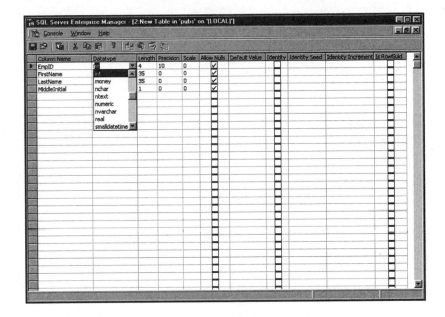

When you're satisfied with your table, select the disk button to save the table. In Figure 6.3, you will see the Properties dialog. Properties are something you should at the very least browse when you're creating or managing a table. Each of the options presented can be changed after the fact, but might require some updating of your table.

FIGURE 6.3
The properties allow you to create indexes and set primary keys.

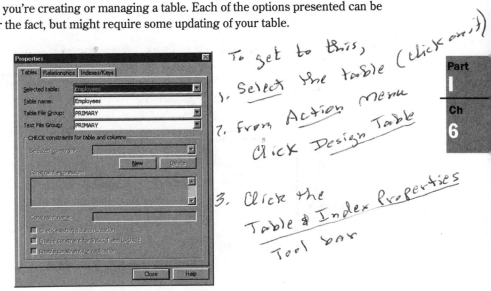

To get to this,
1. Select the table (click on it)
2. from Action menu click Design Table
3. Click the Table & Index Properties Tool bar

Part
I

Ch
6

Other options, for example, in order to indicate the identity column for your table, must be completed when the table is created. They cannot be added after the fact. One way around this is to create a new table, based on the original but with the modifications you need. Then, using the transfer utility, you can copy the contents of the original table into the newly created table.

Finally, rename the original table something like "`old_tablename`" and rename the new table to the original name. This step allows any applications you have that reference the table to keep working with the table without modification. Of course saving the original with the modified name is a safety precaution, and you should extensively test any applications that use the new table prior to dropping the original table.

Understanding Datatypes

The major part of defining a table is specifying the datatypes for the columns of the tables. Transact-SQL allows you to define several datatypes, including those for the storage of characters, numbers, and bit patterns. You can also define your own datatypes for use in stored procedures, tables, and other work that you will be doing with the database tables.

You must define at least one column for a table, and you can define up to 1,024 columns. You're also limited to a maximum row length of 8,060 bytes.

You can use IMAGE, NTEXT, and TEXT datatypes to get around the 8,060-byte limit for rows. Columns that are defined by using the IMAGE and TEXT datatypes are stored outside the table and can store more than two billion bytes of data for text and more than one billion for NTEXT.

You should be careful to follow the rules for relational database design whenever feasible, however, to ensure the optimum response time and use of your SQL Server engine.

▶ For more information on database design, **see** Chapter 4, "Data Modeling and Database Design," **p. 75**

Tables are created by using a unit of measure called an *extent*. When you create a new table, the allocation of space for the table is initially set at one extent, which is eight pages, each of which is 8KB in size. When the table fills the space in the already allocated extents, additional extents are automatically implemented up to the space allocated to the overall database size.

Use the system procedure sp_spaceused to obtain a report on the space allocated to a table or the graphical display in SQL Enterprise Manager. See Chapter 5, "Creating Databases and Transaction Logs," for information on displaying allocated space.

Understanding Unicode

Unicode has been added to SQL Server 7.0. It is a significant step in the internationalization of SQL Server. Unicode is the 16-bit character encoding standard (compared to the 8-bit used for ASCII and ANSI) developed by the Unicode Consortium. By using two bytes, almost all of the character sets of the world languages can be included in one character set. As an example, 21,000 of the possible 65,536 characters are used by the Chinese ideographs. Because each character requires two bytes rather than one, twice the space on disk is required to store the same number of characters. In a practical sense to you and your applications, this means that the Unicode datatypes such as NCHAR have a maximum size of one-half the number of characters of that of the CHAR datatype.

Creating Temporary Tables

Creating a temporary table is a useful technique you should take advantage of. You can create two types of temporary tables in SQL Server: local and global. A *local* temporary table is created if the first character of the table name is a pound sign (#). A local temporary table can be accessed only by the session in which it was created. A local temporary table is automatically dropped when the session in which it was created ends. You can't use more than 116 characters, including the pound sign, to name a local temporary table.

You create a temporary table that can be accessed by any session by defining a table with two pound signs (##) as the first two characters of the table name. Each session can be created by a different user on a different client system. A temporary table that's accessible from multiple sessions is called a *global* temporary table and is automatically dropped when the last session that's using it ends.

T I P Constraints can be defined for temporary tables but foreign key constraints are not enforced.

You can use temporary tables to store sets of data that have to be operated on before permanently storing. For example, you can combine the results of the data from multiple data sets into a temporary table, then access the combined data in the temporary table throughout your session. Data that has already been combined in a temporary table can be accessed faster than data that must be dynamically accessed from multiple tables. A temporary table that combines the results of two tables is faster to access because SQL Server doesn't need to reference the database tables to retrieve the information.

▶ **See** the section titled "Performing Relational Joins" in Chapter 8, "Adding, Changing, and Deleting Information in Tables," **p. 210**

N O T E Sessions are established differently depending on how you will be accessing the server. A session is associated with a live connection to the database. For example, if you query a table and use a Dynaset type of dataset, that is, one that's active and updateable, the session will remain active. If you then connect to the database for another dataset inquiry, a separate and distinct session will be opened. Information in the temporary tables from the first session won't be available to the second session. ■

You might also find it convenient to use a temporary table to make a set of data available to a stored procedure that's invoked from another procedure. You will find it easier to make data

Part

I

Ch

6

available to another procedure within a temporary table rather than pass data as a set of parameters.

▶ **See** Chapter 14, "Managing Stored Procedures and Using Flow-Control Statements," **p. 355**

Selecting Datatypes

The datatype is the first characteristic you define for the column of a table. The *datatype* of a column controls the type of information that can be stored within the column. Define the datatype by following the column name with a keyword that might also require some parameters. After you define the datatype of a table column, it's stored as a permanent characteristic and can't be changed.

You can also use datatypes to define other data-storage structures, such as parameters and local variables. Parameters and local variables are storage structures defined in RAM rather than on disk. You're limited to a subset of the datatypes for the definitions of parameters and variables.

▶ See the Chapter 14 sections titled "Using Parameters with Procedures," **p. 359** and "Defining and Using Variables" **p. 377**

The next sections review each of the different system-defined datatypes that you can use in the definition of your SQL Server tables and stored procedures.

Numeric Integer Datatypes

Numeric integers are the first of several datatypes that you can use to define storage objects. Integer datatypes allow you to store whole numbers. You can directly perform arithmetic operations on integers without using functions. Numbers stored in integer datatypes always occupy the same amount of storage space, regardless of the number of digits within the allowable ranges for each of the integer datatypes.

N O T E   The name of a datatype, such as INTEGER, is case-insensitive. ■

INT or INTEGER   INT (or INTEGER) is the first of three integer datatypes. You can store negative and positive whole numbers within the range of $-(2^{**}31)$ to $2^{**}31$—approximately 4.3 billion numbers. The range is $-2,147,483,648$ to $2,147,483,647$. Each value that's stored in an INT datatype is stored in 4 bytes, using 31 bits for the size or magnitude and 1 bit for the sign.

N O T E   A set of two asterisks is used to denote exponentiation. The range of numbers for numeric digits is frequently referenced using a base number raised to a power because it allows the range to be specified precisely and compactly. ■

SMALLINT   SMALLINT is the second integer datatype. You can store whole numbers within the range -32768 to $+32767$. Each value that's stored in a SMALLINT datatype occupies two bytes and is stored as 15 bits for the magnitude and one bit for the sign.

TINYINT You can store only whole positive numbers in a storage structure defined as TINYINT within the range 0 to 255. Each value stored as a TINYINT occupies one byte.

The following example shows the creation of a table with three columns. The columns are defined as the INT, SMALLINT, and TINYINT datatypes. A single row is inserted into the number_example table with values within the acceptable range for storage of each datatype. Select is subsequently used to retrieve the row.

> **CAUTION**
>
> Database languages and programming languages have keywords. Keywords are the words that force an action to occur in an environment. To avoid confusion and error, avoid using keywords when naming tables, columns, and so on.

```
create table number_example
(int1 int,int2 smallint,int3 tinyint)
insert into number_example
values (400000000,32767,255)
(1 row(s) affected)

select * from number_example
int1       int2    int3
---------- ------- ----
400000000  32767   255
(1 row(s) affected)
```

Enforcing Value Ranges SQL Server automatically enforces the insertion of values within the range of each datatype. In the following two examples, values are inserted into columns that are defined as SMALLINT and TINYINT, although the values are outside the range of acceptable values.

The column values are specified in the values clause of the insert statement in the same order in which the columns were defined in the table. SQL Server returns an error message that describes the reason for the failed row insertion, such as the attempted insertion of a value that is outside the allowable range for the datatype.

```
insert into number_example
values (1,32768,1)
Msg 220, Level 16, State 1
 Arithmetic overflow error for type smallint, value =  32768.
insert into number_example
values (1,1,256)
Msg 220, Level 16, State 2
 Arithmetic overflow error for type tinyint, value =  256.
```

 T I P Use a TINYINT or SMALLINT to store integer values in one-quarter or one-half the storage space used for storing integer values in an INT datatype. These are especially useful for use as flags, status indicators, and so forth.

Part

I

Ch

6

Numeric Floating-Point Datatypes

Floating-point datatypes are the second group of several numeric datatypes you can use to define storage structures such as table columns. Unlike the integer datatypes, floating-point datatypes can store decimal numbers.

Unfortunately, the floating-point datatypes are subject to the rounding error. The storage of a value in a numeric datatype that's subject to the rounding error is accurate only to the number of digits of precision that's specified. For example, if the number of digits of precision is 15, a number that's larger than 15 digits can be stored, but the digits beyond 15 might inaccurately represent the initial number inserted into the storage.

Also, the number might inaccurately return results of computations that involve floating-point datatypes. The rounding error affects a number's least-significant digits, the ones at the far right. You can accurately store numbers within the number of digits of precision available in the floating-point datatype.

N O T E Microsoft calls datatypes such as the floating-point datatypes *approximate numeric datatypes* because values stored in them can be represented only within the limitations of the storage mechanism. You should avoid performing comparisons, such as in a WHERE clause, of data that's stored in approximate datatypes because a loaded value that's larger than the number of digits of precision is altered by the rounding effect during storage. ■

The REAL Datatype   The first of the floating-point datatypes is REAL, which is stored in four bytes. You can store positive or negative decimal numbers in the REAL datatype, with up to seven digits of precision. You can store numbers in a column defined as REAL within the range of 3.4E–38 to 3.4E+38.

The range of values and representation is actually platform-dependent. Remember that SQL Server evolved from the original Sybase SQL Server implementation. The REAL datatype stored on each of the several computer systems that a Sybase version was written for varied in the range of allowable characters and the actual representation of characters. For example, the range of decimal numbers stored by OpenVMS on Digital's VAX computers is 0.29E–38 to 1.7E+38.

The underlying operating system that SQL Server runs on is supported on Intel, MIPS, PowerPC, and Alpha AXP systems. You should consider the previously stated value, the range of 3.4E–38 to 3.4E+38, as approximate and check the range of allowable numbers for the floating-point datatype that's stored in four bytes on your Windows NT system.

You should also realize that data stored in floating-point datatypes, which is moved between different NT platforms with different processor architectures, might require conversion to compensate for different representations and range of values.

FLOAT[(n)] Datatypes   The second of the floating-point datatypes is FLOAT, which is stored in eight bytes if a value for *n* is omitted. You can store positive or negative decimal numbers in the FLOAT datatype with as many as 15 digits of precision. You can store numbers in a column defined as FLOAT within the range of 1.7E–308 to 1.7E+308.

If you specify a value for *n* within the range of one to seven, you're actually defining a REAL datatype. If you specify a value within the range of 8 to 15, the datatype has the identical characteristics as if *n* were omitted.

In the following example, a table is created with two columns defined as REAL and FLOAT. A single row is added with identical numbers that are subsequently added to each column of the table. The retrieval of the row from the table shows that the number stored in the REAL column was stored accurately to only seven digits, the maximum number of digits of precision for a REAL datatype. The same 11-digit number was stored correctly in the column defined with the datatype FLOAT because FLOAT allows up to 15 digits to be stored accurately.

```
create table precision_example
(num1 real,num2 float)
insert into precision_example
values (4000000.1234,4000000.1234)
select * from precision_example
num1                    num2
--------------------    --------------------
4000000.0               4000000.1234
(1 row(s) affected)
```

DECIMAL[(p[, s])] and NUMERIC[(p[, s])] Datatypes   You can use either the name DECIMAL or NUMERIC to select a datatype that, unlike FLOAT or REAL, allows the exact storage of decimal numbers. The scale and digits of precision are specified in the arguments *p* and *s*. You can store values within the range $10^{38}-1$ through -10^{38} using 2 to 17 bytes for storage.

Use *p* to define the number of digits that can be stored to the left and right of the decimal point. Use *s* to define the number of digits to the right of the decimal point that must be equal to or less than the value of *p*. If you omit a value for *p*, it defaults to 18; the default of *s* is 0. Table 6.1 shows the number of bytes that are allocated for the specified precision (value of *p*).

Table 6.1   Number of Bytes Allocated for Decimal/Numeric Datatypes

Bytes Allocated	Precision
2	1–2
3	3–4
4	5–7
5	8–9
6	10–12
7	13–14
8	15–16
9	17–19

Part

I

Ch

6

continues

Table 6.1 Continued

Bytes Allocated	Precision
10	20–21
11	22–24
12	25–26
13	27–28
14	29–31
15	32–33
16	34–36
17	37–38

The following example shows the storage and subsequent retrieval of a single row stored with the columns of a table defined as NUMERIC/DECIMAL datatypes. This example shows the default precision and scale and an explicit precision and scale being displayed.

```
create table definition_example
(num1 decimal,num2 numeric(7,6))
insert into definition_example
values (123456789123456789,1.123456)
select * from definition_example
num1                    num2
--------------------    ----------
123456789123456789      1.123456
(1 row(s) affected)
```

N O T E The maximum precision permitted in the NUMERIC/DECIMAL datatypes is 28 unless you start SQL Server from the command line and change the precision. Use the command sqlservr with the option /p, which has the following syntax:

sqlservr [/dmaster_device_path][/pprecision_level]

For example, the following command starts SQL Server with a maximum precision of 38:

sqlservr /dg:\sql60\data\master.dat /p38.

If no value is specified after the precision qualifier /p, the precision for the NUMERIC/DECIMAL datatypes is set to the maximum of 38. ■

Character Datatypes

You'll frequently use character datatypes to define table columns or other storage structures. Character datatypes allow the storage of a wider variety of symbols than numeric datatypes. Character datatypes enable you to store letters, numeric symbols, and special characters such as ? and >. You enter character data in either single or double quotation marks (' or ' ') when loading it into a storage area such as the column of a table.

CHAR Datatype CHAR is the first type of character datatypes. When you store data in a CHAR datatype, each symbol or character stored uses one byte. The number in parentheses specifies the size of storage for all sets of characters. For example, if you define a table column as the datatype char(15), each value of the column is 15 bytes in size and can store 15 characters. If you enter fewer than 15 characters, SQL Server adds blanks after the last specified character.

You can define a char(*n*) datatype to contain up to a maximum of 8,000 ANSI characters. Remember, the column value always contains the specified number of characters. SQL Server automatically adds spaces to the end of a char value to fill the defined length of space.

N O T E If a column is defined CHAR and allowed to be NULL it will be treated as a VARCHAR column. ■

NCHAR Datatype The behaviorial characteristics of NCHAR are true of CHAR. The difference is that the maximum number of characters in a column is 4,000 Unicode characters.

VARCHAR Datatype You can use the VARCHAR datatype to store a variable-length string of up to 8,000 characters. Unlike the CHAR datatype, the storage space used varies according to the number of characters stored in each column value of rows of the table.

For example, if you define the table column as varchar(15), a maximum of 15 characters can be stored in the corresponding column of each table row. However, spaces aren't added to the end of the column value until the size of each column is 15 bytes. You can use a VARCHAR to save space if the values stored in a column are variable in size. You can also specify a varchar datatype using the keyword char varying.

NVARCHAR Datatype Again, the behaviorial characteristics of NVARCHAR are true of VARCHAR. The difference is that the maximum number of characters in a column is 4,000 Unicode characters.

Using Character Datatypes In the following examples, a table is created with two columns defined as CHAR and VARCHAR datatypes. The inserted row stores only two characters in each column of the row. The first column is padded with three spaces so that it occupies five bytes of storage. The second column of the row isn't padded and occupies only two bytes of storage to store the two characters. The retrieval of the row in the example displays each column value identically, masking the underlying storage difference.

```
create table string_example
(char1 char(5),char2 varchar(5))
insert into string_example
values ('AB','CD')
select * from string_example
char1 char2
---- ----
AB    CD
(1 row(s) affected)
```

In the following example, a row is inserted into the table that contains column values that are longer by one character than the maximum length of the datatypes of the table columns. The select statement in the example shows that the column values of the inserted row were truncated, or cut off, and contain only the first five characters of the column values. You don't receive a message that the truncation occurs when a row is inserted.

```
insert into string_example
values ('abcdef','abcdef')
select * from string_example
char1 char2
---- ----
AB    CD
abcde abcde
(2 row(s) affected)
```

 TIP Use the TEXT datatype, which allows the storage of more than two billion characters, to store sets of characters that are longer than 8,000 characters.

Here are a few points about TEXT and other character datatypes that will help when you begin using them:

- When a table column is defined using the CHAR or VARCHAR datatype, the maximum length is specified for all values that are later inserted into the column. SQL Server will automatically truncate all characters that are longer than the maximum length that was defined. SQL Server doesn't notify you that the truncation is being performed.

- When you use CHAR datatypes, the fields are padded with extra spaces to fill the entire defined space for the column. If you're referencing these types of columns in reports, the output columns may not line up. If the extra spaces in the field are the problem, either use a trim statement in your query or store the data as a VARCHAR.

DATETIME and SMALLDATETIME Datatypes

The DATETIME and SMALLDATETIME datatypes store a combination of the date and time. You will find it more convenient to store dates and times in one of the date and time datatypes rather than a datatype such a CHAR or VARCHAR. If you store data in one of these datatypes, you can easily display them because SQL Server automatically formats them in a familiar form. You can also use specialized date and time functions to manipulate values stored in this manner.

If you store date and time in CHAR or VARCHAR, or if you store time in numeric datatypes, date and time values aren't automatically formatted in conventional ways when they're displayed.

DATETIME Datatype   DATETIME is the first type of date and time datatypes that you can use to define storage structures such as table columns. In the DATETIME datatype, you can store dates and times from 1/1/1753 AD to 12/31/9999 AD.

The total storage of a DATETIME datatype value is eight bytes. SQL Server uses the first four bytes to store the number of days after or before the base date of January 1, 1900. Values that are stored as negative numbers represent dates before the base date. Positive numbers represent dates since the base date. Time is stored in the second four bytes as the number of milliseconds after midnight.

N O T E DATETIME values are stored to an accuracy of 1/300th of a second (3.33 milliseconds) with values rounded downward. For example, values of one, two, and three milliseconds are stored as zero milliseconds; the values of four through six milliseconds are stored as three milliseconds. ▪

When you retrieve values stored in DATETIME, the default format for display is MMM DD YYYY hh:mmAM/PM, for example, Sep 23 1949 11:14PM. You must enclose DATETIME values in single quotation marks when they're used in an insert or other statement. You can enter either the date or time portion first because SQL Server can recognize each portion and store the value correctly.

You can use upper- or lowercase characters for the date and one or more spaces between the month, day, and year when you enter DATETIME values. If you enter time without a date, the default date is January 1, 1900. If you enter the date without the time, the default time is 12:00AM. If you omit the date and the time, the default value entered is January 1, 1900 12:00 AM.

You can enter the date in several ways. Each is recognized and stored correctly by SQL Server. You can enter the date in an alphabetic format, using either an abbreviation for the month or the full name of the month. You can use or omit a comma between the day and year.

If you omit the century part of the year, decades that are less than 50 are represented as 20 and those that are 50 or more are entered as 19. For example, if you insert the year 49, the complete year stored is 2049. If you enter the year as 94, the complete year stored is 1994. You must explicitly enter the century if you want a century different from the default. You must supply the century if the day is omitted from the date value. When you enter a date without a day, the default entry is the first day of the month.

The set option dateformat isn't used if you specify the month of the year in alphabetic format. If you installed SQL Server with the US_English Language option, the default order for the display of DATETIME values is month, day, and year. You can change the default order for the display of the date portion of a DATETIME value using the set dateformat command.

▶ **See** the section titled "Understanding Query Options" in Chapter 16, **p. 435**

You can enter dates in several ways, including the following examples:

- Sep 23 1949
- SEP 23 1949
- September 23 1949
- sep 1949 23
- 1949 sep 23
- 1949 23 sep
- 23 sep 1949

Part

I

Ch

6

The numeric format for DATETIME values permits the use of slashes (/), hyphens (-), and periods (.) as separators between the different time units. When you use the numeric format with a DATETIME value, you must specify the month, day, and year of the date portion of the value.

In the numeric format, enter a separator between the month, day, and year entered in the order defined for dateformat. If you enter the values for a DATETIME datatype in the incorrect order, the month, day, or year will be misinterpreted and stored incorrectly. If you enter the information in the incorrect order, you may also receive an error message that tells you the date is out of range.

The following is an example of several entries for the numeric form of the date portion of a DATETIME datatype value with set dateformat defined as month, day, and year and the language as US_English:

- 6/24/71
- 06/24/71
- 6-24-1971
- 6.24.1971
- 06.24.71

The last of the possible formats for the date portion of a DATETIME datatype value is unseparated four-, six-, or eight-digit values or a time value without a date value portion. The dateformat controlled through set dateformat doesn't affect DATETIME datatype values referenced as the unseparated digit format.

If you enter a six- or eight-digit unseparated value, it's always interpreted in the order of year, month, and day. The month and day are always interpreted as two digits each. Four-digit unseparated values are interpreted as the year, with the century and the month and day defaulted to the first month and the first day of that month. Table 6.2 lists the possible interpretations of unseparated digit datetime datatype values:

Table 6.2 Interpretation of Unseparated Digit Dates for DATETIME Datatypes

Digits	Equivalent Representation in Alphabetic Format
710624	June 24, 1971
19710624	June 24, 1971
1971	January 1, 1971
71	Not valid
' '	January 1, 1900 12:00AM

When working with the DATETIME datatype, keep in mind that if you insert a column with an empty string as a value and that column is defined as a DATETIME column, you won't get a NULL entry as you might expect. When two single quotation marks are used with no characters inserted between them as the value for either of the date and time datatypes, the entry January 1, 1900 and 12 midnight is always inserted by SQL Server.

You must enter the time with the time units in the following order: hours, minutes, seconds, and milliseconds. You must have a colon as a separator between multiple time units to allow a set of digits to be recognized as a time rather than a date value. You can use AM or PM, specified in upper- or lowercase, to specify before or after midnight.

You can precede milliseconds with a period or a colon, which affects the interpretation of the millisecond unit. A period followed by a single digit specifies tenths of a second; two digits are interpreted as hundredths of a second; three digits are interpreted as thousandths of a second. A colon specifies that the following digits will be interpreted as thousandths of a second. Table 6.3 shows several possible interpretations of the time portion of a DATETIME datatype value.

Table 6.3 DATETIME Datatype Values

Time	Interpretation
11:21	11 hours and 21 minutes after midnight
11:21:15:871	11 hours, 21 minutes, 15 seconds, and 871 thousandths of a second AM
11:21:15.8	11 hours, 21 minutes, 15 seconds, and eight tenths of a second AM
6am	Six AM
7 PM	Seven PM
05:21:15:500 AM	Five hours, 21 minutes, 15 seconds, and 500 milliseconds after midnight

SMALLDATETIME SMALLDATETIME is the second of the date and time datatypes you can use to define storage structures, such as table columns. In the SMALLDATETIME datatype, you can store dates and times from 1/1/1900 AD to 6/6/2079 AD.

The total storage of a SMALLDATETIME datatype value is 4 bytes. SQL Server uses 2 bytes to store the number of days after the base date of January 1, 1900. Time is stored in the other 2 bytes as the number of minutes after midnight. The accuracy of the SMALLDATETIME datatype is 1 minute. You can use SMALLDATETIME to store values that are within its more-limited range and lesser precision when compared to DATETIME.

T I P Use the SMALLDATETIME datatype instead of the DATETIME datatype to store values in half the storage space.

In the following example, one column is defined using the DATETIME datatype and the second column is defined using the SMALLDATETIME datatype. After the table is created, a minimum value is inserted into each column of a single row for the respective datatypes.

Part

I

Ch

6

```
create table date_table
(date1 datetime,date2 smalldatetime)
insert into date_table
values ('Jan 1 1753','Jan 1 1900')
select * from date_table
date1                          date2
---------------------------    ---------------------------
Jan 1 1753 12:00AM             Jan 1 1900 12:00AM
(1 row(s) affected)
```

In the following example, successive insert statements insert a date that's beyond both the range of the columns defined by using the SMALLDATETIME and the range of the DATETIME datatype. An error is returned as a result of both insert statements.

```
insert into date_table
values ('May 19 1994', 'Jun 7 2079')
Msg 296, Level 16, State 3
```

In the preceding example, the conversion of CHAR to SMALLDATETIME resulted in a SMALLDATETIME value out of range:

```
insert into date_table
values ('Jan 1 10000','May 19 1994')
Msg 241, Level 16, State 3
```

The example shows a syntax error converting DATETIME from a character string.

Specialized Datatypes

Transact-SQL contains a set of specialized datatypes for data storage. Most of the time you will store data in more conventional datatypes such as integer, floating-point, and character. You can store dates and times in the DATETIME or SMALLDATETIME datatypes.

Although you will probably find that you can use the integer, floating-point, character, and date/time datatype formats for storing 90 percent of your data, in some cases you will probably need a more custom solution.

In these cases, you can use one or more of the specialized datatypes. For example, you might need to store only data that can be represented as true or false, yes or no. Because this is a binary condition, you might decide to create a custom datatype. As another example, you might need to store sets of data in a column that's larger than the 255-character limitation of the conventional character datatypes. Several additional datatypes are available to allow you to choose the best datatype for storing your information.

BIT You can use the BIT datatype to store information that can be represented in only two states. A BIT datatype is stored in a single bit. As a result, only two possible patterns can be stored, zero(0) or one(1). If you enter any other value than 0 or 1 in a data-storage structure such as a table column, 1 is stored. You can't define the BIT datatype to allow NULL entries.

 TIP Although it is not explicitly stated in the SQL Server documentation, the BIT datatype corresponds to the BOOLEAN datatype in other DBMSes and programming languages.

You can also use a single byte to define up to eight different bit columns of a table by using the BIT datatype. The amount of space allocated for one or more bits is a single byte, and the bit columns don't have to be contiguous. If you define nine columns of a table by using the BIT datatype, two bytes are used for the total of nine BIT datatypes.

N O T E SQL Server stores information about columns defined using BIT datatypes in the syscolumns system table by storing an offset to the bit column in the status column. You can't define an index that uses a column defined as a BIT datatype. ■

TIMESTAMP If you define a column of a table using the TIMESTAMP datatype, a counter value is automatically added to the TIMESTAMP column whenever you insert a new row or update an existing row. You can't explicitly enter a value into the column defined as a TIMESTAMP.

The counter value inserted by SQL Server into a TIMESTAMP column specifies the sequence of operations that SQL Server has performed. Values entered into a TIMESTAMP column are stored in a VARBINARY(8) format, not a DATETIME or SMALLDATETIME format. NULL values are permitted in a TIMESTAMP column by default. A TIMESTAMP value isn't a date and time, but it's always unique within the table and database. You can define only a single column of a table as a TIMESTAMP.

N O T E Timestamps are often used to ensure that a row can be uniquely identified. If you're updating columns in a row, it's a common practice to specify the timestamp field in the where clause of your update statement. This ensures that you update only one row of the table. You can be assured of the uniqueness of the value because the server will maintain and update it any time you insert or update a row.

Timestamps are also used, again, as part of the where clause, to prevent two people from updating the same row. Because the timestamp is updated automatically whenever an update is made to the row, you can be sure that you're not going to overwrite someone else's information. If someone else updates a row you're now working on, when he or she saves the update, the row's timestamp will be updated, no longer matching your copy. When you issue the update command to save your changes, the where clause will fail because it can't find the specific row that you retrieved. Timestamps are excellent, server-maintained ways to make sure that you have a unique row identifier. ■

If you define a column with the column name timestamp and don't specify a datatype, the column is defined using the TIMESTAMP datatype. You can display the current TIMESTAMP value that's applied to the next timestamp column of a row that's updated or to a new row added using the global system variable @@dbts.

N O T E You can use a select statement to reference the global variable @@dbts by using the syntax

```
select @@dbts
```

For example, the execution of this statement during the preparation of this chapter returned the following current TIMESTAMP value:

```
0x01000000a3d2ae08
```

UNIQUEIDENTIFIER The UNIQUEIDENTIFIER datatype is a 16-byte globally unique identifier (GUID). The primary use for the UNIQUEIDENTIFIER is to maintain uniqueness among all records when data is collected from many different tables in many different databases.

The only operations that are allowed against a UNIQUEIDENTIFIER datatype are equality comparison operators (= and <>) and the IS NOT NULL and IS NULL operators. No other inequality comparison or arithmetic operators are allowed. All column constraints and properties except IDENTITY are allowed on the UNIQUEIDENTIFIER datatype. Each GUID has a guaranteed unique value.

A new UNIQUEIDENTIFIER is generated in Transact-SQL with the NEWID() function.

BINARY(n) You can use the BINARY datatype to store bit patterns that consist of up to 8,000 bytes. Use the integer specified in parentheses to define the length of all bit patterns from one (1) to 8,000 bytes. You must specify the size of a binary column to be at least one byte, but you can store a bit pattern of all zeros.

You must enter the first binary value preceded with 0x. You can enter binary data using the characters zero (0) through nine (9) and A through F. For example, enter the value A0 by preceding it with 0x, in the form 0xA0. If you enter values greater than the length that you defined, the values are truncated. Values are also padded with zeros after the least significant digit.

Here's another example. A column defined as BINARY(1) can store up to the maximum value of ff. In the following example, a table is defined with two columns with the datatypes BINARY(1) and BINARY(2). Four insert statements are used to enter successive pairs of values of 0, 1, ff, and fff in both columns.

```
create table binarytable
(x binary(1),y binary(2))
insert into binarytable
values (0x0,0x0)
insert into binarytable
values (0x1,0x1)
insert into binarytable
values (0xff,0xff)
insert into binarytable
values (0xfff,0xfff)
select * from binarytable
...
x    y
---- ------
0x00 0x0000
0x01 0x0100
0xff 0xff00
0x0f 0x0fff
(4 row(s) affected)
```

VARBINARY(n) You can use the VARBINARY datatype to store bit patterns that consist of up to 255 bytes. You use the integer specified in parentheses to define the maximum length of all bit patterns from one to 8,000 bytes. You must specify the size of a binary column to be at least one byte, but you can store a bit pattern of all zeros.

Unlike the BINARY datatype, VARBINARY datatype storage is limited to just enough space for the length of the actual value. Like the BINARY datatype, you must enter the first binary value preceded with 0x. You can enter binary data using the characters zero (0) through nine (9) and A through F. If you enter values that are greater than the maximum length you defined, the values are truncated.

In the following example, a table is defined with two columns with the VARBINARY(1) and VARBINARY(2) datatypes. Four insert statements are used to enter successive pairs of values of 0, 1, ff, and fff in both columns.

```
create table varbinarytable
(x varbinary(1),y varbinary(2))
insert into varbinarytable
values (0x0,0x0)
insert into varbinarytable
values (0x1,0x1)
insert into varbinarytable
values (0xff,0xff)
insert into varbinarytable
values (0xfff,0xfff)
select * from varbinarytable
...
x    y
---- ------
0x00 0x00
0x01 0x01
0xff 0xff
0x0f 0x0fff
```

Unlike the values entered into a table in which the columns are defined as BINARY(1) and BINARY(2), the values are stored in only the amount of space that's required. Values are truncated if they're greater than the maximum space defined when the table is created.

TEXT and IMAGE Datatypes

Use TEXT and IMAGE datatypes to store large amounts of character or binary data. You can store more than two billion data bytes in either a TEXT or IMAGE datatype. It's wasteful to preallocate space for TEXT or IMAGE datatypes to any significant extent, so only a portion of the space is preallocated. The remaining space is dynamically allocated.

NOTE IMAGE datatypes are sometimes used for embedded OLE objects that are part of a row. ■

TEXT Use the TEXT datatype for storing large amounts of text. The characters stored in a text field are typically characters that can be output directly to a display device such as a monitor window or a printer. You can store from 1 to 2,147,483,647 bytes of data in a TEXT datatype.

NOTE You can store an entire résumé in a single column value of a table row. ■

Part

I

Ch

6

Your data is stored in fixed-length strings of characters in an initially allocated 8KB (8,192 bytes) unit. Additional 8KB units are dynamically added and are linked together. The 8KB data pages are logically, but not necessarily physically, contiguous. If you use an `insert` statement to insert data into a column defined as TEXT, you must enclose the data within single quotation marks.

TIP If you define a column using the TEXT datatype and permit NULLs, using an `insert` statement to place a NULL value in the column doesn't allocate even a single 8KB page, which saves space. However, any `update` statement will allocate at least one 8KB page for the text column regardless of any value that may or may not be supplied for that column.

NTEXT   The primary difference between NULL and NTEXT is the 16-bit storage required for Unicode characters. This means that one-half the number of characters, or 1,073,741,823, can be stored in an NTEXT column.

IMAGE   You can use the IMAGE datatype to store large bit patterns from 1 to 2,147,483,647 bytes in length. For example, you can store employee photos, pictures for a catalog, or drawings in a single column value of a table row. Typically, the data stored in an image column isn't directly entered with an `insert` statement.

Your data is stored in fixed-length byte strings in an initially allocated 8KB (8,192 bytes) units. Additional 8KB units are dynamically added and are linked together like the pages for a text column. The 8KB data pages are logically, but not necessarily physically, contiguous.

Using TEXT and IMAGE Datatypes   Values that are stored as TEXT and IMAGE datatypes are displayed just as other columns are when you use a `select` statement. The number of bytes displayed is limited by the global value @@Textsize, which has a default value of 64KB or 64,512 bytes. You can specify the NULL characteristic for text or image columns. A NULL for a text or image column of a table doesn't allocate any 2KB pages of storage, unless an `update` is performed on a row containing the NULL value.

In the following example, two table columns are defined using IMAGE and TEXT. Values are inserted into each column of a single row using an `insert` statement. The row is then retrieved from the table with a `select` statement.

```
create table imagetext_table
(image1 image,text1 text)
insert into imagetext_table
values ('123456789aczx+=\','12345678aczx+=')
select * from imagetext_table
image1                                          text1
-------------------------------------------------------
0x313233343536373839961637a782b3d5c       12345678aczx+=

 (1 row(s) affected)
```

Data in a column defined as an IMAGE datatype isn't translated from its ASCII representation automatically when it's displayed with a `select` statement. Data stored in a column defined as the TEXT datatype is automatically translated to ASCII characters when the data is output with a select statement. An image column isn't meant to be direct output. It can be passed on to another program, perhaps running on a client system that processes the data before it's displayed.

Restrictions on TEXT and IMAGE Columns   You will encounter several restrictions on the use of data stored in TEXT and IMAGE datatypes. You can define only table columns using the TEXT and IMAGE datatypes. You can't define other storage structures, such as local variables or parameters, as TEXT or IMAGE datatypes.

The amount of data that can be stored in a TEXT or IMAGE table column makes each datatype unsuitable for use or manipulation in many Transact-SQL statements. This is simply because the amount of data that would have to be manipulated is too great. You can't specify a table column in an ORDER BY, GROUP BY, or compute clause that's a TEXT or IMAGE datatype. SQL Server won't try to sort or group a table's rows using a column that can contain more than four billion bytes of data because too much data would have to be moved around and too large a space would have to be allocated in which to order the rows.

Here are some things to keep in mind when you create your query:

- You also can't use a text or image column in a union unless it's a union all.
- You can't use a subquery that returns data values from a TEXT or IMAGE datatype.
- You can't use a text or image column in a where or having clause, unless the comparison operator like is used.
- You can't specify distinct followed by a table column that's defined as a TEXT or IMAGE datatype.
- You can't create an index or a primary or foreign key that's defined using a table column that you've defined as an IMAGE or TEXT datatype.

MONEY Datatype

The MONEY datatype stores monetary values. Data values stored in the MONEY datatype are stored as an integer portion and a decimal-fraction portion in two four-byte integers. The range of values that you can store in the MONEY datatype is from –922,337,203,685,477.5808 to 922,337,203,685,477.5807. The accuracy of a value stored in the MONEY datatype is to the ten-thousandth of a monetary unit. Some front-end tools display values stored in the MONEY datatype rounded to the nearest cent.

SMALLMONEY Datatype

The SMALLMONEY datatype stores a range of monetary values that's more limited than the MONEY datatype. The values you can store in the SMALLMONEY datatype range from –214,748.3648 to 214,748.3647. Data values stored in the SMALLMONEY datatype are stored as an integer portion and a decimal-fraction portion in four bytes. Like values stored in a table column defined by using the MONEY datatype, some front-end tools display values stored in the SMALLMONEY datatype rounded to the nearest cent.

TIP You can store your monetary values in half the storage space if you choose the SMALLMONEY datatype rather than the MONEY datatype.

When you add values to a table column defined as MONEY or SMALLMONEY, you must precede the most-significant digit with a dollar sign ($) or a sign of the defined monetary unit.

In the following example, a table is created with two columns that are defined using the MONEY and SMALLMONEY datatypes. In the first insert statement, values are incorrectly added because they aren't preceded with a dollar sign. A select statement shows that the values displayed are identical to those that were stored.

```
create table monetary_table
(money1 money,money2 smallmoney)
insert into monetary_table
values (16051.3455,16051.3455)
select * from monetary_table
money1                    money2
------------------------- -------------------------
16,051.35                 16,051.35
(1 row(s) affected)
```

In a continuation of the same example, a three-digit monetary value is added to both table columns, followed by a value that's outside the storage bounds for the datatype on the computer architecture.

```
insert into monetary_table
values ($123,$123)
insert into monetary_table
values (922337203685477,214748.3647)
Msg 168, Level 15, State 1
```

The integer value 922337203685477 is out of the range of machine representation, which is four bytes.

A large monetary value, which is defined as a MONEY datatype, is added to the first column. It's incorrectly entered because it isn't preceded by a dollar sign ($). The select statements show that the number is stored incorrectly. If you enter a value into a table column that's defined as MONEY or SMALLMONEY, it's stored as a floating-point datatype, which makes it subject to the rounding inherent in the processor.

```
insert into monetary_table
values (922337203685476.,0)
money1                    money2
------------------------- --------
16,051.35                 16,051.35
123.00                    123.00
922,337,203,685,475.98    0.00
```

In the following example, the same large number that was previously entered without a dollar sign has been correctly entered with the dollar sign. A subsequent select statement shows that the large monetary value was correctly stored.

```
insert into monetary_table
values ($922337203685476.,0)
select * from monetary_table
money1                      money2
-------------------------   --------
16,051.35                   16,051.35
123.00                      123.00
922,337,203,685,475.98  0.00
922,337,203,685,476.00  0.00
```

Added to the table are values that contain four digits to the right of the decimal place. When the values are subsequently displayed with a `select` statement, the values are displayed to two decimal places, to the nearest cent.

```
insert into monetary_table
values ($922337203685477.5807,$214748.3647)
select * from monetary_table
money1                      money2
-------------------------   --------
16,051.35                   16,051.35
123.00                      123.00
922,337,203,685,475.98      0.00
922,337,203,005,476.00      0.00
922,337,203,685,477.58  214,748.36
```

SYSNAME Datatype

SYSNAME is a user-defined datatype that's defined as NVARCHAR(128), which means 128 Unicode characters or 256 bytes. NULLs are not allowed. SYSNAME is used for defining columns in system tables. You shouldn't use SYSNAME to define the datatype of columns in your tables. You can use NVARCHAR(128) or you can define your own user-defined datatypes. See the section titled "Creating User-Defined Datatypes" later in this chapter.

Understanding NULL and NOT NULL

Now that you've learned about the additional datatypes that can be defined for Transact-SQL storage structures such as columns, parameters, and local variables, you should understand a second characteristic that you can define. In addition to specifying the datatype of a table column, you can specify an additional characteristic for each datatype: NULL or NOT NULL.

The NULL characteristic for a table column allows you to omit the entry of a column value in the column. If you define the characteristic for a column as NOT NULL, SQL Server won't allow you to omit a value for the column when you insert a row. The NULL characteristic provides a type of validation.

The default characteristic for a column is NOT NULL, which doesn't allow an undefined column value. A NULL that's defined for a column is stored differently than a space, a zero, or a NULL ASCII character, which is all zeros. The interpretation of a NULL entry is undefined or unavailable because no explicit or implicit value is assigned to the column when a row is inserted.

If you reference a row that contains a NULL, the entry (null) is displayed in place of a column value to indicate that there's no entry in the row for that column.

There are two ways to designate that a column or storage structure contains a NULL:

■ If no data is entered in the row for that column and there's no default value for the column or datatype, a NULL is entered automatically. You can define a default value that's inserted automatically into the table column when a column value is omitted. A default value can be added in place of a NULL.

■ You can enter a NULL explicitly by using NULL or NULL without quotation marks when a row is inserted into the table. If you enter NULL within quotation marks, it's stored as a literal string rather than a NULL.

In the following example, a table is created that permits a NULL entry for numeric integer datatypes and character datatypes. A NULL is explicitly inserted into both columns of a single row in the table. In the following example, a select statement displays (null) for both column values of the row.

```
create table nulltable
(x int null, y char(10) null)
insert into nulltable
values (null,null)
select * from nulltable
x          y              1
---------- ----------
(null)     (null)
(1 row(s) affected)
```

> **N O T E** You can specify the keyword NULL in lower- or uppercase when you specify a NULL entry for the column of a row. The default display of a column that "contains" a NULL entry is "(null)". ■

To continue the example, NULL is entered in the second column (y) because only the x column precedes the values clause. A NULL value is added to the second column, y, implicitly because no value is specified in the list port, signified by the values within parentheses separated by a comma, of the values clause.

```
insert into nulltable
(x)
values (5)
select * from nulltable
x                y
-------------------------
5                (null)
(2 row(s) affected)
```

ANSI Support for NULLs

You can change the behavior of SQL Server to automatically permit NULLs on table columns, or user-defined datatypes, if no reference to a the NULL characteristic is specified when a column or user-defined datatype, is defined. You can use a set command to change the NULL characteristic for columns or user-defined datatypes defined during a client session. You can also change the NULL characteristic for an entire database using the system procedure sp_dboption.

Use the following set command to cause NULLs to be permitted automatically in table columns or user-defined datatypes:

```
SET ANSI_null_DFLT_ON
```

Use the following sp_dboption command to cause NULLs to be permitted automatically in table columns or user-defined datatypes:

```
sp_dboption database-name, 'ANSI null default', true
```

ANSI nullability permits SQL Server not only to conform to a standard form of SQL but also to be tailored to match the SQL dialect of other SQL used with other server databases. You can more easily use SQL Server if you can modify the syntax and behavior of Transact-SQL to match a dialect of SQL that you have used previously. For example, if you change the default nullability of SQL Server by defining the sp_dboption option as true, it automatically permits NULLs in column definitions, like in Gupta's SQLBase database.

> **N O T E** If you've changed the NULL characteristic during a session or for a database, you can set it
> back to the default by using the commands

```
SET ANSI_null_DFLT_OFF
```

or

```
sp_dboption database-name, 'ANSI null default', false
```

NULL Manipulation

When you compare a NULL value to any non-NULL value of a column or other data-storage structure, the result is never logically true. If you compare a NULL value to another NULL value, the result is also never a logical true. NULL values don't match each other because unknown or undefined values aren't assumed to be identical.

However, rows that contain multiple NULL values in a column referenced in an ORDER BY, GROUP BY, or DISTINCT clause of a select statement are treated as identical values. All three clauses group together rows with identical values. ORDER BY is used to sort rows, and, in the case of NULLs, all entries in the same column are sorted together. Columns containing NULLs appear at the beginning of a sequence of rows that are sorted in ascending order.

GROUP BY forms groups using identical values and all NULLs of a column are placed in a single group. The distinct keyword used in a select clause removes all duplicates from one or more column values and removes multiple NULL values as well. Columns that contain NULLs are considered to be equal when you define an index that uses a NULL column.

> ▶ **See** the sections in Chapter 7 titled "Using an ORDER BY Clause," "Using a GROUP BY Clause,"
> and "Using DISTINCT to Retrieve Unique Column Values," **pp. 178, 185, 180**

Part

I

Ch

6

If you perform computations with columns or other data structures that contain NULLs, the computations evaluate to NULL. In the following example, the evaluation of the expression x=x+1 evaluates to NULL because the x column contains only a single row with a NULL defined for the x column:

```
select * from nulltable
where x=x+1
x          y
---------- ----------
(0 row(s) affected)
```

The following example returns an error because a column defined as NOT NULL is compared with a NULL expression:

```
select * from employee
where badge=null
Msg 221, Level 16, State 1
```

A column of the datatype INTEGER doesn't allow NULLs. It may not be compared with NULL.

Using ISNULL()

ISNULL() is a system function that returns a string of characters or numbers in place of (null) when a NULL is encountered in a data-storage structure such as a table column. The syntax of the function is as follows:

```
ISNULL(expression,value)
```

The expression is usually a column name that contains a NULL value. The value specifies a string or number to be displayed when a NULL is found. In the following example, ISNULL() is used to return a number when a NULL is encountered in the value of a row, or return the character string 'NO ENTRY' when a NULL is encountered.

```
select x,ISNULL(x,531),y, ISNULL(y, 'NO ENTRY')
from nulltable
x                     y
---------- ---------- ---------- ----------
(null)        531     (null)     NO ENTRY
(1 row(s) affected)
```

N O T E   You might decide that it's easier to avoid using NULL than to deal with the intricacies of working with NULLs. You can decide to use a specific pattern that's entered for a datatype that has the meaning of "no entry" or "undefined," rather than NULL. ■

identity Property

In addition to defining the datatype of a column to allow or disallow NULLs, you can define a column with the property of identity. When you define a column with the identity property, you can specify both an initial value (seed) that's automatically added in the column for the first row and a value (increment) that's added to that last value entered for the column. When you add rows to the table, you omit entering a value for the column defined with the `identity` property. The value for the identity column is automatically entered by adding the increment value to the column value of the last row.

In the following example, the second column is defined with the property `identity`. After two rows are added to the table, a subsequent retrieval of the table rows shows that the identity column values were generated by the `identity` mechanism.

```
create table identity_table
(name char(15),row_number integer identity(1,1))
insert into identity_table
(name)
values ('Bob Smith')
insert into identity_table
(name)
values ('Mary Jones')
select * from identity_table
name              row_number
-------------- ----------
Bob Smith        1
Mary Jones       2

(2 row(s) affected)
```

You can assign the `identity` property only to a column that's defined with the datatypes `INT`, `SMALLINT`, `TINYINT`, `DECIMAL(p,0)`, and `NUMERIC(p,0)`—but not if the column permits `NULL`s. If you omit a seed and increment value when specifying the `identity` property on a table column, they default to 1. Also, only a single column of a table can be defined with the `identity` property. The `identity` property doesn't guarantee that rows will be unique. You must establish a unique index on the identity column to guarantee unique table rows.

 TIP You can use the keyword `identitycol`, as well as the name of the column, to reference the column of a table that's defined with the property identity.

Creating and Using Constraints

Constraints are defined to provide data integrity on a table and individual columns. The `create table` statement allows you to create primary and foreign keys, define unique columns and rows, and specify check and default constraints.

PRIMARY KEY Constraints

You use `PRIMARY KEY` constraints for column integrity as well as referential integrity. The definition of a `PRIMARY KEY` constraint for a table has several effects. The `PRIMARY KEY` constraint ensures that all rows of a table are unique by ensuring that one or more columns doesn't permit duplicate values to be entered.

A PRIMARY KEY constraint also disallows NULL for the column(s) that the constraint is defined on. A PRIMARY KEY constraint creates a unique index on the column(s) defined in the constraint. A secondary effect is that the index can be used for faster retrieval of rows of the table than if no index were defined on the table.

NOTE The definition of a PRIMARY KEY constraint on a single table doesn't by itself permit referential integrity. You must also define corresponding foreign keys in the tables whose rows will be combined with the table in which you define the PRIMARY KEY constraint. ■

The syntax of the PRIMARY KEY constraint is as follows:

```
CONSTRAINT constraint_name PRIMARY KEY CLUSTERED (column_name_1 column_name_n)
```

In the following example, the employees table has a PRIMARY KEY constraint defined on the badge column.

NOTE You will have to add a primary key to the Employee table's Badge column prior to running this command. ■

```
Create table employees4
(name char(20),department varchar(20),badge char(4),
constraint badge_pays2 foreign key (badge) references employee (badge))
```

the column in employees 4.

FOREIGN KEY Constraint

A FOREIGN KEY constraint is used along with a previously defined PRIMARY KEY constraint on an associated table. A FOREIGN KEY constraint associates one or more columns of a table with an identical set of columns that have been defined as a PRIMARY KEY constraint in another table. When the column values are updated in the table in which the PRIMARY KEY constraint is defined, the columns defined in another table as a FOREIGN KEY constraint are automatically updated.

The PRIMARY KEY and FOREIGN KEY constraints ensure that corresponding rows of associated tables continue to match so that they can be used in subsequent relational joins. The automatic updating of the corresponding columns of different tables after they're defined as PRIMARY KEY and FOREIGN KEY constraints is called *declarative referential integrity,* a feature added to SQL Server in version 6.0.

The syntax of the FOREIGN KEY constraint clause is as follows:

```
CONSTRAINT constraint_name FOREIGN KEY (column_name_1 column_name_n) REFERENCES
_table_name (column_name_1 column_name_n)
```

The table named after the keyword REFERENCES is the table in which the corresponding column(s) are defined as a PRIMARY KEY constraint. In the following example, the badge column in the pays2 table is defined as a FOREIGN KEY constraint that is associated with, or references, the badge column in the employees4 table.

N O T E   You will have to add a primary key to the Employee4 table's Badge column prior to running this command. ■

```
Create table pays
        (hours_worked integer, pay_rate integer, badge char(4),
        constraint badge_pays3 foreign key (badge)
        references employees4 (badge))
```

N O T E   The corresponding columns that are defined as PRIMARY KEY and FOREIGN KEY constraints don't have to have the same names. However, it's simpler to understand the columns in different tables that are defined as associated PRIMARY KEY and FOREIGN KEY constraints if their names are identical. ■

Unique Constraint

You apply the unique constraint to any table column to prevent duplicate values from being entered into the column. A restriction is that the column can't be defined as the primary key or part of the primary key of the table. The unique constraint is enforced through the automatic creation of a unique index for the table that's based on the column. In the following example, a unique constraint is applied to the badge column of the employees2 table.

```
Create table employees2
(name char(20), department varchar(20),badge integer,
constraint badge_nodupes unique nonclustered (badge))
```

Check Constraint

A check constraint limits the values that can be entered into one or more columns of a database table. You can use a check constraint, for example, to limit the range of values that can be stored in a column defined as a NUMERIC datatype that's smaller than the range permitted by the datatype.

The process of associating a check with a table column is called *binding*. You can define and associate multiple checks with a single column. A check can be defined for a column even though a rule is already defined on the column. In the following example, a check constraint is defined on the department column to restrict subsequent entries to valid departments.

```
Create table employees5
    (name char(20), department varchar(20) check (department in
    ('Sales','Field Service','Software','Logistics')),badge
    integer)
```

N O T E   Check and other constraints can seem as though they duplicate the function of other mechanisms that exist in SQL Server. If you have this perception, it's accurate. In version 6.0 of SQL Server, Microsoft changed its version of SQL, Transact-SQL, to conform to a standardized

continues

Part

I

Ch

6

continued

form of SQL, ANSI SQL. Although Transact-SQL already had existing ways of performing some operations, such as rules and defaults, the addition of ANSI SQL syntax to Transact-SQL added alternative ways of performing the same operation.

You can often choose to implement a feature such as a restriction on the values that can be entered into a column in the way that you feel is the easiest to set up. For example, you can choose to restrict the values entered into the columns of a table by using a `check` constraint rather than by defining a rule and binding it to the column.

However, you should investigate each alternative mechanism because one might be more appropriate for your use. Although a `check` constraint is quicker and simpler to set up to restrict the column values than a rule, a rule is more flexible in one way. After you define a rule, it can be bound to a column in multiple tables. A rule might prove more useful to you if you're going to use it to restrict column values on columns that are in multiple tables. ■

Default Constraint

You use a `default` constraint to have a value that's automatically added to a table column when no value is entered during an insert. You can define a `default` constraint to the most frequent value that occurs within a table column, thus relieving a user of entering the defined `default` constraint value when a new row is added to the table. The syntax of the `default` constraint clause is as follows:

```
DEFAULT default_name value FOR column_name
```

In the following example, a default value is specified for the department column for the employees6 table:

```
Create table employees6
        (name char(20),department varchar(20) default 'Sales',badge integer)
```

You can also use a `default`, which you must define and then bind to a table column, to have a value automatically added to a table column. Although Microsoft recommends that you use a `default` constraint to add a value automatically to a table column, after a `default` is defined, it can be bound to columns in different tables rather than in a single table.

▶ **See** Chapter 13, "Managing and Using Rules, Constraints, and Defaults," **p. 333**

Microsoft recommends that you use a `default` constraint rather than a `default` when you have defined a default value for a column in a single table because a `default` constraint is stored with the table, rather than as a separate database object. If you drop a table, the constraint is automatically dropped. When a table is deleted, a `default` bound to a column of the table isn't deleted.

N O T E   With a `default` constraint, you can use a set of functions called *niladic functions*. A niladic function inserts a value that's generated by SQL Server.

Pg 254 *(handwritten)*

Niladic functions allow system-supplied information about the current user or a timestamp to be inserted when no value is specified. The ANSI niladic functions that can be used with a `default` constraint are `current_user()`, `session_user()`, `system_user()`, `user()`, and `current_timestamp()`. `current_user()`, `session_user()`, and `user()` return the username stored in the database of the user issuing an `insert` or `update`. The `system_user()` function returns the SQL Server logon ID of the user, and the `current_timestamp()` function returns the date in the same form that's returned by the `getdate()` function. ■

Creating User-Defined Datatypes

You can define your own datatype, which can then be used as a datatype for a storage structure such as a table column. You always define a user-defined datatype as one of the existing system datatypes. A user-defined datatype allows you to define a datatype that can contain a length specification, if necessary, and a NULL characteristic.

You can use a descriptive name for the user-defined datatype that describes the type of data that it contains.

Creating User-Defined Datatypes with `sp_addtype` You can define a user-defined datatype with the system procedure `sp_addtype`, which uses the following syntax:

```
sp_addtype user_defined_datatype_name, system_datatype, null | null
```

After you define a user-defined datatype, you can use it to specify the datatype of a storage structure such as a table column. You can use the system procedure `sp_help` to display a user-defined datatype. You can create and then bind defaults and rules to user-defined datatypes. You bind rules and defaults to user-defined datatypes with the same procedures used for system datatypes `sp_bindefault` and `sp_bindrule`.

An error message is generated if you specify NOT NULL for a column and don't create a default, or specify a value at insertion. You can also change the NULL or NOT NULL characteristic for a user-defined datatype when you define a column in a table.

In the following example, a user-defined datatype is created using `sp_addtype`. The characteristics are displayed with `sp_help`. A new table is created in which the column is defined using the user-defined datatype.

```
sp_addtype names, 'char(15)', null
Type added.
sp_help names
Type_name       Storage_type      Length  Nulls  Default_name    Rule_name
------------    ---------------    ------  -----  -------------   ---------
names           char              15      1      (null)          (null)
create table usertype_table
(charstring names)
```

In the following example, a value is inserted into the table and subsequently retrieved. The insertion of the string results in a truncation of the inserted string to 15 characters. The example also displays the table in which a column is defined by using a user-defined datatype.

```
insert into usertype_table
values ('this is a string')
select * from usertype_table
charstring
-------------
this is a strin
(1 row(s) affected)
sp_help usertype_table
Name                            Owner                          Type
------------------------------- ------------------------------ ------------
usertype_table                  dbo                            user table
Data_located_on_segment         When_created
------------------------------- -------------------------
default                         May 19 1994 12:46PM
Column_name     Type            Length Nulls Default_name    Rule_name
--------------- --------------- ------ ----- --------------- ------------
charstring      names             15    1    (null)          (null)
Object does not have any indexes.
No defined keys for this object.
```

Creating User-Defined Datatypes with the Enterprise Manager   To define a user-defined datatype by using the Enterprise Manager, follow these steps:

1. Expand the databases by clicking on the plus (+) box next to the Databases folder. Click a database to select it. Your user-defined datatype will be created in the selected database.

2. Right-click User Defined Datatypes and choose New User Defined Datatype.

3. Enter a name in the Name field of the User-Defined Datatype Properties dialog box.

4. Choose a system datatype in the Datatype drop-down list box. Enter a length for the datatype in the Length field if you choose a datatype such as CHAR or VARCHAR. You can also decide to allow NULLs, apply a previously defined rule or default value to the user-defined datatype, or specify an owner.

5. Click OK to complete the creation process. See Figure 6.4 for an example of the dialog box that allows you to work with the datatypes.

FIGURE 6.4
You can list the user-defined datatypes from the User-Defined Datatypes dialog.

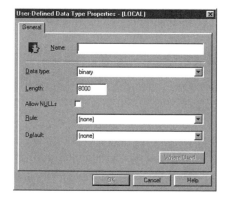

Dropping User-Defined Datatypes   You can use the system procedure sp_droptype to re-move a user-defined datatype. The procedure uses the following syntax:

```
sp_droptype typename
```

You can't drop a user-defined datatype if one or more tables have a column that's defined using it. You can drop the user-defined datatype only if it isn't in use by any tables. In the following example, a user-defined datatype can't be dropped until you first drop the sole table in which a column is defined using the user-defined datatype.

```
sp_droptype names
Type is being used. You cannot drop it.
object                  type owner              column                datatype
---------------------   ---- ----------------   ------------------    --------
usertype_table           U   dbo                charstring            names
(1 row(s) affected)
drop table usertype_table

This command didn't return any data or rows:

sp_droptype names
Type has been dropped.
```

You can also drop a user-defined datatype through the Enterprise Manager. To do so, follow these steps:

1. Expand the databases by clicking on the plus (+) box next to the Databases folder. Open the tree for a database.

2. Select User Defined Datatypes from the tree.

3. Select the user-defined datatype.

4. Right click and select Delete.

Working with Datatypes

You can't name objects with names of commands or other reserved words because datatypes are objects in the database. Datatypes are stored in the Systypes system table along with their coded values. You can use the following select statement to display the datatypes and their code values in the type column:

```
select name,type
from systypes
order by type
name                        type
----------------------      ----
image                       34
ntext                       35
text                        35
uniqueidentifier            36
varbinary                   37
nvarchar                    39
sysname                     39
```

```
varchar              39
binary               45
timestamp            45
char                 47
nchar                47
tinyint              48
bit                  50
smallint             52
int                  56
smalldatetime        58
real                 59
money                60
datetime             61
float                62
decimal             106
numeric             108
smallmoney          122
(24 row(s) affected)
```

Creating Tables and Defining Columns Through the Enterprise Manager

In addition to creating a table with the `create table` statement, you can create a table through the Enterprise Manager. To do so, follow these steps:

▶ **See** the section in Chapter 1, "Understanding Microsoft SQL Server 7.0 Fundamentals," titled "SQL Enterprise Manager," **p. 30**

1. Expand the databases by clicking on the plus (+) box next to the Databases folder. Click a database to select it. Your table will be created in the selected database.

2. Right-click Tables from the tree list and select New Table and enter a name in the Choose Name dialog box. Click OK.

3. Enter a column name in the Column Name field.

4. Use the mouse or Tab key to move to the Datatype field. Select a datatype from the list that appears.

5. If the datatype that you have chosen requires the specification of a length, enter it into the Length field.

6. To allow NULL values, leave the Nulls field selected.

7. If you've previously defined default values, you can choose one in the Default field.

8. Repeat steps 3 through 7 to continue specifying up to 1,024 columns and their characteristics.

Figure 6.5 shows the Manage Tables window after information for four columns is entered.

9. Click the Save icon on the toolbar.

You also can define properties on columns such as an `identity` or `primary key`. For example, in Figure 6.6, a column has been defined as an identity column by checking the Identity Check Box.

FIGURE 6.5

The *NULL* property is automatically enabled for each column that you enter, although you can unselect it.

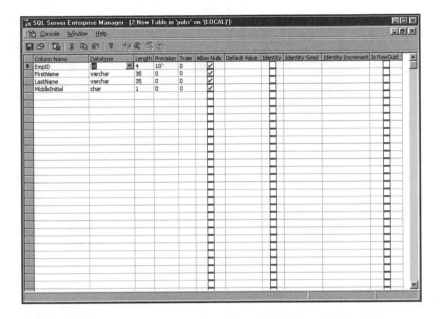

FIGURE 6.6

You can specify an initial value (seed) and increment for your identity column.

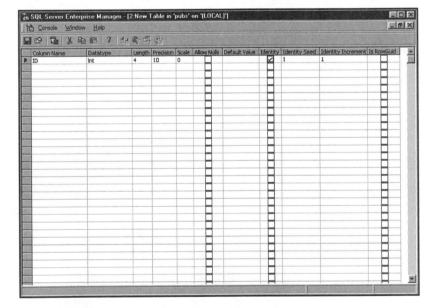

Adding Data to a Table with **insert**

After you create a table, you can add data by using an insert statement. Several forms of the insert statement can be used to add new rows to a table. Each insert statement can add only a single row to a table. The complete form of the insert statement uses the following syntax:

Part

I

Ch

6

```
insert INTO table_name
(column_name_1,...,column_name_n)
VALUES ('string_1',...'lstring_')
```

List the table columns to receive values separately, enclosed by parentheses and separated by commas, after the insert clause. Enter the values that will be added to the table columns in parentheses in the same order as the column names in the previous line. The list of column values is preceded by the VALUES keyword.

You don't have to list the columns and their values in the same order as they were defined in the table. You must, however, enter the values in the VALUES clause in the same order as the column names listed in the previous line. If you do not, data values might be inserted into the wrong columns.

In the following example, the columns are listed in the order in which they were defined in the table, but they don't have to follow the same order. The values are entered in the VALUES clause in an order that corresponds to the order of the columns named in the previous line.

```
insert into employees
(name, department, badge)
values ('Bob Smith', 'SALES', 1834)
```

If you omit one or more column names, a NULL or default value is entered into the table row. In the following example, the name and badge columns are listed in the insert statement. The VALUES clause omits a value for the department.

```
insert into employees
(name, badge)
values ('Bob Mariah', 1999)
```

Table 6.4 shows the resulting entry for a table if an explicit value isn't listed in the VALUES list of an insert statement.

Table 6.4 Effect of NULL and Default Values on Table Column Entries

Column Characteristic(s)	User Entry	Resulting Entry
NULL defined	No default value defined	NULL
NOT NULL defined	No default value defined	Error, no row inserted
NULL defined	Default value defined	Default value
NOT NULL defined	Default value entered	Default value

N O T E Use (null) within the values list to insert a NULL into a column that has been defined to permit the NULL.

From Here...

In this chapter you learned to create database tables. The process of creating a table involves the selection of the appropriate datatypes for your table columns. In addition, you learned to add the additional characteristics that can be defined for a table column including the NULL characteristic and the various constraints. You learned to create, drop, and list the characteristics of a table using Transact-SQL syntax and the Enterprise Manager.

For further discussion about topics mentioned in this chapter, see the following chapters:

- Chapter 7, "Retrieving Data with Transact-SQL," teaches you how to use Transact-SQL syntax to retrieve the data that you've stored in table columns.
- Chapter 11, "Managing and Using Indexes and Keys," teaches you how to create and use keys and indexes and how to constrain rows and columns to unique values.
- Chapter 13, "Managing and Using Rules, Constraints, and Defaults," teaches you how to create and bind rules and defaults to user-defined datatypes and table columns.
- Chapter 14, "Managing Stored Procedures and Using Flow-Control Statements," teaches you how to define storage structures such as parameters and local variables by using system variables. You also learn how to reference global variables.
- Chapter 16, "Understanding Server, Database, and Query Options," shows you how to use query options to control the display of data through set command options.

Part

I

Ch

6

Up and Running with SQL Server

Retrieving Data with Transact-SQL

With all the changes to SQL 7.0, you might be glad to know that the core language elements, the Transact-SQL, are not changing. This is because they are based on industry-standard SQL and will remain constant across revisions of SQL Server, though some extensions to the language are always possible and to be expected.

You usually don't want to access and display all the data stored in a database in each query or report. You might want some, but not all, of the rows and columns of data. Although you can access all the information, you probably don't need to display all rows and columns because it's too much information to examine at one time.

In previous chapters, you learned that the information stored in a relational database is always accessed as a table. If you reference a printed table of information, you usually don't read all the rows and columns. You probably look at only part of the table to obtain the information you need. The table exists in a printed form only because it's a traditional way of storing information.

If you can reconsider your requests for information from the database, you can start to eliminate the queries that produce unwanted or unneeded results. In these cases, you can produce output that presents exactly what's needed and nothing more.

Setting Up a Demonstration Database and Table

The data stored on your database, or the disk of your computer system, is analogous to a set of printed tables. You don't need to retrieve an entire table when you issue queries to display information from the database. You construct a query using a Transact-SQL statement that returns only the relevant number of the column or rows of your database tables.

Table 7.1 shows a sample table structure and its data, which will be used for several examples in this chapter.

▶ For information on creating tables, **see** Chapter 5, "Creating Databases and Transaction Logs" and Chapter 6, "Creating Database Tables and Using Datatypes."

You can find a sample script that will create a small database and this table, and will insert the appropriate values in the table on the CD accompanying this book. The filename for the script is 07_01.SQL.

Table 7.1   A Table Containing 12 Rows

Name	Department	Badge
Bob Smith	SALES	1834
Fred Sanders	SALES	1051
Stan Humphries	Field Service	3211
Fred Stanhope	Field Service	6732
Sue Sommers	Logistics	4411

Name	Department	Badge
Lance Finepoint	Library	5522
Mark McGuire	Field Service	1997
Sally Springer	Sales	9998
Ludmilla Valencia	Software	7773
Barbara Lint	Field Service	8883
Jeffrey Vickers	Mailroom	8005
Jim Walker	Unit Manager	7779

The table is limited to 12 rows to make it easier to work with the examples. A typical table for a production database might have more columns of information and will nearly always have more rows of information. The size of the table won't make any difference in showing the operation of Transact-SQL statements. The statements work identically regardless of the size of the tables they operate on. The examples in this chapter are easier to understand if a small number of rows and columns are present in the table used to show SQL operations.

Retrieving Data from a Table with SELECT

Your queries of a database are a selection process that narrows the information retrieved from the database to those rows that fit your criteria. As you've seen earlier in this chapter and Chapter 4, "Data Modeling and Database Design," your goal as you work with tables should always be to return only the information needed to fulfill the user's request. If you retrieve any extra information, the user will be required to wait for a longer period of time than needed. Any less information than is needed will result in additional queries against the database. This modeling of sets of data is always a balancing act that requires continued refinement.

The SQL SELECT statement is used for the selection process. The various parts of a SELECT statement target the data in the database tables. The complete syntax of the SELECT statement is as follows:

```
SELECT [ALL ¦ DISTINCT ¦ TOP n [PERCENT]] WITH TIES select_list
     [INTO [new_table_name]]
[FROM {table_name ¦ view_name}[(optimizer_hints)]
     [[, {table_name2 ¦ view_name2}[(optimizer_hints)]
     [..., {table_name16 ¦ view_name16}[(optimizer_hints)]]]]
[WHERE clause]
[GROUP BY clause]
[HAVING clause]
[ORDER BY clause]
[COMPUTE clause]
[FOR BROWSE]
```

Part

II

Ch

7

A SELECT statement is like a filter superimposed on a database table. Using SQL keywords, the database is narrowed to target the columns and rows that are to be retrieved in a query. In the filter comparison shown in Figure 7.1, the widest part of the filter selects all the rows and columns of a database for retrieval. The narrowest portion of the filter indicates selection of the smallest cross section of data that can be retrieved from a table, a single row with only one column.

FIGURE 7.1

SELECT queries are used to target specific columns and rows of a database.

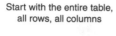
Start with the entire table, all rows, all columns

The select statement narrows the results set, returning only the values needed for processing.

The result can be as narrow as a single row with only one qualifying column.

Most SQL queries retrieve rows and columns that are narrower than the entire table, represented by the base of the filter in Figure 7.1, but wider than the single row and column as shown in the point of the funnel opposite the funnel's base. You'll typically need to retrieve more than a single row and column but fewer than all the rows and columns of the database.

This is where more complicated SELECT statements come in. As you will see in this and the next few chapters, the numbers and types of operations you can perform on your database tables can range from simple selects to complicated, server-resolved queries that provide precisely the information you'll need.

As you read through the different things you can do with SQL, keep in mind that you can, and should, try it out using ISQL, OSQL or SQL Server Query Analyzer against your own tables. That's the quickest way to learn, and the fastest way to get started.

Selecting a Query Tool

There are several different ways you can enter queries to be sent to SQL Server. Although it's beyond the scope and intent of this book to discuss development languages at length, it's likely that, during your testing and experimentation with SQL Server, you'll use one of least three different tools:

- SQL Server Query Analyzer
- OSQL command line version
- ISQL command line version

Initiating the query, sending it to the server, and viewing the results of your query are all covered in the next sections. These sections will serve as the foundation for your use of these tools for the balance of the book.

Using the SQL Server Query Analyzer

SQL Server Query Analyzer is an obvious choice with which to experiment for many different reasons. A primary benefit of this tool is the fact that you can use the functions of the Enterprise Manager to help you work with table structures, other servers, and other features of SQL Server that might not relate to, or be controlled by, your query.

Running queries in SQL Server Query Analyzer is working with a GUI (graphical user interface) that makes revisions of queries much easier. The dialog box you'll use shows the results in one of two optional formats and also displays the query plan.

NOTE Query Analyzer can also be used to see exactly how your query is going to be executed. When you need to find out how SQL Server is going after the data in your tables, this tool can show you the underlying techniques used, possibly pointing out performance bottlenecks. ■

To use the SQL Server Query Analyzer tool from SQL Enterprise Manager, follow these steps:

1. Select the server from the list of available, registered servers.
2. Open the Query window by selecting Tools, SQL Server Query Analyzer.
3. From the resulting dialog box, select the database you want to work with. If you had highlighted a database prior to selecting the tool, that database will already be selected. See Figure 7.2 for an example.

FIGURE 7.2
Be sure to select the database you want to work with prior to entering your query.

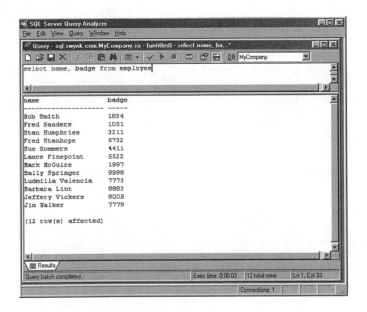

Part II

Ch 7

4. You enter your query in the upper text window portion of the Query tab, then press Control-E, press the green "play" button, or select Query, Execute from the menu. To display the results set in a grid, press Control-R, and then press the green "play" grid button, of select Query, Execute Query Into Grid from the menu.

5. Your results set is automatically displayed in the lower pane of the window. These results are displayed as they are received, so if your query requires processing time on the server for each row, you're likely to see as little information as a single line as each appropriate result is determined.

N O T E   With ISQL, which is a command-line version, you must enter a GO statement after each batch you want to process against the server. Although you can enter these in the Query Tool, it's not necessary. When you select Execute, as in the preceding step 4, all the contents of the query window are sent to SQL Server for processing.

The exception is when you have highlighted one or more sections of the query window. If you have, only the portions that you have highlighted will be sent to SQL Server. This is a good way to test a specific statement out of a batch of statements and a good tool for debugging your queries. ■

Using ISQL from the Command Line

Another commonly used query tool for accessing SQL Server is ISQL from the command line. This type of access is especially helpful in cases where you're running a series of scripts, as you can create a batch file and run the entire series unattended. It's also helpful as a low-overhead approach to testing your queries. The simplest way to start ISQL interactively is

```
isql -Sservername -Uusername -Ppassword
```

Provide the server, username and password that should be used, and you'll be presented with the equivalent to the DOS c> prompt, a 1> prompt, indicating that ISQL is ready and waiting for your input.

From here, you can enter the query you want to run, press Enter, enter a GO statement, and then press Enter. Remember, with the ISQL command-line version, you *must* enter the GO statement, or the query statements you enter will not be executed.

When you run the query, you'll see any messages about the processing as it occurs. This is how you'll find out about any error messages.

N O T E   SQL keywords are case insensitive. SELECT, select, and SeLeCt are all treated the same by SQL Server. ■

```
1> select * from feedback
2> go
Msg 208, Level 16, State 1, Line 1
Invalid object name 'feedback'.
1>
```

Remember, too, you'll need to use the USE statement to select the database you want to access. For example, the following would produce the results desired from the preceding fragment:

```
1> use feedback
2> select * from feedback
3> go
```

NOTE This example assumes you have a database named "feedback" and a table within that database, also named "feedback." ■

TIP You can use the -i option to run ISQL from the command line and pass in a file that contains the SQL statements you want to run. For example:

```
isql -imysql.sql -Sprimary -Uusername -Ppassword
```

will run the mysql.sql file and the results will be displayed to the monitor as they are generated.

In the following sections, you'll learn about all the different portions of the SELECT statement, starting with the basics.

Using OSQL from the Command Line

The newest query tool for accessing SQL Server is OSQL from the command line. The only difference is that OSQL uses ODBC to connect to the database rather than DB-LIB. The syntax is the same except that it uses OSQL rather than ISQL in the opening command.

Specifying the Table with FROM (Required Element)

Different parts of the SELECT statement are used to specify the data to be returned from the database. The first part of the selection process occurs when fewer than all the database tables are referenced. You can retrieve data stored in the database separately by referencing some tables, but not others, in a SELECT statement.

A SELECT statement uses the FROM clause to target the tables from which rows and columns are included in a query. The syntax of the FROM clause is

```
[FROM {table_name ¦ view_name}[(optimizer_hints)]
    [[, {table_name2 ¦ view_name2}[(optimizer_hints)]
    [..., {table_name16 ¦ view_name16}[(optimizer_hints)]]]]
```

In the following complete SELECT statement, the FROM clause specifies that the returned data should include data from the employee table only:

```
SELECT *
FROM employee
```

NOTE In the examples shown in this chapter, the Transact-SQL keywords used to form clauses are written in uppercase. You can, however, use lowercase keywords.

Remember, however, if you installed Microsoft SQL Server with the default binary sort order, the names of your database objects, including the names of tables and columns, must match in case. ■

Part
II

Ch
7

You can also specify multiple tables in the FROM clause, as in the following example:

```
FROM table_name_1,...,table_name_n
```

Each table is separated from the names of other tables with a comma. This is a separator used with lists of information in FROM and other Transact-SQL clauses. The list in a FROM clause often specifies multiple tables rather than a single table.

In the following example of a SELECT statement, the FROM clause references the data from two tables:

```
SELECT *
FROM employee,pay
```

The employee and pay tables are targeted, and all rows and columns are retrieved from these.

N O T E As you'll see later in the section "Using a Wildcard in the SELECT Clause," using SELECT * returns all columns from the requested table or tables. This can produce queries that take quite some time to complete. You should avoid using SELECT * if possible because it does not restrict the returned data set at all. ▤

N O T E In a relational database, you must provide instructions within the SELECT statement to match the rows from two or more tables together. To learn how to match or join rows from multiple tables, see Chapter 8, "Adding, Changing, and Deleting Information in Tables." ▤

The SQL query language enables you to choose tables from different databases. You can specify the name of the database in which the table is located by inserting the database name to the left of the table name. Next, place a period, the database owner name, and another period, followed by the table you need to work with:

```
database_name.owner.table_name
```

In the following example, the employee table in the database company and the owner DBO is specified:

```
SELECT *
FROM company.dbo.employee
```

N O T E The DBO keyword specifies the database owner. You can refer to the DBO at any time. SQL will know that you're referring to the owner of the specific database. ▤

In the previous example, the table was created by using the system administrator's account, so the owner is DBO. If you omit the name of the database and owner when you reference a table, SQL Server looks for the table or tables that you specified in the FROM clause in the current database. You must enter the name of the database in which a table was created, along with its owner, to include the rows and columns from tables in different databases.

Specifying Columns with SELECT (Required Element)

As you work with the SELECT statement, keep in mind that you can control the data elements returned in two different manners. First, you can divide the data vertically, limiting the columns that are returned in your results. This is done with the SELECT statement when you indicate the columns you want to have returned.

The other way you can divide your results set is horizontally, controlling what rows qualify for the results set. You use the WHERE clause, shown in the following sections, to divide your tables in this manner.

The columns of values returned from database tables are specified as part of the SELECT clause immediately following the SELECT keyword. One or more of the columns are entered as a list. Each column, like the tables in a FROM clause, is separated by a comma:

```
select column_name_1,...column_name_n
from table_name_1,...table_name_n
```

In the following code example, the Name and Badge columns are selected for retrieval. The results are shown in Figure 7.2. This example uses the SQL Server Query Analyzer to perform the retrieval of rows.

```
select name, badge
from employee
```

N O T E   The code listings are what should be entered into the query pane of a SQL Server Query Analyzer session. Figures, such as Figure 7.2, will show what the results should look like when the Execute button is selected. ▓

In previous chapters, you learned that one of the basic tenets of a relational database is that operations on database tables always return another table as a results set. The rows and columns of database tables that are targeted for retrieval are always assembled into a temporary table. In most cases, this table is maintained only until the data is provided to the requesting client.

The new temporary table shown in Figure 7.2 was constructed from the three-column employee table. According to the SELECT statement, the temporary table targets all rows of the permanent table's three columns and eliminates the second column, Department. The temporary table is deleted after the rows are provided to the requesting client.

Figure 7.3 shows the query with the employee table performed by the command-line form of ISQL.

T I P   Use the ED command to edit a long statement to be entered at the command line. This will invoke the system editor with the previous command entered. Upon exiting the system editor, it will place the edited statement as the next statement.

FIGURE 7.3
Transact-SQL will produce the same results from a command-line prompt that it will in the GUI environment.

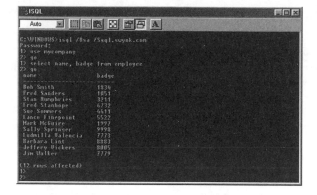

You can display table columns in a different order than you originally defined. To change the default order for the display of table columns, simply list the names of the columns in the order in which you want the columns displayed. In the following example, the order of display for the columns of the employee table is reversed from the order in which they were defined.

```
select badge, department, name
from employee
```

Changing the order of the displayed columns of a database table is consistent with the characteristics of a relational database. You might remember from Chapter 4 that the access of data from a relational database doesn't depend on the manner in which the data is physically stored. You simply specify the names of the columns in the order in which you want them returned in the SELECT clause of the SELECT statement.

 TIP You can display the same column of a table in multiple places if you need to improve the readability of the table, as in a train schedule.

Using a Wildcard in the SELECT Clause

You can use an asterisk (*) in the SELECT clause to specify all columns for inclusion in the retrieval. The following code shows a query that uses an asterisk to reference all columns of the employee table with the results shown in Figure 7.4. The Name, Department, and Badge columns are displayed in the query results.

```
Select *
from employee
```

N O T E Although numerous examples throughout this book show SELECT statements with the asterisk (*) in the SELECT clause, you should always use caution in using the asterisk with production databases.

The asterisk is used in the examples because it's convenient to reference all the columns. In many of the sample queries in which the asterisk is used, it has little effect on the amount of time it takes to perform the query.

You shouldn't use an asterisk with a production database because you probably need to access only some of the table columns in a query rather than all of them. Eliminating some table columns can dramatically reduce the time it takes to retrieve the rows when several rows are retrieved.

You can specify the column names even if all the columns should be retrieved so that the query is more descriptive. If the query is saved and needs revision later, the columns and rows that the query retrieves will be easy to determine by reviewing the query. ■

FIGURE 7.4

You can use the asterisk wildcard character in the SELECT clause of a SELECT statement to return all elements of the table.

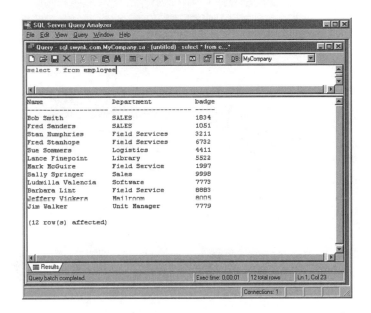

Specifying the Rows of a Table

In the previous examples, all table rows of a database are retrieved. Your goal often will be to retrieve only certain rows rather than all rows. For example, if you have tables that contain millions of rows, you'll probably never execute a query to retrieve all rows from the tables. Every query that you execute specifies a specific results set because it's impractical to retrieve or manipulate all rows in a single query.

The WHERE keyword is used to form a clause that you add to a SELECT statement to specify the rows of a table to be retrieved. A WHERE clause uses the following syntax:

```
SELECT column_name_n,...column_name_n
FROM table_name_1,...table_name_n
WHERE column_name comparison_operator value
```

A WHERE clause forms a row selection expression that specifies, as narrowly as possible, the rows that should be included in the query. A SELECT statement that includes a WHERE clause can return a single row or even no rows if none of the rows matches the criteria specified in the SELECT statement.

Part

II

Ch

7

In the example from the following code (results shown in Figure 7.5) a WHERE clause specifies that only the rows with the sales department are retrieved. All rows that contain the sales department, without regard for the case, are displayed.

```
select *
from employee
where department = "sales"
```

FIGURE 7.5

The sort order that you defined during the installation of SQL Server determines case sensitivity.

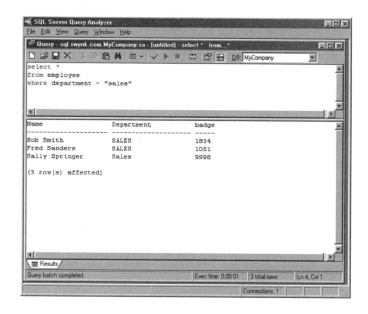

N O T E   The default sort order is defined as case-insensitive during installation. If you change this after installation, you'll need to reinstall SQL Server.

 T I P   If you find that SQL Server returns a message stating that it can't find a column you've indicated, but the column it's calling out is really a value you're passing in, you might have to change a setting. For example, if you issue the following statement

SELECT * from employee where department = "SALES"

and you receive a message that the Sales column was not found, you need to do one of two things. First, you can change the double quotes to single quotes. This will take care of the problem, letting SQL Server treat the information as a constant. Second, you can use the SET QUOTED_IDENTIFIER option. This will tell SQL Server how to work with the information you're passing in. To use the option, simply issue a SET QUOTED_IDENTIFIER ON before your SQL statement.

The following code shows the SELECT statement returns a single row because only one row contains the mailroom department.

```
select *
from employee
where department = "mailroom"
""
```

The query result for a row that contains the Personnel department retrieves no rows, as shown in the following code. The count line, which displays the number of rows retrieved, is at the bottom of the output window.

A retrieval in which no rows match the criteria of the SELECT statement doesn't return an error. Instead, the message (0 row(s) affected) appears.

> **N O T E** If you work with query products other than Transact-SQL, you might receive an error when no rows are retrieved. Transact-SQL, as well as other SQL dialects, considers a query that returns no rows valid. ▪

```
select *
from employee
where department - "personnel"
```

T I P You can refer to the @@ERROR system symbol, which is called a *global variable*, to learn whether the previous operation was successful. SQL Server returns a zero (0) to @@ERROR if the previous operation was successful. After you execute a SELECT query that retrieves zero rows, @@ERROR contains a zero (0), indicating that no error occurred.

```
select @@error
```

A SELECT statement can be used to display the contents of @@ERROR, so the results are returned as rows retrieved from a table. The dashes (-) are displayed underneath the location of where a column header would appear if a column, rather than @@ERROR, was specified. A count message is also displayed for the one value (0) retrieved from the global variable.

▶ For more information on working with @@ERROR, **see** Chapter 14, "Managing Stored Procedures and Using Flow-Control Statements," p. 355

Using Comparison Operators in a WHERE Clause The syntax for the WHERE clause enables the use of a comparison operator following the name of a table column and before a column value.

In the earlier examples, only the comparison operator = (equal) was used. Additional comparison operators can be used to retrieve different rows. Table 7.2 lists the comparison operators that you can use in the WHERE clause.

Part

II

Ch

7

Table 7.2   Comparison Operators

Symbol	Meaning
=	Equal
!=	Not equal
<>	Not equal
<	Less than
>	Greater than
<=	Less than or equal to
>=	Greater than or equal to
LIKE	Equal to value fragment

N O T E   Table 7.2 lists the LIKE keyword as one of the comparison operators. Although LIKE isn't listed as one of the comparison operator symbols in the Microsoft documentation, LIKE is used exactly as a comparison operator. For more information on this operator, see the later section "Using the Comparison Operator LIKE." ▓

The syntax for a WHERE clause that uses a comparison operator is as follows:

```
SELECT column_name_1,...column_name_n
FROM table_name_1,...table_name_n
WHERE column_name comparison_operator value
```

N O T E   You can optionally use spaces around the comparison operations. Your query will execute correctly with or without spaces around the comparison operators. ▓

In addition to the = (equal) comparison operator that was used in the preceding section, you can use the <> (not equal) operator.

You can use the not equal operator to retrieve all rows except those that contain the value to the right of the <> operator. The following code, results shown in Figure 7.6, shows a SELECT statement that contains a WHERE clause for all rows from the employee table except those that contain the sales department.

```
select *
from employee
where department <> "sales"
```

The < (less than) comparison operator can be used to retrieve rows that are less than the value specified for the column in the WHERE clause. In the following code, the rows that contain a badge number less than 5000 are retrieved from the employee table.

```
select *
from employee
where badge < 5000
```

FIGURE 7.6

You can use the comparison operators <> or != for "not equal."

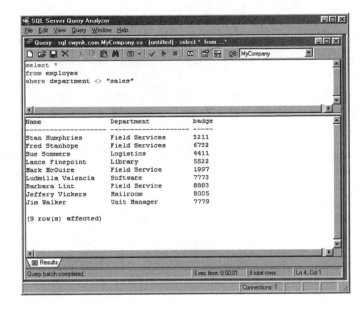

The > (greater than) comparison operator retrieves rows that contain a value greater than the value used in the WHERE clause. In the following code, rows with badge numbers greater than 8000 are retrieved from the employee table.

```
select *
from employee
where badge > 8000
```

The <= (less than or equal to) comparison operator returns rows that have a value equal to or greater than the value in the WHERE statement. The following code returns rows that contain the value less than or equal to badge number 3211.

```
select *
from employee
where badge <= 3211
```

The >= (greater than or equal to) comparison operator returns rows that are greater than or equal to the value in the WHERE clause. Comparison operators can be used with columns that contain alphabetic values as well as numeric values. The following code uses >= in the WHERE clause to retrieve rows that are alphabetically greater than or equal to software for the Department column (see Figure 7.7).

```
select *
from employee
where department >= "software"
```

N O T E When you use comparison operations with columns that are defined as datatypes such as CHAR or VARCHAR, SQL Server uses the binary representation of all characters including

Part
II

Ch
7

continues

continued

alphabetic characters. For example, an uppercase letter A is stored with a lower binary value than an uppercase B. A character value of B is considered greater than the value of an uppercase A using its binary representation.

For values that are more than a single character, each character is successively compared using the binary representation. ■

FIGURE 7.7

The results include rows that contain the software department.

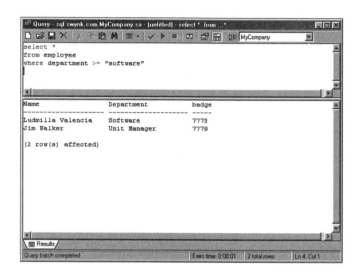

Using the Comparison Operator LIKE The last of the comparison operators is a keyword, rather than one or two special symbols. The LIKE keyword is followed by a value fragment rather than a complete column value. The sample query in the following code retrieves all rows that contain a department name beginning with the alphabetic character S (see Figure 7.8). A wildcard character such as the percent sign (%) can follow the letter S. This wildcard is used to match any number of characters up to the size of the column, minus the number of characters that precede the percent sign.

TIP You can also use the % before a value fragment in the WHERE clause of a SELECT statement, such as 's%'. You can also use wildcards multiple times. The percentage option tells SQL Server to match anything in these positions.

You can use it to find a word within a complete phrase if needed. For example, "%find this%" could be found within the string "The cow asked where he could find this type of fork on the farm" and would be returned.

CAUTION

Use of the LIKE operator typically results in SQL Server not using the indexes associated with a given table. It tells SQL Server to compare the string you indicate and find any occurrence that matches the wildcard string you provide.

For this reason, it's not recommended that you use this type of search or comparison on large tables. At the very least, be sure to warn users that the wait time might be substantial as the system locates the rows that fit their search criteria.

```
select *
from employee
where department like "s%"
```

FIGURE 7.8

The query retrieves only the rows that contain a department starting with the letter S.

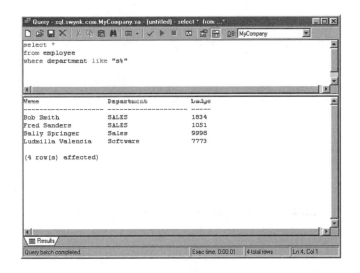

2.

An underscore (_) is another wildcard that you can use to specify a value fragment. Each underscore used in the specification of a value fragment can match any one character. The example shown in the following code uses four underscores following the S to match any rows containing a column value that begins with an S followed by any four characters. Unlike the example shown in Figure 7.8, the query retrieves only the rows that contain Sales or SALES. It doesn't retrieve the rows that include Software.

```
select *
from employee
where department like "s____"
```

3. [-]

You can use square brackets ([]) as wildcards in a WHERE clause that uses the LIKE comparison operator. The square brackets specify a range of values. In the following code, the brackets are used to specify a range of any upper- or lowercase characters as the first character of the Department column (see Figure 7.9).

Part
II

Ch
7

```
select *
from employee
where department like "[a-zA-Z]%"
```

FIGURE 7.9

You can use any wildcard combination in the value fragment.

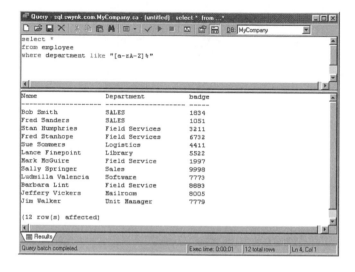

In Figure 7.9, % and [ ] are combined to specify that the rows for retrieval have any upper- or lowercase letter as their first character, as well as any additional characters up to the width of the column. The Department column was created to be wide enough to store 20 characters. Figure 7.9 shows that you can combine wildcards to specify a value fragment.

You can also use a caret (^) after the left bracket to specify a range of values to be excluded from the rows retrieved in a SELECT statement. For example, the SELECT statement shown in the following code retrieves all rows from the employee table except those with first characters that fall within the range F through M.

```
select *
from employee
where department like "[^F-M]%"
```

You can use wildcards only in a WHERE clause that uses the LIKE keyword. If you use the asterisk (*), underscore (_), brackets ([ ]), or caret (^) with any of the other comparison operator symbols, they're treated as literal column values. For example, the following code contains the same query issued earlier, but an equal sign (=) has been substituted for the LIKE query. The identical query with an equal comparison operator, rather than LIKE, doesn't retrieve any rows.

```
select *
from employee
where department = "[^F-M]%"
```

Selecting Columns and Rows with the WHERE Clause   You can retrieve a subset of a table's columns and rows in a SELECT statement by combining the use of specific, called-out columns and the use of a restricting WHERE clause. In the following code, only two columns, Name and

Department, are selected, and only for the rows that contain the Field Service value in the Department column (see Figure 7.10).

```
select name, department
from employee
where department = "Field Service"
```

FIGURE 7.10

A SELECT statement can limit both the rows and columns retrieved.

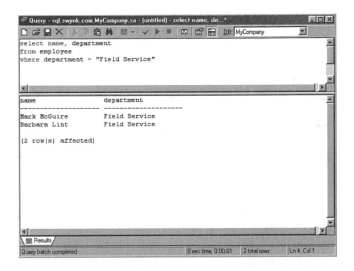

You might remember from Chapter 1 that you can create more than 1,024 columns in a table and an unlimited number of rows. It's almost always impractical, except for small, simple tables, to retrieve all columns and rows of a table. If you correctly construct your query, you can also reference columns from multiple tables in a single query.

The SELECT clause is descriptive because it invokes a selection operation on a table's rows and columns. Keep in mind the analogy of the data retrieval triangle introduced earlier in this chapter. The SELECT statement effectively superimposes a triangle over a table to retrieve some, but not all, columns and some, but not all, rows.

Keep in mind the following tips:

- SQL Server doesn't return an error for a query that results in no returned rows. Although this is not true of other software products, (for example, some programming languages expect an error when no records are retrieved from a file) SQL Server and Transact-SQL consider a query that returns no rows a valid query.

- If you're certain rows exist in the database that match your criteria, try modifying your WHERE clause so only one condition is applied. Run the query with only the first condition. If no rows are returned, you can examine the WHERE clause to determine the problem. If information is returned, add the next portion or portions of the original WHERE clause, running the query after each. You should be able to quickly narrow down which portion of the constricting clause is going awry.

Part

II

Ch

7

Using Boolean Operators and Other Keywords in a WHERE Clause   You can use Boolean operators to retrieve table rows that are based on multiple conditions specified in the WHERE clause. Booleans are used the way conjunctions are used in the English language. Boolean operators are used to form multiple row retrieval criteria. Use Boolean operators to closely control the rows that are retrieved.

The syntax for the use of a Boolean is as follows:

```
SELECT column_name_1,...column_name_n
FROM table_name_1,...table_name_n
WHERE column_name comparison_operator value
Boolean_operator column_name comparison operator
```

You can use several operators with the Boolean option. Each is described in the next sections.

Using the OR Operator   The first of the Boolean operators is OR, which you can use to select multiple values for the same column. In the following code, OR is used to form a WHERE clause to retrieve rows containing two column values(see Figure 7.11). Continue to add ORs to the WHERE clause to select additional values for the same column.

```
select *
from employee
where department = "field service"
or department = "logistics"
```

FIGURE 7.11

You can use any number of ORs with different comparison operators in each statement.

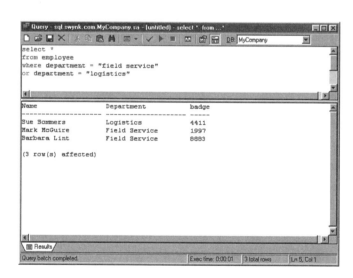

The following query retrieves the rows of the employee table that contain three column values.

```
select *
from employee
where department = "field service"
or department = "logistics"
or department = "software"
```

You can specify different columns in the WHERE clause of a SELECT statement that uses an OR. The query in the following code retrieves rows that either are members of the Field Service department with any badge number or have a badge number that's less than 6000 but are members of any department.

```
select *
from employee
where department = "field service"
or badge < 6000
```

Using the AND Operator   Use the AND Boolean operator if you want the rows returned by the query to meet both comparisons specified in the WHERE clause.

In the following code, a query is used to retrieve a row that contains a specific name and badge combination (see Figure 7.12). If two rows in the table contained Bob Smith, the Boolean AND is used to specify a criterion that requires the row to also contain the badge value 1834. Multiple rows would be returned only if more than one row contained the values Bob Smith and 1834.

```
select *
from employee
where name = "bob smith"
and badge = 1834
```

FIGURE 7.12

You can also use AND and OR together in a WHERE clause.

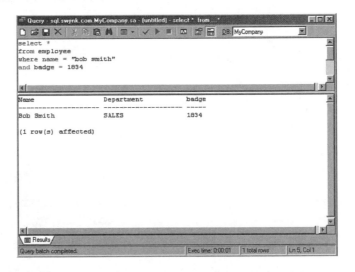

Populating one column of the table with unique values enables individual rows to be retrieved. A unique row is returned if one of the specified columns is the column that contains unique values.

Part
II

Ch
7

> **N O T E**   Defining a column with a unique row or a combination of rows enables individual rows to be retrieved or manipulated. You might remember that SQL Server enables you to store rows that have duplicate values across all table columns. If you allow rows to be individually selected, you establish the capability to reference one table row at a time, if necessary. ∎

▶ **See** the section in Chapter 6, "Creating Database Tables and Using Datatypes," titled "Creating User-Defined Datatypes," **p. 145**

Using the **NOT** *Operator* NOT is an additional Boolean operator that you can use as part of a WHERE clause. Use NOT to specify negation. You use NOT before the column that will be used in the comparison. For example, if you wanted to select based on a value not equaling another value, you'd use the following statement:

```
select *
from employee
where not department = "field service"
```

This query retrieves all rows of the employee table that contain any department except Field Service (see Figure. 7.13).

TIP You can use NOT instead of the not equal comparison operators ! = and <>. A WHERE clause that uses NOT for negation is visually easier to understand than one that uses ! = (not equal).

FIGURE 7.13

You can use NOT for negation the same way the not equal comparison operators (! = and <>) are used.

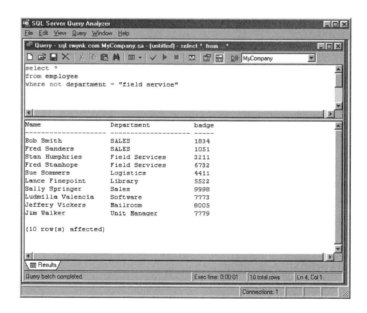

You can also use NOT in a WHERE clause in combination with AND and OR. In the following code, NOT is used to retrieve all rows of the employee table that are members of the Field Service department, except for Mark McGuire.

```
select *
from employee
where department = "field service"
and not name = "mark mcguire"
```

Using BETWEEN to Select a Range of Values Although you can use a number of ORs in a WHERE clause to specify the selection of multiple rows, another construction is available in Transact-SQL. You can use the BETWEEN keyword with AND to specify a range of column values to be retrieved.

In the following code, a WHERE clause that includes BETWEEN is used to specify a range of badge values to be retrieved from the employee table. See Figure 7.14. Use BETWEEN after the name of the column, followed by one end of the range of values, the AND keyword, and the other end of the range of values.

```
select *
from employee
where badge between 2000 and 7000
```

FIGURE 7.14

The table doesn't have to contain rows that are identical to the column values used to specify the range of values referenced by BETWEEN.

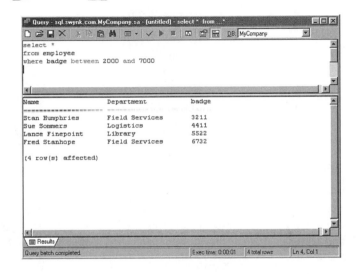

The actual numbers that form the range of values for retrieval don't need to be stored in the table. For example, in Figure 7.15, badge numbers 2000 and 7000 don't have to be stored in the table. Those numbers simply specify a range. Also, a successful query, one that returns an error code of 0, can return zero rows within the range specified by the WHERE clause that contains a BETWEEN. No rows need to be stored in the table for the query to execute correctly.

Using IN to Specify a List of Values You can't always use a WHERE clause with BETWEEN to specify the rows that you want to retrieve from a table in place of a WHERE clause that contains multiple ORs. The rows that contain the column values specified within the range of values will include rows that you don't want. You can, however, use the IN keyword in a WHERE clause to specify multiple rows more easily than if you use multiple ORs with a WHERE clause.

A statement that uses IN uses the following syntax:

```
SELECT column_name_1,...column_name_n
FROM table_name_1,...table_name_n
WHERE column_name IN (value_1, ...value_n)
```

Part

II

Ch

7

In the following code, IN is followed by a list of values to specify the rows to be retrieved (see Figure 7.15).

```
select *
from employee
where badge in (3211,6732,4411,5522)
```

FIGURE 7.15

A WHERE clause that contains IN is simpler to write than a WHERE clause that contains multiple ORs and is more specific than using the BETWEEN operator.

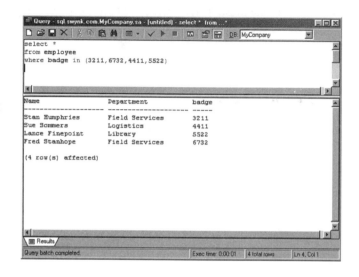

Using an ORDER BY Clause

You might remember that the rows of a relational database are unordered. As part of your SELECT statement, you can specify the order in which you want the rows retrieved and displayed. This is done by adding an ORDER BY clause to sort the table rows that are retrieved by a SELECT statement.

N O T E The rows of a SQL Server database usually will be retrieved in the order in which you inserted the rows into the table. If you create a clustered index for a table, the order of the rows returned by a query is the order of the clustered index. You can't, however, rely on the stored order of rows for two reasons.

- You can create an index for a table that doesn't have a clustered index. After the clustered index is created for the table, the rows will be retrieved in a different order than before the index is created.

- The clustered index for a table can be deleted at any time, which affects the order in which rows are subsequently retrieved.

If you want to return the table rows in a specific order, you must add an ORDER BY clause to a SELECT statement. ■

The syntax of a SELECT statement that contains an ORDER BY clause is as follows:

```
SELECT column_name_1,...column_name_n
FROM table_name_1,...table_name_n
ORDER BY column_name_1,...column_name_n
```

The following code, shown in Figure 7.16, shows a SELECT statement in which the rows are ordered by department. The rows of the employee table are retrieved in ascending order by default.

```
select *
from employee
order by department
```

FIGURE 7.16

You can use multiple columns to determine the order of rows retrieved.

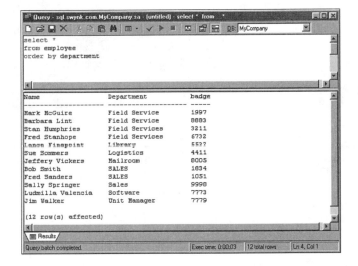

If you include the name of a second column after the name of the first column, the second column orders the rows that are duplicates of the first column. In the following code, ORDER BY is used to order the rows of the employee table first by the department and then by the Badge column.

```
select *
from employee
order by department, badge desc
```

Notice that the DESC keyword is added after the second named column to list the badge numbers in descending badge order. You can also use the keyword ASC to specify explicitly that a column's order in the ORDER BY clause should be ascending. It's unnecessary, however, because the order of a column is ascending by default.

When you use ORDER BY in a SELECT statement, you can specify the columns in the ORDER BY clause by their order number in the SELECT clause. In the following code, the Department and Badge columns from the employee table are referenced in the ORDER BY clause by their order of occurrence from left to right in the SELECT clause.

```
select department, badge
from employee
order by 1, 2
```

Part

II

Ch

7

> **CAUTION**
>
> The number of columns referenced by column number in the ORDER BY clause can't be greater than the number of columns in the SELECT clause of a SELECT statement. If you specify a number that's larger than the number of columns in the SELECT clause, you receive an error message saying that you're out of range of the number of items in the select list.

SQL Server doesn't use the order of the column defined in a table, such as employee in the ORDER BY clause. In a relational database, the syntax of a query language that references database data should be independent of the manner in which the data is stored.

If Transact-SQL used the order of columns as they are defined in the table, the column number would be based as a physical characteristic of the stored data. It's more appropriate to reference the columns using the relative order of the columns in the SELECT clause.

Another problem exists in trying to reference table columns by the order in which the columns are defined in a table. You can specify columns from different tables in the SELECT clause. You can't, for example, reference two columns that are both defined as the third column in two tables, because the column numbers are identical.

You have complete control over specifying columns in the SELECT clause of a SELECT statement. You can reference the same column more than once in a SELECT clause, and the column values will be displayed multiple times. In the following code, the Badge column is referenced twice in the SELECT clause.

```
select badge, name, department, badge
from employee
```

You might not immediately see a reason for displaying the values of a column more than once. If a listing is wide enough, it can be convenient to display a column, often the unique identifier for each row, as the first and last columns of a display A train schedule is an example of a wide output in which the stations often are displayed in the first, center, and last columns to make the output display easier to read.

Using DISTINCT to Retrieve Unique Column Values

You can construct your database table so that it never enables duplicate rows to be stored or so that it allows duplicate rows. Unless you define a constraint on your table, such as a unique key, you can store duplicate rows in the table. Although you can disallow duplicate rows in the table, you can allow duplicates for some columns. You might want to find the unique entries that exist in a table column. The DISTINCT keyword is used to return the unique values of a column.

The following code shows the different departments of the employee table (see Figure 7.17).

```
select distinct department
from employee
```

FIGURE 7.17
You can use DISTINCT with multiple columns to return the unique values of a column.

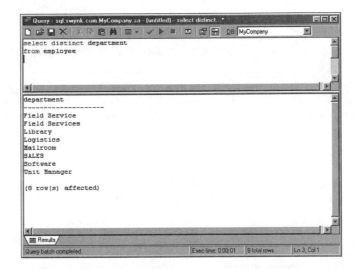

If you use DISTINCT with multiple columns, the rows retrieved are unique by the combination of the columns specified after the DISTINCT keyword. The combination of the values from the Department and Badge columns must return all rows. Whenever you combine a column such as Badge that contains nonduplicate values, with a column such as Department that contains duplicate values, the combination of the two is nonduplicate.

Using Arithmetic Operators

You can use arithmetic operators to form expressions in Transact-SQL. Expressions are evaluated within the statements in which they appear. You need arithmetic operators to manipulate the data retrieved from tables. You can use the arithmetic operators in the SELECT clause to add, subtract, multiply, and divide data from columns that store numeric data.

Table 7.3 shows the arithmetic operators you can use in Transact-SQL.

Table 7.3   Transact-SQL Arithmetic Operators

Symbol	Operation
+	Addition
–	Subtraction
*	Multiplication
/	Division
%	Modulo (remainder)

Part
II

Ch
7

You can form expressions by using arithmetic operators on columns defined with the datatypes TINYINT, SMALLINT, INT, FLOAT, REAL, SMALLMONEY, and MONEY. You can't use the modulo operator (%) on columns defined with the MONEY, SMALLMONEY, FLOAT, or REAL datatypes.

 TIP The modulo operator (%) is used to return an integer remainder that results from the division of two integer values. As a result, it can't be used with datatypes that can contain noninteger values. You'll receive an error message if you try to use the operator on columns defined as other than integer datatypes, even if the column values are whole numbers.

You can use arithmetic operators to form expressions in the SELECT clause of a SELECT statement with both numeric constants and columns. In the following code, an expression is used to increment the badge numbers by five (see Figure 7.18).

```
select badge, badge + 5
from employee
```

FIGURE 7.18

You can use multiple arithmetic operators to operate on column names, constants, or a combination of column names and constants.

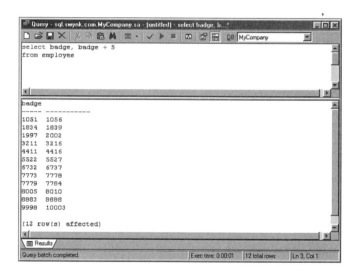

When you use an expression in a SELECT clause, the display for the evaluation of the expression doesn't have a column header. You can specify a column header for the expression by preceding the expression with a text string followed by an equal sign (=). For example, the following code shows the expression preceded by the specified column header in the SELECT clause of the SELECT statement. See Figure 7.19. You can enclose the text string in single or double quotation marks to retain embedded spaces.

NOTE If you perform an arithmetic operation on a column that contains a NULL, the result is NULL. This means that if you're developing an application and an operation is returning NULL as a result, you should check to make sure the values you're using in the equation are valid and not NULL. ■

```
select badge, "badge + 5" = badge + 5
from employee
```

FIGURE 7.19
You can also specify an alternative column header for any column without using the column name in an expression.

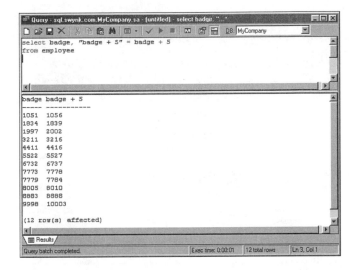

Computed columns are not stored in the database. They might exist in a temporary table that is created during the execution of the SELECT statement. Because the data is not in the database, there is no way to directly verify the results of a computed column. One easy way to compute a value incorrectly is to ignore operator precedence. Arithmetic operators are performed in predetermined order unless parentheses are used to force otherwise. Table 7.4 shows the order in which arithmetic operators are executed.

Table 7.4   Precedence Order of Arithmetic Operators

Operator	Order of Precedence
*	1st
/	1st
%	1st
+	2nd
–	2nd

If you use multiple arithmetic operators with the same order of precedence, the expressions are evaluated from left to right. You can use parentheses to control the order of execution. Expressions in parentheses are evaluated before any other expressions. Use parentheses to evaluate expressions that contain addition and subtraction before the expressions that contain multiplication, division, and modulo operators.

Part
II

Ch
7

The following code shows the use of parentheses in the SELECT clause. The constant 5 is added to each value of the Badge column. After the constant is added to Badge, the sum is multiplied by 2.

```
select "badge + 5 * 2" = (badge + 5) * 2
from employee
```

You can perform arithmetic operations on different numeric datatypes in the same expression, a procedure called *mixed mode arithmetic*. The datatype of the result is determined by the rank of the datatype code stored in a column of a system table.

You can use a SELECT statement to retrieve the datatype names and their code numbers from the Systypes system table. Table 7.5 shows the codes for the numeric datatypes.

Table 7.5   Type Codes for the Numeric Datatypes

Datatype	Code
TINYINT	48
SMALLINT	52
INT[EGER]	56
REAL	59
MONEY	60
FLOAT	62
SMALLMONEY	122

When you write expressions using different datatypes, the results are returned in the datatype of the highest ranked datatype. For example, the values of a column that's defined as either a TINYINT or a SMALLINT datatype are converted to INT if they're evaluated in an expression that contains an INT datatype.

One exception to the datatype code rule applies to expressions that include columns with the FLOAT and MONEY datatypes. The evaluation of an expression that contains FLOAT and MONEY is returned as the MONEY datatype, even though the code number for MONEY (60) is lower than FLOAT (62). You can retrieve the code numbers for all the Transact-SQL datatypes by using the query in following code.

```
select name, type
from systypes
order by type desc
```

This statement retrieves the names and codes for all Transact-SQL datatypes in order by the highest code numbers.

Using a GROUP BY Clause

The GROUP BY clause divides a table into groups of rows. The rows in each group have the same value for a specified column. Duplicate values for each different value are placed in the same group. Grouping enables you to perform the same functions on groups of rows.

You can group by any number of columns in a statement. Columns in the select list must be in the GROUP BY clause or have a function used on it. The syntax of a SELECT statement that contains a GROUP BY clause is as follows:

```
SELECT column 1,...column n
FROM tablename
GROUP BY columnname 1, columnname n
```

GROUP BY targets only unique column values after sorting by ascending column value (default). GROUP BY is unlike the ORDER BY clause, which, although it also sorts records in ascending order, does not remove duplicate column values.

The sample query shown in the following code groups the rows by the Department column (see Figure 7.20). The departments are first sorted to group them together. The duplicate departments aren't displayed because the purpose of the GROUP BY clause in a SELECT statement is to form groups of rows for subsequent action by other clauses.

```
select department, "headcount" = count(*)
from employee
group by department
```

FIGURE 7.20

A SELECT statement containing a GROUP BY clause sorts rows by the columns included.

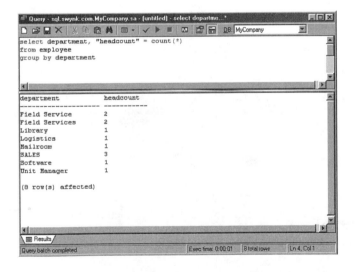

▶ **See** the section in Chapter 9, "Using Functions," titled "Using COUNT()," **p. 229**, for more information on using the function as shown in the example.

Part

II

Ch

7

For example, you can select specific groups with a HAVING clause, which compares some property of the group with a constant value. If a group satisfies the logical expression in the HAVING clause, it's included in the query result. The syntax of a SELECT statement with a HAVING clause is

```
SELECT column 1,...column n
FROM tablename
GROUP BY columnname
HAVING expression
```

The HAVING clause is used to determine the groups to be displayed in the output of the SELECT statement. The following code shows the use of a HAVING clause (see Figure 7.21).

```
select department, "headcount" = count(*)
from employee
group by department
having count(*) = 1
```

FIGURE 7.21

A sample SELECT statement containing a HAVING clause that limits the returned rows.

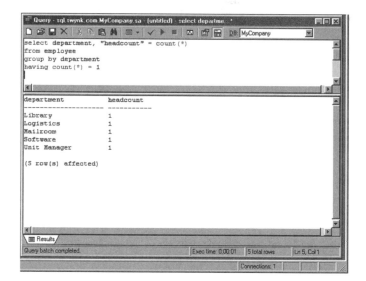

Using a COMPUTE Clause in a SELECT Statement

You can use a COMPUTE clause in a SELECT statement with functions such as SUM(), AVG(), MIN(), MAX(), and COUNT(). The COMPUTE clause generates summary values that are displayed as additional rows. The COMPUTE clause works like a so-called control break, a mechanism used in applications called report writers. You can use the COMPUTE clause to produce summary values for groups as well as calculate values using more than one function for the same group.

N O T E   A *report writer* is an application that permits you to retrieve data from a database without using SQL statements. A report writer is designed with a graphical user interface that permits you to point and click buttons and menu commands to retrieve database data. You might find it useful to purchase a report writer to retrieve data from your database as well as using SQL statements.

You can also use report writers that are built in to some applications, like Microsoft Access, and allow these applications to generate the SQL statements and control breaks for you. ■

The general syntax of the COMPUTE clause is as follows:

```
COMPUTE row_aggregate(column name)
[,row_aggregate(column name,...]
[BY column name [,column name...]
```

▶ **See** Chapter 9, **p. 227**, for more information on the aggregate function shown in the example.

Several restrictions apply to the use of a COMPUTE clause in a SELECT statement. The following list summarizes the COMPUTE clause restrictions:

- You can't include text or image datatypes (or their UNICODE equivalents) in a COMPUTE or COMPUTE BY clause.
- DISTINCT isn't allowed with row aggregate functions.
- Columns in a COMPUTE clause must appear in the statement's SELECT clause.
- You can't use SELECT INTO in the same statement as a COMPUTE clause.
- If you use COMPUTE BY, you must also use an ORDER BY clause.
- Columns listed after COMPUTE BY must be identical to or a subset of those in the ORDER BY clause. They must also be in the same order, left to right, start with the same expression, and not skip any expressions.
- You must use a column name or an expression in the ORDER BY clause, not a column heading.

N O T E You can use a clause that contains the keyword COMPUTE without BY to display grand totals or counts. You can also use both a COMPUTE and a COMPUTE BY clause in a SELECT statement. ■

Using Subqueries

You can nest a complete SELECT statement within another SELECT statement. A SELECT statement that's nested within another SELECT statement is called a *subquery*. The nested or inner SELECT statement is evaluated and the result is available to the outer SELECT statement. To use a subquery, enclose a SELECT statement within parentheses to specify that it should be evaluated before the outer query.

The row or rows returned by the SELECT statement in parentheses are used by the outer SELECT statement. The rows returned by the inner SELECT statement are used in the position of the value in the WHERE clause of the outer SELECT statement. For example, in the following code, all rows are retrieved for the employee table, where the department is equal to the same department to which Bob Smith is a member (see Figure 7.22).

```
select *
from employee
where department =
```

Part

II

Ch

7

```
(
  select department
  from employee
  where name = 'bob smith'
)
```

FIGURE 7.22

You can nest a subquery within the subquery by using an additional set of parentheses around an enclosed SELECT statement.

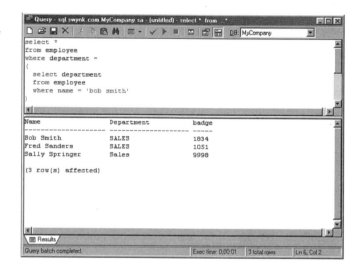

Some restrictions apply to the use of subqueries. The SELECT list of a subquery must return one of two things:

- A single value, as in the example shown earlier. This example selects a value from the second table and uses that value as a parameter to the outer query.

- A count of rows that satisfy an EXISTS test. EXISTS returns the number of rows in which the test value is found. For example,

```
...
if exists select * from mytable where myname="Brennan"
...
```

would be valid as a subquery as long as the table contained at least one row with a value of "Brennan."

This would result in the following error if a comparison operator such as = (equal to) was used in the WHERE clause of the outer query:

```
Msg 512, Level 16, State 1
Subquery returned more than 1 value. This is illegal when the subquery
follows =, !=, <, <= , >, >=, or when the subquery is used as an expression.
Command has been aborted.
```

N O T E Use a NOT IN to eliminate rows that match the results of a subquery. ■

You're restricted in the choice of datatypes within subqueries. You can't use either the IMAGE or TEXT datatypes in the SELECT clause of the subquery. Also, the datatype of the value(s) returned by the subquery must match the datatype used in the WHERE clause of the outer query.

Here are some key points to keep in mind:

- If you try to use the rows returned by a SELECT statement within another SELECT statement and receive an error, your nested SELECT statement probably returned more than one row value to the WHERE clause of your outer SELECT statement.
- Unless you're sure that the inner SELECT statement will return only a single row value, you should use an IN qualifier in the WHERE clause of the outer SELECT statement.

Using ANY and ALL   You can use ANY and ALL to modify the comparison operators that precede a subquery. In Transact-SQL, ANY and ALL don't have the same meaning that they do in the English language. For example, when > (greater than) is followed by ALL, it's interpreted as greater than all values, including the maximum value returned by a subquery. When > (greater than) is followed by ANY, it's interpreted as greater than at least one, which is the minimum.

 If you have difficulty understanding the results of queries that contain one or more nested queries, you can separately execute each subquery. If you record the result of the execution of an inner query, you can use the values to help you interpret the results of the outer queries.

N O T E   The = ANY keyword is evaluated identically to IN. It would be clearer to use an IN instead of = ANY. ■

Specifying Optimizer Hints   The optimizer hints clause is somewhat misleading. You use the optimizer clause of the SELECT statement to override the data retrieval methods that are automatically chosen by the query optimizer. When a query is executed, a portion of SQL Server, called the *query optimizer*, determines how the retrieval of the data from the database is performed.

For example, although an index might exist on a table that's referenced in a query, the query optimizer might determine that it would be faster to retrieve the rows from the table without using the index. The query optimizer might not use an index because the number of rows requested by the query are few in number, and it would be faster to directly access the data rows rather than both the index rows and then data rows.

If multiple indexes exist on a table, the query optimizer will choose to return the rows of the table using the index that would result in the fastest retrieval of information.

You might, however, want to override the way in which the retrieval of rows will be done. For example, if two indexes, one clustered and one nonclustered, exist on a table, the query optimizer might choose to use the nonclustered index for the retrieval of the table rows. You can use the optimizer hints clause in a SELECT statement to force a retrieval using the clustered index. You want the rows to be retrieved by the clustered index because they will automatically be returned in ascending sorted order by the column or columns on which the clustered index was created.

For example, you can use the following optimizer hints clause in a SELECT clause to specify that the rows of a table will be retrieved by the clustered index:

```
select * from employee (index=0)
```

This statement specifies the index name or ID to use for that table. Zero (0) forces the use of a clustered index if one exists. If you use an optimizer hint of one (1), a nonclustered index is used for retrieval of rows targeted in the SELECT statement.

N O T E You can confirm the method that's used to retrieve your rows by using the query option SHOWPLAN. This option returns information about how SQL Server performed your query. For example, if the rows of the query were retrieved without using an index, the method table scan appears in the information returned by SHOWPLAN.

SHOWPLAN also clearly specifies whether a clustered or nonclustered index is used for retrieval in a query. Click the Query Options button on the toolbar to bring up the Query Options dialog box, then select the Show Query Plan check box to return SHOWPLAN information. ■

 TIP You can also use the syntax *index=index_column_name* as an optimizer hint in a SELECT statement in place of the index number.

▶ **See** the section in Chapter 16, "Understanding Server, Database, and Query Options," titled "Interpreting SHOWPLAN Reports," **p. 438**

You can use a second set of optimizer hints to control the synchronization, or locking of the tables in your SELECT statement. You can use the locking optimizer hints to override the way in which SQL Server normally controls access to data from multiple clients.

Using NOLOCK   You use the NOLOCK optimizer hint to permit you to read rows that SQL Server would normally not permit you to access. For example, if you use NOLOCK in a SELECT statement, you can read uncommitted rows.

Using HOLDLOCK   You use HOLDLOCK to prevent other clients from changing rows that are part of your SELECT clause until your transaction is complete. Normally, other clients can modify the rows when they're displayed. One restriction of HOLDLOCK is that you can't use it in a SELECT clause that also contains a FOR BROWSE clause, discussed below.

Using UPDLOCK   You use an UPDLOCK like HOLDLOCK to prevent other clients from changing rows that are part of your SELECT clause. UPDLOCK releases the rows of your table and the end of the command or next transaction, rather than at the end of the transaction only.

Using TABLOCK   You use TABLOCK like HOLDLOCK to prevent other clients from changing rows. TABLOCK, unlike HOLDLOCK, acts on the entire table, rather than just on the rows of your table. You can use TABLOCK along with HOLDLOCK to prevent other clients from changing rows of your entire table until your transaction completes.

Using PAGLOCK   You use PAGLOCK like HOLDLOCK to prevent other clients from changing rows. PAGLOCK prevents other clients from changing rows a table page at a time, rather than the entire table.

Using **TABLOCKx**   You use TABLOCKx to prevent other clients from displaying as well as changing an entire table referenced in your SELECT clause until your command or transaction is complete.

You might implement this option in cases where you're updating a table and it's imperative that the updated information is always displayed at the client. It's simply a way of locking the information until it's certain that you're able to provide complete, updated information to the client applications that might be accessing it.

Using **FASTFIRSTROW**   You use FASTFIRSTROW to retrieve the rows of a table using a nonclustered index. Unlike the index=1 optimizer hint, the first row of the query is returned more quickly through the use of optimized read techniques. The total time it takes to perform the query might be longer than if the nonclustered index were used with the FASTFIRSTROW option. You use FASTFIRSTROW to get better response time by returning the initial results of your query faster.

N O T E   The *response time* for a database such as SQL Server is usually defined as time it takes to display the first row of a query on a client system monitor. *Throughput* is the amount of time that it takes to complete an operation, whether or not part of the operation involves the display of information as feedback to a client.

Using the FOR BROWSE Option

You can use the FOR BROWSE clause in a SELECT statement to read a table that another client is now adding, deleting, or updating rows within. Normally, SQL Server won't permit you to read a table while pending updates, deletes, or inserts are uncommitted. There are restrictions on what other clauses your SELECT statement can use with the FOR BROWSE clause.

To use the FOR BROWSE clause in a SELECT statement, the SELECT statement must contain a table with a timestamp column and a unique index. To use the FOR BROWSE clause in a SELECT statement, the SELECT statement can't contain a UNION clause. FOR BROWSE should be the last clause of a SELECT statement.

Unique indexes and timestamp columns are required attributes of tables to be used with the FOR BROWSE clause. If a table doesn't meet these requirements, a retrieval statement executes as if the FOR BROWSE clause weren't present in the SELECT statement. A SELECT statement that tries to read the rows from a table that's being modified waits up to the default query timeout interval of five minutes.

If the modification is completed within that time, the rows are displayed by the waiting query. If the pending modification doesn't complete within the timeout interval, the query fails. The FOR BROWSE clause in a SELECT statement permits you to read rows of a table while they're being changed.

Part

II

Ch

7

CAUTION

If you use the FOR BROWSE clause in a SELECT statement, remember that you're looking at table rows whose values might not be kept by the user who's modifying the table. You must be willing to take a chance that a change you see in a table using a SELECT statement containing the FOR BROWSE clause might not be kept.

From Here...

In this chapter you learned to write queries for the retrieval of data from a database so the results set contains only the required rows or columns. In addition, you learned to manipulate the returned data, perform arithmetic operations, and sort the rows. Finally, you learned to use optimization techniques to override the default actions of SQL Server to retrieve data faster or different ways.

For more information about the topics mentioned in this chapter, see the following chapters:

- Chapter 1, "Understanding Microsoft SQL Server 7.0 Fundamentals," shows the syntax used for the command-line form of interactive SQL (ISQL).
- Chapter 6, "Creating Database Tables and Using Datatypes," discusses the treatment of NULLs as column values, as well as column datatypes.
- Chapter 8, " Adding, Changing, and Deleting Information in Tables," teaches you how to combine rows from multiple tables in the same query.
- Chapter 11, "Managing and Using Indexes and Keys," teaches you how to create and use keys and indexes and how to constrain rows and columns to unique values.
- Chapter 14, "Managing Stored Procedures and Using Flow-Control Statements," teaches you how to use conditional statements and how to check status in global variables such as @@ERROR.

CHAPTER 8

Adding, Changing, and Deleting Information in Tables

In this chapter

Understanding how to retrieve information from your database, as outlined in the last chapter, is only the start of making full use of SQL Server. As you saw in Chapter 4, it takes some planning to implement a good database structure. In doing so, you'll introduce some intricacies into how you work with the information in the database. This is because, in many cases, you must work with more than one table to retrieve or update the information for a given transaction.

Information that's stored in multiple tables is often combined in a single query, called a join. A *join* lets you combine rows logically across tables, producing a single output table.

The tables must be created with related columns of data, typically by creating a common key between the tables. You must be able to issue queries that not only combine but also eliminate values from multiple tables. This is where the restrictive clauses of the SELECT statement come into play. The goal is always that only the requisite rows appear in the resultant record set.

The typical database operations, add, change, and delete, are accomplished with INSERT, UPDATE, and DELETE statements, respectively. These statements can operate on one or more rows in your table, and can be directed against a logical view across multiple tables.

In addition to changing the values contained in existing columns within table rows, you'll find that you might need to add additional columns of information to a database table. You use the ALTER TABLE statement to add one more columns to an already existing table, as well as change other characteristics of the table.

In this chapter, you'll learn to write queries that retrieve rows of related information from multiple tables. You'll also learn to update and delete the rows of a database table. Also, you'll learn to change the characteristics of database tables, including how to add columns to a table.

Adding Rows

Of all the operations you'll perform on your database tables, the act of adding information to your database is probably most basic. After all, you have to have the information in the system before you can write the really great client/server application.

To add information to your tables, you use the INSERT statement. The INSERT statement lets you indicate the table and columns you're inserting information against, and the values that are to be inserted. The syntax of the INSERT statement is as follows:

```
INSERT [into] [target] [(columns)] [DEFAULT ¦ values ¦ statement]
```

The INTO clause is optional, but you might want to consider including it because it makes it a bit easier to read. It's sort of like commenting your code. It won't positively or negatively impact performance, so the added clarification on the statement might prove useful at a later time.

The TARGET parameter can refer to one of two things:

Table—Indicates the name of the table you want to insert the values into. This can also take the form of specifying the database.owner.tablename you want to insert into, as indicated in the SELECT Chapter. This is the option you'll likely use most often.

View—Inserts information into the underlying tables. For more information about this technique of updating your tables, see Chapter 10, "Managing and Using Views."

In most cases, you'll be calling out the name of the table you'll be inserting into, but you must indicate one of the two options, or SQL Server won't know where to store the information you're inserting.

Columns tell SQL Server what columns you'll be inserting into, as you might guess. More importantly, however, it specifies the order of the incoming information, and whether any columns are being excluded from the incoming data.

For example, if you have a table with Name, Address, and Phone as columns, your insert statement might begin with

```
insert into addresses (Name, Phone)...
```

This example would let you insert two values, but would skip the Address column.

> **CAUTION**
>
> If you call out the columns in your insert statement and fail to provide information for a column that does not allow NULLs, the insert will fail, indicating that you must provide values for that column.
>
> You can work around this by using the DEFAULT option, indicating a value that should be used if a value is not provided in the INSERT statement. The easier approach is to define a default constraint on the table. You can find out more about this option in Chapter 6, "Creating Database Tables and Using Datatypes," in the "Default Constraint" section and in Chapter 13, "Managing and Using Rules, Constraints, and Defaults."

The last option gives the values to SQL Server that should be placed in the database. For example, to insert a record with the partial field listing used in the last code snippet, the statement would look like the following:

```
insert into addresses (Name, Phone) values ("Caitlin Wynkoop", "520-555-1212")
```

This would result in the single row being inserted, with the name and phone number being updated. The Address column would be NULL, or would be populated by the default value assigned to it.

If you want to insert a row that simply contains all of the default values that you've defined as DEFAULT constraints for the table, you can use the DEFAULT VALUES clause on the INSERT statement. When you do, the values for the columns in the table are all set up to contain the defaults or NULL, whichever is defined for the table you are working with.

The final option for inserting information into your tables is to use a SELECT statement to gather the values to be inserted. This might seem a bit strange at first, but you'll use this often when you consider moving information from one table to another be it for backup purposes, structure changes, or simply so you can work with the data on a test table, rather than on the production tables.

Here's a simple example of this type of INSERT statement:

```
insert into addresses
    (name, phone, address)
    values (select name, phone, address
    from prod_addresses)
```

*NO.
"VALUES"
MUST NOT
BE USED.*

In this example, the Prod_Addresses table contains the source information. Of course, it could also contain other columns beyond those being pulled as the source for the Addresses table, but, in this example, it's only required that you insert the three columns indicated.

What happens is that a single new row is created in the Addresses table for each row in the Prod_Addresses table. Note that, as an example of indicating the columns from the earlier sample, the columns are specified out of the physical order on the addresses table.

The same is true of the Prod_Addresses table. The columns are indicated in the order in which they are needed to populate the first table. Keep in mind that the order, although not important in and of itself, *must* match between the tables. If it doesn't, one of two things will happen. First, you'll have values from the source table showing up in the wrong columns in your target table. This can be a real bear to track down as it generates no error indication from SQL Server.

Second, the insert will fail because the datatypes are not correct from one table to the other. For example, if you try to insert a CHAR type from the second table into an INT in the target, SQL Server will be unable to copy the information into the target.

In the next section, you'll see how you can use the UPDATE statement to make changes to values in your database tables.

Making Changes to Existing Information

An update or change can be performed in SQL Server in two ways. Under certain conditions, changes can be made directly to the rows of database tables. When a direct update of the table row can be made, the operation is done quickly with little overhead to perform the operation. An update directly to the rows of a table is referred to as an *update in place.*

A second way in which you can change the rows of a table is an *indirect* or *deferred* update. In such an update, the change is made by deleting the row to be modified and then inserting the row as a new row with the new values in place. Though it will typically still occur very quickly, a deferred update is slower because two operations are required to change the row of a table, delete and insertion.

The conditions under which a direct update can be performed are primarily determined by restrictions set on the database table. The following conditions must be met for a direct update to be performed on a table:

- The updated column can't be part of a clustered index.
- An update trigger can't be defined on the table.
- The table can't be set up for replication.

Also, a number of conditions must be met for an update in place to be performed on updates that change a single row:

- For a table column that's defined using a datatype of variable length, such as VARCHAR, the updated row must fit in the same database page. In general, this means that the information you're inserting can't be larger than the information you're replacing.
- If a non-clustered index that allows duplicates is defined for the column, the updated column must be a fixed-size datatype or composed of multiple fixed datatypes.
- If a unique, non-clustered index is defined on the column and the WHERE clause of the UPDATE statement uses an exact match for a unique index, the updated column must be a fixed-size datatype or composed of multiple fixed datatypes. The column in the WHERE clause can be the same column as the updated column.
- The byte size of the updated row value can't be more than 50 percent different from the original row, and the total number of new bytes must be equal to or fewer than 24.

The following set of conditions must be met for updates that change multiple rows to be performed in place:

- The updated column must be defined as a fixed-length datatype.
- The updated column can't be part of a unique, non-clustered index.
- If a non-unique, non-clustered index is defined on the column, and the WHERE clause of the UPDATE statement isn't the same column as the updated column, an updated column must be a fixed-size datatype or composed of multiple fixed datatypes.
- The table can't include a timestamp column.

▶ When you do updates against a table, SQL Server will begin locking rows based on several different factors. **See** the section in Chapter 12 , "Understanding Transactions and Locking," titled "Understanding Locks," **p. 323**, for more information.

▶ You can help SQL Server optimize operations with appropriate indexes on your tables. **See** the section in Chapter 11, "Managing and Using Indexes and Keys," titled "Defining Indexes," **p. 288**, for help about creating indexes.

▶ **See** the section in Chapter 15, "Creating and Managing Triggers," titled "Using INSERT and UPDATE Triggers," **p. 399**, to learn more about other factors that might come into play when you update your tables. For example, triggers can be set up to automatically start a process when you do an update. It is important to understand this functionality as you design your system.

If needed, perhaps because you'll be making many subsequent updates on your database tables, you can plan the table design so that all updates are direct. You can consider all the restrictions for direct updates to ensure that your updates are performed as quickly as possible.

T I P You can use the query option SHOWPLAN to determine whether an update was direct or deferred. SHOWPLAN will show you exactly what SQL Server is doing behind the scenes when you execute a query. For example, for a simple query, this is what SHOWPLAN indicates:

```
STEP 1
The type of query is SELECT (into a worktable)
GROUP BY
Vector Aggregate
FROM TABLE
wwwlog
Nested iteration
Table Scan
TO TABLE
Worktable 1
STEP 2
The type of query is SELECT
FROM TABLE
Worktable 1
Nested iteration
```

You turn on SHOWPLAN as a toggle. By issuing a SET SHOWPLAN_TEXT ON or SET SHOWPLAN_ALL ON command, all queries for that session with SQL Server will include the information about what was done for the query. Absolutely key items of note include Table Scan entries. Table scans are nearly never a good thing and can be downright crippling on large tables. What a table scan means is that SQL Server couldn't use any existing index to retrieve the information in the manner you requested. Instead, SQL Server read each and every row in the table to determine how it compared to your criteria. This is a much slower process than that of working an index on a table.

There will be cases where you cannot prevent a table scan, but if you can add an index that makes sense, you should consider doing so. It will improve your performance, sometimes dramatically, and will make your users much happier with you.

The Process of Updating Rows

Obviously, it's likely that the information in your database will change after it is entered in most cases. You use an UPDATE statement to modify the existing column values of table rows. The simplified syntax of an UPDATE statement is as follows:

```
UPDATE table_name
SET column_name_1 = value,......column_name_n = value
WHERE column_name comparison operator value
```

The first thing you need to indicate is the table name. As you probably suspect, this can be specified with the database and owner as prefixes to the table name.

As with the SELECT statement, you use the WHERE clause to identify the rows to be changed. The WHERE clause, used as part of a SELECT statement, narrows the scope of your selection of rows that will be returned or affected by the query. In an UPDATE statement, the WHERE clause is used to identify the rows that are changed, rather than the rows to be displayed.

You can use the UPDATE statement to change erroneous entries or misspellings for the column values of existing rows of a table.

In the following example, the values for the department and badge columns of the Employees table are changed for the employee Bob Smith. If more than one row has an employee named Bob Smith, the department and badge number of each row is changed.

```
update employees
set department = 'SALES', badge = 1232
where name = 'Bob Smith'
```

N O T E   You can also update views as well as tables with the UPDATE statement. You simply use the name of the View in place of the table name in the UPDATE clause of the UPDATE statement. In many different operations, views are treated the same as tables. For more information on working with views in this manner, see Chapter 10, "Managing and Using Views." ▮

You can use UPDATE to change multiple rows that match the criteria specified by the WHERE clause. In the following example, all rows that contain the department SALES are changed to MARKETING.

```
update employees
set department = 'MARKETING'
where department = 'SALES'
```

> **CAUTION**
>
> You must be careful that you specify only the rows you want changed. If you omit a WHERE clause from an UPDATE statement, the change specified in the SET clause is made to every row of the table. The following example shows a change that's made to all rows of a table:
>
> ```
> update employees
> set wageclass = 'W0'
> ```
> There are usually two reasons why an UPDATE statement wouldn't contain a WHERE clause. The first is if the WHERE was inadvertently omitted; the second because you purposely want to change a column for all rows of a table. For example, when you add a new column to a table with the ALTER TABLE command, you might have assigned a NULL value for the new column for all existing rows of the table. You can use an UPDATE statement without a WHERE clause to add a non-NULL value to the new column for all rows.

 You can use a SELECT count(*) statement with the same criteria; specifically, your WHERE clause that you plan to use in your UPDATE statement to learn the number of rows that will be subsequently changed by your UPDATE statement. By first determining the number of rows that will be affected by your UPDATE, you're more likely to notice any mistakes in your criteria.

▶ For more information on using the COUNT function, **see** the section in Chapter 9, "Using Functions," titled "Using COUNT," **p. 229**

SET Clause Options

You can also use an expression or the keywords DEFAULT and NULL in the SET clause of an UPDATE statement. If you use an expression in a SET clause rather than a constant value, the expression is first evaluated, and its result is assigned to the rows that are specified in the UPDATE statement.

In the following example, a raise in the hourly rate is given to all employees by updating the rate column of the Pays table.

```
update pays
set rate=rate+2
```

You can use the keyword NULL to change the column value of the specified rows of a table to NULLs. The table column that's to be assigned a NULL value must have been created with the NULL characteristic originally. In the following example, an employee who has been moved out of his current department, but not yet assigned to another department, has his department changed to a NULL.

```
update employees
set department=null
where name='Bob Smith'
```

You can also use the UPDATE statement to assign a DEFAULT value if a default value has been associated with the table column. In the following example, the department for an employee is changed to the default value that was previously established and associated with the department column.

```
update employees
set department=default
where name ='Sally Springer'
```

▶ For more information on how you can create values that are used as defaults, **see** the sections in Chapter 13, "Managing and Using Rules, Constraints, and Defaults," titled "Creating Defaults" and "Binding Defaults," **p. 347**

N O T E As indicated in the earlier section on using the INSERT statement, if a default doesn't exist for the column and the column permits NULLs, the column value is changed to a NULL. ■

Deleting Rows

Removing rows from a database table is another operation that you must be able to perform to maintain a database. Use a DELETE FROM statement to remove table rows. The syntax of a DELETE [FROM] statement is as follows:

```
DELETE [FROM] table_name
WHERE column_name = 'value'
```

CAUTION

The DELETE statement is one to be taken seriously and cautiously. It's extremely easy to remove all rows from a table and, before you know it, you'll be looking for your most recent backup to restore your table values. There are few, if any, cases where you'll not want a very explicit WHERE clause with your DELETE statement, and you should always re-read your statement prior to clicking the EXECUTE button.

You don't need to use the keyword FROM. It's optional in the DELETE statement. You can delete rows from tables, as well as update tables, through views. ^Also

In the following example, the operation of the DELETE statement removes all rows that match the criteria specified in the WHERE clause of the DELETE statement. In this case, you're removing all rows that contain the department "SALES."

```
delete from employees
where department = 'SALES'
```

T I P You can first use a COUNT function in a SELECT statement that has an identical WHERE clause to your DELETE statement to determine the number of rows that will be subsequently removed.

Keep in mind when you are using the DELETE statement that the sort order that was selected when you installed SQL Server is very important. If you find that upper- and lower-case specifics as part of the WHERE clause don't seem to have any effect on the criteria, it's likely that the sort order is case-insensitive. If you want all your subsequent DELETE and UPDATE statements to be case-sensitive, you might want to update SQL Server using SQL Setup from the SQL Server program group to effectively reinstall SQL Server with a case-sensitive sort order specified.

▶ For more information on setting SQL Server options, **see** Chapter 3, "Installing and Setting Up the Server and Client Software," **p. 63**

You can use a DELETE FROM statement to remove multiple rows as well as individual rows. However, use the DELETE FROM statement carefully. If you don't use a WHERE clause in a DELETE FROM statement, all table rows are removed, leaving you with an empty table. You'll receive no warning before the DELETE FROM statement is executed. In the following example, all rows of the specified table are deleted:

```
delete from employees
```

N O T E The execution of a DELETE statement without a WHERE clause that removes all rows of a table is most often an accident. If you want to delete all rows of a table, but still keep the table intact, you should use the TRUNCATE statement. The syntax of TRUNCATE TABLE is:

```
Truncate Table table_name
```

The advantage of using a TRUNCATE TABLE statement is that the removal of rows is completed faster than an equivalent DELETE statement. The truncate statement is faster because it removes pages of information that contain multiple tables rows at a time rather than the DELETE statement, which

continues

continued

removes individual rows at a time. You can't, however, recover table rows with the TRUNCATE TABLE statement. Unlike the DELETE statement, the TRUNCATE statement does not maintain a copy of the deleted rows even if it's part of a defined transaction.

TRUNCATE TABLE and DELETE TABLE retain the database table. If you want to permanently remove a table, as well all rows that it contains, you can use the DROP TABLE statement, which uses the following syntax:

```
DROP TABLE table_name
```

After you drop a table, you can't recover the rows that it contained except from a previously made backup copy of the table. ▓

TIP Another advantage of the TRUNCATE statement is that it won't log the removal of the information in the transaction log. If you have a situation where your transaction log has become full, you can still use the TRUNCATE statement to remove rows and free up space in the database.

Adding Columns with ALTER TABLE

You primarily use the ALTER TABLE command to add more columns to an existing table.

NOTE In previous versions of SQL Server, you were limited in what could be done with an alter table statement. In SQL Server 7.0, you can now drop columns, change datatypes, or increase the size of a column. These operations do still have restrictions imposed upon them as will be noted later in the section titled "Changing the Width of a Table Column" and "Removing a Column from a Table." ▓

The syntax of the ALTER TABLE statement is as follows:

```
ALTER TABLE table
{ [ALTER COLUMN column_name
{ new_data_type [ (precision[, scale] ) ]
[ NULL ¦ NOT NULL ] ¦ {ADD ¦ DROP} ROWGUIDCOL}] ¦ ADD
{ [ <column_definition> ] ¦ column_name AS computed_column_expression}[,...n]
¦ [WITH CHECK ¦ WITH NOCHECK] ADD{ <table_constraint> }[,...n]
¦ DROP { [CONSTRAINT] constraint_name ¦ COLUMN column}[,...n]
¦ {CHECK ¦ NOCHECK} CONSTRAINT {ALL ¦ constraint_name[,...n]}
¦ {ENABLE ¦ DISABLE} TRIGGER {ALL ¦ trigger_name[,...n]}}
<column_definition> ::= { column_name data_type }[ [ DEFAULT constant_expression
]
¦ [ IDENTITY [(seed, increment ) [NOT FOR REPLICATION] ] ]][ ROWGUIDCOL ]
[ <column_constraint>] [ ...n] <column_constraint> ::= [CONSTRAINT
constraint_name]
{[ NULL ¦ NOT NULL ] ¦ [ { PRIMARY KEY ¦ UNIQUE } [CLUSTERED ¦ NONCLUSTERED]
[WITH FILLFACTOR = fillfactor]
[ON {filegroup ¦ DEFAULT} ]]] ¦ [ [FOREIGN KEY] REFERENCES ref_table
[(ref_column) ]
[NOT FOR REPLICATION]] ¦ CHECK [NOT FOR REPLICATION]
```

```
(logical_expression)}
<table_constraint> ::= [CONSTRAINT constraint_name]
{ [ { PRIMARY KEY ¦ UNIQUE } [ CLUSTERED ¦ NONCLUSTERED]{ ( column[,...n] ) }
[ WITH FILLFACTOR = fillfactor][ON {filegroup ¦ DEFAULT} ]]
¦ FOREIGN KEY[(column[,...n])]REFERENCES ref_table [(ref_column[,...n])][NOT FOR
REPLICATION]
¦ DEFAULT constant_expression [FOR column]¦ CHECK [NOT FOR
REPLICATION](logical_expression)}
```

When ALTER TABLE is executed, it doesn't expand existing rows. It changes only the internal description of the added columns in the system tables. Each time an existing row is read from the disk, SQL Server adds the additional NULL entry for the new column or columns before it's available to a user.

When a new row is written to the disk, SQL Server creates the new row with the additional column and its value. SQL Server writes the row with the additional column unless no value is specified for the new row and its value remains a NULL. In the following example, sp_help is used to display the existing characteristics of a table in which three columns are defined:

```
sp_help employees3
Name                                 Owner                          Type
-------------------------------      ----------------------------   -----------------
employees3                           dbo                            user table
Data_located_on_segment              When_created
-------------------------------      ----------------------------
default                              Jul 5 1999 10:08PM
Column_name     Type                 Length Nulls
Default_name    Rule_name
--------------- ---------------      ------ -----  ---------------  ------
name            char                 30     0      (null)           (null)
department      char                 30     0      (null)           (null)
badge           int                  4      0      (null)           (null)
Object does not have any indexes.
No defined keys for this object.
```

ALTER TABLE is used to add a new column to the table. You use the sp_help procedure to verify that the new columns have been added to the table. In the following example, SELECT displays all rows of the new table, including NULLs in the new column for all rows:

```
alter table employees3
add wageclass char(2) null
sp_help employees3
Name                                 Owner                          Type
-------------------------------      ----------------------------   -----------------
employees3                           dbo                            user table
Data_located_on_segment              When_created
-------------------------------      ----------------------------
default                              Jul 5 1999 10:08PM
Column_name     Type                 Length Nulls
Default_name    Rule_name
--------------- ---------------      ------ -----  ---------------  ------
name            char                 30     0      (null)           (null)
department      char                 30     0      (null)           (null)
```

```
badge              int         4      0      (null)          (null)
wageclass          char        2      1      (null)          (null)
Object does not have any indexes.
No defined keys for this object.
select * from employees3
name                          department                    badge   wageclass
-------------------------     ------------------------      -------  --------
Stan Humphries                Field Service                 3211    (null)
Fred Stanhope                 Field Service                 6732    (null)
Sue Sommers                   Logistics                     4411    (null)
Lance Finepoint               Library                       5522    (null)
Mark McGuire                  Field Service         1997    (null)
Sally Springer                Sales                 9998    (null)
Ludmilla Valencia             Software              7773    (null)
Barbara Lint                  Field Service         8883    (null)
Jeffrey Vickers               Mailroom              8005    (null)
Jim Walker                    Unit Manager          7779    (null)
Bob Smith                     SALES                 1234    (null)
(11 row(s) affected)
```

You can use an UPDATE statement to define values for new columns that are added to a table with ALTER TABLE.

The NULL values are inserted when a new column is added to the table with the ALTER TABLE statement. In the following example, all table rows have a new value added to the column that was added with an earlier UPDATE TABLE statement. A subsequent SELECT statement is used to display all rows of the table, which includes the new column values.

```
update employees3
set wageclass='w4'
(11 row(s) affected)
select * from employees3
name                          department              badge        wageclass
---------------------         ---------------------   ----------   --------
Stan Humphries                Field Service           3211         w4
Fred Stanhope                 Field Service           6732         w4
Sue Sommers                   Logistics               4411         w4
Lance Finepoint               Library                 5522         w4
Mark McGuire                  Field Service           1997         w4
Sally Springer                Sales                   9998         w4
Ludmilla Valencia             Software                7773         w4
Barbara Lint                  Field Service           8883         w4
Jeffrey Vickers               Mailroom                8005         w4
Jim Walker                    Unit Manager            7779         w4
Bob Smith                     SALES                   1234         w4
(11 row(s) affected)
```

You can also define a new column that you've added to a table with the identity characteristic. In Chapter 6, you learned that the identity characteristic permits you to define an initial value for the first row of the table, the seed, and a value that's added to each successive column to automatically generate a new column value, the increment.

N O T E You can't assign the identity characteristic to an existing column. Only new columns
that are added to a table with the ALTER TABLE command can be defined with the
identity characteristic. Also, if the value automatically generated for a new column by the identity
mechanism exceeds the allowable values for the column's datatype, the ALTER TABLE statement fails
and an error is displayed. ■

▶ For more information on establishing an identity column, **see** the Chapter 6 section titled "Identity Property," **p. 140**

In the following example, an additional column is added to table Pays, which is defined with the identity characteristic and can be subsequently used as a row number.

```
Alter table pays
add row_number int identity(1,1)
```

You can also add one or more columns to a table using the SQL Enterprise Manager.

To add a column to an existing table through the SQL Enterprise Manager, follow these steps:

1. Right-click a selected table to which you want to add a column.
2. Choose Design Table from the menu.
3. Enter one or more columns in the Design Table dialog box. You enter a column name, choose a datatype, and choose a size for the datatype.
4. Click the Save Table icon on the Design Table dialog to keep the additional columns that you've added to a table. In Figure 8.1, an additional column, wageclass, is added to the Employees table.

FIGURE 8.1

You can't deselect the NULL property on a column added to an existing table. If you do, when the new table design is saved, Enterprise Manager will issue an error message.

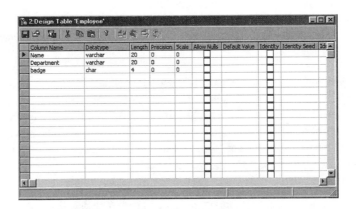

 T I P You can double-click a table to open it and see the structure of the table. You can also update the permissions associated with the table.

Changing the Width of a Table Column

Unlike in previous versions of SQL Server, the alter table statement can now be used to change the width of a column.

The following command will change the datatype of the wageclass column added in the previous example to a 3 character column.

```
alter table employees3 alter column wageclass varchar(3) null
```

Datatype modifications are not allowed in the following conditions:

- 65 compatibility level
- Text, image, ntext, or timestamp
- ROWGUIDCOL for a table
- Computed column or used in a computed column
- Replicated column
- Involved in a index unless the datatype is varchar or varbinary, the datatype does not change, and the length is the same or greater
- Part of a primary key or references constraint
- Used in a check or unique constraint
- Has a default associated with it

Due to these restrictions imposed on changing a column's datatype or length, it is recommended that you use the following procedure.

N O T E   You can also use the Design View in Enterprise Manager to work with columns in your database tables. ▪

In the following example, a new table is created in which the name and datatype of the first column are identical to the first column in an existing table, but the first column in the new table is smaller in size. In the new table, the second column is defined as VARCHAR instead of CHAR, as it's defined in the second column of the existing table. The new table's third column is defined as SMALLINT instead of INT, as it's defined in the corresponding Badge column in the existing table. The SMALLINT datatype uses half the storage space of INT.

After the new table is created, all rows of the older table are loaded into the new table with an INSERT statement. A SELECT statement is then used to display the rows of the new table.

```
create table employees4
(name char(15), department varchar(20),badge smallint)
insert into employees4
select name,department,badge from employees
(11 row(s) affected)
```

```
select * from employees4
name             department          badge
---------------- -------------------- ------
Stan Humphries   Field Service        3211
Fred Stanhope    Field Service        6732
Sue Sommers      Logistics            4411
Lance Finepoint  Library              5522
Mark McGuire     Field Service        1997
Sally Springer   Sales                9998
L. Valencia      Software             7773
Barbara Lint     Field Service        8883
Jeffrey Vickers  Mailroom             8005
Jim Walker       Unit Manager         7779
Bob Smith        SALES                1234
(11 row(s) affected)
```

The sp_help procedure shows the difference between datatypes in the corresponding columns of the two tables used in the example. The example shows only the relevant parts of the display returned by sp_help.

```
sp_help employees
Name                              Owner                            Type
--------------------------------- -------------------------------- ------
employees                         dbo                              user table
...
name            char              20    0    (null)        (null)
department      char              20    0    deptdefault   (null)
badge           int               4     0    (null)        (null)
...
sp_help employees4
Name                              Owner                            Type
--------------------------------- -------------------------------- ------
employees4                        dbo                              user table
---------------- ---------------- ------- ----- -------------- --------
...
name            char              15    0    (null)        (null)
department      varchar           20    0    (null)        (null)
badge           smallint          2     0    (null)        (null)
...
```

The INSERT table statement successfully completes because the data from the earlier table is compatible with the columns defined for the new table. If the data isn't compatible between the tables, you'll receive an error. In the following example, a new table is created that defines a column as a character datatype. The attempted insertion of the corresponding column from one table results in an error because the datatypes can't be implicitly converted.

```
create table onecolumn
(badge char(4))
insert into onecolumn
select badge from employees
Msg 257, Level 16, State 1
Implicit conversion from datatype 'int' to 'char' is not allowed.
Use the CONVERT function to run this query.
```

N O T E If you're transferring a large number of rows between tables, you can first set a database option called `select into/bulkcopy`. If the `select into/bulkcopy` option is set, your rows are copied into a new table faster because SQL Server keeps less information in its transaction logs about your operation. The lack of complete log information about your operation, which prevents an undo or rollback operation to be done later, is probably not important because you still have the rows in the original table should the need arise to undo any operations.

From an ISQL command line, the `select into/bulk copy` option can be set on or off by issuing the following command:

```
sp_dboption database_name, 'select into/bulkcopy', TRUE¦FALSE
```

For example, the following command turns on `select into/bulkcopy` for the database Employees:

```
sp_dboption database_employees, 'select into/bulkcopy', true ▪
```

T I P You can also change a database option using the graphical interface of the MMC rather than a command line. To access this dialog, right-click the database, then select Options.

N O T E This procedure is known as an extended alter. ▪

Removing a Column from a Table

SQL Server 7.0 now allows you to remove a column from a table using the ALTER TABLE command. To remove a column, you will use the DROP COLUMN portion of the ALTER TABLE syntax. To drop the column added in the previous example, use the following statement.

```
alter table drop column wageclass
```

N O T E Dropping a column from a table can be an extremely destructive process for your data. If you are unsure as to whether you will need that data again, use the procedure below to remove the column instead. This will still preserve the old table in case you need to restore the data. ▪

First, create a new table that you define with all but one of the columns in an existing table. Then use an INSERT statement to copy rows from the original table to the new table, minus the column that you didn't define in the new table.

In the following example, a new table is defined that contains only two of the three columns defined in an existing table. INSERT is used with a SELECT statement that references only two of the three columns of the original table in the SELECT clause.

```
create table employees5
(name char(20), badge int))
insert into employees5
select name,badge from employees
```

Adding Constraints with ALTER TABLE

You can also use the ALTER TABLE command to add, drop, apply, or bypass constraints or checks on existing table. Constraints are defined to provide data integrity on added columns. The ALTER TABLE statement, like the CREATE TABLE statement, allows you to add a column to a table with primary and foreign key, unique, and check and default constraints. You can add or drop constraints to or from a table without adding a new column. The syntax for constraints is identical to the syntax used for defining constraints in the CREATE TABLE statement.

▶ For more information about defining constraints, **see** the Chapter 6 section titled "Creating and Using Constraints," **p. 141**

In the following example, a unique CONSTRAINT is added to the badge column for the table Employees2.

```
ALTER TABLE employees2
ADD
CONSTRAINT badgeunc UNIQUE NONCLUSTERED (badge)
```

You can easily drop a constraint from a table using the DROP CONSTRAINT clause of the ALTER TABLE statement. You simply specify the name of the constraint to be removed from a table after the keywords DROP CONSTRAINT. For example, to remove a DEFAULT constraint on the department column for the Employees table, enter the following statement:

```
alter table employees
drop constraint department_default
```

Using the WITH NOCHECK Clause

You can add a NOCHECK clause to an ALTER TABLE statement to specify that a CHECK or FOREIGN KEY constraint shouldn't be applied on the existing rows of a table. The constraints added with the ALTER TABLE statement that contain the WITH NOCHECK clause are in effect only for rows that are subsequently changed or inserted. You can use a NOCHECK clause in an ALTER TABLE statement when you're certain that the existing data doesn't violate the constraints to speed up the execution of the ALTER TABLE statement.

You can't use WITH NOCHECK to override the initial checking of PRIMARY KEY and UNIQUE constraints. By default, SQL Server applies the constraints to existing rows in the table as well as new rows that are added or changed later. You'll receive an error message and the ALTER TABLE statement will fail if existing data violates your constraint.

You can also specify that a CHECK constraint that's added to a table through the ALTER TABLE statement isn't applied to the existing rows of a table through the NOT FOR REPLICATION clause. NOT FOR REPLICATION operates as though the WITH NOCHECK clause was added to the ALTER TABLE statement. The NOT FOR REPLICATION clause is added to an ALTER TABLE statement for a different purpose than the WITH NOCHECK clause.

If you set up the automatic copying of a table and table rows from one server system to another, the actual work of ensuring the server system that receives a copy of the data is done by an intermediate server. The NOT FOR REPLICATION clause is added to an ALTER TABLE statement to prevent the table copy on the intermediate server from being checked, an unnecessary operation.

▶ For more information, **see** the section in Chapter 17 titled "Setting Up and Managing Replication," **p. 443**

Adding Constraints Through the SQL Enterprise Manager

You can add table and column constraints through the SQL Server Enterprise Manager.

To add a constraint to a table or column through the Enterprise Manager, follow these steps:

1. Right-click selected tables that you want to add a constraint to in the main window of the Enterprise Manager.

2. Choose Design Table from the menu.

   Click the Table and Index Properties icon which is the second button. You can click the Tables, Relationships, and Indexes/Keys tabs to create each type of constraint.

3. Enter the requisite information in the Constraint Expression box that appears after you click a tab. For example, in Figure 8.2 a Check Constraint is entered on the au_id column for the authors table in order to prevent any author ID that does not match a social security number format.

FIGURE 8.2

The Enable Constraint for Replication check box can also be checked when the Check Constraint option is defined.

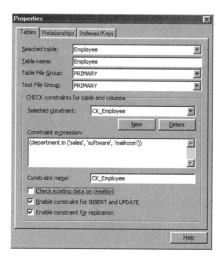

4. When you exit the Table Design dialog, the constraint is applied to the table and saved.

Performing Relational Joins

The rows of different tables can be combined to display and operate on the data using the same statements used in single tables. The rows of multiple tables can be combined in various ways.

The first way is called an *equi-join or natural join*.

You perform a natural join or equi-join by matching equal values for rows in shared columns between multiple tables. You must define one of the two tables so that a column from one of the tables is duplicated in the second table. The column from the original table can be its primary key if it also is a column with values that make the rows of the table unique. The duplicate column that's added to a second table is referred to as a *foreign key*.

You define a foreign key to permit rows from different tables to be related. In a sense, the matching columns are used to form virtual rows that span a database table. Although each table is limited to 1024 columns, matching columns to combine rows from multiple tables can result in almost an unlimited number of columns that can be combined across tables.

You use a standard SELECT statement with a WHERE clause to retrieve data from two or more tables. The syntax of a SELECT statement that's used to join two tables is as follows:

```
SELECT column_name_1,...column_name_n
FROM table_name_1, table_name_2
WHERE primary_key_column=
      foreign_key_column
```

The following CREATE TABLE and INSERT statements are used to create a new table in the same database to be used for subsequent relational join examples. Each row that's added to the Pays table matches one row of the Employees table.

```
create table pays
(hours_worked int, rate int,badge int)
go
insert into pays
values (40,10,3211);
go
insert into pays
values (40,9,6732);
go
insert into pays
values (52,10,4411);
go
insert into pays
values (39,11,5522);
go
insert into pays
values (51,10,1997);
go
insert into pays
values (40,8,9998);
go
insert into pays
values (55,10,7773);
go
insert into pays
values (40,9,8883);
go
insert into pays
values (60,7,8005);
```

```
go
insert into pays
values (37,11,7779);
go
```

In the following example, three columns from two tables are displayed after the Badge column is used to combine the rows that have matching Badge numbers.

```
select name, department,hours_worked
from employees,pays
where employees.badge=pays.badge
name                     department
hours_worked
------------------- -------------------- --
Stan Humphries      Field Service        40
Fred Stanhope       Field Service        40
Sue Sommers         Logistics            52
Lance Finepoint     Library              39
Mark McGuire        Field Service        51
Sally Springer      Sales                40
Ludmilla Valencia   Software             55
Barbara Lint        Field Service        40
Jeffrey Vickers     Mailroom             60
Jim Walker          Unit Manager         37
(10 row(s) affected)
```

An equi-join doesn't eliminate any of the table columns from the temporary tables that are formed by the join of tables. You must use a WHERE clause to match the corresponding rows of the tables. You also shouldn't use the asterisk wildcard character to reference all columns of the combined tables. If you use an asterisk, the columns with matching values are displayed twice.

In the following example, the rows of two tables are accessed without using a WHERE clause. SQL Server forms a cross-product of the rows in both tables. If you don't try to combine the rows using matching columns, each row of the second table in the FROM clause is added to every row of the first table. The Badge column is displayed from both tables because the asterisk wildcard is used in the SELECT clause.

```
select *
from employees,pays
name               department      badge  hours_worked rate   badge
------------------ --------------- ------ ------------ ------ ----
Stan Humphries     Field Service   3211   40           9      6732
Stan Humphries     Field Service   3211   40           10     3211
Stan Humphries     Field Service   3211   52           10     4411
Stan Humphries     Field Service   3211   39           11     5522
Stan Humphries     Field Service   3211   51           10     1997
Stan Humphries     Field Service   3211   40           8      9998
Stan Humphries     Field Service   3211   55           10     7773
Stan Humphries     Field Service   3211   40           9      8883
Stan Humphries     Field Service   3211   60           7      8005
Stan Humphries     Field Service   3211   37           11     7779
Fred Stanhope      Field Service   6732   40           9      6732
...
(100 row(s) affected)
```

The combination of all rows of the second table with the first table results in a *cross-product*, also called a *Cartesian Product,* of the two tables. In the example, the Employees table and the Pays table each contain 10 rows, so the resultant cross-product create 100 rows in the temporary table. However, only 10 of the 100 rows belong together. The badge numbers match in one out of every 10 rows between the two tables.

 TIP

The SELECT statement operates on multiple tables whether or not they were designed to be combined with a relational join. It's important to always use a WHERE clause, which eliminates rows that don't have matching column values.

If you don't use a WHERE clause, you'll receive a temporary table that contains the cross-product of the number of rows in the first table multiplied by the number of rows in the second table. For example, two tables that each contains only 100 rows joined without a WHERE clause will return 10,000 rows.

If you reference one of the columns used to match the rows across both tables, you must indicate the table in which the column is defined. Any time you reference a column that has the same name in multiple tables, you must somehow specify which column is from which table to prevent ambiguity. The following example displays an error because SQL Server doesn't know from which table to display the Badge column.

```
select badge
from employees,pays
where employees.badge=pays.badge
Msg 209, Level 16, State 1
Ambiguous column name badge
```

To avoid ambiguity, the table columns used for matching rows are preceded by the table in which they're defined and separated by a period (.). In the following example, the Badge column is displayed from the first table by preceding the name of the Badge column with its table name.

```
select employees.badge
from employees,pays
where employees.badge=pays.badge
badge
----------
3211
6732
4411
5522
1997
9998
7773
8883
8005
7779
(10 row(s) affected)
```

Using Range Variables

In the previous example, the name of the table is used to prevent ambiguity when referencing table columns in a SELECT statement when multiple tables are referenced. In fact, what appears in the examples to be the name of the table preceding the column name actually is a *range variable.*

N O T E   Other dialects of SQL refer to a range variable as an *alias.*

Range variables are symbolic references for tables that are specified in the FROM clause of a SELECT statement. You can use a range variable in a preceding clause, such as the SELECT clause, or in a clause that comes after the FROM clause, such has a WHERE clause. Define a range variable by specifying a character constant following the name of a table in the FROM clause of a SELECT statement, as in the following syntax:

```
...
From table_name_1 range_name_1, ...,table_name_n range_name_n
...
```

You can define a range variable for each table that's specified in the FROM clause. You can use as many as 128 characters, the limit for any permanent or temporary object in Transact-SQL, to define the range variable. A range variable can be defined to provide a shorter reference to a table in a SELECT statement. In the following example, a range variable is defined for each table. The range variables are used in both the SELECT and WHERE clauses.

```
select e.badge,p.id
from employees e,pays p
where e.badge=p.id
badge      id
---------- ----
3211       3211
3211       3211
3211       3211
3211       3211
6732       6732
4411       4411
5522       5522
1997       1997
9998       9998
7773       7773
8883       8883
8005       8005
7779       7779
3211       3211
3211       3211
3211       3211
3211       3211
(17 row(s) affected)
```

Range variables are called this because after they're defined, the symbolic reference applies to, or ranges through, the table. As in the previous example, you can define a range variable to be a single character and use it as a short nickname for a table.

Range variables can be quite handy because several tables with long names can be specified in a SELECT statement. You can combine rows from as many as 32 tables in SQL Server using Transact-SQL. If you don't explicitly define range variables in the FROM clause, they're implicitly created using the complete name of each table.

In the following example, the rows from three tables are combined using the Badge columns that are defined in all the tables. The range variables are implicitly defined to the table names and are used in both the SELECT and WHERE clauses. The WHERE clause first combines the first and second tables. The first and third tables use the AND Boolean operator.

```
select pays.badge, name,department, payrate
from employees,pays, salaries
where employees.badge = pays.badge
and employees.badge=salaries.badge
```

N O T E Transact-SQL automatically establishes range variables for use in queries. If you don't specify a range variable for the name of a table in the FROM clause, a range variable is created with the same name as the table, as in the following example:

```
select name
```

```
from employees
```

is internally rewritten as:

```
select employees.name
```

```
from employees employees
```

Although it seems unnecessary to create range variables when only a single table is named in the query, they are mandatory when you reference tables that contain columns with the same names in the same query. ■

Using Many-to-One and One-to-Many Joins

You can not have tables that have only one corresponding row in each table. In previous examples, only a single row in the Employees table matches the value of a single row in the Pays table. It's possible that you'll have to create or work with existing tables in which more than one entry is a match for the entries in another table.

In the ensuing examples, rows have been added with identical badge numbers in the Employees table. Three employees have been added, each with a last name of Smith and each with the same badge number. In the tables referenced in the following examples, badge isn't defined as a primary key, so duplicate badge numbers can be present. Three employees with last names of Humphries have also been added, each with the same badge number as the original employee, Stan Humphries. The following example shows the rows of the Employees table after the additional seven rows are added.

N O T E   Although you usually define a primary and foreign key using the corresponding columns of tables that you subsequently want to combine rows from for display, you aren't required to define the columns as keys. SQL Server will permit you to perform joins on tables that don't have primary or foreign key definitions. You should realize that the assignment of primary and foreign keys to a table isn't required, though it's often desirable, if you combine data from different tables. ■

```
select * from employees
order by badge
name                    department            badge
--------------------    --------------------  ----
Bob Smith               SALES                  1234
Henry Smith             Logistics              1234
Susan Smith             Executive              1234
Mark McGuire            Field Service          1997
Gertie Humphries        Sales                  3211
Stan Humphries          Field Service          3211
Stan Humphries Jr       Sales                  3211
Winkie Humphries        Mailroom               3211
Sue Sommers             Logistics              4411
Lance Finepoint         Library                5522
Fred Stanhope           Field Service          6732
Ludmilla Valencia       Software               7773
Jim Walker              Unit Manager           7779
Jeffrey Vickers         Mailroom               8005
Barbara Lint            Field Service          8883
Sally Springer          Sales                  9998
(16 row(s) affected)
```

The Pays table is unaltered and contains only the original ten rows, as shown in the following example:

```
select * from pays
order by badge
hours_worked rate         badge
------------ -----------  ----
51           10           1997
40           10           3211
52           10           4411
39           11           5522
40           9            6732
55           10           7773
37           11           7779
60           7            8005
40           9            8883
40           8            9998
(10 row(s) affected)
```

You can combine tables that have an unequal number of matching rows. The following example joins the Employees table, in which two sets of entries match a single entry for the badge column in the Pays table. The join of the Employees table with the Pays table is called *many-to-one*.

[Handwritten margin notes: 1. Take an entry from "employees" 2. use "badge" as the match criterion 3. look for all entries in "Pays" with a matching "badge" #]

```
select name,pays.badge,hours_worked,rate
from employees,pays
where employees.badge=pays.badge
name                 badge      hours_worked     rate
----                 -----      ------------     ----
Fred Stanhope        6732       40               9
Stan Humphries       3211       40               10
Gertie Humphries     3211       40               10
Stan Humphries Jr    3211       40               10
Winkie Humphries     3211       40               10
Sue Sommers          4411       52               10
Lance Finepoint      5522       39               11
Mark McGuire         1997       51               10
Sally Springer       9998       40               8
Ludmilla Valencia    7773       55               10
Barbara Lint         8883       40               9
Jeffrey Vickers      8005       60               7
Jim Walker           7779       37               11
(13 row(s) affected)
```

If you switch the order of the joined tables, it becomes a *one-to-many* join. The following example returns the same rows that were returned in the previous example:

```
select name,pays.badge,hours_worked,rate
from pays,employees
where pays.badge=employees.badge
name                 badge      hours_worked     rate
----                 -----      ------------     ----
Fred Stanhope        6732       40               9
Stan Humphries       3211       40               10
Gertie Humphries     3211       40               10
Stan Humphries Jr    3211       40               10
Winkie Humphries     3211       40               10
Sue Sommers          4411       52               10
Lance Finepoint      5522       39               11
Mark McGuire         1997       51               10
Sally Springer       9998       40               8
Ludmilla Valencia    7773       55               10
Barbara Lint         8883       40               9
Jeffrey Vickers      8005       60               7
Jim Walker           7779       37               11
(13 row(s) affected)
```

Using Many-to-Many Joins

You might also want to join tables where more than one row matches more than one row in a second table, which is referred to as a *many-to-many join*. In the following example, two tables are combined after one row is added to Pays with a 3211 badge number, 73 hours_worked, and rate of 31.

```
select name,pays.badge,hours_worked,rate
from employees,pays
where employees.badge=pays.badge
name                 badge      hours_worked     rate
----                 -----      ------------     ----
```

```
Fred Stanhope        6732      40        9
Stan Humphries       3211      40        10
Gertie Humphries     3211      40        10
Stan Humphries Jr    3211      40        10
Winkie Humphries     3211      40        10
Sue Sommers          4411      52        10
Lance Finepoint      5522      39        11
Mark McGuire         1997      51        10
Sally Springer       9998      40        8
Ludmilla Valencia    7773      55        10
Barbara Lint         8883      40        9
Jeffrey Vickers      8005      60        7
Jim Walker           7779      37        11
Stan Humphries       3211      73        31
Gertie Humphries     3211      73        31
Stan Humphries Jr    3211      73        31
Winkie Humphries     3211      73        31
(17 row(s) affected)
```

The additional row is added to the temporary table that's displayed. If the row value is restricted to the badge number 3211 only, eight rows are returned.

Many-to-many queries are often not desirable and can produce results that are difficult to follow. In most cases, it's best to implement either a one-to-many or a many-to-one relationship, even if it entails adding an intermediary table.

▶ For more information on database design approaches, **see** Chapter 4, "Data Modeling and Database Design," **p. 75**

```
select name,pays.badge,hours_worked,rate
from employees,pays
where employees.badge=pays.badge
and pays.badge=3211
name                 badge      hours_worked  rate
----                 -----      ------------  ----
Stan Humphries       3211       40            10
Gertie Humphries     3211       40            10
Stan Humphries Jr    3211       40            10
Winkie Humphries     3211       40            10
Stan Humphries       3211       73            31
Gertie Humphries     3211       73            31
Stan Humphries Jr    3211       73            31
Winkie Humphries     3211       73            31
(8 row(s) affected)
```

Using Outer Joins

In the previous join examples, rows were excluded in either of the two tables that didn't have corresponding or matching rows.

Previous examples, in which the rows of two tables were joined with a WHERE statement, included all rows of both tables. However, a query that includes all rows from both tables is probably never useful, except to understand the way in which SQL Server combines the rows. You can combine any two or more tables with a WHERE clause and receive a set of rows that were never meant to be combined and thus receive a meaningless result.

In practice, you'll combine only the rows from tables that have been created to be matched together. Tables that are designed to be combined have common columns of information so that a WHERE clause can be included in a query to eliminate the rows that don't belong together, such as those that have identical values.

> **N O T E** You must ensure that the information used to combine tables, the corresponding values in common columns, remain valid. If the value in one table is changed, the corresponding identical value, or values, if a one-to-many relationship exists, must also be updated in other tables.
>
> *Referential integrity* involves ensuring that you have valid information in common columns across tables used to join tables. You'll read more about referential integrity in subsequent chapters. Chapter 15, "Creating and Managing Triggers," discusses the mechanism for maintaining referential integrity and Chapter 11, "Managing and Using Indexes and Keys," discusses the common table columns on which joins are based. ▨

Use outer joins to return table rows that have both matching and non-matching values. You might need to return the rows that don't contain matching values in the common table columns for either one table or the other tables specified in the SELECT statement.

If, for example, you join the Employees table with the Pays table used in the previous examples, you can specify the return of rows with matching values along with rows without matching values. The specification of the outer join is positional, which means that you use a special symbol the precedes or follows the comparison operator in the WHERE clause of a SELECT statement.

An outer join references one of the two tables joined using the table's position in the WHERE clause. A *left-outer join* specifies the table to the left of a comparison operator and a *right-outer join* specifies the table to the right of a comparison operator. The following table shows the symbol combination used for outer joins.

Symbol Combination	Join
*=	Left-outer join
=*	Right-outer join

A left-outer join (*=) retains non-matching rows for the table on the left of the symbol combination in a WHERE statement. A right-outer join (=*) retains non-matching rows for the table on the right of the symbol combination.

In the following example, a SELECT statement specifies a join in the WHERE clause to return only rows that contain matching values in a common column for the two tables:

```
select *
from employees,pays
where employees.badge=pays.badge
name              department      badge   hours_worked rate      badge
---------------   -------------   ------  ------------ --------  -----
Stan Humphries    Field Service   3211       40          10      3211
Gertie Humphries  Sales           3211       40          10      3211
```

```
Stan Humphries Jr.  Sales          3211    40      10      3211
Winkie Humphries    Mailroom       3211    40      10      3211
Fred Stanhope       Field Service  6732    40       9      6732
Sue Sommers         Logistics      4411    52      10      4411
Lance Finepoint     Library        5522    39      11      5522
Mark McGuire        Field Service  1997    51      10      1997
Sally Springer      Sales          9998    40       8      9998
Ludmilla Valencia   Software       7773    55      10      7773
Barbara Lint        Field Service  8883    40       9      8883
Jeffrey Vickers     Mailroom       8005    60       7      8005
Jim Walker          Unit Manager   7779    37      11      7779
Stan Humphries      Field Service  3211    73      31      3211
Gertie Humphries    Sales          3211    73      31      3211
Stan Humphries Jr.  Sales          3211    73      31      3211
Winkie Humphries    Mailroom       3211    73      31      3211
(17 row(s) affected)
```

In the next example, a left-outer join is used in the WHERE clause of a SELECT statement to specify that both rows containing matching values for a common column and the rows from the left table, Employees, are included in the rows returned. This might be the case when you need to find out what employees don't have a pay rate associated with them.

Before the following query was executed, additional rows were added to the Employees table that don't have corresponding values in a common column in the Pays table:

```
select *
from employees,pays
where employees.badge*=pays.badge
name                department     badge   hours_worked rate    badge
-------------------- -------------- ------- ------------ ------- -----
Stan Humphries      Field Service  3211    40           10      3211
Stan Humphries      Field Servic   3211    73           31      3211
Fred Stanhope       Field Service  6732    40            9      6732
Sue Sommers         Logistics      4411    52           10      4411
Lance Finepoint     Library        5522    39           11      5522
Mark McGuire        Field Service  1997    51           10      1997
Sally Springer      Sales          9998    40            8      9998
Ludmilla Valencia   Software       7773    55           10      7773
Barbara Lint        Field Service  8883    40            9      8883
Jeffrey Vickers     Mailroom       8005    60            7      8005
Jim Walker          Unit Manager   7779    37           11      7779
Bob Smith           SALES          1234    (null)       (null)  (null)
Bob Jones           Sales          2223    (null)       (null)  (null)
Gertie Humphries    Sales          3211    40           10      3211
Gertie Humphries    Sales          3211    73           31      3211
Stan Humphries Jr.  Sales          3211    40           10      3211
Stan Humphries Jr.  Sales          3211    73           31      3211
Winkie Humphries    Mailroom       3211    40           10      3211
Winkie Humphries    Mailroom       3211    73           31      3211
Susan Smith         Executive      1234    (null)       (null)  (null)
Henry Smith         Logistics      1234    (null)       (null)  (null)
(21 row(s) affected)
```

NOTE Recall that NULL values don't match, so rows that contain NULLs in the primary and foreign key columns are displaying with outer joins only and won't be seen with equi-joins. ▓

In the next example, a right-outer join is used in the WHERE clause of a SELECT statement to specify that both rows that contain matching values for a common column and the rows from the right table, Pays, are included in the rows returned. Two additional rows are first added to the Pays table that don't have corresponding values in a common column in the Employees table.

```
insert into pays
values (40,10,5555)
insert into pays
values (40,10,5555)
select *
from employees,pays
where employees.badge=*pays.id
```

? badge

name	department	badge	hours_worked	rate	id
Stan Humphries	Field Service	3211	40	10	3211
Gertie Humphries	Sales	3211	40	10	3211
Stan Humphries Jr.	Sales	3211	40	10	3211
Winkie Humphries	Mailroom	3211	40	10	3211
Fred Stanhope	Field Service	6732	40	9	6732
Sue Sommers	Logistics	4411	52	10	4411
Lance Finepoint	Library	5522	39	11	5522
Mark McGuire	Field Service	1997	51	10	1997
Sally Springer	Sales	9998	40	8	9998
Ludmilla Valencia	Software	7773	55	10	7773
Barbara Lint	Field Service	8883	40	9	8883
Jeffrey Vickers	Mailroom	8005	60	7	8005
Jim Walker	Unit Manager	7779	37	11	7779
Stan Humphries	Field Service	3211	73	31	3211
Gertie Humphries	Sales	3211	73	31	3211
Stan Humphries Jr.	Sales	3211	73	31	3211
Winkie Humphries	Mailroom	3211	73	31	3211
(null)	(null)	(null)	40	10	5555
(null)	(null)	(null)	40	10	5555

```
(19 row(s) affected)
```

TIP Left- and right-outer joins can be used to show rows that contain NULLs that won't have corresponding entries across tables, and will *only* be displayed with other non-matching entries.

Combining Query Results with UNION

Use a UNION to combine the results of two or more queries. A UNION merges the results of the first query with the results of a second query. UNION implicitly removes duplicate rows between the queries. A UNION returns a single results set that consists of all the rows that belong to the first table, the second table, or both tables.

You should define the queries that contain a UNION clause so that they're compatible. The queries should have the same number of columns and a common column defined for each table. You also can't use a UNION within the definition of a view.

The syntax for queries that include a UNION clause is as follows:

```
SELECT column_name_1, ..., column_name_n
FROM table_name_1, ... , table_name_n
WHERE column_name comparison_operator value
[GROUP BY...]
[HAVING ...
UNION
SELECT column_name_1, ..., column_name_n
FROM table_name_1, ... , table_name_n
WHERE column_name comparison_operator value
[GROUP BY...]
[HAVING...]
[ORDER BY...]
[COMPUTE...
```

In the following example, the badge numbers that are common to both tables are displayed using two select statements that are bound with a UNION clause. The ORDER BY clause is used after the last query to order the final results. The ORDER BY clause appears only after the last SELECT statement. Recall that UNION implicitly removes duplicate rows, as defined by the query.

```
select badge from employees
union
select badge from pays
order by badge
badge
----------
1234
1997
3211
4411
5522
6732
7773
7779
8005
8883
9998
(11 row(s) affected)
```

In the following example, the same set of queries is used except the ALL keyword is added to the UNION clause. This retains query-defined duplicates, from the Badge column only, in the resultant rows. The duplicate rows from both tables are retained.

```
select badge from employees
union all
select badge from pays
order by badge
badge
------
1234
```

```
1234
1234
1997
1997
3211
3211
3211
3211
3211
3211
4411
4411
5522
5522
6732
6732
7773
7773
7779
7779
8005
8005
8883
8883
9998
9998
(27 row(s) affected)
```

In the following example, the datatypes referenced in the query for one of the two columns aren't compatible. Because of this, the execution of the example returns an error.

```
select name,badge from employees
union
select hours_worked,badge from pay
Msg 257, Level 16, State 1
Implicit conversion from datatype 'char' to 'int' is not allowed.
 Use the CONVERT function to run this query.
```

You can use a UNION clause with queries to combine the rows from two compatible tables and merge the rows into a new third table. To illustrate this merge, in which the results are kept in a permanent table, a new table is created that has the same datatypes as the existing Employees table. Several rows are first inserted into the new table.

```
create table employees2
(name char(20),department char(20),badge int)
go
insert into employees2
values ('Rod Gilbert','Sales',3339)
go
insert into employees2
values ('Jean Ratele','Sales',5551)
go
insert into employees2
values ('Eddie Giacomin','Sales',8888)
```

Each table now has rows that contain employee records. If you use a UNION clause to combine the SELECT statements along with INSERT INTO, the resultant rows can be retained in a new table.

The SELECT statement that references the Employees table uses WHERE to restrict the rows returned to only those with the Sales department. All three rows of the Employees2 table are in the Sales department, so no WHERE clause is necessary.

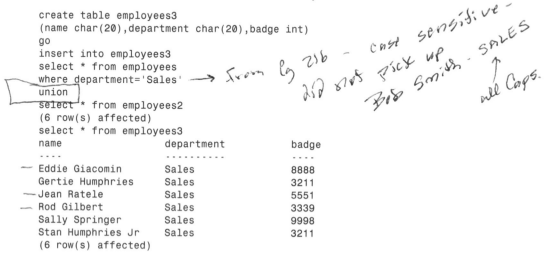

```
create table employees3
(name char(20),department char(20),badge int)
go
insert into employees3
select * from employees
where department='Sales'
union
select * from employees2
(6 row(s) affected)
select * from employees3
name                  department           badge
----                  ----------           ----
Eddie Giacomin        Sales                8888
Gertie Humphries      Sales                3211
Jean Ratele           Sales                5551
Rod Gilbert           Sales                3339
Sally Springer        Sales                9998
Stan Humphries Jr     Sales                3211
(6 row(s) affected)
```

As in the previous example, you can use UNION to combine multiple tables or combinations of selected columns and rows from tables into an existing or new table. You can have tables with identical columns at different office locations in which rows are added throughout the day.

At the end of the work day, you can use a set of SELECT statements with a UNION clause to add the separate collection tables to a master table at a central location. After the rows are copied to the master table, the rows of the collection tables can be removed using a DELETE FROM statement without a WHERE clause, or a TRUNCATE statement as mentioned earlier in this chapter.

You can combine up to sixteen SELECT statements by adding additional UNION clauses between each set of SELECT statements. You can use parentheses to control the order of the UNIONs. The SELECT statements within parentheses are performed before those that are outside parentheses. You don't need to use parentheses if all the UNIONs are UNION ALL. You also don't need parentheses if none of the UNIONs is UNION ALL.

In the following example, three tables are combined using a UNION clause. IN is used with the first table to specify multiple forms of one department. The second table doesn't use WHERE and all rows are selected. The third table specifies only a single case-sensitive department name, assuming the sort order is case sensitive.

You don't need parentheses to control the order of the merges because no UNIONs use ALL. The resultant rows are ordered by Badge and Name using an ORDER BY clause that can appear only after the last SELECT statement.

```
select name,badge
from employees
where department in ('SALES','Sales','sales')
union
select name,badge
from employees2
union
select name,badge
from employees3
where department='Sales'
order by badge,name
name                   badge
----                   ----
Bob Smith              1234
Gertie Humphries       3211
Stan Humphries Jr      3211
Rod Gilbert            3339
Jean Ratele            5551
Eddie Giacomin         8888
Sally Springer         9998
(7 row(s) affected)
```

Reality Check

There are some techniques you can use to help safeguard your applications against the changes that you'll be implementing using ADD, CHANGE, and DELETE operations as outlined here. For example, you can do the old standby: Back up the table to another table until you're certain all changes are appropriate and no applications have been changed.

You can also use transactions if you're writing an application to complete these tasks. By putting a transaction around these types of update statements, you can rollback the transaction if you later determine that you don't need to make the changes after all. Of course, the scope of the transaction is only as good until a COMMIT is reached, but you do have at least some leeway.

▶ For additional information about transactions, **see** the section in Chapter 12, "Understanding Transactions and Locking," titled "Creating and Working with Transactions," **p. 317**

Another thing that happens frequently is finding out that several users are using your database system from applications and systems you might not have been aware of. Remember, the whole point of ODBC and especially SQL Server as an intelligent server engine is to enable open access to your databases. To that end, a user could be coming in to your database and using the structures there from Excel, Access, Visual Basic or other application environments—all in addition to any applications developed specifically to use the database.

When you change the structure of a table, you run the risk of breaking the structures that these individuals are using in their tools. One way to avoid this is to provide your users with views on the database. Have them link their applications to these views and you'll be able to provide a level of abstraction between the user and the underlying database tables. It can be just the ticket to keep from breaking applications just to make simple database table structure changes.

▶ For more information about using views, **see** Chapter 10, "Managing and Using Views," **p. 257**

In short, keep a close eye on who is using your database and how. You can do this by locking down the security and by requiring logins that you control. Don't be a control freak, but be sure you know whom to consider for any proposed changes.

From Here...

In this chapter you learned to add rows and delete rows from a database table, as well as change the characteristics of a table. You also learned how to perform operations on multiple tables using relational joins and UNION statements. Additional related information can be found in the following chapters:

- Chapter 4, "Data Modeling and Database Design," teaches you how you can create tables that logically lend themselves to the types of joins covered here.
- Chapter 11, "Managing and Using Indexes and Keys," teaches you how to define the common columns in tables that are used to perform joins.
- Chapter 12, "Understanding Transactions and Locking," teaches you how to set up a query so that you can undo it.
- Chapter 15, "Creating and Managing Triggers," teaches you how to maintain referential integrity, which ensures that correct rows are joined between tables.

Using Functions

There are many cases in which you'll need to have an operation performed on the information in your table prior to returning it to a SELECT request or using it in another project. When this happens, you can either write some logic yourself and use it to work with the information coming back or you can look to SQL Server to provide some of this functionality for you.

An example of this type of approach is the COUNT() function, probably one of the most used functions provided with SQL Server. COUNT does just what its name implies: It counts the rows that you indicate in your query. While you'll find out more about this specific function later, it's important to understand some key elements of functions. First, functions execute on the server, saving on bandwidth. Second, functions run faster than if they were executing on your local system because they have immediate access to your database information.

Functions execute a section of code that performs an operation that returns a desired value. For the function to perform its operation, you must usually supply the required data as a list in which each element is called a parameter. You can use functions with columns of data and other storage structures of Transact-SQL. You can also use functions in the SELECT or WHERE clause of Select statements, in expressions, and, for selected functions such as system and niladic functions, in constraints defined in tables or views.

NOTE *Niladic functions* are special functions that you can use with constraints you set up for your tables. Niladic functions return a user or timestamp value and are useful for inserting a default value in the table. ■

Basic SQL Functions

A small subset of Transact-SQL functions illustrates how functions are typically used in Transact-SQL statements. Also, the subset of SQL functions is generic and is typically available in any dialect of SQL.

NOTE If you've worked with another dialect of SQL, you're probably familiar with the handful of basic functions. Unfortunately, the set of functions that is used across different vendors' dialects of SQL is extremely small. The remaining functions may be comparable across server database SQL dialects, although they aren't identical. ■

Some of the basic Transact-SQL functions are shown in Table 9.1.

Table 9.1 Basic Transact-SQL Functions

Function	Operation
AVG	Average
SUM	Sum
MIN	Minimum value
MAX	Maximum value
COUNT	Count

These functions, and others in a SELECT clause, are used as if they were column identifiers. They return their results as columns in the resulting data set.

The objects or arguments of a function must be enclosed in parentheses. If the function requires more than a single argument, the arguments are separated by a comma (,).

The syntax for the use of functions in the SELECT clause of a SELECT statement is as follows:

```
SELECT function (column_1 or *),...function (column_n)
FROM table
```

Note that NULL values aren't used for computation of AVERAGE, SUM, MIN, or MAX. If all elements of a set are NULL, the function return is NULL. COUNT, when used with an asterisk (*), determines the number of rows in a column, even if it contains NULL values.

Using AVG

The AVG function returns the arithmetic average of the column values referenced. In the following example, AVG is used to return the average of the Pay Rate column for all rows of the Pays table.

```
select avg(pay_rate)
from pays
```

Using COUNT

The COUNT function returns the numbers of columns that match the selection expression. The asterisk wild card (*) is used as an argument for the COUNT function. If * is used in place of the column name in a SELECT clause, the asterisk specifies all rows that meet the criteria of the SELECT statement. The COUNT function counts all table rows that meet the criteria. The following syntax is used with the COUNT function:

```
SELECT COUNT(column_name)
FROM table_name
```

For example, the following SELECT statement returns the number of rows in the Employees table.

```
select count(*)
from employees
```

If a WHERE clause is used in your SELECT statement, the COUNT function applies to only the rows that match the criteria specified in the WHERE clause. For example, the following COUNT statement returns the number of employees in the Sales department.

```
select count(*)
from employees
where department='Sales'
```

 TIP You can improve the performance of the COUNT function by specifying a column name to count, and making sure that the column you specify is both indexed and not NULL. By doing so, SQL Server can use its optimization techniques to return the count of the rows more quickly.

Using MAX

MAX returns the largest value in a column. The syntax of MAX is as follows:

```
SELECT MAX(column_name)
FROM table_name
```

In the following example, MAX is used to return the maximum, or greatest number of hours_worked, for all rows of the Pays table.

```
select max(hours_worked)
from pays
```

Using MIN

MIN returns the smallest value in a column. In the following example, MIN is used to return the minimum number of hours_worked for all rows of the Pays table.

```
select min(hours_worked)
from pays
```

In the next example, MIN is used to return the lowest rate of pay for employees in the Field Service department. Both the Pays and Employees tables must be referenced in the SELECT statement because the Department column is in the Employees table, whereas the Rate column is in the Pays table. The corresponding badge numbers in each table are used to combine the appropriate rows.

```
select min(rate)
from employees,pays
where employees.badge=pays.badge
and department='Field Service'
```

Using SUM

SUM returns the summation of such entities as column values. The SUM function returns the total of the non-NULL values in the numeric expression, which is often just a column name, that follows the SUM keyword. The syntax for SUM is as follows:

```
SUM([DISTINCT] <expression>)
```

In the following example, the displayed result would be the sum of the hours_worked for all rows of the Pays table.

```
select sum (hours_worked)
from pays
```

 TIP   Rows that contain a NULL value in the column referenced by the SUM function are automatically skipped in the calculation.

You can use multiple functions within a single statement. The following example returns the average, minimum, and maximum of the hours_worked column in the Pays table:

```
select avg(hours_worked), min(hours_worked), max(hours_worked)
from pays
```

In the more complicated example that follows, a SELECT statement is used to return the maximum and average rate, minimum hours_worked, and the count of all rows of the Employees table.

```
select max(rate),min(hours_worked),avg(rate),count(*)
from employees,pays
where employees.badge=pays.badge
```

Using DISTINCT with COUNT

If the COUNT function is used to reference a column-name, it returns the number of values. The COUNT function includes duplicates in its count, but it doesn't include NULL values. If you add the keyword DISTINCT, the COUNT function returns the number of each unique value. The following syntax for the COUNT function is used with the keyword DISTINCT in a SELECT statement:

```
SELECT COUNT(DISTINCT column_name)
FROM table_name
```

In the following example, the keyword DISTINCT is used with the COUNT function in a SELECT statement to display the number of different departments in the Employees table:

```
select count(distinct department)
from employees
```

Using CUBE and ROLLUP

The CUBE and ROLLUP operators were added to SQL Server 6.5 to make it easier to access large amounts of data in a summary fashion. When a SELECT statement is cubed, aggregate functions are transformed into super-aggregate functions that return only the rows necessary to report a summary of the information requested. The ROLLUP operator differs from CUBE only because it is sensitive to the order of columns in the GROUP BY clause.

> **N O T E** There are several things to be aware of when using the CUBE and ROLLUP operators. First, a GROUP BY column list can be no more than 900 bytes. Second, there is a maximum of 10 columns. Next, columns or expressions must be specified in the GROUP BY clause. GROUP BY ALL can't be used. Finally, these operators are disabled when trace flag 204 is on. ▪

Book sales are a perfect example. A query that returns a book title and the number of books ordered for each invoice in a database would return a row for each invoice. If the CUBE operator were applied to this query, it would only return a row for each title and the total quantity ordered for that title.

 T I P If you're using the CUBE and ROLLUP functions, you'll also want to investigate and consider using the Decision Support Services (DSS) that are part of SQL Server 7.0. These services support the many aspects of data warehousing that CUBE and ROLLUP were initially designed to begin to address.

Part II

Ch 9

Using String Functions

Functions are used to perform various operations, including string concatenation, on binary data, character strings, and expressions. String functions are used to return values commonly needed for operations on character data. The following list shows the set of string functions:

ASCII	QUOTENAME	SPACE
CHAR	REPLACE	STR
CHARINDEX	REPLICATE	STUFF
DIFFERENCE	REVERSE	SUBSTRING
LOWER	RIGHT	UPPER
LTRIM	RTRIM	+
PATINDEX	SOUNDEX	

String functions are usually used on CHAR, VARCHAR, BINARY, and VARBINARY datatypes as well as datatypes that implicitly convert to CHAR or VARCHAR. For example, you can use the PATINDEX function on CHAR, VARCHAR, and TEXT datatypes.

You can nest string functions so that the results returned by an inner function are available for the operation performed by the outer function. If you use constants with string functions, you should enclose them in quotation marks. String functions are usually used in SELECT or WHERE clauses.

> **CAUTION**
>
> You should ensure that the result returned by a nested function is compatible as input to the function in which it's embedded. In other words, if your function is expecting a string variable, be sure that the nested function returns a string, not a numeric value. Check your functions and datatypes carefully to determine if they're compatible. Otherwise, the set of functions can't function correctly.

Using ASCII

ASCII returns the ASCII code value of the leftmost character of a character expression. The syntax of the ASCII function is as follows:

```
ASCII(<char_expr>)
```

> **N O T E**   Remember that ASCII only returns the code associated with the leftmost character. If you need to have the ASCII value associated with the remaining portion of the string, you'll need to write a function that can walk down the string and return each value in succession. ▪

Using CHAR

CHAR converts an ASCII code into a character. If you don't enter the ASCII code within the range of values between zero and 255, a NULL is returned. The syntax of the CHAR function is as follows:

```
CHAR(<integer_expr>)
```

In the following example, the ASCII and CHAR functions are used to convert a character to the decimal ASCII value, and the decimal ASCII value to a character:

```
select ascii('Able'),char(65)
----------- -
65          A
```

Using SOUNDEX

SOUNDEX returns a four-digit, or SOUNDEX, code that is used in comparing two strings with the DIFFERENCE function. SOUNDEX can be used to search for duplicates with similar spellings in a mailing list. SOUNDEX can also be used in a word processor to return words that are similar to one that is misspelled.

The syntax for use of the SOUNDEX function is as follows:

```
SOUNDEX(<char_expr>)
```

SOUNDEX ignores all vowels unless they're the first letters of a string. In the following example, SOUNDEX is used to return evaluation values for a series of strings.

```
select soundex ('a'),soundex ('aaa'),soundex ('b'),soundex ('red'),
 soundex ('read')
----- ----- ----- ----- -----
A000  A000  B000  R300  R300
select soundex ('right'),soundex ('write')
----- -----
R230  W630
```

Using DIFFERENCE

DIFFERENCE returns the difference between the values of two character expressions returned by SOUNDEX. The difference is rated as a value from zero to four, with a value of four as the best match. Define the threshold within the range zero to four and perform subsequent operations defined by your criteria. The syntax of the DIFFERENCE function is as follows:

```
DIFFERENCE(<char_expr1>, <char_expr2>)
```

In the following example, the difference between "the" and "teh" is four, a value that is considered a good match. If you were using DIFFERENCE along with SOUNDEX in a program such as a spell checker, "teh" could be treated as a misspelling of "the."

```
select difference(soundex('the'),soundex('teh'))
----------
4
```

Part

II

Ch

9

N O T E The value returned by the DIFFERENCE function is fixed according to the design of the DIFFERENCE function. You must decide how you use the value returned. In the example, a value of four means that the two character strings, the and teh, are as alike as they can be using the SOUNDEX scale of values.

If you're looking for a misspelling for the name of a department stored in the Department column of a table such as Employees, a value of three or less might be a different department or a misspelling of a department. ■

Using LOWER

LOWER, which converts uppercase strings to lowercase strings, uses the following syntax:

```
LOWER(<char_expr>)
```

Using UPPER

UPPER, which converts lowercase strings to uppercase strings, uses the following syntax:

```
UPPER(<char_expr>)
```

In the following example, UPPER and LOWER are used to convert a mixed-case string to all upper-case and all lowercase:

```
select upper('Bob Smith1234*&^'),lower('Bob Smith1234*&^')
---------------- ----------------
BOB SMITH1234*&^ bob smith1234*&^
```

Using LTRIM

LTRIM removes leading spaces from a string. To save space, you can remove leading spaces from a string before it's stored in the column of a table. The leading spaces can also be removed before you perform additional processing on the string. LTRIM uses the following syntax:

```
LTRIM(<char_expr>)
```

In the following example, LTRIM is used to remove leading spaces from a string:

```
select ltrim('    middle    ')
-------------
middle
```

N O T E In this example, the returned value of ('   middle   ') still contains trailing spaces. You need to use the next function, RTRIM, to remove trailing spaces. ■

Using RTRIM

RTRIM removes trailing spaces from a string. As with LTRIM, trailing spaces can be removed before you store the string in the column of a table. Like LTRIM, RTRIM can be used to remove trailing spaces before you perform further processing on the string. RTRIM uses the following syntax:

```
RTRIM(<char_expr>)
```

N O T E In many cases, you'll want to work with the string without any leading or trailing spaces. Remember that you can nest these functions, so you can use the syntax as indicated in the following example:

```
select RTRIM(LTRIM('    middle    '))
```

This example returns only the word "middle" with no spaces surrounding it. ▦

Using CHARINDEX

CHARINDEX returns the starting position of the specified character expression within a specified string. The first parameter is the character expression and the second parameter is an expression, usually a column name, in which SQL Server searches for the character expression. CHARINDEX cannot be used with TEXT and IMAGE datatypes. The syntax of the CHARINDEX function is as follows:

```
CHARINDEX(<'char_expr'>, <expression>)
```

In the following example, CHARINDEX returns the starting character position of the word "Service" in a row of the Department column of the table Employees. An uppercase S, the first letter in Service, is the seventh character in the Field Service department.

```
select charindex('Service',department)
from employees
where name='Stan Humphries'
----------
7
```

N O T E CHARINDEX can be used with other functions. The value returned by CHARINDEX can be used with other functions to extract parts of strings from within other strings. For example, CHARINDEX could be used within the string expression in the second argument of SUBSTRING. ▦

Using PATINDEX

PATINDEX returns the starting position of the first occurrence of a substring in a string such as the value of a table column. If the substring isn't found, a zero is returned. You can use the PATINDEX function with data stored as CHAR, VARCHAR, and TEXT datatypes.

Wild-card characters can be used in the substring as long as the percent sign (%) precedes and follows the substring. The syntax PATINDEX is as follows:

```
PATINDEX('%substring%', <column_name>)
```

In the following example, PATINDEX returns the character position for the first character of the substring within the string of characters stored in the Department column for the employee Stan Humphries. Stan Humphries is a member of the Field Service department.

```
select patindex('%erv%',department)
from employees
where name='Stan Humphries'
----------
8
```

Using REPLICATE

REPLICATE returns multiple sets of characters specified in the first argument of the function. The second argument specifies the number of sets to be returned. If the second argument, an integer expression, is a negative number, the function returns a NULL string. The syntax of REPLICATE is as follows:

REPLICATE(*character_expression, integer_expression*)

In the following example, REPLICATE returns a string of identical characters and also returns two iterations of the same sequence of two characters:

```
select replicate ('a',5),replicate('12',2)
----- ----
aaaaa 1212
```

Using REVERSE

REVERSE returns the reverse order of a string of characters. The character string argument can be a constant, a variable, or a value of a column. The syntax of REVERSE is as follows:

REVERSE(*character_string*)

In the following example, the example would return the two constant strings that are enclosed in quotation marks, but their contents would be reversed:

```
select reverse('12345678910'),reverse('John Smith')
----------- ----------
01987654321 htimS nhoJ
```

In the following example, the result is a table column displayed without REVERSE. The same column is displayed in a different order using the REVERSE attribute. Finally, the same string that is the name of the column of the Employees table is processed as a constant because it's enclosed in parentheses:

```
select name,reverse(name),reverse('name')
from employees
where name='Bob Smith'
name
------------------- ------------------- ----
Bob Smith           htimS boB           eman
```

Using RIGHT

RIGHT returns part of a character string, starting at the number of characters from the right as specified in the function argument. If the number of characters in the integer expression argument is negative, perhaps as the result of a nested function, `RIGHT` returns a `NULL` string. The syntax of the `RIGHT` function is as follows:

```
RIGHT (character_expression, integer_expression)
```

The following example shows two identical strings, one that is displayed with a `RIGHT` function and one without a function. The second parameter of the `RIGHT` function, `4`, specifies to return from four characters from the end of the string to the rightmost character of the string.

```
select '12345678', right ('12345678',4)
-------- ----
12345678 5678
(1 row(s) affected)
```

Part

II

Ch

9

> **CAUTION**
>
> You can't use a function such as the `RIGHT` function on `TEXT` and `IMAGE` datatypes. You must use the specialized set of string handling functions with `TEXT` and `IMAGE` datatypes. These special functions are discussed later in this chapter in the section titled "Using `TEXT` and `IMAGE` Functions."

Using SPACE

`SPACE` returns a string of spaces for the length specified by the argument to the function. If the argument integer value is negative, `SPACE` returns a `NULL` string. The `SPACE` syntax is as follows:

```
SPACE(<integer_expr>)
```

In the following example, `SPACE` returns multiple spaces between two string constants:

```
select 'begin',space(15),'end'
---- -------------- --
begin                end
```

Using STR

`STR` converts numeric data to character data. The `STR` syntax is as follows:

```
STR(<float_expr>[, <length>[, <decimal>]])
```

You should ensure that both the *length* and *decimal* arguments are non-negative values. If you don't specify a length, the default *length* is `10`. The value returned is rounded to an integer by default. The specified length should be at least equal to or greater than the part of the number before the decimal point plus the number's sign. If `<float_expr>` exceeds the specified length, the string returns `**` for the specified length.

In the following example, a series of constant numbers is converted to strings. The first number is completely converted because the second argument, the length, specifies the correct size of the resultant string, five numeric digits, the minus sign (–), and the decimal place (.). When the same constant value is converted using a length of six, the least-significant digit is truncated.

The third constant is correctly displayed using a length of six because it's a positive number. The same constant can't be displayed with a length of two, so two asterisks (**) are displayed instead.

```
select str(-165.87,7,2)
go
select str(-165.87,6,2)
go
select str(165.87,6,2)
go
select str(165.87,2,2)
go
-------
-165.87

------
-165.9
------
165.87

--
**
```

Using STUFF

STUFF inserts a string into a second string. The *length* argument specifies the number of characters to delete from the first string, beginning at the starting position. You can't use STUFF with TEXT or IMAGE datatypes. The STUFF syntax is as follows:

```
STUFF(character_string_1,starting_position,length,character_string_2)
```

In the following example, the string abcdef is inserted into the first string beginning at the second character position. The string abcdef is inserted after the number of characters specified by the *length* argument are deleted from the first string:

```
select stuff('123456',2,4,'abcdef')
---------
1abcdef56
```

If the starting position or length is negative, or if the starting position is larger than the first *character_string*, STUFF displays a NULL string. In the following example, a NULL is the result of the code shown because the starting position is a negative value:

```
select stuff('wxyz',-2,3,'abcdef')
(null)
```

If the length to delete is longer than the length of the first character string, the first character string is deleted to only the first character. In the following example, only the first character of the first character string remains after the second character string is inserted:

```
select stuff('123',2,3,'abc')
----
1abc
```

Using SUBSTRING

You can use SUBSTRING to return a part of a string from a target string. The first argument can be a character or binary string, a column name, or an expression that includes a column name. The second argument specifies the position at which the substring starts. The third argument specifies the number of characters in the substring.

Like several other string-only functions, you can't use SUBSTRING with TEXT or IMAGE datatypes. The SUBSTRING syntax is as follows:

```
SUBSTRING(character_string, starting_position,length)
```

In the following example, multiple SUBSTRINGs are used along with the SPACE function to separate the first name from the last name, each of which is stored in a single column of the Employees table.

```
select substring(name,1,3),space(4),substring(name,5,5)
from employees
where badge=1234
--- ---- -----
Bob     Smith
```

Unlike earlier examples, the following example uses a function in several SQL statements. Multiple functions are often used in stored procedures or other batch objects. See Chapter 14, "Managing Stored Procedures and Using Flow-Control Statements," for more information about the use of local variables and the SELECT statement in the following example. Like the previous example, the first name is separated from the last name with multiple spaces added between the names, which is done by using multiple functions.

```
declare @x int
select @x=charindex(' ',(select name from employees where name='Bob Smith'))
select @x=@x-1
    select substring(name,1,@x), right(name,@x+2)
from employees
where badge=1234
-------------------
Bob                Smith
```

+ (Concatenation)

The concatenation operator symbol (+) concatenates two or more character or binary strings, column names, or a combination of strings and columns. Concatenation is used to add one string to the end of another string. You should enclose character strings within single quotation marks. The syntax of the concatenation operator is as follows:

```
<expression> + <expression>
```

Conversion functions are used to concatenate datatypes that could not be concatenated without a change in datatype. CONVERT is one of the functions that you can use for datatype conversion. In the following example, a string constant is concatenated with the current date returned using the GETDATE date function. GETDATE is nested within CONVERT to convert it to a datatype, in this case VARCHAR, that is compatible with the string constant.

Part

II

Ch

9

```
select 'The converted date is ' + convert(varchar(12), getdate())
-----------------------------------
The converted date is Jul 11 1994
(1 row(s) affected)
```

Using Arithmetic Functions

Arithmetic functions operate on numeric datatypes such as INTEGER, FLOAT, REAL, MONEY, and SMALLMONEY. The values returned by the arithmetic functions are six decimal places. If you encounter an error while using an arithmetic function, a NULL value is returned and a warning message appears.

Two query processing options can be used to control the execution of statements that include arithmetic functions. The keyword for each of the two arithmetic operations is preceded by the SET keyword. You can use the ARITHABORT option to terminate a query when a function finds an error. ARITHIGNORE returns NULL when a function finds an error. If you set both ARITHABORT and ARITHIGNORE, no warning messages are returned.

There are numerous mathematical functions available in Transact-SQL. See Table 9.2.

Table 9.2   Transact-SQL Mathematical Functions

Function	Parameters	Return
ACOS	(float_expression)	Angle in radians whose cosine is a FLOAT value.
ASIN	(float_expression)	Angle in radians whose sine is a FLOAT value.
ATAN	(float_expression)	Angle in radians whose tangent is a FLOAT value.
ATAN2	(float_expr1,float_expr2)	Angle in radians whose tangent is float_expr1/floatexpr2.
COS	(float_expression)	Trigonometric cosine of angle in radians.
COT	(float_expression)	Trigonometric cotangent of angle in radians.
SIN	(float_expression)	Trigonometric sine of angle in radians.
TAN	(float_expression)	Trigonometric tangent of expression in radians.
DEGREES	(numeric_expression)	Degrees converted from radians returned as the same datatype as expression. Datatypes can be INTEGER, MONEY, REAL, and FLOAT.

Function	Parameters	Return
RADIANS	*(numeric_expression)*	Radians converted from degrees returned as the same datatype as expression. Datatypes can be INTEGER, MONEY, REAL, and FLOAT.
CEILING	*(numeric_expression)*	Smallest INTEGER >= expression returned as the same datatype as expression. Datatypes can be INTEGER, MONEY, REAL, and FLOAT.
FLOOR	*(numeric_expression)*	Largest INTEGER <= expression returned as the same datatype as expression. Datatypes can be INTEGER, MONEY, REAL, and FLOAT.
EXP	*(float_expression)*	Exponential value of expression.
LOG	*(float_expression)*	Natural log of expression.
LOG10	*(float_expression)*	Base 10 log of expression.
PI()		Value is 3.1415926535897936.
POWER	*(numeric_expression,y)*	Value of expression to power of *y* returned as the same datatype as expression. Datatypes can be INTEGER, MONEY, REAL, and FLOAT.
ABS	*(numeric_expression)*	Absolute value of expression returned as the same datatype as expression. Datatypes can be INTEGER, MONEY, REAL, and FLOAT.
RAND	*([integer_expression])*	Random float number between zero and one using optional *[integer_expression]* as seed.
ROUND	*(numeric_expr,integer_expr)*	Rounded value to precision of *integer_expr* returned as the same datatype as expression. Datatypes can be INTEGER, MONEY, REAL, and FLOAT.
SIGN	*(numeric_expression)*	One, zero, or –1 returned as the same datatype as expression. Datatypes can be INTEGER, MONEY, REAL, and FLOAT.
SQRT	*(float_expression)*	Square root of expression.

Part
II

Ch
9

The following example shows the use of ABSOLUTE, RAND, SIGN, PI, and ROUND within an expression:

```
Select abs(5*-15),rand(),sign(-51.23),pi(),round((10*rand()),0)
----- ------------------  ----------  ----------------------  ----
75    0.3434553056428724  -1.0        3.141592653589793         8.0
(1 row(s) affected)
```

In another example of the use of mathematical functions, FLOOR and CEILING are used to return the largest and smallest integer values that are less than or equal to, or greater than or equal to, the specified value.

```
select floor(81),ceiling(81),floor(81.45),
ceiling(81.45),floor($81.45),ceiling(-81.45)
-------- -------- ------------- ------------- ----------- ------
81       81       81.0          82.0          81.00        -81.0
 (1 row(s) affected)
```

ROUND always returns a value, even if the length is invalid. If you specify that the length is positive and longer than the digits after the decimal point in ROUND, a zero is added after the least-significant digit in the returned value. If you specify that the length is negative and greater than or equal to the digits before the decimal point, 0.00 is returned by ROUND.

The following example shows the effects of using ROUND functions on various values. In the first example, the decimal number is rounded to two decimal places. The second number is displayed as 100.0 because the length is negative.

```
select round(81.4545,2), round(81.45,-2)
----------------------- --------------
81.45                   100.0
(1 row(s) affected)
```

In the following example, the first number is rounded down to three decimal places but the second number is rounded up to a whole number because it's more than half the value of the least-significant digit.

```
select round(81.9994,3),round(81.9996,3)
----------------------- -----------------------
81.999                  82.0
(1 row(s) affected)
```

Using TEXT and IMAGE Functions

In addition to PATINDEX, you can use several functions for operations on TEXT and IMAGE datatypes. You can also use relevant SET options and global variables with TEXT and IMAGE datatypes.

Using SET TEXTSIZE

SET TEXTSIZE specifies the number of bytes that are displayed for data stored as TEXT or IMAGE datatypes with SELECT statements. The SET TEXTSIZE syntax is as follows:

```
SET TEXTSIZE n
```

Use *n* to specify the number of bytes to be displayed. You must specify the value of *n* in the function SET TEXTSIZE as an INTEGER. If you specify *n* as zero (0), the default length in bytes, up to 4K bytes, is displayed. The current setting for TEXTSIZE is stored in the global variable @@TEXTSIZE.

In the following example, the TEXTSIZE default is first used to display a table column defined as the datatype TEXT. SET TEXTSIZE is defined as two (2), and as a result only two bytes of the table-column test are displayed. Finally, TEXTSIZE is reset to the default of 4K using a value of zero (0).

```
select * from imagetext_table
image1              ...                                      text1
------------------------   ...   -------------------------------------
0x3132333435363738396163 7a782b3d5c   ... 12345678aczx+=
(1 row(s) affected)
set textsize 2
go
select text1 from imagetext_table
go
set textsize 0
go
select * from imagetext_table
go
text1
-----------  ...  -------------------------------------
12
(1 row(s) affected)

image1              ...                                      text1
------------------------   ...   -------------------------------------
0x3132333435363738396163 7a782b3d5c   ... 12345678aczx+=
(1 row(s) affected)
```

Using TEXTPTR

TEXTPTR returns a value in VARBINARY format as a 16-character binary string. The value returned is a pointer to the first database page of stored text. The text pointer is used by the SQL Server system rather than by you, although the value is accessible by using TEXTPTR.

SQL Server automatically checks whether the pointer is valid when the function is used. The system checks that the return value points to the first page of text. The TEXTPTR syntax is as follows:

TEXTPTR(*column_name*)

Using READTEXT

READTEXT is a statement rather than a function. It is used along with the TEXT and IMAGE functions. READTEXT extracts a substring from data stored as a TEXT or IMAGE datatypes. You specify the number of bytes to include in the substring that follows an offset. The READTEXT syntax is as follows:

```
READTEXT table.column
 textptroffset size
```

In the following example, TEXTPTR retrieves the pointer to the first page of text for the one-and-only row of the table. The pointer is stored in a local variable @v. READTEXT is then used to extract a substring starting at the third byte, using an offset to skip past the first two bytes and retrieve the specified four bytes.

```
declare @v varbinary(16)
select @v=textptr(text1) from imagetext_table
readtext imagetext_table.text1 @v 2 4
(1 row(s) affected)
text1
--------------------------------------------....-----------------------------
3456
```

Using TEXTVALID

TEXTVALID returns either zero (0) or one (1), depending on whether a specified text pointer is valid or invalid. You must include the name of the table as part of your reference to the column defined as the datatype TEXT. The TEXTVALID syntax is as follows:

```
TEXTVALID('table_name.column_name', text_ptr)
```

In the following example, TEXTVALID determines the validity of a pointer to a data column stored as the datatype TEXT. Recall that the output of one function can be used as the input to another function, as is the following example:

```
select textvalid('imagetext_table.text1',(select textptr(text1)
from imagetext_table))
go
----------
1
(1 row(s) affected)
```

In the next example, a SELECT statement that contains a WHERE clause returns a table row. As a result, TEXTVALID returns a zero, which is an invalid value because no row column was located.

```
select textvalid('imagetext_table.text1',(select textptr(text1)
from imagetext_table where text1 like '5'))
----------
0
(1 row(s) affected)
```

Using Conversion Functions

You often don't have to explicitly perform conversions because SQL Server automatically performs them. For example, you can directly compare a character datatype or expression with a DATETIME datatype or expression. SQL Server also converts an INTEGER datatype or expression to a SMALLINT datatype or expression when an INTEGER, SMALLINT, or TINYINT is used in an expression.

▶ For more information on datatypes, **see** the Chapter 6 section titled "Numeric Integer Datatypes," **p. 120**

Use a conversion function if you're unsure whether SQL Server will perform implicit conversions for you or if you're using other datatypes that aren't implicitly converted.

Using CONVERT

As mentioned earlier, CONVERT performs the explicit conversion of datatypes. CONVERT translates expressions of one datatype to another datatype as well as to a variety of special date formats. If CONVERT can't perform the conversion, you'll receive an error message. For example, if you attempt to convert characters contained in a column defined as a CHAR datatype to an INTEGER datatype, an error message will appear.

The CONVERT syntax is as follows:

```
CONVERT(<datatype> [(<length>)], <expression> [, <style>])
```

You can use CONVERT in SELECT and WHERE clauses or anywhere an expression can be used in a Transact-SQL statement.

You'll want to keep the following key concepts in mind when you use the CONVERT function:

- If you omit a length specification, it defaults to a value of 30.
- Any unrecognized values that appear in DATETIME-to-SMALLDATETIME conversions aren't used.
- Any conversions of BIT datatypes convert non-zero values to one (1) in keeping with the usual storage of BIT datatypes.
- Integer values that you convert to MONEY or SMALLMONEY datatypes are processed as monetary units for the defined country, such as dollars for the United States.
- If you convert CHAR or VARCHAR datatypes to INTEGER datatypes such as INT or SMALLINT, the values must be numeric digits or a plus (+) or minus (-) sign.
- Conversions that you attempt to make to a datatype of a different size can truncate the converted value and display + after the value to denote that truncation has occurred.
- Conversions that you attempt to make to a datatype with a different number of decimal places can also result in truncation.
- Conversions that you specify as TEXT datatypes to CHAR and VARCHAR datatypes can be up to only 8000 characters, the maximum length for CHAR and VARCHAR datatypes. The default of 30 characters is used if an explicit length is not supplied.
- The conversion of data stored as IMAGE datatypes to BINARY and VARBINARY datatypes can also be up to only 8000 characters with a default of 30 characters.

In the following example, a numeric constant is converted to a CHAR datatype, a decimal constant is converted to an INT datatype, and a decimal constant is converted to a BIT datatype:

```
select convert(char(4),1234),convert(int,12.345),convert(bit,87453.34)
---- ----------- --
1234 12          1
(1 row(s) affected)
```

In the next example of using CONVERT, several table columns are converted from an INT datatype to a CHAR datatype. The attempted conversion of the same table column to a VARCHAR datatype of an inadequate length results in truncation of each column value.

```
select badge,convert(char(4),badge),convert(varchar(2),badge)
from employees
badge
----------- ---- --
3211        3211 *
6732        6732 *
4411        4411 *
...
```

You can use the *style* argument of the CONVERT function to display the date and time in different formats. You can also use the *style* argument as part of a CONVERT function when you convert dates and times to CHAR or VARCHAR datatypes. Table 9.3 shows the different style numbers that can be used with CONVERT.

Table 9.3   Style Numbers for the CONVERT Function

Without Century (yy)	With Century (yyyy)	Standard	Display
-	0 or 100	default	mon dd yyyy hh:miAM (or PM)
1	101	USA	mm/dd/yy
2	102	ANSI	yy.mm.dd
3	103	English/French	dd/mm/yy
4	104	German	dd.mm.yy
5	105	Italian	dd-mm-yy
6	106		dd mon yy
7	107		mon dd, yy
8	108		hh:mi:ss
9	109		mon dd yyyy hh:mi:sssAM (or PM)
10	110	USA	mm-dd-yy
11	111	Japan	yy/mm/dd
12	112	ISO	yymmdd
13	113	Europe	dd mon yyyy hh:mi:ss:mmm (24h)

Without Century (yy)	With Century (yyyy)	Standard	Display
14	114	-	hh:mi:ss::mmm (24h)
20	120	ODBC Canonical	yyyy-mm-dd hh:mi:ss(24h)
21	121	ODBC Canonical with milliseconds	yyyy-mm-dd hh:mi:ss.mmm (24h)

In the following example, the current date and time are implicitly displayed using GETDATE, and GETDATE appears within CONVERT using different style numbers.

```
select getdate(),convert(char(12),getdate(),3),convert(char(24),
getdate(),109)

------------------------ ----------- ----------------------
1998-08-25 22:43:26.753    25/08/98    Aug 25 1998 10:43:26:753

(1 row(s) affected)
select convert(char(24),getdate(),114),convert(char(24),getdate(),112)

------------------------ ----------------------
22:43:49:363             19980825

(1 row(s) affected)
```

Using Date Functions

You can use several functions to perform operations with DATE datatypes. Use date functions to perform arithmetic operations on DATETIME and SMALLDATETIME values. Like other functions, date functions can be used in the SELECT or WHERE clauses, or wherever expressions can be used in Transact-SQL statements.

Using DATENAME

DATENAME returns a specified part of a date as a character string. DATENAME uses the following syntax:

```
DATENAME(<date part>, <date>)
```

Using DATEPART

DATEPART returns the specified part of a date as an integer value. DATEPART uses the following syntax:

```
DATEPART(<date_part>, <date>)
```

Using GETDATE

GETDATE returns the current date and time in SQL Server's default format for DATETIME values. Use a NULL argument with GETDATE. GETDATE uses the following syntax:

```
GETDATE()
```

Using DATEADD

DATEADD returns the value of the date with an additional date interval added to it. The return value is a DATETIME value that is equal to the date plus the number of the date parts that you specify. DATEADD takes the date part, number, and date arguments in the following syntax:

```
DATEADD (<date part>, <number>, <date>)
```

Using DATEDIFF

DATEDIFF returns the difference between parts of two specified dates. DATEDIFF takes three arguments, which are the part of the date and the two dates. DATEDIFF returns a signed integer value equal to the second date part, minus the first date part, using the following syntax:

```
DATEDIFF(<date part>, <date1>, <date2>)
```

Table 9.4 shows the values used as arguments for the date parts with the date functions.

Table 9.4   Date Parts Used in Date Functions

Date Part	Abbreviation	Values
Year	yy	1753-9999
Quarter	qq	1-4
Month	mm	1-12
Day of Year	dy	1-366
Day	dd	1-31
Week	wk	1-54
Weekday	dw	1-7 (Sun-Sat)
Hour	hh	0-23
Minute	mi	0-59
Second	ss	0-59
Millisecond	ms	0-999

The following examples show the use of several of the date functions. In the first example, the columns of a table that are defined as DATETIME and SMALLDATETIME datatypes are displayed without any functions.

```
select * from date_table
date1                      date2
-------------------------- --------------------------
Jan 1 1753 12:00AM         Jan 1 1900 12:00AM
(1 row(s) affected)
```

In the following example, the keyword year is used with DATENAME to return the year with the century from a DATETIME value:

```
select datename(year,date1) from date_table

1753
(1 row(s) affected)
```

In the following example, hour is used with DATENAME to return the hour from a DATETIME datatype value:

```
select datename(hour,date1) from date_table
----------------------------
0
(1 row(s) affected)
```

In the following example, month is used with DATENAME to return the number of the month from a DATETIME datatype value:

```
select datepart(month,date1) from date_table
----------
1
(1 row(s) affected)
```

In the following example, the GETDATE function is used in a SELECT statement to display the current date and time:

```
select now=getdate()
now
--------------------------
1998-08-25 22:46:26.150

(1 row(s) affected)
```

In the following example, GETDATE is nested within DATEPART to display only the current day as part of a SELECT statement:

```
select datepart(day,getdate())
----------
19
(1 row(s) affected)
```

In the following example, GETDATE is nested within DATENAME to display only the name of the current month as part of a SELECT statement:

```
select datename(month,getdate())
----------------------------
May
(1 row(s) affected)
```

In the following example, the current date and the date stored in a DATETIME column are first displayed for reference. DATEDIFF is then used to display the number of days between the two DATETIME values.

```
select getdate()
-------------------------
May 19 1994  2:12PM
(1 row(s) affected)
select date1 from date_table
date1
-------------------------
Jan 1 1753 12:00AM
(1 row(s) affected)
select new=datediff(day,date1,getdate())
from date_table
new
----------
88161
(1 row(s) affected)
```

Using System Functions

You can use system functions to obtain information about your computer system, user, database, and database objects. The system functions enable you to obtain information such as the characteristics of database objects within stored procedures and, using conditional statements, perform different operations based on the information returned.

You can use a system function, like other functions, in the SELECT and WHERE clauses of a SELECT statement as well as in expressions. If you omit the optional parameter with some system functions, as shown in Table 9.5, information about your computer system and the current user database is returned.

Table 9.5   System Functions

Function	Parameter(s)	Information Returned
HOST_NAME()		The name of the server computer
HOST_ID()		The ID number of the server computer
SUSER_ID	(['login-name'])	The login number of the user
SUSER_NAME	([server_user_id])	The login name of the user
USER_ID	(['user_name'])	The database ID number of the user

Function	Parameter(s)	Information Returned
USER_NAME	([user_id])	The database username of the user
DB_NAME	(['database_id'])	The name of the database
DB_ID	(['database_name'])	The ID number of the database
GETANSINULL	(['database_name'])	Returns 1 for ANSI nullability, 0 if ANSI nullability not defined
OBJECT_ID	('object_name')	The number of a database object
OBJECT_NAME	(object_id)	The name of a database object
INDEX_COL	('table_name', index_id, key_id)	The name of the index column
COL_LENGTH	('table_name', 'column_name')	The defined length of a column
COL_NAME	(table_id, column_id)	The name of the column
DATALENGTH	('expression')	The actual length of an expression of a datatype
IDENT_INCR	('table_or_view')	The increment (returned as numeric(@@MAXPRECISION,0)) for a column with the identity property
IDENT_SEED	('table_or_view')	The seed value, returned as numeric(@@MAXPRECISION,0), for a column with the identity property
STATS_DATE	(table_id, index_id)	The date that the statistics for the index, index_id, were last updated
COALESCE	(expression1, expression2, ... expressionN)	Returns the first non-NULL expression
ISNULL	(expression, value)	Substitutes value for each NULL entry
NULLIF	(expression1, expression2)	Returns a NULL when expression1 is NULL when expression1 is equivalent to expression2

Part
II

Ch
9

In the following example, system function the HOST_ID is used to return the name of the Windows NT Server system to which a user is connected.

```
select host_name ()
----------------------------
NT1

(1 row(s) affected)
```

In the following example, multiple system functions are used to return information about the Windows NT Server system, the current database and the current user.

```
select host_name (),host_id (),db_name (), db_id (), suser_name ()
---------- -------- ---------- -------------------------
NT1        0000005e employees          6       sa

(1 row(s) affected)
```

N O T E You may not have reason to use any of the system functions. You may only need to use the system functions if you're performing some administrative operation with the database. Several of the system functions require that you have access to the system tables in order to return useful information. Access to these will depend on the security of your login ID.

You would not usually use the system functions in the SELECT clause of a SELECT statement that displays the information on your monitor. Rather, system functions, like other functions, can be used within other functions, and the information returned is recorded in local variables or a temporary or permanent table. System functions provide information that is usually used for advanced programming or administrative operations. Administrative operations can be performed within stored procedures as well as in an interactive session.

For example, the system function STATS_DATE returns the date the last time that statistics were updated for an index on a table. The database administrator must ensure that statistics for a table are periodically updated so that the query optimizer has valid information to use to decide whether to use an index for the retrieval of rows from a table. SQL Sever automatically updates the table statistics used by the query optimizer, but this should still be checked until you are comfortable with the interval SQL Server updates statistics.

For example the following SELECT statement returns the statistics update date for two indexes on the table Company.

```
select 'Index' = i.name,
       'Statistics Update Date' = stats_date(i.id, i.indid)
             from sysobjects o, sysindexes i
                  where o.name = 'company' and o.id = i.id
Index                               Statistics Update Date
------------------------------      -------------------------
badge_index                         Sep 18 1995   3:24PM
department_index                    Sep 18 1995   3:27PM

(2 row(s) affected)
```

You can use a system function such as STATS_DATE, as shown in the previous example, to determine if it's time to update the statistics for the indexes of a table so the query optimizer will work properly.

You can also combine the system function STATS_DATE with the GETDATE and DATEDIFF functions to return the update statistics date, the current date, and the difference between the two dates. Using these three functions and a conditional statement in a procedure, you can run the procedure periodically to determine whether the statistics for a table index have been updated within some period of time, for example, a week.

If the difference between the STATS_DATE and the GETDATE is more than seven days, an UPDATE STATISTICS command should be issued. Other system functions can also be used to determine whether a needed system operation on the database or its objects needs to be performed. ■

▶ For more information, **see** the section titled "Using Date Functions" earlier in this chapter.

▶ For more information about working with stored procedures, **see** Chapter 14, "Managing Stored Procedures and Using Flow-Control Statements," **p. 355**

Using ISNULL and NULLIF

ISNULL is a system function that returns a string of characters or numbers in place of (NULL) when a NULL is encountered in a data-storage structure such as a table column. The syntax of the function is as follows:

```
ISNULL(expression,value)
```

The *expression* is usually a column name that may contain a NULL value. The *value* specifies a string or number to be displayed when a NULL is found. In the following example, the ISNULL function is used to return the character string No entry when a NULL is encountered.

```
select ISNULL(y, 'No entry') from nulltable
y
----------
      No entry
(1 row(s) affected)
```

The NULLIF function returns a NULL if the two expressions are identical. If they are not, the second expression is returned. The NULLIF function is usually used with the CASE statement. In the following example, a NULL is returned for identical strings while the first parameter is returned when the strings don't match.

```
select nullif ('same','same'),space (2),nullif ('same','different')
---- -- ----
(null)   same
 (1 row(s) affected)
```

N O T E The space function is used in the example of the NULLIF function to provide a visual separation between the values returned by the use of the function twice in the SELECT statement. ■

Using COALESCE

The form of the COALESCE function that uses the syntax COALESCE (*expression1,expression2*) is similar to the NULLIF statement. Unlike the NULLIF statement, the COALESCE statement with two parameters returns *expression2* when a NULL is returned and returns *expression1* if NOT NULL is encountered.

You can also use COALESCE with more than two parameters. COALESCE returns the first non-NULL expression in the list of parameters when no NULL is used. If no non-NULL values are present, when COALESCE is used with more than two parameters, the function returns a NULL.

NOTE The COALESCE function is designed for use in a CASE statement that is discussed in the chapter on stored procedures. Consult Chapter 14 on stored procedures for additional information on the COALESCE function. ▧

▶ **See** the Chapter 14 section titled "Using CASE Expressions." **p. 387**

Using Niladic Functions

Niladic functions return a user or timestamp value that is automatically placed in the row of a table when the value is omitted from an INSERT or UPDATE statement. Niladic functions are defined as part of a DEFAULT constraint in a CREATE or ALTER TABLE statement. You can use any of the following niladic functions:

    USER

    CURRENT_USER

    SESSION_USER

    SYSTEM_USER

    CURRENT_TIMESTAMP

    APP_NAME

The niladic functions USER, CURRENT_USER, and SESSION_USER all return the database username of the user executing an INSERT or UPDATE statement. The function SYSTEM_USER returns the user's login ID. CURRENT_TIMESTAMP returns the current date and time in the same form as the GETDATE function. APP_NAME returns the program name for the current session if one has been set.

Niladic functions cannot be used outside the DEFAULT CONSTRAINT of a CREATE or ALTER TABLE statement. For example, you cannot use the niladic functions in the SELECT clause of a SELECT statement.

▶ For more information on setting up these options, **see** Chapter 13 "Managing and Using Rules, Constraints, and Defaults," **p. 333**

Reality Check

Remember that the goal of your implementation needs to be to return the fewest number of rows possible in each query you submit to the server. To that end, the set of SQL functions you use can be very helpful.

In many cases, you will find that if you are working with information from the database in your application, you can consider carefully how you are using it, and what the end goal is for the information. If you are trying, for example, to analyze a set of numbers and use the result to show the user of the application, consider using server-side functions, those outlined in this chapter, to help mold the information as you need it.

When you use these functions, you create a true client/server application, one that allows the server to do the database-information manipulation that it's so good at. You also optimize things for the client. Because the client won't have to perform the manipulation of the information returned from the database, response time to the user will be faster.

This directly impacts systems that you convert from older database types. For example, in one project that was completed, the database was converted to SQL Server from Btrieve. In Btrieve, the data manipulation, relationships, and so on are managed by the application.

When the database was converted, it was necessary to re-architect the system to allow the back-end system a more active role in the manipulation of the information in the system. This meant removing some functionality from the client side and implementing it on the server. Of course, this led to code changes in the application, potentially impacting the schedule to cut over the application.

One approach you might want to take with legacy systems is to first convert the database, leaving the processing assignments between the client and server side as they were in the original system. After the system is online and you have worked out the kinks in the data conversion, you can begin writing the stored procedures to automate the processes on the server.

Because you won't be impacting the database, only providing a new way to get information from it, the application will still work during the creation of the stored procedures. When you're ready on the database side, you can go back into the code and make the changes, one by one, to use the stored procedures instead of the client-side processing. Because you are doing a controlled cut-over on the client application, you can test each change carefully.

At the same time, you are controlling the risk to the client application by only implementing a single new function at a time.

From Here...

In this chapter you learned the use of various functions that return information about your system and characteristics of SQL Server. In addition, you learned how to use functions to perform operations on table data. Functions can be used both in an interactive session and in stored procedures.

For information about selected aspects of the topics mentioned in this chapter, review the following chapters:

- Chapter 6, "Creating Database Tables and Using Datatypes," discusses the values that can be stored in various Transact-SQL datatypes.
- Chapter 14, "Managing Stored Procedures and Using Flow-Control Statements," discusses the variables used for the temporary storage of values returned by functions as well as the global variables used to store information relevant to the use of functions.
- Chapter 16, "Understanding Server, Database, and Query Options," shows you how to use SET options to control the display of data through the use of functions used in SELECT statements.

Managing and Using Views

Views are static definitions for the creation of dynamic tables, constructed from one or more sets of rows according to predefined selection criteria. Views can be used to define numerous combinations of rows and columns from one or more tables. A defined view of the desired combination of rows and columns uses a simple SELECT statement to specify the rows and columns included in the view.

Understanding Views

Simply put, a view is a sort of bookmark on your table, or a way of returning to a window of information. This window is actually a set of instructions that tells SQL Server how you want to see the information in your view. This includes the parameters, formatting, and other information SQL Server will use to query the database and retrieve your information.

Technically, a view is a stored definition of a SELECT statement that specifies the rows and columns to be retrieved when the view is later referenced. You can define up to 1,024 columns of one or more tables in a view. The number of rows that you can define is limited only by the number of rows in the tables referenced.

NOTE   If you're familiar with the Access environment, you'll know views as queries. You can manipulate, change, update, or delete rows from an Access query, depending on its makeup, just as you can a table. In fact, you can specify a query nearly anywhere you'd indicate a table.

In SQL Server, queries are called views, but the balance of the information you already know from working with queries remains accurate. You can update views because they're based on simple or complex SELECT statements or functionality, and your application can refer to them in statements just as it would the underlying tables. ■

Views are aptly named because they function as the set of rows and columns that you can see through their definition. After the view is defined, you reference it as if it is a table. Although a view appears as a permanent set of rows and columns stored on a disk in a database, it's not. A view doesn't create a permanent copy of the selected rows and columns of a database.

A view performs the SELECT statement contained within its definition when the view is later referenced, just like a table. The temporary table that is created and returned to the monitor is unavailable after the display of its rows is complete. A view enables you to execute a SELECT statement when you reference the view as a table.

CAUTION

It's easy to be misled and believe that a view is a table. After the view is defined, you always access data through it as if it's a table. Try to remember that the data referenced through a view is always coming from its underlying table. Also, if you add columns to the underlying table that the view is defined on, the new columns don't appear in the view, unless the view is first dropped and recreated.

One thing that you can do to help in this area is to keep consistent naming conventions. One example of this might be to add a prefix to all views, perhaps starting each with "vw_." This will let you know that the underlying object is a view as soon as you see the name.

A view can be used to access an entire table, part of a table, or a combination of tables. Because the portion of a table you access is defined within the view, you don't have to repeat the selection statements. You can use views to simplify access to the database. If you create even complicated views that use multiple clauses, you can perform the SELECT statement in the view just as easily as a view that contains a simple SELECT statement.

▶ For more detailed information about creating and working with SELECT statements, see Chapter 7, ""Retrieving Data with Transact-SQL," **p. 155**

You can also use views to provide security in the database. You can grant permissions on a view that are different from the permissions granted on the tables the view is based upon. You can provide access to only the rows and columns referenced through a view, but not to all rows and columns directly through the table.

▶ For more information about SQL Server security, see the Chapter 20, "SQL Server Security" section titled "Understanding the Types of Security," **p. 520**

Part

II

Ch

10

Creating a View

You can create a view either through a command-line ISQL session, an ISQL/w session, or through the SQL Enterprise Manager using the Create View Wizard. A view is stored as a separate object in your database through which you have an alternative way of viewing and, with limitations, modifying a table. You should remember that you can only create a view in the current database. The syntax to create a view in an ISQL or ISQL/w session is as follows:

```
CREATE VIEW view_name [WITH ENCRYPTION] AS
SELECT statement...
FROM table_name | view_name
 [WHERE clause] [WITH CHECK OPTION]
```

You can also create a new view with the SQL Enterprise Manager Create View Wizard by performing the following steps:

1. Within the current database, select Tools, Wizards, expand the databases item, and select Create View Wizard.

2. Follow the Wizard steps, selecting tables and columns. Figure 10.1 shows the Create View Wizard dialog box for the newly created view.

After the view is created using the Create View Wizard, you may edit it. To open the Design View Window as shown in Figure 10.2, right-click the view name and choose Design View.

FIGURE 10.1

SQL Server generates all
the statements required
for the view.

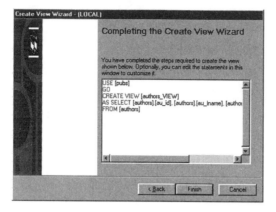

FIGURE 10.2

You can use the View list
box to select other views
for display or subse-
quent editing.

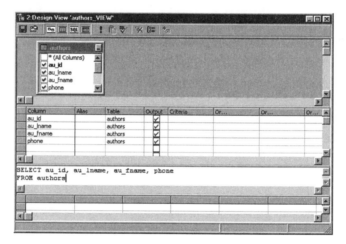

Selective Columns

You can define a view that is made up of some, but not all, of the columns of a table. In the
following example, a view is defined as a pseudotable that has two of the three columns of the
Employees table:

```
create view twocolumns as
select name, badge
from employees
```

After you've defined the view, you can use a SELECT statement to access it just like a table. For
example, the view created in the previous example can be referenced in the following manner
to display the name and badge for all rows:

```
select *
from twocolumns
```

Selective Rows

You can also define a view that references some, but not all, of the rows of a table. In the following example, the sales1 view is defined to contain only the rows in which the department is equal to Sales from the Employees table:

```
create view sales1 as
select name, department, badge
from employees
where department='SALES'
```

You can also use one or more Boolean operators in the WHERE clause of a SELECT statement to specify the rows contained through the view. In the following example, a view is defined that contains all columns from the table that are members of the Sales department and have a badge number greater than 1000.

▶ For more information about Boolean operators, see Chapter 7, **p. 155**

```
create view sales2 as
select name, department, badge
from employees
where department='Sales'
and badge>1000
```

 TIP You can use a WHERE clause in the SELECT statement that references a view even though the SELECT statement view within the view definition can include a WHERE clause. The view is treated just like an actual table.

Selective Columns and Rows

You can also define a view that comprises a combination of only some columns and rows of a table. In the following example, the view is defined and provides access to only two of the three columns, and only for the rows that contain the Sales department:

```
create view twocolumnsales as
select name,badge
from employees
where department='SALES'
```

You can continue to use a simple SELECT statement to reference the view, just like you use a table to retrieve the set of columns and rows defined in the view. For example, to show all rows and columns that are defined in the three previous views, you can use the following three SELECT statements:

```
select *
from twocolumns
select *
from sales1
select *
from twocolumnsales
```

Part

II

Ch

10

T I P You don't necessarily need to specify all the columns in the table within the view. You can specify certain columns, calling each out as a specific part of the SELECT statement. It's not a requirement to use an asterisk (*) to reference all columns defined in the view.

You can't distinguish a view from a table by the way you use a view. You have to see the view definition to distinguish a view from a table. You can create views for all the combinations of rows and columns that you access together from database tables.

N O T E You can establish a naming convention for views and tables so that the name of each is self-descriptive as a table or view. For example, the table Employees could be instead named Employees_table, and the view Sales could be named Sales_view. Remember that you can use up to 30 characters for the name of an object such as a view or table. You can also use a single character within the name of a view or table, such as a *v* for a view and a *t* for a table, if you run short of characters. ▪

CAUTION

If you define views and tables so that each is obviously a table or view, (for example, Employees_table or Sales_view) you can defeat the purpose of a view. A feature of the view is that it is nearly indistinguishable from a table. You work with a view in the same way that you work with a table.

It can be an advantage to permit views and tables to be indistinguishable from one another to database users who don't need to perform complicated queries. A complicated query can be defined within the view and the user told to use a simple SELECT statement to access the new "table," which is actually the view.

You can encounter some restrictions when you define a view. You can't define a view on a temporary table. Temporary tables are transitory database structures and exist only until data retrieved from a permanent table is displayed to an output device, such as a monitor.

If you were allowed to define a view that is based on a temporary table, the data may not be available when you reference it through the view. The temporary table on which the view was defined was automatically deleted.

▶ For more information on temporary tables, see the section in Chapter 6, "Creating Database Tables and Using Datatypes," titled "Creating Temporary Tables," **p. 119**

You also can't define a trigger on a view. A trigger can be defined on a permanent table only. It makes sense to define a trigger on only a table because a table is the permanent underlying source of the data for all views. If you were permitted to define a trigger on a view, SQL Server would still have to reference the underlying table to locate the data specified by the trigger. It's simpler to establish triggers that are based directly on tables.

N O T E A *trigger* is a database object that is automatically executed when a table row is inserted, updated, or deleted. It's primarily designed to maintain referential integrity. See Chapter 15, "Creating and Managing Triggers," for more information. ▪

In addition, you can't include ORDER BY in the definition of a view. The rows of a view are unordered like the rows of a database table. If you were permitted to use a SELECT statement that includes an ORDER BY clause in a view, the rows would be ordered and a view would have different characteristics than a database table.

If a view is to be used like a permanent table, it must have similar or identical characteristics. You can use an ORDER BY clause when you retrieve rows from a view, just as you would if you retrieve rows from a table. Remember, using views is a two-step process. First, you define the view and save it in the system. This is exactly like creating a table in the system for future use.

Second, you SELECT information from the dataset that is created by the view. Two steps give you two opportunities to manage the return information.

When you work with the view, you can also further restrict the values that are returned. For example you could have a view that limits the results set of a name and address database to doctors only. When you select from the view, you can further limit the results by indicating that you want only the general practitioners.

Think of views and selecting information from them as coin sorters. (You know, the kind where you drop a coin in the top slot, it rattles around in the bank, and then comes to rest in the proper location for that denomination in the bank—quarter, dime, nickel, and penny.) The bank is your view—it sorts and presents the information.

Now, in this example, you have two options. You can say "Give me all the dimes," or you can say "Give me all the dimes with a date of 1969." This is the SELECT statement against the view. You're deciding which parts of the information are represented by the view you're interested in.

▶ For more information on using the ORDER BY clause, see the section in Chapter 7, "Retrieving Data with Transact-SQL," titled "Using an ORDER BY Clause," **p. 178**

You also can't use COMPUTE in a view. COMPUTE creates a virtual column for the actual columns of a table or view.

▶ For more information on the COMPUTE clause, see the section in Chapter 7 entitled "Using a COMPUTE Clause in a SELECT Statement," **p. 186**

You can't use INTO as part of a SELECT statement within a view. INTO redirects rows into another table rather than to a monitor. In the following example, a view can't successfully be created because it contains an INTO clause in its SELECT statement.

```
sp_help two
Name              Owner            Type
------------------------------------------------------
two               dbo              user table
Data_located_on_segment        When_created
------------------------------   ------------------------
default                         Oct 2 1994  1:33PM
Column_name    Type    Length Nulls Default_name   Rule_name
-------------- -------------- ------ ---- --------------
name           char      25    0     (null)        (null)
badge          int        4    0     (null)        (null)
```

```
Object does not have any indexes.
No defined keys for this object.
create view selectinto as
select name,badge
into two
from employees
Msg 154, Level 15, State 3
An INTO clause is not allowed in a view.
```

Simple and Complex Views

To understand views, you might find it helpful to further categorize them. Recall that you can define views that access multiple tables as well as individual tables. *Simple views* are those you define that access any combination of rows and columns from which single tables are called. *Complex views* are those that provide access to the rows and columns of multiple tables.

The syntax for a complex view uses the same syntax in the SELECT statement that is directly used for the retrieval of rows and columns. Use the following syntax to specify the rows and columns from multiple tables of a database:

```
CREATE VIEW view_name AS
SELECT column_1,...column_n
FROM table_1,...table_n
WHERE table_key_1=table_key_2
,...AND table_key_1=table_key_n
```

In the following example, the Name and Department columns are referenced from the Employees table, and the Hours_Worked column is selected from the Pays table in the definition of the view. The WHERE clause is used to match the rows from the Employees table with the corresponding rows in the Pays table.

The Badge column is used in each table to match the rows in the same way in which a corresponding column can be used to match rows from a SELECT statement that is used outside a view.

```
create view combo as
select name,department,hours_worked
from employees,pays
where employees.badge=pays.badge
```

You access the rows and columns through a complex view the same way that you access rows and columns in a simple view. For example, you can reference the rows and columns defined in the combo view with the following SELECT statement:

```
select *
from combo
```

 TIP Rather than require a user to perform a complicated SELECT statement, you can place the complex query within the view and have the user reference the view.

Displaying Views

When you create a view, the definition of a view is stored in the syscomments system table. One way that you can display the stored definition of a view from the syscomments table is by using the sp_helptext stored system procedure.

TIP You can also use sp_helptext to display the text of a stored procedure, trigger, default, or rule as well as a view. Use sp_help to list the characteristics of a view or other objects.

In the following example, a simple view that selects all rows of the Sales department is defined. The rows of the Employees table are retrieved through the Sales view. The sp_helptext sales procedure is used to display the definition of the view.

```
sp_helptext sales1
text
-----------------
create view sales as
select * from employees
whoro dopartment='Sales'
(1 row(s) affected)
```

The view definition that is stored in the syscomments table is retrieved by sp_helptext and displays the view definition as the row of a table. The column header is text, the view definition is the row, and the count message specifies the count of the one row retrieved.

TIP If you find that a view has seemingly vanished when you return to SQL Server after you've created the view, make sure you're in the right database. Views are, by definition, database-specific and won't be visible unless you're using the right database.

You can also display the definition of a view through the SQL Enterprise Manager by performing the following steps:

1. Select the SQL Server Views folder in the database in which the view was created. Notice that an icon of a pair of eyeglasses appears to the left of each view to distinguish views from other objects. Figure 10.3 shows the expanded list of views that are currently defined for the pubs database.

2. Click the right mouse button and choose Design View. Figure 10.4 shows the definition of the view Titleview displayed through the Enterprise Manager.

Editing Views

You must use the SQL Enterprise Manager to edit an existing view. You cannot edit a view from a command-line ISQL or ISQL/w session. You would edit a view in order to change the columns or rows that are referenced by the view. For example, you'll need to add the name of a column that you inadvertently omitted when you originally defined the view.

FIGURE 10.3
You can also double-click the selected view to display it.

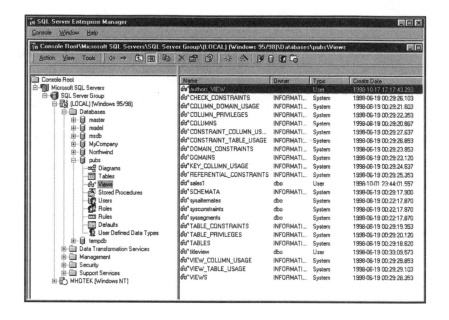

FIGURE 10.4
You can edit the view displayed in the Design View dialog box of the SQL Enterprise Manager.

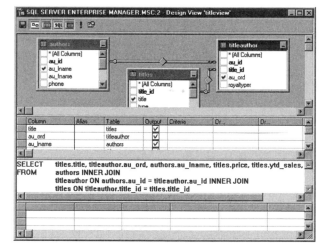

To edit a view through the SQL Enterprise Manager, perform the following steps:

1. Select the Views folder under the database in which the view was created.

2. Click the right mouse button and choose Design View.

3. Make your changes to the SQL SELECT statement in the SQL pane of the Design View window.

4. Click the Save icon.

Figure 10.5 shows the view Titleview after it has been changed. The view now shows only titles with a price greater than 50.

FIGURE 10.5

You can execute the view by clicking the Execute icon, which is the exclamation point, to see the results in the Results pane.

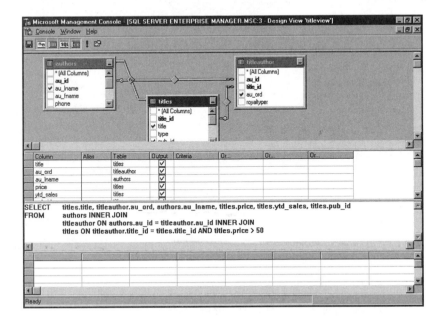

When you save the changed view, the existing view is dropped and replaced with the new view.

You can effectively edit an existing view from ISQL or ISQL/w only by deleting the existing view and creating a new one using the same name as the view that you deleted. You'll find it much easier to change views through the SQL Enterprise Manager.

Adding the WITH ENCRYPTION Clause

You might not want users to be able to display the definition of a view from the syscomments table. If you add the WITH ENCRYPTION in the CREATE VIEW statement, you can't subsequently list the definition of the view. In the following example, a view is created whose definition can't be subsequently displayed with the procedure sp_helptext.

```
create view test_view_encryption with encryption as
select * from company
go
sp_helptext test_view_encryption
go
The object's comments have been encrypted.
```

You also can't view the definition of an encrypted view from the SQL Enterprise Manager. Figure 10.6 shows the error message returned when an encrypted view is accessed errone-ously.

FIGURE 10.6

The owner of an encrypted view can still drop it and create a new view with the name of the dropped view.

> **CAUTION**
>
> A disadvantage of encrypting view definitions is that views can't be recreated when you upgrade your database or SQL Server. During an upgrade, the definitions of a view are used to recreate the view, which can't be done if the view definition is encrypted. You would also be unable to upgrade a database if you delete the view definition stored as a row in the syscomments table.

NOTE You can also encrypt procedures and triggers. The reason for encryption is security. You can prevent users from displaying the objects, such as a table or view, that an object references to prevent them from directly accessing the objects. You can use encryption and object permissions to control access to objects and object definitions. ▪

Displaying View Associations

One way to display the tables or views upon which a view is defined is to use the system procedure sp_depends. You might need to display the tables or views that a view references in order to discover and correct problems that you might encounter when you use the view.

In the following example, sp_depends shows that the Sales view is defined from the Employees table user.

```
sp_depends sales
In the current database, the specified object references the following:
name                    type               updated selected column
-------------------     ---------------    ------- -------- -------
dbo.employee            user table         no      yes      emp_id
dbo.employee            user table         no      yes      fname
dbo.employee            user table         no      yes      minit
dbo.employee            user table         no      yes      lname
dbo.employee            user table         no      yes      job_id
dbo.employee            user table         no      yes      job_lvl
dbo.employee            user table         no      yes      pub_id
dbo.employee            user table         no      yes      hire_date
```

NOTE You can also use sp_depends to display information about tables and views that are dependent upon procedures. Sp_depends references the sysdepends system table to locate dependencies. Sp_depends shows only references to objects within the current database. ▪

You can also display dependencies through the SQL Enterprise Manager. To display the dependencies of a view, click the right mouse button and choose All Tasks, Display Dependencies from the menu. For example, in Figure 10.7, the dependencies of the view Titleview are displayed in the Object Dependencies dialog box. The Object Dependencies dialog box shows that the view is defined based on the four tables.

FIGURE 10.7

The same icons used for tables and views in the Server Manager window of the SQL Enterprise Manager are used in the type column of the Object Dependencies dialog box.

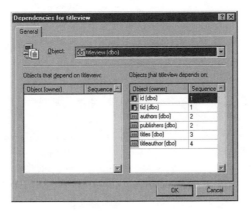

Creating Views of Views

You can define a view that references a view rather than a table. You can also create a view that references several views or a combination of views and tables. In the following example, the first view that is created is based on a table. A second view is created that references the first view. No matter how many views are defined, they must all eventually reference a table because it is the permanent source of data.

```
create view salesonly as
select name,department,badge
from employees
where department='Sales'
go
This command did not return data, and it did not return any rows
create view salespersons as
select name
from salesonly
```

In a continuation of the previous example, the following example retrieves rows from the permanent table through a view that was defined on a previously created view. Sp_depends is used to confirm that the second view was defined based on the first view.

```
select * from salespersons
name
--------------------
Bob Smith
Mary Jones
```

Part

II

Ch

10

```
John Garr
(3 row(s) affected)
sp_depends salespersons
go
In the current database the specified object references the following:
name                 type            updated selected  column
---------------------------- ----------------- ----------
dbo.salesonly        view              no       no      name
```

Sp_depends doesn't iterate through views that are defined using other views. If a view references another view rather than a table, sp_depends shows the view rather than the original table. The sp_depends procedure shows only the view or table that the view directly references in the view definition.

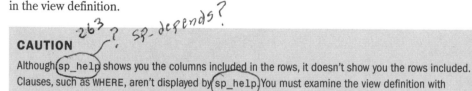

CAUTION

Although sp_help shows you the columns included in the rows, it doesn't show you the rows included. Clauses, such as WHERE, aren't displayed by sp_help. You must examine the view definition with sp_helptext.

If you want to see the columns of rows that are included in a view that is defined on one or more views, you'll have to use sp_helptext to display all the view definitions. If a view is defined on tables only, the definition of the view displayed by sp_helptext specifies the rows and columns that are included. It's better to directly define views on tables rather than on other views.

You should use the Object Dependencies dialog box in the SQL Enterprise Manager to display object dependencies. Unlike sp_depends, the listing of object dependencies in the Object Dependencies dialog box shows the multiple level of views and tables that a view is based upon. For example, it shows that the view Lowtitleview is defined directly based on the view Titleview, and indirectly to four tables. In Figure 10.8, this is indicated with the Eyeglass icon in the type column for sequence number five, and the Table icon in the type column for sequence number four. The sequence numbers are used to illustrate level or depth of objects that the view is defined on.

FIGURE 10.8
Object dependencies have levels indicated by the sequence number.

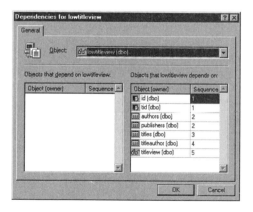

Renaming Columns in Views

You can also rename the columns of the base tables in the view. Define the list of alternative column names following the name of the view and preceding the keyword, as in the view definition. Use the following syntax to assign alternative names for the columns referenced in a view:

```
CREATE VIEW view_name [ (view_column_1,...view_column_n) ] AS
SELECT statement...
FROM table_name or view_name
[WHERE clause]
```

In the following example, alternative names for the columns of the Employees table are specified as part of the view definition. A single letter is used for the alternative column name in the view. After the list of column names for the view is defined, the alternative column names appear as new column headers as well as in other clauses, such as a WHERE clause.

```
create view view8 (a,b,c)
as
select name,department,badge from employees
(1 row(s) affected)
select * from view8
a                       b                      c
--------------------    -------------------    ----------
Mary Jones              Sales                  5514
Dan Duryea              Shipping               3321
John Garr               Sales                  2221
Mark Lenard             Sales                  3331
Bob Smith               Sales                  1
Minty Moore             Sales                  7444
(6 row(s) affected)
```

N O T E You don't have to create a view to rename the column of a table during retrieval. Instead, you can rename a column with a SELECT clause outside a view using the following syntax:

```
SELECT column_name=renamed_name
...
```

A new name that contains embedded spaces can be enclosed within single quotation marks. The new name isn't permanent. It only applies within the SELECT statement. ■

Renaming Views

You can use sp_rename to rename a view. The system procedure uses the following syntax:

```
sp_rename old_name, new_name
```

Use a comma (,) between the old_name and the new_name to separate the parameters from the procedure name. In the following example, the Sales view is renamed sales2. After the view is renamed, sp_depends shows that the renamed procedure is still based upon the permanent Employees table.

Part

II

Ch

10

```
sp_rename sales, sales2
Object name has been changed.
sp_depends sales2
In the current database, the specified object references the following:
name                     type              updated selected column
------------------------ ----------------- ------- -------- ---------
dbo.employee             user table        no      yes      emp_id
dbo.employee             user table        no      yes      fname
dbo.employee             user table        no      yes      minit
dbo.employee             user table        no      yes      lname
dbo.employee             user table        no      yes      job_id
dbo.employee             user table        no      yes      job_lvl
dbo.employee             user table        no      yes      pub_id
dbo.employee             user table        no      yes      hire_date
```

You can also rename a view using the SQL Enterprise Manager. To rename a view through the Enterprise Manager, perform the following steps:

1. Left-click the view to select it.

2. Click the right mouse button. Choose Rename.

3. Enter a new name for the view in the Rename Objects dialog box.

4. Click OK.

TIP You can use `sp_rename` to rename other database objects, including tables, columns, stored procedures, triggers, indexes, defaults, rules, and user-defined datatypes.

CAUTION

Although you can rename views with the `sp_rename` procedure, SQL Server does not change the name of a table or view in the stored definition of a view in the table syscomments. It warns you of this when you rename a view or similar objects. In the following example, a warning is displayed when the Employees table is renamed with the procedure `sp_rename`. The procedure `sp_helptext` shows that the old name of the table, Employees, is retained in the definition of the view based on the renamed table.

```
Caution: Changing any part of an object name could break scripts and stored
⇒procedures. The object was renamed to 'vw_emp_dept'.
```

However, both the `sp_depends` procedure and the Object Dependencies dialog box will display the updated name of renamed tables and views.

You should try not to rename objects unless it's absolutely necessary.

Dropping Views

You can use the `DROP VIEW` command to remove a view from a database. Dropping a view has no effect on the permanent table that the dropped view is based upon. The definition of the view is simply removed from the database. The `DROP VIEW` syntax is as follows:

```
DROP VIEW view_name_1, ... view_name_n
```

You can drop multiple views in a single DROP VIEW by using a list of views separated by commas after the DROP VIEW keywords. The following example drops the Sales2 view:

```
drop view sales2
This command did not return data, and it did not return any rows.
```

You can also use the SQL Enterprise Manager to drop views by performing the following steps:

1. Left-click the view to select it.

2. Click the Delete icon on the Enterprise Manager Toolbar.

3. Click the Drop All button.

Figure 10.9 shows the Drop Objects dialog box. The view that was selected in the Server Manager dialog box is automatically selected in the Drop Objects dialog box.

FIGURE 10.9
You can use the Show Dependencies button to display the object dependencies before you drop the view.

CAUTION

If you drop a view in which another view is defined, the second view returns the following error when you reference it, such as in a SELECT statement.

```
Msg 208, Level 16, State 1
Invalid object name 'name_of_dropped_view'.
Msg 4413, Level 16, State 1
```

View resolution was unsuccessful because the previously mentioned objects, upon which the view directly or indirectly relies, don't currently exist. These objects need to be re-created in order to use the view.

You should consider defining views directly on tables rather than other views. Tables are less likely to be dropped than views because tables are the objects in which rows are actually stored unlike views, which are simply a different way of looking at the data in a table.

Inserting Rows Through Views

In addition to retrieving rows of data through a view, you can also use the view to add rows to the underlying table on which the view is defined. To easily add a row, reference all table columns in the view. In the example shown next, a new row is added to the permanent Employees table through an INSERT statement that specifies the sales view.

After you've created the view, reference it in an INSERT statement to add rows just as if you've referenced a table in the INSERT statement. The rows inserted through the view are added to the underlying table that the view was defined on.

In the following example, the view definition is first displayed to demonstrate that the view references the underlying table, Employees, and is restricted only to rows that contain the department, Sales. After a new row is inserted through the view, the row is subsequently retrieved from both the view and the table.

```
sp_helptext sales
go
text
-----------------
create view sales as
select * from employees
where department='Sales'
go
insert into sales
values ('Mark Lenard','Sales',3331)
select * from sales
where badge=3331
go
name                    department              badge
------------------      --------------------    -----
Mark Lenard             Sales                   3331
(1 row(s) affected)
go
select * from employees
where badge=3331
name                    department              badge
------------------      --------------------    -----
Mark Lenard             Sales                   3331
(1 row(s) affected)
```

In the previous example, the row that was inserted through the view matched the criteria specified in the WHERE clause of the view. For example, the inserted row contained the department, Sales. Although you might find it odd, SQL Server will permit you to insert a row through a view even though it doesn't match the criteria of WHERE clauses defined within the view.

After a row is inserted through a view that does not match the criteria specified in the WHERE clause of the view, you can't retrieve the row through the view. The criteria for rows defined in the WHERE clause prevents you from retrieving the new row that you've just inserted. For example, in the following INSERT statement, a row is inserted through a view into the Employees table on which the view Sales is defined. As you'll recall from the definition of the Sales view in the previous example, rows can have only the Sales department.

A subsequent SELECT statement is unable to retrieve the newly inserted row through the view. However, the row was added to the underlying table Employees. A SELECT statement that references the table retrieves the new row that was added through the view. Both examples are shown here:

```
insert into sales
values ('Fannie Farmer','Logistics',6689)
go
select * from sales
where badge=6689
name                    department           badge
-------------------- -------------------- ----------
(0 row(s) affected)
go
select * from employees
where badge=6689
go
name                    department           badge
-------------------- -------------------- ----------
Fannie Farmer        Logistics            6689
(1 row(s) affected)
```

You can become confused when you add a row to the underlying table through a view in which the row doesn't match the criteria for inclusion in the view. The row can be inserted through the view, but it cannot be retrieved and subsequently displayed through the same view. The row effectively disappears when retrieved through the view, but it still can be accessed through the table on which the view is based.

Fortunately, you can add the WITH CHECK OPTION clause to your view definition to prevent an operation, such as the insertion of a row through a view, that can't be subsequently displayed through the view.

The WITH CHECK OPTION, which is applied to the SELECT statement that is defined within the view, restricts all changes to the data to conform to the row selection criteria defined within the SELECT statement. For example, if a view is defined based on the Employees table that contains a WHERE clause that specifies only the Sales department, only rows that contain the Sales department can be inserted in the Employees table through the view. WITH CHECK OPTION is illustrated in the following example:

```
create view check_with_check as
select * from company
where department='Sales' with check option
go
This command did not return data, and it did not return any rows
insert into check_with_check
values ('Bob Matilda','Field Service',3325,2)
go
Msg 550, Level 16, State 2
The attempted insert or update failed because the target view
either specifies WITH CHECK OPTION or spans a view which specifies
WITH CHECK OPTION and one or more rows resulting from the operation
did not qualify under the CHECK OPTION constraint.
Command has been aborted.
update check_with_check
set department='Hardware Repair' where department='Field Service'
```

```
go
(0 row(s) affected)
delete from check_with_check
where department='Field Service'
go
(0 row(s) affected)
```

TIP   If you find that, after adding a row to a view, the row seems to disappear, you might have added a row that doesn't meet the criteria for the View. Another reason for this is if the view has changed since you added the row, making the row no longer part of the view's dataset.

You can prevent the first instance of this by using the WITH CHECK OPTION, keeping rows that don't match the criteria for the view from being inserted through the view. Of course, this won't help in the second case where the view was changed after the row was inserted, but it's a good measure nonetheless.

In the previous example, a view was created that included all columns of the underlying table on which it was defined. If one or more columns of the underlying tables aren't present in the view, the missing columns must be defined to allow a NULL or have a default value bound to the missing columns. If not, you can't add the row to the table through the view.

In the following example, a view is created that includes two columns of the Employees table. The insertion of a row through the view is unsuccessful because the Department column was defined with NOT NULL.

```
create view namebadge as
select name,badge
from employees
go
insert into namebadge
(name,badge)
values ('Russell Stover',8000)
Msg 233, Level 16, State 2
The column department in table employees may not be null.
```

After a default is defined for the Department column and bound to the column in the Employees table, a new row can be inserted through the namebadge view. The addition of the default for the Department column in the Employees table permits a value to be applied by default when a new row is inserted through the namebadge view. An example is shown in the following code:

```
create default deptdefault
as 'Sales'
go
sp_bindefault deptdefault, 'employees.department'
Default bound to column.
go
insert into namebadge
(name,badge)
values ('Russell Stover',8000)
(1 row(s) affected)
```

N O T E A default can be bound to a user-defined datatype or column of a table. A default can't be bound to the column of a view. However, the defaults bound to table columns that are referenced in a view are applied to the columns if a new row is inserted through the view. ■

The following example shows that after the row is inserted into the underlying Employees table through the namebadge view, successive SELECT statements are used to retrieve the new row through the view and the table:

```
select * from namebadge
where name='Russell Stover'
go
name                    badge
-------------------- ----------
Russell Stover          8000
(1 row(s) affected)
select * from employees
where name='Russell Stover'
go
name                    department           badge
-------------        -------------------- ----------
Russell Stover          Sales                8000
(1 row(s) affected)
```

▶ For more information about defaults, see the section in Chapter 13, "Managing and Using Rules, Constraints, and Defaults," titled "Defining Defaults," **p. 347**

▶ For more information about different datatypes, see the section in Chapter 6, "Creating Database Tables and Using Datatypes," titled "Creating User-Defined Datatypes," **p. 145**

Using Views to Delete Rows

You can delete rows through views even though all columns are not referenced in the view. In the following example, a row that was previously added to the Employees table through the Namebadge view is deleted by using the Namebadge view. A subsequent SELECT statement demonstrates that the row is deleted.

```
delete from namebadge
where name='Russell Stover'
go
(1 row(s) affected)
select * from namebadge
where name='Russell Stover'
go
name                    badge
-------------------- ----------
(0 row(s) affected)
```

You can't delete a row if the criterion specified in the SELECT clause doesn't include the row specified for deletion. It isn't necessary to add the WITH CHECK OPTION to the definition of the view to prevent the deletion of rows that don't match the criteria specified by the WHERE clause of the view. In the following example, one or more rows of the Shipping department are specified for deletion through the Sales view. Even if multiple rows were stored in the underlying permanent Employees table upon which sales are based, the rows can't be deleted through the Sales view.

```
delete from sales
where department='Shipping'
go
(0 row(s) affected)
```

You also can't delete a row from the underlying table of a view if the column that you specify in the WHERE clause of a DELETE statement specifies a column that isn't specified in the view. The following example returns an error because the column specified in the WHERE clause isn't present in the Namebadge view used in the DELETE statement:

```
delete from namebadge
where department='Shipping'
go
Msg 207, Level 16, State 2
Invalid column name 'department'.
```

You can, however, delete the row through a view that was defined with a WHERE clause that specifies criteria that includes the row or rows specified in the DELETE statement. You can also delete one or more rows directly through the table in which the view was defined. In the following example, a row is deleted by using a DELETE statement that references the table containing the row:

```
delete from employees
where department='Shipping'
go
(1 row(s) affected)
```

Using Views to Update Rows

You can use an UPDATE statement to change one or more columns or rows that are referenced through a view. You can change one or more columns of the view. Any changes that you specify through the view are made to the underlying table in which the view is defined. In the following example, a single row is updated through the Sales view:

```
select * from sales
go
name                    department              badge
-------------------- -------------------- ----------
Bob Smith               Sales                   1234
Mary Jones              Sales                   5514
John Garr               Sales                   2221
Mark Lenard             Sales                   3331
(4 row(s) affected)
update sales
set badge=0001
where name='Bob Smith'
go
(1 row(s) affected)
select * from sales
```

```
where name='Bob Smith'
name                     department           badge
-------------------      -------------------  ----------
Bob Smith                Sales                1
(1 row(s) affected)
```

You can change one or more columns or rows so that they no longer meet the criteria for inclusion in the view. In the following example, a row is updated through a view and a column value is changed so that the row no longer matches the criteria defined in the view:

```
update sales
set department='Field Service'
where name='Bob Smith'
go
(1 row(s) affected)
select * from sales
where name='Bob Smith'
go
name                     department           badge
-------------------      -------------------  ----------
 (0 row(s) affected)
```

You can also update the underlying table by updating it through a view that is defined on a view. In the following example, the update to the Employees table is performed through a view that is defined using the Sales view.

```
select * from onlyname
name
go
----------------------
Bob Smith
Fred Sanders
(2 row(s) affected)
update onlyname
set name='Bob Orieda'
where name='Bob Smith'
go
(1 row(s) affected)
select * from onlyname
go
name
----------------------
Fred Sanders
Bob Orieda
(2 row(s) affected)
select * from employees
where name like 'Bob%'
go
name                     department           badge
-----------------------  -------------------  ------
Bob Orieda               SALES                1834
(1 row(s) affected)
```

The updated row that was changed through the name Onlyname view, which was based on the underlying Employees table through the Sales view, is displayed through both the Nameonly view and the Employees table. The updated row is also displayed through the Sales view. Here are the results:

```
select * from sales
where name like 'Bob%'
go
name                          department           badge
------------------------      -------------------  ------
Bob Orieda                    SALES                1834
(1 row(s) affected)
```

Any changes to the data that you make by updates through views are always reflected in the underlying tables. Views permit you to establish virtual tables with data rows organized like tables, though they are dynamically created as the view is referenced. It's convenient to use views as the only access to data. They offer greater control and a layer of insulation between the user and the database tables. The best-case scenario is to not allow tables to be directly referenced.

N O T E Users of older databases, such as hierarchical or network databases, might remember that their databases could only be manipulated through entities equivalent to views. Network databases were indirectly accessed through an entity called a *subschema*. A subschema functioned like a view.

The usual definition of a subschema is that it serves as the entity through which a programmer or user views the database. In the past, you always had to use a subschema to access a network database. Usually, a default subschema was created for a network database that permitted access to the entire database if necessary. ▪

You can update underlying tables through multitable views if the updated columns are part of the same table. The following example shows a row is successfully updated through the multitable combo view.

```
create view combo (a,b,c) as
select name,employees.badge,pays.badge
from employees,pays
where employees.badge=pays.badge
go
This command did not return data, and it did not return any rows
update combo
set a='Jim Walker II'
where b=3211
go
(1 row(s) affected)
select * from combo
where b=3211
go
a                             b           c
------------------------      ----------  ----------
Jim Walker II                 3211        3211
(1 row(s) affected)
```

You can't, however, update the view columns that are used to match rows between the tables because they're part of separate tables. In the next example, the column b and column c views are based on the Badge columns in the Employees and Pays tables. An error is returned that cites an unsuccessful update because the columns are from two tables.

```
update combo
set c=1111, b=1111
where b=8005
go
Msg 4405, Level 16, State 2
View 'combo' is not updatable because the FROM clause names multiple tables.
```

You can update a value in a single column directly through the view, and you can use a trigger to update the corresponding value in a related table. In the following example, a trigger has been defined to automatically update the Badge column in the Pays table if the Badge column in the Pays table is changed. When the badge is changed through the b column in the combo view, the trigger automatically activates to change the corresponding value in the Pays table.

```
update combo
set b=9999
where c=4411
go
(1 row(s) affected)
select * from combo
where b=9999
go
a                             b           c
------------------------- ----------- ----------
Sue Sommers                 9999        9999
(1 row(s) affected)
```

Part
II
Ch
10

Exploring Other View Characteristics

A view remains defined in the database if you drop the table upon which it's based. However, an error is returned when the view is referenced if its underlying table is undefined. If you create a new table with the same name as the one referenced by the view that was dropped, you can again retrieve data from the underlying new table through the view.

The following example drops a table upon which a view is based. As shown in the following example, sp_help confirms that the view remains defined even though you have deleted the table upon which it's based. When the view is used in a SELECT statement, an error is returned because the table doesn't exist. After the table is recreated and rows are loaded from an existing table, the view is used to reference rows for the underlying new table.

```
drop table employees3
go
This command did not return data, and it did not return any rows
sp_help namebadge3
go
```

```
Name                Owner             Type
- - - - - - - - - - - - - - - - - - - - - - - - - - - - - - - - -  - - - - - - - - - - - - - - -
namebadge3          dbo               view
Data_located_on_segment When_created
- - - - - - - - - - - - - - - - - - - - -  - - - - - - - - - - - - - - - - - - - - - - - - - -
not applicable           Oct 2 1994 11:45AM
Column_name Type Length Nulls Default_name Rule_name
- - - - - - - - - - - - - - - - - - - - - - - - - - - - - -  - - - - - - - - - - - - - - - -
name        char    25      0     (null)       (null)
badge       int     4       0     (null)       (null)
No defined keys for this object.
select * from namebadge3
go
Msg 208, Level 16, State 1
Invalid object name 'employees3'.
Msg 4413, Level 16, State 1
View resolution could not succeed because the previously mentioned
objects, upon which the view directly or indirectly relies, do not
currently exist.  These objects need to be re-created for the view
 to be usable.
create table employees3
(name char(25),department char(20),badge int)
go
This command did not return data, and it did not return any rows
insert into employees3
select * from employees
go
(12 row(s) affected)
select * from namebadge3
where name='Sally Springer'
go
name                        badge
- - - - - - - - - - - - - - - - - - - - - - - -  - - - - - - - - - -
Sally Springer              9998
(1 row(s) affected)
```

If you use a SELECT clause in a view with an asterisk (*) to specify columns, the new columns added to the table with an ALTER TABLE statement won't be available in the old view. The new table columns are made available only if the view is dropped and recreated.

In the following example, a view is defined that uses an asterisk (*) in the SELECT clause of a SELECT statement to reference all columns of the Employees table. After an additional column is added to the table with an ALTER TABLE statement, the view doesn't display the NULL entries in the new column that was added to the table. The new Wageclass column is available through the view only after the view is dropped and recreated.

```
sp_helptext sales3
go
text
- - - - - - - - - - - - - - - -
create view sales3
as
select * from employees3
where department='SALES'
```

```
go
(1 row(s) affected)
select * from sales3
go
name                    department      badge
------------------------------------- ----------
Fred Sanders            SALES           1051
Bob Orieda              SALES           1834
(2 row(s) affected)
alter table employees3
add wageclass int null
go
This command did not return data, and it did not return any rows
select * from sales3
go
name                    department      badge
------------------------------------- ----------
Fred Sanders            SALES           1051
Bob Orieda              SALES           1834
(2 row(s) affected)
select * from employees3
where department='SALES'
go

------------------------- --------------- ----------
Fred Sanders            SALES           1051    (null)
Bob Orieda              SALES           1834    (null)
(2 row(s) affected)
drop view sales3
go
This command did not return data, and it did not return any rows
create view sales3 as
select * from employees3
where department='SALES'
go
This command did not return data, and it did not return any rows
select * from sales3
go
name                    department      badge  wageclass
----------------------- ---------- ----------
Fred Sanders            SALES           1051    (null)
Bob Orieda              SALES           1834    (null)
(2 row(s) affected)
```

Understanding the Advanced Use of Views

After you've worked through views for a bit, you should consider some additional helpful, though perhaps less obvious, uses for them. Views are a powerful component of SQL Server and they offer you the capability to really leverage your SQL Server implementation by enhancing everything from the user experience to security on the system.

In the following sections, you'll see how you can implement views to achieve more advanced cuts of your information, and how you can use them to enhance the security of the information on your system.

Security Management with Views

It might not seem like security comes into play too much with views, but indeed it's one of the most frequent uses you'll have for them. Whether your intent is to protect the data from users or users from themselves, you'll do well to look into implementing a solid array of views and supporting functionality.

The first approach to SQL Server security is, of course, the setting of permissions on the user and group level. This allows you to lock down specific tables and columns, giving you a great deal of protection for the system. One of the drawbacks to this is that if users are accessing your database with a method other than your expected applications, they might run into trouble. This trouble comes in the form of an error message when you've protected a table's columns.

When you do a SELECT against a table and you're just starting the information analysis of that table, you'll often find that you issue a SELECT * FROM *tablename* statement. This statement will typically retrieve all rows and all columns from the table so you can determine how to lay out and request the information you need from the table.

If you issue this type of statement against a table that has permissions denied on a given column or columns, you'll receive an error message and no information will be returned.

```
SELECT permission denied on column...
```

This can be really frustrating for the users if they receive this message and are not aware of the columns that are in the table. If they don't know the columns, they'll be forced to refer to your documentation, or they'll need to talk with support staff to determine the columns available and the correct statement to retrieve them.

You can avoid all this by creating views and letting users gain access to information by using the views, rather than directly querying the underlying tables. As you've seen throughout this chapter, the views have the added advantage of being able to hide database relationship complexities from the user as well.

When you create a view, and only select the columns that should be shown so that the view accurately reflects their privilege level, the users will be able to use the SELECT * approach. This will keep the error message away, and will keep your database information most accessible to the user.

You can further lock down the security by mixing a series of views and stored procedures. By creating views as read-only, you can then force users to do updates and new record insertions by using stored procedures. Because they're using stored procedures, you can control how records are modified, perform checks on the incoming information, and more.

▶ For additional information about creating and managing stored procedures, see Chapter 14, "Managing Stored Procedures and Using Flow-Control Statements," **p. 355**

For extreme situations, you can actually create stored procedures that act as views on your tables. These stored procedures are simple, and take the form of your select statement as the content of the stored procedure. When you do this, you can even remove the SELECT permissions on the table. Users will only need to have EXECUTE permissions for the stored procedures. This is the ultimate lock-down approach for your tables, but it doesn't come without a price.

For example, you'll have to create stored procedures to do all operations that relate to the tables in your system. This means even the simple things like standard insert operations and allowable browsing of the tables will have to be programmatically supported. In most installations, this isn't necessary, but there will undoubtedly be extreme cases where you will need absolute control.

One drawback to this is that your users will have a much more difficult time just browsing the tables from other applications. For example, in Excel, without some alternative approaches, you won't be able to use the powerful features that are built into the application that enable browsing of ODBC databases, and the same might be true of other third-party applications.

TIP When you're creating a tightly managed, secure system, you can test user rights by using the SETUSER statement to impersonate another user. By doing so, you can "pretend" you're that user, test access points, then return to your typical developer role and fine-tune the process.

In order to use this statement, you must be the SA or the DBO.

The SETUSER statement has the following syntax:

SETUSER *username* [with noreset]

When you execute this statement, the rights associated with the username you specify will become your rights. You can create objects, test your access levels, and so on. Anything this user can or cannot do, you'll be able to mimic.

The statement remains in effect until you issue a SETUSER statement for either a different user or with no parameters, or until you USE a different database, whichever comes first.

Reality Check

Views are a powerful component available to you for use in many different circumstances. Views are inexpensive resource-wise because they don't store information other than the statements that control the content represented by the view. At IKON, we use views daily in our applications as a way of eliminating the need to do a join at the application level. Because we can use the view to accomplish the join, it saves coding in the application, and our application can be consistent in the way it works with the database tables.

One of the key applications we've used views for is the timekeeping system. This system uses SQL Server as the backend database engine and it has Web, Visual Basic, and Access components on the client side. The client applications are used to enter time slips and query the user's database of past slips. The Access application uses different views in presenting users the information in the system at the administrative reporting level. The view makes it possible to create relatively simple applications for users without regard for the underlying relationships between the tables.

Additionally, new views have been created to make it easier to query the database with other applications. From Excel to custom-built Visual Basic applications, the view ensures that the database information is selected in the most expeditious manner and that it uses all available indexes. There are some drawbacks to views; namely, if they contain columns not required for the calling routines, they can bog down the processing unnecessarily.

For example, in one instance, a view took a substantial amount of time to produce the desired dataset. When we created a new view with a smaller target dataset, we found that the original dataset contained several columns that were not needed. When we removed the columns, there was no longer any need for joins to support the columns, which speeded up the query and the return of results.

In short, don't hesitate to create a new view to support a specific program or query process, within reason. The overhead is low, the performance payback is potentially high, and you can always drop the view later without impacting your data.

From Here...

In this chapter, you've learned to create virtual tables that use a stored SELECT statement to create a subset of the rows, columns, or a combination of the rows and columns of one or more database tables. You've also learned to change previously defined views using the Enterprise Manager and display and remove views when they're no longer needed. Finally, you learned to add, update, and delete rows through views, applying the changes to the underlying tables from which the views are defined.

For information about selected aspects of the topics mentioned in this chapter, see the following chapters:

- Chapter 6, "Creating Database Tables and Using Datatypes," discusses the treatment of NULLs as column values, as well as the column datatypes.
- Chapter 7, "Retrieving Data With Transact-SQL," teaches you how to combine rows from multiple tables in the same query, including the use of COMPUTE and COMPUTE BY.
- Chapter 11, "Managing and Using Indexes and Keys," teaches you how to create and use keys and indexes and how to constrain rows and columns to unique values.
- Chapter 15, "Creating and Managing Triggers," teaches you how to create and use triggers to maintain referential integrity in the database.

Managing and Using Indexes and Keys

One of the most important responsibilities of a database designer is to correctly define a database table for optimal performance. SQL Server's basic design of a table doesn't define how data is to be accessed or stored physically, beyond the datatype constraints and any referential constraint placed on a column or columns designated as primary key. Instead, SQL Server provides a mechanism of indexes or keys to a table that help SQL Server optimize responses to queries.

Without an index, SQL Server must *table scan*, or read every row in a table, before it can answer any given query. In large tables, this is obviously an expensive option for the server to take. Indexes provide a way for SQL Server to organize pointers to the data required. An index in a database works the same way as an index in a reference book. Like an index in a book, an index in a database is a list of important values that have references to pages in the database table containing the information that matches the index value. This enables the database to read from a typically smaller list of index pages that will, in turn, point to the data to answer any given request.

Defining Indexes

Indexes are SQL Server's internal method of organizing the data in a table in such a way that it can be retrieved in an optimal fashion. *Optimal*, in this case, refers to the quickest way. Indexes are collections of unique values in a given table and their corresponding list of pointers to the pages of data where those values are physically represented in a table.

At a high level, indexes are a shorthand way for the database to record information that it's storing in tables. Indexes are just another kind of object in the database and have storage needs like tables. Just as tables require pages of data to store their rows in, indexes require pages to store their summary data in. The advantage of an index is that, generally, it reduces the number of I/Os required to reach any given piece of data in a table.

When you create an index in SQL Server, you tell the database to scan the table, gather the discrete values in the particular column(s) being indexed, and then write a list of data pages and row identifiers to the index page that matches the value being indexed. This enables the server to scan a list of index pages, before scanning the whole table to look for matchingdata.

Understanding General Index Guidelines

Working with indexes is a test-and-test-again proposition. You're faced with many different variables that you'll need to weigh against one another in terms of performance and the end-user experience. For example, the indexes you create will generally be driven by the data-retrieval habits of the applications on the system. These approaches to gathering up information from your tables will certainly be a key factor in which columns you index.

Optimizing Indexes Based on Usage Patterns

Just when you thought this might be easy, along comes the problem of analyzing only the retrieval situations you'll be supporting. Not only must you consider retrieval, but also insertion and update processes. This might seem strange at first, but when you think about what's happening behind the scenes, you'll see that the difference between a query, update, and insert application and an application that is query only is night and day.

When indexes are updated, that's when the work happens. This is a simple, but very important, rule of thumb. Therefore, if your system does a lot of inserts, you'll do well to limit the indexes that are active on the database tables. When records are inserted or updated, the indexes must be updated as well. In fact, when you update a record in SQL Server, you have the same amount of overhead associated with the transaction as you do with an insert. In general, the magic number on these types of systems is five indexes. As you move beyond this, the performance hit you'll take can be excessive.

On the other hand, if you have a query-centric system, one where few inserts are happening and the focus is more on the analysis of existing information, you can implement all the indexes you need to improve query performance. Your limiting factor in this case becomes disk space because each index will require additional database space.

Keys to a Successful Index

If you take the time to create an index, make sure you also take the time to determine what you are targeting with the index. This means that you should understand what types of queries will be going against the database. Specifically, this means understanding what columns will be in the WHERE clauses of the SELECT statements.

As you'll see when you create one, an index is created by indicating what fields you want to include in it. The key is that when SQL Server considers an index, one of the field qualifiers to the SELECT statement *must* be the first column in the index. If not, the index will simply not be used.

For example, if you have an index on the ZIP code and state fields of your database, in that order, and you query the database for a record based on state, the index will not be used. SQL Server will have to work out a different means of retrieving the row(s) that meet your request. Depending on a number of factors, this can mean a table scan, the enemy of performance.

On the other hand, if your select statement queries only on ZIP code, it can use the index. This is regardless of the fact that the index also includes the state. SQL Server will ignore that component of the index and work on without it. Your application will still benefit greatly from the index.

TIP SQL Server manages the decision about what indexes to use to fulfill a given query in a series of pages that summarize the distribution of information in the table. SQL Server uses this summary information to determine whether a table scan or an indexed query will be the fastest and best way to satisfy a query.

If you create your table *with* data, this summary information is automatically established for you. If, on the other hand, you create the table and then add data to the table, the summary page will not be updated. In this case, and any case when you're adding, changing or deleting 10-20% of the information in a given table, you need to update the summary information. You do this by issuing an UPDATE STATISTICS command.

▶ For more information on UPDATE STATISTICS, **see** the section titled "Understanding and Using UPDATE STATISTICS and RECOMPILE," in Chapter 19, **p. 502**

This command is never a destructive step, and can help performance significantly by enabling SQL Server to learn from the real data in your database.

Choosing a Good Index Candidate

First, it's important to understand that you cannot create an index on a column with a datatype of BIT, TEXT or IMAGE. That said, what general things are helpful to look for in determining what columns to index?

The maximum size of an index is 900 bytes, so using large char, varchar, nchar, nvarchar, binary, and varbinary columns is not allowed.

Here are some good general rules to follow in looking for good index candidates:

Table 11.1 Good Index Candidates

Description	Notes
Foreign keys	Tables with foreign keys are prime candidates for indexes. There are very few cases where you should *not* have an index on a primary key. It helps the lookup times immensely.
Large results set queries	For the queries that will be returning a large data set, you should index whenever possible. Note that this typically breaks the rules according to good client/ server methodology. You want to always be looking for ways to decrease the size of the results set, not support large data sets. Nonetheless, the requirement will undoubtedly arise and you'll want to support it well with an index.
Order by and group by support	Columns that are referenced in these clauses will benefit greatly from an index.

Query Optimizer Enhancements

SQL Server 7.0 has provided significant improvements to the query processor and its handling of indexes. One of the most significant improvements is the capability of using multiple indexes per table in a single query. This has a significant performance impact when locating data because scans of data pages are virtually eliminated.

However, this new methodology complicates the database designer's decisions on which indexes to create. Should she create a small number of composite indexes or should multiple indexes consisting of a single column be defined? For those indexes that are used to enforce uniqueness, a composite index is required if multiple rows are involved. At the time of this writing, the jury is still out on creating multiple indexes consisting of a single column in all other cases.

SQL Server handles multiple indexes per table, per query via two new methods called index intersection and index union.

Every row inside a SQL Server table has an associated rowid. During a query that uses an index, SQL Server gathers the rowids from the index pages. After it has all the rowids, it uses these pointers to return the actual data. When using multiple indexes, this same method is used, except rowids are now gathered from multiple indexes. If you have specified an AND condition in your query, an index intersection is applied. The rowids that lie at the intersection of the individually accumulated rowids are used to return the result set. In plain English, this means that only those rowids that were found in every index are used. If an OR condition is applied in the query, an index union occurs. This means that all the individual rowids are accumulated and the data corresponding to those rows are returned to the client

Part
II

Ch
11

Creating Indexes

SQL Server has two methods of creating indexes. There is a graphical method provided in SQL Enterprise Manager, and a Transact-SQL interface using the CREATE INDEX statement. Only the table's owner can create an index on a table.

> **N O T E** When you create indexes through SQL Enterprise Manager, you can't specify a data segment for the index to be created on. Moving indexes on to different data segments can significantly improve performance on non-clustered indexes because multiple I/O threads can be used to read the data from the index and data pages concurrently. Use the CREATE INDEX statement in ISQL/w to create an index if you need to specify a segment for the index data.

Creating an Index with SQL Enterprise Manager   To create an index using SQL Enterprise Manager, follow these steps:

1. Run SQL Enterprise Manager from the Microsoft SQL Server 7.0 group. Figure 11.1 shows the main screen shortly after the startup of SQL Enterprise Manager.

2. Select the server, database, and table that you want to work on (see Figure 11.2).

FIGURE 11.1

SQL Enterprise Manager's Explorer view after having just being started. Note that no server is selected.

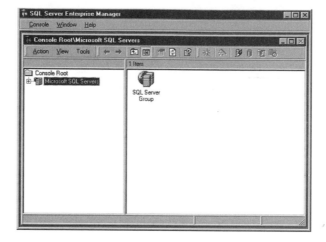

FIGURE 11.2

You use the Explorer-type view from within the Enterprise Manager to select the table objects you want to work with.

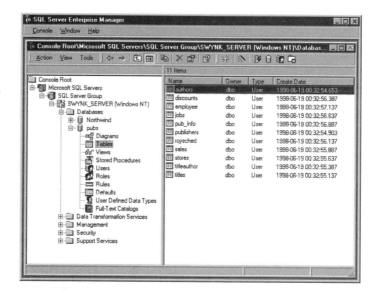

3. Select Action, All Tasks, Manage Indexes. The Manage Indexes dialog box, shown in Figure 11.3, appears.

4. Click New to clear the Index combo box, enabling you to enter the new index name and indicate the columns for the index.

5. Enter fk_au_id as the index name, check the au_id column, select the check boxes Unique Values and Ignore Duplicate Values. See Figure 11.4.

FIGURE 11.3

The authors table is selected in the combo box, and the `aunmind` index is shown in the lower list box.

FIGURE 11.4

The Create New Index dialog box is ready to build a new index.

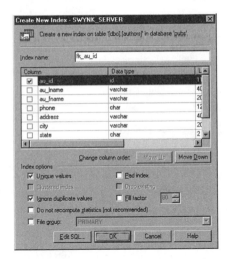

 TIP Prefacing index names with `pk` for primary key or `fk` for foreign key makes it easier to identify the index type without having to inspect its properties.

6. Click the OK button to build the index.

Creating an Index with `CREATE INDEX` The Transact-SQL command `CREATE INDEX` is used by SQL Enterprise Manager to perform the index creation when the Build button is clicked in the Manage Indexes dialog box. The syntax for `CREATE INDEX` is as follows:

```
CREATE [UNIQUE] [CLUSTERED ¦ NONCLUSTERED]
    INDEX index_name ON table (column [, ...n])
[WITH
```

Part

II

Ch

11

```
              [PAD_INDEX]
              [[,] FILLFACTOR = fillfactor]
              [[,] IGNORE_DUP_KEY]
              [[,] SORTED_DATA_REORG]
              [[,] {IGNORE_DUP_ROW ¦ ALLOW_DUP_ROW}]
              [[,] DROP_EXISING]
              [[,] STATISTICS_NORECOMPUTE]
[ON filegroup]
```

The options for the Transact-SQL command CREATE INDEX are covered in the following sections.

UNIQUE   If an index is created as UNIQUE, SQL Server disallows duplicate values in the index and, therefore, stops a client from inserting a record into the base table. This is the most common use of an index to enforce integrity on a table. Unique indexes can't be created on tables that have duplicate values in the columns being indexed. The duplicate data must be removed first. If enabled, the IGNORE DUP KEY option, described in the following section, enables UPDATE or INSERT statements, affecting several rows that modify index keys to complete, even if the new index key values become duplicates. The duplicate values will be rolled back and the transaction will continue. No error will be generated.

> **N O T E**   If you define an index as being unique, and you're declaring it on a column that allows NULL values, you'll run into problems as the table becomes populated. This is because SQL Server will allow a single NULL value in the column during indexing, but when the second NULL column value is inserted, it will fail. This is because the column will only allow one value (UNIQUE) and in this case, NULLs are consider a distinct and unique value, of which there can only be one.
>
> In short, if you're defining a UNIQUE key, be sure that none of the columns that comprise the key allow NULLs. ■

CLUSTERED   A *clustered index* is a special index that forces SQL Server to store the table data in the exact order of the index. Using a clustered index to physically store the data in the table in a particular way can greatly improve access performance to the table. Data requested from tables that are scanned repeatedly by the index key value for an individual record or set of records in a range can be found very quickly, because SQL Server knows that the data for the index page is right next to it. Any further values are guaranteed to be in the following data pages.

> **T I P**   You should always have an index on the table defined as CLUSTERED. This will greatly improve performance by keeping the database in a managed state; moreover, it enables you to reuse space from deleted rows. This is because a clustered index will reclaim space in the index and data pages as new rows are inserted.
>
> Because you can only have one clustered index per table, you should carefully weigh on which column(s) you will place this index in order to get the maximum benefit. Columns that you do range searches on are generally good candidates for a clustered index.

If CLUSTERED isn't specified in the CREATE INDEX statement, the index is assumed to be NONCLUSTERED.

There can be only one CLUSTERED index per table because the data can be in only one physical order.

> **CAUTION**
>
> When you create a CLUSTERED index, because the information in the table is physically moved, the entire table is locked, preventing access from any client application. If you're indexing a production table, consider running the creation of the index after hours as a scheduled task.

> **CAUTION**
>
> Specifying a filegroup for a CLUSTERED index to be placed on will actually move the table data too. Be careful using the ON *filegroup* keyword when creating a CLUSTERED index. You must have approximately 1.2 times the space required for the entire table available on the target filegroup for the CLUSTERED index and data.

NONCLUSTERED This is the default index type. It means that SQL Server will create an index whose pages of index data contain pointers to the actual pages of table data in the database. You can create up to 249 non-clustered indexes in a table.

index_name An index name must be unique by table. This means that the same index name can be given to two indexes, provided that they're indexing different base tables in the database. Index names must follow standard SQL Server naming conventions for objects.

table_name *table_name* is the table that's going to be indexed.

column_name This is the column that's being indexed. If more than one column is placed here, a composite or compound index is created. Multiple columns should be separated by spaces. You can specify up to 16 columns to create a composite key, but the maximum width of the datatypes being combined can't exceed 900 bytes.

PADINDEX This option specifies the number of rows to maintain on an interior node of an index. This is never fewer than two rows. PADINDEX is only useful when a FILLFACTOR has also been specified, because it uses the same percentage as the FILLFACTOR.

FILLFACTOR = x Specifying a FILLFACTOR on an index tells SQL Server how to "pack" the index data into the index data pages. FILLFACTOR tells SQL Server to preserve space on the index data page for other similar rows that are expected for the same index keys or similar index key values.

> **CAUTION**
>
> The FILLFACTOR should rarely be used. It is included solely for fine-tuning purposes. Even for fine-tuning, it should only be used if future changes in the data can be made with accuracy.

Part

II

Ch

11

Specifying a FILLFACTOR for frequently inserted database tables can improve performance because SQL Server won't have to split data onto separate data pages when the index information is too big to fit on a single page. Page splitting is a costly operation in terms of I/O and should be avoided, if possible.

The number of the FILLFACTOR refers to the percentage of free space that should be preserved on each index page.

A small FILLFACTOR is useful for creating indexes for tables that don't contain their complete dataset yet. For example, if you know that a table is going to have many more values than it does now and you want SQL Server to preallocate space in the index pages for those values so that it won't need to page split, specify a low FILLFACTOR of about 10. A *page split* occurs when the index fills up so that no further values will fit in the current 2 KB data page. Consequently, SQL Server splits the page in two and puts references to the newly created page in the original page.

A high FILLFACTOR will force more frequent page splits because SQL Server will have no room on the index page to add any additional values that might be necessary if a record is inserted into the table. A FILLFACTOR of 100 will force SQL Server to completely fill the index pages. This option is good for highly concurrent, read-only tables. It's inadvisable, however, for tables that are inserted or updated frequently. Every insert will cause a page split, and many of the updates will also cause page splits if key values are updated.

If no FILLFACTOR is specified, the server default, usually 0, is used. To change the server default, use the system-stored procedure sp_configure.

▶ For more information on setting defaults, **see** the section titled "Displaying and Setting Server Options" in Chapter 16, **p. 412**

Be careful when specifying a FILLFACTOR for a clustered index. It will directly affect the amount of space required for the storage of the table data. Because a clustered index is bound to a table, as the physical order of the table data is mapped to the order of the clustered index, a FILLFACTOR on the index will space each data page of the table apart from the others according to the value requested. This can consume substantial amounts of disk space if the FILLFACTOR is sparse.

N O T E   Specifying a FILLFACTOR when creating an index on a table without data has no effect because SQL Server has no way of placing the data in the index correctly. For tables that have dynamic data sets that need to be indexed with an index specifying a FILLFACTOR, you should rebuild indexes periodically to make sure that SQL Server is actually populating the index pages correctly. ■

IGNORE_DUP_KEY   When SQL is executed, this option controls SQL Server's behavior that causes duplicate records to exist in a table with a unique index defined on it. By default, SQL Server will always reject a duplicate record and return an error. This option enables you to get SQL Server to continue processing as though this isn't an error condition.

This configuration option can be useful in highly accessed tables where the general trend of the data is more important than the actual specifics. It shouldn't be used for tables where each individual record is important, however, unless application code is providing appropriate referential constraints to the data. If multiple records are affected by an update or insert statement, and the statement causes some records to create duplicates, the statement will be allowed to continue. Those records that created duplicates will be rolled back with no error returned.

> **CAUTION**
>
> When enabling IGNORE_DUP_KEY, be careful that you don't lose required data due to unwanted updates occurring. If IGNORE_DUP_KEY is enabled for a unique index and an update is done to data that causes duplicate records to exist, not only will the duplicates be rejected by the update, but the original records will also be removed. This is because SQL Server performs updates by deleting the record and then reinserting it. The reinsertion will fail, due to the duplicity of the record, so neither the original record nor the updated record will exist.

SORTED_DATA SQL Server uses the SORTED_DATA keyword to speed up index creation for clustered indexes. By specifying SORTED_DATA, you're telling SQL Server that the data to be indexed is already physically sorted in the order of the index. SQL Server will verify that the order is indeed correct during index creation by checking that each indexed item is greater than the previous item. If any item isn't found to be sorted, SQL Server will report an error and abort index creation. If this option isn't specified, SQL Server will sort the data for you as it would do normally.

Using the SORTED_DATA keyword greatly reduces the amount of time and space required to create a clustered index. The time is reduced because SQL Server doesn't spend any time ordering the data. The required space is reduced because SQL Server no longer needs to create a temporary workspace to place the sorted values before creating the index.

SORTED_DATA_REORG SORTED_DATA_REORG is similar to SORTED_DATA in that it helps SQL Server's overall performance by making the data physically reside in the database table in the order of the index. The SORTED_DATA_REORG keyword tells SQL Server to physically reorder the data in the order of the index. This can be especially useful on nonclustered indexed tables when you want to reduce the amount of page splits due to data no longer being in adjacent data pages. This will put the data physically adjacent in the database and will reduce the number of nonsequential physical I/Os required to fetch data—that, in turn, improves performance.

IGNORE_DUP_ROW This option is for creating a nonunique clustered index. If enabled at index creation time on a table with duplicate data in it, SQL Server will

- Create the index.
- Delete the duplicate values.
- Return an error message to the calling process indicating the failure. At this point the calling process should initiate a ROLLBACK to restore the data.

If data is inserted into or updated in the table after the index is created, SQL Server will

- Accept any non-duplicate values.
- Delete the duplicate values, and possibly the original record, if a duplicate occurs during an update.
- Return an error message to the calling process indicating the failure. At this point the calling process should initiate a ROLLBACK to restore the data.

▶ For more information on rolling back transactions, see the section titled "ROLLBACK TRAN," in Chapter 12, **p. 318**

N O T E   This option has no effect on nonclustered indexes. SQL Server internally assigns identifiers to the records being indexed and doesn't have to manage the physical order of the data according to the clustering. ■

ALLOW_DUP_ROW   This option can't be set on an index that's allowed to IGNORE_DUP_ROW. It controls behavior for inserting or updating records in a nonunique clustered index. If ALLOW_DUP_ROW is enabled, no errors are returned and no data is affected if multiple duplicate records are created in a clustered index.

DROP EXISTING   This option specifies that the clustered index should be dropped and recreated. The nonclustered indexes are then rebuilt. This prevents a double update of the nonclustered indexes.

STATISTICS_NORECOMPUTE   This option specifies that distribution statistics are not automatically updated. To enable this again, you will need to issue and update statistics on that table.

ON filegroup   Specifying a filegroup for the index to reside on enables the placement of an index on a different filegroup from the data. This will improve performance of nonclustered indexes because multiple I/O handlers can be used to read and write from the index and data filegroups concurrently.

Clustered indexes that have a filegroup specified will move the data that's being indexed, as well as the index, to the indicated filegroup.

Forcing the Use of a Particular Index   If SQL Server fails to pick an index that you know would provide better performance than the index it chose, you can force the use of an index by specifying it in the FROM clause. To force an index, use the optimizer hints or (INDEX = ...) section of the SELECT statement's syntax. In simplified syntax, here's a SELECT statement:

```
SELECT ...
FROM table_name (INDEX = n) /* optimizer hints are placed after the table */
...
```

▶ For more information on the syntax of SELECT statements, **see** Chapter 7, "Retrieving Data with Transact-SQL," **p. 155**

The INDEX keyword tells SQL Server to use the index specified by the numeric *n*. If *n* equals zero (0), SQL Server will table scan. If *n* equals one (1), SQL Server will use the clustered index if one is in the table. The other values of *n* are determined by the number of indexes on the table.

 TIP An index name can also be used in the optimizer hint instead of an identifying id number.

Listing 11.1 shows SQL Server using the optimizer hints when selecting from the authors table.

Listing 11.1   11_01.SQL—The Same SELECT Statement Performed Four Times to Demonstrate the Use of a Forced Index

```
/* Turn on statistics IO, so that the results can be seen */
set statistics io on
go

/* Basic Select with no hints to show the optimizer
   choosing the clustered index */
Select      AU_ID, AU_FNAME
From   AUTHORS
Where AU_ID between '172-32-1176' and '238-95-7766'
Order By AU_ID
go

/* Force a table scan */
Select      AU_ID, AU_FNAME
From   AUTHORS (INDEX = 0)
Where AU_ID between '172-32-1176' and '238-95-7766'
Order By AU_ID
go

/* Force the clustered index */
Select      AU_ID, AU_FNAME
From   AUTHORS (INDEX = 1)
Where AU_ID between '172-32-1176' and '238-95-7766'
Order By AU_ID
go

/* Force the first alternate index */
Select      AU_ID, AU_FNAME
From   AUTHORS (INDEX = 2)
Where AU_ID between '172-32-1176' and '238-95-7766'
Order By AU_ID
go
```

Part
II

Ch
11

The output is as follows:

```
AU_ID        AU_FNAME
----------   --------------------
172-32-1176  Johnson
213-46-8915  Marjorie
238-95-7766  Cheryl
```

```
(3 row(s) affected)

Table: authors  scan count 1,  logical reads: 1,  physical reads: 0
AU_ID       AU_FNAME
----------- --------------------
172-32-1176 Johnson
213-46-8915 Marjorie
238-95-7766 Cheryl

(3 row(s) affected)

Table: authors  scan count 1,  logical reads: 1,  physical reads: 0
Table: Worktable  scan count 0,  logical reads: 4,  physical reads: 0
AU_ID       AU_FNAME
----------- --------------------
172-32-1176 Johnson
213-46-8915 Marjorie
238-95-7766 Cheryl

(3 row(s) affected)

Table: authors  scan count 1,  logical reads: 2,  physical reads: 0
AU_ID       AU_FNAME
----------- --------------------
172-32-1176 Johnson
213-46-8915 Marjorie
238-95-7766 Cheryl

(3 row(s) affected)

Table: authors  scan count 1,  logical reads: 29,  physical reads: 0
Table: Worktable  scan count 0,  logical reads: 4,  physical reads: 0
```

> **CAUTION**
>
> The effects of forcing an index are clearly shown in these examples. The last example shows an extremely expensive option being forced on the server. You can cause major performance problems by forcing index use, and so it's generally not recommended that you update the indexes.
>
> Forcing index selection in a query is also dangerous if the application code is left unchanged and the indexes are changed or rebuilt. Changing the indexes can cause severe performance degradation due to the forcing of indexes that no longer provide optimal performance.

Displaying Index Information

SQL Server has two ways to show information about indexes. The graphical method is via SQL Enterprise Manager's Index Manager. The command-line method is via the system stored procedure sp_helpindex and the ODBC stored procedure sp_statistics.

sp_helpindex   The system stored procedure sp_helpindex has been provided to get information about indexes. The syntax for the procedure's use is

```
sp_helpindex table_name
```

table_name should be replaced with an unqualified table name. If the table you want to inquire on isn't in the current database, you must change to the required database before executing this procedure.

`sp_helpindex` will return the first eight indexes that are found on a database table. In the following example, `sp_helpindex` shows all the indexes on the authors table:

```
/*--------------------------
sp_helpindex authors
--------------------------*/
index_name            index_description
index_keys
------------------------------------------
UPKCL_auidind         clustered, unique, primary key located on default
au_id
aunmind               nonclustered located on default
au_lname, au_fname

(1 row(s) affected)
```

sp_statistics `sp_statistics` is a special stored procedure that has been created to help Microsoft "publish" information for the ODBC interface to the database. Microsoft created this stored procedure so that an ODBC driver could retrieve all the relevant information about an index with a single call to the database. The information returned can be gathered in a number of other ways, but it's often convenient to use `sp_statistics` to summarize all the relevant information on a table. The syntax for `sp_statistics` is as follows:

```
sp_statistics {'name'} [, 'owner'] [, 'qualifier'] [, 'index_pattern']
➥ [, 'is_unique'][, 'accuracy']
```

The options for the system stored procedure `sp_statistics` are as follows:

- *name*—This is the name of the table that you require the index information on.
- *owner*—This is the owner of the table.
- *qualifier*—This is the name of the database in which the table resides.
- *index_pattern*—This is the specific index that's being requested.
- *is_unique*—If this parameter is set to Y, SQL Server will return only unique indexes on the table.
- *accuracy*—This is the level of cardinality and page accuracy for statistics. To ensure that the statistics and cardinality are accurate, use a value of E for this parameter.

TIP Many stored procedures have many parameters. To save time, rather than specify all the parameters, you can indicate a particular one by placing an @ sign in front of the parameter name. An example is

```
sp_statistics authors, @is_unique = 'Y'
```

Part

II

Ch

11

Dropping Indexes

SQL Server has two ways of dropping indexes on a table. The graphical interface can be performed by using SQL Enterprise Manager. The command-line interface is accessed by using the SQL statement DROP INDEX.

Using SQL Enterprise Manager to Drop an Index

To use SQL Enterprise Manager to drop an index, follow these steps:

1. Launch SQL Enterprise Manager from the Microsoft SQL Server 7.0 group.
2. Select the server, database, and table that you want to work on.
3. Select Action, All Tasks, Manage Indexes.
4. Select the index you want to remove and click Delete. Click the Remove button to drop the index required. A message box asks for confirmation.

Using the DROP INDEX Command

To remove an index using Transact-SQL, use the DROP INDEX statement. The syntax for DROP INDEX is as follows:

```
DROP INDEX [owner.]table_name.index_name
[, [owner.]table_name.index_name...]
```

The options for the Transact-SQL command DROP INDEX are as follows:

- *table_name*—The name of the table that the index resides on. If the user running DROP INDEX is the DBO or SA and the table isn't owned by that user, *table_name* can be prefaced with the *owner* of the table.
- *index_name*—The name of the index to be removed. You can remove multiple indexes by indicating them in the same statement, separated by commas.

The following example drops the barny index on the authors table:

```
Drop Index authors.barny
```

No output is generated after executing this command.

Defining Keys

Keys and indexes are often synonymous in databases, but in SQL Server a slight difference exists between them. In SQL Server, keys can be defined on tables and then can be used as referential integrity constraints in the same fashion as the ANSI standard for SQL.

A *primary key* is a unique column or set of columns that defines the rows in the database table. In this sense, a primary key performs the same integrity role as a unique index on a table. Keep in mind though, that SQL Server allows only one primary key to be defined for a table. On the other hand, there can be many unique indexes. Primary keys enforce uniqueness by creating a unique index on the table on which they're placed. Even though a unique index is created when a primary key is defined, there is a slight difference. A primary key will not allow a NULL value, whereas a unique index does allow a single NULL value.

TIP Even though a unique index does allow a NULL value, it is a bad practice to place a unique index on a column that allows NULLs.

Foreign keys are columns in a table that correspond to primary keys in other tables. The relationship of a primary key to a foreign key defines the domain of values permissible in the foreign key. The domain of values is equivalent to a distinct list of values in the corresponding primary key. This foreign key domain integrity is a useful way of enforcing referential integrity between associated sets of columns. Foreign keys don't create indexes on the table when the key is created.

Starting in version 6.0, primary and foreign keys in SQL Server offer much of the functionality that had to be coded with triggers in previous versions of SQL Server. In prior versions of SQL Server, primary and foreign keys weren't much more than documentation and were useful to third-party programs that needed to know key information about a table. Keys provide needed functionality and should be used as a referential integrity enforcer.

Adding Primary and Foreign Keys

In SQL Server you can add primary and foreign keys in two ways. Using SQL Enterprise Manager performs the graphical method. The command-line method is done by using Transact-SQL commands ALTER TABLE...ADD CONSTRAINT, or by specifying PRIMARY/FOREIGN KEY in the CREATE TABLE statement.

Using SQL Enterprise Manager to Add Primary and Foreign Keys To use SQL Enterprise Manager to add a primary key, follow these steps:

1. Launch SQL Enterprise Manager from the Microsoft SQL Server 7.0 group.

2. Select the server, database, and table that you want to work on.

3. From the Action menu, choose Design Table. The Design Tables screen, shown in Figure 11.5, appears.

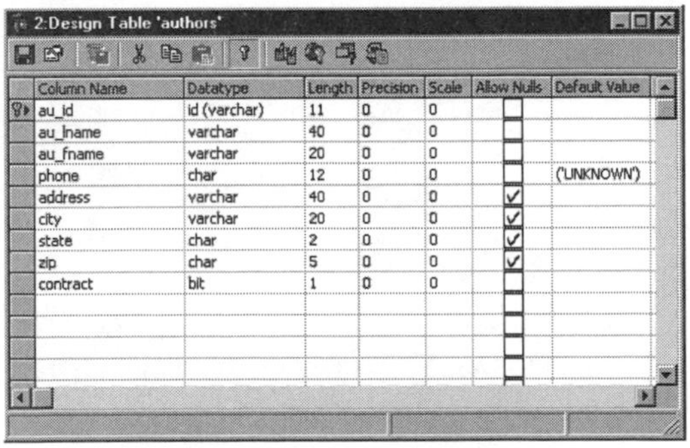

FIGURE 11.5

A key icon appears in the Key column of the au_id row and nulls are not allowed.

4. Highlight the rows you want to define as the primary key by shift-selecting the different rows, including the au_id row. Right-click and select Set Primary Key or click the key icon in the toolbar. For the purposes of this exercise, you will get an error message because there is a foreign key defined for that column. Select OK to delete the relationship.

5. Click the Save button to save the changes to the table.

Using CREATE TABLE...PRIMARY KEY   The CREATE TABLE syntax has a place for adding a PRIMARY KEY or a FOREIGN KEY in the CONSTRAINT section. A simplified syntax of the CREATE TABLE is shown as follows:

```
CREATE TABLE table_name
( column_name data_type CONSTRAINT ...,...)
```

In Listing 11.2, you'll see tables created in different styles with different types of CONSTRAINTs.

Listing 11.2   11_02.SQL—Creating Tables with Different CONSTRAINTs

```
/* create a table where the primary key name is not
   specified, and the database will assign it */

Create TABLE TABLE_A
( COLUMN_A smallint PRIMARY KEY)
go

/* Now create a primary key specifying the name */
Create TABLE TABLE_B
( COLUMN_B smallint CONSTRAINT PK_COLUMN_B PRIMARY KEY)
go

/* Now create a foreign key referencing TABLE_A */
Create TABLE TABLE_C
( COLUMN_C smallint FOREIGN KEY (COLUMN_C) REFERENCES TABLE_A(COLUMN_A))
go

/* Now Create a multi-column primary key */
Create TABLE TABLE_D
( COLUMN_D1 smallint CONSTRAINT PK_D_COLUMNS PRIMARY KEY
(COLUMN_D1, COLUMN_D2), COLUMN_D2 smallint)

go

/* now create a foreign key referencing the multi-column
   primary key */
Create TABLE TABLE_E
( COLUMN_E1 smallint FOREIGN KEY (COLUMN_E1, COLUMN_E2)
                REFERENCES TABLE_D( COLUMN_D1, COLUMN_D2),
  COLUMN_E2 smallint)
Go
```

N O T E When you add a PRIMARY KEY to a table with the ALTER TABLE...ADD CONSTRAINT
syntax or in the CREATE TABLE statement, a clustered, unique index is created on the
table if you don't indicate any parameters for the key. To specify a non-clustered index, add
NONCLUSTERED immediately after PRIMARY KEY to the statement. ■

Using ALTER TABLE...ADD CONSTRAINT The ALTER TABLE...ADD CONSTRAINT syntax is
very similar to the CREATE TABLE logic. In Listing 11.3, the same tables are created, but the
ALTER TABLE syntax is used to add the keys.

On the CD

Listing 11.3 11_03.SQL—Altering Tables to Add Primary and Foreign Keys

```
/* create the table */
Create TABLE TABLE_A
( COLUMN_A smallint not null)
go

/* add the basic primary key without specifying the name */
Alter Table TABLE_A ADD PRIMARY KEY (COLUMN_A)
go

/* create the table */
Create TABLE TABLE_B
( COLUMN_B smallint not null)
go

/* add the primary key specifying the name */
Alter Table TABLE_B ADD CONSTRAINT PK_COLUMN_B PRIMARY KEY (COLUMN_B)
go

/* create the table */
Create TABLE TABLE_C
( COLUMN_C smallint not null)
go

/* Now create a foreign key referencing TABLE_A */
Alter Table TABLE_C ADD FOREIGN KEY (COLUMN_C) REFERENCES TABLE_A(COLUMN_A)
go

/* create the table */
Create TABLE TABLE_D
( COLUMN_D1 smallint not null,
  COLUMN_D2 smallint not null)
go

/* Now add the multi-column primary key */
Alter Table TABLE_D ADD CONSTRAINT PK_D_COLUMNS PRIMARY KEY
(COLUMN_D1, COLUMN_D2)
go

/* create the table */
Create TABLE TABLE_E
```

Part
II

Ch
11

continues

Listing 11.3   Continued

```
( COLUMN_E1 smallint not null,
  COLUMN_E2 smallint not null)
go

/* now add the foreign key referencing the multi-column
   primary key */
Alter Table TABLE_E ADD CONSTRAINT FK_E_COLUMNS FOREIGN KEY
(COLUMN_E1, COLUMN_E2)
REFERENCES TABLE_D( COLUMN_D1, COLUMN_D2)
Go
```

▶ For more information on constraints, **see** the section titled "Creating and Using Constraints," in Chapter 6, **p. 141**

Displaying Key Information

SQL Server has two ways to show information about keys. The graphical method is via SQL Enterprise Manager's Table Manager. The command-line method is via the system stored procedures sp_help and sp_helpconstraints, and the ODBC stored procedures sp_pkeys and sp_fkeys.

SQL Enterprise Manager's Table Manager has been discussed in detail in previous sections in this chapter. Please refer to the preceding section entitled "Using SQL Enterprise Manager to Add Primary and Foreign Keys" for information on how to view the constraints on a table.

sp_helpconstraint   SQL Server's primary way of displaying information about keys is through the system stored procedure sp_helpconstraint. Its syntax is as follows:

```
sp_helpconstraint table_name
```

sp_help   sp_help is a generic system stored procedure that returns information about database tables. Part of the output from sp_help is information on keys on a table. The syntax for sp_help is

```
sp_help table_name
```

sp_pkeys and sp_fkeys   SQL Server provides two system stored procedures, sp_pkeys and sp_fkeys, that can be used to view key information stored in the database. sp_pkeys and sp_fkeys are procedures that have been created to help ODBC implementers access SQL Server's system catalog tables easily.

The syntax for the two procedures is identical and is as follows:

```
sp_pkeys ¦ sp_fkeys table_name
```

table_name is the table for which the keys need to be found.

Dropping Keys

SQL Server has two methods for dropping primary and foreign keys. The graphical method uses SQL Enterprise Manager. The command-line method is done by using the Transact-SQL command ALTER TABLE...DROP CONSTRAINT.

Using SQL Enterprise Manager To use SQL Enterprise Manager to drop a key, follow these steps:

1. Launch SQL Enterprise Manager from the Microsoft SQL Server 7.0 group.

2. Select the server, database, and table that you want to work on.

3. From the Action menu, choose Design Table. The Design Tables dialog box appears.

4. Remove the existing primary key by highlighting the rows that are defined as the primary key. Right-click and select Set Primary Key. This will deselect the check mark and cause the primary key to be dropped.

5. Click the Save button, which looks like a diskette, to save the changes to the table. If you get any referential constraint errors, you'll need to go to those tables and remove the primary/foreign keys that are causing the problem.

Using `ALTER TABLE...DROP CONSTRAINT` To drop a foreign key using SQL, use the `ALTER TABLE...DROP CONSTRAINT` statement. The syntax for this SQL statement is as follows:

```
ALTER TABLE table_name DROP CONSTRAINT constraint_name
```

The `table_name` is the name of the table that the constraint applies to. The `constraint_name` is the name of the constraint.

N O T E You can't drop a primary key if other tables reference it as a foreign key. You must drop those foreign keys first. ■

Part
II

Ch
11

Reality Check

If a list of double-edged swords relating to SQL Server configuration and management is ever created, indexes are likely to be very close to the top of the list. The typical system cycle appears to be that of creating an index to individually satisfy each and every select statement, then realizing that performance is taking a serious hit from the indexing. From that point on, the consensus about indexes is the fewer the better, but the ones implemented should count.

The model data you had in the system for testing might, in actuality, bear little resemblance to the real-life data in the system. From the pattern of information entered, to the values in the columns, there's nothing like real-life use to determine real-life data patterns. After you've had the system up for a bit, make *sure* you update statistics. This is critical. In many systems I've done in my integration work, this step alone boosts performance by an amazing amount. Consider making the update process a scheduled process, perhaps once every six months at sites where data distribution is relatively stable, more often at sites where the mix of information is more dynamic.

How?

If you're creating a system that is built to support more query options, consider indexing every column on which you allow queries. Now, before a bunch of email is sent out, be sure that systems you consider this option for are query-only type systems, not update systems. As indicated earlier, query-related systems don't suffer from too many different indexes. Don't do this on tables where you are inserting information, as well as updating it.

From Here...

In this chapter you learned how to create, view, and manage indexes on your data tables. This information is very important in helping you to create an optimized database that won't be bogged down by user queries that force table scans.

From here you should look at the following chapters for more information:

- Chapter 7, "Retrieving Data with Transact-SQL," shows how you can examine your queries to make sure that they're hitting the indexes defined on the tables.

- Chapter 16, "Understanding Server, Database, and Query Options," explains how to make changes to your global server, database, and query configurations to further optimize your queries.

Understanding Transactions and Locking

A good understanding of transactions and locking is essential for anybody who is going to write database applications for more than one user. Even single-user applications require some understanding of locking, though the impact of locking your own application is not nearly as drastic as that of locking an enterprise network of hundreds of users.

SQL Server has a number of different styles of locking available to the programmer. This chapter will provide you with the information required to make an accurate assessment of what is needed for your application in terms of transaction control and locking.

As a programmer you should always concentrate on attempting to minimize the amount of locking that occurs so that there is less chance of users interfering with each other.

The basics of a transaction, whether it is imposed implicitly by SQL Server, or explicitly by your application, are outlined in Table 12.1.

Table 12.1   The ACID Requirements for Transactions

Atomicity	A transaction is assumed to be complete, or not. This seems obvious, but it's important to understand that either all or none of the transaction becomes final. For example, if you're posting transfer of funds from one account to another, the funds are deposited into the target account *and* they are removed from the original account, as in a commit, or nothing happens at all, as in an abort.
Consistency	A transaction should leave things as it found them. In other words, when a transaction starts, the system is in a known state. When a transaction commits, the system must once again be in a known, consistent state. You cannot leave anything hanging from a transaction. It must be a full and complete operation. Of course, by definition, an aborted transaction will also fulfill these requirements because it will revert to the state of the system prior to opening the transaction.
Isolation	Transactions must stand alone and have no effect or dependence on other transactions. Dependence on another transaction is what causes deadlocks, resulting in unpredictable rollback operations. This attribute has also been referred to serializability.
Durability	When completed, the transaction's objective has been met and there is no further reason that the operation would be undone. In other words, when a transaction is completed, it will stay that way, even if something happens to the system. This is typically why you wrap an important operation in one large transaction, ensuring that all or nothing is applied to the database tables.

This is not to say that a transaction in and of itself enforces these rules. Instead, these are things that you, the developer, must keep in mind. You should strive to meet each of these objectives for each and every transaction you create. There should be no exceptions. If it doesn't measure up to the ACID test, don't continue coding until the operation meets the requirements. You won't be sorry later.

Defining Transactions

A *transaction* is a logical unit of work that you want the SQL Server to perform for you. That unit of work can include one or many SQL statements, provided the unit of work is delineated appropriately to the server as far as which statements within a batch are part of a transaction.

Single-statement transactions can be executed in ISQL by entering their text and typing go. Single-statement transactions are ideal where the results required are simple and self-contained. For example, the following statement will return a list of tables from the database currently being used. The text for this statement can be found in 12_01.SQL on the CD-ROM.

On the CD

```
Select      *
From  SYSOBJECTS
Where TYPE = 'U'  /* user defined tables */
Order By NAME
```

There are instances, however, when you need to do more than one thing in a transaction and conditionally undo it if something goes wrong. This is where multistatement transactions come into play. Multistatement transactions enable you to put two or more SQL statements together and send them to the server for processing. Then on some basis that you decide, you might choose to undo the work submitted. An example of a multistatement transaction is as follows. The text for this statement (Listing 12.1) can be found in 12_02.SQL on the CD-ROM.

On the CD

Listing 12.1   Performing Multiple Updates in a Single Transaction

```
Create Table TABLE_A(
      X     smallint null,
      Y     smallint null)
Go
Create Table TABLE_B(
      Z     smallint null)
Go

Begin Tran
      Update      TABLE_A
      Set   X = X + 1
      Where       Y = 100

      Update TABLE_B
      Set   Z = Z + 1

      If @@rowcount = 0 or @@error !=0 /* no rows where hit by our update */
      Begin
            Rollback Tran
            Print 'Error Occurred, no rows were updated'
            Return
      End
Commit Tran
```

Part
II

Ch
12

TIP   To make your scripts and stored procedures easier to read, format them with indented sections inside transaction blocks.

You can also set up SQL Server to automatically start transactions when certain operations are performed. Although this isn't recommended in a production environment because it's better to have your application declare explicit transactions, the IMPLICIT_TRANSACTIONS option can be helpful in a development or testing environment. You set this option with the SET statement as follows:

```
set IMPLICIT_TRANSACTIONS ON | OFF
```

CAUTION

Be warned—if you set this option, you are still required to issue corresponding COMMIT statements, or the transactions will remain open and can bog down, if not lock up, your system. This option should not be used in a production environment. Instead, set your transactions explicitly in your routines.

When set, the following operations will automatically begin transactions:

- ALTER TABLE
- CREATE
- DELETE
- DROP ...
- FETCH
- GRANT
- INSERT
- OPEN
- REVOKE
- SELECT
- TRUNCATE TABLE
- UPDATE

Limitations on Transactions

There are some things that you cannot do within a transaction, though after some consideration, they'll probably seem somewhat obvious. These are general things that you cannot undo, or at least not without significant repercussions to major components of the system. Keep in mind that transactions are meant to be protection for groups of processing statements, not so much as a backup to the management of your system. If you're looking to protect yourself from a potential system-damaging change, consider doing a dump of the database and transaction log prior to the operation you want to perform.

The following actions are not allowed within a transaction:

- ALTER DATABASE
- CREATE DATABASE
- CREATE INDEX
- CREATE PROCEDURE
- CREATE TABLE
- CREATE VIEW
- DISK INIT
- DROP ...
- DUMP TRANSACTION
- GRANT
- LOAD DATABASE
- LOAD TRANSACTION
- RECONFIGURE
- REVOKE
- SELECT INTO
- TRUNCATE TABLE
- UPDATE STATISTICS
- SP_DBOPTION or other procedures that modify the master database

N O T E   A new type of transaction has been added that allows transactions to be distributed. The Distributed Transaction Coordinator controls such transactions. This type of transaction is very useful for transactions that occur at remote locations but affect centralized inventory levels.

For more information on the Distributed Transaction Coordinator, see Chapter 18, "Using the Distributed Transaction Coordinator." ■

Optimistic Versus Pessimistic Locking

When you write multiuser database applications, you can take one of two approaches to transaction control: optimistic or pessimistic locking. *Optimistic locking* assumes that you are going to do nothing in your application code to explicitly enforce locks on records while you work on them. Instead, you will rely on the database to manage this on its own while you concentrate on application logic. *Pessimistic locking* assumes that the application code will attempt to enforce some type of locking mechanism.

Part
II

Ch
12

To implement optimistic locking in your application, without having it grind to a halt under excessive locks on the server, you must take care to observe some simple rules, as follows:

- Minimize the amount of time that a transaction is held open by limiting the amount of SQL that occurs inside a BEGIN TRAN...COMMIT TRAN section.
- Rely on application code to guarantee that updates are hitting the right record rather than holding locks while a user browses data.
- Ensure that all application codes update and select from tables in the same order. This will stop any deadlocks from occurring.

N O T E   One very good way to ensure that insert, update, delete, and select statements are always processed in the same order is to place all this code in stored procedures.

For more information on stored procedures, see Chapter 14, "Managing Stored Procedures and Using Flow-Control Statements." ▪

To assume that SQL Server will manage locking and that there is nothing to worry about is a *very* optimistic locking approach. Unfortunately, it is not very pragmatic because it assumes that there is nothing a programmer or user can do to explicitly cause locking. In fact, there are many situations that will cause a large amount of locking to occur on a server, potentially disabling it for the enterprise that it is supporting.

Background Information on Locking

Some background on the basics of locking as they pertain to, and are implemented by, SQL Server will be covered here. This is so that some of the more detailed items discussed in the following sections are not without a basis of understanding. Specifically, this area will focus on the following two key areas of locking:

- Page sizes and granularity of data
- Types of locks

Page Sizes and Granularity of Data   SQL Server's internal basic unit of work is an 8 KB data page. What this means is that any activity that is executed on the server will generally do work on at least 8 KB of data. To further explain, a table has a number of pages of data associated with it. Depending on the number and size of rows that it contains, SQL Server can only reference data in that page a row at a time. If an update hits a single record in a table and a lock is held for some period of time, it is more than likely that another process will need access to that row.

How does this affect a database application? One of the most important considerations when writing a multiuser application is that there must be a way for multiple users to work independently of one another. For example, two users must be able to update customer records at the same time while answering phone calls from customers. The greater the capability to manipulate data in the same table without affecting other users by locks, the greater the concurrency of an application and the greater the chance of being able to support a lot of users.

A highly accessed table, such as a table of unique values for the rest of the system, should be made as concurrent as possible by forcing users' transactions to be kept to a minimum duration when hitting these tables.

Three other types of locks can occur that lock data more greatly than a singe row: page, table and extent.

Page locks can occur when a user accesses many rows on a single data page. This has the effect of locking a much larger amount of data than would be normally locked during a single row access.

N O T E   Page level locks were the lowest level of granularity in previous versions of SQL Server. ▪

Table locks occur because a user issued a query to update a table without including a WHERE clause, thereby implicitly saying "I want to update every row." In addition, it can occur when the number of data pages locked exceeds the Lock Escalation threshold.

Extent locks occur when SQL Server needs to create a new database extent, eight pages of data, to respond to a user query. Unfortunately, there are no controls at your disposal to handle or deal with extent locks, so you simply should know that they occur and what they mean.

Types of Locks   SQL Server can place several types of locks on database rows, pages, and tables. The locks that are possible are SHARED, EXCLUSIVE, and UPDATE. SHARED locks and EXCLUSIVE locks are reasonably self-explanatory in that they either enable another process to acquire a lock on the same row or page or they don't.

Multiple processes can have SHARED locks on the same data page, and they are usually acquired when data is being read. Importantly, though, no other process can take an EXCLUSIVE lock, to perform statements within the Data Manipulation Language or DML, until all SHARED locks have been released.

EXCLUSIVE locks of a table's rows and pages are given to a process that is updating a record on a page, inserting a new record at the end of a page, or when a process deletes a record from a page. EXCLUSIVE locks disallow any other process from accessing the row or page.

The UPDATE lock type is somewhere between a SHARED and EXCLUSIVE lock. It will enable a process to acquire a SHARE on the page until an update has occurred on it. UPDATE locks are acquired when a CURSOR is being built in the server. UPDATE locks are automatically promoted to EXCLUSIVE when an update occurs on one of the rows or pages associated with the cursor.

At the table level, SQL Server has SHARED and EXCLUSIVE locks that work in the same fashion as the page level. SQL Server also has INTENT locks. INTENT locks indicate that a table has a number of pages on it that SQL Server is intending to lock at the page level in response to a user process. This might be the case as SQL Server walks down through a table, but your specific query is ahead of the query that is locking pages in the table.

At a database level, SQL Server has SCHEMA locks that work for modifications to a database's schema. A SCHEMA STABILITY lock is used to ensure that a table or index is not dropped or altered while another process is accessing it. A SCHEMA MODIFICATION lock is placed during schema manipulations such as dropping or altering a table or index.

SQL Server 7.0 now supports full row level locking. This allows data manipulations to have less impact on other users as a much smaller amount of data can be locked at any given time. This is a significant benefit in heavy processing environments where locking an entire page at a time can cause significant contention between users.

▶ For additional information on cursors, **see** Chapter 24, "Creating and Using Cursors," **p. 619**

Defining Isolation Levels

There are a number of ways in SQL Server that you can cause locks to be held or released while querying the database. One method is by setting a transaction's isolation level. As its name implies, an *isolation level* specifies to the database how "protected" to keep the data that is currently being worked on by the other users and requesters of data on the server.

SQL Server has four different types of isolation levels and they are documented in the following four sections.

> **N O T E** Transaction isolation levels are set for the entire time that a session is connected to the database. If you change isolation levels for a specific part of your application, do not forget to change back to the default so that other parts of the application are not adversely affected.
>
> Although you can change the isolation level, this is generally not recommended.
>
> To achieve the same effects as isolation levels for a single SELECT statement, refer to the later section, "Holding a Lock Explicitly," for more information. ■

Read Committed Read Committed is the default method of operation for SQL Server. It does not enable you to have data returned from the database that is "dirty" or *uncommitted*. Read Committed acquires SHARE locks on all the pages it passes over inside a transaction. It is possible that due to another user performing a delete or insert that is committed or rolled back during the life of your query, you might receive some data pages that are not rereadable or that might contain values that only temporarily exist in the database.

If it is important that the query's results be completely unaffected by other users during the life of a particular transaction, make sure that you use the Repeatable Read isolation level.

To set your isolation level to Read Committed, perform the following SQL:

```
Set Transaction Isolation Level Read Committed
Go
```

Read Uncommitted Read Uncommitted is the same as the NOLOCK keyword on an individual SELECT statement. No SHARED locks are placed on any data that you pass over in the query. Additionally, no locks held by other users are observed. For example, if another user has deleted a whole table that you are about to select from, but has yet to COMMIT a transaction, you will still be able to read the data from it and not receive any error conditions.

> **CAUTION**
>
> The Read Uncommitted transaction isolation level is not recommended for any applications that require data integrity because you cannot be guaranteed that the data you are working with is the same, or, indeed, in the database at all. Use Read Uncommitted sparingly in your applications and possibly only for procedures such as reporting applications on tables that are statistically unaffected by the average transactions that post against your server.

To set your isolation level to Read Uncommitted, perform the following SQL transaction:

```
Set Transaction Isolation Level Read Uncommitted
Go
```

Repeatable Read   Repeatable Read guarantees that the data you are reading will be unaffected by other transactions issued from other users during the life of a given transaction that you are working on. Because of Repeatable Read's explicit locking of data from other users, Repeatable Read reduces the concurrency of the database. It reduces the number of different users that can access data at the same time without affecting each other. Take care that you do not use Repeatable Read unwisely in your application. There are not that many places where it is actually required.

To set your isolation level to Repeatable Read, perform the following SQL transaction:

```
Set Transaction Isolation Level Repeatable Read
Go
```

Serializable   Serializable is the most exclusive type of locking that you can force SQL Server to maintain. Serializable contains all the restrictions of Repeatable Read while also preventing phantom reads. Take care that you do not use Serializable unwisely in your application. There are not many times when it is actually required.

To set your isolation level to Serializable, perform the following SQL transaction:

```
Set Transaction Isolation Level Serializable
Go
```

Creating and Working with Transactions

In the opening section of this chapter, you saw how to delineate a transaction using BEGIN, COMMIT, and ROLLBACK. SQL Server's keywords or Transact-SQL statements that are required for transaction control are described below for clear definition.

> **CAUTION**
>
> It is very important to remember that every BEGIN TRAN must be followed at some point in the code by a matching COMMIT TRAN or ROLLBACK TRAN. Transactions must begin and end in pairs, or the server will continue holding locks until the client is disconnected.

Part
II
Ch
12

BEGIN TRAN   When you issue a BEGIN TRAN to the database, SQL Server marks a point in the database's transaction logs identifying a point to be returned to in the event of a ROLLBACK TRAN. BEGIN TRAN explicitly tells SQL Server that all the work following, until a COMMIT or ROLL-BACK is encountered, should be treated as one logical unit. This is true despite the fact that it might contain many operations.

It is possible to issue operations without a BEGIN TRAN statement, and they will affect a database. You will not, however, be able to conditionally undo the work that you sent to the server if it is not preceded by a BEGIN TRAN so that SQL Server knows to what state the database must be returned.

N O T E   SQL Server's transaction logs monitor those transactions that are contained inside of BEGIN and COMMIT statements. In the event of a media failure on a database before data is physically changed on the database, SQL Server will recover or ensure that those changes are applied by "rolling forward" those unapplied transactions to the database when the server is next brought back online. ▪

COMMIT TRAN   Issuing a COMMIT TRAN to the database signals SQL Server that the work was successful and no longer want to group any additional work inside the transaction.

By definition, a COMMIT TRAN also implies that you've fulfilled the requirements of the ACID test, presented at the beginning of this chapter.

ROLLBACK TRAN   ROLLBACK TRAN is SQL Server's equivalent of the Edit, Undo menu option in your favorite word processor. Sending a ROLLBACK to the database server will cause it to undo all the work to the most recent BEGIN TRAN statement. Typically, a ROLLBACK TRAN would be issued during a long transaction if any particular part of it encountered a SQL error of some kind.

> **CAUTION**
>
> SQL Server will enable you to call remote stored procedures inside a transaction. Because of the nature of the *Remote Procedure Call* (RPC) interface with the other server upon which the RPC executed, however, SQL Server will not be able to ROLLBACK any such calls. Take care when writing applications that require RPCs that there are additional RPCs to programmatically undo the work you did previously.

DDL and Database Statements

DDL, or Data Definition Language, and database modification statements are now allowed inside a transaction. The following statements can appear in transactions:

ALTER TABLE	CREATE DEFAULT	CREATE INDEX
CREATE PROCEDURE	CREATE RULE	CREATE TABLE
CREATE TRIGGER	CREATE VIEW	DROP DEFAULT
DROP INDEX	DROP PROCEDURE	DROP RULE
DROP TABLE	DROP TRIGGER	DROP VIEW
GRANT & REVOKE	SELECT INTO	TRUNCATE TABLE

These are important statements because they enable the database schema management features to function. You can see that many of these are statements whose purpose is to modify the table structures on the system, or are used to create new ways to access the information.

Using Named Transactions and SavePoints

One thing that becomes obvious during the writing of large stored procedures and applications with large bodies of SQL code is that the code is pretty unreadable. It is text-based and there is a great reliance on programmers all working with the same style of format and layout.

For this reason, it's a good tip to keep in mind that when transactional programming is involved, it becomes even more important to use good indenting to clearly mark blocks of code.

However, even the most careful programmer will find that it becomes a bit of a nightmare to remember how many indents to ROLLBACK out of in the event of an error condition or some programmatic constraint. Named transactions and SavePoints are used for just this purpose. They provide a way of rolling back work to a given *named* or *saved* portion of the code that has been executing, even if it is at a higher nesting level.

Named Transactions   Named transactions provide a convenient way of attaching an identifier to a whole body of work. Use named transactions to make it easier to undo large portions of code. To create a named transaction, add the name of the transaction to the BEGIN TRAN statement, as follows. The text for Listing 12.2 can be found in 12_03.SQL on the CD-ROM.

On the CD

Listing 12.2   Creating a Named Transaction

```
/* Open outer transaction */
Begin Tran UPDATE_AUTHORS
     Update AUTHORS
     Set   CONTRACT = 1
     Where AU_ID = '341-22-1782'

     /* Open inner transaction */
     Begin Tran UPDATE_TITLEAUTHOR
          Update TITLEAUTHOR
          Set   ROYALTYPER = ROYALTYPER + 25
          Where AU_ID = '341-22-1782'
          If @@error != 0
          Begin
               Rollback Tran UPDATE_TITLEAUTHOR
               Print 'Failed to update Royalties'
               Return
          End
     Commit Tran UPDATE_TITLEAUTHOR
Commit Tran UPDATE_AUTHORS
```

Part
II

Ch
12

N O T E   If you omit the transaction's identifier or name when committing a transaction, SQL Server will simply undo the work to the most recent BEGIN TRAN regardless of its name. If you rollback without using an identifier, all work in all open transactions will be undone. Take care that when using named transactions, all work is coded in a consistent manner; that is, either using names or not. If you do not, programmers might end up stepping on each other's transactions inadvertently. ■

Using SavePoints   SavePoints are really just another way of doing a named transaction. They provide a method of marking a place in the code to which a ROLLBACK can be used to undo work. To create a SavePoint, issue the SQL command

```
SAVE TRANSACTION <TRAN_NAME>
```

You then simply use the identifier, <TRAN_NAME>, when performing your ROLLBACK. For example:

The text for Listing 12.3 can be found in 12_04.SQL on the CD-ROM.

On the CD

Listing 12.3   Rolling Back to a Named SavePoint

```
Begin Tran
     Update AUTHORS
     Set    CONTRACT = 1
     Where  AU_ID = '341-22-1782'

     /* save our work to this point */
     Save Transaction AuthorDone

     Update TITLEAUTHOR
          Set    ROYALTYPER = ROYALTYPER + 25
          Where  AU_ID = '341-22-1782'
     If @@error != 0 Or @@RowCount > 1
     Begin
          /* rollback and exit */
          Rollback Tran AcctDataDone
          Print 'Error occurred when updating TitleAuthor'
          Return
     End
Commit Tran
Print 'Transaction Committed'
```

? correct ? (handwritten annotation)

CAUTION

Despite the fact that the preceding transaction rolled back the UPDATE on TITLEAUTHOR, SQL Server will hold locks on the TITLEAUTHOR table until the entire transaction is completed by either COMMIT or ROLLBACK. This is a side effect of using a SavePoint and might cause unexpected locking in an application.

TIP

If you find that you have an application that seems to continuously hold locks after the first transaction executes, the most likely scenario is that you have issued more BEGIN TRANs than you have corresponding COMMIT TRANs or ROLLBACK TRANs.

Remember that transactions must be enclosed in pairs of BEGIN and COMMIT/ROLLBACK. If you fail to do so, SQL Server will think that you want to keep the transaction open for a longer period.

To help identify your code problems, do a walkthrough of your application, and monitor error conditions carefully. Chances are that an error condition is occurring and some code is returning control before closing an open transaction. Also, check the value of the system variable @@trancount to tell you how deeply nested in transactions you really are.

Serialized Columns Without `IDENTITY`

SQL Server 6.0 introduced a new *serial* datatype, called the `IDENTITY`, in which SQL Server will automatically assign the next sequential value to a column in a table. `IDENTITY`s are very valuable in applications that have high transaction volume and want to identify each record uniquely.

For some applications that must support multiple database back ends and for those applications that require SQL Server 4.*x* compatibility, it is possible to implement the same kind of feature as an `IDENTITY` column by performing the steps shown in Listing 12.4:

On the CD

Listing 12.4   12_05 SQL—Creating an SQL-based Identity Column

```
/* create the table */
Create Table Record_IDs(
     Table_Name  varchar(30),
     Current_ID  int)
     Go

/* add a primary clustered index */
Create     Unique Clustered Index PK_Record_IDs
     on Record_IDs( Table_Name ) with FILLFACTOR = 1
Go
Insert Record_IDs
     Select   Name,     1
     From   Sysobjects
     Where  Type = 'U' /* user defined tables */
Create Procedure up_GetID                  /* up = user procedure */
     @psTableName     varchar(30),         /* p = parameter */
     @rnNewID     int OUTPUT        /* r = receive or output
➥parameter */
As
Declare
     @nSQLError int,
     @nRowCount int

Begin Tran
     /* First update the record to acquire the exclusive lock on the
➥page */
     Update Record_IDs
     Set    Current_ID = Current_ID + 1
     Where  Table_Name = @psTableName

     /* Check for errors */
     Select    @nSQLError = @@error,
         @nRowCount = @@rowcount
     If @nSQLError != 0 OR @nRowCount != 1
     Begin
         Rollback Tran
         Return -999 /* failed to update record correctly */
     End
```

continues

Part

II

Ch

12

Listing 12.4   Continued

```
        /* Select back the value from the table that we've already locked */
        Select     @rnNewID = Current_ID
        From   Record_IDs
        Where  Table_Name = @psTableName

        /* Check for errors */
        Select     @nSQLError = @@error,
            @nRowCount = @@rowcount
        If @nSQLError != 0 OR @nRowCount != 1
        Begin
            Rollback Tran
            Return -998 /* failed to select record correctly */
        End
Commit Tran
Return 0
Go
Declare
    @nRecordID  int,
    @nRC        int,
    @sMsg       varchar(255)

/* Fetch a record ID for use in inserting new record */
Exec @nRC = up_GetID 'table_A', @nRecordID OUTPUT

If @nRC != 0
    Print 'An error occurred fetching new Record ID'
Else
Begin
    Select @sMsg = 'New Record value is ' + Convert( varchar(4),
➥@nRecordID )
    Print @sMsg
End
Go
```

1. Create a table with columns in it to store a table name and the current value. The text for all the following statements can be found in 12_06.SQL on the CD-ROM.

2. Insert records into the table that correspond to tables in the target database.

3. Create a stored procedure that will have a consistent access interface to the table and will lock the table so that no other users can modify the data while a given process is accessing it.

4. Test the new procedure.

 T I P Always use the new IDENTITY column to create identifying columns instead of the TIMESTAMP datatype. The IDENTITY column is far easier to reference and use in application code and can impose less data overhead if you use a small datatype for it, such as TINYINT or SMALLINT.

Version 7.0 introduces a new datatype of uniqueidentifier. This is a globally unique value that can be used just as an identity. The difference is that an identity is localized to a table, whereas the uniqueidentifier is applied to the entire database. The uniqueidentifier is a 16-bit binary value that is guaranteed to be unique across the database.

For more information on how the uniqueidentifier is constructed, please refer to the Books Online.

Understanding Locks

In addition to the background information provided previously, it is important to know how to handle locking when it occurs in your database.

Displaying Lock Information

There are two ways to review information about locks held in the database: using the SQL Enterprise Manager, or through the execution of the system stored procedure, sp_lock. SQL Enterprise Manager, under the covers, is calling sp_lock to get the information to display.

Using SQL Enterprise Manager　To view information that is being locked using the SQL Enterprise Manager, perform the following steps:

1. Run SQL Enterprise Manager from the Microsoft SQL Server 7.0 group.

2. Select the server on which you want to work.

3. Open the Management tree and select Current Activity. (see Figure 12.1).

Part

II

Ch

12

FIGURE 12.1

The tree view that makes up the Current Activity for your server includes information on several different types of activity and locks.

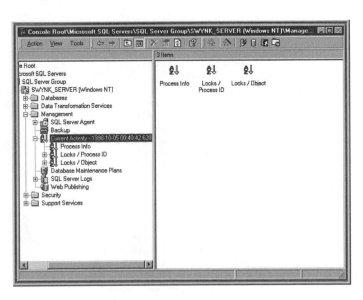

To get more information about what individual statement is causing locking, you can click the process that is in the respective tree.

Using sp_lock   The sp_lock system stored procedure will return a list of processes and the types of locks that they are holding on the system. To get the locks held by a particular process, add the process ID to the command (sp_lock *spid*). Here is some sample code, shown in Listing 12.5, to show you the output of sp_lock:

[handwritten: Server Process Id]

Listing 12.5   Transactions to Show a Lock on the Table, and the Resulting Output from sp_lock.Begin Tran

```
        Update authors
        set au_id = au_id
go
sp_lock
go
rollback tran
go
```

spid	dbid	ObjId	Type	Resource	Mode	Status
1	1	0	DB		S	GRANT
6	5	0	DB		S	GRANT
7	1	0	DB		S	GRANT
8	5	0	DB		S	GRANT
8	5	0	DB		S	GRANT
8	5	117575457	PAG	1:296	IX	GRANT
8	5	117575457	PAG	1:440	IX	GRANT
8	5	117575457	TAB		IX	GRANT
8	5	117575457	KEY	(150b091e0136)	X	GRANT
8	5	117575457	KEY	(1a0b0d1e0138)	X	GRANT
8	1	5575058	TAB		IS	GRANT
8	5	117575457	KEY	(1907091d0d36)	X	GRANT
8	5	117575457	KEY	(1900041c0837)	X	GRANT
8	5	117575457	KEY	(1f090a1c0136)	X	GRANT
8	5	117575457	KEY	(1a000a1b0335)	X	GRANT
8	5	117575457	KEY	(1f040f1b0f35)	X	GRANT
8	5	117575457	KEY	(140a0d1b0032)	X	GRANT
8	5	117575457	KEY	(1c06031a0532)	X	GRANT
8	5	117575457	KEY	(1b05001a0b32)	X	GRANT
8	5	117575457	KEY	(190501190b37)	X	GRANT
8	5	117575457	KEY	(1b0400190e31)	X	GRANT
8	5	117575457	KEY	(180105190132)	X	GRANT
8	5	117575457	KEY	(150802180f32)	X	GRANT
8	5	117575457	KEY	(150601180d31)	X	GRANT
8	5	117575457	KEY	(1a0706180131)	X	GRANT
8	5	117575457	KEY	(190901150439)	X	GRANT
8	5	117575457	KEY	(150307150f32)	X	GRANT
8	5	117575457	KEY	(1e0506150032)	X	GRANT
8	5	117575457	KEY	(1c0404150d35)	X	GRANT
8	5	117575457	KEY	(1a0b07140930)	X	GRANT
8	5	117575457	KEY	(1f0e07140930)	X	GRANT
8	5	117575457	KEY	(1a0205140230)	X	GRANT
8	5	117575457	KEY	(1f0404140031)	X	GRANT
8	5	117575457	KEY	(0a246f707070)	X	GRANT

TIP Many system procedures return an OBJECT_ID column to identify a database object. To quickly get the name of that object, use the system function OBJECT_NAME ( ). For example, select OBJECT_NAME (1232324).

Killing a Locking Process

Before killing a process that is holding locks on the database, verify with the sp_who and sp_lock system procedures that the server process id (spid) you are targeting to kill is in fact the user holding the locks.

When reviewing the output from sp_who, look at the blk spid column to identify a user that is blocked. Trace the tree of the blocks back to the parent spid, and kill that user process. To kill a user process you can either use SQL Enterprise Manager, or execute the Kill command.

You can also use DBCC to check the status of transactions open against a given database. *also Pg 497* Using the OPENTRAN statement for DBCC, you can determine what transactions are open and when they were started. The syntax for the command is

```
dbcc opentran [(database ¦ databaseID)] [WITH TABLERESULTS]
```

If you don't specify the database name or ID, the command runs against the current database, listing open transactions. If you specify the WITH TABLERESULTS option, you will receive a listing of the same results, but with output formatted a bit more to enable you to save it for use in a workbook or in another table. This can be a big help if you're troubleshooting a problem and want to look for trends that are occurring for the transactions.

Using SQL Enterprise Manager Using SQL Enterprise Manager to kill a process involves first finding the process that is causing locking, and the steps to do this are outlined previously in the section entitled "Using sp_lock."

Having found a process that needs to be killed, you can right-click the process you want to kill and select Kill Process from the resulting menu. This is shown in Figure 12.2.

A warning dialog box appears so you can change your mind and undo your action (see Figure 12.3).

Using Kill Having identified the user process (spid) that you want to kill, execute the following SQL to kill it:

```
KILL spid
```

This will kill most processes that are existing on the server. Under some circumstances, it is possible to have processes that can't be killed. Usually this occurs when it is in an Extent or Resource lock awaiting the underlying operating system to complete a task. Monitor the process with sp_who until it leaves this condition and then execute the KILL command.

FIGURE 12.2

The Kill Process menu option enables you to halt an activity.

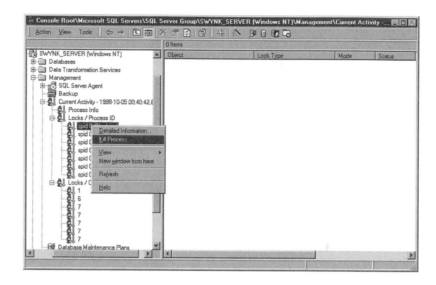

FIGURE 12.3

The warning dialog box enables you to confirm whether or not you really want to kill a process.

Holding a Lock Explicitly

If you have application code that really needs to explicitly hold locks on particular sets of data, SQL Server provides you with extensions to the basic SELECT statement that perform this functionality. SQL Server enables you to add *optimizer hints* or keywords to your SELECT statements that tell it how to process the data that matches your results. There are several kinds of hints that you can place on a set of data affected by a SELECT statement: NOLOCK, HOLDLOCK, UPDLOCK, TABLOCK, PAGLOCK, or TABLOCKX.

The following table explains the two more obscure options. The balance of these are explained in the next sections.

Table 12.2   Explicit Lock Conditions

UPDLOCK	Locks the values in the table for a future update, but allows other users to read the information in the table. This can help prevent delays users might typically experience in simply browsing or reviewing the data in tables while updates are going on. By using this option, the users will still be able to review the database contents, but they won't be able to update the rows you have locked.

PAGLOCK On by default, this explicitly tells SQL Server that you want to use shared page locks. The only time you'd use this option is if you had issued a TABLOCKX lock on a table, preventing all other reads. See the coming sections for additional information about TABLOCKX locks.

NOLOCK NOLOCK is an option that enables the query to read from dirty data. *Dirty* data is data that might have been affected by other user's updates and deletes. Selecting records from a table with the NOLOCK keyword ignores any other user's EXCLUSIVE locks, indicating that they had updated a record, and does not place any locks on the data itself.

NOLOCK is a very useful option for those people writing applications in which the data is statistically unaffected by a small sample of records having fluctuating values; that is, if programmers are more interested in trends of data than in the actual values themselves. Care should be taken—it is important to clearly differentiate between data fetched with the NOLOCK keyword and data that is legitimately accurate according to the known condition of the database as a whole.

> **CAUTION**
>
> When selecting data with the NOLOCK keyword, it is possible that another user has affected your data in such a way as to make it invalid during the time you are reading from the data page in which it resides. For example, another user could have deleted a record that you are reading, and while you are reading it, their COMMIT is processed and the record is removed.
>
> If you are reading data and it is no longer available, you will receive error messages 605, 606, 624, or 625. It is recommended that you process these errors in the same way that you process a deadlock condition. That is, inform the users that an error has occurred and ask them to retry their operations. Advanced applications might want to auto retry the first time to avoid confusing the users unnecessarily.

HOLDLOCK Normal SELECTs on tables acquire a SHARED lock on a page while the SELECT is passing through the data. A SHARED lock does not prohibit another user from updating a record or attempting to gain an EXCLUSIVE lock on the data page that is currently being processed by the SELECT. In addition, the SHARED lock expires on a data page as the next page is being read. If you want to maintain data integrity for the life of the SELECT because you might need to scroll backwards and forwards through the result set, use the HOLDLOCK command to force SQL Server to hold the SHARED lock until the transaction is complete.

TABLOCK and TABLOCKX As its name implies, TABLOCK forces a SELECT statement to lock the entire table or tables affected by the SELECT for the duration of the statement. TABLOCKX forces an exclusive table lock for the life of the transaction, denying any other user access to the table until the transaction has been completed.

 Do not place a table lock (TABLOCK) on a table unless you have a good programmatic reason. TABLOCKs often create unnecessary overhead and undue locking in the server. Instead, rely on lock escalation (LE) thresholds to manage TABLOCKs for you.

Lock Escalation Options

SQL Server locks data on the row, page, or table level. Any query that you execute on the server will hold locks on at least one row. If you start updating or locking multiple rows on a page, SQL Server starts consuming resources to manage your requests. At a certain point, based on a percentage of rows locked per page, it becomes more efficient for the database to lock the entire page than to keep managing the individual row being locked by a given transaction. A similar method is used when page locks are acquired.

Management of lock escalation and thresholds is now automatic inside SQL Server 7.0.

T I P   As seen in the preceding section, despite the LE thresholds it is possible to force locking on pages and tables by using the HOLDLOCK and TABLOCK keywords when issuing a SELECT statement to the server.

Reality Check

The Transaction Log can quickly become your mortal enemy when you first start working with transactions. This comes from those times that you inadvertently leave transactions open, issue many, many transactions, and so on. You might recall that when you truncate a transaction log, it dumps the contents of the log, but only to include all committed transactions. Obviously if you have a whole slew of uncommitted transactions, the log won't be freed up much at all.

This is a traditional problem and can be solved with the DBCC OPENTRAN approach mentioned earlier. Of course you'll still have to troubleshoot your code to determine what went wrong, but at least you can start to free up the processes that have the transaction log full.

In one especially interesting case, a transaction was opened, the operations performed, and the code was verified to have performed correctly. Strangely enough, when the transaction never showed up in the database table itself, the developer decided a server re-start was in order. When SQL Server came back up, had finished recovering the database, and allowed the developer back in to the system, the data was unchanged. This, even though the routine had apparently executed correctly.

Of course, what had happened is that the transaction was left open. When the server restarted, it rolled back the operations that were performed within the transaction, restoring the database to the state it was in prior to the routine being run by the developer. There weren't any syntax errors in the code of the stored procedure, only a missing COMMIT statement at the termination of the processing.

When in doubt, check for open, pending processes. Check out your locks and pending processes as well. You can save a lot of trouble by installing a small bit of error control and referencing the @@trancount intrinsic SQL Server variable to confirm that, as you leave a stored procedure, the relevant transactions have been completed and committed.

From Here...

In this chapter you learned about the fundamentals of locking and transactions and how they will affect your application. In addition, you learned about the internals of SQL Server and how it manages many users hitting the same table.

Take a look at the following chapters to further develop your SQL Server and application programming knowledge:

- Chapter 6, "Creating Database Tables and Using Datatypes," tells you how you can redefine some of your tables to enable better concurrency.
- Chapter 11, "Managing and Using Indexes and Keys," shows you how you can optimize table access through the creation of a clustered index with a sparse FILL FACTOR.
- Chapter 16, "Understanding Server, Database, and Query Options," provides an understanding of how the options you set up for the server affect database applications and transaction locks.

Part
II

Ch
12

Server-Side Logic and Capabilities

Managing and Using Rules, Constraints, and Defaults

You'll recall from previous chapters that maintaining referential integrity in your database tables is one of the biggest benefits of using SQL Server. It has the capability to manage the information flow into and out of the system by enforcing your criteria on the database side, rather than expecting the application to control this type of information. This leads to data independence from applications, making an open database system possible.

To make this possible, SQL Server implements several tools that help you manage the information in your system. In this chapter, you'll find out about three of these tools—Rules, Constraints, and Defaults. In addition, you can use Triggers to manage information as it flows through your system. Be sure to read up on and understand Triggers as you design your system.

▶ For more information about Triggers, **see** Chapter 15, "Creating and Managing Triggers," **p.395**

Here's an overview of what these terms mean and how you use them in your systems:

- Rule—Rules control the values that can be stored within table columns and within user-defined datatypes. Rules use expressions that are applied to columns or user-defined datatypes to restrict the allowable values that can be entered. A rule is stored as a separate database object. This independence enables the user to apply a rule not only to columns of a table but also to user-defined datatypes. Also, because a rule is stored separately from the table on which it's imposed, if a table on which a rule is applied is dropped, the rule remains available to be applied against other tables. A table can have only one rule.

- Constraints—Constraints are defined on a table column when the column is defined in a CREATE TABLE statement. Microsoft considers constraints preferable to rules as a mechanism for restricting the allowable values that can be entered into a table column because you can define multiple constraints on a column although you can only define a single rule for a column. The type of constraint that is comparable to a rule is a CHECK constraint. When a table is dropped, its CHECK constraints are no longer available. A table can have more than one constraint applied to it.

- Default—Defaults supply a value for an inserted row when users do not supply one with the information to be inserted.

N O T E   You should consider the advantages of using both constraints and rules. For example, a table column can have only one rule but several CHECK constraints defined on it. A table column is restricted by the combination of a rule and one or more CHECK constraints that apply to the column. ▪

▶ For more information on constraints, **see** the section in Chapter 6, "Creating Database Tables and Using Datatypes," titled "Creating and Using Constraints," **p. 141**

Defining Rules

A rule provides a defined restriction on the values for a table column or a user-defined datatype. Any data that you attempt to enter into either a column or a user-defined datatype must meet the criteria defined for the user-defined datatype or column. You should use rules to implement business-related restrictions or limits.

Rules allow you to specify the test they will perform in one of several different ways. First, you can use a function to perform a test on the information. Functions are used to return a comparison value that you can use to validate the value in the column.

Alternatively, you can use comparison operators like BETWEEN, LIKE and IN to complete the test on the value in the new data. Once again, your point is to test the new value and make sure it falls within the bounds you've set for it.

For example, you can use a rule that is defined on a column to limit the values added into a column that records the departments of the company to only the allowable departments. If there are only four departments of which an employee can be a member, you can define a rule to limit the values entered into the Department column to only the four department names. Use a rule to specify the range of allowable values for a column of user-defined datatype.

N O T E   SQL Server provides an automatic validation for datatypes. You'll receive an error if you enter a value that is outside the range of allowable values for the datatype and if you enter a value that is incompatible with the datatype. For example, you can't enter alphabetic or special characters, such as an asterisk (*) and question mark (?) in an int integer datatype.

You should keep this in mind when you define a column or user-defined datatype. If you choose a correct datatype for a column or user-defined datatype, it may make the definition of the rule simpler or even unnecessary. ■

Remember, you can use a user-defined datatype to define a new datatype based on one of the system datatypes, such as char and int, or specialized datatypes. User-defined datatypes for table columns must be identically defined across tables. In addition, you can't define a rule for a system datatype, only for a user-defined datatype.

For example, instead of redefining a column, such as Badge Number that is defined in multiple tables to be used for relational joins, you can define a user-defined datatype and use it as the datatype of badge in each table for which it's defined. If the range of values can be identical for the Badge Number columns, you can define a rule for a user-defined datatype called badge and use it as the datatype for all Badge columns across tables.

Part
III

Ch
13

Creating Rules

Remember, rules are a separate object in your database. Because of this, you have to first create the rule, then bind it to a column. You create a rule with a CREATE RULE statement. The syntax of the CREATE RULE statement is as follows:

```
CREATE RULE rule_name
AS condition_expression
```

If you create a rule in the current database, it applies only to columns or user-defined datatypes within the database in which it is defined. You can use any expression in a rule that is valid in a WHERE clause, and your rule can include comparison or arithmetic operators.

The conditional expression you use in a rule must be prefaced with the symbol @ (at). Use @ to specify a parameter that refers to the value later entered into a table column with either an UPDATE or INSERT statement.

N O T E   When you create a rule, be sure to pay close attention to the datatypes you use within it for the comparison. SQL Server does no datatype checking against the values that are using the rule, so you must ensure that the datatype is compatible with the values you'll be checking. Errors that result from datatype mismatches will not be evident until the rule runs for the first time, and you' receive an error message. ▪

In the following example, CREATE RULE is used to create a list of values using an IN keyword to form a condition expression. Although the parameter used in the condition expression is descriptively identical to the column name in the table to which it's later bound, the parameter can be defined using any set of alphanumeric characters.

```
create rule department_values
as @department in ('Sales','Field Service','Logistics','Software')
```

N O T E   If you add a rule and other database objects to the database MODEL, the rule will be automatically available in any database that is created subsequently. When you create a new database, it's created using the MODEL database as a template. Any objects that are in the MODEL database are automatically duplicated in new database.

If you create a set of rules that can and should be used throughout all your databases, create the rules first in the MODEL database using the database administrator's account (sa) for access before you create your databases. ▪

The rule must restrict values to those that are compatible with the column datatype. You can't use constants within a condition expression that aren't compatible with the column or user-defined datatype to which the rule is subsequently applied. You can make the name of a rule descriptive by defining it so that it includes the name of the column or user-defined datatype to which it will be bound.

You can also create a rule through the SQL Enterprise Manager by performing the following steps:

1. After your start the SQL Enterprise Manager, select the server and the database in which the rule is to be defined.
2. Expand the Objects folder and select Rules.
3. Right-click Rules, select New Rule to bring up the Rule Properties dialog box.
4. Enter the name for the rule in the Rule field, the SQL for the rule in the text box.
5. Click OK to create the new rule.

Figure 13.1 shows the Rule Properties dialog box for the creation of the rule, Jobs_list, through the SQL Enterprise Manager.

FIGURE 13.1
The Rules page of this dialog box creates the rule but does not bind it to a column or user-defined datatype.

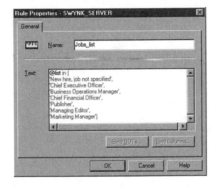

Binding Rules

The definition of a rule doesn't include the specification that applies the rule to either a table column or user-defined datatype. If you only define a rule, it's never in effect; it's only created as an object in the database.

After you define a rule, you must bind it to a column or user-defined datatypes. A rule bound to a column or user-defined datatype specifies that the rule is in effect for the column or user-defined datatype. All values that you enter into a column or user-defined datatype must satisfy the criteria defined by the rule.

You use sp_bindrule to bind a rule to a column or user-defined datatype, as shown in the following syntax:

```
sp_bindrule 'rulename', 'table_name.column_name', ['futureonly']
```

After you bind a rule to a column or user-defined datatype, information about the rule is entered into system tables. A unique rule ID number is stored in the syscolumns and systypes system tables. A rule has a row in syscolumns if it is bound to a column and in systypes if it is bound to a user-defined datatype.

The first parameter of sp_bindrule specifies the name of the rule. You can use as many as 30 characters for the name of the rule, so you may be able to include the name of the table column or user-defined datatype within the name of the rule.

Enter the name of either the table column or the user-defined datatype to which the rule will be applied. You must enter the name of the table column preceded by the name of the table in which it's defined. The table name must be enclosed in single quotation marks. If you enter only the name of an object, SQL Server interprets it as the name of a user-defined datatype. When you enter a column name, use a period (.) to separate the table name from the column name to which the rule is to be bound. A rule that is bound to a datatype restricts the values that can be added to the table column that is defined using the user defined datatype.

The third parameter, futureonly, is used only for the management of user-defined datatypes. Futureonly prevents the rule from being applied to columns that are already defined using the user-defined datatype. Use futureonly to specify that the rule only applies to columns that are subsequently created using the user-defined datatype to which the rule is bound.

You can also bind a rule to a table column or user-defined datatype using the SQL Enterprise Manager by performing the following steps:

1. After your start the SQL Enterprise Manager, select the server and the database in which the rule is defined.

2. Expand the database folder and select Rules.

3. Double-click the rule to be bound.

4. Click the Column Bindings or DataType Bindings tab. For a column binding, select the name of the table in the Table field and add the column(s) you want to bind the rule to by using the Add>> button.

   For a datatype binding, select the user-defined datatype in the User-Defined Datatype field and the rule in the Binding column.

5. Click OK.

6. Click Close to close the Rule Properties dialog box.

Figure 13.2 shows the Rule Properties dialog box for the binding of the Jobs_list rule to the Department column in the Employee table.

 TIP You can double-click the left mouse button on a selected rule to bring up the Rule Properties dialog box.

FIGURE 13.2

You can bind a rule to the columns of multiple tables.

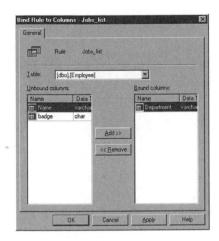

You may have already realized that conflicts can occur with rules, and there are some precedence conventions that are used to resolve the conflicts. You might encounter a situation in which you have a table column that is defined using a user-defined datatype, and both the datatype and column have rules that are bound to them. The following list includes three precedence rules that apply to rule binding:

- Rules that you've bound to columns take precedence over rules bound to datatypes. If rules are bound to both a table column and the user-defined datatype with which the column is defined, the rule that is bound to the table column is used. If you bind a new rule to a table column, it also overrides a rule bound to the user-defined datatype to which the column is defined.

- If you bind a new rule to a column or datatype, the new rule replaces the old one. You can have only a single rule bound to a column or user-defined datatype.

- If you bind a rule to a user-defined datatype, it doesn't replace a rule bound to a column of that datatype. Table 13.1 summarizes rule precedence.

Table 13.1   Rule Precedence

New Rule Bound to...	Old Rule Bound to User Datatype	Old Rule Bound to Column
User datatype	Replaces old rule	No change
Column	Replaces old rule	Replaces old rule

Rules don't apply to the data that has already been entered in the table. Values that are currently in tables don't have to meet the criteria specified by rules. If you want a rule to constrain the values entered in the table, define a rule directly or indirectly through a user-defined datatype before you allow data to be entered into a table.

Part

III

Ch

13

> **CAUTION**
>
> When you copy information into your database using the BCP utility, and in some cases the Data Transformation Services, rules are not enforced. These utilities are meant to complete changes in a bulk fashion as quickly as possible. If you are concerned about incoming information integrity, consider importing the information into a working table, then write and application that will insert each row into your production table, leaving the rules in force for the insertions.

In Listing 13.1, the procedure, `sp_bindrule`, is used to bind the rule, Jobs_list, to the column department in the Employees table. A subsequent INSERT statement fails in its attempt to enter a value in the table column that doesn't meet the criteria defined by the rule. SQL Server returns a descriptive error message that specifies that the attempted INSERT violates the rule bound on the table column.

Listing 13.1 Binding a Rule to a Column

```
sp_bindrule department_values, 'employees.department'
go
Rule bound to table column.
insert into employees
values ('Dan Duryea','Shipping',3321)
go
Msg 513, Level 16, State 1
A column insert or update conflicts with a rule imposed by a previous
CREATE RULE command. The command was aborted. The conflict occurred in
database 'master', table 'employees', column 'department'
Command has been aborted.
```

Listing 13.2 defines a new user-defined datatype and rule that is later bound to the datatype:

Listing 13.2 Binding a Rule to a User-Defined Datatype

```
sp_addtype badge_type2, int, 'not null'
go
Type added.
create rule badgerule2
as @badge_type2 >000 and @badge_type2 <9999
go
This command did not return data, and it did not return any rows
sp_bindrule badgerule2, badge_type2
Rule bound to datatype.
```

T I P You can restrict the range of allowable values by using the appropriate system datatype, such as `smallint` instead of integer.

N O T E Microsoft says that there are three types of rules that you can define: rules with a range, a list, or a pattern. The two previous examples use a range (...@badge_type2 >000 and @badge_type2 <9999) and a list (...@department in ('Sales','Field Service','Logistics')) to restrict values for the rule. The following example shows the third type of rule, which is a rule that uses a pattern to restrict values. The example restricts values to any number of characters that end with S through U.

```
Create rule pattern_rule
As @p like '%[S-U]'
```

You may find it easier to define and use rules if you understand the types of rules that you can create. ■

Displaying Rule Bindings

You can use the system procedure, sp_help, to display information about the user-defined datatypes or table columns that have rules bound to them. In Listing 13.3, information displayed about the user-defined datatype created in an earlier example includes the rule that is bound to the datatype:

Listing 13.3   Reviewing the Rule Assignments

```
sp_help employee

...
RULE on column Department (bound with sp_bindrule)
Jobs_list (n/a) (n/a)
create rule [Jobs_list] as @list in (
'New hire, job not specified',
'Chief Executive Officer',
'Business Operations Manager',
'Chief Financial Officer',
'Publisher',
'Managing Editor',
'Marketing Manager')
...
```

As mentioned earlier, you can also display rule-binding information by clicking Bindings in the Rule Properties dialog box. In Figure 13.3, the dialog box shows a rule bound to a table column.

Part

III

Ch

13

FIGURE 13.3

You can also unbind a rule from the Rule Properties dialog box.

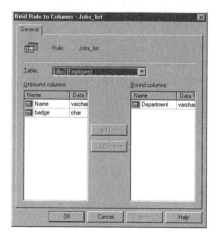

Displaying Rules

Sp_help displays information about a database object, such as a user-defined datatype or column, including the name of a rule that is bound to the datatype or column. Sp_help doesn't show the rule itself when information about the object to which it's bound is shown.

You can use sp_help to display information about a rule. It doesn't, however, return much information about a rule. Sp_help returns information about the rule, badgerule2, and shows only its owner, the type of object, and the date and time it was created.

You are probably more interested in displaying the rule itself rather than the characteristics of the rule as an object. To display the definition of a rule itself, use sp_helptext. The definition of a rule is saved as the row of a system table, so the definition of a rule is returned as the row of a table. The following example shows the rule that is used to constrain the range of allowable badge numbers:

```
sp_helptext badgerule2
text
---------------------------
create rule badgerule2
as @badge_type2 >000 and @badge_type2 <9999
```

You can also use the SQL Enterprise Manager to display rules. A rule definition is shown in the Description field of the Manage Rules dialog box. Double-click a selected rule or right-click and select Properties to bring up the description of a rule in the Rule Properties dialog box. Figure 13.1 shows the Rule Properties dialog box with the description of the rule within the description field.

Finally, keep in mind that rules are defined within a set of system tables that is local to each database. The rules defined within one database aren't available within another database. You can select the rule definition within a Query Analyzer session, store it as a file, and then open the file to recover the rule. You can define the rule after you use a USE command to position yourself in the database in which the rule will be used.

Unbinding Rules

At some point, you may no longer want the values that are entered into a column or user-defined datatype to be constrained by a rule. You can unbind a rule using `sp_unbindrule`, which removes the constraint from a bound column or user-defined datatype. Unbinding a rule makes it nonapplicable to a column or user-defined datatype. The sp_unbindrule syntax is as follows:

```
sp_unbindrule table_name.column or user_datatype [, futureonly]
```

As with `sp_bindrule`, if the first parameter of `sp_unbindrule` is a column, it must be preceded by the name of the table in which it's defined and entered in single quotation marks. Otherwise, the first parameter is interpreted as the name of a user-defined datatype.

Use `futureonly`, the optional third parameter, only with rules that are bound to user-defined datatypes. Table columns that are already defined using the user-defined datatype have the rule applied to the columns unless the `futureonly` optional parameter is present. The `futureonly` option prevents existing columns from inheriting the rule. Only new columns that are defined using the user-defined datatype are affected by the rule.

You can also use the SQL Enterprise Manager to unbind a rule from a table column or user-defined datatype by clicking Remove after opening the Rule Properties dialog box. See Figure 13.4.

FIGURE 13.4

The name of the rule is removed from the Bound Columns field of the Rule Properties dialog box.

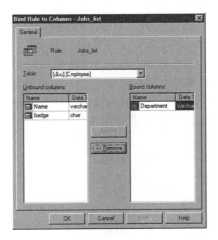

In the following example, `sp_help` displays the Employees table, which has a rule that is defined on the Department column. `Sp_unbindrule` unbinds the rule from the Department column of the Employees table. If you then query the table with sp_help as covered earlier, you'll find that the rule has been unbound from the Table column.

```
sp_help employees
go
Name            Owner                    Type
------------------------------  -----------
employees       dbo                      user table
Data_located_on_segment         When_created
```

Part III

Ch 13

```
------------------------------- -----------
default                 May 12 1994 10:15AM
Column_name Type Length Nulls Default_name  Rule_name
------------- -------------- ------ ---- ------
name       char   20    0     (null)        (null)
department char   20    0     (null) department_values
badge      int    4     0     (null)        (null)
Object does not have any indexes.
No defined keys for this object.
sp_unbindrule 'employees.department'
go
Rule unbound from table column.
sp_help employees
go
Name                Owner              Type
---------------------------- -----------
employees           dbo               user table
Data_located_on_segment      When_created
---------------------------- -----------
default                 May 12 1994 10:15AM
Column_name  Type Length Nulls Default_name Rule_name
------------- -------------- ------ ---- --------
name        char  20    0     (null)     (null)
department  char  20    0     (null)     (null)
badge       int   4     0     (null)     (null)
Object does not have any indexes.
No defined keys for this object.
```

You can also unbind a rule by replacing the current rule with a new one. Sp_bindrule binds a new rule to that column or datatype. The old rule is automatically unbound from the user-defined datatype or table column.

In Listing 13.4, the attempted redefinition of the existing department_values rule is unsuccessful because a rule can't be replaced by one with the same name. A new rule is created, and it's bound to the same column to which the department_values rule is bound. The new rule replaces the old department_values rule.

Listing 13.4 Creating and Binding a Rule

```
create rule department_values
as @department in ('Sales','Field Service','Logistics','Shipping')
go
Msg 2714, Level 16, State 1
There is already an object named 'department_values' in the database.
create rule depart2
as @department in ('Sales','Field Service','Logistics','Shipping')
go
This command did not return data, and it did not return any rows
sp_bindrule depart2, 'employees.department'
go
Rule bound to table column.
```

In Listing 13.5, which is a continuation of the previous example, an INSERT into the Employees table demonstrates that the new rule has been bound to the Department column. The old rule for Department would have disallowed the addition of a row that contains the Shipping department. A SELECT statement shows that the new row was added to the table. Finally, sp_help shows that the new depart2 rule is bound to the Department column of the Employees table and replaces the old department_values rule.

Listing 13.5 Inserting Rows into a Table Controlled by Rules

```
insert into employees
values ('Dan Duryea','Shipping',3321)
go
(1 row(s) affected)
select * from employees
go
name                 department          badge
-------------------- -------------------- ----------
Bob Smith            Sales               1234
Mary Jones           Sales               5514
Dan Duryea           Shipping            3321
(3 row(s) affected)
sp_help employees
go
Name                         Owner                           Type
---------------------------- ------------------------------- ------------
employees                    dbo                             user table
Data_located_on_segment      When_created
---------------------------- -------------------------------
default                      May 12 1994 10:15AM
Column_name    Type           Length Nulls Default_name    Rule_name
-------------- -------------- ------ ----- --------------- --------------
name           char              20     0  (null)          (null)
department     char              20     0  (null)          depart2
badge          int                4     0  (null)          (null)
Object does not have any indexes.
No defined keys for this object.
```

Renaming Rules

You can rename rules, like other objects, using sp_rename. You can also use sp_rename to rename other user objects, such as tables, views, columns, stored procedures, triggers, and defaults. The sp_rename syntax is as follows:

```
sp_rename object_name, new_name
```

In Listing 13.6, an existing rule is renamed. After the rule is renamed, a display of the Employees table shows that the new name of the rule is in effect for the Department column.

Part
III

Ch
13

Listing 13.6   Renaming a Rule

```
sp_rename depart2, depart3
go
Object name has been changed.
```

You can also rename a rule using the SQL Enterprise Manager by right-clicking a selected rule and selecting Rename. Enter the new name for the rule and press Enter.

Dropping Rules

You can use the DROP RULE statement to permanently remove a rule from a database. The rule is immediately removed if it's not bound to any columns or user-defined datatypes. If the rule is bound to a column or a datatype, you must first unbind the rule from all columns and user datatypes to be able to drop the rule. You can drop multiple rules with a single DROP RULE statement. The DROP RULE syntax is as follows:

```
DROP RULE rule_name_1[,…rule_name_n]
```

In Listing 13.7, an initial attempt to remove a rule is unsuccessful because the rule is bound to a table column. After the rule is unbound from the table column, it's successfully removed. Sp_helptext demonstrates that the object is gone.

Listing 13.7   Dropping a Rule

```
drop rule depart3
go
Msg 3716, Level 16, State 1
The rule 'depart3' cannot be dropped because it is bound to one or more column.
sp_unbindrule 'employees.department'
go
Rule unbound from table column.
drop rule depart3
go
This command did not return data, and it did not return any rows
sp_helptext depart3
go
No such object in the current database.
```

You can also drop rules through the SQL Enterprise Manager. Select the name of the rule in the Results pane of the SQL Enterprise Manager with the Rules object selected. Next, click the delete icon on the tool bar.

TIP   Keep in mind that you can only have a single rule bound to either a user-defined datatype or a table column. If you have a rule defined and then bind a new rule to the same column as the first, the first rule will be replaced.

In addition, if you bind a rule to a user-defined datatype without using `futureonly`, it effectively replaces the rule for all table columns defined from the user-defined datatype.

Defining Defaults

You can use defaults to define a value that is automatically added to a column if no value is explicitly entered. You bind a default to a column or user-defined datatype using sp_binddefault. You must define a default value that is compatible with the column datatype. A default also can't violate a rule that is associated with a table column.

Default definitions are stored in the syscomments table like rule definitions. Also as with rules, if you bind a new default to a column, it automatically overrides an old rule. A default bound to the column takes precedence over a default bound to the user-defined datatype.

Creating Defaults

You can define a default using the CREATE DEFAULT statement. The name used in the second parameter of the sp_bindefault is interpreted as a user-defined datatype unless it's preceded by the table name. It must be preceded by the name of a table to be interpreted as a column of a table. The CREATE DEFAULT syntax is as follows:

```
CREATE DEFAULT default_name AS constant value
```

> **CAUTION**
>
> If you define a default with a value that's longer than the table column to which it's subsequently bound, the default value entered into the column is truncated. Make sure the datatype and size of your column matches that of the default you're trying to establish.

You can also create a default using the SQL Enterprise Manager by performing the following steps:

1. After you start the SQL Enterprise Manager, select the server and the database in which the default is to be created.
2. Expand the Objects folder and select Defaults.
3. Right-click and select New Default to bring up the Default Properties dialog box.
4. Enter a name and value for the default and click OK.

Figure 13.5 shows the Manage Defaults dialog box for the creation of the default Department through the SQL Enterprise Manager.

FIGURE 13.5
You can also manage existing defaults using the Manage Defaults dialog box.

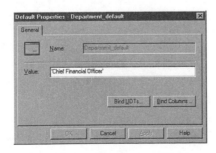

Binding Defaults

You can use the system procedure, sp_bindefault, to bind a default to a user-defined datatype or table column. The second parameter can be the name of a table column or a user-defined datatype. Use the third parameter to specify that the default value should only be applied to new columns of tables that are defined, not to existing columns of tables. The sp_bindefault syntax is as follows:

```
sp_bindefault default_name, table_name.column_name, [futureonly]
```

Listing 13.8 shows a default defined and bound to the Department column of the Employees table. A row is inserted into the table that omits a value for the Department column in the list of values. A subsequent SELECT statement demonstrates that the default value was added to the Department column for the newly inserted row.

Listing 13.8 Applying Defaults

```
create default Department_default as 'Sales'
go
sp_bindefault Department_default, 'employees.department'
go
Default bound to column.
insert into employees
(name, badge)
values ('John Garr',2221)
go
(1 row(s) affected)
select * from employees
where badge=2221
go
name                    department              badge
------------------      ------------------      ---------
John Garr               Sales                   2221
(1 row(s) affected)
```

In the following example, a default is defined and bound to a user-defined datatype. The second parameter of sp_bindefault is interpreted as a user-defined datatype because no table name precedes the object name. The third parameter isn't specified, so the default value is applied to any table columns that are defined using the user-defined datatype.

```
create default badge_default
as 9999
sp_bindefault badge_default, badge_type2
Default bound to datatype.
```

> **N O T E** If you define a table column that permits NULL values, a NULL is added to a row when the column isn't referenced when a row is inserted into the table. A NULL entry is automatically inserted, just as a default value is automatically inserted. The definition of a NULL remains the same. Its meaning, however, is still undefined. Undefined is different from the automatic insertion of an actual value. ■

▶ For more information on NULLs, **see** the Chapter 6 section entitled "Understanding NULL and NOT NULL," **p. 137**

You can also bind a default to a table column or user-defined datatype using the SQL Enterprise Manager by performing the following steps:

1. After your start the SQL Enterprise Manager, select the server and the database in which the default is defined.

2. Expand the Objects folder and select Defaults.

3. Double-click the default to be bound.

4. Click the Column Bindings or Datatype Bindings tab.

5. For a column binding, use the Add >> button to select the columns to bind to. Select OK to apply the binding.

   For a datatype binding, select the user-defined datatype in the User-Defined Datatype field and the default in the Binding column.

6. Click Close to close the Manage Defaults dialog box.

Figure 13.6 shows the Manage Defaults dialog box for the binding of the department_default default to the Department column in the Employee table.

FIGURE 13.6
You can bind a default to the columns of multiple tables.

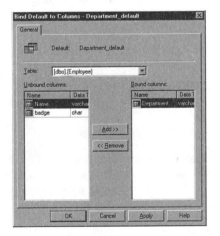

You can only bind a single default value to a given column. If you try to bind a default to a column on which one already exists, you'll receive an error message from SQL Server. Use the sp_unbindefault statement to remove the existing default and then apply the new default to the column.

Unlike rules, defaults are applied during bulk copy operations. Also, if you have both a default and a rule on a given column, the default is applied first. Then the rule is checked. This helps keep your rule from having to be aware of NULL values, because the default will have already updated the value appropriately.

In the next section you will find out how to determine what defaults are already in place for a given column.

Displaying Bindings

You can use sp_help to display the defaults bound to either table columns or user-defined datatypes. In Listing 13.9, sp_help displays the default that's bound to the Badge column:

Listing 13.9   Showing Bindings

```
sp_help employees
go
Name                                    Owner                              Type
------------------------------------    ----------------------------      ----------
employees                               dbo                               user table
Data_located_on_segment                 When_created
------------------------------------    ----------------------------
default                                 Oct 18 1994 12:52PM
Column_name      Type           Length Nulls Default_name      Rule_name
--------------   --------------  ------ ----- ---------------   ---------
name             char              20    0       (null)           (null)
department       char              20    0       (null)           (null)
badge            int               4     0     badge_default      (null)
Object does not have any indexes.
No defined keys for this object.
```

 TIP A default bound to a table column is also displayed in the Default file of the Manage Table dialog box in the SQL Enterprise Manager.

Displaying Defaults

You can use the procedure sp_helptext to display the value that's defined for a default. The definitions of defaults are stored as rows in the syscomments system table. The display of a default definition is shown as the row of a table. In the following example, the default for a table column is shown using sp_helptext:

```
sp_helptext Department_default
go
text------------------------------------------
create default Department_default as 'Sales'
```

You can also use the SQL Enterprise Manager to display a default. A default definition is shown in the Description field of the Manage Defaults dialog box. Double-click a selected rule or right-click and select Edit to bring up the description of a default in the Manage Defaults dialog box.

Unbinding Defaults

When you no longer want the default value automatically entered into a column or user-defined datatype, you must unbind the default by using sp_unbindefault, which removes the default from a bound column or user-defined datatype. Unbinding a default makes it nonapplicable to a column or user-defined datatype. The sp_unbindefault syntax is as follows:

```
sp_unbindefault table_name.column_name [,futureonly]
```

Use the third parameter, which is optional, to specify that only new columns defined using the user-defined datatype aren't bound using the default. You only use the third parameter for user-defined datatypes. You don't use it for table columns. In the following example, a default is unbound from a table column. Sp_help is first used to verify that the default is bound to the table column. Thereafter, sp_help is used after the default is unbound to verify that the default was unbound from the table column.

```
sp_unbindefault 'employees.badge'
go
Default unbound from table column.
```

Renaming Defaults

You can use system procedure, sp_rename, to rename a default. In Listing 13.10, a default is renamed using sp_rename. After the default is renamed, the table in which the default is bound to a column is displayed using sp_help to confirm that the default was renamed.

Listing 13.10   Renaming a Default and Verifying the Name Change

```
sp_rename Department_default, dept_default
go
Object name has been changed.
sp_help employees
go
Name                            Owner                           Type
----------------------------    ----------------------------    ---------- 
employees                       dbo                             user table
Data_located_on_segment         When_created
----------------------------    ----------------------------    ------------
default                         May 12 1994 10:15AM
Column_name     Type            Length Nulls Default_name     Rule_name
-------------   -----------     ------ ----- --------------   ----------
name            char            20     0     (null)           (null)
department      char            20     0     dept_default     (null)
badge           int            4      0     (null)           (null)
Object does not have any indexes.
No defined keys for this object.
```

N O T E   All database objects can be renamed using the sp_rename system procedure of the Rename Object dialog box in the SQL Enterprise Manager. ∎

Dropping Defaults

You can permanently remove a default with the DROP DEFAULT statement. The default is immediately removed if it's not bound to any columns or user-defined datatypes. If the default is bound to a column or a datatype, you must first unbind the default from all columns and user datatypes to be able to drop the default. You can drop multiple defaults with a single DROP DEFAULT statement. The DROP DEFAULT syntax is as follows:

```
DROP DEFAULT default_name_1 [,...default_name_n]
```

In Listing 13.11, an attempt to drop a default is unsuccessful because the default is bound to a table column. After the column is unbound from a table column, the default is successfully dropped.

Listing 13.11   Dropping a Default

```
drop default dept_default
go
Msg 3716, Level 16, State 1
The default 'dept_default' cannot be dropped because
it is bound to one or more columns.
sp_unbindefault 'employees.department'
go
Default unbound from table column.
drop default dept_default
go
This command did not return data, and it did not return any rows
sp_helptext dept_default
No such object in the current database.
```

You can also drop defaults through the SQL Enterprise Manager. Select the name of the default in the Default field of the Manage Defaults dialog box. Click Delete to remove the default. Click Close to close the Manage Defaults dialog box.

Reality Check

ODBC is both a blessing and a curse. With ODBC, you can query and work with databases from nearly any Microsoft Office application, from Web sites and more. This is now especially true with Office 97's capability to connect directly to database sources from within each of the applications. This is great for the user. This can be disastrous for the developers, though, as they no longer control the client-side application that is used to manipulate the database.

This is where rules, defaults, and constraints come in. By implementing this low-level checking on the database side of the equation where the information is ultimately stored, you remove the dependence on the client application. You also make your database strong enough to guarantee the relationships between tables.

In large-scale applications, rules and these types of server-side constraints play another, just as important, role. You should consider having a person or team of people that is responsible for the database engine and for implementing the rules you're defining here. You can save yourself a good deal of heartache if you have the responsibility for managing the database controls in a centralized party.

In large development teams, it's difficult to make sure all the developers know all the rules that pertain to the database they're working on. Because you can implement these rules separately from the development work they're doing, you'll still be assured of a well-mannered application, even if many different developers write the code to access the database. By delegating the management of the database to a central person or team, you can assure that no duplication will occur, and you'll be able to optimize the database to reflect the requirements of the teams as a whole.

From Here...

Rules are very powerful tools used to enforce limitations on column and user-defined datatype values. After a rule is created it must be bound to columns or datatypes. Rules and datatypes can be bound to multiple table columns or user-defined datatypes. Defaults provide a way to provide an initial value to columns. Initial values can be used as suggestions or as a way to enable users with a limited view of a table to insert rows that will contain data in columns to which they do not have access.

For information about the type of restrictions that are provided by constraints, see the following chapters:

- Chapter 6, "Creating Database Tables and Using Datatypes," teaches you how to define data columns and user-defined datatypes. You'll also learn the allowable range of values for each system datatype.

- Chapter 15, "Creating and Managing Triggers," shows how you can add more control to the database back end, reacting programmatically to data changes in your tables.

Part
III

Ch
13

Managing Stored Procedures and Using Flow-Control Statements

As your systems become more complex, you will need to spend more time carefully integrating SQL code with your host application code. In this chapter, you will review the logic and flow control statements that you have available to you in your SQL code.

At a high level, stored procedures are a way that you can create routines and procedures that are run on the server, by server processes. These routines can be started by an application calling them or called by data integrity rules or triggers.

The benefit of stored procedures comes from the fact that they run within the SQL Server environment on the server. While at first this might not seem to be any obvious advantage, it goes to the heart of the client/server model. Remember the rule of thumb that the system doing the work to satisfy a given situation should be the system most suited for that work? Because SQL Server manages the databases in your system, it makes sense that it is the best place to run the stored procedures against that data.

Stored procedures can return values, modify values, and can be used to compare a user-supplied value against the prerequisites for information in the system. Stored procedures run quickly with the added horsepower of the average SQL Server hardware, and they are database-aware, able to take advantage of SQL Server's optimizer for best performance at runtime.

You can also pass values to a stored procedure, and it can return values that are not necessarily part of an underlying table, but are, instead, calculated during the running of the stored procedure.

The benefits of stored procedures on a grand scale include:

- Performance—Because stored procedures run on the server, typically a more powerful machine, the execution time is generally much less than at the workstation. In addition, because the database information is readily at hand and on the same physical system, there is no wait for records to pass over the network for processing. Instead, the stored procedure has immediate, ready access to the database to make working with the information extremely fast.

- Client/server development benefits—By breaking apart the client and server development tasks, you can sometimes help to decrease the schedule needed to bring your projects to completion. You can develop the server-side pieces separately from the client-side, and you can re-use the server-side components between client-side applications.

- Security—As mentioned earlier in Chapter 10, "Managing and Using Views," you can use stored procedures as a tool to really clamp down on security. You can create stored procedures for all add/change/delete/list operations and programmatically control each of these aspects of information access.

- Server-side enforcement of data-oriented rules—Finally, one of the end-all reasons for using an intelligent database engine, stored procedures let you put into place the rules and other logic that help control the information put into your system.

N O T E   It's important to keep in mind the client/server model when you're building your systems. Remember that data management belongs on the server, and data presentation and display manipulation for reports and inquiries should reside on the client in the ideal model. As you build systems, be on the lookout for those items that can be moved to the different ends of the model to optimize the user's experience with your application. ■

Although SQL is defined as a non-procedural language, SQL Server permits the use of *flow-control keywords*. You use the flow-control keywords to create a procedure that you can store for subsequent execution. You can use these stored procedures instead of writing programs using a conventional programming language, such as C or Visual Basic, to perform operations with a SQL Server database and its tables.

Some of the advantages that stored procedures offer over dynamic SQL statements are the following:

- Stored procedures are compiled the first time they're run and are stored in a system table of the current database. When they are compiled, they are optimized to select the best path to access information in the tables. This optimization takes into account the actual data patterns in the table, indexes that are available, table loading, and more. These compiled stored procedures can greatly enhance the performance of your system.

- Another benefit is that you can execute a stored procedure on either a local or remote SQL Server. This enables you to run processes on other machines and work with information across servers, not just *local* databases.

- An application program written in a language, such as C or Visual Basic, can also execute stored procedures, providing an optimum solution between the client-side software and SQL Server.

Defining Stored Procedures

You use the CREATE PROC[EDURE] statement to create a stored procedure. Permission to execute the procedure that you create is set by default to the owner of the database. An owner of the database can change the permissions to allow other users to execute the procedure. The maximum stored procedure name length is 128 characters. The syntax that you use to define a new procedure is as follows:

```
CREATE PROCEDURE [owner,] procedure_name [;number]
[@parameter_name datatype [=default] [OUTput]
[...]
[@parameter_name datatype [=default] [OUTput]
[FOR REPLICATION] ¦ [WITH RECOMPILE] , ENCRYPTION
AS sql_statements
```

CAUTION

Be sure you reload your stored procedures again after information has been saved in the database tables that represents, both in volume and content, the information that your application can expect to see. Because stored procedures are compiled and optimized based on the tables, indexes, and data loading, your query can show significant improvement just by reloading it after "real" information has been placed in the system.

Part
III

Ch
14

In the following example, a simple procedure is created that contains a SELECT statement to display all rows of a table. Once the procedure is created, its name is entered on a line to execute the procedure. If you precede the name of a stored procedure with other statements, you use the EXEC[UTE] *procedure-name* statement to execute the procedure.

```
create procedure all_employees
as select * from employees

exec all_employees

name                    department              badge
-------------------     -------------------     ----------
Bob Smith               Sales                   1234
Mary Jones              Sales                   5514
( 2 row(s) affected)
```

TIP   If your call to the stored procedure is the first in your batch of commands, you don't have to specify the EXEC[UTE] portion of the statement. You can simply call the procedure by name and it will be executed automatically.

N O T E   As mentioned earlier, naming conventions for SQL objects are an important part of your implementation plan. In a production system, you will often have hundreds of stored procedures, many tables, and many more supporting objects. You should consider coming up with a naming convention for your stored procedures that will make it easy to identify them as procedures and will make it easier to document them. In many installations, a common prefix for the stored procedure name is sp_. ▩

You can create a new procedure in the current database only. If you're working in ISQL or ISQL/W, you can execute the USE statement followed by the name of the database to set the current database to the database in which the procedure should be created. You can use any Transact-SQL statement in a stored procedure with the exception of CREATE statements.

When you submit a stored procedure to the system, SQL Server will compile and verify the routines within it. If any problems are found, the procedure is rejected and you will need to determine what the problem is prior to re-submitting the routine. If your stored procedure references another, as yet unimplemented stored procedure, you will receive a warning message, but the routine will still be installed.

If you leave the system with the referred-to stored procedure uninstalled, the user will receive an error message at runtime.

N O T E   Stored procedures are treated like all other objects in the database. They are, therefore, subject to all of the same naming conventions and other limitations. For example, the name of a stored procedure cannot contain spaces, and it can be accessed using the *database.<object>* convention. ▩

Using Parameters with Procedures

Stored procedures are very powerful, but to be most effective, the procedure must be somewhat dynamic, allowing you, the developer, to pass in values to be considered during the functioning of the stored procedure. Here are some general guidelines for using parameters with stored procedures:

- You can define one or more parameters in a procedure.
- You use parameters as named storage locations just as you would use the parameters as variables in conventional programming languages, such as C and VB.
- You precede the name of a parameter with an *at* symbol (@) to designate it as a parameter.
- Parameter names are local to the procedure in which they're defined.

You can use parameters to pass information into a procedure from the line that executes the parameter. You place the parameters after the name of the procedure on a command line, with commas to separate the list of parameters if there is more than one. You use system datatypes to define the type of information to be expected as a parameter.

In the following example, the procedure is defined with three input parameters. The defined input parameters appear within the procedure in the position of values in the VALUE clause of an INSERT statement. When the procedure is executed, three literal values are passed into the INSERT statement within the procedure as a parameter list. A SELECT statement is executed after the stored procedure is executed to verify that a new row was added through the procedure.

 TIP Be sure to check the documentation for the host language you are using with SQL Server to determine the correct calling sequence for the host language. Actual calling syntax varies by language.

```
create procedure proc4 (@p1 char(15), @p2 char(20), @p3 int) as
insert into Workers
values (@p1, @p2, @p3)

proc4 'Bob Lint',Sales,3333

select * from Workers
where Badge=3333
```

```
Name                             Department      Badge
-----------------------------    --------------  ----------
Bob Lint                         Sales           3333
```

```
(1 row(s) affected)
```

The semicolon and integer after the name of a procedure enable you to create multiple versions of a procedure with the same name. In the following example, two procedures with the same name are created as version one and two. When the procedure is executed, the version number can be specified to control the version of the procedure that is executed. If no version

Part
III

Ch
14

number is specified, the first version of the procedure is executed. This option is not shown in the example above, but is available if needed by your application. Both procedures use a PRINT statement to return a message that identifies the procedure version.

```
create procedure proc3;1 as
print 'version 1'

create procedure proc3;2 as
print 'version 2'

proc3;1

version 1

proc3;2

version 2

proc3

version 1
```

In the previous example, proc3 is executed without preceding it with the keyword EXECUTE because it is executed as the first statement on a line.

 TIP You can use the SET NOEXEC ON command the first time you execute a procedure to check it for errors. This will prevent you from executing it when errors may cause it to fail.

You can create a new stored procedure through the SQL Enterprise Manager as well as in ISQL or ISQL/W.

Perform the following steps to create a new stored procedure through the SQL Enterprise Manager:

1. Select Stored Procedures under the Objects of the selected database in the Server Manager window.

2. Right-click Stored Procedures and select New Stored Procedures from the menu. You can enter Transact-SQL statements in the dialog box. Figure 14.1 shows the New Stored Procedures dialog box before any statements are typed into the dialog box.

3. You must overwrite <PROCEDURE NAME> in the New Stored Procedures dialog box with the name of your new procedure.

4. Click the OK button to create and store your procedure. Figure 14.2 shows a simple Transact-SQL statement and a new procedure name entered in the Stored Procedures Properties dialog box.

FIGURE 14.1
You can also edit an existing stored procedure in the Stored Procedure Properties dialog box.

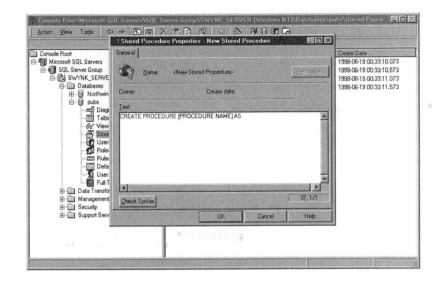

FIGURE 14.2
Click the Check Syntax button to check the syntax of the procedure.

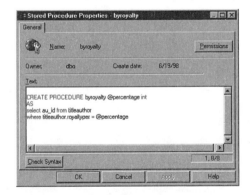

Calling Stored Procedures from Your Application

When you call stored procedures from other applications environments, there are a few tricks you'll want to know about. For starters, when your stored procedures take parameters, you have a couple of different options.

First, you can always provide all parameters in the order in which they are declared. While this is easiest to develop for at first blush, consider carefully whether this makes sense in the long run. There will probably be cases in which you want to make a multi-purpose stored procedure that calls for more parameters than would be required, on the whole, for any given call. In those cases, you're *expecting* to have some parameters that are not specified in each call.

You use a test for NULL on a parameter to determine whether it was provided. This means you can test directly against NULL, or you can use the ISNULL comparison operator.

▶ For more information about ISNULL **see** the "Using ISNULL and NULLIF" section, **p. 253**, in Chapter 9, "Using Functions."

Part
III

Ch
14

On the application side, it can be quite cumbersome to have to specify each value on every call to the stored procedure, even in cases in which the value is NULL. In those cases, the calling application can use *named arguments* to pass information to SQL Server and the stored procedure. For example, if your stored procedure allows up to three different arguments, name, address, and phone, you can call the routine as follows:

```
Exec sp_routine @name="blah"
```

By providing the name of the argument being passed, SQL Server will be able to map it to its corresponding parameter. This is typically the best way to pass information to SQL Server, and it also helps make the code more readable because you can tell what the passed parameters are.

Displaying and Editing Procedures

You use the system procedure sp_helptext to list the definition of a procedure and sp_help to display control information about a procedure. The system procedures sp_helptext and sp_help are used to list information about other database objects, such as tables, rules, and defaults, as well as stored procedures.

Procedures with the same name and version number are displayed together and dropped together. In the following example, the definition of procedure proc3, versions one and two, are both displayed when the procedure is specified with the sp_helptext system procedure.

```
sp_helptext proc3

text
-------------------------------------------
create procedure proc3;1 as
print 'version 1'
create procedure proc3;2 as
print 'version 2'

(1 row(s) affected)
```

In the next examples, the system procedure sp_help is used to display information about the procedure proc3. If the version number is used with the sp_help system procedure, an error is returned.

```
sp_help proc3

Name                          Owner                                Type
--------- ----------          ---------------------------- ------  ----------------
proc3                         dbo                                  stored procedure
Data_located_on_segment When_created
-------------------- ----------------------------
not applicable          Dec 7 1994  1:50PM
```

You can use an additional system procedure just to return information about stored procedures. The system procedure sp_stored_procedures is used to list information about stored procedures. In the following example, the procedure sp_stored_procedures is used to display information about a previously stored procedure.

```
sp_stored_procedures procall

procedure_qualifier  procedure_owner  procedure_name  num_input_params
→num_output_params num_result_sets remarks
--------------------------------------------------------------------------
master  dbo  procall;1  -1  -1 -1  (null)

(1 row(s) affected)
```

 TIP You can use the command SET SHOWPLAN ON before you execute a procedure to see the way in which SQL Server will perform the necessary reads and writes to the database tables when the statements in your procedure are executed. You can use this information to help determine whether additional indexes or different data layout would be beneficial to the query.

You use the SQL Enterprise Manager to list and edit existing procedures. Double-click the procedure to be edited in the list of stored procedures in the main window of the Server Manager. The selected procedure is displayed and can be changed in the Stored Procedures Properties dialog box that is brought up.

Making Changes and Dropping Stored Procedures

Two closely related tasks that you will no doubt have to work with are the ability to make changes to existing stored procedures and the need to remove no longer used stored procedures. In the next two sections, you will see exactly how you accomplish both of these tasks and you will understand why they are so tightly related.

Changing an Existing Stored Procedure   Stored procedures cannot be modified in place, so you're forced to first drop the procedure, then create it again. Unfortunately, there is no ALTER statement that can be used to modify the contents of an existing procedure. This stems largely from the query plan that is created and the fact that stored procedures are compiled once they are initiated.

Because the routines are compiled, and because the query plan relies on the compiled information, SQL Server uses a binary version of the stored procedure when it is executed. It would be difficult or impossible to convert from the binary representation of the stored procedure back to "English" to allow for edits. For this reason, it's imperative that you maintain a copy of your stored procedures in a location other than SQL Server. While SQL Server can produce the code that was used to create the stored procedure, you should always maintain a backup copy.

You can pull the text associated with a stored procedure by using the sp_helptext system stored procedure.

Sp_helptext *procedure name*

For example, pulling the text associating with the all_authors stored procedure would result in the display shown in Figure 14.3.

FIGURE 14.3

You can review the text associated with a stored procedure with the `sp_helptext` statement.

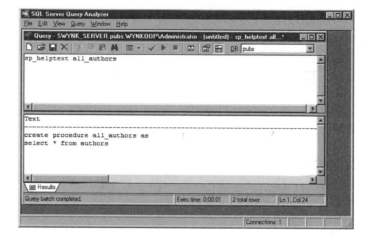

Alternatively, if you want to review a stored procedure in the Enterprise Manager, you can do so by selecting the database, stored procedures and then double-clicking on the stored procedure you want to view. The result, shown in Figure 14.4, is a listing of the stored procedure.

FIGURE 14.4

The Enterprise Manager allows checking the permissions and syntax of the stored procedure.

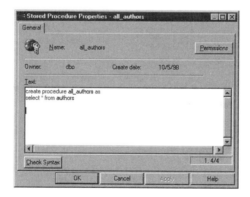

Once you have the text, you can re-create the routine with the changes you need.

Removing Existing Stored Procedures   You use the `DROP PROCEDURE` statement to drop a stored procedure that you've created. Multiple procedures can be dropped with a single `DROP PROCEDURE` statement by listing multiple procedures separated by commas after the keywords `DROP PROCEDURE` in the syntax:

```
DROP PROCEDURE procedure_name_1, ...,procedure_name_n
```

Multiple versions of a procedure can't be selectively dropped. All versions of a procedure with the same name must be dropped at the same time by using the `DROP PROCEDURE` statement that specifies the procedure without a version number. All versions of a procedure with the same name must be dropped together.

In the following example, the two versions of the procedure proc3 are dropped.

```
drop procedure proc3
This command did not return data, and it did not return any rows
```

You can also drop a selected procedure in the SQL Enterprise Manager. Click the right mouse button for the selected procedure and choose Delete from the menu that is brought up.

Understanding Procedure Resolution and Compilation

The benefit of using a stored procedure for the execution of a set of Transact-SQL statements is that it is compiled the first time that it's run. During compilation, the Transact-SQL statements in the procedure are converted from their original character representation into an executable form. Also during compilation, any objects that are referenced in procedures are converted to alternative representations. For example, table names are converted to their object IDs and column names to their column IDs.

An execution plan is also created just as it would be for the execution of even a single Transact-SQL statement. The execution plan contains, for example, the indexes to be used to retrieve rows from tables that are referenced by the procedure. The execution plan is kept in a cache and is used to perform the queries of the procedure each time it's subsequently executed.

 You can define the size of the procedure cache so that it is large enough to contain most or all the available procedures for execution and save the time that it would take to regenerate the execution plan for procedures.

Automatic Recompilation

Normally, the procedure's execution plan is run from the memory cache of procedures that permits it to execute rapidly. A procedure, however, is automatically recompiled under the following circumstances:

- A procedure is always recompiled when SQL Server is started, usually after a reboot of the underlying operating system, and the procedures are first executed.

- A procedure's execution plan is also automatically recompiled whenever an index on a table referenced in the procedure is dropped. A new execution plan must be compiled because the current one references an object that doesn't exist—the index—for the retrieval of the rows of a table. The execution plan must be redone to permit the queries of the procedure to be performed.

- Compilation of the execution plan is also re-initialized if the execution plan in the cache is currently in use by another user. A second copy of the execution plan is created for the second user. If the first copy of the execution plan weren't in use, it could have been used rather than a new execution plan being created. When a user finishes executing a procedure, the execution plan is available in the cache for reuse by another user with appropriate permissions.

Part

III

Ch

14

■ A procedure is also automatically recompiled if the procedure is dropped and re-created. All copies of the execution plan in the cache are removed because the new procedure may be substantially different from the older version and a new execution plan is necessary.

N O T E It's often the case that SQL Server remains up and running on the server system continuously. As a database server, it must be available whenever users on client PC workstations must access the SQL Server databases. The server computer and SQL Server need never be stopped and restarted unless a major error occurs, hardware malfunctions, or there is an update to a new version of SQL Server, Windows 9x, or Windows NT. The recompilation of stored procedures would not be done frequently on systems that run non-stop. ■

Note that because SQL Server attempts to optimize stored procedures by caching the most recently used routines, it is still possible that an older execution plan, one previously loaded in cache, may be used in place of the new execution plan.

To prevent this problem, you must both drop and re-create the procedure, or stop and restart SQL Server to flush the procedure cache and ensure that the new procedure is the only one that will be used when the procedure is executed.

You can also create the procedure using a WITH RECOMPILE option so that the procedure is automatically recompiled each time it's executed. You should do this if the tables accessed by the queries in a procedure are very dynamic. Tables that are very dynamic have rows added, deleted, and updated frequently, which results in frequent changes to the indexes that are defined for the tables.

In other cases, you may want to force a recompilation of a procedure when it would not be done automatically. For example, if the statistics used to determine whether an index should be used for a query are updated or an entire index is created for a table, recompilation is not re-done automatically. You can use the WITH RECOMPILE clause on the EXECUTE statement when you execute the procedure to do a recompilation. The syntax of the EXECUTE statement with a recompile clause is as follows:

```
EXECUTE procedure_name AS
.Transact-SQL statement(s)
...
WITH RECOMPILE
```

If the procedure you're working with uses parameters and these parameters control the functionality of the routine, you might want to use the RECOMPILE option. This is because if the routine's parameters determine the best execution path, it might be beneficial to have the execution plan determined at runtime, rather than determining it once and using that plan for all accesses to the stored procedure.

N O T E It might be difficult to determine whether a procedure should be created with the WITH RECOMPILE option. If in doubt, you will probably be better served by not creating the procedure with the RECOMPILE option. This is because if you create a procedure with the RECOMPILE option, the procedure is recompiled each time the procedure is executed and you might waste valuable CPU time to perform these compiles. You can still add the WITH RECOMPILE clause to force a recompilation when you execute the procedure. ■

You can't use the WITH RECOMPILE option in a CREATE PROCEDURE statement that contains the FOR REPLICATION option. You use the FOR REPLICATION option to create a procedure that's executed during replication.

▶ For more information about replication, **see** Chapter 17, "Setting Up and Managing Replication," **p. 443**

You can add the ENCRYPTION option to a CREATE PROCEDURE statement to encrypt the definition of the stored procedure that is added to the system table syscomments. You use the ENCRYPTION option to prevent other users from displaying the definition of your procedure and learning what objects it references and what Transact-SQL statements it contains.

> **CAUTION**
>
> Unless you absolutely must encrypt procedures for security reasons, you should leave procedures unencrypted. When you upgrade your database for a version change or to rebuild it, your procedures can only be re-created if the entries in syscomments are not encrypted.

Defining Procedure Auto Execution

You can use the system stored procedure sp_makestartup to define a procedure to execute automatically when SQL Server is started up. You can mark any number of procedures to execute automatically at start up. The syntax sp_makestartup is as follows:

sp_makestartup *procedure_name*

The procedures that are defined to execute automatically at startup execute after the last database has been automatically started and recovered at startup of SQL Server. You can use the system procedure sp_helpstartup to list the procedures that are defined to execute at startup. You use the system procedure sp_unmakestartup to prevent a procedure from executing automatically.

In the following example, a new procedure is created that is marked for automatic execution when SQL Server is started. In addition, the list of startup procedures is also listed before and after the procedure is removed from automatic execution at startup.

```
create procedure test_startup as
print 'test procedure executed at startup'
go
sp_makestartup test_startup
go
Procedure has been marked as 'startup'.
sp_helpstartup
go
Startup stored procedures:
----------------------------
test_startup
```

Part
III

Ch
14

```
(1 row(s) affected)
sp_unmakestartup test_startup
go
Procedure is no longer marked as 'startup'.
sp_helpstartup

Startup stored procedures:
```

Understanding Procedure and Batch Restrictions

Sets of Transact-SQL statements are referred to as batches and include stored procedures. The rules or syntax for the use of Transact-SQL statements in batch apply to the following list of objects:

- Procedures
- Rules
- Defaults
- Triggers
- Views

The syntax is primarily a set of restrictions that limit the types of statements that can be used in batch. Most of the restrictions are on the statements that create objects or change the database or query environment, which don't take effect within the current batch.

For example, although rules and defaults can be defined and bound to a column or user-defined datatype within a batch, the defaults and rules are in effect until after the completion of the batch. You also can't drop an object and reference or re-create it in the same batch.

Some additional SET options that are defined with a batch don't apply to queries contained in the batch. For example, the SET option SET NOCOUNT ON will affect all queries that follow it with a stored procedure and suppress the count line for the execution of SELECT statements. The SET SHOWPLAN ON option does not affect the queries used within a stored procedure, and a query plan isn't displayed for the queries in the procedure.

Understanding the End-of-Batch Signal GO

As you've seen throughout this book, if you use the command line ISQL for the execution of a set of Transact-SQL statements, the GO command is used to specify the end of the set of statements. GO is used on a line by itself. The GO command is required if you interactively use a set of statements or read in statements from an input file to ISQL.

The GO command is not required to execute a set of Transact-SQL statements in the Windows GUI application form of ISQL, ISQL/W. GO is also not required in a series of Transact-SQL statements that are executed within batch objects, such as stored procedures, rules, defaults, triggers, or views. In the following example of an interactive ISQL session, the GO command is used first to cause the execution of the USE command and then to signal the end of the second batch, two SELECT statements.

```
C:>isql/U sa
Password:
1>use employees
2>go
1>select * from Workers
2>select count(*) from Workers
3>go

Name                            Department      Badge
- - - - - - - - - - - - - - - - - - - - - - - - -   - - - - - - - - - - - -   - - - - - - - - - -
Bob Smith                       Sales           1234
Sue Simmons                     Sales           3241
Mary Watkins                    Field Service   6532
Linda Lovely                    Library         7888

(4 row(s) affected)
- - - - - - - - - -


- - - - - - - - - -
4

(1 row(s) affected)
```

In the following example, the GO command is used with the file query1.sql, which contains the following commands:

```
use employees
go
select * from Workers
select max(Rownum) from Rownumber
go
```

The Transact-SQL statements within the file are executed with the invocation of ISQL, which returns the following display:

```
isql /U /i query1.sql /n /P ''
Name                            Department              Badge
- - - - - - - - - - - - - - - - - - - - - - - - - -   - - - - - - - - - - - - - - - - - - - - - -   - - - - - - - - - - - -
Bob Smith                       Sales                   1234
Sue Simmons                     Sales                   3241
Mary Watkins                    Field Service           6532
Linda Lovely                    Library                 7888

(4 rows affected)

- - - - - - - - - - - -
        19

(1 row affected)
```

TIP You can also use /o file-spec to direct the output of the execution of ISQL to a file rather than to your monitor and to capture the output of any statements executed during the ISQL session.

Using Flow-Control Statements

Transact-SQL contains several statements that are used to change the order of execution of statements within a set of statements such as a stored procedure. The use of such flow-control statements permits you to organize statements in stored procedures to provide the capabilities of a conventional programming language, such C or COBOL. You may find that some of the retrieval, update, deletion, addition, and manipulation of rows of database tables can more easily be performed through the use of flow-control statements in objects such as stored procedures.

Using IF...ELSE

You can use the keywords IF and ELSE to control conditional execution within a batch, such as a stored procedure. The IF and ELSE keywords permit you to test a condition and execute either the statements that are part of the IF branch or the statements that are part of the ELSE branch. You define the condition for testing as an expression following the keyword IF. The syntax of an IF...ELSE statement is as follows:

```
IF expression
    statement
[ELSE]
    [IF expression]
    statement]
```

N O T E It's impossible to show examples of the use of conditional statements that can be formed with the keywords IF and ELSE without using other keywords. The examples shown next use the keywords PRINT and EXISTS. In the subsequent examples, the keyword PRINT is used to display a string of characters. ▪

The keyword EXISTS is usually followed by a statement within parentheses when used in an IF statement. The EXISTS statement is evaluated to either True or False, depending upon whether the statement within the parentheses returns one or more rows, or no rows, respectively.

You needn't use an ELSE clause as part of an IF statement. The simplest form of an IF statement is constructed without an ELSE clause. In the following example, a PRINT statement is used to display a confirmation message that a row exists in a database table. If the row doesn't exist in the table, the message No entry is displayed. Unfortunately, the message is also displayed after the verification message is displayed because you're not using the ELSE option.

```
if exists (select * from Workers
where Badge=1234)
    print 'entry available'
print 'No entry'

entry available
No entry
```

In the following example, the row isn't found in the table so only the PRINT statement that follows the IF statement is executed.

```
if exists (select * from Workers
where Badge=1235)
     print 'entry available'
print 'No entry'
```

```
No entry
```

The previous two examples show the problem of using an IF statement that doesn't contain an ELSE clause. In the examples, it's impossible to prevent the message No entry from appearing. You must add an ELSE clause to the IF statement to print the message No entry if a row isn't found and the condition after the IF isn't True.

In the following example, our previous examples are rewritten to use an IF and ELSE clause. If a row that is tested for in the IF clause is in the table, only the message employee present is displayed. If the row isn't found in the table, only the message employee not found is displayed.

```
if exists (select * from employees
where name='Bob Smith')
     print 'employee present'
else print 'employee not found'
```

> **CAUTION**
>
> Unlike some programming languages you might have used, when used alone, the Transact-SQL IF statement can have only one statement associated with it. As a result, there is no need for a keyword, such as END-IF, to define the end of the IF statement. See the next section, "Using BEGIN...END," for information on grouping statements and associating them with an IF...ELSE condition.

Using BEGIN...END

You use the keywords BEGIN and END to designate a set of Transact-SQL statements to be executed as a unit. You use the keyword BEGIN to define the start of a block of Transact-SQL statements. You use the keyword END after the last Transact-SQL statement that is part of the same block of statements. BEGIN...END uses the following syntax:

```
BEGIN
     statements
END
```

You often use BEGIN and END with a conditional statement such as an IF statement. BEGIN and END are used in an IF or ELSE clause to permit multiple Transact-SQL statements to be executed if the expression following the IF or ELSE clause is True. As mentioned earlier, without a BEGIN and END block enclosing multiple statements, only a single Transact-SQL statement can be executed if the expression in the IF or ELSE clause is True.

In the following example, BEGIN and END are used with an IF statement to define the execution of multiple statements if the condition tested is True. The IF statement contains only an IF clause; no ELSE clause is part of the statement.

```
if exists (select * from employees
where badge=1234)
    begin
            print 'entry available'
            select name,department from employees
            where badge=1234
    end
```

```
entry available
name                        department
------------------- -------------------
Bob Smith                   Sales
```

```
(1 row(s) affected)
```

In the second example, an ELSE clause is added to the IF statement to display a message if the row isn't found.

```
if exists (select * from employees
where department='Sales')
    begin
            print 'row(s) found'
            select name, department from employees
            where department='Sales'
    end
else print 'No entry'
```

```
row(s) found
name                        department
------------------- -------------------
Bob Smith                   Sales
Mary Jones                  Sales
```

```
(2 row(s) affected)
```

The third example returns the message that follows the ELSE clause because no row is found.

```
if exists (select * from employees
where department='Nonexistent')
    begin
            print 'row(s) found'
            select name, department from employees
            where department='Nonexistent'
    end
else print 'No entry'
```

```
No entry
```

Using WHILE

You use the keyword WHILE to define a condition that executes one or more Transact-SQL statements when the condition tested evaluates to True. The statement that follows the expression of the WHILE statement continues to execute as long as the condition tested is True. The syntax of the WHILE statement is as follows:

```
WHILE
    <boolean_expression>
    <sql_statement>
```

N O T E As with the IF...ELSE statements, you can only execute a single SQL statement with the
WHILE clause. If you need to include more than one statement in the routine, you'll need
to use the BEGIN...END construct as described earlier. ▪

In the following example, a WHILE statement is used to execute a SELECT statement that displays
a numeric value until the value reaches a limit of five. The example uses a variable that is like a
parameter in that a variable is a named storage location. You define the datatype of a variable
using a DECLARE statement to control the way information is represented in the variable. Like a
parameter, a variable is always referenced preceded by an *at sign* (@).

In the example, the value stored in the variable is initialized to 1 and subsequently
incremented. The statements associated with the WHILE execute until the variable x reaches a
value of 5.

```
declare @x int
select @x=1
while @x<5
begin
print 'x still less than 5'
select @x=@x+1
end
go
(1 row(s) affected)
x still less than 5
(1 row(s) affected)
x still less than 5
(1 row(s) affected)
x still less than 5
(1 row(s) affected)
x still less than 5
(1 row(s) affected)
```

A more meaningful example of the use of a WHILE statement can be shown after two additional
keywords are introduced and explained. An example using WHILE along with the keywords
BREAK and CONTINUE will be shown a little later in this section.

Using BREAK

You use the keyword BREAK within a block of Transact-SQL statements that is within a conditional WHILE statement to end the execution of the statements. The execution of a BREAK results
in the first statement following the end of block to begin executing. The syntax of a BREAK
clause is as follows:

```
WHILE
    <boolean_expression>
    <sql_statement>
BREAK
    <sql_statement>
```

Part
III

Ch
14

In the following example, the BREAK within the WHILE statement causes the statement within the WHILE to terminate. The PRINT statement executes once because the PRINT statement is located before the BREAK. Once the BREAK is encountered, the statements in the WHILE clause aren't executed again.

```
declare @x int
select @x=1
while @x<5
begin
     print 'x still less than 5'
     select @x=@x+1
     break
end

(1 row(s) affected)
x still less than 5
(1 row(s) affected)
```

Using CONTINUE

You use a CONTINUE keyword to form a clause within a conditional statement, such as a WHILE statement, to explicitly continue the set of statements that are contained within the conditional statement. The syntax of the CONTINUE clause is as follows:

```
WHILE
 <boolean_expression>
 <statement>
BREAK
 <statement>
CONTINUE
```

In the following example, a CONTINUE is used within a WHILE statement to explicitly define that execution of the statements within the WHILE statement should continue as long as the condition specified in the expression that follows WHILE is True. The use of CONTINUE in the following example skips the final PRINT statement.

```
declare @x int
select @x=1
while @x<5
begin
     print 'x still less than 5'
     select @x=@x+1
     continue
     print 'this statement will not execute'
end

(1 row(s) affected)
x still less than 5
(1 row(s) affected)
x still less than 5
(1 row(s) affected)
x still less than 5
(1 row(s) affected)
x still less than 5
(1 row(s) affected)
```

Examples of Using WHILE, BREAK, and CONTINUE

Although the two previous examples use BREAK and CONTINUE alone, you don't typically use either CONTINUE or BREAK alone within a WHILE statement. Both BREAK and CONTINUE are often used following an IF or ELSE that is defined within a WHILE statement, so an additional condition can be used to break out of the WHILE loop. If two or more loops are nested, BREAK exits to the next outermost loop.

In the following example, a BREAK is used with an IF statement, both of which are within a WHILE statement. The BREAK is used to terminate the statements associated with the WHILE if the condition specified by the IF statement is True. The IF condition is True if the value of the local variable, @y, is True.

```
declare @x int
declare @y tinyint
select @x=1, @y=1
while @x<5
begin
    print 'x still less than 5'
    select @x=@x+1
    select @y=@y+1
    if @y=2
    begin
        print 'y is 2 so break out of loop'
        break
    end
end
print 'out of while loop'

(1 row(s) affected)
x still less than 5
(1 row(s) affected)
(1 row(s) affected)
y is 2 so break out of loop
out of while loop
```

In the following example, a WHILE statement is used to permit only the rows of a table that match the criteria defined within the expression of the WHILE statement to have their values changed.

```
begin tran
while (select avg(price)from titles) < $30
begin
    select title_id, price
    from titles
    where price >$20
    update titles set price=price * 2
end

(0 row(s) affected)
```

```
title_id price
-------- ------------------------
PC1035   22.95
PS1372   21.59
TC3218   20.95

(3 row(s) affected)
(18 row(s) affected)
(0 row(s) affected)

title_id price
-------- ------------------------
BU1032   39.98
BU1111   23.90
BU7832   39.98
MC2222   39.98
PC1035   45.90
PC8888   40.00
PS1372   43.18
PS2091   21.90
PS3333   39.98
TC3218   41.90
TC4203   23.90
TC7777   29.98

(12 row(s) affected)
(18 row(s) affected)
(0 row(s) affected)
```

You must be careful in defining the WHILE statement and its associated statements. As shown in the following example, if the condition specified with the WHILE expression continues to be True, the WHILE loop will execute indefinitely.

```
while exists (select hours_worked from pays)
print 'hours worked is less than 55'

(0 row(s) affected)
hours worked is less than 55
(0 row(s) affected)
...
```

If the evaluation of the expression following the WHILE returns multiple values, you should use an EXISTS rather than any comparison operators. In the following example, the error message that is returned is descriptive of the problem.

```
while (select hours_worked from pays) > 55
print 'hours worked is less than 55'

Msg 512, Level 16, State 1
Subquery returned more than 1 value.  This is illegal when the
➥subquery follows =, !=, <, <= , >, >=, or
➥ when the subquery is used as an expression.
Command has been aborted.
```

In this case, you'll want to use EXISTS to determine the comparison value.

Defining and Using Variables

You may recall that earlier in this chapter variables were described as similar to parameters in that they are named storage locations. Variables in Transact-SQL can be either local or global. You define local variables by using a DECLARE statement and assigning the variable a datatype. You assign an initial value to local variables with a SELECT statement.

You must declare, assign a value, and use a local variable within the same batch or stored procedure. The variable is only available for use within the same batch or procedure, hence the name *local* variable.

You can use local variables in batch or stored procedures for such things as counters and temporary holding locations for other variables. Recall that local variables are always referenced with an @ preceding their names. You can define the datatype of a local variable as a user-defined datatype as well as a system datatype. One restriction that applies to local variables is that you can't define a local variable as a TEXT or IMAGE datatype.

The syntax of a local variable is as follows:

```
DECLARE @variable_name datatype [,variable_name datatype...]
```

The SELECT statement is used to assign values to local variables, as shown in the following syntax:

```
SELECT @variable_name = expression |select statement
[,@variable_name = expression select statement]
[FROM list of tables] [WHERE expression]
[GROUP BY...]
[HAVING ...]
[ORDER BY...]
```

If the SELECT statement returns more than a single value, the variable is assigned to the last value returned. In the following example, two local variables are defined and used to return the number of rows in the table. The CONVERT function must be used to convert the numeric format of the number of rows to a text datatype for the PRINT statement. The message that is displayed by the PRINT statement is first built and assigned to a local variable because the concatenation can't be done within the PRINT statement.

```
declare @mynum int
select @mynum = count(*)from Workers
declare @mychar char(2)
select @mychar = convert(char(2),@mynum)
declare @mess char(40)
select @mess ='There are ' + @mychar + 'rows in the table Workers'
print @mess

(1 row(s) affected)

(4 row(s) affected)

(1 row(s) affected)

There are 4 rows in the table Workers
```

Part
III

Ch
14

Each SELECT statement in the previous example returns a count message. If you want the count message suppressed, you must first execute the SET NOCOUNT statement. In the following example, the same statements that were executed in the previous example are re-executed with the count turned off.

```
declare @mynum int
select @mynum = count(*)from Workers
declare @mychar char(2)
select @mychar = convert(char(2),@mynum)
declare @mess char(40)
select @mess ='There are ' + @mychar + 'rows in the table Workers'
print @mess

There are 4 rows in the table Workers
```

Using PRINT with Variables

You'll recall that in examples shown earlier in this chapter, PRINT was used to display a message to the assigned output device. You use the keyword PRINT to display ASCII text or variables up to 8,000 characters in length. You can't use PRINT to output other than CHAR, nCHAR, VARCHAR, or nVARCHAR datatypes or the global variable @@VERSION.

Recall that you can't concatenate string data in a PRINT statement directly. You must concatenate text or variables into a single variable and output the results with the PRINT statement. The syntax of the PRINT statement is as follows:

```
PRINT 'text' ¦@local_variable ¦ @@global_variable
```

Using Global Variables

Though your stored procedure parameters are limited in scope to the procedure in which they are defined, SQL Server has several intrinsic global variables. These variables, defined and maintained by the system, are available at any time within your stored procedures. Keep the following guidelines in mind when you work with global variables:

- Global variables are not defined by your routines; they are defined at the server level.
- You can only use the pre-declared and defined global variables.
- You always reference a global variable by preceding it with two at signs (@@).
- You shouldn't define local variables with the same name as system variables as you may receive unexpected results in your application.

You reference a global variable to access server information or information about your operations. Table 14.1 lists the names of all Microsoft SQL Server global variables and a brief description of the information that's contained within them.

Table 14.1 Global Variables for Microsoft SQL Server

Global Variable	Description
@@CONNECTIONS	total logons or attempted logins
@@CPU_BUSY	cumulative CPU server time in ticks
@@CURSOR ROWS	as of the last time the cursor was opened, the number of rows associated with the cursor
@@DATEFIRST	indicates the first day of the week — Sunday, Monday, and so on
@@DBTS	value of unique timestamp for database
@@ERROR	last system error number, 0 if successful
@@FETCH_STATUS	status of the last FETCH statement
@@IDENTITY	the last inserted identity value
@@IDLE	cumulative CPU server idle time
@@IO_BU3Y	cumulative server I/O time
@@LANGID	current language ID
@@LANGUAGE	current language name
@@LOCK_TIMEOUT	the milliseconds setting that controls timeouts for locking operations
@@MAX_CONNECTIONS	maximum number of simultaneous connections
@@MAX_PRECISION	precision level for decimal and numeric datatypes
@@MICROSOFTVERSION	internal version number of SQL Server
@@NESTLEVEL	current nested level of calling routines from 0 to 16
@@OPTIONS	returns settings of the current SET options
@@PACK_RECEIVED	number of input packets read
@@PACK_SENT	number of output packets written
@@PACKET_ERRORS	number of read and write packet errors
@@PROCID	current stored procedure ID
@@REMSERVER	name of the remote server
@@ROWCOUNT	number of rows affected by last query
@@SERVERNAME	name of local server
@@SERVICENAME	name of the running service

Part
III

Ch
14

continues

Table 14.1 Continued	
Global Variable	**Description**
@@SPID	current process server ID
@@TEXTSIZE	current of max text or image data with default of 4K
@@TIMETICKS	number of microseconds per tick—machine independent; one tick is 31.25 milliseconds or 1/32 of one second
@@TOTAL_ERRORS	number of errors during reads or writes
@@TOTAL_READ	number of disk reads (not cache)
@@TOTAL_WRITE	number of disk writes
@@TRANCOUNT	current user total active transactions
@@VERSION	date and version of SQL Server

In the following example, a global variable is used to retrieve the version of SQL Server, which is concatenated with a string literal and the contents of a second global variable.

```
PRINT @@VERSION
declare @mess1 char(21)
select @mess1 = 'Server name is ' + @@servername
PRINT @mess1

SQL Server for Windows NT 4.20 (Intel X86)
    Aug 24 1993 00:00:00

(1 row(s) affected)

Server name is BOB486
```

Using Additional Procedure and Batch Keywords

Several additional keywords can be used within stored procedures or batches of Transact-SQL commands. These additional keywords don't fall into a single descriptive category of similar function. Some of these keywords are GOTO, RETURN, RAISERROR, WAITFOR, and CASE.

Using GOTO

You use a GOTO to perform a transfer from a statement to another statement that contains a user-defined label. A GOTO statement used alone is unconditional. The statement that contains the destination label name follows rules for identifiers and is followed by a colon (:).

You only use the label name without the colon on the GOTO line. The syntax of the GOTO statement is as follows:

label:

GOTO *label*

The following example shows the use of the GOTO statement that is used to transfer control to a statement that displays the word yes until the value of a variable reaches a specified value. The COUNT was turned off prior to execution of the statements in the example.

```
declare @count smallint
select @count =1
restart:
print 'yes'
select @count =@count + 1
while @count <= 4
goto restart

yes
yes
yes
yes
```

Using RETURN

You use the RETURN statement to formally exit from a query or procedure and optionally provide a value to the calling routine. A RETURN is often used when one procedure is executed from within another. The RETURN statement, when used alone, is unconditional, though you can use the RETURN within a conditional IF or WHILE statement. The syntax of the RETURN statement is as follows:

RETURN [*integer*]

You can use a RETURN statement at any point in a batch or procedure. Any statements that follow the RETURN are not executed. A RETURN is similar to a BREAK with one difference. A RETURN, unlike a BREAK, can be used to return an integer value to the procedure that invoked the procedure that contains the RETURN. Execution of statements continues at the statement following the statement that executed the procedure originally.

To understand the use of the RETURN statement, you must first understand the action performed by SQL Server when a procedure completes execution. SQL Server always makes an integer value available when a procedure ends. A value of 0 indicates that the procedure executed successfully. Negative values from -1 to -99 indicate reasons for the failure of statements within the procedure. These integer values are always returned at the termination of a procedure even if a RETURN statement isn't present in a procedure.

You can optionally use an integer value that follows the RETURN statement to replace the SQL Server value with your own user-defined value. You should use non-zero integer values so that your return status values don't conflict with the SQL Server status values. If no user-defined

Part
III

Ch
14

return value is provided, the SQL Server value is used. If more than one error occurs, the status with the highest absolute value is returned. You can't return a NULL value with a RETURN statement. Table 14.2 shows several of the return status values that are reserved by SQL Server.

Table 14.2   Selected Microsoft SQL Server Status Values

Return Value	Meaning
0	successful execution
-1	missing object
-2	datatype error
-3	process was chosen as a deadlock victim
-4	permission error
-5	syntax error
-6	miscellaneous user error
-7	resource error, such as out of space
-8	nonfatal internal problem
-9	system limit was reached
-10	fatal internal inconsistency
-11	fatal internal inconsistency
-12	table or index is corrupt
-13	database is corrupt
-14	hardware error

You must provide a local variable that receives the returned status in the EXECUTE statement that invokes the procedure that returns status. The syntax to specify a local variable for the returned status value is the following:

```
EXEC[ute] @return_status=procedure_name
```

The following example shows a return value from a called procedure that executes successfully and returns zero (0). The example shows the definition of the called procedure proc1. This stored procedure is executed from a set of Transact-SQL statements entered interactively.

> **N O T E**   When a set of Transact-SQL statements executes together, whether the statements are part of a procedure or not, the rules for batch operations apply. This is true even if the set of statements is typed in interactively. ■

N O T E A procedure that is invoked within another procedure with an EXECUTE statement is most often referred to as a *called procedure*. "Called" refers to an equivalent operation used in some programming languages. The keyword used in these languages to invoke the equivalent of a section of code from a program is CALL. This is the same as running a subroutine or function in these other languages. ■

Although the called procedure doesn't contain a RETURN statement, SQL Server returns an integer status value to the procedure that called proc1.

```
create procedure proc1 as
select * from employees

declare @status int
execute @status = proc1
select status = @status
```

```
name                    department            badge
-------------------     -------------------   ----------
Bob Smith               Sales                 1234
Mary Jones              Sales                 5514

(2 row(s) affected)

status
----------
0

(1 row(s) affected)
```

In the following example, proc2 is identical to the procedure proc1 that was used in the previous example except that proc2 contains a RETURN statement with a user-defined positive integer value. A SELECT statement is used to display the returned status value from proc2 to confirm that the specified value in the RETURN statement in proc2 is returned to the next statement after the statement that executed proc2.

```
create procedure proc2 as
select * from employees
return 5

declare @status int
execute @status = proc2
select status = @status
```

```
name                    department            badge
-------------------     -------------------   ----------
Bob Smith               Sales                 1234
Mary Jones              Sales                 5514

(1 row(s) affected)

status
----------
5

(1 row(s) affected)
```

Part

III

Ch

14

In the following example, the returned value is checked as part of a conditional statement and a message is displayed if the procedure executed successfully. This third example of Transact-SQL RETURN statements is more typical of the usage of return status in a production environment.

```
declare @status int
execute @status = proc1
if (@status = 0)
begin
    print ''
    print 'proc1 executed successfully'
end
```

name	department	badge
Bob Smith	Sales	1234
Mary Jones	Sales	5514

proc2 executed successfully

TIP You can nest procedures within other procedures up to 32 levels in Transact-SQL.

Using RAISERROR

You use the RAISERROR statement to return a user-specified message in the same form that SQL Server returns errors. RAISERROR also sets a system flag to record that an error has occurred. The syntax of the RAISERROR statement is as follows:

```
RAISERROR (<integer_expression>¦<'text of message'>, [severity]
➥ [, state[, argument1] [, argument2] )
[WITH LOG]
```

The *integer_expression* is a user-specified error or message number and must be in the range 50,000 to 2,147,483,647. The *integer_expression* is placed in the global variable, @@ERROR, which stores the last error number returned. An error message can be specified as a string literal or through a local variable. The text of the message can be up to 255 characters and is used to specify a user-specified error message. A local variable that contains an error message can be used in place of the text of the message. RAISERROR always sets a default severity level of 16 for the returned error message.

In the following example, a local variable is defined as a character datatype that is large enough to receive the error number specified in the RAISERROR statement after the error number is converted from the global variable, @@ERROR. The RAISERROR statement first displays the message level, state number, and the error message, Guru meditation error. The error number 99999 is then displayed separately using a PRINT statement.

```
declare @err char(5)
raiserror 99999 'Guru meditation error'
select @err=convert(char(5),@@ERROR)
print @err
```

```
go
Msg 99999, Level 16, State 1
Guru meditation error
```

```
(1 row(s) affected)
```

```
99999
```

You can also add your message text and an associated message number to the system table sysmessages. You use the system stored procedure sp_addmessage to add a message with a message identification number within the range 50,001 to 2,147,483,647. The syntax of the sp_addmessage system procedure is as follows:

```
sp_addmessage message_id, severity, ëmessage text'
➥ [, language [, {true ¦ false} [, REPLACE]]]
```

> **CAUTION**
>
> If you enter a user-specified error number that has not been added to the sysmessages table and do not explicitly specify the message text, you'll receive an error that the message can't be located in the system table as shown in the following example:

```
raiserror (99999,7,2)
go
Msg 2758, Level 16, State 1
RAISERROR could not locate entry for error 99999 in Sysmessages.
```

User-defined error messages that are generated with a RAISERROR statement without a number in the sysmessages table return a message identification number of 50,000.

The severity level is used to indicate the degree or extent of the error condition encountered. Although severity levels can be assigned in the range of 1 through 25, you should usually assign your system message a severity level value from 11–16.

Severity levels of 11–16 are designed to be assigned through the sp_addmessages statement and you can't assign a severity level of from 19–25 unless you're logged in as the administrator. Severity levels 17–19 are more severe software or hardware errors, which may not permit your subsequent statements to execute correctly.

Severity levels of 20–25 are severe errors and won't permit subsequent Transact-SQL statements to execute. System messages that have severity levels over 19 can be such problems as connection problems between a client system and the database server system or corrupted data in the database.

> **N O T E** Microsoft suggests that severe errors—those that have a severity level of nineteen or higher—should also notify the database administrator. The database administrator needs to know of these problems because such problems are likely to impact many different users and should be attended to as soon as possible. ■

Part
III

Ch
14

When specifying messages, you enter an error message within single quotes of up to 255 characters. The remaining parameters of the sp_addmessage procedure are optional. The *language* parameter specifies one of the languages SQL Server was installed with. U.S. English is the default language if the parameter is omitted.

The next parameter, either True or False, controls whether the system message is automatically written to the Windows NT application event log. Use True to have the system message written to the event log. In addition, True results in the message being written to the SQL Server error log file.

The last parameter, REPLACE, is used to specify that you want to replace an existing user-defined message in the sysmessages table with a new entry.

The following example shows the use of the sp_addmessage system stored procedure that adds a system message with an associated identification number and severity. A subsequent SELECT statement retrieves the message from the system table sysmessages. Finally, the RAISERROR statement is used to return the user-defined system message.

```
sp_addmessage 99999,13,'Guru meditation error'
go
select * from sysmessages where error=99999
go
raiserror (99999, 13,-1)
go
New message added.
error       severity dlevel description          languid
----------- -------- ------ -------------------- -------
99999       13       0      Guru meditation error    0

(1 row(s) affected)

Msg 99999, Level 13, State 1
Guru meditation error
```

You can use the system stored procedure, sp_dropmessage, to remove a user-defined message from the system table sysmessages when it is no longer needed. The syntax of the sp_dropmessage is as follows:

```
sp_dropmessage [message_id [, language | 'all']]
```

You're only required to enter the message number to drop the message. The two additional optional parameters permit you to specify the language from which the message should be dropped. You can use the keyword all to drop the user-defined message from all languages.

In the following example, a user-defined message in the default language of U.S. English is removed from the system table, sysmessages.

```
sp_dropmessage 99999
go
Message dropped.
```

Using WAITFOR

You use a WAITFOR statement to specify a time, a time interval, or an event for executing a statement, statement block, stored procedure, or transaction. The syntax of the WAITFOR statement is as follows:

```
WAITFOR {DELAY <'time'> ¦ TIME <'time'> ¦ ERROREXIT ¦ PROCESSEXIT ¦ MIRROREXIT}
```

The meaning of each of the keywords that follows the WAITFOR keyword is shown in the following list:

- DELAY—Specifies an interval or time to elapse
- TIME—A specified time, no date portion, of up to 24 hours
- ERROREXIT—Until a process terminates abnormally
- PROCESSEXIT—Until a process terminates normally or abnormally
- MIRROREXIT—Until a mirrored device fails

In the following example of a WAITFOR statement, a DELAY is used to specify that a pause of 40 seconds is taken before the subsequent SELECT statement is executed.

```
waitfor delay '00:00:40'
select * from employees
```

In the second WAITFOR example, a TIME is used to wait until 3:10:51 PM of the current day until the subsequent SELECT statement is executed.

```
waitfor time '15:10:51'
select * from employees
```

Using CASE Expressions

You can use a CASE expression to make an execution decision based on multiple options. Using the CASE construct, you can create a table that will be used to look up the results you are testing and apply them to determine what course of action should be taken. The syntax of the CASE expression is as follows:

```
CASE [expression]
WHEN simple expression1¦Boolean expression1 THEN expression1
[[WHEN simple expression2¦Boolean expression2 THEN expression2] [...]]
    [ELSE expressionN]
END
```

If you use a comparison operator in an expression directly after the CASE keyword, the CASE expression is called a *searched expression* rather than a *simple* CASE expression. You can also use a Boolean operator in a searched CASE expression.

In a simple CASE expression, the expression directly after the CASE keyword always exactly matches a value after the WHEN keyword. In the following example, a CASE expression is used to substitute alternative values for the column Department in the table Company. In the following example, a CASE expression is used to return a corresponding set of alternative values for three department values of the table Company.

```
select name,division=
case department
     when "Sales" then "Sales & Marketing"
     when "Field Service" then "Support Group"
     when "Logistics" then "Parts"
     else "Other department"
end,
badge
from company
go
name                     division         badge
-------------------      ----------------  ----------
Fred Sanders             Sales & Marketing 1051
Bob Smith                Sales & Marketing 1834
Mark McGuire             Support Group     1997
Stan Humphries           Support Group     3211
Sue Sommers              Parts             4411
Lance Finepoint          Other department  5522
Fred Stanhope            Support Group     6732
Ludmilla Valencia        Other department  7773
Jim Walker               Other department  7779
Jeffrey Vickers          Other department  8005
Barbara Lint             Support Group     8883
Sally Springer           Sales & Marketing 9998

(12 row(s) affected)
```

If you don't use an ELSE as part of the CASE expression, a NULL is returned for each non-matching entry, as shown in the following example.

```
select name,division=
case department
when "Sales" then "Sales & Marketing"
when "Field Service" then "Support Group"
when "Logistics" then "Parts"
end,
badge
from company
go
name                     division         badge
-------------------      ----------------  ----------
Fred Sanders             Sales & Marketing 1051
Bob Smith                Sales & Marketing 1834
Mark McGuire             Support Group     1997
Stan Humphries           Support Group     3211
Sue Sommers              Parts             4411
Lance Finepoint          (null)            5522
Fred Stanhope            Support Group     6732
Ludmilla Valencia        (null)            7773
Jim Walker               (null)            7779
Jeffrey Vickers          (null)            8005
Barbara Lint             Support Group     8883
Sally Springer           Sales & Marketing 9998

(12 row(s) affected)
```

You will recall that a searched CASE expression can include comparison operators and the use of AND as well as OR between each Boolean expression to permit an alternative value to be returned for multiple values of the column of a table. Unlike a simple CASE expression, each WHEN clause is not restricted to exact matches of the values contained in the table column.

In the following example, comparison values are used in each WHEN clause to specify a range of values that are substituted by a single alternative value.

```
select "Hours Worked" =
case
when hours_worked < 40 then "Worked Insufficient Hours"
when hours_worked = 40 then "Worked Sufficient Hours"
when hours_worked > 60 then "Overworked"
else "Outside Range of Permissible Work"
end
from pays
go
Hours Worked
--------------------------------
Worked Sufficient Hours
Worked Sufficient Hours
Overworked
Worked Insufficient Hours
Overworked
Worked Sufficient Hours
Overworked
Worked Sufficient Hours
Outside Range of Permissible Work
Worked Insufficient Hours
Worked Sufficient Hours
Worked Sufficient Hours

(12 row(s) affected)
```

N O T E When a CASE construct is executed, only the first matching solution is executed.

> **CAUTION**
>
> You must use compatible datatypes for the replacement expression of the THEN clause. If the replacement expression of a THEN clause is a datatype that is incompatible with the original expression, an error is returned.
>
> For example, a combination of original and replacement datatypes is compatible if one is a variable length character datatype (varchar) with a maximum length equal to the length of a fixed length character datatype (char). In addition, if the two datatypes in the WHEN and THEN clauses are integer and decimal, the resultant datatype returned will be decimal in order to accommodate the whole and fractional portion of the numeric value.

Part
III

Ch
14

You can also use both the COALESCE and NULLIF functions in a CASE expression. You use the COALESCE function to return a replacement value for any NULL or NOT NULL values that are present in, for example, the column of a database table. The syntax of one form of the COALESCE function is as follows:

```
COALESCE (expression1, expression2)
```

In the following example, the COALESCE function is used to display either the product of hours_worked times rate or a zero if the columns hours_worked and rate are NULL.

```
select badge, "Weekly Pay in Dollars"=coalesce(hours_worked*rate,0)
from pays2
go
badge      Weekly Pay in Dollars
---------- --------------------
3211           400
6732           360
4411           520
5522           429
1997           510
9998           320
7773           550
8883           360
8005           420
7779           407
1834           400
1051           360
3467           0
3555           0
7774           0

(15 row(s) affected)
```

N O T E A COALESCE function is equivalent to a searched CASE expression in which a NOT NULL *expression1* returns *expression1* and a NULL *expression1* returns *expression2*. An equivalent CASE expression to a COALESCE function is as follows:

```
CASE
     WHEN expression1 IS NOT NULL THEN expression1
     ELSE expression2
END
```

You can use a COALESCE function as part of a SELECT statement simply as an alternative way of returning an identical display or because you find the COALESCE function simpler to use. ▨

You can also use a NULLIF function with or in place of a CASE expression. The NULLIF function uses the following syntax:

```
NULLIF (expression1, expression2)
```

In the following example, a simple SELECT statement is first used to display the table without using a NULLIF function to show all column values for all rows. A second SELECT statement is used to operate on the columns badge and old_badge.

```
select * from company2
go
name                    department            badge       old_badge
------------------      ------------------    ----------  ----------
Mark McGuire            Field Service         1997        (null)
Stan Humphries          Field Service         3211        (null)
Sue Sommers             Logistics             4411        (null)
Fred Stanhope           Field Service         6732        (null)
Ludmilla Valencia       Software              7773        (null)
Jim Walker              Unit Manager          7779        (null)
Jeffrey Vickers         Mailroom              8005        (null)
Fred Sanders            SALES                 1051        1051
Bob Smith               SALES                 1834        1834
Sally Springer          Sales                 9998        9998
Barbara Lint            Field Service         8883        12
Lance Finepoint         Library               5522        13

(12 row(s) affected)

select name,nullif(old_badge,badge)
from company2
go
name
------------------      ----------
Mark McGuire            (null)
Stan Humphries          (null)
Sue Sommers             (null)
Fred Stanhope           (null)
Ludmilla Valencia       (null)
Jim Walker              (null)
Jeffrey Vickers         (null)
Fred Sanders            (null)
Bob Smith               (null)
Sally Springer          (null)
Barbara Lint            12
Lance Finepoint         13

(12 row(s) affected)
```

The example only returns non-NULL values for rows that contain old_badge values that are different than new column values. In addition, a NULL is returned if no old column values were present. You can combine the use of the NULLIF and COALESCE functions to display the returned information in a more organized way.

The following example combines a COALESCE and NULLIF function to return an old badge number only if it was different than the current badge number or if it was defined. If not, a new badge number is displayed.

```
select name,badge=coalesce(nullif(old_badge,badge),badge)
from company2
go
name                    badge
------------------      ----------
Mark McGuire            1997
Stan Humphries          3211
```

```
Sue Sommers          4411
Fred Stanhope        6732
Ludmilla Valencia    7773
Jim Walker           7779
Jeffrey Vickers      8005
Fred Sanders         1051
Bob Smith            1834
Sally Springer       9998
Barbara Lint         12
Lance Finepoint      13

(12 row(s) affected)
```

Reality Check

Stored procedures are nearly always the backbone of your system. You'll find that they make a good scaling point to move functionality from the client to the server. In cases in which you find that you're repeating a SQL Server access over and over, consider moving it to a stored procedure and calling it from the application.

Perhaps one of the biggest benefits to a software development house in using stored procedures is the division of work between the development of the client application and the development of the server-side components. This was especially true in one case in which an application was developed for an insurance company. Both the user interface and the database management were challenging in how they needed to perform.

By breaking development between the database and the client-side UI, it was possible to bring the project in on time, but still maintain experts in the development of the respective sides. For example, the only thing that the UI development team knew about the database was the set of calls it needed to make (stored procedures) to get access to the information it needed. The team didn't worry about the complicated search algorithms, the database management, nor did it have to worry about the rules implementations that were necessary behind the scenes.

On the other hand, the only thing the database team had to know about the user interaction with the application was the required response time and what the incoming information would look like. It didn't need to worry about what the dialog boxes looked like, how the user set up the application, and so on.

If you think about it, you're breaking the development cycle into components as you do your application: client and server. You should use client-development experts for the tasks at which they are best — designing the interface, developing reports, and.working with the users. Use the server-side developers for tasks they are best at, such as developing a solid database plan, implementing the server-side enforced rules, and so on. It provides you with real leverage on the personnel and project development cycles.

From Here...

In this chapter, you've seen how you can use Transact-SQL to control the flow of your SQL Server–based application. Remembering to use these techniques to manipulate information on the server can significantly improve performance for your application.

Here are some other areas of interest relating to the materials covered here:

- Chapter 5, "Creating Databases and Transaction Logs," teaches you how to create and use user-defined datatypes.
- Chapter 13, "Managing and Using Rules, Constraints, and Defaults," teaches you how to create and use rules and defaults.
- Chapter 15, "Creating and Managing Triggers," teaches you how to use triggers to maintain referential integrity in the database.
- Chapter 21, "Optimizing Performance," teaches you ways to optimize the operation of SQL Server, including the correct sizing of the procedure cache.

Part
III

Ch
14

Creating and Managing Triggers

Triggers are methods that SQL Server provides to the application programmer and database analyst to ensure data integrity. Triggers are very useful for those databases that will be accessed from a multitude of different applications because they enable business rules to be enforced by the database instead of relying on the application software.

Understanding SQL Server Triggers

The ability of SQL Server to effectively manage your information stems from its ability to help you control the data in your system as it flows through the tables and application logic you build into your application. You have seen how stored procedures let you execute logic on the server and how you can implement rules and defaults to further help manage the information in the database.

SQL Server considers rules and defaults *before* information is written to the database. They are a sort of "pre-filter" for information and can prevent the action against the data item based on their role in controlling the database activity.

Triggers are "post-filters" and are executed after the data update has passed all considerations with rules, defaults, and so on.

A trigger is a special type of stored procedure that is executed by the SQL Server when an insert, modify, or delete operation is performed against a given table. Because triggers are run after the operation would take effect, they represent a sort of final word on the modification. If the trigger fails the request, the information update is refused and an error message is returned to the application attempting the transaction.

The most common use of a trigger is to enforce business rules in the database. Triggers are used when the standard constraints or table-based declarative referential integrities (DRI) are not adequate.

N O T E Because triggers are run after rules and other referential integrity checks, if an operation fails these other checks, the trigger will not be run. An operation must not have otherwise failed in order for the conditions or operations of a trigger to be considered or executed. ▪

Triggers have a very low impact on performance to the server and are often used to enhance applications that have to do a lot of cascading operations on other tables and rows.

▶ **See** Chapter 11, "Managing and Using Indexes and Keys," **p. 287**, and Chapter 13, "Managing and Using Rules, Constraints and Defaults," **p. 333**, for more information about DRI.

As of SQL Server 6, Microsoft added ANSI-compliant DRI statements that can be used in the CREATE TABLE statement. The sorts of rules that can be enforced by them are relatively complex. It can make the understanding of the table creation quite difficult.

Besides the inability to perform complex business rule analysis based on values that are supplied when a trigger is executed, DRI has one important limitation. The current implementation does not permit referencing values in other databases. Although this might seem a relatively insignificant problem, it has a substantial impact on those people trying to write distributed applications that might need to check data constraints and values on other databases and servers.

Creating Triggers

When you create a trigger, you must be the owner of the database. Although this might seem odd at first, if you consider what's happening, it really makes a lot of sense. When you add a trigger to a column, row, or table, you're changing how the table can be accessed, how other objects can relate to it, and so on. This means that in actuality you're changing the database schema. Of course this type of operation is reserved for the database owner, protecting against someone inadvertently modifying the layout of your system.

Creating a trigger is much like declaring a stored procedure and it has a similar syntax.

```
CREATE TRIGGER [owner.]trigger_name
ON [owner.]table_name
FOR {INSERT, UPDATE, DELETE}
[WITH ENCRYPTION]
AS sql_statements
```

The options for the Transact-SQL command CREATE TRIGGER are as follows:

- *trigger_name*—The name of the trigger must conform to standard SQL Server naming conventions.

- INSERT, UPDATE, DELETE—With these keywords, the trigger's scope is defined. This determines which actions will initiate the trigger.

- WITH ENCRYPTION—This option is provided for developers to prevent users in their environment from being able to read the text of the trigger after it has been loaded onto the server. This is very convenient for third-party application developers who embed SQL Server into their products and do not want their customers to be able to disassemble the code and modify it.

   SQL Server stores the text of a trigger in the system catalog table syscomments. Use the WITH ENCRYPTION option with care because if the original trigger text is lost, it will not be possible to restore the encrypted text from syscomments.

CAUTION

SQL Server uses the unencrypted text of a trigger stored in syscomments when a database is upgraded to a newer version. If the text is encrypted, it will not be possible for the trigger to be updated and restored into the new database. Make sure that the original text is available to upgrade the database when necessary.

N O T E To provide a good level of recovery for your applications, you should always maintain an offline copy of your stored procedures, triggers, table definitions, and overall structure of the server side of your SQL Server application. This information can be used to reload the server in case of any problems. ■

■ *sql_statements*—A trigger can contain any number of SQL statements in Transact-SQL, provided they are enclosed in valid BEGIN and END delimiters. Limitations on the SQL permitted in a trigger are described in the next section.

> **N O T E** When a trigger is executed, SQL Server creates a special table into which the data that caused the trigger to execute is placed. The table is either INSERTED for INSERT and UPDATE operations or DELETED for DELETE and UPDATE operations. Because triggers execute after an operation, the rows in the INSERTED table are always a duplicate of one or more records in the trigger's base table. Make sure that a correct join identifies all the characteristics of the record being affected in the trigger table so that the trigger does not accidentally modify data itself. The following examples show how to construct a trigger. ■

Examining Limitations of Triggers

SQL Server has some limitations on the types of SQL statements that can be executed while performing the actions of a trigger. The majority of these limitations are because the SQL cannot be rolled back, which may need to occur if the UPDATE, INSERT, or DELETE that caused the trigger to execute in the first place is also rolled back.

> **N O T E** Prior to version 7.0 of MS SQL Server, if a trigger modified a table on which it was defined, the trigger would not be invoked recursively for that modification. In version 7.0, you can use sp_dboption to set the recursive trigger option to True for a database, in which case the trigger will be recursive. You can also set this option on the Property pages for the database.
>
> Also as of SQL 7.0, you can have more than one trigger defined for a given operation. In other words, you can have more than one trigger that is fired for the INSERT operation, more than one for DELETE, and so on. ■

The following is a list of Transact-SQL statements that are not permitted to be in the body text of a trigger. SQL Server will reject the compilation and storage of a trigger with these statements:

■ All database and object creation statements: CREATE DATABASE, TABLE, INDEX, PROCEDURE, DEFAULT, RULE, TRIGGER, and VIEW

■ All DROP statements

■ Database object modification statements: ALTER TABLE and ALTER DATABASE

■ TRUNCATE TABLE

> **N O T E** DELETE triggers will not be executed when a TRUNCATE operation is initiated on a table. Because the TRUNCATE operation is not logged, there is no chance for the trigger to be run. Permission to perform a TRUNCATE is limited to the table owner and sa and it cannot be transferred. ■

■ Object permissions: GRANT and REVOKE

■ UPDATE STATISTICS

- RECONFIGURE
- Database load operations: LOAD DATABASE and LOAD TRANSACTION
- All physical disk modification statements: DISK...
- Temporary table creation: either implicit through CREATE TABLE or explicit through SELECT INTO

Additionally, the following are limitations that should be clearly understood:

- A trigger may not be created on a view, but only on the base table or tables that the view was created on.
- Any SET operations that change the environment, while valid, are only in effect for the life of the trigger. All values return to their previous states once the trigger has finished execution.
- Manipulating binary large object (BLOB) columns of datatype TEXT or IMAGE, whether logged or not by the database, will not cause a trigger to be executed.
- SELECT operations that return result sets from a trigger are not advised because of the very special handling of result sets that is required by the client application code, whether in a stored procedure or not. Make sure that all SELECT operations read their values into locally defined variables available in the trigger.

Using Triggers

In this section you will see several types of triggers being created for use. These examples aren't very sophisticated but should give you ideas on how you might implement triggers in your own environment.

Triggers are fired or executed whenever a particular event occurs. In the following sections you will see the different events that can cause a trigger to be executed and get some idea of what you might want to do on those events.

Using INSERT and UPDATE Triggers

INSERT and UPDATE triggers are particularly useful because they can enforce referential integrity constraints and make sure that your data is valid before it enters the table. Typically INSERT and UPDATE triggers are used to verify that the data on the columns being monitored by the trigger meets the criteria required or to update timestamp columns. Triggers are used when the criteria for verification are more complex than what can be represented in a declarative referential integrity constraint.

In Listing 15.1, the trigger is executed whenever a record is inserted into the Sales table or when it is modified. If the order date is not during the first 15 days of the month, the record is rejected.

Listing 15.1 15_01.SQL—Sales Trigger Disallowing Specified Records

```
Create Trigger Tri_Ins_Sales
On     SALES
For    INSERT, UPDATE
As
/* declare local variables needed */
Declare    @nDayOfMonth      tinyint
/* Find the information about the record inserted */
Select     @nDayOfMonth = DatePart( Day, I.ORD_DATE )
From   SALES S, INSERTED I
Where  S.STOR_ID = I.STOR_ID
And    S.ORD_NUM = I.ORD_NUM
And    S.TITLE_ID = I.TITLE_ID
/* Now test rejection criteria and return an error if necessary */
If @nDayOfMonth > 15
Begin
       /* Note: always Rollback first, you can never be sure what
       kind of error processing a client may do that may force locks
       to be held for unnecessary amounts of time */
       ROLLBACK TRAN
       RAISERROR ( 'Orders must be placed before the 15th of
                     the month', 16, 10 )
End
Go
```

N O T E Notice the way the INSERTED table is referred to in the previous join. This logical table is created specially by SQL Server to allow you to reference information in the record being modified. Using an alias, I, as shown makes it easy to reference the table in the join criteria specified in the Where clause. ▪

You will notice in the code segment that a new table is referenced, one not included in the database if you simply review the list of tables present. In this case, the INSERTED table contains a copy of every row that would be added if the transaction were allowed to complete. You use the values of the INSERTED table to feed the information to any comparisons you want to make to validate the transaction.

The columns in the INSERTED table will exactly match those in the table you're working with. You can perform comparisons on them, as in the example, in which they're compared against the Sales database to verify that the sales date is valid.

You can also create triggers that are able to do their work only if a given column is updated. The If Update statement can be used in your trigger to determine whether the trigger processing should continue.

```
...
if update(au_lname)
    and (@@rowcount=1)
    begin
    ...
    ...
    end
...
```

In this case, the only time the code within the segment will be executed is if the specific column au_lname is updated. One thing to keep in mind here is that just because a column is being updated, doesn't mean that it's being changed. There are a number of applications out there, including most proprietary systems, that simply update the entire record if any change is made whatsoever.

It might be helpful to compare the new value against the old value, which will be stored in the INSERTED table, and see if it indeed changed prior to taking further action in the trigger.

Using DELETE Triggers

DELETE triggers are typically used for two reasons. The first reason is to prevent deleting records that will have data integrity problems if they are deleted. An example is if the records are used as foreign keys to other tables.

The second reason for a DELETE trigger is to perform a cascading delete operation that deletes children records of a master record. This might be used to delete all the order items from a master sales record.

TIP When you create a trigger, remember that the trigger can impact more than one row. This must be a consideration by your procedure that is run by the trigger. Be sure you check the @@rowcount global variable to see exactly what is happening before you start work with the information.

Triggers take into account the sum total of all rows impacted by the requested operation, meaning that they must be able to consider the different combinations of information in the table and respond according to what you need. For example, if a DELETE * from Authors statement is issued, the trigger has to work with the fact that all records from the Authors table would be deleted.

In the example in Listing 15.2, the @@rowcount variable is used to prevent the deletion of more than one row at a time.

In Listing 15.2, the trigger is executed whenever a user attempts to delete a record from the Stores table. If there are sales at that store, the request is denied.

Listing 15.2 15_02.SQL—Stores Trigger Disallowing Removal of More Than One Store

```
Create Trigger Tri_Del_Stores
On    STORES
For   DELETE
As
/* First check the number of rows modified and disallow
anybody from deleting more than one store at a time */
If @@RowCount > 1
Begin
      ROLLBACK TRAN
      RAISERROR ( 'You can only delete one store at a time.', 16, 10 )
End
```

continues

Listing 15.2   Continued

```
/* declare a temp var to store the store
that is being delete */
Declare     @sStorID char(4)
/* now get the value of the author being nuked */
Select      @sStorID = D.STOR_ID
From  STORES S, DELETED D
Where S.STOR_ID = D.STOR_ID
If exists (Select *
           From   SALES
           Where  STOR_ID = @sStorID )
Begin
     ROLLBACK TRAN
     RAISERROR ( 'This store cannot be deleted because there are
                 still sales valid in the SALES table.', 16, 10 )
End
Go
```

 T I P   Use RAISERROR as an easy way to send detailed and specific information about the error to the calling process or user. RAISERROR allows you to specify error text, severity levels, and state information, all of which combine to make for more descriptive errors for the user. It also makes it easy to write generic error-handlers in your client applications.

▶ The code sample shows several transaction management statements that allow you to prevent the operation from happening. For more information about transactions, please **see** Chapter 12, "Understanding Transactions and Locking."

You will notice in the code segment that a new table is referenced, one not included in the database if you simply review the list of tables present. In this case, the DELETED table contains a copy of every row that would be deleted if the transaction were allowed to complete. You use the values of the DELETED table to feed the information to any comparisons you'll want to make to validate the transaction.

The columns in the DELETED table will exactly match those in the table that you're working with. You can perform comparisons on them, as in the example, in which they're compared against the Sales database to verify that the store has no sales outstanding.

Special Transaction Management with Rollback Triggers

If you are working with triggers and transactions, you might want to consider working with a special trigger option, the rollback trigger. The rollback trigger option is, in essence, an "abort all" statement. When encountered, the processing of the trigger is stopped and the data modification that caused the trigger to execute in the first place is not allowed.

```
Rollback trigger  [with raiserror errornumber [message]]
```

When you use the `rollback trigger` statement, you have the option, and some would say the responsibility, to indicate an error number and optional message. Except in very rare situations, you should *always* use the RAISERROR option, as it is how the calling routines will know that you have stopped the action from occurring. The rollback trigger statement will not stop processing for a batch of updates; instead, it will only fail the current item. Because this is true, it's important that the code you develop to be update the database checks the return state of the update to make sure the update was successful.

When the routine returns from the update operation, always be sure to check the @@error global variable to ensure that the updates happened as planned.

Using Triggers That Send Email

One of the better features of SQL Server is its ability to invoke behavior directly from the operating system. This sort of behavior must be predefined through SQL Server's extended procedures, but it allows you to create incredibly powerful trigger operations. SQL Server is relatively unique in its ability to support operating system–specific features. This is achieved because it runs only on Windows NT, which has a very standardized programming interface across all of its supported hardware platforms such as Intel, MIPS, Alpha, and PowerPC.

Triggers can call any of the extended procedures (xp_*) available to the server and any external procedures that you add to the server with the sp_addextendedproc command. In Listing 15.3, the trigger demonstrates sending email when a record is deleted from the underlying Authors table.

On the CD

Listing 15.3 15_03.SQL—Trigger Sending Email to ChiefPublisher Indicating That Author Deleted from System

```
Create Trigger Tri_Del_Authors_Mail
On     AUTHORS
For    DELETE
As
/* declare some variables to store the author's name */
Declare    @sLName varchar(40),
      @sFName varchar(20),
      @sMessage varchar(50),
      @sAuthor varchar(60)
/* now get the value of the author being removed */
Select     @sLName = D.AU_LNAME,
      @sFName = D.AU_FNAME
From   AUTHORS A, DELETED D
Where A.AU_ID = D.AU_ID
/* Send mail message */
Select @sAuthor = @sLName + ', ' + @sFName
select @sMessage = 'deleted ' + @sAuthor
exec master.dbo.xp_sendmail @recipient = 'ChiefPublisher', @message = @sMessage
Go
```

Using Nested Triggers

Triggers can be nested up to 16 layers deep. If it is not desirable to have nested trigger operations, however, SQL Server can be configured to disallow them. Use the nested trigger option of sp_configure to toggle this option.

▶ **See** the Chapter 16 section titled "Displaying and Setting Server Options," for more information on sp_configure and other options **p. 412**

Triggers become nested when, during execution, one trigger modifies a table on which there is another trigger, which is therefore executed.

T I P   You can check your nesting level at any time by inspecting the value in @@NestLevel. The value will be between 0 and 16.

SQL Server cannot detect nesting that causes an infinite loop during the creation of a trigger until the situation occurs at execution time. An infinite loop could be caused by having a trigger, TRIGGER_A, on TABLE_A that executes on an update of TABLE_A, causing an update on TABLE_B. TABLE_B has a similar trigger, TRIGGER_B, that is executed on an update and causes an update of TABLE_A. Thus, if a user updates either table, the two triggers keep executing each other indefinitely. If SQL Server detects such an occurrence, it shuts down or cancels the trigger.

N O T E   If a trigger causes an additional modification of the table from which it was executed, it does not cause itself to executed recursively. SQL Server has no support for re-entrant or recursive stored procedures or triggers in the current version. ▨

As an example, suppose there are two triggers. There is one on the Sales table and one on the Stores table. The two triggers are defined in Listing 15.4.

On the CD

Listing 15.4   15_04.SQL—Two Triggers Nested If Delete Occurs on Sales Table

```
/* First trigger deletes stores if the sales are deleted */
Create  Trigger Tri_Del_Sales
On      SALES
For     DELETE
As
/* Announce the trigger being executed */
Print "Delete trigger on the sales table is executing..."
/* declare a temp var to store the store
that is being deleted */
Declare @sStorID char(4),
        @sMsg    varchar(40)
/* now get the value of the store being deleted */
Select  @sStorID = STOR_ID
From    DELETED          /* DELETED is a fake table created
                            by SQLServer to hold the values of
                            records deleted */
```

```
Group By STOR_ID
/* Now delete the store record */
Select @sMsg = "Deleting store " + @sStorID
Print @sMsg
Delete      STORES
Where       STOR_ID = @sStorID
Go
/* Second trigger deletes discounts if a store is deleted */
Create  Trigger Tri_Del_Stores
On      STORES
For     DELETE
As
/* Announce the trigger being executed */
Print "Delete trigger on the Stores table is executing..."
/* declare a temp var to store the store
that is being deleted */
Declare @sStorID char(4),
        @sMsg    varchar(40)
/* now get the value of the store being deleted */
Select  @sStorID = sTOR_ID
From    DELETED             /* DELETED is a fake table created
                               by SQLServer to hold the values of
                               records deleted */
Group By STOR_ID
If @@rowcount = 0
Begin
        Print "No Rows affected on the stores table"
        Return
End
/* Now delete the store record */
Select @sMsg = "Deleting discounts for store " + @sStorID
Print @sMsg
Delete  DISCOUNTS
Where   STOR_ID = @sStorID
Go
```

If a Delete is executed on the Sales table, as shown in Listing 15.5, the trigger is executed on the Sales table, which in turn causes a trigger to execute on the Stores table.

Listing 15.5 Results of Executing Delete on Sales Table

```
/*---------------------------
Delete from sales where stor_id = '8042'
---------------------------*/
Delete trigger on the sales table is executing...
Deleting store 8042
Delete trigger on the Stores table is executing...
Deleting discounts for store 8042
```

 TIP Triggers and DRI don't typically work together very well. For example, in Listing 15.5, you must first drop the foreign key constraint on the Discounts table for it to actually complete the delete. It is recommended that wherever possible you implement either triggers or DRI for integrity constraints.

Displaying Trigger Information

If you need to view the behavior that is being enforced on a table due to a trigger, you must display the information that describes the triggers, if any, that a table owns. There are a number of ways of obtaining information about a trigger that is on any given table. In this section, the two most common methods, using SQL Enterprise Manager (SQL EM) and the system procedures sp_help and sp_depends, will be demonstrated.

Using SQL Enterprise Manager

To view information about a trigger using the SQL Enterprise Manager, perform the following steps:

1. Run SQL Enterprise Manager from the SQL Server 7.0 group.

2. Select the Server that you want to work on.

3. Select the table that you want to work on and select the database and table you need. See Figure 15.1.

N O T E You must select down to the table that you want to work with. Remember that SQL Server menus are context-sensitive and change based on your current selection. If, when you select All Tasks, you don't see the Manage Triggers option listed, check to make sure you're highlighting the table, not the database or some other object. ■

FIGURE 15.1

After a table is highlighted, you can click the right mouse button and use the quick menu to perform common operations that are also available on the Action menu.

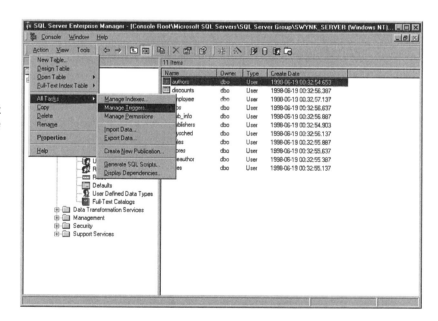

4. From the Action menu, select All Tasks, Manage Triggers. See Figure 15.2.

FIGURE 15.2

In the Trigger Properties window of SQL Enterprise Manager, the combo box on the toolbar lists the triggers that are active on the table in the first combo box.

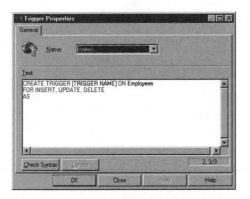

Using sp_help, sp_depends, and sp_helptext

The system procedures sp_help, sp_depends, and sp_helptext will provide valuable information in determining whether a trigger exists, what it references, and what its actual text or source code looks like. This is all provided the ENCRYPTION option was not used during trigger creation.

Using sp_help   sp_help is a generic system procedure that reports information about any object in the database. The following syntax is used:

```
sp_help [object_name]
```

If the object_name is omitted, SQL Server will report information on all user objects found in the sysobjects system catalog table.

sp_help is useful to determine who created a trigger and when it was created. Here is an example of the output from sp_help when used on the trigger created below, Tri_Del_Authors:

Listing 15.6   Using sp_help to View Information About Tri_Del_Authors

```
/*----------------------------
sp_help Tri_Del_Authors
----------------------------*/
Name                    Owner         Type                 When_created
-----------------       -----------   ------------------   --------------
Tri_Del_Authors         dbo           trigger              Nov 26 1995  4:37PM
Data_located_on_segment
----------------------
not applicable
```

Listing 15.7 shows a more advanced trigger that will be used in the following sections.

Listing 15.7   15_05.SQL—Advanced Trigger Demonstrating Information Returned from sp_helptext

```
/* create a basic trigger to stop anyone deleting an
author that still has records titleauthor table */
Create Trigger Tri_Del_Authors
On      AUTHORS
For     DELETE
As
/* First check the number of rows modified and disallow
anybody from removing more than one author at a time */
If @@RowCount > 1
Begin
        ROLLBACK TRAN
        RAISERROR ( 'You can only delete one author at a time.', 16, 10 )
End
/* declare a temp var to store the author
that is being deleted */
Declare     @nAuID id
/* now get the value of the author being deleted */
Select      @nAuID = D.AU_ID
From  AUTHORS A, DELETED D     /* DELETED is a fake table created
                                  by SQL Server to hold the values of
                                  records deleted */
Where A.AU_ID = D.AU_ID
If exists (Select       *
           From   TITLEAUTHOR
           Where AU_ID = @nAuID )
Begin
        ROLLBACK TRAN
        RAISERROR ( 'This author cannot be deleted because he/
                     she still has valid titles.', 16, 10 )
End
Go
```

Using sp_depends   sp_depends is a useful system stored procedure that will return a database object's dependencies, such as tables, views, and stored procedures. The syntax is as follows:

```
sp_depends object_name
```

After adding the trigger shown in Listing 15.7, Listing 15.8 shows the output from sp_depends when run on the Authors table.

Listing 15.8   Using sp_depends to View Dependency Information on the Authors Table

```
/*---------------------------
sp_depends authors
--------------------------*/
In the current database the specified object is referenced by the following:
name                                     type
---------------------------------------- ---------------
dbo.reptq2                               stored procedure
dbo.titleview                            view
dbo.Tri_Del_Authors                      trigger
```

Using sp_helptext User-defined objects, such as rules, defaults, views, stored procedures, and triggers store their text in the system catalog table syscomments. This table is not very easy to read, so the sp_helptext procedure is provided to enable easier access.

The syntax for sp_helptext is as follows:

```
sp_helptext object_name
```

If you are unable to read the text returned, the trigger was probably stored as ENCRYPTED. In this format, you cannot read the trigger's associated commands. You will need to contact the original author of the trigger and request the text file for the procedure.

Dropping Triggers

There are a number of reasons why you might want to remove triggers from a table or tables. You might, for example, be moving into a production environment and you want to remove any triggers that were put in place to enforce good quality assurance but that were costing performance. Another possibility is that you simply might want to drop a trigger so that you can replace it with a newer version.

To drop a trigger, use the following syntax:

```
DROP TRIGGER [owner.]trigger_name[,[owner.]trigger_name...]
```

Dropping a trigger is not necessary if a new trigger is to be created that will replace the existing one. Note also that by dropping a table, all its child-related objects, such as triggers, will also be dropped.

The following example drops the trigger created above:

```
Drop Trigger Tri_Del_Authors
```

Reality Check

Triggers are both powerful and dangerous. SQL Server 7.0ís recursive triggers open up all sorts of possibilities, both good and bad.

For example, on swynk.com, triggers are used in the discussion forums to update the threads that show responses, last reply date, and so on. Here's the trigger that fires when a new message is posted:

```
CREATE      TRIGGER trigMsgInsert ON dbo.Message
FOR INSERT, UPDATE
AS
        declare @PrevID Int;
begin
      set nocount on
       select @PrevID = prevref from inserted
       if @PrevID > 0
                update message set lastupdate = getdate(), hasreplies=-1 where id
= @PrevID
end
```

This trigger walks down the tree of messages, updating as it goes. If you look closely, you'll see that it really *doesn't* do that, but instead updates only rows that reference the current row. How could this walk down a tree of messages?

If you think about how triggers work, you'll begin to understand. Since the trigger is bound to the update or insert event for any given row, the trigger actually causes a trigger to fire when it updates the next row in the tree. That trigger in turn updates another row, and so on. Until the PrevID is zero, there are referring rows.

Triggers calling triggers is recursion. It sounds nice until you realize how quickly you could walk the entire database and update rows all over the place. This could happen because of an errant trigger firing in an unexpected manner. Make sure you test your triggers extensively before you deploy. Keep in mind that triggers are, by definition, behind-the-scenes tools, so you'll have limited indication of updates gone crazy.

Triggers are one of the fundamental pieces of the N-tier architecture—they represent the server-side part of the equation, giving you server-enforced rules and integrity validation. Use them, but test them too.

From Here...

In this chapter, you learned about the values of triggers and how they can be applied to enforce referential integrity in your application. In addition, you learned that triggers can be nested and that they can be used to provide more complex business rule validation than constraints that can be defined during table creation.

Look at the following chapters for more information that may be useful in helping you write effective triggers:

■ Chapter 11, "Managing and Using Indexes and Keys," discusses how to enforce integrity constraints through table-based declarative referential integrity and unique indexes.

■ Chapter 13, "Managing and Using Rules, Constraints, and Defaults," shows a different way to enforce integrity constraints on table columns through rules and bound table defaults.

■ Chapter 14, "Managing Stored Procedures and Using Flow-Control Statements," provides information on how to create stored procedures that you can execute as triggers.

Understanding Server, Database, and Query Options

Defining Server Options

SQL Server provides a number of configuration options to enable varied and different installations of the server. These options are used to customize the way SQL Server's resources are managed. The sorts of resources that are available for management are the following:

- Memory
- User and logon handling
- Sizes of objects
- Network and physical I/O handling
- Symmetric multi-processing (SMP) management and parallelism

N O T E Symmetric multi-processing (SMP) conform to a published standard for incorporating more than one CPU in the system unit. SMP computers typically offer substantial performance improvements over single CPU boxes because they can distribute the processing workload to as many CPUs as are available. Windows NT has been shown to provide near-linear performance improvements on computers with as many as four CPUs. This means that for every processor you add to the server, you can expect to see a 100% performance increase.

SQL Server has two sets of server configuration options available. The default or basic server options contain the day-to-day sort of things that need to be managed. The advanced server options are provided to allow tuning of things in the server not generally considered necessary. Unless you have been advised by a technical support center to specifically configure one of the advanced options, it is not recommended that you change any of the advanced options.

The advanced options can be enabled by turning on the configuration option Show Advanced Option. For detailed instructions on how to set this and any option, see the section titled "Displaying and Setting Server Options" later in this chapter.

CAUTION

Changing server configurations can sometimes make a server unable to be restarted after the change. An example of this might be over-committed memory. To restart a server in this situation, it might be necessary to start the server in minimal configuration mode, which enables you to bring up the server without it attempting to apply the configurations that you set. For more information on starting the server in minimal configuration mode, see the section called "Starting the Server in Minimal Configuration Mode from the Command Line," later in this chapter.

Displaying and Setting Server Options

SQL Server provides two ways to display and set configuration options for the server. The graphical method is via SQL Server Enterprise Manager. The Transact-SQL method uses the system stored procedure sp_configure.

NOTE The SQL Server Enterprise Manager gives you access to a few of the common configuration options. To access all of the options, you will need to use the sp_configure system stored procedure. ▨

Using SQL Enterprise Manager SQL Enterprise Manager is a very convenient tool for the DBA to use when changing server options. The user interface makes it unnecessary to remember the syntax required for sp_configure or to know all the different options.

To use the SQL Enterprise Manager to display and set server options, perform the following steps:

1. Run SQL Enterprise Manager from the Microsoft SQL Server 7.0 group. See Figure 16.1.

FIGURE 16.1
After being started, SQL Enterprise Manager shows that no server is selected.

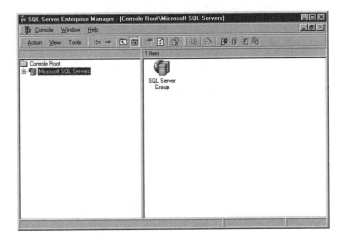

2. Select the server that you want to work on. See Figure 16.2.

FIGURE 16.2
After selecting a particular server, SQL Enterprise Manager shows all of its properties and objects folders.

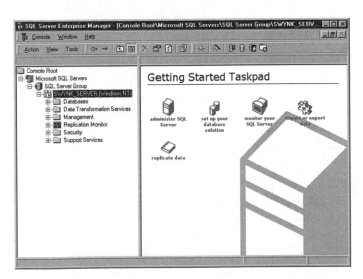

3. From the MMC toolbar select Action, Properties. The Properties dialog appears as shown in Figure 16.3.

FIGURE 16.3

SQL Enterprise Manager's Properties dialog box shows the available configuration categories.

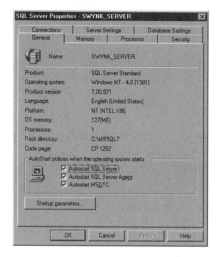

4. To change any of the available settings for the server, enter the required value on the appropriate tab.

The options available on each tab are as follows:

- General—Autostart policies and startup parameters
- Memory—Memory management mode (static or dynamic) and the maximum amount of memory
- Processor—Dedicated processors in an SMP environment, maximum worker threads, the number of processors to utilize for parallel queries, and the parallel query threshold
- Security—Security mode (standard, integrated, or mixed) as well as the account SQL Server will start under
- Connections—Number of users, connection options, and remote connections
- Settings—Language, direct updates to system tables, nested triggers, and SQL Mail
- Database Settings—Database size, fill factor, backup options, and recovery interval

 Press the F1 key on any SQL Enterprise Manager dialog box to bring up context-sensitive help that explains the different objects/options available.

Using the System Stored Procedure sp_configure sp_configure is a system stored procedure provided to allow the changing of settings on the server. sp_configure is useful for writing automated scripts that update the server without user intervention.

sp_configure's syntax is as follows:

```
sp_configure [configuration option, [configuration value]]
```

The *configuration option* is the value that is needed to change in the server. SQL Server uses a LIKE operator on the text that is supplied so that any unique set of characters is recognized without requiring the full text value. SQL Server requires that any text with spaces or other formatting in the *configuration option* parameter be enclosed in quotation marks.

Listing 16.1 shows that all of the sp_configure statements perform the same function, because they are resolved using this "closest match" approach.

Listing 16.1 sp_configure **Requires Only That the Option Being Changed Is Uniquely Identified**

```
sp_configure "nested Triggers", 0
go
sp_configure "nested", 1
go
sp_configure "triggers", 0
go
sp_configure "trig", 0
go
```

N O T E If no parameters are supplied to sp_configure, the resulting output is the current status of the server. Listing 16.2 shows an example of the results returned when sp_configure is used without a parameter.

The sp_configure information produced below includes the advanced options. Notice that the run value for show advanced options is 1.

Listing 16.2 Executing sp_configure **Without Any Options Returns the Current Server Configuration**

name	minimum	maximum	config_value	run_value
affinity mask	0	2147483647	0	0
allow updates	0	1	0	0
cost threshold for parallelism	0	32767	5	5
cursor threshold	-1	2147483647	-1	-1
database size	2	10000	2	2
default comparison style	0	2147483647	1	1
default language	0	9999	0	0
default locale id	0	2147483647	1033	1033
default sortorder id	0	255	52	52
fill factor	0	100	0	0
language in cache	3	100	3	3

continues

Listing 16.2 Continued

locks	5000	2147483647	0	0
max additional query mem.	0	2147483647	1024	1024
max async IO	1	255	32	32
max degree of parallelism	0	32	0	0
max query wait	0	2147483647	2147483647	2147483647
max text repl size	0	2147483647	65536	65536
max worker threads	10	1024	255	255
media retention	0	365	0	0
memory	0	3072	0	0
nested triggers	0	1	1	1
network packet size	512	32767	4096	4096
open objects	100	2147483647	500	500
priority boost	0	1	0	0
procedure cache	1	99	30	30
recovery interval	1	32767	5	5
remote access	0	1	1	1
remote login timeout	0	2147483647	30	30
remote proc trans	0	1	0	0
remote query timeout	0	2147483647	0	0
resource timeout	5	2147483647	10	10
set working set size	0	1	0	0
show advanced options	0	1	1	1
sort pages	32	511	64	64
spin counter	1	2147483647	10000	0
time slice	50	1000	100	100
user connections	5	32767	30	30
user options	0	4095	0	0

If you're having problems using sp_configure and are getting the following error message:

```
Msg 15125, Level 16, State 1
Only the System Administrator (SA) may change configuration parameters.
```

then you're not logged in to the database as SA. Only SA can change a server configuration. Log off from the SQL Server Query Analyzer or the database tool that you are using, and re-connect to the database as the SA user.

Understanding the RECONFIGURE Command   After executing sp_configure, the server might return the following:

```
Configuration option changed. Run the RECONFIGURE command to install.
```

This means that the server has changed the internal value of the configuration, but has not yet applied it. The output shown in Listing 16.3 shows that the configuration before and after is changed in the config value column, but the run value column remains unchanged.

Listing 16.3 Some `sp_configure` Options Require Reconfiguration of the Server

```
/*--------------------------
sp_configure "nested"
go
sp_configure "nested", 0
-------------------------*/
name                     minimum    maximum    config_value run_value
------------------       ---------- ---------- ------------ ----------
nested triggers          0          1          1            1
Configuration option changed. Run the RECONFIGURE command to install.
name                     minimum    maximum    config_value run_value
------------------       ---------- ---------- ------------ ----------
nested triggers          0          1          0            1
Executing the RECONFIGURE command applies the change to the server as shown in
Listing 16.4.
Listing 16.4--RECONFIGURE Forces SQL Server to Adjust the Run Value of a Server
Option
/*--------------------------
reconfigure
go
sp_configure "nested"
-------------------------*/
name                     minimum    maximum    config_value run_value
------------------       ---------- ---------- ------------ ----------
nested triggers          0          1          0            0
```

`RECONFIGURE` is available only to dynamic configuration options. These are options that can be changed without requiring the server to be shut down and restarted. The following is a list of the dynamic options that can be set with `sp_configure` and then applied dynamically with `RECONFIGURE`:

```
allow updates                     nested triggers

cursor threshold                  network packet size

max degree of parallelism         recovery interval

max additional query mem          max query wait

max text repl size                max worker threads

remote query timeout              resource timeout

show advanced options             spin counter

user options

cost threshold for parallelism

remote login timeout option
```

Server Options Explained

The following is a comprehensive list of all the available server options. If the word "advanced" appears in parentheses to the right of the keyword, this option is available only if you have turned on the configuration value Show Advanced Options. If the word "dynamic" appears in parentheses to the right of the keyword, this option can be changed without shutting down and restarting the server. See the section on the RECONFIGURE command earlier in this chapter for more information.

In each item that follows, there are indications of the minimum, maximum, and default values. These values indicate the range of values that the item can have and the default value to which SQL Server is configured when first installed.

affinity mask (advanced)

Minimum: 0

Maximum: 0x7fffffff

Default: 0

On SMP machines, affinity mask allows a thread to be associated with a processor. This is done using a bit mask. The processors on which the processes run are represented by each bit. Decimal or hexadecimal values can be used to specify values for this setting. This is done to improve performance on machines that generally have more than four processors under heavy load by confining processes to a particular set of processors. This reduces the amount of reloading of the processor cache that is needed.

Affinity is a process of attaching threads on a particular processor. By attaching a thread to a particular processor, the thread no longer migrates, and the cache reloading associated with such migration is eliminated, which improves performance.

allow updates (dynamic)

Minimum: 0

Maximum: 1

Default: 0

The allow updates configuration option allows the system catalog to be updated. If the value is set to 1, the system catalog is updateable. Stored procedures created while the system catalog is updateable will be able to update the system catalog even when this value is returned to 0.

> **CAUTION**
>
> Allowing updates on the system catalog is an extremely dangerous decision. It should only be done under very controlled situations and should probably be done with the server in single-user mode to prevent other users from accidentally damaging the system catalog.
>
> To start the server in single-user mode, execute sqlservr -m from the Win32 command prompt.

Because this option can cause so much harm, it requires an additional keyword, WITH OVERRIDE, when executing the RECONFIGURE command. The following is the correct syntax to enable allow updates:

```
sp_configure "allow updates", 1
go
reconfigure with override
go
```

cost threshold for parallelism (dynamic, advanced)

> Minimum: 0
>
> Maximum: 32767
>
> Default: 5

This configuration option determines the point at which SQL Server will perform parallel queries on SMP machines. The cost is based upon the number of seconds a serial query would take to execute. If max degree of parallelism is set to 1 or it is a single processor machine, this option is ignored.

cursor threshold (dynamic, advanced)

> Minimum: -1
>
> Maximum: 2147483647
>
> Default: -1

This configuration option controls how SQL Server decides to build the results to answer a request for a cursor by a client. The value corresponds to the number of rows expected in the cursor's result set. The accuracy of the cursor threshold is largely based on the currency of the INDEX statistics on the tables for which a cursor is being built. To ensure more accurate picking of the synchronous/asynchronous cursor build, make sure that the statistics are up-to-date on the base tables.

If set to -1, SQL Server will always build the cursor results synchronously, meaning that the server will attempt to build the cursor immediately upon receiving the OPEN CURSOR command. Synchronous cursor generation is usually faster for small result sets.

If set to 0, SQL Server will always build the cursor results asynchronously, meaning that the server will spawn an additional thread to answer the client and it will return control to the client while still processing other client requests. For large result sets this is the preferred option because it will stop the server from being bogged down answering a single client's request for a large cursor result.

Note that if the value is set to other than 0 or –1, the query optimizer compares the number of expected rows in the cursor to the number in the setting. If the expected number of rows is higher, it builds the cursor asynchronously.

database size

> Minimum: 1
>
> Maximum: 10000
>
> Default: 2

This option controls the default number of megabytes to reserve for a new database being created. If the majority of the databases being created on a given server are greater than 2MB, it is advisable to change this value. Also, if the model database grows to be greater than 2MB, you will have to adjust this value.

TIP Because the minimum database size is 1MB, SQL Server databases can exist on floppy disks. See the Chapter 5 section titled "Using Removable Media for Databases" for more information on this option.

default comparison style (advanced)

> Minimum: 0
>
> Maximum: 2147483647
>
> Default: 0

This option controls the sorting options within a locale used for Unicode character sets.

default language

> Minimum: 0
>
> Maximum: 9999
>
> Default: 0

This option controls the default language ID to be used for the server. US English is the default and is always 0. If other languages are added to the server, they will be assigned different language IDs.

default locale id (advanced)

> Minimum: 0
>
> Maximum: 2147483647
>
> Default: 1033

This option specifies the locale to use for sorting Unicode character data.

default sortorder id (advanced)

> Minimum: 0
>
> Maximum: 255
>
> Default: 52

This option controls the sort order that the server will use. The sort order controls the way SQL Server sorts data and returns it to the client. The default is Dictionary, Case Insensitive.

CAUTION

Do not use sp_configure to change the sortorder. Use the SQL Server setup program if you wish to change this value. Changing the sortorder will require that you unload and reload the database because the data will need to be stored in a different format.

See Chapter 3, "Installing and Setting Up the Server and Client Software," for additional information on using the setup program to make changes or re-install SQL Server.

Part III
Ch
16

fill factor

> Minimum: 0
>
> Maximum: 100
>
> Default: 0

This configuration option controls the default fill factor to use when creating indexes. The fill factor refers to how much space SQL Server reserves in an index page for the potential growth of key values on the index. This option is overridden if a fill factor is specified when the CREATE INDEX command is executed.

A fill factor of 100 forces SQL Server to fill the index pages completely and should only be used for extremely static tables whose key values never change, grow, or are inserted into. Smaller fill factor values allow/force SQL Server to reserve space on the index page for new values that may be added to the table or index after the initial table load.

▶ For more information on indexes, **see** the Chapter 11 section titled "Creating an Index with CREATE INDEX," **p. 293**

language in cache

> Minimum: 3
>
> Maximum: 100
>
> Default: 3

This configuration option controls the number of languages that SQL Server can store in the language cache simultaneously.

locks (advanced)

> Minimum: 5000
>
> Maximum: 2147483647
>
> Default: 0

This configuration option controls the number of locks that the SQL Server can maintain at any time. Each lock consumes 32 bytes of RAM, so increasing this value to a large number will most likely require that more RAM be made available to the server. For example, setting this value to 20000 will result in 20,000 * 32 bytes = 640,000 bytes or 625KB of RAM consumed just by the lock manager.

Setting this value to 0 allows the lock manager to dynamically allocate memory for locks as needed. When SQL Server is started with `locks` set to 0, 2% of the memory is allocated to lock structures. Once this is used up, more space is allocated. The maximum space the lock manager will dynamically allocate is 40% of the configured memory.

max async io

> Minimum: 1
>
> Maximum: 255
>
> Default: 8

This configuration option controls the maximum number of asynchronous I/O requests that the SQL Server can make to the hardware devices. This value should only be changed from the default on systems that have more than eight physical disks with database devices on them or on systems that are using disk striping to improve performance.

max degree of parallelism (dynamic, advanced)

> Minimum: 0
>
> Maximum: 32
>
> Default: 0

This option controls the threads allocated to parallel query processing on SMP machines. A value of 0 will use all available processors. If this value is set to 1, parallel queries are disabled even on SMP machines.

max additional query mem (dynamic, advanced)

> Minimum: 0
>
> Maximum: 2147483647
>
> Default: 1024

This option is to specify the maximum amount of memory, in KB, that is allocated per user for queries above the memory required for the query. This generally improves the performance for queries that use hashing or perform sort operations.

max query wait (dynamic, advanced)

> Minimum: 0
>
> Maximum: 2147483647
>
> Default: 65536

This option controls the timeout period in seconds for long-running queries.

max text repl size (dynamic)

> Minimum: 0
>
> Maximum: 2147483647
>
> Default: 65536

This option specifies the maximum amount of data in bytes that can be added to a replicated column in a single `insert`, `update`, `writetext`, or `updatetext` command.

max worker threads (dynamic)

> Minimum: 10
>
> Maximum: 1024
>
> Default: 255

This configuration option controls the maximum number of threads that SQL Server spawns to handle database operations. By default, SQL Server spawns at least one thread for each listener service that is installed. In addition, a thread is spawned for database checkpointing, lazywriting, and for the read ahead manager. The checkpointing process is a process or server operation that writes dirty, or changed, pages of data that are currently cached from memory directly to disk. The lazywriting process manages cached writes to disk and allows transactions to be batched together for a single I/O to disk containing multiple items instead of writing every transaction to disk as it occurs.

The rest of the available threads are allocated for user processes that are making requests. If the number of users is greater than the number of available threads allocated by the server, up to the maximum configured, SQL Server uses the available threads in a pooling fashion. The next request by a user process received at the server will be assigned to the first thread that becomes available after it has completed its assigned task.

media retention (advanced)

> Minimum: 0
>
> Maximum: 365
>
> Default: 0

This configuration option controls the number of days that a given backup is expected to be retained before it can be reused. If this value is other than 0, SQL Server warns the user that he or she is performing a backup over an existing backup that has not gone past its number of retention days.

This is a useful configuration for SQL Servers that are in remote areas where a full-time administrator is not available to manage the environment and where it is likely that the user might incorrectly re-use backup tapes that should be kept for a prescribed period. A good setting is 7, which stops the tape from being used more than once a week.

memory (advanced)

> Minimum: 1000
>
> Maximum: 1048576
>
> Default: 0

This configuration option controls the maximum amount of memory that is allocated to SQL Server in MB.

The default setting is 0, which allows SQL Server to dynamically manage memory requirements. The lazywriter periodically queries the system for free memory. It expands or shrinks the buffer cache to maintain the free memory on the system at 5MB +/– 200KB. This prevents NT from paging.

If free memory falls below 5MB, the lazywriter releases memory from the buffer cache to bring the free memory back above the threshold. This process only occurs for a server under load. If there is no activity on the server, the buffer cache is not expanded as memory is freed on the system.

You can also manually configure memory although it is not recommended. The maximum amount of memory that SQL Server can currently address is 3072 regardless of the amount of memory available.

> **CAUTION**
>
> If you over-commit the amount of available memory, SQL Server will not start. See the section later in this chapter titled "Starting SQL Server in Minimal Configuration Mode" to fix a server that is no longer starting because memory was overcommitted.

N O T E In previous versions of SQL Server, you could place the tempdb database into RAM. This needed to be accounted for when configuring memory requirements. This configuration option is no longer available. ▪

To help tune the amount of memory being consumed by SQL Server, you can use the DBCC MEMUSAGE command, which reports the top 20 data pages and stored procedures that have been executed.

nested triggers (dynamic)

> Minimum: 0
>
> Maximum: 1
>
> Default: 1

When this option is set to 1, a trigger can call another trigger, which can call another trigger, up to 32 levels of cascading (nesting). To disable nesting (cascading) triggers, set the value of this option above to 0.

network packet size (dynamic)

> Minimum: 512
>
> Maximum: 32767
>
> Default: 4096

This configuration option controls the server-wide maximum network packet size that is requested by a client. If the client requests a size less than the value specified in the current value, SQL Server accepts it. Greater values than the current value are negotiated to the maximum value specified here, however.

This option can improve performance on networks whose base topology supports wider or larger packets than TCP/IP's default of 4096 bytes. This is especially useful if you are running over a satellite service and want to batch large packets of data to send through the satellite packet service.

Increasing the value of this option may be beneficial in BCP operations where a large amount of data, test, or images needs to be moved across the network.

This option should be adjusted to a higher value for reporting databases that are not acquiring any locks on the datasets because it will allow larger batches of data to be sent to the client at one time, improving network throughput.

> **CAUTION**
>
> Setting the packet size too high can cause locking problems on databases with many transactions. This is because SQL Server holds locks for an unnecessarily long time in order to fill up a network packet to send to the client. Take care when adjusting this value and perform statistical analysis to prove that the values you have chosen are providing benefits to you.
>
> ▶ For additional information on locking, **see** Chapter 12, "Understanding Transactions and Locking," **p. 309**

open objects

Minimum: 100

Maximum: 2147483647

Default: 0 (Dynamic)

This configuration option controls the maximum number of objects that SQL Server can hold in memory at one time. An object can be a table page, a stored procedure that is executing, or any other object in the database. Increase this value if the server reports that the maximum number of objects has been exceeded.

Take care when assigning values to this option because it may be necessary to allocate more memory to the server due to the consumption of memory resources by the open objects configuration option. By default, allocation of this option is dynamically changed by SQL Server, based on the current needs of the system.

priority boost (advanced)

Minimum: 0

Maximum: 1

Default: 0

This configuration option controls the priority SQL Server will run at under Windows NT. The default is 0, meaning that SQL Server runs at a normally high priority, but allows other tasks to request high threading priority, too. If set to 1, SQL Server runs at the highest priority under the Windows NT scheduler.

A default setting of 0 corresponds to priority base 7 on a single processor computer, and at priority base 15 on an SMP computer.

It is not recommended to set this option as it can cause bottlenecks for the operating system.

recovery interval (dynamic)

> Minimum: 1
>
> Maximum: 32767
>
> Default: 5

This configuration option controls the number of minutes that SQL Server requires to recover a database in the event of a system failure of some kind. This option combined with the amount of activity that is occurring on the server controls the amount of time between database CHECKPOINTS.

A database CHECKPOINT forces the writing of all the changes to dirty data pages from the transaction log information to disk instead of residing in the transaction log buffers or lazywriter buffers. A CHECKPOINT can take considerable time if there has been a lot of activity on the server, but frequent checkpointing reduces the amount of time required to restart the server because it will not have to ROLLFORWARD as much work from the transaction log. If the Truncate on Checkpoint option is enabled for the database, a checkpoint is issued every minute regardless of this setting.

remote access

> Minimum: 0
>
> Maximum: 1
>
> Default: 1

This configuration option controls whether remote SQL Servers are allowed logon access to the server. If set to 0, SQL Server will deny access to remote SQL Servers.

remote logon timeout option (dynamic, advanced)

> Minimum: 0
>
> Maximum: 2147483647
>
> Default: 5

This configuration option controls the amount of time, in seconds, that SQL Server waits before returning an error to the client process that was requesting the logon to a remote server. Setting this value to 0 causes the SQL Server to wait indefinitely.

remote proc trans

> Minimum: 0
>
> Maximum: 1
>
> Default: 0

This feature allows users to protect the actions of a server-to-server procedure through a DTC-coordinated distributed transaction. When set to True, it provides a DTC transaction that protects certain properties of transactions. After this option is set, new sessions will inherit the configuration setting as their default.

remote query timeout (dynamic, advanced)

> Minimum: 0
>
> Maximum: 2147483647
>
> Default: 0

This configuration option controls the amount of time, in seconds, that SQL Server waits before returning an error to the client process that was requesting the execution of a query on a remote server. Setting this value to 0 causes the SQL Server to wait indefinitely.

resource timeout (dynamic, advanced)

> Minimum: 5
>
> Maximum: 2147483647
>
> Default: 10

This configuration option controls the amount of time, in seconds, that SQL Server waits before returning an error to the client process requiring a server resource. A server resource could be access to a memory buffer, a disk I/O request, a network I/O request, or a log I/O request. This option should be increased if a large number of logwait or bufwait timeout warnings are in the SQL Server error log.

set working set size (advanced)

> Minimum: 0
>
> Maximum: 1
>
> Default: 0

This configuration option controls whether SQL Server requests that Windows NT physically allocate and lock memory to the SQL Server. The amount allocated will be equal to the memory configuration. Do not set this to 1 if you are using dynamic memory allocation. Doing so prevents the dynamic swapping of memory pages.

show advanced option (dynamic)

> Minimum: 0
>
> Maximum: 1
>
> Default: 1

Part III

Ch 16

This configuration option controls whether SQL Server displays and allows the configuration of other advanced options through sp_configure. If set to 0, SQL Server responds that an option does not exist if an attempt is made to change an advanced option.

Remember, you must first enable the show advanced option using sp_configure before you will be allowed to configure advanced options.

spin counter (dynamic, advanced)

> Minimum: 1
>
> Maximum: 2147483647
>
> Default: 10000

This configuration option controls the maximum number of attempts SQL Server makes to acquire a resource from the SQL Server service manager. This option defaults to 10 for a single processor system and 10000 for a multiprocessor system.

This is an advanced option and should not be altered except in extreme situations where it's likely that you will be working with a support center to troubleshoot your system.

time slice (advanced)

> Minimum: 50
>
> Maximum: 1000
>
> Default: 100

This configuration option limits the amount of time in milliseconds that a user process can pass through a yield point without voluntarily yielding. The SQL Server kernel is not preemptive and doesn't control the amount of time a process runs. Instead SQL Server is controlled by the amount of time a process spends on a CPU before yielding.

If a process exceeds this limit, SQL Server assumes the process is locked and kills it. Setting this option too low can cause the system to slow down as processes frequently swap out. Setting this option too high can allow a process to monopolize the processor(s).

user connections

> Minimum: 5
>
> Maximum: 32767
>
> Default: 20

This configuration option controls the maximum number of user processes that can connect to the server at one time. The logical limit is 32767, but it is very likely that practical limits of server hardware will be exceeded before this limit is ever achieved.

There is a minimum fixed overhead for each user connection of about 40KB. If this value is set to a large value it may be necessary to allocate more memory to the SQL Server. If you find that users are reporting that they cannot connect, it's possible that you are running out of available user connections on the server. Use sp_configure to increase the number of user connections to a higher value so that more concurrent users are permitted.

user options

> Minimum: 0
>
> Maximum: 4095
>
> Default: 0

The user options are used to set global defaults for users logging into the system. After a change is made, all new logins are affected but existing logins are not changed. Users can override these values by using the SET statement.

SYSCONFIGURES and SYSCURCONFIGS: System Catalog Tables

SYSCONFIGURES and SYSCURCONFIGS are system catalog tables that SQL Server uses to store information about the configuration options in use on the server. They are stored in the master database.

SYSCONFIGURES has information about the available options and their defaults that the server has created. Note that the sp_configure option that you see comes from the spt_values table in the master database. Rather than relying on the formatted results returned from sp_configure, it's sometimes necessary to be able to select back and process in a result set the configurations available and configured on the server. The query below shows you the defaults for all the configurable options in the server.

On the CD

The CD contains the query 16_01.SQL below to select all of the information from the sysconfigures table.

```
/*---------------------------
Select V.NAME,   COMMENT = substring( C.COMMENT, 1, 60 ),
        "DEFAULT" = c.value
From    MASTER.DBO.SPT_VALUES V,
        MASTER.DBO.SYSCONFIGURES C
Where   V.NUMBER = C.CONFIG
And     V.NAME is not null
Order by V.NAME
---------------------------*/
```

TIP In the above query, the reserved SQL Server keyword DEFAULT was used as a column title. To use any reserved word as text in a column title, enclose it in quotation marks.

SYSCURCONFIGS stores the currently configured values being used by the server. The query below shows how to get the current values for each of the configurable options in the server. Using SYSCONFIGURES and SYSCURCONFIGS together allows you to write your own programs to dynamically set options and report options on the server.

On the CD

The CD contains the query below to select all of the information from the syscurconfig table.

Listing 16.5   16_02.SQL—Querying the SYSCURCONFIGS Table to Review the Current Server Configurations

```
/*---------------------------
Select V.NAME,   COMMENT = substring( C.COMMENT, 1, 60 ),
       "CURRENT VALUE" = c.value
From   MASTER.DBO.SPT_VALUES V,
       MASTER.DBO.SYSCURCONFIGS C
Where  V.NUMBER = C.CONFIG
And    V.NAME is not null
Order by V.NAME
---------------------------*/
```

N O T E   Both queries above are joined to the SQL Server system table spt_values. This is a special table that SQL Server uses for displaying value/configuration data. ■

Defining Database Options

SQL Server has several options available at a per-database level that enable the database administrator, DBA, to configure how different databases perform and act on a given server.

N O T E   In versions prior to SQL Server 6.0, it was necessary to do a CHECKPOINT command in the modified database after performing a change to a database option. In SQL Server 6.0, Microsoft added the dynamic interpretation of procedural logic to stored procedures, making it possible for Microsoft to update the sp_dboption system-stored procedure to automatically do the CHECKPOINT for you. ■

Displaying and Setting Database Options

SQL Server provides two ways to display and set configuration options for the database. The graphical method is via SQL Server Enterprise Manager. The command-line method is by using the system stored procedure sp_dboption.

Using SQL Enterprise Manager   To configure a database using SQL Enterprise Manager, follow these steps:

1. Run SQL Enterprise Manager from the Microsoft SQL Server 7.0 group.

2. Select the server and database that you want to work on.

3. Either click the right mouse button and select Properties from the menu or select Actions, Properties. When the Database properties dialog box is displayed, click the Options page. See Figure 16.4.

FIGURE 16.4
SQL Enterprise
Manager's Database
Properties dialog box
shows the Options
page.

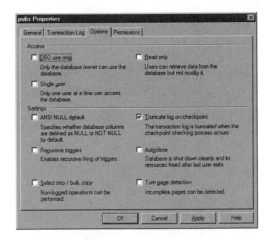

4. To change any of the settings for the database, click the required options and press OK to apply the changes and return to the main SQL Enterprise Manager window. These options are explained in the next sections.

Using sp_dboption The system stored procedure sp_dboption can be used instead of the SQL Enterprise Manager to set options for the database. The syntax for sp_dboption is as follows:

```
sp_dboption [database name, database option, database value]
```

database name is the name of the database that is being viewed or changed.

database option is the name of the option being viewed or changed. Place quotation marks around the option being set if it contains any embedded spaces.

database value is the new value for the option.

If no parameters are supplied to sp_dboption, it returns the available parameters that can be set for any current database. In Listing 16.6, you can see sp_dboption being executed without parameters.

Listing 16.6   Using sp_dboption to Report All the Configurable Database Options

```
/*---------------------------
sp_dboption
--------------------------*/
Settable database options:
---------------------------------
ANSI empty strings
ANSI null default
dbo use only
default to local cursor
merge publish
```

continues

Listing 16.6   Continued

```
no chkpt on recovery
offline
published
read only
recursive triggers
select into/bulkcopy
single user
subscribed
trunc. log on chkpt.
```

If a database is supplied as a parameter, but no configuration option is supplied, sp_dboption returns the currently active configuration options for the indicated database. For an example of this, see Listing 16.7.

Listing 16.7   Seeing the set Option on a Database Using sp_dboption

```
/*...........................
sp_dboption pubs
..........................*/
The following options are set:
...........................
select into/bulkcopy
trunc. log on chkpt.
```

sp_dboption is similar to sp_configure in that, for the option being set, it performs a wildcard-style search on the passed-in option parameter so that dbo, dbo use, and dbo use only are the same parameter.

Database Options Explained

The following is a list of all the database options that are available for configuration in user databases. In parentheses following the option name is the equivalent name that SQL Enterprise Manager uses for the option if it's different from the standard option name. Note that options listed here that are not part of the Enterprise Manager dialog box and must be set with sp_dboption. Refer to Figure 16.4.

N O T E   The only option that is user configurable for the master database is the Truncate Log on Checkpoint (Trunc. Log on Chkpt) option. SQL Server requires that all other configurations be left in their default setup to operate correctly. ■

ANSI empty strings   This database option enables empty strings to be stored in the database. By default this is off. If you attempt to store an empty string when this is not enabled, SQL Server puts a space in that column instead. With this option enabled, an empty string is stored in the column.

N O T E This option should not be used unless necessary to get around the limitations of a front-end development tool. Storing an empty string or a blank in a column instead of the expected NULL is problematic at best. At worst it can cause you to "lose" data. ■

ANSI null default

This database option controls the way the CREATE TABLE statement is parsed by the SQL interpreter when defining columns. By default, if the NULL keyword is omitted in SQL Server, the SQL interpreter assumes that the column is supposed to be NOT NULL. The ANSI standard specifies the reverse, however, that if not specified a column is NULL.

If the database scripts being used to create a table or set of tables have been created for an ANSI-compatible database, it will be necessary to have this option turned on so that the tables generated or created behave the same way as they would on another ANSI-compatible database.

If, when you define a table, you specify the nullability for a given column, your indication will override this setting.

DBO use only   This database option controls the user access to the database. If set to True, the only user who may access the database is the database owner, dbo. If this option is turned on while existing users are connected, their connections are not killed. They are allowed to stay on the database until they disconnect voluntarily.

Default to local cursor   This database option, when enabled, sets the cursor scope of all declared cursors to local.

Merge publish   This database option, when enabled, allows a database to be published for merge replication.

N O T E The fact that you enable the merge publish option does not cause the database to be replicated. For information about replication and setting up the publisher, subscriber relationship between databases, see Chapter 17, "Setting Up and Managing Replication." ■

no chkpt on recovery (No Checkpoint on Recovery)   This database option controls the behavior on recovery of a database. The default is False, meaning that after a recovery of database or transaction log, a CHECKPOINT operation will occur.

If multiple databases are being used in a primary and secondary fashion and transaction logs are being rolled forward from one database to another, this option should be turned on, or True. It stops the database from rejecting further transaction logs being applied.

offline   This database option, if enabled, brings a database "down" into an offline condition. This option is most often used with removable media, such as floppy diskette or CD-ROM based databases that need to be "swapped out" at any given time.

Databases that have currently connected or active users cannot be placed offline until those users disconnect. An offline database is not recovered when the server is restarted.

published   This database option controls whether a database is available for publishing and subscribing based replication. If enabled, a `repl_subscriber` user is added to the database and the transaction log is monitored for transactions that need to be replicated to other databases.

> **N O T E** The fact that you enable the `published` option does not cause the database to be replicated. For information about replication and setting up the publisher and subscriber relationship between databases, see Chapter 17. ■

read only (Read Only)   This database option, if enabled, places a database in read-only mode, making it impossible for any Insert**s**, Update**s**, Delete**s**, or DDL to be issued in the database. This is a useful option to turn on for reporting databases. For example, if you are writing an application that creates a lot of reports for your users, the `read only` flag guarantees that the data does not change. This is also useful when you want to keep a "clean" copy of a database schema for use when deploying database modifications.

> **N O T E** If you use this option, don't forget to reverse it in your applications that populate the tables in the database. You need a way to get information into the database before you can mark it read only, so your routines that place this information online must disable, then re-enable the option during processing. ■

recursive triggers (Recursive Triggers)   This database option, if enabled, allows recursive firing of triggers. This option is the same as the server-level option of nested triggers. Enabling this at a database level allows trigger nesting to be controlled at a more granular level.

select into/bulkcopy (Select Into/Bulk Copy)   This database option controls whether non-logged database operations are permitted in the current database. A non-logged operation, such as the SELECT INTO... command, is highly optimized and does not write any entries to the database transaction log, making it unrecoverable.

> **CAUTION**
>
> If you set this option to `True`, you won't be able to use the transaction log for recovery of a problem database. Be certain you set this option to `False` to ensure your ability to use the transaction dump and restore capabilities of SQL Server if that is your backup approach.

This option must be enabled if bulkcopy (BCP) operations are to be executed against a database table without indexes. However, if a table has indexes, SQL Server always uses the slow load algorithm so that it has a chance to update the indexes.

single user (Single User)   This database option limits database access to a single user. If enabled and a user connects, that user can stay connected, but any other user will be denied access.

If single-user mode is turned on, `trunc. log on chkpt.` is disabled because it requires an additional user connection to the database to act as a monitor. This option cannot be over-ridden by the dbo or sa. If another user is logged on to a given database, he or she will not even be able to access the database.

subscribed This database option controls whether the database can be part of a subscription-based replication. If set to `True`, a private account, `repl_publisher`, is given access as a DBO to the database and the replication services are activated.

trunc. log on chkpt. (Truncate Log on Checkpoint) This database option controls whether the database logs will be truncated when a checkpoint activity occurs. By default this option is off and it should always be off in production when it may be necessary to use the transaction logs for replication, backup, or recovery.

If you find that you're executing the checkpoint frequently but still fill up your transaction logs, you will need to either perform more frequent manual dumping of the transaction logs, enlarge your logs, or use Performance Monitor to run a batch file that dumps the logs when the logs are approaching a full state.

▶ For information on Performance Monitor, **see** Chapter 21, "Optimizing Performance," **p. 539**

Note that if you have this option enabled, or set to `True`, you cannot dump the transaction log. It only exists between checkpoints, so you will receive an error message indicating that the transaction log cannot be dumped.

One important consideration in using this option is the fact that you cannot use the transaction log as part of your backup approach. Because you cannot dump the transaction log, you will not be able to back it up. In this case, you will need to do complete database backups to ensure the safety of the information in your database.

Understanding Query Options

SQL Server has a number of individual options that can be set while querying the database. These options control the behavior of queries when they are executed. They are also useful statistical and informational gatherers. They can be helpful in diagnosing query problems, such as queries that run very slow for no apparent reason.

Displaying and Setting Query Options

SQL Server provides two ways to display and set configuration options for a query. The graphical method is via SQL Server Query Analyzer or through the Query Analyzer of SQL Server Enterprise Manager. The command-line method is by using the system keyword `SET`.

Using Query Analyzer To use the Query Analyzer to set or view query options, perform the following steps:

1. Run SQL Server Query Analyzer from the Microsoft SQL Server 7.0 group, and logon to the required server. See Figure 16.5.

FIGURE 16.5

Select the pubs database in the drop down list after starting the Query Analyzer.

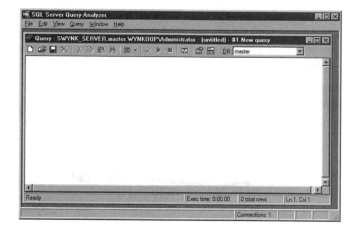

2. From the Query menu, select Set Options to display the Current Connections Options dialog box, shown in Figure 16.6.

FIGURE 16.6

Query Analyzer's Query Options section of the Current Connection Options dialog box shows the various execution options.

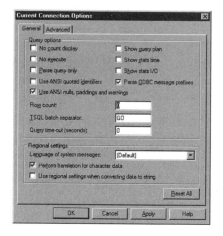

3. To change any of the settings for the query, click the required options and then click OK to apply the changes and return to the main ISQL/w.

SET   SQL Server provides a SQL keyword, the SET statement, that can be used to set any query option. If used in a stored procedure, the SET statement is in effect for the life of the procedure and overrides any previous settings. The syntax for the SET statement is as follows:

```
SET Option On ¦ Off
```

Option is any valid SQL Server query option.

Query Options Explained

The following is a list of all the query options that are configurable and what they do. In parentheses following the SET option is the equivalent in Query Analyzer.

***Arithabort* (Abort on Arithmetic Error)**   This option controls what SQL Server does when an arithmetic error occurs. If set to True, SQL Server aborts any query that causes a divide by zero error or numeric overflow condition, in which the value is greater than the defined datatype. There is no opportunity to capture this error at runtime, so if this option is not set, the resulting output could be NULL results.

In Listing 16.8, Arithabort is used to stop a command batch from continuing with invalid data:

Listing 16.8   16_03.SQL—Using the Arithabort Option

```
/* Declare working variables */
Declare @nDecimal Decimal( 8, 2 ),
        @nInteger Integer
/* ensure that the error does not cause an abort */
Set ArithAbort off
/* do a division that is going to cause an error
   note that the print statement doesn't
   get executed because this is a special error
   condition that SQL Server doesn't "publish"
   for handling */
Select @nDecimal = 8 / 0
If @@error != 0
     Print 'Error'
/* abort processing if the error occurs again */
Set ArithAbort on
/* This time the division will cause an error and
   the SQL command batch will be terminated, note
   that the termination stops any further activity
   and the print statement again is ignored */
Select @nDecimal = 8 / 0
If @@error != 0
     Print 'Error'
```

Here is the output:

```
Division by zero occurred.
Server: Msg 8134, Level 16, State 1
[Microsoft][ODBC SQL Server Driver][SQL Server]Divide by zero error
➥ encountered.
```

NOCOUNT (No Count Display)   This option disables the display of the number of rows processed by any SQL statement. The @@ROWCOUNT global variable is still maintained even though this option is turned off. The output in Listing 16.9 shows the effect of NOCOUNT.

On the CD

> **Listing 16.9   16_04.SQL—Using NOCOUNT to Stop the Reporting of Rows Affected by SQL**

```
/* Make sure that NoCount is Off (the default) */
Set NoCount Off
/* Do some SQL */
Select  "# Authors" = Count(*)
From    AUTHORS
/* Now turn on NoCount */
Set NoCount On
/* Do the same SQL and observe the different results */
Select  "# Authors" = Count(*)
From    AUTHORS
```

Here is the output:

```
# Authors
- - - - - - - - - -
23
(1 row(s) affected)
# Authors
- - - - - - - - - -
23
```

NOEXEC (No Execute)   This option controls whether SQL Server actually executes a SQL statement. If you turn this option on, SQL Server will not execute the query, but will perform only the work to determine how the query would have been answered. This option is most commonly used when viewing the SHOWPLAN that a query generates without fetching the data.

N O T E

SQL Server processes queries in two phases: compilation and execution. In the compilation phase, SQL Server validates that the query is OK, checks that all the objects exist and are readable, and generates the query plan or best path to the actual data. In the execution phase, SQL Server starts performing the query, which could be updating the records, fetching the data, and so on. ▪

PARSEONLY (Parse Query Only)   This option is like NOEXEC except that SQL Server does not compile the query or generate the access path to the data. It merely checks that the query is syntactically accurate.

SHOWPLAN (Show Query Plan)   This option shows the query plan that SQL Server generated to answer a query. The query plan can be interpreted by the Query Analyzer or by SQL Enterprise Manager, and a graphical representation will be seen as shown in Figure 16.7.

STATISTICS TIME (Show Stats Time)   This option shows the amount of time the server spent in different areas of parsing, compilation and execution, and answering a query. This information can be very useful in helping to tune queries. The data, however, can be skewed because of server caching.

FIGURE 16.7
ISQL/w's graphical *SHOWPLAN* output can help you understand how a query is being performed.

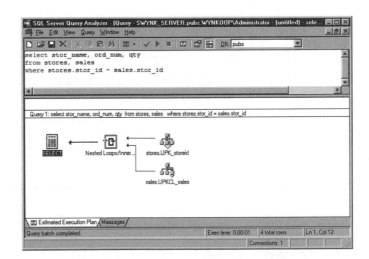

Part
III

Ch
16

Starting the Server in Minimal Configuration Mode

Minimal configuration mode is a mode of last resort that should only be used when the server fails to start because of an invalid configuration specified with sp_configure. Minimal configuration mode starts the minimum number of services to allow reconfiguration of the server. Minimal configuration mode is provided in SQL Server 6.0 and later in place of SQL Server 4.2's and Sybase's bldmaster executable. Prior to version 6.0 of SQL Server the configuration options were written to the bldmaster file and, if the server was not able to be started, it was necessary to edit this file manually.

> **CAUTION**
> This chapter applies only to SQL Server 6.x and later. The instructions here are not effective against prior releases. See the Microsoft SQL Server documentation on bldmaster to restart a server prior to SQL Server 6.x.

A server started in minimal configuration mode has the following limitations:

- All configuration values that affect memory, database, and server are set to their minimums as shown in sp_configure.
- The stored procedure cache is set to 50 percent of available memory as configured in the minimums of sp_configure. Memory, therefore, is set to 1000 2KB pages, or 2MB, and procedure cache is 500 pages, or 1MB.
- SQL Server is started in single-user mode at the server level, which is equivalent to the -m command-line option of SQL Server. Because the server is in single-user mode, the CHECKPOINT service is not started. This service is required to guarantee that transactions are written to disk.

T I P The CHECKPOINT service behaves like a user in the system and is assigned spid 3. You can check that the service is running by executing an sp_who command in ISQL.

- Remote access is disabled because the Remote Access service that acts as a user is not able to connect to the server due to single-user limitations.

- Read-ahead paging is disabled because the Read Ahead service that acts as a user is not able to connect to the server due to single-user limitations.

- SQL Enterprise Manager cannot be used because it requires more than one connection to the server and consumes more resources than are available during minimal configuration mode. You must use ISQL to fix the configuration option that is causing the server to be unable to be started.

- No autoexec procedures are run on server startup. Again, these procedures rely on being able to connect to the database and this connection is reserved for the user to correct the server configuration problem through ISQL.

Starting SQL Server in Minimal Configuration Mode from the Command Line

To start the server in minimal configuration mode from the command line, perform the following steps:

1. Start a command prompt by double-clicking the Command Prompt icon in the Main group of Program Manager.

2. Type start sqlservr -f.

 T I P The start command launches a separate process thread in which SQL Server is executed. This allows you to continue using the same command prompt to do other things. Any Windows NT task can be started.

N O T E To start SQL Server independently of the Windows NT Service Control Manager, use the -c command line switch. A server started in this fashion starts more quickly and allows more rapid fixing of the server in an emergency situation. ■

Starting SQL Server in Minimal Configuration Mode with the Services Application in Control Panel

To start the server in minimal configuration mode from using the Services application in Control Panel, perform the following steps:

1. Start Control Panel by double-clicking the Control Panel icon in the Main group of Program Manager.

2. Start the Services application by double-clicking the Services icon in the Control Panel window.

3. Type start `sqlservr -f`.

Repairing a Server Started in Minimal Configuration Mode

There might be several things you will need to do to repair a server that needs to be started in minimal configuration mode.

If you started your server in minimal configuration mode to reset a configuration, this is what you should do:

1. Start the server in minimal configuration mode.

2. Run SQL Server Query Analyzer.

3. Execute `sp_configure` to change the offending configuration value.

4. Execute `reconfigure` to change the server value.

5. Execute `shutdown` with `nowait` to shut down the server.

6. Restart the server as you normally would and confirm that it starts OK. If the server still does not start, follow these guidelines again and adjust another configuration value.

From Here...

In this chapter you learned how to configure your server, database, and queries to get optimal performance and to maximize your use of the server. Take a look at the following chapters for more information:

- See Chapter 7, "Retrieving Data with Transact-SQL," to take advantage of some of the configuration options discussed in this chapter and improve the performance of your SELECTs.

- See Chapter 14, "Managing Stored Procedures and Using Flow-Control Statements," to take advantage of the new options to stop your stored procedures from getting error conditions and aborting.

Setting Up and Managing Replication

In this chapter, the fundamentals of replication, including how to install and use it and how it might be a good fit for your projects, will be covered. Replication is an intricate feature of SQL Server. The boundaries of it have not been defined yet, and there will be innovative projects still to come that stretch these boundaries.

Replication is a broad term. To understand how to install and use it, you first need to understand what it is and is not. To help with this, I'll first look at some of the terms that Microsoft is using, how they implement the replication capabilities, and what this means to your system.

Understanding the Basics

Replication with SQL Server provides you with the ability to duplicate information between servers. This enables you to synchronize information sources for multiple domains, even in cases where those domains are physically separated by distance and possibly poor communications links. Replication, at its most fundamental level, recognizes changes made to information in a database and sends these changes to a remote system or systems for their use.

Microsoft has employed what is called *loose integration* in its replication model. You might have heard of the phrase *real-enough time* in systems implementation. Loose integration follows the real-enough time model. This means that information will flow across the system of servers not in real-time and not necessarily in batch mode, but as quickly as it can. The phrase, *real-enough time,* was first introduced when information was being distributed by email to remote locations. It was certainly not real-time, as no live connection was maintained between sites.

Using email didn't implement a batch approach because transactions were often still addressed on a transaction-by-transaction basis. With the email system, you're certain that your transactions are going to make it to the destination when a connection is completed between that system and yours.

SQL Server synchronizes the database tables almost immediately in many cases, but not concurrently with the transaction that makes the original change that is to be replicated.

Certainly there are pros and cons to this approach. On the positive side, the user of the system is not waiting for a remote server to respond before the application can continue. This alone can be a big timesaver. Another benefit is that the system can manage some fault-tolerance in the queue of things to be done.

If you have a transaction that is going to a remote server and the remote system is down, the transaction can be queued for later processing. The server engine on the local side, the distribution engine, can retry the connection to and update of the remote server at regular intervals and make sure the transaction happens as soon as possible.

Another positive side effect of this approach is a realistic approach to wide-area networks that might need to be connected over slow links. Transactions can be handled as quickly as the connection allows, without bogging down applications that are using the database tables that are to be replicated.

On the negative side, in two databases that are using this schema, it's possible to have information that is out of date or different on different sides of the replication equation. With true replication as implemented in SQL Server at this time, this is a situation that you cannot control but might have to address if this presents a problem. Remember, there are limited situations where this might occur, such as when a scheduled connection is unavailable or a server goes down. In either case, as soon as the connection is available, the databases resynchronize at the next communication with each other.

N O T E   If you have multiple databases, tables, or other entities that must be absolutely in sync, you'll need to work with the two-phase commit capabilities of SQL Server. This entails custom development on your part using the C API and working with DB-Library. Be sure to review Chapter 21, "Optimizing Performance," and Chapter 22, "Backward Compatibility Options for Developers," for more information about developing applications for use with SQL Server. ■

There are three key physical layer components to the SQL replication model. They are subscriber, publisher, and distributor. Each of these components must be in place in order to have a functioning replication model.

Is It Distributed or Replicated Information?

There is a distinct implementation difference between *distributing* your information and *replicating* it. In many installations, you'll probably find that you have both scenarios. When you decide to implement a system based on multiple SQL Servers, you'll need to be very careful to define what information will reside on which SQL Servers. This sounds obvious, but you need to take it to the next step, which is beyond just determining functional requirements.

In many disbursed systems, the requirement to implement replication comes from the desire to have information available at a central location. This requirement, combined with the remote starting location of the information to be centralized, provides the foundation for a replication scenario.

This is certainly a system that can be automated using the replication capabilities of SQL Server. The primary requirements are that you put a SQL Server at each location and initiate the replication from the remote locations to the central location. An alternative might be available if you reverse the flow of information shown in Figure 17.1.

FIGURE 17.1
Basic replication model shows information flowing between different points in your system.

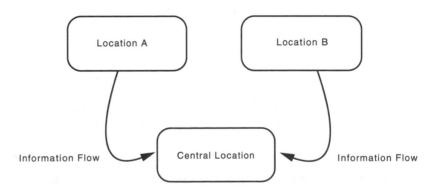

Adding a distributed approach to this scenario might be helpful to enhance your application's performance. Distributed systems or components of systems lend themselves to situations that include some or all of the following attributes:

- The information required at each individual location is different and distinct.

- The information from one location does not need to be available in its most up-to-date form at other locations. Somewhat aged information, if it's needed at all, will suffice at the alternative locations.

- There is an intelligent agent running at the remote locations, and that agent must be able to respond to basic data requests and manipulation requirements, such as copying working sets to a temporary database, and so forth.

A good example of a distributed system is a point-of-sale (POS) system. In a POS system, sales information exists at each individual location, but other locations do not have access to that sales information until it has been posted to a central location. See Figure 17.2.

FIGURE 17.2

A typical wide area network point-of-sale system lends itself to a mixed distribution-based and replication-based system.

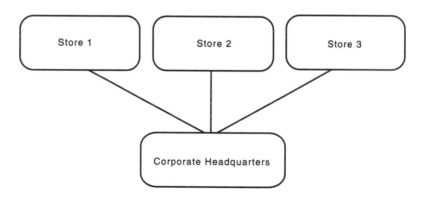

In this configuration, you can see that the information flow between the store locations is minimal, and when it does occur, it's likely to come from the corporate headquarters. Systems like this lend themselves to both a distributed information approach and a replicated scenario.

N O T E   In version 6.5, SQL Server's replicated tables were read-only on the subscribing system. This option is now configurable at the time you set up a publication. The new merge replication now supports the capability of a subscriber to modify data and have it propagated back to the publisher. ■

In our POS example, you can use replication to send all inventory information, including pricing, store inventory levels, and other stores' sales information, to different remote locations. Because this information is reasonably static, you can use a scheduled exchange of this information, rather than a continuous update. Keep this in mind as the process of setting up replication is discussed in the coming sections.

Distributed information can be maintained at the stores. This information will include sales information, customer-update information about purchases, credit payments, and so on. You can refer to this as distributed because the stores operate on this information separately from the corporate headquarters. They can create, update, delete, and otherwise manage this information on their own.

 TIP Using SQL Server to manage distributed information at the remote locations is not a requirement. You can consider using less expensive options if needed. Other databases that use ODBC are key candidates for the remote locations, as they'll be able to connect most easily to SQL Server later to update the main database systems.

In short, you should use a distributed environment to provide a fault-tolerant, independent system. The information produced under these routines and the routines designed to create the distributed information may or may not be required at the central location. Replicated systems are ideal for information that doesn't change very frequently at the recipients' locations. Keep this in mind as you review the different replication and installation options throughout this chapter.

Part
III

Ch
17

N O T E The processes that make up the replication model are all managed by the SQL Server Agent service. If you experience problems with replication, one of the things you'll want to check out is whether the userid and password used by the SQL Server Agent are still available and have not been changed. You specified these values during the installation process. ■

SQL Server Replication Fundamentals

SQL Server's replication features follow a magazine-type analogy to relate the different roles that are parts of the equation. The model follows an "I'll Publish, You Subscribe" approach that's easy to follow and implement. In the next sections, I cover setting up the different options for replication on both sides of the equation.

N O T E Beginning in version 6.5, SQL Server added the capability to replicate to ODBC subscribers, such as Access and Oracle. As stated in the SQL Server documentation, the ODBC subscriber must meet the following criteria:

- Must be ODBC Level 1 compliant.
- Must be 32-bit, thread safe, and for the processor architecture that the distribution process runs on, such as Intel, PPC, MIPS, Alpha.
- Must be transaction-capable.
- Must support the Data Definition Language (DDL).
- Cannot be read-only. ■

One last consideration is the replication between a SQL Server version 7.0 environment and one running version 6.x of SQL Server. A SQL Server 6.5 publisher can use a 7.0 distributor, but they must reside on different systems. SQL Server 7.0 supports push subscriptions to 6.x servers, but not pull subscriptions.

The final step in getting the down-level server ready is to install the replp70.sql script and run `sp_addpublisher70`. This script makes the replication possible, and it enables you to use Enterprise Manager from 7.0 against the 6.x server. This script is found in the \<platform> subdirectory on your SQL Server 7.0 CD.

Before You Start—Test the Connection

Before you proceed, test your connection to remote servers to make sure you can connect to them appropriately. Microsoft provides a utility, located in your BINN subdirectory on the server, that will help you test the ODBC connection between your server and the remote system.

TIP Even if you're not using an ODBC connection directly to work with the other server, as would be the case with a remote SQL Server 7.0 system, it's still a good idea to check your connection with this fast test. It will remove a variable later should you encounter any problems.

As you can test a TCP/IP connection with the PING utility, you can test an ODBC connection with the ODBCPING utility. ODBCPING has the following syntax:

```
odbcping [-s servername] [-d dsn] [-u username] [-p password]
```

Though the utility is a command line, DOS window utility, it provides a solid test of the connection between your servers.

When you run the utility, you can do so to check both a direct login, by specifying the server name, or to test a DSN that you've set up by indicating the DSN. Either way, provide the username and password for the connection.

When the utility runs, you should receive a message similar to the following:

```
M:\I386>odbcping -S Primary -U SA
CONNECTED TO SQL SERVER

ODBC SQL Server Driver Version: 03.70.0517

SQL Server Version: Microsoft SQL Server  7.00 - 7.00.517 (Intel X86)
        Jun 19 1998 17:06:54
        Copyright (c) 1988-1998 Microsoft Corporation
        Standard version on Windows NT
M:\I386>
```

If you cannot connect successfully, you'll receive an error message that resembles the following:

```
COULD NOT CONNECT TO SQL SERVER
SQLState: 08001  Native Error: 6
Info. Message: [Microsoft][ODBC SQL Server Driver]
    [dbnmpntw]Specified SQL server not found.
SQLState: 01000  Native Error: 53
Info. Message: [Microsoft][ODBC SQL Server Driver]
    [dbnmpntw]ConnectionOpen (CreateFile()).
```

In this case, consider the following:

- Confirm that the remote server is available.

- Make sure the DSN you've defined for the ODBC connection is a *System* DSN. This means that you should not be able to see it when you first start up the ODBC manager from the control panel.

- Make sure you've indicated the right server name on the command line for the ODBCPING command.

- Make sure the user name you provided exists on the remote server, not just the local server, and that it has permissions to log in to the server.

If all else fails, consider re-creating the connection in ODBC and try connecting to the server using standard network drive mapping conventions. Chances are good that the server is unavailable or the SQL Server process on the remote server has not yet been started.

Publishing: Providing Information to Other Systems

When you decide to use replication to provide information to other systems, you, in effect, become a publisher. You'll be publishing your information for other systems to receive. At the highest level, the information you provide to other systems is called a *publication*. Publications consist of *articles,* which are the items that will be provided to the other systems. Articles are discrete pieces of information that range from the entire contents of a database to a single row or the result of a query. As you'll see later in the chapter, there are several different ways to dissect the information you'll be providing via replication, as follows:

- Entire databases
- Entire tables
- Horizontal partitions of information
- Vertical partitions of information
- Custom views of information

Each of these has its advantages and disadvantages. Which you use will depend entirely on what types of information you're replicating and how it will be used by the remote system.

N O T E   Any table you want to replicate must have a primary key defined for it. If you don't have one defined, it will not show up in the list of available tables when you define the publication. It is also not possible to publish from the desktop version of SQL Server. Publications can only originate from the standard and enterprise versions. Also, the desktop version cannot participate in merge replication. ▨

After you've installed and configured the necessary components of replication, consider the following troubleshooting tips if you have problems:

- Replication might be established on a scheduled basis. It might be that you set up the replication to occur, at least for synchronization tasks, during the night or some other off-peak time. Check the publication setup options on the publication server to verify when you expect table synchronization tasks to be performed.

- It's also possible that enough time hasn't passed since the publication and subscription was set up. By default, synchronization occurs every five minutes. If your table is large, it might take some time to physically transfer the information to the subscription system, or it might be that the initial five minutes has not yet passed.

- Finally, the connection might be down between the two servers. Check to see that you can otherwise connect to the servers and make sure that they are up, running, and allowing logons. You'll also want to check utilization on the servers. Microsoft recommends 32MB of RAM on the publication system. With less RAM, it's possible that you're running into memory constraint issues and that the server is swapping more information than necessary while performing the operations demanded of it with replication.

Entire Databases   When you provide entire database articles to the remote system, you'll be asking SQL Server to monitor all activity for that database and update the users of the information with any changes that occur. This is probably the simplest form of replication to administer, as you're telling SQL Server to send everything.

N O T E   If you're creating a *data warehousing* application, one in which you simply provide snapshot type information to other locations, this might be just the ticket. In these types of applications, you want to provide a picture of the information at a given time. You can create a database of information that can be queried, provide it to these remote users, and not need to worry about the information being changed. You can also be assured of the most recent and updated information at these locations, as SQL Server will be monitoring it for you and initiate updates on the schedule you designate.

The replication of tables and specific partitions of tables is often the way to go when you have a modifiable, production environment to which you're exporting information.

Entire Tables   When you replicate entire tables, you specify a table that is monitored and sent out by the replication engine whenever changes are made. This table will be kept up-to-date based on the export timing and criteria you establish in setting up the publication article.

N O T E   You can establish more than one article for a given table. This might be helpful if you want to provide all information to a production, administrative server, but only limited information to a reports-only server that is used by non-administrative personnel. Be aware, though, that each publication you establish will require resources on the server to process the replication event. If possible, consider publishing the table once. After doing this, you can create a view or other protected viewing mechanism on the receiving server as it works with the client-side software.

Horizontal and Vertical Partitions of Information, Custom Views   When you publish horizontal partitions, you're using a SELECT statement that will provide all columns of information, but is selective on the rows of information that will be considered. For example, consider the following simple SELECT statement:

```
Select * from Authors where au_lname like "W%"
```

This would select only those authors whose last name started with a *W.* These are the authors that would be included in published information.

You might want to only publish certain columns of information to the remote system. For example, the Authors table in the Pubs database installed by default with SQL Server will include a Contract field indicating whether the author is under contract. If you're replicating a list of authors to a remote location, the users might not need to know whether you've established a contract with the author. In that case, you can select all fields except the Contract field to be included in the replication article.

You can also export a combination of a vertical and horizontal partition, or you can replicate the results of a view. The selective replication capabilities of SQL Server are the power behind the tool that really begins to broaden the appeal of replication.

▶ For additional information on setting up and managing views, **see** Chapter 10, "Managing and Using Views," **p 257**

Subscribing: The Recipients of Information

After you've set up what information you'll be publishing with the articles and other information covered earlier, move to the subscription system and let it know where to find the information that it will receive. The recipient is called the *subscriber* in the replication scenario. The subscriber sets up a connection to the distribution server and receives the information at the intervals you establish when you create the article to be replicated.

Subscriptions include the capability to designate where the information will go. This enables you to control who has access to it by using the standard NT and SQL security capabilities.

The Log Reader Process

There are two silent partners in the replication process that are always running and performing their tasks, but are much less visible when compared to the subscriber and publisher roles. These are the log reader process and the distribution database.

Replication in SQL Server is transaction log-based. As changes are made to articles that are declared for replication, they show up in the transaction log. The log reader process, an automatic background task on the server, detects these changes, and logs them to the distribution server's distribution database.

After a transaction has been processed for replication and put in the distribution database, the replication engine will publish it and make it available to the other servers that need it. You can see the log reader process if you look at the running processes in SQL Server. You'll see the process in the list of active connections.

N O T E If there are any synchronization jobs pending, you'll also see those jobs listed in the pending tasks area of the running tasks list. ■

Distribution Server: The Source of Information

The distribution server and database serve as the go-between for the publication server and the subscription server. When you set up the system, as you'll see when you go through the installation process, you'll have the option to set up a local distribution server or a remote system.

Although the distribution database is separate from the other databases in your SQL Server system, it can still be on the same physical server. When you set up a local distribution database on the publication server, SQL Server will use this new database as the mechanism to keep track of the different items that need to be provided to the subscription servers on the network.

The distribution database is also the storage location for the different stored procedures that make up the replication engine. These stored procedures are automatically called when you use replication and are used to automate the different processes that happen under the covers when replication is running.

If you choose to use a remote system as your distribution database, the database is created or referenced on a different server from the publication server. This can be beneficial on a system where you might have high transaction volumes or where a server is bogged down in just the normal processing of transactions or network requests. In these situations, it can be beneficial to have this other system, the distribution database hosting system, manage the replication of information to the subscription servers.

> **CAUTION**
>
> You must have 32M of RAM on the server that will be the distribution system if you combine the distribution and publication operations on a single server. In addition, you might need to install additional memory if a given distribution server is to be used by more than one publication server. It might also be beneficial to implement a multi-processor server in cases where workload on the server is substantial.

You generally won't be working directly with the log reader processes or the distribution database, but it's important to understand their functions in order to correctly set up your system.

Different Server Configurations for Replication

When you establish replication, you will save yourself time later if you take some time now to figure out exactly how to best lay out your system. As with database definitions and ERDs discussed in Chapter 2, planning early in the development process will really pay off when it comes time to move your system into production.

The configuration options for replication, at least on a physical implementation level, boil down to four different approaches, although there are certainly variations on these that might work well for some situations. The following are the basic five topologies:

- Central publisher
- Central subscriber (centralized data warehousing)
- Publisher with remote distributor
- Publishing subscriber (distributed data warehousing)
- Merge replication

Each of these is briefly described in the upcoming sections.

Central Publisher   The most basic type of installation is the combined publisher/distribution server and a single subscriber system. This enables you to configure a server where the transactions for your system take place and the information is replicated to the subscribing server. Figure 17.3 shows a simple replication configuration.

FIGURE.17.3

This is a simple system using a single server as the publication and distribution system and a single subscriber.

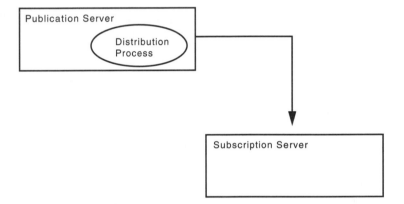

> **N O T E**   The figures and examples indicate a one-way flow of information. You can also install replication's publication features on a subscribing server and effectively replicate other information back to the original publication server. To put it another way, because a system can be both a publication and a subscription server, information can flow in both directions. In this case, you just need to establish appropriate articles for publication. ▩

It's likely that many systems that are not extremely high-volume will fall into this category, as it's the most straightforward to set up and maintain. Be sure, however, to consider moving the distribution processes if your transaction volume begins to cause the server to become bogged down in processing both application and replication requests.

Central Subscriber   This topology is almost identical to the central publisher with one exception. Multiple publishers now send data to a single subscriber. This model is generally used for centralized data warehousing.

> **N O T E**   The most important single feature of the data model for this topology is that each table being replicated to the central site will contain an identifier column that contains an ID for the source of the data. This avoids conflicts of data during the consolidation. ▩

Central Publisher with Remote Distributor   By splitting apart the publication and distribution model, you can begin to address specific performance bottlenecks that might be apparent in your system. If you implement a model of this type, you'll be able to add processors, memory, or other resources to systems as they become over-utilized. As you can see in Figure 17.4, it might be helpful to distribute the configuration of your servers.

FIGURE 17.4

Moving the distribution processes enables you to optimize system configurations for optimum performance.

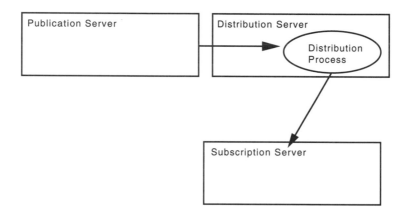

This system topology is also the first step toward a data warehousing system. By copying the information to the intermediary server, if you implement multiple subscription servers using this information, you'll be able to ensure that accurate, timely information is distributed without an overwhelming impact on the initial publication system.

In systems where you are publishing to multiple subscribers, especially in cases where the publications might be going out over a slow or remote link, you should carefully consider a separate distribution server. In each of these situations, more server attention will be required to complete the replication and that is best handled by a separate system.

N O T E   If you do implement this type of scenario, each system, the publication server, the distribution server, and each of the subscribers, is required to obtain separate SQL Server licenses. This cost will be part of the analysis when you are considering using a distribution server in this manner. ■

Publishing Subscriber   A big topic in the database world right now is distributed *data warehousing*. As mentioned in the last section, replication lends itself well to data warehousing implementations, as it provides you with an automated way to provide read-only access to users of your system. You know the information will be correct and as up to date as you need, and because no intervention will be required, SQL Server's replication engine can be set up to update the remote systems at intervals required by your application.

In this scenario, you are publishing the information to an intermediary server that is responsible for secondary replication to subscribers. This is an excellent way to leverage your servers for their distribution to the users of your information. As you can see in Figure 17.5, one approach might be to link servers to further distribute information.

FIGURE. 17.5

Republishing informa-
tion leverages your
resources and can be
helpful in mass
distribution or slow-link
to multiple subscriber
installations.

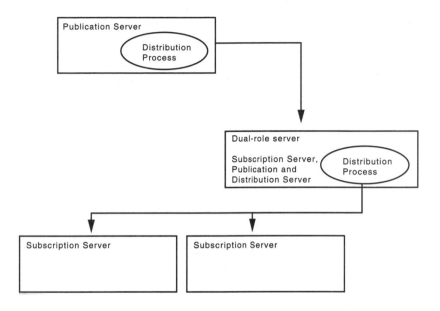

This type of installation is also a good candidate for a separate distribution server if there are
other operations that are required of the initial subscription and republication server. It's also
important to keep in mind that memory requirements might increase on the republication
server to work with the increased number of subscribers.

Merge Replication   Merge replication is essentially a combination of the central publisher
and multiple publishers of a single table topology. Although it is not true bidirectional replication, there are similarities. The basic topology is shown in Figure 17.6.

FIGURE 17.6

This is a system using a
single server as the
publication and
distribution system, and
multiple subscribers
with one subscriber set
up under merge
replication.

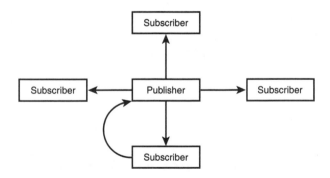

N O T E   The figure indicates a one-way flow of information to three of the subscribers. You can also
setup merge replication to all of the subscribers. ▪

In a central publisher topology, a central server is in charge of replicating all transactions to the
subscribing servers. In this type of topology, the subscribers are normally read-only and all

Part
III

Ch
17

transactions are processed on the publication server. The publisher is solely responsible for ensuring that all subscribers are properly updated with all transactions.

The merge replication topology works very similar to the central publisher topology. The main difference is that the subscribers are not read-only and transactions are processed on the subscribing SQL Servers. When a transaction occurs on a subscribing server, this transaction is transmitted back to the publisher via the merge agent. After the publisher receives the transaction, the subscriber is notified that a commit of the transaction can take place. The publisher then becomes responsible for updating all of the subscribers. However, the transaction is not replicated to the subscriber that initiated the transaction.

> **CAUTION**
>
> This replication topology should not be attempted unless you have significant replication experience. The interaction between publishers and subscribers is very blurred within this model and warrants much great care. This is an administration-intensive topology, because collisions can and do occur between publishers and subscribers that must be immediately resolved. In addition to that, merge replication places many more design considerations upon your database(s), application(s), and network.

Installing the SQL Server Replication Services

The first o installing replication is registering the remote server in the Enterprise Manager. There is nothing unique that you'll need to do to accomplish this, but you must have the server predefined prior to beginning the installation of the replication and subscription services.

> **N O T E**   When you define servers in the Enterprise Manager, it's important that you select the correct type of security to be installed at each server. Selecting the Trusted Connection indicates that Integrated Security is in use. If you select the standard logon connection, you'll need to be sure to specify a user that is a valid user on the remote system and one that has sufficient rights to work with the database tables you are replicating. If you do not, you'll receive errors when the replication service tries to connect to the remote server. ▪

When you start the replication installation process, one of the first things SQL Server will do is to verify that you've declared enough memory for SQL Server processes. The minimum required memory available to SQL Server is 8MB.

> **TIP**   It's generally recommended that you allocate as much RAM as possible to SQL Server. This is best accomplished by allowing SQL Server to dynamically manage memory. For more information about this option, see the section "Server Options Explained" in Chapter 16, "Understanding Server, Database, and Query Options."

The next step starts the process of installing replication as a publishing server on your system. Prior to setting up the distribution database, you'll need to ensure there is sufficient disk space to support the database that you'll be replicating. The recommended minimum size for these items is 30M, but your size will depend significantly on several different factors, as follows:

- What is the size of the databases you'll be replicating? Remember, for each subscriber, there is an initial synchronization that must take place. This means that your distribution database must be able to accommodate the combined maximum table size for each table that will be replicated. This size represents the size to support a single article. If you will be publishing multiple articles, you will want to figure out a total size based on all articles combined.

- What will the traffic be like on your system? More transactions mean more staging of information as it's passed along to the subscribing servers. This will impact the database size requirements.

- How many different articles will you be publishing? Try to avoid using several different articles against a single information source. If you have a table that you need to provide to multiple subscribers, it's worth the effort to try to use only one publication/article combination to fulfill their needs. This is better utilization of disk resources, processing resources and general processing bandwidth at the server.

▶ For more information about setting up databases in SQL Server, **see** Chapter 5, "Creating Databases and Transaction Logs," **p. 93**

With the server where you want replication set up, select Tools, Replication, Configure Publishing, Subscribers. This will begin the process of setting up the distribution database and other options that govern the server's operation for replication. Figure 17.7 shows the dialog box that you'll use to set up replication options.

Part

III

Ch

17

FIGURE. 17.7

Set the options for the distribution database and processes for replication, including device sizes and naming.

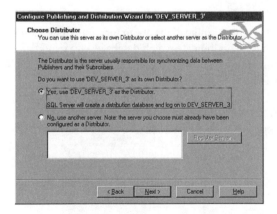

This dialog box enables you to define whether the distribution process will be local or located on a remote system. If you select local, you'll need to indicate where the distribution database will be installed. If you indicate a remote server, you'll need to know the server name. The SQL Server process must be already running on that system.

When you click Next, you will be able to select the default or Customize the setup. For this exercise, select the default. Select Finish on the next screen. If all goes well, you'll receive a prompt, as shown in Figure 17.8, enabling you to go directly to setting up publications on your system.

FIGURE 17.8

After the distribution database is created, you can go directly to the definition of your publications and subscriptions.

N O T E   If the installation of the distribution database fails for any reason, you'll need to address the problem before you can continue. A possible reason for a problem here is that you've registered a server with a user that is nonexistent or has insufficient rights on the remote system. Make sure you create an appropriate user prior to continuing if this is the problem you experience.

After you've addressed any system problems that are presented, you need to completely uninstall replication before you can continue. For more information, see the "Uninstalling Replication" section at the end of this chapter. ■

Enabling Publishing

The steps to creating your own publications are to turn on publication services, designate a frequency for the services, and indicate which databases are candidates for replication. You can get to the configuration options, shown in Figure 17.9, by selecting Replication, Create and Manage Publications from the Tools menu.

FIGURE 17.9

With the Create and Manage Publications dialog box, you create new publications for databases you want to replicate.

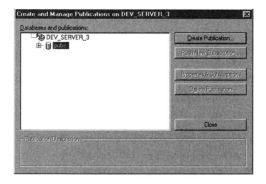

You can now see a distribution database that has been created. This is where all of the information will reside as it is moved from the publisher to the subscriber.

The next step is to check the configuration options. You can get to the configuration options by selecting Replication, Configure Publishers, Subscribers, and Distribution from the Tools menu.

On the distributor tab, shown in Figure 17.10, you can set up several distribution options.

FIGURE 17.10

Distributor configuration options.

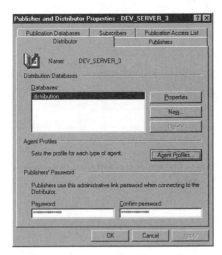

By selecting the properties button, you call up the screen shown in Figure 17.11 where you are able to set the default options for storage of transaction and the length of the history.

FIGURE 17.11

Distributor storage options.

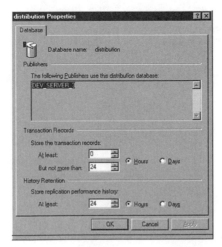

Part

III

Ch

17

By selecting the New button, you are able to create an additional distribution database to support replication operations, as shown in Figure 17.12. At the time of creation, you can also specify the length of time transactions are held in the distribution database and how long the performance history is maintained.

FIGURE 17.12

Defining an additional distribution database.

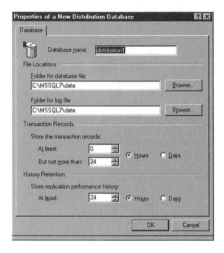

NOTE For systems that will support a variety of connected, disconnected, and anonymous subscribers, it can be advantageous to set each one up with a separate distribution database. This will enable you to balance the size of the distribution database with the needs of these very different scenarios and minimize the impact throughout your environment. ▨

The Agent Profiles button enables you to set a multitude of options, as shown in Figure 17.13 to support the Distributor, Log Reader, Snapshot and Merge replication. All of these options are found under the Profile Details button and include such things as network packet size, login time out, batch size, and polling interval.

FIGURE 17.13

Defining the distribution agent profiles.

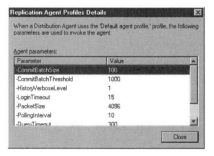

The Publishers tab, as shown in Figure 17.14, gives you access to adding remote servers, enabling publishing on all registered servers, and setting the location of the snapshot folder.

FIGURE 17.14

Setting publisher options.

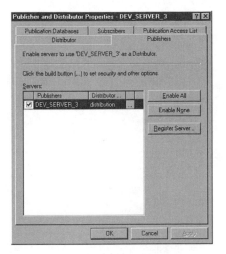

If you select the Build button on the Publishers tab in the Configure dialog, you will see the working directory option shown in the dialog box just following the designation of the distribution database. This directory is where information is kept and staged as it is sent out to the subscription servers. You can change this directory if needed. When SQL replicates a database, it is using a method somewhat like a BCP to copy the data from one system to another. This directory is where the data files are built.

N O T E   You might want to indicate a secured location for this directory if you have concerns about other users modifying or reviewing this information when it's staged. The information is not readily discernible, but should be protected nonetheless. ▪

From the Publication Databases tab, as shown in Figure 17.15, you can enable or disable merge and transactional replication for any of the databases on the servers declared as publishers.

FIGURE 17.15

Setting up the databases that will publish.

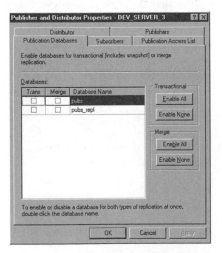

The Subscribers tab, shown in Figure 17.16, enables you to define subscribing servers and also set the replication scheduling.

FIGURE 17.16

Setting up the subscription options.

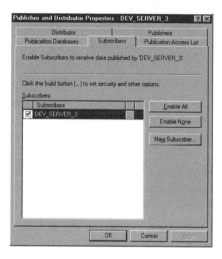

For each server you allow to subscribe, you can indicate at what frequency you'll be replicating information to the server. The default is to replicate information continuously starting at 12:00 AM and continuing throughout the day.

If you are using a remote link or are only providing snapshot information to the subscription servers, you might want to change this value to a time when the system is generally under less of a load. This can help decrease the impact on network traffic that will be incurred when the replication process kicks off. Of course, this places your data in a batch type mode and might not be acceptable at the end user's application.

If you want to create a custom distribution schedule or control how often information is sent based on transaction volume, you can click the Properties button on the Subscribers tab and select the Schedule tab in the resulting dialog. Figure 17.17 shows the setup options for this tab.

If you do opt to establish a custom distribution schedule, a separate dialog box enables you to change a number of options. As shown in Figure 17.18, you'll be able to set up how often, on a macro level, the replication will take place. This option allows values that range from daily to monthly. As you select this highest level interval, the balance of the options will change to reflect values that enable you further to define how you would like to have the replication carried out.

The Publication Access List tab, as shown in Figure 17.19, enables you to specify which logins will have access to the publications on the publisher defined.

FIGURE 17.17

You can create custom distribution schedules on a server-by-server basis. This can be helpful to take into account time zone changes and other loading factors.

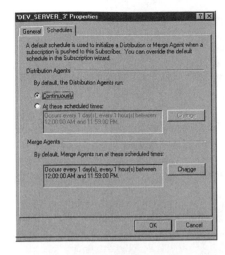

FIGURE 17.18

Custom timing for replication can be defined for a number of time intervals.

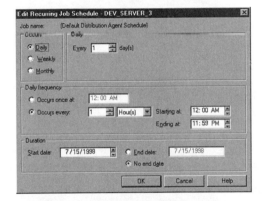

FIGURE 17.19

Defining the users allowed to access the publications.

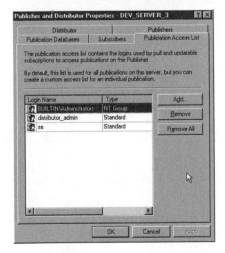

At this point, you're now ready to set up the specific publications and articles that you'll be making available to other systems. You've defined the servers that have access to the information, the frequency at which it will be provided, and you've indicated where the information will come from in your system. The next step is to create the publications that will be replicated.

 If you find that you're having trouble getting information to the subscribing systems, make sure the replication users, `repl_publisher` and `repl_subscriber` are still defined on the systems that are taking part in the replication.

Publishing Databases: How to Replicate Entire Databases

You may recall that you have two different options for replicating information on your system. You can either publish the entire database or you can select specific information in the database to replicate. In this section, setting up replication for an entire database will be covered. In the coming sections, setting up targeted articles will be discussed.

Select Tools, Replication, Create and Manage Publications from the menus to begin working with the different publications that are on your system. This will take you to the dialog boxes that enable you to define and configure the publications and articles that you will be offering.

The dialog box will show each database for which you've enabled replication during the setup phase. Of course, there will not be any publications listed initially because you've not defined them yet. You use the Create Publication, Push New Subscription, Properties and Subscriptions, and Delete Publication buttons to manage the different replications in your system. The tree display will expand under each database, showing the different publications that are available after they are defined. Under each publication, you'll be able to see the articles that have been created. From this display, you'll be able to manage all active publications.

Selecting the Tables to Be Published   In the first example, an AllPubs publication will be set up to replicate all eligible tables in the PUBS database. Remember, you must have a primary key defined for each table that you need to replicate. You can use the Alter Table command to institute a primary key if needed.

▶ For information about modifying table definitions, please **see** Chapter 6, "Creating Database Tables and Using Datatypes," **p. 113**

When you select Create Publication, you're presented with the dialog box that enables you to set up the publication and indicate the information that should be replicated. Figure 17.20 shows the dialog box that enables you to define the type of replication that will be performed. In this chapter we work largely with transactional replication as it is the most commonly implemented approach.

When you click the next button, you will be presented with the dialog as shown in Figure 17.21.

SQL Sever is able to replicate information to both SQL Server and non-SQL Server destinations. The non-SQL Server destinations are enabled for replication through either ODBC or OLE-DB connections.

FIGURE 17.20

Choose the type of replication you'll be establishing for your system.

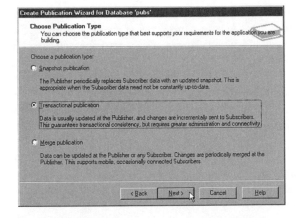

FIGURE 17.21

Defining the destination for the replication.

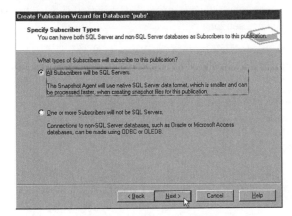

After clicking the next button, you will finally be presented with a list of tables to publish. Figure 17.22 shows an example of these options.

FIGURE 17.22

Selecting tables to publish.

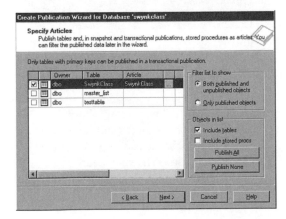

By default, when you select the table to publish, an article name will be created that matches the name of the table. You can accept this name or create your own. When you create your own, make sure you do not include spaces or wild-card characters, such as an asterisk, in the name.

N O T E   You might want to create a naming convention for your publications to make it easier to know what information they provide. This is completely optional, but if you're publishing numerous articles, this information will help the subscription systems determine which publications they need to be working with. ▪

As this publication publishes all eligible tables from the PUBS database, you can simply click the Publish All button for the definition. Each table is selected for publication and an article name is created.

Next, you can customize each article as needed. The options button for each article will be covered in detail in a later section.

Clicking the Next button will take you to the dialog as shown in Figure 17.23, where you can name the publication. Click Next to continue.

FIGURE 17.23

Naming the publication.

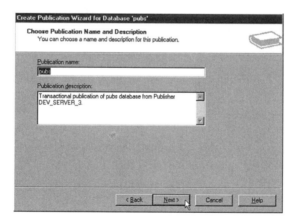

You have the option to define filters for the data. This will be covered in a later section. Because you want to publish all data at this point, simply select the default of No as shown in Figure 17.24.

Clicking the Next button will take you to the final step where the publication you have defined will be set up. When the creation completes successfully and you close the notification dialog, you will be returned to the Manage Publications dialog. You should now have a publication entitled Pubs beneath the Pubs database as shown in figure 17.25.

FIGURE 17.24

Defining data filter
options.

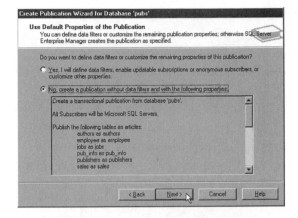

FIGURE 17.25

Managing a pub-
lication.

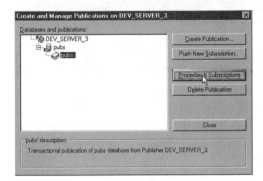

If you highlight the publication and select the Properties and Subscriptions button, you will be presented with a dialog that contains all information concerning the publication: who is subscribed to it, subscription options, and status. You will use this dialog to fine-tune a publication and manage it over time.

Establishing Table Synchronization   When you establish a publication, you are guaranteed that the subscribing system's tables will be initialized to contain the same information as the replicated table. To do this, complete an initial synchronization step. You can control how and when this step occurs by selecting the General tab from the Publications Properties dialog box shown in Figure 17.26.

If you are replicating information between SQL Servers, you'll want to make sure you leave the default copy method, using Native Format data files, selected. This will enable SQL Server to save the information in as optimized a format as possible when it creates the export file used to initialize the subscriber's database tables. The other option, Character format, will save the exported information in a format that you can use if you are importing to the receiving database using other utilities, or if you're using the information produced by the initial synchronization in a third-party system.

FIGURE 17.26

Selecting the format and time limit for synchronization.

TIP

If the transaction log fills up and you're forced to dump and truncate it, you should first unsubscribe any replication servers. After you have done this, dump and truncate the log, then resubscribe the servers. When you do, they will automatically resynchronize with the publishing server.

You can also set up the schedule of times that controls when the synchronization will occur by selecting the Status tab and clicking the Agent Properties button. Establishing these times is very similar to setting up the time frames during the initial configuration of the replication services.

Controlling the Recipients of Subscriptions   A key feature and concern regarding replication of databases is security. When you set up your system for replication, you can determine what subscribing systems will have overall access to your replication services. This presents a possible challenge, though, when you need to provide access to some, but not all, publications that reside on your replication server.

SQL Server enables you to indicate, on a case-by-case basis, what servers will have access to any given publication. By default, when you set up a new subscription, SQL Server will make it available to any server with overall access to the replication system of your server. To change this, as indicated in Figure 17.27, select the Subscribers tab of the Configure Publishing, Subscribers, and Distributor dialog box.

When a server looks to your system to select available publications, if its system has not been authorized to use a given publication, that publication will not show up in the list of available items. You can change this option later to allow or disallow access to a publication by selecting the Subscribers tab of the Configure Publishing, Subscribers, and Distributor dialog box.

Making Changes to Publications   After you've set up publications, you can review them from the Manage Publications window. Select Tools, Replication, Manage and Create Publications. In Figure 17.28, you can see that each database will show its related publications and articles as they've been defined on the server.

FIGURE 17.27

You can easily prevent access to specific publications depending on what servers are requesting the information.

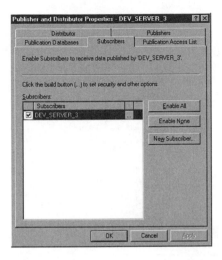

FIGURE 17.28

You can use the tree view of the replication system to select a publication to review or modify.

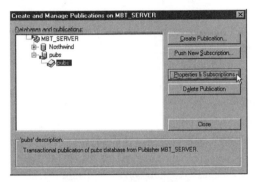

If you want to make a change to a publication, simply highlight it and select Properties, then Subscriptions. You'll be able to modify the tables that are included, how the information is synchronized, and the security aspects of the publication.

Publishing Partial Databases and/or Tables

Now that you understand how to publish entire databases, this section will review how to selectively publish information from your replication server. As you might imagine, publishing select information can be quite complicated, although it will depend a great deal on how you're trying to limit the information being replicated and how you go about defining that information.

Limiting Publications to a Single Table   The first and most basic selective publication is limiting the publication to a single table. You might have noticed that each table available for replication is listed when you define a given publication. In the first example, the entire database is published by selecting the Publish All button. The alternative to this is to select the individual tables that you want to include in the subscription from the Database Tables list. See Figure 17.29.

FIGURE 17.29

You can select one or more individual tables to be included in the publication.

If you do nothing more for this publication, the entire table will be monitored and replicated as part of this publication. You have the same options for managing how the publication will be synchronized and what servers will have access to it as you do when setting up a full-database replication.

The alternative to publishing the entire database table is to partition it. You might recall from an earlier section in this chapter, "Publishing Partial Databases or Tables," that you can partition a table in one of two ways: either horizontally or vertically. The next section shows how you can control this functionality with your publication.

Partitioning Information to Be Included in a Publication   The two partitioning options, horizontal and vertical, correspond to looking at views of your information based on selectively retrieving rows (horizontal) or columns (vertical) from your database tables. Of course, you can combine these two techniques as well to provide a concise view of the information in the table if needed.

To establish a partition of information to be used in the article, you select the Filter Columns tab on the Manage Publications dialog box. See Figure 17.30.

In the example, as discussed earlier in this section, the Contract column information shouldn't be included in the replicated information that is provided to other sites with this publication. By scrolling down the list of columns, you can select and deselect the columns that you want to include. After you complete the selection, you have vertically partitioned the database if you've deselected any columns because the publication includes only those fields that you allowed.

Normally, the SQL Server replication process manages insert, delete, and update operations automatically. This might be a problem if, for example, you're inserting information and want another process kicked off by the action of inserting a new row. In these cases, you can click the Build button within the grid on the Articles tab and specify the Insert, Update, and Delete scripts that you can run when records are modified with these operations. See Figure 17.31.

FIGURE 17.30

You can select which columns you want to be included in the replication process.

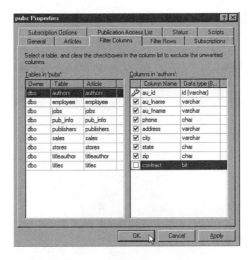

FIGURE 17.31

You can specify custom scripts to run as part of the replication process for each article.

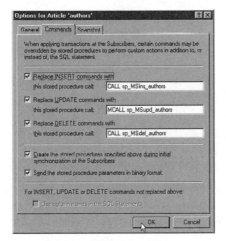

In addition, you can provide a table-creation script that you can use in initializing tables. This script will be run instead of the standard table script generated by SQL Server based on the source table's definition. This can be helpful if you're defining tables that will receive replicated data, but perhaps not all columns that need to be in a table.

By default, when the table is created, it will be created with columns to match the article's definition. This means that, in the example where you did not choose to copy the Contract column, the column would not exist at all in the recipients' databases. You can modify the creation script here and make sure all appropriate information and columns are included. Figure 17.32 shows how you can modify these values.

FIGURE 17.32
You can override SQL's default methods that are used to implement changes to the underlying database tables.

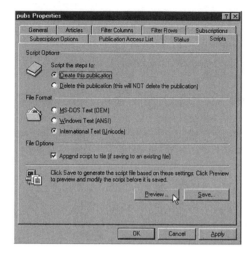

CAUTION

Unless you are very comfortable with modifying these types of SQL scripts, you should consider alternative means of making the changes you need. For example, perhaps you could create a series of triggers on the subscriber that institute changes needed in the storage of the information so that only certain columns are reused in the end user's system. Remember that changes made here will impact all subscribing systems, and you should ensure that this will not cause unforeseen problems on systems that might vary in their implementation of database structures and table layouts.

▶ For more information on triggers, **see** Chapter 15, ""Creating and Managing Triggers," **p. 395**

You also have the option of controlling the synchronization scripts that will be run by SQL Server. Clicking the Build button on the Articles tab will let you edit what actions are taken on synchronization of tables between the publication and subscription systems. The Snapshot shown in Figure 17.33.

 TIP   If there is a chance that the table might already exist on the user's system, be sure to check the DROP Table First option. If you don't, you might have a database table in an unknown state.

If you want to see or edit the actual script that will be created when the table is synchronized, you can click the Save button on the Scripts tab. You'll be presented with the listing that will be used to create the table when it's initialized.

After you've completed your changes, click OK from the Manage Publication dialog box, and you'll be ready to allow other users to start accessing the publications on your system.

In the next section, I will discuss setting up subscriptions on the recipient side of the equation. Now that you've set up the publications, it's a straightforward process to indicate which publications any given subscription server needs to begin receiving replication updates.

FIGURE 17.33
You have full control over how indexes and existing tables will be managed during the synchronization process.

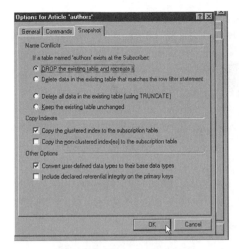

Enabling Subscribing

After the publications have been set up on the publication server, it's a simple task to set up the subscription server to begin receiving the information. Before you can subscribe to a given article, you must follow the same installation steps outlined earlier in this chapter. These steps set up the distribution database and prepare your system to begin working with the replicated information. The only difference is that, when it comes to specifying which databases are visible to the replication process, you'll be specifying which ones can be the recipients of information rather than the source of the information.

▶ For installation instructions, **see** the previous section of this chapter, "Installing SQL Server's Replication Services," **p. 456**

When you're ready to initiate subscriptions, select Tools, Replication, Push Subscriptions to Others from the menu in Enterprise Manager. As shown in Figure 17.34, this brings up the Manage Publications dialog box used to define and create publications.

FIGURE 17.34
Select the publication that you want to subscribe to from the list of available items for the server and database you are interested in.

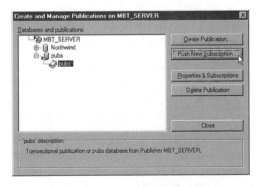

After you've found the publication you want to subscribe to, highlight it and select Push New Subscription. This will launch the Push Subscription Wizard. See Figure 17.35.

FIGURE 17.35
The New Push Subscription Wizard.

Click the Next button and highlight the server in the list that will be the target for this publication. Click the Next button.

Here you will be able to specify the database that you want to replicate to. See Figure 17.36.

FIGURE 17.36
Select the target database for the publication.

Notice that you are able to create a new database at this point. If you do not have a database already setup to accept the information, click the Create New button. This will launch the database creation dialog.

▶ For database creation instructions, **see** Chapter 5,"Creating Databases and Transaction Logs," **p. 93**

When you have the database selected, click OK and then the Next button.

You are now presented with the Distribution Schedule options as shown in Figure 17.37. You can have replication run continuously or on a scheduled basis. If you select the continuous option, each transaction is replicated as soon as possible to the subscriber. If you select a schedule option, all transactions are held until that specified time.

FIGURE 17.37
Scheduling distribution.

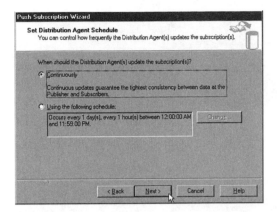

N O T E If you are using a remote link or are only providing snapshot information to the subscription servers, you might want to change this value to a time when the system is generally under less load. This can help decrease the impact on network traffic that will be incurred when the replication process kicks off. If you are subscribing over a dial-up connection, this enables you to move the replication process to a time when phone rates are much lower. ■

For this exercise, we will set up replication on a continuous basis.

In the next dialog, you'll notice that there are three different options available to you for the initial synchronization of the database. The last option is to turn off the synchronization altogether. This means that you know for a fact that the database and the concerned tables are in sync with the master system by some other means.

> **CAUTION**
>
> If you are at all unsure about the validity of the information in the database, it's best to allow the system to perform an initial synchronization on the database.

 TIP Remember, you can schedule the time at which synchronization takes place. Moving it to off-hours can ease network loading significantly.

Monitoring Replication

Monitoring replication was one of the most time-consuming tasks in previous versions due to the lack of monitor tools. In this version of SQL Server, a monitor is included to help you track the health of the replication system.

The Replication Monitor, as shown in Figure 17.41, is used to track each publication and all of the associated agents that move information throughout the system. Selecting an Agent displays the active publications that it is currently managing. If you right-click and select Agent History, you are presented with the dialog in Figure 17.38.

FIGURE 17.38

The Snapshot Agent history.

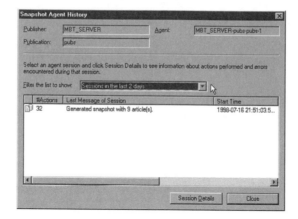

You have the option to filter the processed snapshot processes by a series of timelines and also all those that had errors. Highlighting one of the instances and clicking the Agent Details button, as shown in Figure 17.39, will show you the exact series of steps that occurred during that procedure.

FIGURE 17.39

Details of the initial snapshot operation.

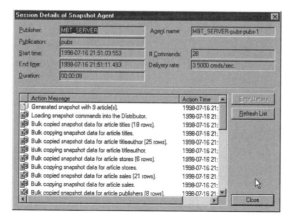

Finally, a set of alerts with customized actions can be configured to monitor the replication process. This enables you to do such things as page, send an email to an operator in the case of specified problems, or execute custom tasks to bring replication back up. When you link the alerts with tasks run by the SQL Server Agent, you get a very powerful system for detecting and fixing problems without requiring the intervention of an operator.

> **CAUTION**
>
> Although this provides a powerful, automated mechanism to maintain and monitor replication, it should be used very carefully. You should thoroughly test any automated procedures before implementing them in a production environment to ensure the data is always protected. In all cases when the server takes an action based upon an alert, an operator should be notified either via email, pager, or network message.

Uninstalling Replication

There might be times when you need to uninstall replication, either on a server-specific basis or on an overall basis. Examples include a case where a server is changing physical locations and no longer needs access to sensitive information, or where you've installed several test scenarios and simply want to start over.

The next two sections will show how you can cover both of these situations using facilities within SQL Server.

Disallowing Specific Servers

If you find that you want to remove a server from the list of servers that are eligible to receive information from your publication server, you must first determine whether you need to restrict only individual publications or if you want to revoke access altogether. If your intent is to remove access completely, you simply remove the server from the list of eligible candidates that can see the publications on this server.

From the Tools menu, select Replication, Configure Publishing, Subscribers, and Distribution. You'll be able to indicate which servers are able to subscribe to your server. Figure 17.40 shows the server selection dialog box that will appear.

Part
III

Ch
17

FIGURE 17.40

Deselect any servers to which you no longer want to make publications available.

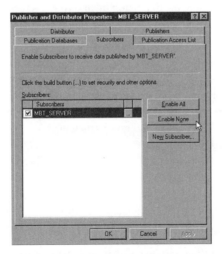

You'll be presented with a list of subscriptions that are about to be removed and be asked to confirm that you want to remove the server from the list of eligible systems. After you confirm, the server will still show up on the list, but the server will not be able to select publications on the publication server.

Uninstalling Replication Completely

Carefully consider all options before you opt to remove replication entirely from the system. This operation will shut down *all* replication to *all* subscribing servers, and it does so in a somewhat brute force manner by removing the replication option from the server and deleting the distribution database.

In version 6.5, this process was rather long and tedious and consisted of manually removing or disabling multiple options. Finally, you had to execute a stored procedure to ensure everything was cleaned up. SQL Server 7 makes this process much easier. If you haven't noticed by now, this is accomplished by yet another of the numerous wizards available in this version. Select Tools, Replication, Disable Publishing. This wizard will walk you through the steps of removing publishing and distribution and will finally remove all traces of replication from the system.

Reality Check

Probably one of the most frequently encountered problems with a replication installation is that, when SQL Server is installed, the administrator account is used for the SQL Server Agent service. Later, when the password is changed on the Administrator account, the replication services stop working, seemingly without cause.

The fact that the SQL Executive must be able to log in, and that it's set up with the Administrator account when you run setup, makes it easy to forget that the account and the process are linked.

One performance area that has helped in implementations has been to use stored procedures in the replication process. Remember, you can indicate the SQL Statement that is used to divide up the information that you work with in the replication process by using a stored procedure in place of the SQL statement. This takes advantage of the fact that SQL Server compiles stored procedures. This makes them faster and more efficient.

From Here...

Replication is a powerful tool, especially in distributed environments. By putting replication into your systems, you can provide an excellent level of usability for applications, a great security layer for the underlying database tables, and better overall data availability.

For additional information about the topics covered in this chapter, please refer to the following chapters:

- Chapter 5, "Creating Databases, and Transaction Logs," provides additional information about creating the databases that you'll be using in the replication process. It also includes information about the management of the transaction log for your applications.

- For information on managing databases and creating databases and tables, see Chapter 6, "Creating Database Tables and Using Datatypes."

- In Chapter 10, "Managing and Using Indexes and Keys," information about defining primary keys is provided. You'll need this information to enable replication for your tables.

- Chapter 15, "Creating and Managing Triggers," includes information that might help you automatically create subsystems for further distributing information that has been replicated.

- Chapter 25, "Using the SQL Server Agent," includes information for automating and managing the administration of your servers.

Part
III

Ch
17

Using the Distributed Transaction Coordinator

In this chapter

With SQL Server 6.5, Microsoft began supporting distributed transactions, which are transactions that span more than one server. There are many times when you need to update more than one source of information and to apply transaction technologies to the update to ensure that all or none of the changes are made against the database tables. The Distributed Transaction Coordinator (DTC) is the tool that will provide this functionality as well as utility functions that help you manage the process.

N O T E The DTC is the start to a more comprehensive transaction system built on the Component Object Model (COM) architecture. While DTC is largely SQL Server–oriented at this writing, other types of systems are expected to use this same technology for their work—from workflow to transactional systems based in other technologies. ■

As with standard transactions, distributed transactions must follow the ACID rules. For more information on this, be sure to read Chapter 12, "Understanding Transactions and Locking." In short, the transaction must be self-contained and must be autonomous, meaning it can be reversed without impacting other processes. As you might imagine, distributed transactions add a whole new layer of variables to the development and deployment process.

With a typical system, you don't have to work with server-to-server issues, network problems or other issues that can become a part of the transaction process. Remember that transactions must be completely self-contained and able to be completed without intervention. With a distributed transaction, you might face issues with hardware failures, server availability, or different loading and performance patterns between the participating servers. As you configure the DTC, you'll need to keep these in mind and make sure you set appropriate time out and latency options.

You can think of the DTC as an extension of standard transactions. The DTC simply enables you to build transactions across servers, rather than containing them within a given server.

DTC is broken up into two different components. The first, the Transaction Manager, is responsible for overall coordination of the transactions. The Transaction Manager is responsible for enforcing the ACID rules and for making sure the transaction objects are complete and that they are addressed as needed to complete the transaction.

The other component, the Resource Manager, has the role of setting up the transaction and making it happen. The Resource Manager's role is to carry out the statements that make up the transaction and make sure the updates happen as requested. More on these components is covered in the next two sections.

Resource Manager

The Resource Manager has the task of carrying out the distributed transaction's mission. This means that the commands requested are performed by the Resource Manager against the different tables as needed.

The application doesn't work directly with the Resource Manager, but the transaction objects are submitted to the Transaction Manager. The Transaction Manager sets up the transaction and works with the Resource Manager to make it happen. All of this is transparent to the application, which must only issue the appropriate BEGIN and END transaction statements to ensure a complete distributed transaction.

The Resource Manager is also responsible for making sure that the transaction can be recovered, even in cases of power failure during the resolution of the transaction.

Transaction Manager

The Transaction Manager responds when a new distributed transaction is begun. With the transaction BEGIN statement, the Transaction Manager sets up the transaction object and works through two distinct phases of the transaction. These are the PREPARE phase, and the COMMIT phase. This is what is referred to as a two-phase commit, which is something not possible with SQL Server prior to the implementation of the Transaction Manager and the DTC overall.

In the PREPARE phase, the Transaction Manager works with the Resource Manager to complete the operations, but not commit them to the databases involved. You'll recall that, with a standard transaction, you open a transaction, perform the actions you need, then commit the transaction, saving the changes to the tables. With distributed transactions, you do basically the same thing. First, you begin the distributed transaction, perform the actions you need to perform, and then commit the changes to the respective database tables.

The Transaction Manager is responsible for making sure that, each step along the way, the proper logging is done, and that the Resource Manager is able to obtain the information and responses it needs to be able to ultimately fulfill the request. The Transaction Manager logs all activity to the msdtc.log file, which is what is used to roll back transactions if needed.

The Transaction Manager steps in when a BEGIN DISTRIBUTED TRANSACTION request is issued. This statement tells the Transaction Manager to set up a new transaction object and get ready to work through the distributed transaction as needed. The Transaction Manager uses the proper Resource Managers on the different servers that will be needed to complete the transaction.

When completed, the application issues a COMMIT TRANSACTION or a ROLLBACK TRANSACTION, and the Transaction Manager works with the Resource Manager to complete or abort the task.

Part
III

Ch
18

Building Distributed Transactions

As with a typical transaction, you bracket distributed transactions between BEGIN and COMMIT or ROLLBACK transaction statements. The SQL statements between the two are carried out, then committed or rolled back as a whole depending on the completion of the series of statements.

Configuring Remote Servers for Use with the Distributed Transaction Coordinator

When you start a distributed transaction, you indicate the name of the remote server in the transaction's execute statements where you call the stored procedures on the remote system.

You need to define those server names before you can reference them in the execute state-ments. If you don't, SQL Server won't be able to resolve where to look for the stored procedure you're executing.

You set up the server in the Remote Server Properties dialog box. You access this dialog by expanding the tree view for the server you are working on, right-clicking the Remote Servers item, and selecting New Remote Server from the pop-up menu. See Figure 18.1 for an example.

FIGURE 18.1

You must define the servers that will be accessed by the DTC by providing the server name and selecting the RPC check box.

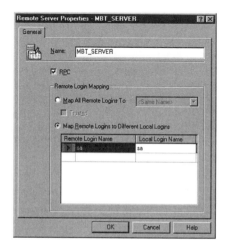

Provide the name of the server and be sure to select the Remote Procedure Calls (RPC) check box. RPC is the method that is used by the DTC to communicate with the remote servers. If you don't check this option, the DTC will not be able to work with the other servers.

You'll also need to provide the login information. The easiest and most direct route is to select the Map All Remote Logins To: option button and leave <Same Name> selected. This will use the current user's name as the login on the remote system. Keep in mind that the user must be a valid user on the remote system as well as the local system.

Once these are defined, select the Add button to save the update. Be sure to complete this information for each server that will be working with DTC.

N O T E   If you have any trouble connecting over RPCs, check the network protocols on the server and make sure the RPC service is loaded and available. If it's not, add it to the server. You will probably have to reboot your system to have the changes take effect. ▪

Installing and Configuring the Distributed Transaction Coordinator

There are two steps to setting up the DTC component of SQL Server. First, you need to set up the server-side components. Those components make the DTC available to your applications.

The second step is to set up is the client interface to the server, which enables you to work with the server-based DTC and specifies the protocol that is used to work with the server.

In the next sections, you'll learn how to set up these components on your network.

Setting Up the Server Components of DTC

When you install SQL Server, it automatically installs the Distributed Transaction Coordinator. It's not an automatically started option, though, so you won't see it in the Enterprise Manager until you start it. To start the service, select Services from the Control Panel and then find the MSDTC service. See Figure 18.2.

FIGURE 18.2

By default, the service does not start automatically when the server is started unless you've installed the NT4 Option Pack or MTS.

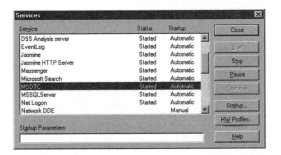

Part

III

Ch

18

If you'll be using the service regularly, you want to set it up to start automatically when your server is started. To set this up, click the Startup button. The service dialog, shown in Figure 18.3, lets you provide information about several of the options of the DTC server component startup. The two key items are:

- Startup Type—Select automatic to have the service start automatically each time the server is restarted. If you leave the setting at Manual, you can still use the DTC, but you'll have to start the service either from the Service Manager, or from the Enterprise Manager, each time you need to use the DTC.

- Log on As—This option is used to indicate the account that should be used by the service when it starts. Remember, if you set up the service to use a non-system account, you'll need to make sure you assign the "Log on as a service" right to the account you select.

FIGURE 18.3

You should select automatic start and log on as a system account for the most trouble-free installation.

Once you've set up the service, be sure you start it manually the first time. If you do not, DTC won't start until the next time you reboot your server. Note that you can start this service both from within the Control Panel and from within the SQL Server Service Manager.

Select Start, Programs, Microsoft SQL Server 7.0, MSDTC Administrative Console to display the console as shown in Figure 18.4.

FIGURE 18.4

You can work with many of the options associated with the DTC from the MS DTC Administrative Console.

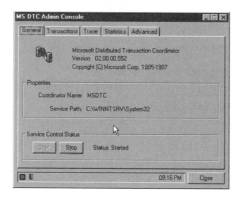

The Administrative Console contains five tabs which will be discussed in the next five sections.

General   This tab enables you to start and stop the service. You cannot, however, set up the service for automatic startup when NT Server starts. To set this up, you'll need to see the section earlier entitled "Setting Up the Server Components of DTC."

Transactions   The Transactions tab shows any open transactions at the time you request the option. Each transaction is listed in a table and the DTC shows trace information for each transaction so you can track it down should the need arise.

Trace...   As with SQL Trace, you can set up filters on DTC transactions. These traces can help you determine where a transaction has gone wrong and how to track it down to correct the situation. The trace tab shows a table of the transactions that you're monitoring and provides the information you'll need to work with them.

TIP When you're running the DTC, it logs its messages to the Windows NT Server's Event Logs, as well as any trace facilities you might have implemented. You should always review the Event Logs as well as the trace facilities if you're experiencing trouble with a distributed transaction.

Tracing produces messages with four different severity levels:

■ Error—This indicates a fatal error has occurred in the DTC. This might point to other problems in your SQL Server. Be sure to check the errorlog. file in the LOG directory, and also be sure to restart the DTC service. In addition, if you have transactions open at the time you receive this error, be sure you don't remove the msdtc.log file as it will contain the information needed by DTC to reconstruct the data in your system to the state prior to the failure, after you restart the service.

■ Information—This is somewhat like the information notices in the event log. The information presented won't take down the server, but it might be of use to you in debugging or tracing a transaction. This includes starting and stopping the DTC services.

■ Trace—Information produced as part of the trace process.

■ Warning—These items either might possibly happen or have happened. They are bad, but not bad enough to cause the DTC to go down. Be sure to review all warning messages and make sure you understand what happened to cause them. You should not put into production any system that generates warning messages.

In addition, the Trace display will show one of several different status states for each transaction:

■ Aborted—The transaction has been aborted to the best capability of the DTC in the current system state. What this means is that the DTC has notified, or attempted to notify, each participating system that the transaction should be aborted. This is a final state and only shown as the transaction is flushed from the trace display. Once in this state, the transaction state cannot be changed.

■ Aborting—The transaction is in the process of aborting. During this time, the Resource Manager is notifying all participating DTCs that the transaction should be aborted. During this time, you cannot change the state of the transaction.

■ Active—The resource manager is actively working the transaction, but it is not yet committed.

■ Committed—The transaction completed successfully.

■ Forced Commit, Forced Abort—These states are the result of a forced transaction that had previously been marked In-Doubt.

■ In-Doubt—After the DTC on a system other than the coordinating system has been notified that all other systems are prepared, if it determines that the coordinating system becomes unavailable, the transaction state changes to In-Doubt. You can force a transaction in this state to complete, and it will do so based on the information for that specific system. If the transaction fails, the transaction is marked as Forced Abort. If it succeeds, it will be marked Forced Commit. Remember, if you commit a transaction in this manner, other participating systems might or might not be up-to-date with the system on which you force the transaction.

■ Notifying Committed—The coordinating DTC is notifying the various participating systems that the transaction should be committed. Between the time that the DTC is notifying other systems, and the time when they respond with success, this state is in effect. You cannot manually change the state of a transaction when this status is displayed.

■ Only Fail Remain to Notify—For some reason, one or more participating servers have failed to notify the coordinating system that they've properly committed the transaction as requested during Notifying Committed state. At this point, you can wait to allow the transaction to clear, or you can force the issue, taking into account that those remote, unavailable systems will not be updated unless you force each of them to commit as mentioned earlier under the In-Doubt status.

■ Prepared—All participating systems have acknowledged that they are ready and able to commit the transaction.

■ Preparing—The DTC has been told to commit the transaction and is now checking with each of the other participating systems to ensure that all involved in the transaction are ready and able to commit the transaction.

Three different subsystems generate messages to the logs and the trace facility. These are CM for the connection manager and its related activities, LOG for the logging mechanisms, and SVC for the overall DTC service.

Statistics   The statistics tab will show you the volume and types of transactions you're processing through the DTC. The dialog box shows the current and overall total or aggregate values for your distributed transactions. See Figure 18.5 for an example.

FIGURE 18.5

If you think distributed transaction performance might not be up to par, be sure to review the statistics on each of the servers involved in the distributed transactions on your system.

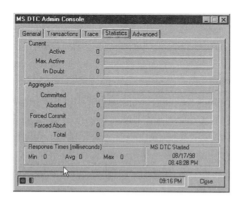

A key value to watch is the Response Times frame. These values represent a good view on how your DTC is doing in working through transactions. If you start to see these values jump, you'll need to review activity on the servers involved in the transactions, and you'll want to make sure the transactions aren't reliant on some factor that creates a bottleneck for the transactions to complete.

Remember, the response times listed are overall response times. To find out about specific transactions, you'll need to use the trace facility.

Advanced   There are several different options you can set up for the DTC on the server to help in the monitoring of the server. If you are tracing transactions, and you find that performance has been significantly impacted, be sure you've set the Trace settings to the "Faster MS DTC" side of the equation. See Figure 18.6 for an example of the configuration dialog box.

FIGURE 18.6

Be careful not to make the trace frequency too small as it can impact overall DTC performance on the server.

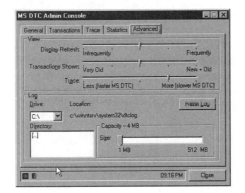

The display refresh values range from one to 20 seconds. This is another item that can impact the server performance, but it's likely you'll want to set this rather low to see transactions more readily if you're debugging a known issue.

Transaction aging runs from one second to five minutes. This controls the age of transactions that are shown. Transactions falling outside this range are still being processed, just not displayed. In the normal course of business, it's unlikely you'll need to see transactions that are only a few seconds old. On the other hand, transactions that approach even one minute are surely suspect and need to be reviewed and modified if possible. Remember that the user of your application won't want to sit and wait for a transaction to commit, regardless of the technology happening behind the scenes.

The log options let you dictate how large the log file will be allowed to get and where it should be located. You can select the directory, drive and size for the file. To make changes to the log file settings, you'll need to first stop the DTC services. After you've completed your changes, you can restart the services and the new settings will be in effect.

The Reset Log option will clear the log file and let you start anew. As with the other log file options, you'll need to have the DTC stopped prior to using this option.

Part

III

Ch

18

Defining Distributed Transactions

As mentioned in the opening section of this chapter, distributed transactions are extensions to the standard transactions that you found out about in Chapter 12, "Understanding Transactions and Locking." Distributed transactions add the DISTRIBUTED keyword to the BEGIN TRANSACTION statement and enable you to indicate different server names on the execute instructions, but otherwise are identical to more typical transactions.

For example, if you have two servers, SQL1 and SQL2, you can create a distributed transaction with the following code snippet:

```
BEGIN DISTRIBUTED TRANSACTION
    insert into localtable values ('These', 'are', 'inserted', 'locally')
    exec sql2.testdb.dbo.sp_addvalues 'these', 'are', 'inserted', 'remotely'
COMMIT TRANSACTION
```

> **N O T E** You can also indicate two additional option parameters when you start the transaction: the transaction name and a variable. Use these to better manage and trace your transactions when you're debugging or troubleshooting your systems. ■

The two SQL statements doing the value insertions are nothing that you can't accomplish without the use of the DTC. The catch, of course, is what context they are executed within and the amount of control you have should a problem occur.

Without the DTC, these statements would be executed as two separate and distinct requests. If one failed, it would not necessarily impact the second. This would even be true if you had enclosed the two statements in the standard BEGIN TRANSACTION and COMMIT statements. Since they are running on different servers, the only thing that is seen by the transaction and considered a part of it is the actual execution of the INSERT statement, and the execution of, but not successful completion of, the stored procedure call. Regardless of success or failure programmatically of the stored procedure, the transaction succeeds.

With the DTC, the problem of the remote operation is handled, and you'll know for sure the operation succeeded. The DTC effectively extends the reach of the transaction to the second system. With the DTC in effect by using the DISTRIBUTED keyword when you declare the transaction, you'll be able to ensure that all aspects of the transaction succeed, not just the local portions of it.

Debugging Distributed Transactions

If you find that you have transactions remaining on your SQL Server in a pending state, you have a few options available to you that will help to track down the problem area. In general, you can review the statistics that are gathered by the DTC and see how long transactions are taking overall, and you can start to see trends between your servers.

One of the first areas to look at if you find that transactions are slow to complete is the connectivity between your local server and the remote system. If the connection speed is slow, or if either of the servers is being heavily used, it will help explain the execution time of the transactions.

You can also force a transaction to commit by selecting the Trace tab, right-clicking the transaction, and selecting the Resolve option. You'll be able to commit, abort, or forget the transaction.

If you have a transaction that is runaway, don't forget that you can run the different components of the logic through ISQL and watch a little more carefully, considering each value and logic step along the way. In the worst case scenario, consider adding logic to your stored procedures that call the DTC and have them drop values for your variables into a working table along the way, along with checkpoint notations so you will know where in your code you are when the value is written. In pseudo-code:

```
Start procedure
    Write initial value to work table, along with start of routine
    Statement 1
    Write state values to work table, along with before DTC call
    call the DTC participants and start your transaction
```

This admittedly goes back to the debugging days of using message boxes to show information to the developer during the execution of code. The difference, of course, is that you don't have the luxury of the msgbox when working in this environment without moving to an alternate development environment.

 TIP If you use this approach, be sure you don't put your debugging code inside the transaction. If you do, when the transaction rolls back, you'll also lose your debugging information in the work table as it is reversed out of the system.

Reality Check

In the systems that have been completed using the DTC, the biggest stumbling blocks are how to see what's really going on, and how to determine what you need to do to fix any problems that arise. This is where the debugging "droppings" mentioned in the last section come into play. They can save you many hours of test time. Keep in mind that you can have each of your participating servers log information to work tables, providing you with an overall picture of what's happening on your system.

The other thing that you should be sure to do with DTC-based applications is to test what happens in your application if a distributed transaction either takes too long to complete or is rolled back for whatever reason. Be sure your application is able to recover gracefully from the situations that are sure to arise as you add more variables to your development picture.

Part
III

Ch
18

From Here...

The DTC capabilities of SQL Server can be an excellent addition to your system, especially in cases where you're involving several servers with different roles in the processing picture. As with most development issues, there is more than one way to approach moving information around the system and protecting it during that process. Consider the following additional areas of information as you design your system:

- Chapter 12 details how you work with transactions, what the ACID properties of a valid transaction are, and how you use them in your applications.

- Chapter 17, "Setting Up and Managing Replication," will give you one alternative to moving information between servers—replication. With replication you can make sure copies of data are up to date at the publisher and subscriber systems for the information. Different capabilities exist with replication when compared to the DTC approach, so be sure to consider both for your application.

IV

SQL Server Administration Topics

SQL Server Administration

In this chapter

In this chapter you'll be presented with several issues to keep in mind as you administer your SQL Server system. There are many different concepts, routines, and ideas that you need to know for the day-in and day-out management of SQL Server.

The everyday operation of SQL Server will require some of your time to manage the database engine to its fullest potential. By staying on top of the system, you'll be able to ensure the optimum response times for users, and you'll be able to prevent some common system problems.

Some of the concepts in this chapter refer to strictly administrative tasks, and some are related more to the management of performance and system tuning. Taken as a whole, these topics and the correct definition of your system will make sure you have a successful SQL Server installation.

Understanding and Performing Checkpoints

Checkpoints are a function incorporated by SQL Server to commit changes to a database or configuration option at a known, good point in time. As you work to configure the server or make modifications to the server that require a restart of the server, you may want to initiate the checkpoint process manually.

When a checkpoint is issued, whether by a manual intervention process or by naturally occurring server-based processes, all dirty pages are saved to disk. A *dirty page* is one containing updates that have not yet been applied to the disk image of the database. Without intervention on your part, checkpoints normally occur approximately every 60 seconds. The actual time frame in which they are called will depend on server loading, recovery options you've set, and general performance tuning that SQL Server will be looking after, but it should be very close to 60 seconds.

You may have noticed that if your SQL Server goes down unexpectedly, it can take longer to startup the next time. This is because SQL Server will roll back and roll forward transactions to the last checkpoint. When SQL Server does this, it is restoring the database to the last known good state, which is the one recorded when the last checkpoint was issued and successfully carried out.

N O T E You can also manually shutdown the server by issuing the SHUTDOWN command. By issuing CHECKPOINT followed by a SHUTDOWN, you can ensure that all transaction information is saved appropriately. ▪

If you know that you're shutting down the server (especially if you're using the WITH NOWAIT option), you can avoid the longer startup times by manually issuing the CHECKPOINT command. This will accomplish the same thing as enabling the server to issue the command automatically. All information will be saved to disk, and the system will be able to simply start up and "turn on" the databases for access by your client applications. This is helpful if you're shutting down a server quickly, perhaps in a case where you've had power failure and the UPS that is sustaining the server is nearing its life cycle.

N O T E The CHECKPOINT command is issued at a database level and is applied against the current database. If you have more than one database in your system, you need to issue the command against each database. In order to issue the CHECKPOINT command, you must be the database owner. ■

Another option that will prove quite helpful is the Truncate Log on Checkpoint option. This option will automatically truncate the transaction log whenever a checkpoint is reached. To set this option, select the database in the Enterprise Manager and right-click it. Select Properties from the menu, then select the Options tab. Figure 19.1 shows the options that are available.

FIGURE 19.1
You can control the
interval in which the
transaction log is
truncated from the
Enterprise Manager.

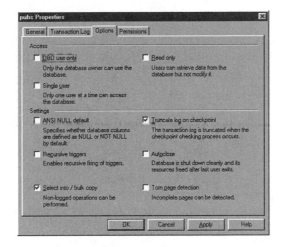

N O T E If you set Truncate Log on Checkpoint as an option, you won't be able to back up the transaction log during the course of standard backups. This may not present a problem in your installation, as you can still do database backups, but you should consider your overall backup plan prior to setting this option. See the sections later in this chapter for more information on backup and restore operations. ■

If you have Truncate Log on Checkpoint enabled for a database, the transaction log will be truncated up to the point of the last successfully committed transaction, provided replication is not in use. If replication is in use, the log is truncated up to the last successfully replicated and committed transaction. Because replication is transaction-log based, the log will not be truncated in cases where replication has not been propagated to the subscribers for a given publication. More information on replication is presented in Chapter 17, "Setting Up and Managing Replication."

Using the Database Consistency Checker

The *Database Consistency Checker* (DBCC) is a tool that you use for detailed information about the database objects that SQL Server manages. Because there are so many different facets to the SQL Server system and its handling of tables, objects, rules, triggers, stored procedures, and so on, it is helpful to be able to go into the server and run a "sanity check" to make sure all is well. The DBCC statement provides this functionality.

Setting Up to Ensure the Best Results: Single-User Mode

Before getting into the use and utility of DBCC, it's important to understand two different conditions that are generally in effect any time you want to use this statement. First, as a rule, you should try to make sure that as little activity as possible is impacting the SQL Server. If people are accessing the server to make updates or changes, you may receive errors when DBCC runs. This is due to the nature of the calls that DBCC will perform. They are very low-level and require near-exclusive use of the database in many cases.

Second, you'll often have to ensure exclusive access to the database. In these cases, use the sp_dboption statement to set the database to single-user mode. The following is the syntax of that command:

```
sp_dboption <database name>, 'single user', True
```

For example, if you want to run some checks on the PUBS database, you'll use the following command:

```
sp_dboption 'pubs', 'single user', True
```

This will prevent others from using the system while you perform your checks.

> **N O T E** You'll need to be in the Master database prior to updating the options for the system. Be sure you issue a Use Master prior to attempting to set options using sp_dboption. ▪

Once you've turned on single-user mode, you can perform the checks you need to make sure the database is running in top shape. When you've completed your work with DBCC, you can set the database back to multi-user mode by changing the True noted earlier in the sp_dboption command to False. For example:

```
sp_dboption 'pubs', 'single user', False.
```

Using the DBCC Options

As mentioned earlier, DBCC supports many different options. In the next few sections, I will discuss the most often used options and what they can do to help in your administration of your SQL Server.

Using DBCC CHECKALLOC—In 6.5 NEWALLOC replaced CHECKALLOC. With CHECKALLOC, the system process stops if an error is found. This sometimes obscures other problems with the database. NEWALLOC does not stop when an error is found, but continues on and reports all errors that it finds in the database structures. In 7.0, NEWALLOC is provided for backward compatibility only. CHECKALLOC has been resurrected to replace NEWALLOC. It has the following syntax:

```
DBCC CHECKALLOC [('database_name'[, NOINDEX])] [WITH NO_INFOMSGS]
```

If you leave out the <database name> parameter, SQL Server will check the current database.

When CHECKALLOC runs, it will return detailed information about your system and its database objects. This information can be used to point you in the direction of any problems that may be occurring on the system. The next listing shows a portion of a report run against the standard pubs database. This sample indicates the type of information you can expect to receive from the CHECKALLOC option.

Listing 19.1—Sample Output from the NewAlloc Statement

```
Checking pubs
*****************************************************************
TABLE: sysobjects         OBJID = 1
INDID=1         FIRST=(1:5)    ROOT=(1:16)    DPAGES=3    SORT=0
    Data level: 1.   4 Data  Pages in 2 extents.
INDID=2         FIRST=(1:112)  ROOT=(1:112)   DPAGES=1    SORT=0
    Indid     : 2.  1 Index Pages in 1 extents.
INDID=3         FIRST=(1:120)  ROOT=(1:120)   DPAGES=1    SORT=0
    Indid     : 3.  1 Index Pages in 1 extents.
TOTAL # of extents = 4
*****************************************************************
TABLF: sysindexes         OBJID = 2
INDID=1         FIRST=(1:24)   ROOT=(1:56)    DPAGES=1    SORT=0
    Data level: 1.   2 Data  Pages in 2 extents.
INDID=255       FIRST=(1:96)   ROOT=(1:96)    DPAGES=0    SORT=0
    Indid     : 255.  5 Index Pages in 1 extents.
TOTAL # of extents = 3
...


...
*****************************************************************
TABLE: dtproperties        OBJID = 933578364
INDID=1         FIRST=(1:536)  ROOT=(1:544)   DPAGES=1    SORT=0
    Data level: 1.   2 Data  Pages in 2 extents.
INDID=255       FIRST=(1:516)  ROOT=(1:516)   DPAGES=0    SORT=0
    Indid     : 255.  1 Index Pages in 0 extents.
TOTAL # of extents = 2
*****************************************************************
Processed 42 entries in Sysindexes for dbid 5.
Alloc page (1:2) (# of extent=71 used pages=161 ref pages=114)
          (1:2) (# of mixed extents=10  mixed pages=74)
    OBJID 1 INDID 1 data extents=2 pages=4 mixed extent pages=2
    OBJID 1 INDID 2 index extents=1 pages=1 mixed extent pages=0
    OBJID 1 INDID 3 index extents=1 pages=1 mixed extent pages=0
    OBJID 2 INDID 1 data extents=2 pages=2 mixed extent pages=0
    OBJID 2 INDID 255 index extents=1 pages=5 mixed extent pages=4
    OBJID 3 INDID 1 data extents=2 pages=8 mixed extent pages=6
    OBJID 4 INDID 1 data extents=2 pages=2 mixed extent pages=0
    OBJID 4 INDID 2 index extents=1 pages=1 mixed extent pages=0
...


...
OBJID 933578364 INDID 255 index extents=0 pages=1 mixed extent pages=1
Total (# of extent=71 used pages=161 ref pages=114) in this database
```

continues

Part

IV

Ch

19

Listing 19.1 Continued

```
        (# of mixed extents=10  mixed pages=74) in this database
CHECKALLOC found 0 errors in database
DBCC execution completed. If DBCC printed error messages,
see your System Administrator.
```

You can see that a great deal of information is returned. Usually, you'll need to look at the report returned and search only for the exceptions. Focus on problems that are reported, if any, and work with them. The balance of the information is provided to confirm database table structures, page allocations, and so on. If you do receive an error message, you should also receive specific instructions on what must be done to correct the problem. The report for the pubs database is relatively short. For production environments, this can span hundreds of pages. The easiest way to scan your DBCC outputs is by using the search functionality. Running a search on the following strings will take you to any errors: "Msg", "dbprocess", "Level", "error:". Using this list is not bulletproof. If you have used any of these words in the names of your tables, a search will also find them even though they are not errors. However, this technique will save you many hours of searching large outputs for errors.

N O T E If there are objects on removable devices, CHECKALLOC might return warning message 2558. This warning can be ignored. It is caused by a necessary setting for objects residing on removable devices. ▪

Using DBCC CHECKDB When you run CHECKDB, each table and its associated data pages, indexes, and pointers are all validated. Indexes and data pages are checked to ensure they are properly linked and indexes are in proper sorted order. It also checks to ensure that the data on each page is reasonable, pointers are consistent, and page offsets are valid. CHECKDB also checks to ensure that text, image, and ntext pages are linked properly and the size is correct. If you run CHECKDB, you do not need to run CHECKALLOC or CHECKTABLE. CHECKDB has the following syntax:

```
DBCC CHECKDB [('database_name'[, NOINDEX])] [WITH NO_INFOMSGS]
```

If you leave out the <database name> parameter, SQL Server will check the current database.

The following excerpts from the resulting listing show what you can expect to see from the CHECKDB option:

Listing 19.2 Sample Output from the CheckDB Statement

```
Checking pubs
Checking sysobjects
There are 117 rows in 3 pages for object 'sysobjects'.
Checking sysindexes
There are 47 rows in 1 pages for object 'sysindexes'.
Checking syscolumns
There are 531 rows in 7 pages for object 'syscolumns'.
Checking systypes
```

```
There are 27 rows in 1 pages for object 'systypes'.
Checking syscomments
There are 156 rows in 28 pages for object 'syscomments'.
Checking sysfiles1
There are 2 rows in 1 pages for object 'sysfiles1'.
Checking syspermissions
There are 77 rows in 1 pages for object 'syspermissions'.
Checking sysusers
There are 13 rows in 1 pages for object 'sysusers'.
Checking sysdepends
There are 290 rows in 1 pages for object 'sysdepends'.
Checking sysreferences
There are 10 rows in 1 pages for object 'sysreferences'.
Checking sysfilegroups
There are 1 rows in 1 pages for object 'sysfilegroups'.
Checking sysallocations
There are 1 rows in 1 pages for object 'sysallocations'.
Checking authors
There are 24 rows in 1 pages for object 'authors'.
...


...
Checking employee
There are 43 rows in 1 pages for object 'employee'.
Checking dtproperties
There are 0 rows in 1 pages for object 'dtproperties'.
CHECKDB found 0 errors in database pubs
DBCC execution completed. If DBCC printed error messages,
see your System Administrator.
```

You'll notice that the option will also check system tables. When you run the command, you'll be checking all tables in all aspects of the database you specify in the command.

 TIP

If you find that it takes too long to check the entire database, you can use the CHECKTABLE option. Like CHECKDB, you simply specify CHECKTABLE as the DBCC option, and then list the table name you want to check. Only that table will be examined, possibly saving significant time on the analysis steps.

Using DBCC CHECKFILEGROUP When you run CHECKFILEGROUP, each table and its associated data pages, indexes, and pointers are all validated. Indexes and data pages are checked to ensure they are properly linked and indexes are in proper sorted order. It also checks to ensure that the data on each page is reasonable, pointers are consistent, and page offsets are valid. CHECKFILEGROUP also checks to ensure that text, image, and ntext pages are linked properly and the size is correct.

CHECKFILEGROUP has the following syntax:

```
DBCC CHECKFILEGROUP [( [ {'filegroup_name' ¦ filegroup_id} ]
[, NOINDEX] ) ] [WITH NO_INFOMSGS]
```

Using DBCC SHRINKDATABASE When SHRINKDATABASE is run, any used data pages above the target percentage are relocated into free space within the part of the file that is to be retained.

If you run SHRINKDATABASE without a target percentage, SQL Server will seek to shrink the database as much as possible. To shrink a database a certain percentage, specify a target percentage. If the NOTRUNCATE option is specified with a target percentage, the space freed is not released back to the operating system.

N O T E   You cannot shrink a database past the size it takes to store the data. It also cannot be shrunk past the size of the model database. The database does not have to be in single-user mode to run SHRINKDATABASE. ▪

SHRINKDATABASE has the following syntax:

```
DBCC SHRINKDATABASE (database_name [, target_percent]
[, {NOTRUNCATE ¦ TRUNCATEONLY} ] )
```

Using DBCC SHRINKFILE   SHRINKFILE is applied to the files in the current database. When SHRINKFILE is run, any used data pages above the target percentage are relocated into free space within the part of the file that is to be retained. If you run SHRINKFILE without a target percentage, SQL Server will seek to shrink the database as much as possible. To shrink a database a certain percentage, specify a target percentage. If the NOTRUNCATE option is specified with a target percentage, the space freed is not released back to the operating system.

N O T E   You cannot shrink a file past the size it takes to store the data. It also cannot be shrunk past the size of the model database. The database contained in the file does not have to be in single-user mode to run SHRINKFILE. ▪

SHRINKFILE has the following syntax:

```
DBCC SHRINKFILE ( {file_name ¦ file_id }[, target_size]
[, {NOTRUNCATE ¦ TRUNCATEONLY} ] )
```

N O T E   In the past, DBCCs had to be run on a regular basis to ensure the health of your databases. SQL Server 7.0 includes powerful error-correcting routines that can automatically detect and correct errors as they occur. While this will not completely eliminate the need to run DBCCs, they are no longer as necessary as in previous versions. It is recommended that you continue to run regular DBCCs until you are comfortable with this. From there, you can run DBCCs less frequently simply to verify that SQL Server is doing its job. ▪

Understanding and Using UPDATE STATISTICS and RECOMPILE

SQL Server gains much of its performance from intelligent processing of data stored in the tables. This analysis comes in different forms, but the most significant is the examination of real data in the system to determine the optimal path for retrieving the information.

To make this clearer, consider the route to your house. You've likely figured out the best, fastest way to get to your house from your office. Once you've found the best route, it's a safe bet that you're more likely to take that route, even if someone were to suggest that you select a different route, because you've taken the time to consider the different roads available and selected the best one possible.

In order for you to seriously consider a new route home, there would need to be a new road offering a better route to your house, or there would have to be construction on the existing road that makes it an inefficient road home.

With SQL Server, this analogy holds true. When you implement a stored procedure, SQL Server reviews the SELECT logic of the stored procedure, along with any other data-impacting events. It figures out the best route to take in fulfilling the stored procedure's function. Once this is selected, it remembers this information so that the next time you run the stored procedure, it's optimized for the data it impacts. SQL Server's "roads" consist of the indexes on the data in the system. These are the paths that will be considered when analyzing the best way to retrieve a given value set.

If you've added a number of rows to the table, for example, more than 20 percent of the original table size, you should consider updating the statistics associated with the table. The syntax for updating a table is as follows:

```
UPDATE STATISTICS {table} [index ¦ (index_or_column [, ...n])]
[WITH  [[FULLSCAN] ¦[[,] SAMPLE number {PERCENT ¦ ROWS}]]
[[,] NORECOMPUTE] [[,] [INDEX ¦ COLUMNS ¦ ALL]]
```

As an example,

```
update statistics authors
```

N O T E There are no quotes around the table name you want to update. ■

You can specify that only a given index or column be updated or that the information concerning the entire table be updated. If you specify the index or column, you must specify it as shown, indicating the table in which the index or column can be found.

SQL Server 7.0 provides a needed enhancement to statistics. Not only is it a much more efficient sampling technique used to gather statistics, but statistics are automatically kept up to date. Periodically SQL Server will take advantage of idle processor time to sample tables and keep the statistics up to date, thus ensuring continued efficient operation.

You can still run update statistics manually and a variety of additional parameters have been included. If you specify the FULLSCAN option, SQL Server will perform a full scan of the index or table with updating the statistics. Using the SAMPLE option informs SQL Server to use a sampling technique based upon the specified number of rows or percentage of rows. SQL Server will ensure that a statistically significant number of values are sampled. If the number of rows or the percentage is not large enough to meet this requirement, SQL Server will automatically increase the number of rows or the percentage. The last option for INDEX, COLUMN, ALL specifies if statistics should be gathered for indexes, columns, or both. If this is not specified, statistics are gathered only for indexes.

To override the automatic gathering of statistics, although I'm not sure why someone would do this, issue an UPDATE STATISTICS with the NORECOMPUTE option. This disables SQL Server's automatic statistics gathering.

Statistics can be removed for a table, index, or column using the DROP STATISTICS command:

```
DROP STATISTICS table.column [, ...n]
```

The final step to implement these updated indexes and make the stored procedures aware of them is to indicate to the SQL Server that it should reconsider the route to take when retrieving the information from the database. To do this, you'll need to recompile the different stored procedures that are impacted by the UPDATE STATISTICS you just ran.

In general, stored procedures are compiled the first time they're called after SQL Server is started. There are other instances that stored procedures are automatically recompiled, but simply issuing the UPDATE STATISTICS will not cause an automatic recompile. An example of this is when an index on which a stored procedure is based is dropped. You've probably noticed that the first time you call a particular stored procedure, the execution is a bit slower. Subsequent calls to the stored procedure are often noticeably faster. This is because the optimizer is compiling the stored procedure based on the current statistics of the database tables and any relevant indexes.

You recompile a stored procedure by setting a flag on a table that will basically invalidate any copies of stored procedures that are in procedure cache. This causes SQL Server to reload and recompile the affected stored procedures the next time they are accessed if they reference the table you flagged. To set the flag, the following command is used:

```
sp_recompile <table name>
```

where `<table_name>` is the table that will be marked for all referencing stored procedures to be recompiled. If successful, the command returns a simple acknowledgment message indicating that the stored procedures will be reloaded and recompiled.

```
sp_recompile "authors"
go
Each stored procedure and trigger that uses table authors
will be recompiled the next time it is executed.
```

 T I P If you don't recompile the stored procedures impacted by UPDATE STATISTICS, the performance gain you seek will not be realized until the server is stopped and restarted again. This is the next time that the procedures will be reloaded and compiled.

You can't hurt anything by starting the UPDATE STATISTICS and RECOMPILE operations, but you should run them when the fewest users are on the system. This is especially true if your databases are large. The time it takes to update these parameters can be quite a hit on the system performance for users of your system. It's a good idea to make updating statistics a part of your regular ongoing maintenance, perhaps running the process on each of your high-use tables approximately once a month during high database throughput. When you're first bringing up a system and when you're adding information at a high rate, you may want to consider frequent calls to this procedure, perhaps as often as once per day of heavy, new-data input.

Backing Up and Restoring Databases and Transaction Logs

One of the most dreaded things to hear when you call for help with your application is, "Well, when was your last backup?" It usually only happens once, but when it does, and you're caught without a backup, it can be very painful.

Protection of data is often many times more important with SQL Server than it is on a standalone system. You'll often be supporting a database that is used by many, many people. Having the information on the system held in good standing is very important. Data loss may incur costs across departments and may involve significant data reentry. In serious situations, some of this data is very difficult to reenter, such as in databases supporting stock markets.

SQL Server provides several different ways to protect from data loss or at least minimize it, should the worst happen. These techniques range from physical duplication of the information to backing up the databases and transaction logs at specific intervals during the course of business.

In the upcoming sections, you'll see how to back up the system and what tradeoffs to consider in determining your optimum backup scenario.

Part
IV
Ch
19

How Often to Back Up?

One of the first things that a new SQL Server customer will ask is, "How often do I need to back up?" The answer is simple, but seems sarcastic when it's first given. Quite simply, how much data can you afford to lose?

The first answer to this is usually, "None." This is fine, but now sit down and determine what the impact will be on the system plan if you want to incur no loss of data should a catastrophic system failure occur. Typically, this involves mirroring the disks on which your databases are stored. This incurs hard dollar costs to implement. Because the cost to mirror a system can be quite steep, the next step is to determine what amount of data can truly be at risk at any given time. To determine this, it's important to first understand that you'll be backing up two different components to the system. As you've seen throughout this book, the database contains the different tables and all other objects associated with the database. The transaction log contains an incremental log of the things that change a database. In essence, the transaction log contains before-and-after pictures of the data that is changed with each block of work performed by the server.

The key thing to remember is that the database backup is a snapshot in time, and the transaction logs contain all of the changes after that snapshot was taken. At a minimum, you'll want to back up the database once a week with daily backups of the transaction log.

The best plan is to have a system of rotating backups. This is the safest and most secure way to ensure that you have the correct fault tolerance for any system failures you may experience. If you consult computer professionals, you'll find that they all agree on one thing: your system will fail; it's only a question of when. You should have complete, concise, and accurate backups. They are the only lifeline you have in times of hardware failure.

Table 19.1 shows a suggested backup schedule. Over the course of a year, assuming you're backing up to tape, this approach will require 29 tapes. Fourteen tapes are used in the weekly backup of your system and 13 are used to maintain monthly archives. The remaining two tapes are used as 1) working transaction log backups, and 2) as an initial, baseline backup of the database. Remember, your purpose is to maintain backups, not to retain historical data on the system. You should not count on backups for retention and research on historical information. You'll need to rely on alternative backups for that purpose.

Number the tapes sequentially on a permanent label on each tape cassette.

N O T E If your database is large, you may need more than one tape per day, week, or month. In this case, consider the tape numbering scheme to be a *tape set* numbering approach. ■

Table 19.1 Suggested Backup Approach

Tape #	Used For	Comments
1	Monday backup	Backup for the first Monday of two-week cycle
2	Tuesday backup	
3	Wednesday backup	
4	Thursday backup	
5	Friday backup	
6	Saturday backup	
7	Sunday backup*	
8	Monday backup	Backup for the second Monday of cycle
9	Tuesday backup	
10	Wednesday backup	

Tape #	Used For	Comments
11	Thursday backup	
12	Friday backup	
13	Saturday backup	
14	Sunday backup*	

These tapes should be removed from the physical site and placed in a separate location.

With this backup schedule, you'll have a full two weeks of backups to rely on should a problem arise. A two-week backup cycle is recommended because you might determine that you have a problem you did not recognize immediately. Perhaps a program change or other system event caused the problem, and it was undetected for a few days. By having the two weeks of backups, the odds are good that you have a clean copy of the information in these recent archives.

Backing Up and Restoring Databases

When you back up your databases and transaction logs, you do so by dumping the information in your system to a *dump device,* which is recognized by SQL Server as a repository for information and can be either a disk file or a tape device. Once SQL has dumped information to the device, the file it creates, in the case of a disk-based device, can be backed up to tape, another server, or some other location where you are managing the backup files.

The best way to manage the backup of information is with the SQL Enterprise Manager. With the database you want to backup, select Action, All Tasks, Backup Database to start working with the backup subsystem. When you do, you'll be presented with the main SQL Server Backup dialog box shown in Figure 19.2.

FIGURE 19.2

The main control panel for backup and restore operations enables you to select and create devices.

Setting Up Backup Devices The first step in setting up backup devices is to establish the backup devices to be used as the destination for information dumped from the working databases and tables. Devices that are already known to the system are listed in the dialog box in the Backup Devices window. You can accept one of these devices or create your own device.

To create a device, select the backup icon under the Management item, right click, and select New Backup Device, as shown in Figure 19.3.

FIGURE 19.3

You can create new devices that will identify a tape or disk destination for backups.

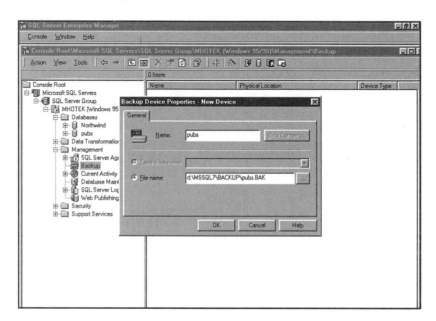

Notice that as you type in the name for the device, the location will be updated to include the name you use.

TIP You can specify a path that points to another physical system when you indicate the backup devices that you want to use. By doing so, you can provide good backup coverage without the need for additional storage media.

Consider creating a new device for each day in the 14-day cycle mentioned earlier. Then, when you create a scheduled backup, you won't necessarily have to use a tape to store the information. If you point to the device on the remote system, you can use the device as a backup destination. If you set up the system to back up to the devices without the append flag, each of the devices you create will be only as big as needed for a single copy of the database you're backing up.

Also, because the likelihood that both your core SQL Server system and the remote system will experience downtimes simultaneously is quite small, you are assured of solid backups for your system.

The downside points to remember for this approach include the following:

- The remote system must always be accessible to the backup and restore process.

- The remote system must have enough disk space to support the dump devices.

- If your building burns down and both systems are in the same building, you've lost your backup system. This is a major reason for using off-site tape or other media backups.

Keeping these rules in mind, you can see that a solution that offers the best of both worlds would be a combination of remote system backups and off-site storage for tape backups made somewhat less frequently.

N O T E Be sure to take note of the file name if you're backing up to a file on disk instead of tape. This file name is the name you'll need to back up to tape or elsewhere on the system when you want to copy the backup file off the system for storage. ■

After you've indicated the name of the device you want to create, simply press OK. SQL Server will create the new device and you'll see it listed in the Backup Devices dialog box. You're all set to start creating the backups you'll need to support your SQL Server as shown in Figure 19.4.

FIGURE 19.4

The pubs database now has a backup device for each day of a two week backup cycle.

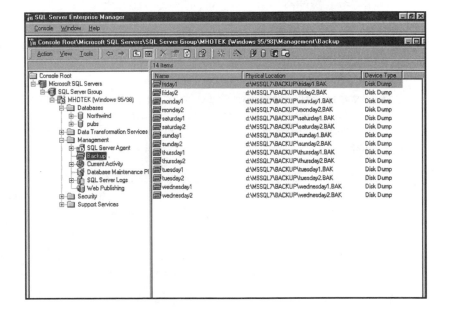

Part

IV

Ch

19

T I P The Master database does not have an explicit transaction log as it always has the Truncate Log on Checkpoint option set. For this reason, when you're backing up this database, you cannot do a transaction log backup. You must do a database backup.

The next sections will detail what's involved in setting up the backups on the system.

Running the Backup   After you've created the devices you need to support the backups, you need to do the actual backup. To that end, you have two options available. The first option is to run backups on demand. Although this will work fine, it will require manual intervention each time you want to back up the system. This approach is more likely than the second approach, an automated solution, to fall victim to the your forgetfulness, unexpected meetings, and the like.

The following are some general points you need to keep in mind as you determine your backup strategy:

- Be sure you back up the transaction logs between backups of the databases. Backing up the transaction log is no different than backing up a database. It's simply an option you select during the definition of the backup.

- Be sure you back up each database that you want to protect. There is no command that backs up the entire system, so create backup processes for all databases you are concerned with.

- Be sure you back up the Master database. Because this database includes all information about the other database objects that are in the system, it's very important to have this information in case you need to restore the entire system and rebuild from scratch.

- Be sure you back up the msdb database. Because this database includes all information about the backups, tasks, alerts, and replication information, it's very important to have this information in case you need to restore the entire system and rebuild from scratch.

Select the type of backup, either manual or scheduled/automatic, that will best fit the systems you are supporting.

Completing Manual Backups—Manual backups are quite straightforward and are a good way to get a feel for how the system works, the time it takes to back up, and how much impact a database backup will have on your system if other users are on the system at the time that a backup is started.

N O T E   When a backup is first run, the device must be initialized. This is done by selecting the Initialize Media Radio button in the Action section of the Backup page. If a backup is attempted without initializing the device, you will be prompted with a warning stating that the device is either offline or uninitialized.

To complete the backup, select the device you want to back up to and click OK. The Backup Volume Labels dialog box appears if you are dumping to tape.

Once you select the device and click OK, the backup will be completed. You'll be presented with a status indicator showing the progress of the backup. Finally, you'll be presented with a dialog box confirming that the backup was successful.

Here are several items to keep in mind as you run your backups of the system:

- If you experience difficulty completing a backup, examine the free space on the dump device you've created. Make sure you have enough free space for the device to grow to accommodate the information you're saving. Remember, too, that if you have the Append option selected, the information you save will be added to the prior information each time you run a backup. This will eventually lead to some very sizable dump devices. By using the rotating tapes, as noted earlier, you can safely back up to separate dump devices each time you back up because you'll have the prior backup information stored safely away.

- If you have the Truncate Log on Checkpoint option set, you won't be able to backup the transaction log. You might recall from the earlier section, "Understanding and Performing Checkpoints," that one way of helping to manage transaction log size is to turn on the Truncate Log on Checkpoint option. Another way to manage the size of the log is to dump the transaction log to a backup device. SQL Server will, by default, also truncate the log at that point after a successful backup. Because both operations take control over truncating the log, they are mutually exclusive. You'll need to turn off the option to truncate the log on checkpoint before you can successfully back up the transaction log.

Don't forget that you need to be absolutely certain you've backed up all the following:

- The Master database
- The msdb database
- All databases that you would be sorry to lose
- All transaction logs for each database you have in production or which is undergoing significant testing

Using and Understanding Information Restoration from Backups

Once you've created the backups and have faithfully been backing up your database, how do you recover the database if something does go wrong? This is where you'll be glad you put into place a formal backup plan, as it will guide you to restoring your system to full functionality in the least amount of time possible.

The following are the steps for restoring your system:

1. Install SQL Server if needed.
2. Restore the Master database if needed.
3. Restore the msdb database if needed.
4. Restore the last full database backups you completed.
5. Restore the transaction logs that were backed up after the database was backed up.

At the completion of this process, you'll have a fully functional system that will be up to date as of the last transaction log backup.

Part
IV

Ch
19

You've already learned about installing SQL Server and creating databases, so that won't be covered here, but if you'd like more information on this, see Chapter 5, "Creating Databases, and Transaction Logs."

NOTE You no longer have to create a database before restoring. If you specify the REPLACE option for the RESTORE DATABASE command, this causes SQL Server to re-create the database as well as restore the information.

When you select the Action, All Tasks, Restore Database command, you are first presented with a dialog box containing all the valid backups available. This listing will show the date and time of the backup, the type of backup, database or transaction log, and so on. Figure 19.5 shows the options available on the Restore tab.

FIGURE 19.5

The restore options enable you to designate the source and destination for restoration efforts.

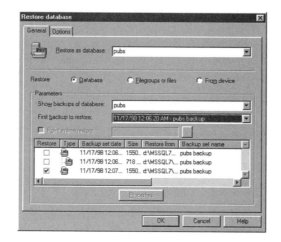

SQL Server will automatically present the list of databases for which a database backup has been completed. This enables you to select the different backups that you want to apply to the database you designate in the drop-down list box.

If you know that the information on a given backup is good until a certain time, you can indicate that in the Point in Time Restore text box. Note that any pending transactions at the time you specify will be rolled back, and it will be as if they never occurred. In most cases, you'll need to restore the database and transaction logs in their entirety, so default options will be fine.

Click OK and the database and transaction log(s) will be restored.

If you created the new database with the Create for Load option, you'll need to update the database options before anyone else can use the database. You'll notice that, until you do this, the database you're working with will be flagged in the Enterprise Manager's display as loading. During this time, no user except the DBO can use the database. To update the options and enable other users access to the database, select Action, Properties. You'll see a dialog box similar to the one shown in Figure 19.1.

Once you've completed this step, you're restored to the point of the most recent transaction log backup and should be ready to begin some quick testing to see that everything restored correctly to boost your confidence in the process. At this point, the data is restored, all objects in the database are restored, and there should be no change in operation whatsoever for the users.

Practice will certainly play a key role in helping you recover from a system failure. As a test of this process, consider using the PUBS database as a Guinea pig. Follow these steps:

1. Perform a database backup of the PUBS database.

2. Make a change to one of the authors in the Authors table. The specifics of the change don't matter. You can add a row, change a name, or whatever you will be able to easily recognize later.

3. Perform a transaction log backup of the database. You've now backed up the basic database, and you've backed up the change you made as a sort of "delta," or difference, backup.

4. Create a new database, such as RestoreTest. The name does not matter. What matters is that it has sufficient size to support the PUBS database. Make the database size 33MB, and the transaction log size 30MB. Restore *only* the database to your system. You'll have to deselect the Transaction Log Restoration option.

5. Go into ISQL/W and select the rows from the Authors table. They should be all represented correctly, as they existed prior to your change. Your changes won't yet appear because the changes occurred after the database was backed up. In a traditional backup scenario, this was as good as it got for recovery.

6. Restore the transaction log only now. Requery the Authors table, and your changes will be there. This proves that the transaction log changes were correctly logged against the database table.

You can and should experiment with different scenarios using the test database approach. If you do this, when it comes time to restore your database in a real crisis, you can rest assured things will go smoothly. Think of these tests as the fire drill for database recovery.

Another method to use, if you can find a spare server, is to create an entire test server that mirrors one of your production databases. This server can be used to perform a variety of tests before applying it to the production environment. However, the largest benefit is that you can use this server to practice backups and restores. Test servers are used extensively by DBAs. They give you the ability to validate your backup and recovery strategies during a variety of staged disasters. They can identify any problems with your current strategy. You also get practice in restoring from a failure. The question of having to restore is not if, but when. The day when your production database goes down, your phone is ringing off the hook, and the CEO is standing over your shoulder is not the best time to be performing your first restore.

Transferring Information to and from SQL Server

Data Transformation Services provides an excellent way to move information between databases on your system. To start the Transfer, select the source database. Select Action, All Tasks, Export Data. This will launch the Data Transformation Wizard. Click next to be taken to the source definition as shown in Figure 19.6.

FIGURE 19.6

Define the source database, login, and connection method for the transfer.

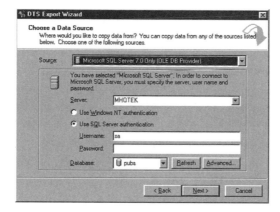

Click the Next button to define the destination database. Here you specify much the same information as for the source database. Additionally, you can create a new database to transfer into. This is shown in Figure 19.7.

FIGURE 19.7

Create a new database to transfer data and objects into.

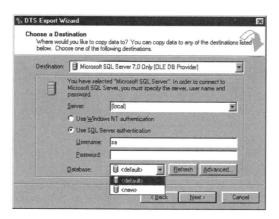

By clicking the next button, you can specify whether you want to transfer the tables, objects, or specify a query to restrict the data being transferred.

N O T E You can transfer data and tables to any destination that has an OLEDB provider such as Oracle, Excel, or a text file. You can only transfer objects such as triggers, indexes, and stored procedures to another SQL Server 7.0 database. ∎

FIGURE 19.8

Indicate the initial properties for the database you'll be using for the destination.

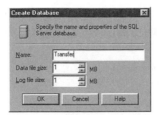

For this exercise, select the Transfer Objects and Data option and click next. You will then be presented with a screen as shown in Figure 19.8 where you can specify how the transfer should proceed.

FIGURE 19.9

You can specify how existing objects are treated, how data is transferred, transfer for all or only certain objects, and a location for the script directory.

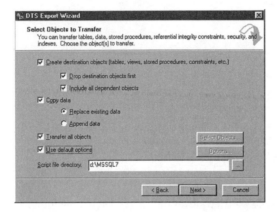

By deselecting the Default Options box, you can access the screen as shown in Figure 19.10.

FIGURE 19.10

You can specify how permissions, indexes, and DRI is transferred.

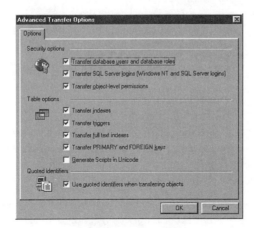

Once you are done specifying options, click the Next button. Here you can specify whether you want to run the transfer immediately or whether you want to schedule it. Any scheduled transfers will be added as jobs in the SQL Agent. You can also save the transfer package to a file, repository, or SQL Server. When you complete the options, click the next button. At the final screen, click the Finish button to execute the transfer.

You will see a screen similar to Figure 19.11 that will show the progress of the transfer.

FIGURE 19.11

Shows the progress of the transfer.

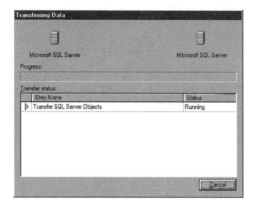

You can use the Transfer utility to make rudimentary backups of your system by copying databases to backup devices, even databases located on a different server altogether. You should, however, avoid using the Transfer process as a production means of backing up your system. It's not meant to be an end-all solution to the backup needs for your system and will not support the same level of logging or critical processing checks that the backup process affords. There is, for example, no way to transfer only a transaction log for a given database.

Data Transformation Services is a good companion to the backup feature you've seen earlier in this chapter. By putting these to use in your installation, you'll be able to ensure a maximum amount of up time for your user base. Use Data Transformation Services to make copies of critical system components, then use backups for ongoing protection against catastrophic system failures.

Reality Check

In real life, you're forced to weigh the costs involved with running backups, monitoring your system, and providing the best possible performance for your user base. The cost of not running backups comes down to two things. First, recovery from a catastrophic failure is going to cost you a lot, possibly your job. If you run a large production system and have not provided for the recovery of it, when something in the database breaks, you are in hot water at best.

Second, depending on how you set up your database and the logging associated with it, not backing up your system causes your transaction log to continue to grow, and therefore, to require additional disk space. You'll have to decide where the balance is between frequent backups and physical hardware requirements.

With regards to backups, it's not *if*, but *when* you'll need to restore to address a database problem. It's a fact of life that hard drives fail, bugs in software exist, and people want to revert from that latest and greatest change you installed. Figure out your backup schedule and stick to it. In systems I set up, the dump process is added as a scheduled task, making the dump file always available on the system. After this, from a workstation designated to perform the backups, you can run consistent, scheduled backups and always know how to get the dump file or files for your SQL Server systems by pointing your backup software to the location of your dump files.

Put simply, there is no excuse for not having a backup. The only thing you should be explaining to your users when the system fails is how you determined the timeframe between backups, which translates to the amount of information they'll need to reenter in the system.

From Here...

In this chapter, we've explored some very important administrative utilities that provide the support for good, solid, fault-tolerant system design for your users. Now is the time to implement these items, not later. If you wait until you need them, it will be too late. Keep in mind the old computer-support adage mentioned earlier: Components will fail, it's only a matter of time. Plan for it; be ready for it, and it will be far less painful and less difficult to recover from it. The other thing to remember is rule number 1 for any DBA: "Protect the data at all costs."

The following are some additional sources for some of the topics covered in this chapter that will help you in your administration of SQL Server:

- Chapter 5, "Creating Databases, and Transaction Logs," covers the specifics of setting up the different components for your system.
- Chapter 16, "Understanding Server, Database, and Query Options," explains the configuration options that can effect recoverability of your databases.
- Chapter 25, "Using the SQL Server Agent," explains how to use the SQL Agent to automate your database maintenance tasks.
- Que's *Special Edition Using Microsoft Windows NT Server* covers more specifics about disk-based recovery and fault-tolerant systems. Be sure to check into striped disk drive configurations and how you can work with backup devices.

Part

IV

Ch

19

SQL Server Security

In this chapter

Just about everyone is concerned with the security of data. If you're not, you might not have considered how easy it is to get access to sensitive data on your server. One thing to remember, however, is that sometimes too much security can get in the way of productivity. Make sure that you achieve a balance between your need to manage access to data and monitor users and the users' need to *use* the data.

No document can categorically define every possible security option. This chapter's purpose is to illustrate the features that SQL Server offers and to offer suggestions on what you can do to secure your environment from unauthorized access.

Understanding the Types of Security

Securing your data from internal and external attacks is an important job for you as a database administrator. It is important that you control who accesses data on your server and how that data is accessed. Security in SQL Server helps you manage the access that you give to your users.

Securing your data from internal attacks is probably your primary concern for most corporate environments. This security involves the monitoring and managing of corporate databases at the direction of the managers of your company. Security is often designed to limit the sorts of data that your employees can see and when they can see it.

Securing your data from external attacks, such as over the Internet, is much more complicated, and is applicable to those companies that have an Internet presence with their SQL Server databases.

This chapter focuses more on internal security. This security operates in a layered approach, starting with logins and user permissions that secure the basic access to the server. The second layer adds views and stored procedures that limit data access. Finally, the third layer is external security through things such as physical LAN access, firewalls, and so on.

SQL Server's security system can be implemented in two ways on any server: SQL Server and Windows NT ("standard") and Windows NT Only ("integrated"). These security methods control how SQL Server manages user accounts on the server and how it interacts with Windows NT's own security system.

To configure a database server's security type for standard or integrated security, follow these steps:

1. Run SQL Enterprise Manager from the Microsoft SQL Server 7.0 group. See Figure 20.1.
2. Select the server that is going to be managed and from the Scrver menu, select Actions, Properties. After this, activate the Security tab as shown in Figure 20.2.

FIGURE 20.1

After being started, SQL Enterprise Manager shows that no server is selected.

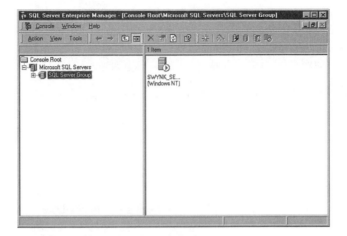

FIGURE 20.2

Configure SQL Server to use standard or integrated security.

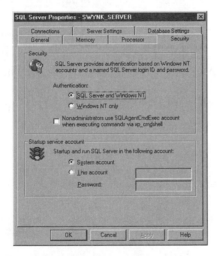

N O T E When you install SQL Server, two users are installed automatically. The system administrator account is set up for the user SA and the Guest user is set up for default access to the system.

As you've seen throughout this book, the SA account is a special account, allowing you to fully control the different aspects of your system. For this reason, it is extremely important that you change the default blank password to one that is more secure. You should never leave a production system with a blank password. ▣

Using Standard Security

In standard security mode, SQL Server is wholly responsible for managing and maintaining accounts on the server. In this case, SQL Server is responsible for authenticating a user and for enforcing password/login restrictions. This is the most common way of configuring SQL

Server because it behaves identically to Sybase on any hardware platform and to SQL Server 4.2, 6.0, and 6.5. The majority of the rest of this chapter will discuss the features of standard security. For more information on Windows NT's integrated security system, refer to Que's *Special Edition Using Windows NT Server.*

N O T E   Standard security should be used when there are no Windows NT servers being used for logon authentication duties. In this case, NT's integrated security mechanisms provide no benefit to the SQL Server. Also, standard security should be used when you expect that various protocols will be used to attach to the server. ■

Using Integrated Security

Because SQL Server runs on Windows NT, Microsoft could take advantage of, and integrate into, Windows NT's excellent security system. When operating in integrated security mode, Windows NT is responsible for managing user connections through its Access Control List (ACL). The advantages of integrated security include single-password access to all resources on a Windows NT domain and password aging and encryption across the network.

A login to the Windows NT server is either granted or denied connection to the SQL Server based on attributes of the user's login account to the NT server. This granting of permission or authentication between client and server creates a trusted login to the server. At this point, NT only validates that the login name is valid for accessing any particular resource available on the network or server.

N O T E   Trusted connections are only available via the Multi-Protocol NetLibrary (MPNL) or via Named Pipes communications protocols, so there might be networking reasons that make integrated security unfeasible in your environment. MPNL is discussed in the section in this chapter titled "Encrypted Multi-Protocol NetLibrary." ■

When a user establishes a trusted connection to the SQL Server, the user is

- Mapped to an existing SQL Server login if a name match is found, or
- Connected as the default login (usually Guest), or
- Connected as SA if the user is the administrator on the NT system

SQL Server manages all other database-based permissions, such as permissions on tables, views, and other objects, in the same way as a server running in standard security mode. These security permissions are discussed next.

N O T E   Keep in mind that when running under integrated security, any administrator, local or domain, has access to the SQL Server as sa. This can be both good and bad. One good point to this is if you forget the sa password. If you are running in standard security, most people mistakenly think you need to reinstall SQL Server. This is not the case! Simply follow these steps:

- Switch the security mode of the server to integrated
- Stop and start SQL Server

- Make sure you are logged into the NT Server as an administrator
- Start Enterprise Manager
- Select the SA login, right click, and change the password. (We use EM to do this, because it doesn't require that you know the old password.)
- Switch the security mode back to standard
- Stop and start SQL Server ■

Creating and Managing User Accounts

SQL Server has two levels of a user that are important to understand. The first level of a user is a login. A *login* is the ability to attach to the SQL Server itself. SQL Server manages logins on a server-wide basis. All logins are stored in the SYSLOGINS table of the master database. The second level of a user is a *user*. Users are SQL Server's way of managing who has permissions to interact with resources, such as tables and stored procedures, in a given database. A user can be in one or many databases. All users are stored in the SYSUSERS table of each database for which they have permission to access.

SQL Server uses these distinctions to allow a single user to have different levels of access based on the database that they are connecting to, and yet retain the same password. To support this, a user has a login or connection permission to the server. That login is what SQL Server associates a password to. Without a valid login to the server, a user will not have access to any of the server's databases, with the possible exception of remote systems using remote stored procedures.

When a login is created, it is necessary to create a user of a database on that server. This process is very similar to creating a SQL Server system login and is described in the following sections.

Using SQL Enterprise Manager to Create a Login

The SQL Enterprise Manager provides a simple way of creating a login to the database. You perform the following steps:

1. Run SQL Enterprise Manager from the SQL Server 7.0 group.
2. Select the server that you want to add a login to, select the Logins object in the Security Folder. Select Action, New Login. This is shown in Figure 20.3.
3. Enter the information for the new login and, optionally, indicate the databases that the login will be allowed to access on the Database Access tab. See Figure 20.4.
4. Enter the password and click OK to verify that the information is correct and to create the login. Verify the password assigned to the user to ensure that the information was entered correctly. This screen is shown in Figure 20.5.

Part
IV

Ch
20

FIGURE 20.3

The Login Properties dialog box enables you to grant access to all the databases on the server by selecting the required access level in the table at the bottom of the dialog box.

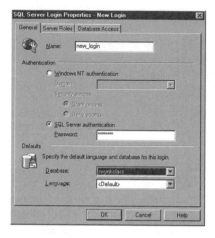

FIGURE 20.4

The Database Access tab box shows a new login being created with user access to the master database.

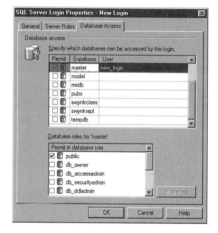

FIGURE 20.5

The Confirm Password dialog box requires verification of password information.

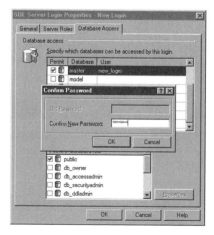

T I P When creating a new login, set the password to be the same as the login name so that it is easy to remember.

Server Roles In previous versions of SQL Server, a user could be assigned to one group within a database along with the default public group. Being able to join only one group was seen as a severe limitation. Groups have been eliminated in SQL Server 7.0.

In place of groups, SQL Server now supports roles. This is a major step forward in terms of manageability. A user can be assigned any number of roles.

At the server level, there are a variety of roles a login can take on as shown in Figure 20.6.

FIGURE 20.6

The Enterprise Manager shows various roles and descriptions.

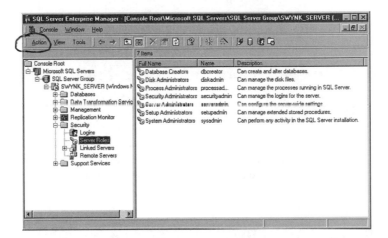

The judicious use of roles can ease the administrative burden of managing multiple SQL Servers. This can also centralize control of certain resources within your company. For example, in some companies, security is centrally maintained by a specific person or group. Granting that person or the members of that group the Security Administrator role allows them to manage all of the SQL Server logins and frees up the system administrator to handle other tasks.

If, at a later time, it is necessary to add a user to a database, highlight the database in the SQL Enterprise Manager and then select New, Database User from the Action menu. The New User dialog box will appear, as shown in Figure 20.7.

Select the user to be added to the database from the Login drop-down list box and enter the name by which the user is to be identified. Select any database roles the user will have. Finally, click OK.

Part
IV

Ch
20

FIGURE 20.7

The New User dialog box shows a new user being created.

Dropping Logins and Users with SQL Enterprise Manager

Dropping a login from within Enterprise manager is as simple as highlighting the login and selecting Action, Delete.

> **N O T E**   SQL Server Enterprise Manager is *right-click aware,* which means that you can right-click just about anything in the tree and bring up a context-sensitive menu about that object. To quickly drop a user or login, find the user or login in the tree and right-click it. Click Delete to remove the user or login. ■

Using `sp_addlogin` to Add Logins to a Server

The `sp_addlogin` stored procedure is provided to add a login to the server using Transact-SQL statements. The syntax for `sp_addlogin` is as follows:

```
sp_addlogin login_id [, password [, defaultdb [, defaultlanguage]]]
```

The elements of the statement are described in the list below.

- *login_id* is the name of the login being added. A login follows standard SQL Server naming conventions.

- *password* is the password to be assigned to the login. Passwords are optional but are highly recommended as the most basic of security measures.

- *defaultdb* is the default database in which the SQL Server should place the login after connecting to the database. If left NULL, SQL Server leaves the login in the master database. You should always assign a default database for your users, and you should avoid making it the master database. This ensures that objects are not inadvertently created in the master database.

- *defaultlanguage* is the default language that should be assigned to the login. If left NULL, SQL Server assigns the default language for the server.

The user can change his or her password at any time using the sp_password stored procedure. For example, sp_password 'Agent99', 'MaxwellSmart' changes the currently connected user's password from Agent99 to MaxwellSmart. It's a good idea to have users change their password after their first login and regularly thereafter.

The following is an example of creating a login to the server with the default database of pubs and a password of Allen.

```
sp_addlogin 'Ronald', 'Allen', pubs
```

Using sp_adduser to Add New Users to Databases

sp_adduser is similar in style to the sp_addlogin procedure. It takes an existing login and adds it to the currently active database. Note that you must issue a use *databasename* and be in the required database to add a user to before running the sp_adduser stored procedure.

```
sp_adduser login_id [, username [, rolename]]
```

The elements of the statement are described in the following list:

- ▓ login_id is the name of the login being added as a user to the database. Invalid logins will not be added to the database.

- ▓ username is provided to allow logins to be "aliased" in a database. This allows the same login to connect to different databases on the same server and have a different name in each database. User names cannot be null or blank.

- ▓ rolename allows the specification of a role to which the user will be assigned. Using roles simplifies security because instead of granting permissions to individual users, permissions can be granted to the role and all members of the role receive them.

 Roles can be confusing until you get used to them. For those already familiar with SQL Server, it might be easier to think of roles in the same way as you are used to thinking of groups. The biggest difference is that a user can be assigned multiple roles.

Below is an example of adding a user to the currently active database. Because no username is supplied, the *login_id* is assumed for the username.

```
sp_adduser 'Ronald'
```

sp_droplogin and sp_dropuser

To remove a login or user from the server or database, execute the system procedure sp_droplogin or sp_dropuser. Their syntax is very similar, especially when the username chosen for a given login to a database is the same as the *login_id*.

```
sp_droplogin login_id
```

and

```
sp_dropuser username
```

Creating and Using Roles

SQL Server provides the ability to create roles so that security permissions granted to all members are the same. This provides far better simplicity and is a more practical approach to security than granting individual users specific permissions on any particular set of tables.

SQL Server installs with a wide range of roles. One of these roles is called PUBLIC. All users created in your system belong to the PUBLIC role and it drives the default permissions sets of your users.

Users can belong to as many additional roles on your system as are needed. This lets you associate custom rights with their accounts. Also, remember that roles are defined on a database-by-database basis. This means that when you define a role in one database, it's not available in others. You'll have to create the role anew in each database as needed. To get around this, you can use the model database. Create the roles you need in that database. Then when a new database is created, it's used as the template for new databases.

Using SQL Enterprise Manager to Add Roles

SQL Enterprise Manager provides an easy method for adding roles to the database. You should perform the following steps:

1. Start SQL Enterprise Manager and highlight the database in the server tree for which you want to create a role. See Figure 20.8.

FIGURE 20.8

The SQL Enterprise Manager shows the pubs database highlighted.

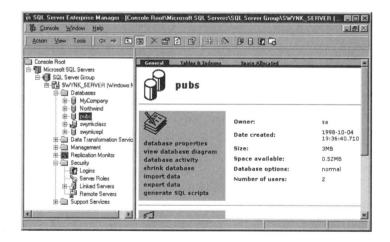

2. From the Action menu, select New, Database Role and enter the information and name of the new group. Select any users who are required members of the group as shown in Figure 20.9.

FIGURE 20.9

In the New Role dialog box, a new role—test—is created with Guest as its only member.

3. Click OK to add the role to the database.

Types of Database Roles Database roles are of two different types: standard and application.

A standard role is exactly what most people are used to thinking of as a group. Users are assigned to the role and the role is granted permissions on database objects.

Application roles are much more complicated. Application roles, as their name implies, are activated by an application. These roles are inactive by default and do not contain any users. In addition, application roles require a password to activate them.

Application roles, just like standard roles, are assigned permissions to database objects. When an application logs on to SQL Server using one of the application roles, all security authentication is bypassed and access is granted to the database by the password for the role.

This can significantly reduce the number of needed logins to the server to only those users who need direct access to tables. All other users who are going to access the database on an ad hoc basis can simply utilize an application role set up specifically to facilitate that particular access.

In the past, elaborate systems were created to limit access to tables through ad hoc tools such as Access because each user had a single login to the server to which all rights were assigned. With the inclusion of application roles, access can now be granted on an application-by-application basis.

Dropping Roles with SQL Enterprise Manager

Dropping roles with SQL Enterprise Manager involves performing the same steps as dropping users or logins. You simply highlight the role, right-click, and select Delete from the popup menu. Removing a role does not remove any users associated with that role. Any permissions granted to users because they were members of the role are revoked.

Part

IV

Ch

20

Using Permissions and SQL Server

Permissions are the rights to access an object, such as a table, in the database. Permissions are granted to a user or role to allow that user or role to perform functions such as selecting data, inserting new rows, and updating data. Several permissions exist on objects in the database and their descriptions follow.

Permissions are implicitly granted to the owner or creator of an object. The owner can then decide to grant permissions to other users or groups as that user sees fit.

- The *database owner* (DBO) has full permissions on all objects in the database that he owns.
- The *system administrator* (SA) has full permissions on all objects in all databases on the server.

SQL Server provides the GRANT and REVOKE commands to give permissions to and take permissions away from a user. SQL Enterprise Manager also provides an easy way to add and remove permissions. These commands are discussed in the following sections.

Object Permissions

Object permissions are the permissions to act on tables and other objects in the database, such as stored procedures and views.

The following is a list of permissions available on tables and their descriptions:

- SELECT enables a user to select or read data from a table or view. Note that a SELECT permission can be granted to individual columns within a table or view, not just the entire table.
- INSERT enables a user to add new data to a table or view.
- UPDATE enables a user to change data in a table or view. Note that an UPDATE permission can be granted to individual columns within a table or view, not just the entire table.
- DELETE enables a user to remove data from a table or view.
- EXECUTE enables a user to execute a stored procedure.
- DRI/REFERENCES enables a user to add foreign key constraints on a table.
- DDL/Data Definition Language enables a user to create, alter, and drop objects in the database. Examples are CREATE TABLE, DROP DATABASE, ALTER TABLE.
- ALL enables the user full permissions on the object. Note that only the SA can use ALL when DDL statements are being used.

Using SQL Enterprise Manager to Manage Permissions

SQL Enterprise Manager provides an easy way of managing permissions for users and groups in a database. Perform the following steps:

1. Start SQL Enterprise Manager and highlight the database in the server tree for which you want to manage permissions. Refer to Figure 20.8.

2. From the Action Menu, select Properties.

3. Select the Permissions tab from the database properties dialog. Highlight the user or role and select the permissions you want to apply to that user or role. This is shown in Figure 20.10.

FIGURE 20.10

Changing permissions by checking any of the columns does not take effect until you click the Apply or OK buttons.

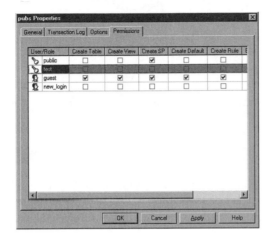

N O T E Because administering permissions on a role is much simpler and more standardized than assigning permissions directly to a user, we will use a role for this example. ■

Using GRANT and REVOKE

SQL Server's Transact-SQL interface to permissions is through the GRANT and REVOKE statements.

The Transact-SQL GRANT command is used to give a permission or permissions to a user or group in SQL Server. Granting a permission allows the user or group to perform the granted permission.

The syntax for using GRANT is as follows:

```
GRANT permission_list
ON object_name
TO name_list
```

Use REVOKE to revoke permissions from a user. It's the opposite of GRANT and is designed to undo or remove any permissions granted from a user or group.

The syntax for REVOKE is as follows:

```
REVOKE permission_list
ON object_name
FROM name_list
```

permission_list is a list of permissions being granted or revoked. A comma should separate multiple permissions. If ALL is specified, all permissions that the grantor has are granted to the grantee.

Part

IV

Ch

20

`Object_name` is a table, view, or stored procedure for which permissions are being granted or revoked.

`name_list` is a list of usernames or roles for which permissions are being granted or revoked. Commas should separate multiple names. Specifying `PUBLIC` will include all users.

N O T E If `WITH GRANT OPTION` is appended to a `GRANT` statement, it will allow the grantee to grant his rights to other users. This is a nice option, but it should be used very sparingly. It probably is best if it is used only by the system administrator because of security reasons. You can also take advantage of the `db_securityadmin` role. ▨

The following example grants `SELECT` and `UPDATE` permissions on the Authors table:

```
Grant   SELECT, UPDATE
On      AUTHORS
To      PUBLIC
Go
```

The following example revokes `DELETE` permissions on the Employee table:

```
Revoke  DELETE
On      EMPLOYEE
From    PUBLIC
Go
```

Using Views to Enhance Security

Views provide a great way to enhance security because they limit the data that is available to a user. For example, you can have a group of users in junior_emp that is not allowed to view any of the authors that receive more than 50 percent royalties because these are to be available only to the senior managers or other employees within the company. In Listing 20.1, the Transact-SQL shows how this can be achieved.

▶ **See** Chapter 10, "Managing and Using Views," **p. 257**, to learn more about creating views with SQL Server.

On the CD

Listing 20.1 20_01.SQL—Using Roles and Views to Create a Well-Secured Environment

```
/* First add the role */
sp_addrole junior_emp
go
/* now revoke select on the base tables from the public role */
Revoke Select on TitleAuthor from public
go
Revoke Select on Authors from public
go
/* now create the view that limits access */
Create View V_Authors
As
```

```
        Select      *
        From  AUTHORS
        Where AU_ID in (Select AU_ID
                   From TITLEAUTHOR
                   Where ROYALTYPER <= 50)
Go
/* grant select on the view to the members of the role */
grant select on V_Authors to junior_emp
go
```

Using Stored Procedures to Conceal Underlying Data Objects and Business Rules

Stored procedures can be used in a very similar fashion to views to provide a level of security on the data that completely conceals the data available to a user and the business processes involved in manipulating the data.

In Listing 20.2, you can see the same data concealment as demonstrated in using the view in Listing 20.1 except that it is achieved through the use of a stored procedure.

On the CD

Listing 20.2 20_02.SQL—Using Roles and Stored Procedures to Conceal Data Structures on the Server

```
/* First add the role */
sp_addrole junior_emp
go
/* now revoke select on the base tables from the public role */
Revoke Select on TitleAuthor from public
go
Revoke Select on Authors from public
go
/* now create the stored procedure that limits access */
Create Procedure up_SelectAuthors
As
        Select      *
        From  AUTHORS
        Where AU_ID in (Select AU_ID
                   From TITLEAUTHOR
                   Where ROYALTYPER <= 50)
Go
/* grant execute on the view to the members of the role */
grant execute on up_SelectAuthors to junior_emp
go
```

Part

IV

Ch

20

In Listing 20.3, the junior employees are allowed to update the contract flag on the Authors table without having permission to update anything else on the table. This is the sort of procedure that enables you to hide data manipulation from the users while still giving them limited power to work on the data available to them in the server.

Listing 20.3 20_03.SQL—Stored Procedure That Allows Updating of the Authors Table

```
/* First add the role */
sp_addrole junior_emp
go
/* now revoke select on the base table from the public role */
Revoke Update, Delete, Insert on Authors from public
go
/* now create the stored procedure that limits access */
Create Procedure up_SetContractForAuthor
     @nAu_Id id,
     @bContract bit
As
     Update       AUTHORS
     Set   CONTRACT = @bContract
     Where AU_ID = @nAu_Id
     Print "Author's contract flag set."
Go
/* grant execute on the view to the members of the role */
grant execute on up_SetContractForAuthor to junior_emp
go
```

Using Security Beyond SQL Server

A number of steps can be taken to provide a more secure environment in which SQL Server will operate. Some of the sections below might seem obvious, but are worth thinking about. It is recommended that you designate a person to be responsible for system security at your workplace. This person will live, breathe, and eat security and should be clearly empowered to implement any of the steps outlined below. System Security Officers (SSO) are becoming more and more common within organizations due to the highly accessible nature of public access networks such as the Internet. Their roles are that of company custodians.

Physical Security

Often overlooked when designing the security of a system is the physical security of the server itself. Granted, it is unlikely that the average hacker will spend all day sitting on the system console hacking into a server trying various passwords without being noticed. If the server can physically be removed from its location, however, many unscrupulous users will be prepared to spend more time in the comfort of their homes. This also includes the server's mass data storage devices, such as tapes and hard drives.

Ensure that physical access to the server is limited. Provide locked doors, preferably with electronic locks, that secure the server, and optionally bolt the server to the structure on which it resides. Remember that in these days of smaller and smaller hardware, the server can be a laptop or similar small device. This makes it easier to steal the box.

Because Windows NT provides excellent remote administration capabilities, you can remove monitors and keyboards from servers that must be placed in high-access areas. This will stop the idle person from walking by and examining the server. As an alternative, there are plenty of hardware manufacturers that provide secure casings for server boxes to provide better security for your server.

It is assumed that the same level of physical security applied to the SQL Server will also be applied to the following:

- The network file servers
- The network hubs and routers
- Any other shared network devices, such as bridges and remote WAN linkup devices

Local Area Network Access

A common mistake on Local Area Networks (LANs) is to have unmonitored network nodes that allow access. Ensure that all nodes on the network that do not have computers actually attached to them have been disconnected from the hub so that no one can bring in a laptop and access the LAN at a physical level.

For highly secure environments, provide all users with SecureID cards or similar devices. These devices generate passwords that are authenticated by the network file server and change constantly. This will stop users without valid identification cards from having access to the LAN, even if they have physical access to a node.

At a LAN software level, ensure that all the features of the LAN's software are being utilized. Most network operating systems provide at least government–approved C2 level of security, but only if you turn it on. Unlike the B2 standard of security, C2 provides the features but does not enforce their use. Windows NT, NetWare 4.1, and some versions of UNIX support C2 security. Make sure that you are doing all the basics of good user management on your local area network, as follows:

- Enforce password aging with a maximum life of 30 days.
- Require unique passwords.
- Require long, eight-character passwords that are validated against a list of invalid passwords. Third-party applications exist to ensure that a client is using good passwords.
- Enforce security block-outs on logins that fail due to invalid passwords.

Remote or Wide Area Network Access

It's much harder to control Wide Area Network (WAN) and remote access to a network than the local access provided through the LAN. Some of the steps that you can take are as follows:

- Assign IP addresses to all external users and do not allow them to connect with their own addresses. This enables you to monitor closely all remote connections to your LAN.
- Implement a software- or hardware-based firewall that physically limits external packet traffic on the server's network.
- Enforce routine password changing per the files server guidelines outlined above.

- Audit all remote transactions/IP traffic and scan it for invalid requests.
- Implement secure WAN protocol transport by using hardware-based compression on either end of WAN bridges.

Application Security

There are a number of steps you can take to make your applications secure independent of the security applied at the SQL Server level. Some things that you might want to consider are as follows:

- Permission trees that allow users access to Windows within your application program. You might want to break down access into three levels: view, new, and edit.
- Application-based audit trails that track the changes of fields and the amount of time spent on any given window in the system.
- Application-based limits on the amount of money that can be posted for financial systems.

Remember, if the security of your database is important to you, you should always ensure that the database itself is secure with or without application programs. You must do this because sophisticated users on your network and on the Internet, if you are connected, will always be able to use a different application to work with your data if they wish. This would bypass any application-only security that was being enforced.

Encrypted Multi-Protocol NetLibrary

If security is a serious concern in the environment in which SQL Server is being used, it is possible to implement the SQL Server Multi-Protocol NetLibrary (MPNL). This feature is available in version 6.0 and higher. MPNL provides a Remote Procedure Call (RPC)-based interface from clients to the SQL Server. MPNL requires that the protocol be added as a listener service to the engine, although MPNL is not actually a listener because it is RPC-based.

One key advantage of MPNL is that it can be encrypted. The encryption algorithm used can be enabled for individual clients. The server, however, must be enabled for encrypted traffic. Support for clients varies. Check your SQL Server documentation for the client support available in your version.

Server enumeration via the dbserverenum call in NetLibrary is not supported on servers that are MPNL-enabled. Clients must know the name of servers that are operating in this mode.

Reality Check

Security is one of those things that changes from installation to installation. What works best for you might not be the best thing for others, so you'll have to consider carefully before you select integrated, mixed, or standard security for your SQL Server installation. The most common installation choice is one of mixed security. This gives you the most flexibility, but still allows you to use the features of the NT user base as the foundation for your SQL Server users.

Leaving the SA user with no password is, by far, the most common mistake made by system administrators. Take the time, immediately after installation, to put a password on this account. You should never allow your developers to use the account for standard maintenance. They can use a permission-based account in the database or databases as they need to make necessary changes to their project databases. No matter how small your shop is, it's just not a good idea to use the SA account for anything other than administration.

CAUTION

The SA account holds a lot of power both within the database and also on the machine or potentially the domain the SQL Server resides in.

By a rather innocuous extended stored procedure called xp_cmdshell, anyone with the SA password can cause severe damage not only to the SQL Server, but also to the physical server and the domain it resides in. This procedure opens a command-line shell running under the account the SQL Server service is logged in under. It is perfectly capable of executing something like: exec xp_cmdshell 'format c:'. This will do exactly what you think it will: format the hard drive of the machine SQL Server is running on. If the SQL Server is running under a domain admin account instead of a local admin account, this damage can be extended to any server that resides in the same or a trusting domain as the SQL Server. ALWAYS change the SA logon, lock it up, and only allow those who will need to administer the SQL Server access to the password. As an additional protection, assign the system administrator role to each administrator's personal SQL Server login and do not use the SA login for anything.

SQL Server security is a complex matrix of options. You have the ability to control database access on many different levels. Remember that you can control access to information with views as well as security implemented as outlined in this chapter. Combine the different techniques to make the system as secure, or as open, as you need. When you're designing your system, keep in mind what types of access are possible, even when they're not probable. This means that if your server resides on a system that is also connected to the Internet, be sure to take into account that you should enhance security to prevent unknown users from accessing the system. Your security should be extremely tight if your system is available to the Internet or other outside sources in any way.

From Here...

Having discovered the many facets of SQL Server security, it is most likely that you will spend the next few months trying to fill the holes that you now know exist. If you are lucky enough to be reading this book before you implement SQL Server in your environment, take advantage of what you have learned and apply as many security features as necessary to provide the appropriate control needed.

Part
IV

Ch
20

Optimizing Performance

In this chapter

Performance tuning in the client/server world is something of a magical art. A combination of so many factors causes an application to perform well, and knowing where to focus your time is what's most important.

The most critical part of optimizing performance is good documentation. Document statistically how the system works or performs before even starting any performance tuning. As the performance tuning cycle begins, you should monitor and document the effects of all the changes so that it's easy to determine what changes were positive and what were negative. Never assume that all the changes made for one application automatically apply to another application. Remember, you're ultimately tuning a product for the user, not just a database that's being accessed by some unknown client.

SQL Server provides tools and wizards that can help in this process; this chapter focuses on monitoring and understanding what is happening in SQL Server as a foundation for optimizing the overall performance of the database. The index tuning wizard, SQL profiler and query optimizer are all tools that you can use to tune your database system.

Sizing a Database

Estimating the size of a SQL Server database is relatively straightforward and can be done with a good level of accuracy. The principle of space calculation is that all the bytes of data per table should be added together along with the associated overhead per row and page of data.

N O T E   In previous versions of SQL Server, it was necessary to monitor and manually expand databases when they needed more room. SQL Server 7.0 has eliminated this burden and made sizing a SQL Server much easier. Databases and transaction logs dynamically resize in version 7.0. The only concern you now have is being able to fit your databases on the physical hardware. ■

When you have this information calculated, you will use it to determine the different sizing aspects of your database, including page fill percentages, table sizes and ultimately, the amount of disk space that you'll need to have on your system.

You'll use these values as a divisor to the page size (8KB) to determine how many rows of data will fit in a page. The actual available space of a page is 8060 bytes because 132 bytes are reserved for fixed overhead to manage the rows on the page. In general terms, these calculations are affected by the placement and use of FILL FACTORS on indexes and whether a clustered index is on the table.

After you've created your initial database, you can use the stored procedure sp_spaceused to monitor the size of your database and tables. The syntax of sp_spaceused is:

```
sp_spaceused object [, @updateusage = 'TRUE|FALSE'
```

For example, if you wanted to check both the entire Pubs database and the Authors table, you could submit the following query:

```
sp_spaceused
go
sp_spaceused authors
```

N O T E The GO is required to separate the two queries when they are submitted to SQL Server. ■

When you submit this query, you'll get the following results, indicating the space used and the space remaining for each of the respective objects:

```
database_name database_size     unallocated space
--------------------------------------------------
pubs           2.31 MB          1.02 MB


reserved       data             index_size   unused
--------------------------------------------------
1328 KB        592 KB           704 KB       32 KB

name     rows  reserved  data index_size  unused
--------------------------------------------------
authors   23   48 KB    8 KB 32 KB        8 KB
```

With this information, you can determine where you stand on utilization of existing database space.

You can also use sp_helpdb to get information about the size, owner, ID, date of creation, and current status for databases in the system. The following shows sample output from calling sp_helpdb:

```
name    db_size   owner  dbid  created      status
------- -------- ------ ----  -----------  --------------------
master  20.00 MB  sa     1     Dec 13 1997 trunc. log on chkpt.
model    3.50 MB  sa     3     Jun  3 1998 no options set
msdb     4.75 MB  sa     4     Jul 27 1998 select into/bulkcopy, trunc. log on
                                           ➥chkpt.
pubs    12.50 MB  sa     5     Jun  3 1998 no options set
tempdb  10.00 MB  sa     2     Dec 13 1997 select into/bulkcopy
```

In the coming sections, you'll see how to project how much space your tables will require in hopes of preventing errors when the database attempts to grow beyond its current confines.

Datatype Sizes

Each SQL Server datatype consumes a certain amount of bytes based on the storage of the data. The following list defines the amount of storage that each datatype uses:

Datatype	Size
Char/Binary	The size indicated in the definition
VarChar/VarBinary	The actual data size—use an average estimate
Int	4 bytes
SmallInt	2 bytes
TinyInt	1 byte
Float	8 bytes

Float(b)	4 bytes (numbers with precision of 1-7 digits)
Float(c)	8 bytes (numbers with precision of 8-15 digits)
Double Precision	8 bytes
Real	4 bytes
Money	8 bytes
SmallMoney	4 bytes
Datetime	8 bytes
SmallDatetime	4 bytes
Bit	1 byte
Decimal/Numeric	2-17 bytes depending on the precision
Text/Image	16 bytes per table row plus at least one 2KB page per NOT NULL column
Timestamp	8 bytes

SQL Server internally defines any NULLable column as a *var* datatype. So a Char(12) NULL column is actually a Varchar(12) column. Therefore, for any columns that permit NULL values, the average expected column size should be used.

Decimal and numeric precision affects the amount of storage required for these datatypes. The following table indicates the amount of bytes required for each range of precision:

Numeric Precision	Size
0–9	5 bytes
10–19	9 bytes
20–28	13 bytes
29–38	17 bytes

Calculating Space Requirements for Tables

The method of calculating a table's space requirements differs based on whether the table has a clustered index or not. Both calculation methods are shown here, and examples will be drawn from the Pubs database to illustrate their use.

Some things to be aware of when calculating table and index sizes are

- Performing UPDATE STATISTICS on an index adds an extra page for that index to store the distribution statistics of the data that it contains. Performing UPDATE STATISTICS on the table will add one data distribution page per index on the table.

- For tables with variable-length columns, you should try to average the length of the row by estimating the anticipated average size of the columns on the table.

Tables with Clustered Indexes   The Publishers table has a clustered index. This example will estimate the space required for 5,000,000 rows, and will assume that the average length of the varchar columns is 60 percent of the defined length:

1. Calculate the row length. If the row contains only fixed-length, NOT NULL columns, the formula is

```
2 + (Sum of column sizes in bytes) = Row Size
```

If the row contains mixed variable-length fields and/or NULL columns, the formula is

```
2 + (Sum of fixed-length column sizes in bytes) + (Sum of average
    ➥of variable-length columns) = Subtotal
Subtotal  + (Number of variable-length
    ➥ columns +_ 1) + 2 = Row Size
```

For the Publishers table, the second formula is required:

```
2 + 4 + (60% of 92) = 55.2
55.2  + 5 + 2 = 63
```

2. Calculate the number of rows that will fit on a page. The formula is

```
8060 / (Row Size) = Number of rows per page
```

In this case,

```
8060 / 63 = 127
```

 TIP For more accurate calculations, round *down* any calculations for number of rows per page.

3. The number of rows required/number of rows per page = number of 8K data pages.

In this case:

```
5,000,000 / 127 =  39,371
```

 TIP For more accurate calculations, round up any calculations for number of pages required.

4. Next, calculate the space required for the clustered index. The size of the clustered index depends on whether the key columns are variable or fixed-length. For fixed-length keys, use this formula:

```
5 + (Sum of column sizes in bytes) = Clustered index size
```

For variable-length keys, use this formula:

```
5 + (Sum of fixed-length column sizes in bytes) + (Sum of average
    ➥ of variable-length columns) = Subtotal
Subtotal + (Number of variable-length
    ➥ columns +_ 1) + 2 = Clustered index size
```

For publishers, the key is a single fixed-length column, so the formula is

```
5 + 4 = 9
```

5. Calculate the number of clustered index rows that will fit on a page. The formula is:

```
(8060 / (Clustered index size)) - 2 = Number of rows per page
```

In this case:

```
(8060 / 9) - 2 = 894
```

Part
IV

Ch
21

6. Next, calculate the number of index pages by using the following formula:

```
(Number of data pages) / (Number of clustered index rows per page)
= Number of index pages at index level N
```

For this example,

```
39371 / 894 = 45
```

Index pages are at multiple levels. To compute all the levels of the index, continue to divide the resulting number of index pages by the number of clustered rows per page until the result is one (1) or fewer. In this case:

```
45 / 894 = 1,
```

which means that one index page is at the top of the index and all the other pages are actual pointers to data pages.

7. Compute the total number of 8KB pages required for the database table:

Data Pages: 39,371

Index Pages (level 1): 1

Index Pages (level 0): 45

Total number of 8KB pages: 39,417 (or about 308MB)

Tables with Nonclustered Indexes   Tables with Nonclustered indexes are calculated in size the same way as a clustered index table, except for the sizing of the index itself. In this example, assume that a non-clustered index has been added to the Roysched table on the title_id column, and that 7,000,000 rows are in the table. The following steps will help you size a nonclustered index:

1. The first step is to calculate the length of the leaf row in the index. A *leaf row* is the bottom row of an index tree and points to the data page. The leaf row's size is the size of the index's columns summed together and is affected by variable or fixed-length columns. Use this formula if you have only fixed-length columns in the index:

```
7 + (Sum of fixed-length keys) = Size of index row
```

Use this formula if you fixed and variable-length columns in the index:

```
9 + (Sum of length of fixed-length keys) + (Sum of length of
   ➥ variable-length keys) + (Number of variable-length keys)
   ➥ + 1 = (Size of leaf index row)
```

In the Roysched table, the primary key is fixed-length and isn't NULL, so the formula is

```
7 + 6 = 13
```

2. Next, calculate the number of leaf pages that will be required by using the following formula:

```
8060 / (Size of leaf index row) = Number of leaf rows per page
```

for example: `8060 / 13 = 620`

```
(Number of rows in table) / (Number of leaf rows per page) =
   ➥ Number of leaf pages
```

for example: `7,000,000 / 620 = 11,291`

3. Next, calculate the size of the non-leaf row and calculate the number of non-leaf pages. The size of non-leaf row is calculated according to this formula:

`(Size of leaf index row) + 4 = Size of nonleaf row`

In this case, it would be 13+4=**17**

```
(8060 / Size of nonleaf row) - 2 = Number of nonleaf index rows
    ➥ per page
```

In this example, (8060/17)-2=**473**

```
(Number of leaf pages / Number of nonleaf index rows per page)
    ➥ = Number of index pages at Level N
```

or 11,291/473=**24** pages at level 1

Like the clustered index, result division determines the levels of the index until the result is one (1) or fewer.

24/ 473 = **1,** which means that one index page is at the top of the index and all the other pages are actual pointers to data pages.

4. Finally, compute the size of the Index by summing the number of pages at the various levels of the index.

Leaf Pages: 11,291

Level 1 Pages: 24

Level 2 Pages: 1

Total number of 8KB pages: 11,316, or about 89MB

Effects of FILL FACTOR

FILL FACTOR alters the number of rows that SQL Server will place on a page. The most likely configuration of FILL FACTOR is to assume that the table will never change its dataset and therefore needs a FILL FACTOR of 100% to maximize the use of data pages. If you're sizing an index with a FILL FACTOR of 100 percent, don't subtract two (2) from the result of the number of rows per page because SQL Server won't preallocate these rows for page growth, but will instead put user data there.

Any other value of FILL FACTOR alters the size of the page itself. For example, a FILL FACTOR of 70 percent reduces the amount of available space on the page to 5642 bytes.

 When you build a data warehouse, you may want to consider setting this value to 100%, indicating little or no ongoing changes to the data in the tables. This can help performance by lessening the number of pages required to store the data.

The inverse is also true. If you have data that changes very frequently, you may want to make the fill factor smaller, making the impact on data pages smaller.

Using the Windows NT Performance Monitor

Windows NT's Performance Monitor is an advanced tool that provides statistics about the operation of the NT environment. One of the unique properties of the performance monitor is its capability to install performance heuristics and callbacks from other executables in the Windows NT system and report their statistics.

SQL Server's performance monitor is just a set of hooks for the core Windows NT Performance Monitor to call. SQL Server groups the statistics that can be displayed into objects. These objects group the logical similar statistics.

SQL Server Statistics Objects

The following sections list the objects that SQL Server Performance Monitor can report on. Some of the counters within the objects can be applied to particular instances of activity on the server. For example, the `Database Manager` object's Percent Log Used counter can be applied to each database on the server. This process of configuring instances to the particular counter enables you to customize the statistics that you want to monitor.

Access Methods The `Access Methods` object enables you to track things such as the number of index searches, page splits, and full scans. Normal monitoring will track page splits and full scans.

The access methods information is available as follows:

- *Extents Allocated*: This statistic gives you the number of extents allocated to database objects for storing index or data records.
- *Forwarded Records:* This statistic gives you the number of records fetched through forwarded record pointers.
- *FreeSpace Page Fetches:* This statistic gives you the number of pages returned by free space scans to satisfy requests to insert record fragments.
- *FreeSpace Scans:* This statistic gives you the number of scans initiated to search for free space in which to insert a new record fragment.
- *Full Scans:* This statistic gives you the number of unrestricted full scans on either the base table or indexes. A high rate of full scans can indicate the need for additional indexes.
- *Index Searches:* This statistic gives you the number of index searches. Index searches are used to start range scans and single index record fetches and to reposition in an index.
- *Mixed Page Allocations:* This statistic gives you the number of pages allocated from mixed extents. This is used for storing the first eight pages that are allocated to an index or table.

N O T E In SQL Server 6.5 and earlier, each object was required to reside in its own extent. SQL Server 7.0 now gives you the ability to have multiple objects in a single extent, which can save space.

Extents can be either mixed or uniform. Objects will occupy mixed extents when they are created. As soon as the allocation for an object reaches eight pages, the extent is converted to a uniform extent which will only contain that object and its associated data and index pages. ■

■ *Page Merge:* This statistic gives you the number of pages merged as the result of index pages being shrunk.

■ *Page Requests:* This statistic gives you the number of logical page requests issued by access methods code.

■ *Page Splits:* This statistic gives you the number of page splits that occur due to index pages overflowing. A high rate of page splits usually indicates the need to reorganize the table to reestablish a FILL FACTOR.

■ *Pages Allocated:* This statistic gives you the number of pages allocated to database objects for storing index or data records.

■ *Probe Scans:* This statistic gives you the number of probe scans. A probe scan is used to find rows in an index or base table directly.

■ *Range Scans:* This statistic gives you the number of qualified range scans through indexes.

Block I/O   The Block I/O object enables you to track the number of pages being read and written to SQL Server.

The block I/O information is available as follows:

■ *Page Reads:* This statistic gives you the number of database page reads that are issued.

■ *Page Writes:* This statistic gives you the number of database page writes that are issued.

Buffer Manager   The Buffer Manager object enables you to track such things as cache hit ratio, procedure cache size, and stolen pages. Normal monitoring will track the cache hit ratio and stolen page counters.

The buffer information is available as follows:

■ *Cache Hit Ratio:* These statistics give you the percentage of pages that were found in the buffer cache without having to read from disk. You want to maximize this number in all systems. A low cache hit ratio indicates that you need to add more RAM to the server.

■ *Committed Pages:* This statistic gives you the number of buffer pages committed.

■ *Free Buffers:* This statistic gives you the number of free buffers available. You want to ensure that there is a ready supply of free buffers for use in processing. If no free buffers are available, SQL Server is forced to search through allocation buffers to find a large enough set to perform the requested operation.

■ *Lazy Writes:* This statistic gives you the number of buffers written by Buffer Manager's lazy writer. The lazy writer seeks to keep a set of buffers free for new requests. When the number of free buffers falls below a certain threshold, the lazy writer will clean out some of the least frequently used buffers until the number of free buffers rises above this threshold.

Part

IV

Ch

21

- *Page Requests:* This statistic gives you the number of requests for a buffer page.
- *Procedure Cache Pages in Use:* This statistic gives you the number of pages in the procedure cache marked as in use.
- *Procedure Cache Size (pages):* These statistics give you the size of procedure cache, in pages.
- *Readahead Pages:* This statistic gives you the number of requests to asynchronously prefetch pages before they are actually encountered. The Readahead Manager seeks to minimize the impact of disk reads by prefetching pages during sequential scans.
- *Reserved Page Count:* This statistic gives you the number of buffer cache reserved pages.
- *Stolen Page Count:* This statistic gives you the number of buffer cache pages that have been stolen to satisfy other server memory requests. Having a high number of stolen pages indicates that you either need to add more RAM or are running too many applications that are conflicting with SQL Server on the server.
- *ExtendedMem Cache Hit Ratio:* These statistics give you the percentage of page requests that were satisfied from the Extended Memory cache.
- *ExtendedMem Cache Migrations:* This statistic gives you the number of pages migrated into the Extended Memory cache region.
- *ExtendedMem Requests:* This statistic gives you the number of requests for pages from large memory region.

Database Manager   The `Database Manager` object enables you to track such things as active transactions and pending replication transactions. Normal monitoring in a replication system will track Repl(replication). Pending Xacts (transactions).

The database information is available as follows:

- *Active Transactions:* This statistic gives you the number of active transactions for the database. When performance on the server markedly declines, you should monitor this statistic. A high number of active transaction does not necessarily mean a problem. If you consistently have a very high number of transactions and slow performance, you should add more RAM to the machine because this indicates that the current transaction volume on the server has exceeded its current capacity.
- *Percent Log Used:* These statistics give you the percentage of space in the log that is in use.
- *Log Cache Hit Ratio:* These statistics give you the percentage of log cache reads that were satisfied from the log cache.
- *Log Cache Reads:* This statistic gives you the number of reads performed through the log manager cache.
- *Repl. Pending Xacts:* This statistic gives you the number of pending replication transactions in the database. A high number of pending replication transaction normally indicates that you have a problem in your replication system. This could either be caused by replication "going down" or the network connection becoming a bottleneck.

- *Repl. Trans. Rate:* This statistic gives you the number of replicated transactions/second. A very high number here indicates a very fast and healthy replication system.
- *Total Transactions:* These statistics give you the cumulative number of transactions for the database.

General Statistics   The General Statistics object enables you to monitor counters such as user connections and server memory. Normal monitoring will track user connections.

The general statistics information is available as follows:

- *Total Server Memory (KB):* This statistic gives you the total amount of dynamic memory SQL Server is currently using. This number should always be a significant portion of the total server memory available. If your counters do not reflect this, consider adding additional RAM or relocating some applications to other servers.
- *User Connections:* This statistic gives you the number of users connected to the system. You should normally set up an alert on this counter. When it rises above about 75% of the number of user connections you have configured for the server, you will need to add more connections. Failure to do this will prevent new users or connections to your SQL Server when the maximum number of connections has been reached.

Latches   The Latches object enables you to monitor counters related to internal SQL Server resources such as data and index pages.

The latches information is available as follows:

- *Average NP Latch Wait Time (ms):* This statistic gives you the average unprotected latch wait time (in milliseconds) for latch requests that had to wait.
- *Latch Releases:* This statistic gives you the number of NP latch releases that have been issued since the server was started.
- *Latch Requests:* This statistic gives you the number of NP latch requests that have been issued since the server was started.
- *NP Latch Waits:* This statistic gives you the number of NP latch requests that could not be granted immediately and had to wait.
- *NP Total Latch Wait Time (ms):* This statistic gives you the NP total latch wait time (in milliseconds) for latch requests that had to wait.

Lock Manager   The Lock Manager object enables you to monitor such counters as lock blocks and table lock escalations. Normal monitoring will track table lock escalations.

The lock manager information is available as follows:

- *Lock Blocks:* This statistic gives you the current number of lock blocks that are in use on the server. This represents an individual locked resource, such as a table, page, or row.
- *Lock Blocks Allocated:* This statistic gives you the current number of allocated lock blocks. At server startup, the number of allocated lock blocks plus the number of allocated lock owner blocks depends on the SQL Server.

Part
IV

Ch
21

- *Locks:* This statistic gives you the current number of locks allocated or the number configured, whichever is greater.

- *Lock Owner Blocks:* This statistic gives you the number of lock owner blocks that are currently in use on the server (refreshed periodically). A lock owner block represents the ownership of a lock on an object by an individual thread. This counter tracks the total number of locks currently in use by all connection threads.

- *Lock Owner Blocks Allocated:* This statistic gives you the current number of allocated lock owner blocks. At server startup, the number of allocated lock owner blocks plus the number of allocated lock blocks depends on the SQL Server locks configuration option. If more lock owner blocks are needed, the value dynamically increases.

- *Table Lock Escalations:* This statistic gives you the number of times locks on a table were escalated. If you are experiencing a large amount of blocking, you should consider monitoring this counter. A table lock is the most restrictive lock possible and should be minimized. A large number of table lock escalations can indicate an improperly coded application or a large number of unrestricted queries being run in the SQL Server.

Locks   The Locks object enables you to monitor counters such as average wait time, lock waits, and number of deadlocks. Normal monitoring should always track number of deadlocks.

The locking information is available as follows:

- *Average Wait Time:* This statistic gives you the average amount of wait time (in milliseconds) for each lock request that resulted in a wait.

- *Lock Requests:* This statistic gives you the number of new locks and lock conversions that are requested from the lock manager.

- *Lock Timeouts:* This statistic gives you the number of lock requests that timed out. This includes internal requests for NOWAIT locks. This number should be minimized as it indicates that a connection could not place a lock on a resource in order to fulfill a user request.

- *Lock Wait Time:* This statistic gives you the total wait time (milliseconds). This number should be minimized. Having a high lock wait time will cause user requests to take longer to complete.

- *Lock Waits:* This statistic gives you the number of lock requests that could not be satisfied immediately and required the caller to wait. This indicates the number of locks that had to wait for system resources to be freed up to service a request. A large number of lock waits can indicate that you need to add more RAM to the server.

- *Number of Deadlocks:* This statistic gives you the number of lock requests that resulted in a deadlock. A deadlock is a very serious situation and can cause a big performance problem as well as create unpredictable results in a client application. You should set up an alert for this counter that will be triggered when a deadlock occurs. These should be immediately investigated to prevent any future occurrences.

Log Manager   The Log Manager object enables you to monitor such counters as log flush wait time and log flush waits.

The log manager information is available as follows:

- *Log Bytes Per Flush:* This statistic gives you the number of bytes in the log buffer when buffer is flushed.
- *Log Flushes:* This statistic gives you the number of log flushes.
- *Log Flush Wait Time:* This statistic gives you the total wait time (milliseconds). A large wait time indicates that checkpoint process had to wait for resources to be freed on the server. A large wait time can indicate the need to add more RAM to the server.
- *Log Flush Waits:* This statistic gives you the number of commits that are waiting on log flush. If you see your transaction log steadily increasing in size all of a sudden, you should monitor this statistic. A large and continually increasing value means that a transaction has been left open which will prevent subsequent transactions from being flushed to disk.

N O T E Every transaction that occurs to a database is written to the transaction log. (A transaction never writes directly to the disk.) A process called checkpointing periodically occurs within SQL Server, normally once per minute. The purpose of the checkpoint process is to write the committed transactions to disk.

As a transaction is flushed to disk, an entry is written in the transaction log to indicate this. The checkpoint process sequentially reads the transaction log. It begins at the first entry in the transaction log and skips ahead through all committed transactions it has already processed. It then begins flushing committed transaction to disk. The checkpoint process ends when the first open transaction is encountered.

Normal processing will occur on the server and write committed transactions into the log after this open transaction. Leaving a transaction open prevents the checkpoint process from flushing any subsequent committed transactions to disk. ■

Procedure Cache The Procedure Cache object enables you to monitor counters such as procedure cache hit ratio and procedure cache object counts.

The procedure cache information is available as follows:

- *Procedure Cache Hit Ratio:* This statistic gives you the ratio between procedure cache hits and lookups. Having this value maximized means that SQL Server is finding the procedures already available in memory and does not have to read them in from disk.
- *Procedure Cache Object Counts:* This statistic gives you the number of cache objects in the procedure cache.
- *Procedure Cache Pages:* This statistic gives you the number of pages that are used by cache objects.
- *Procedure Cache Use Counts:* This statistic gives you the number of times each type of cache object has been used.

Replication Agents   The `Replication Agents` object enables you to monitor the number of replication agents active.

The replication agents information is available as follows:

- *Running:* This statistic gives you the number of instances of a given replication agent that are currently running.

Replication Distribution   The `Replication Distribution` object enables you to monitor counters related to the replication distribution process. Normal monitoring in a replicated system should track the delivery latency counter.

The distribution information is available as follows:

- *Delivered Commands:* This statistic gives you the number of distribution commands that were delivered in the last batch. Having a low number of commands could indicate that you need to increase the batch size.

- *Delivered Transactions:* This statistic gives you the number of distribution transactions that were delivered in the last batch. Having a low number of transaction could indicate that you need to increase the batch size.

- *Delivery Latency:* This statistic gives you the amount of time the commands were in the distribution database before being applied to the subscriber. Tracking this counter will reveal bottlenecks. A high delivery latency usually means that you are experiencing a network bottleneck. A large and increasing latency indicates that the subscriber is no longer able to receive replicated transactions. This situation demands immediate attention.

- *Delivery Rate:* This statistic gives you the number of distribution commands that are delivered per second. A high number indicates an efficient replication system.

Replication Logreader   The `Replication Logreader` object enables you to track counters related to transactions delivered to the distribution database such as the delivery rate and delivery latency. Normal monitoring should track the delivery latency.

The logreader information is available as follows:

- *Delivered Commands:* This statistic gives you the number of commands that were delivered in the last batch.

- *Delivered Transactions:* This statistic gives you the number of transactions that were delivered in the last batch.

- *Delivery Latency:* This statistic gives you the amount of time in seconds that it took the `logreader` to deliver transactions to the distributor . A large number indicates a network bottleneck. A large and increasing number indicates that the distributor or distribution database has gone offline. This situation demands immediate attention.

- *Delivery Rate:* This statistic gives you the number of `logreader` commands that were inserted per second. A high number indicates an efficient distribution mechanism.

Replication Merge The Replication Merge Object provides counters such as conflicts and merge rate for merge replication. In a merge replication architecture, the conflicts counter should always be monitored.

The replication merge information is available as follows:

- *Conflicts:* This statistic gives you the number of conflicts that occurred in the publisher/subscriber upload and download changes. This value should always be zero. A nonzero value demands immediate attention. This will require the subscriber to be notified that the merged transaction conflicted with data on the publisher. This will also require that the transaction conflict be resolved before proceeding.

- *Download Changes:* This statistic gives you the number of changes (inserts, updates, and deletes) sent from the publisher to the subscriber.

- *Merge Rate:* This statistic gives you the number of changes sent from the publisher to the subscriber divided by the duration of the merge run. A high value indicates an efficient merge architecture.

- *Upload Changes:* This statistic gives you the number of changes (inserts, updates, and deletes) that are sent from the subscriber to the publisher.

Replication Snapshot The Replication Snapshot object provides counters for monitoring the snapshot portion of replication such as the bulk copy rate. The replication snapshot information is available as follows:

- *Bulk Copy Rate:* This statistic gives you the number of rows bulk copied per second.

- *Rows Bulk Copied:* This statistic gives you the number of rows bulk copied. You should track this counter during snapshot operations. If the number of rows transferred does not match the number that should have been, you could have a data problem or improperly defined synchronization.

SQL Statistics The SQL Statistics object enables you to track counters related to queries such as number of batch requests and SQL compilations. The SQL statistics information is available as follows:

- *Number of Auto-Param Attempts:* This statistic gives you the number of auto-parameterization attempts.

- *Number of Batch Requests:* This statistic gives you the number of SQL batch requests that are received by server.

- *Number of Failed Auto-Params:* This statistic gives you the number of failed auto-parameterizations.

- *Number of Safe Auto-Params:* This statistic gives you the number of safe auto-parameterizations.

- *Number of Unsafe Auto-Params:* This statistic gives you the number of unsafe auto-parameterizations.

Part

IV

Ch

21

- *SQL Compilations:* This statistic gives you the number of SQL compilations. A very high number indicates a large amount of ad hoc querying occurring. You could enhance performance by moving some of this to stored procedures.

- *SQL Recompilations:* This statistic gives you the number of SQL recompiles. This should be minimized. A high number indicates a large number of stored procedures being recompiled. When this occurs, you should reevaluate your stored procedures to determine why they need to be frequently recompiled.

- *SQL SQL Manager Memory:* This statistic gives you the number of pages used by the SQL Manager

User Settable   The User Settable object is a catch-all bag that provides a counter for monitoring a stored procedure or TSQL statement. The custom monitoring information is available as follows:

- *Query:* Defined by the user.

Creating and Using Chart Views

Chart views are often the easiest statistical viewing mechanism for a database administrator. With a chart you can track periodic performance in a number of criteria and see prior history in the same view.

To use the SQL Performance Monitor to chart statistics for view, follow these steps:

1. Run Performance Monitor from the Microsoft SQL Server 7.0 group (see Figure 21.1).

FIGURE 21.1
Windows NT's Performance Monitor runs the SQL Server control file (SQLCTRS.PMC) while the default objects are monitored.

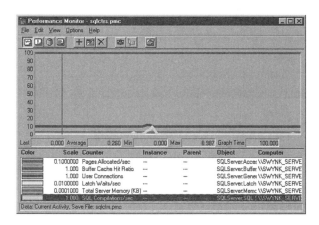

2. From the View menu, select Chart.
3. From the Edit menu, select Add To Chart. This opens the Add To Chart dialog box shown in Figure 21.2.

FIGURE 21.2

You use the Add to Chart dialog box to select the counters you want to have displayed in Performance Monitor.

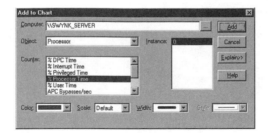

 Click the Explain button to get a short explanation of each counter as you select it.

---

4. Select the object from which you want to monitor a counter.

5. Select one or many counters from the Counter list box and, if necessary, specify what instances you want to apply the counters to in the Instance list box.

6. Specify the required line attributes for the item(s) being added. Some of these might be color, line style, and so on.

7. Click Add to add the items to the current Performance Monitor Chart, shown in Figure 21.3.

FIGURE 21.3

The Add To Chart dialog box is ready to add SQL Server-Log Manager counters for the master database.

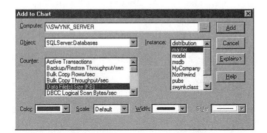

8. Add any other statistics that you want to chart and then click Done to close the dialog box. The Cancel button changes to a Done button after you add the first item to the chart.

Creating and Using Reports

Performance Monitor can create basic reports of data that's being gathered. These reports show the current, or most recent, values gathered from the statistics of the selected counters.

To use the SQL Performance Monitor to create a report of system statistics, follow these steps:

1. Run Performance Monitor from the Microsoft SQL Server 7.0 group.

2. From the View menu, choose Report.

3. From the Edit menu, select Add To Report (see Figure 21.4).

Part
IV

Ch
21

FIGURE 21.4

The Add To Report dialog box has the SQL Server Replication Logreader object as well as all the counters to be added to the report selected.

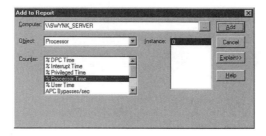

4. Select the object that you want to report a counter from.

5. Select one or many counters from the Counter list box and, if necessary, go to Instance and specify the number of instances on which you want to apply the counters.

6. Click Add to add the items to the current Performance Monitor Report.

7. Add any other statistics that you want to report on and click Done to close the dialog box. The Cancel button changes to a Done button after you add the first item to the chart.

Creating and Using Alerts

Alerts are one of the most useful features of Performance Monitor. Performance Monitor not only can gather statistics from various system objects, but it can also monitor the values of those statistics. If they reach predetermined levels, Performance Monitor can execute a program that can, for example, dial a pager or alert the DBA in some other fashion.

To use the SQL Performance Monitor to create a statistical alert, follow these steps:

1. Run Performance Monitor from the Microsoft SQL Server 7.0 group.

2. From the View menu, select Alert.

3. From the Edit menu, select Add To Alert (see Figure 21.5).

FIGURE 21.5

The Add To Alert dialog box is ready to add an alert that will send a mail message to the DBA if the used log space on the Pubs database exceeds 75 percent.

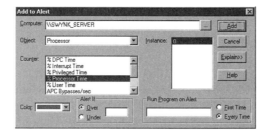

4. Select the object that you want to add an alert counter from.

5. Select one or many counters from the Counter list box. If necessary, go to Instance and specify the instances on which you want to apply the counters.

6. Click Add to add the items to the current Performance Monitor Alert list.

7. Add any other statistics for which you want to create alerts and click Done to close the dialog box. The Cancel button changes to a Done button after you add the first item to the chart.

Reality Check

On the CD

On the CD accompanying this book you'll find an Excel workbook that will help in your sizing efforts. This workbook enables you to indicate the columns, their associated datatype, and the indexes that you're defining against a table. If you complete one worksheet for each table in your database, you can easily add together the resulting sizes and have a good idea of the sizing requirements for your database.

If you have a dedicated server, as it's likely you will in a production environment, you should consider running the performance monitor at all times, though with an infrequent timing interval. A good interval might be in the five to ten minute range. In actual use, consider also monitoring the counter for swap file usage. Using this counter, along with the other counters outlined here that are specific to SQL Server, you can see trends in system usage that might indicate a change in usage patterns which would adversely impact your system.

From Here...

In this chapter you learned how to identify and manage statistics that will help you determine the performance characteristics of your server. You also learned how to size a database and how to size the procedure cache.

Consider looking at the following chapters to further develop your SQL Server knowledge:

- Chapter 16, "Understanding Server, Database, and Query Options," teaches you to further tune the server after analyzing the information provided by the SQL Performance Monitor.

- Chapter 25, "Using the SQL Server Agent," teaches you how automate server tasks and configure alerts for Performance Monitor counters.

- Appendix A, "Mail-Enabling Your SQL Server," teaches you how to set up SQL Mail and to use it to help monitor your server.

Part
IV

Ch
21

Developing Applications and Solutions

Backward Compatibility Options for Developers

Developing applications for SQL Server has taken many different forms as the product has evolved. As you have seen throughout this book, queries executed by the server are at the heart of the system. The queries you have worked with thus far are all based in the SQL language and are generally entered or executed from the Query Analyzer utilities.

This approach won't prove very useful, however, when you're developing an application to work with SQL Server information. The client application, that portion of the program responsible for information formatting, presentation, and other user interaction, is where the power of SQL Server is presented to the average user. The way your application interfaces with the SQL Server can be just as important as all of the hard work you have done behind the scenes in defining the tables, creating the stored procedures, and optimizing the system to work at its peak.

In this chapter, we will review a few of the best historical methods of working with SQL Server from an application development perspective. Note that projects developed today typically use Advanced Data Objects, ADO. This approach applies to Active Server Pages development (Web development) as well as Visual Basic and C implementations.

▶ Additional information on this approach is provided in Chapter 27, "Using Advanced Data Objects with SQL Server 7.0," and updates are provided on the http://www.swynk.com web site for this increasingly comprehensive technology and its applications.

Each of these technologies is a comprehensive environment for working with SQL Server and each warrants far more coverage than is afforded here. This information is provided so you will have a starting point of knowledge for selecting the method that is right for you.

The most common methods of working with SQL Server are as follows:

- DB-Library
- ODBC and the Data Access Objects (DAO)
- SQL OLE

The coming sections will review the basics of each of these options and explain how they may be useful in your work with SQL Server.

Understanding the DB-Library Interface

DB-Library, or DB-LIB, is an API for both C and Visual Basic (VB) that allows you to work directly with SQL Server. The API provides you with the different tools you need for sending queries to and receiving information from SQL Server. It also provides the means for working with that information by allowing you to extract information from the result sets returned from your queries.

> **CAUTION**
>
> DB-LIB is a technology that Microsoft has indicated will not be improved. It's included here because a huge array of legacy systems use the technology, but if you're developing new applications, you should be looking to OLE-DB for your connectivity to the server.

Required Components for DB-LIB

To use DB-LIB, you need to include several different supplemental files with your project. Table 22.1 shows the different files you will need in the VB and C environments.

N O T E Some of the files listed in the following tables might not have been included with your version of SQL Server. If this is the case and the files are necessary, they can be obtained through the SQL Server SDK from Microsoft. ▓

Table 22.1   Required Components for DB-LIB

C	Visual Basic
SQLDB.H	VBSQL.OCX
SQLFRONT.H	VBSQL.BAS

Table 22.2 shows the different components you will be working with as you develop applications with Borland's developer tools, including C++. Be sure to use the memory model that matches your application development environment.

Table 22.2   Borland DB-LIB Components

Component File	Description
BLDBLIB.LIB	Large memory model static library
BMDBLIB.LIB	Medium memory model static library

You will use slightly different components when developing with Microsoft environments. Table 22.3 shows the required elements in this environment.

Table 22.3   Microsoft-Oriented Components (C++, and so on)

Element	Description
MSDBLIB3.LIB	Windows: Import library
NTWDBLIB.LIB	Win32: Import library
RLDBLIB.LIB	DOS: Large memory model library
RMDBLIB.LIB	DOS: Medium memory model library

Concepts and Characteristics

Working with DB-LIB typically follows a standard cycle of calls. The cycle usually includes logging on, performing one or more actions against the server, and then logging off from SQL Server.

Two structures are used to establish your connection to the server. Both dbproc and login are used to establish and continue communications between your application and the SQL Server.

You use the DBOpen API call to initiate the connection to the server. DBOpen will initialize the DBProcess structure, giving you the information you need to continue working over the same connection to the server. Table 22.4 shows the different ways you accomplish these steps in the VB and C languages.

Table 22.4   Basic Components for SQL Server Communications with DB-LIB

Description	Visual Basic	C
Initialize new loginrec structure	SqlLogin%	dblogin
Set username for login	SqlSetLUser	DBSTLUSER
Set user password for login	SqlSetLPwd	DBSTLPWD
Set client application descriptive name	SqlSetLApp	DBSTLAPP
Open the connection to SQL Server	SqlOpen%	dbopen
Close the connection to SQL Server	SqlClose	dbclose
Close all connections	SqlExit	dbexit

Using these statements, you create a new login structure and populate the required fields. There are other properties of the login structure, but the username and password are the only required items.

N O T E   If you are using integrated security, these fields are required, but the server ignores them when the connection is made. The server will use the user's credentials from the currently logged-on user. In this situation, if you know ahead of time that integrated security is used, you might want to pass in arbitrary information in these fields. For example, a username and password of "blah" will suffice. Because the users will be authenticated by their network sign on, the user ID and password are not needed. The sign-on presents the user with an additional dialog box.

The descriptive name is not required, but it is strongly recommended. The reason for supplying this information is simple. If you have a system administrator working with the SQL Server and reviewing the open connections, the name you provide here will be shown in the connection listing. By providing meaningful information, the administrator will know who is on the server at any given point. Because of that, you should avoid the temptation to sign in all users on an application as the application name. If you can provide the application name and the station ID or user ID, you will be adding some key identifying elements that the administrator can use. ■

Using the login structure and the server name, the call to open the connection is made and the server connection is opened. When you issue the Open command, a structure is established and returned by the call. In future calls to the server, you will be using this structure pointer whenever you issue a command to the server.

TIP SQL Server login and logout operations are among the most costly transactions in terms of performance. If you log in each time you need to make a call or series of calls and then log out, you will find that your application can be slower than you would expect.

To remedy this, consider using a separate connection for each major classification of work that is to be done. For example, if you have a point-of-sale system at the front counter, you might want to develop a system to maintain the open connection to the Inventory table and the Accounts Receivable and Cash Drawer tables to help performance.

By doing so, you can take the time up front, during the loading of the application, to create your connections to SQL Server. Because the connections will already exist, the amount of time to access the separate tables will be minimized, and the users will be able to initiate transactions more quickly.

One consideration in this scenario can be the number of licensed connections you have to SQL Server. You need to make sure you are running the number of licenses you have purchased for your SQL Server. If you use more, you might have to re-think your application, purchase additional licenses, or do both in order to have an optimal price-performance installation.

Sending Commands to SQL Server

When nd statements to SQL Server, you first build them in the SQL command buffer. Putting the commands into the buffer is done by calling SqlCmd with the parameters you need to place in the buffer.

N O T E The examples provided here are largely VB-related. Although the actual statement varies in C, the calling conventions are similar and require many of the same approaches that apply to VB. ■

The syntax for SqlCmd() in VB is as follows:

```
Status% = SqlCmd(MyConnection%, "<statement>")
```

Each statement is appended to the previous statement, if any, currently in the SqlCmd structure. Be careful building your statement if it requires more than one line. Remember that the string you specify is simply concatenated with any prior information in the buffer. Consider the following example:

```
...
Status% = SqlCmd(MyConnection%,"Select * from pubs")
Status% = SqlCmd(MyConnection%,"where author like 'A%'")
...
```

Why will this statement provide a syntax error and fail? There would not be any resulting spaces between "pubs" and "where" in the example. Be sure to provide spaces in these situations or you will generate syntax errors as shown.

Once you have created the buffered statement, you need to send it to SQL Server to be executed. You use the `SqlExec` statement to accomplish this.

```
Status% = SqlExec(MyConnection%)
```

Because you have queued up the commands and associated them with the particular connection, `SqlExec` knows exactly what you are executing. It sends the buffered statement to SQL Server and allows SQL to translate and run your request. In this example, the entire command sent to SQL Server would be `SELECT * from pubs where author like 'A%'` (adding in the required spaces as indicated earlier).

> **N O T E** If you want to call a stored procedure, you can create your command and preface it with `Execute`. For example:
>
> ```
> ...
> Status% = SqlCmd(MyConnection%,"Execute GetAuthors 'A%'")
> ...
> ```
>
> In this case, you are executing the stored procedure `GetAuthors` and passing the parameter `'A%'` to the stored procedure, presumably to be used as a search value. Executing the call and processing the results that are returned are the same as if you had issued a `select` statement.
>
> ▶ For additional information on creating and working with Stored Procedures, **see** chapter 14, "Managing Stored Procedures and Using Flow-Control Statements". ■

Working with Result Sets

Once you have sent your request to SQL Server, you need to be able to work with the information returned from the query. To do so, you need to use two constants to monitor your work with the data sets. These constants are defined in the .BAS files, which are required to develop with the DB-LIB libraries. The constants are as follows:

- SUCCEED
- NOMOREROWS

What you're doing when you process returned result sets from SQL Server is to walk down through the rows returned until you receive NOMOREROWS, indicating that all returned rows have been accessed by your application. You can retrieve the current status of the record set by using the `SqlResults%` function. This function will return either SUCCEED or NOMOREROWS, and your application can determine what to do next based on this information.

```
Status% = SqlResults%(MyConnection%)
```

You should call `SqlResults` before launching into any processing loops. This will ensure that you're not working with an empty data set. If you have successfully returned information from your query, you can loop through the results by using `SqlNextRow%`. `SqlNextRow`, as the name suggests, works down through the rows in your results, one at a time. The results are placed into the working buffer so you can work with them. When `SqlNextRow` hits the end of the data set, it will return NOMOREROWS, allowing your application to stop processing the data set.

N O T E Results returned from DB-LIB's functions are enumerated, rather than named, properties. As you work with columns returned, you will indicate the column by number, not name. You need to keep in mind the order in which you specify the columns in your `select` statement or stored procedure. If you do not, the information column you requested might not return what you expect, as it would be returning a different column's information. ■

The final step in working with the information is to retrieve it from the buffer. `SqlData` and `SqlDatLen` are the functions that are regularly used to work with this information. The code sample below shows how a sample processing loop would be implemented, allowing you to print the author name.

```
...
Status% = SqlCmd(MyConnection%,"Select au_lname from authors")
Status% = SqlExec(MyConnection%)
While SqlNextRow%(MyConnection%) <> NOMOREROWS
    Print SqlData$(MyConnection%,1)
Wend
Print "No more information to present."
...
```

Closing the SQL Connection

After you have finished working with a given connection, you should make sure to close the connection, freeing up the memory associated with it and releasing the connection to the server. The `SqlClose` function will close an associated connection for just this purpose.

```
Status% = SqlClose%(MyConnection%)
```

You have to close each connection you open for access to the server. Alternatively, you may wish to call `SqlExit`, which will close all currently open connections to the server. If your application has completed and is exiting, it might be easier to use the `SqlExit` statement to ensure that all connections are closed properly.

Client Configuration

Aside from distributing the OCX with your client application, no other external modules are required with the client application (you still have to provide the code modules you write, of course). The functionality of the DB-LIB add-in is provided in the OCX and .BAS files.

In the C environment, you have to include the appropriate DLLs with your application and network environment. The DLLs will vary depending on the LIBs you employ, as mentioned previously. Please refer to Table 22.2 and Table 22.3 for more information.

Advantages and Disadvantages of Using DB-Library

DB-LIB is a SQL Server–specific interface layer. This means that of the three different options presented here, this is the least "portable" between back-end database servers but also one of the faster ways to access information. This is due not only to the fact that it's an optimized interface, but also that you're developing directly in the host language. The other options,

ODBC and SQL OLE, offer similar services but also impose an abstraction layer between your application and the calls to SQL Server.

You might notice that DB-LIB is very manual in how it is implemented. This is because you create and issue the Select statements, you create and issue the Update statements, and so on. There is no concept of bound, or automatically updating, values. This can be good in that you can control the interface to the server, optimizing the connections and making sure that all data meets your criteria. In addition, you have complete control over the error trapping associated with the transactions.

DB-LIB is an API-level interface to SQL Server. Keep in mind that this is not the method you will be using to work with SQL Server through more user-oriented tools such as Access and Excel. Those types of tools use an abstraction layer, Open Database Connectivity (ODBC) or OLE-DB, to make working with the database less developer-intensive.

Understanding Open Database Connectivity (ODBC)

If you have been working in the personal computer industry for any length of time, you know that there are a significant number of database applications that different people have installed to address different needs. Gone are the days when you could count on a specific database type at an installation site. This is especially true if you're developing a utility program, such as one that is expected to query a database, regardless of where that database came from, who designed it, and so on.

ODBC attempts to rectify this, although, as you will see, there are some costs involved with this approach. Your best-case solution will depend on a number of factors, including how diverse the database types are in the location or locations where you plan to deploy any given solution.

Where Do SQL-DMO Objects Fit In?

With the introduction of Visual Basic 4, Microsoft also introduced the new SQL Data Management Objects (SQL-DMO). These make it easier to work with the different objects associated with a database, including the database, table, rules, and so on.

SQL-DMO is created by working with objects in Visual Basic. If you're not familiar with objects, make sure you understand the concepts of creating new objects, working with properties in general, working with collections, and so forth.

N O T E   The SQL-DMO object model has completely changed from version 6.5 to version 7.0. If you have any applications written using the previous object model, they must be rewritten using sqldmo.dll instead of the outdated sqlole.dll. ■

You also need to understand how to set up the references from within Visual Basic to point to the SQL object. You set up the object type by using the following statement:

```
Dim objSQLServer as New SQLDMO.SQLServer
```

Once established, you can work with the different objects associated with SQL Server by referencing them as you would other properties, methods, and collections associated with other objects. For example, to work with tables in a given database, you can reference them as follows:

```
Dim objSQLServer as NEW SQLDMO.SQLServer
dim objDatabase as SQLDMO.Database
objSQLServer.Connect "sqlserver1", "dbdev", "devpw"
For Each objDatabase in objSQLServer.Databases
     Msgbox "Database name: " & objDatabase.Name
Next
Set oSQLServer = Nothing
```

You can see several things at work here. First, the declaration of the SQL Server object makes the connection to the server possible. Next, using the Connect method, the connection to the server is established. The server name in this example is SQLSERVER1 and the user ID and password are DBDEV and DEVPW, respectively.

N O T E   If you leave out the reference to the username and password, you will be prompted for them when the application runs. ■

Next, during the for...next loop, the database object's NAME property is displayed in the message box, showing each database available on the server.

Finally, the connection to SQL Server is dropped when the object is set to NOTHING. This releases the connection and the objects associated with it on the client system.

The balance of the objects you will be working with are objects, collections, properties, and methods on the SQL-DMO object. You can access them as you do any other automated object. In addition, you can send commands to SQL Server using the ExecuteImmediate and ExecuteWithResults methods. These allow you to send SQL statements directly to the server.

▶ For additional information about developing database applications with Visual Basic, see Que's *Platinum Edition Using Visual Basic 5.*

Where Do the Data Access Objects (DAO) Fit In?

▶ **See** Chapter 27, **p. 673**, for additional information on Advanced Data Objects—a technology that fits tightly into the Web development and database access model developed by Microsoft.

The Data Access Objects (DAO) are objects, methods, and properties that make it easier to work with your database. While they still use the Jet and ODBC access layers for the transactions with SQL Server, they add an abstract layer between you, the developer, and the ODBC calls needed to accomplish your requests.

With the DAO, you use collections of objects to work with databases, tables, views, and so on. It's a simple thing to refer to an .ADD method on an object to add a new table than it is to use the standard ODBC approach and reference stored procedures. As another example, most collections will have standard property sets. In the code shown next, you can see that the .COUNT property shows the number of TableDefs, or table definitions, in the current database.

```
'Determine how many tables there are and then print
'the results.
i = db.TableDefs.Count
Debug.Print "There are " & Str$(i) & " table(s) in this database."
```

By using these standardized approaches in working with the database, you can leverage your knowledge to work with just about any data source accessible by ODBC. In addition, these approaches work in other languages and other environments. For example, the DAO are accessible in Visual Basic for all versions currently available and will be supported into the future.

The examples in the balance of this chapter will often reference the DAO form of accessing the feature covered. This will help outline how you use the different properties and methods to work with SQL Server.

Concepts and Characteristics

To address the concern of connectivity to, and between, database systems, Microsoft developed the ODBC approach. ODBC is a layer of abstraction between the application and the underlying database system. This layer allows you to issue one `Select` statement and have that statement run against any supported database, including some cases in which the databases do not directly support the SQL language.

ODBC serves as the access layer to the database files. ODBC is responsible for taking your request for information and changing it into the language the database engine understands and uses for retrieving the information in the database.

ODBC presents a common interface to your application. This allows you to develop to a common set of calls and methodologies without worrying about the subtleties of the underlying database. You can see an excellent example of this in Microsoft Access. In Access, you can choose to link or attach a table to a database. When you do, Access will prompt you for the type of database table you want to work with. You have the option of selecting from several formats that Access works with directly or you can simply select ODBC. When you do, you are presented with the different ODBC configurations you have established. Therefore you are able to select any one of them without regard to database engine.

Access will be able to attach the table to the database because it won't know or care about the database. It knows only that it can use the database table with standardized SQL statements, which is the key to ODBC.

Because the main purpose of ODBC is to abstract the conversation with the underlying database engine, the use of ODBC is somewhat transparent once you're connected. This is different when compared with DB-LIB reviewed earlier. DB-LIB required special syntax to buffer statements and work directly with the server. ODBC, on the other hand, requires only that you create the standardized SQL statement and then pass that statement to ODBC.

Understanding ODBC Sessions

When you work with ODBC in your application, you are working with a data source and the database engine it references. As you will see in the "Client Configuration" section later in this chapter, when you install ODBC, you should install not only the overall ODBC subsystem, but also driver-to-database combinations. These combinations are given names and then used in your connection request when you want to access the database they refer to. These database-and-driver combination definitions are called *Data Source Names* (DSNs). When you open an ODBC connection and don't otherwise specify this information, ODBC steps in and prompts you for it.

In most languages, when you specify the connect string for ODBC, you have a couple of options. First, you can specify only that it's an ODBC connection you want to open, in which case ODBC will step in and prompt you for the DSN to use.

```
Set db = OpenDatabase("",,"odbc;")
```

In this case, the information provided by the user determines the database that is opened. You can also specify the connection to use by indicating the DSN, user ID, and password for the connection, as applicable.

```
Set db = OpenDatabase("",,"odbc;<DSN Info>")
```

CAUTION

If you allow your user to specify the ODBC connection to use, you might end up working against a database that you have not planned to interact with. In nearly all cases, your application should provide the DSN information that will allow ODBC to connect to the database, ensuring that you know the database schema for the information sources you're accessing.

Your second option is to indicate the details for the connection in the connection string itself. In this type of connection, <DSN Info> represents any of the different items you can specify as part of the DSN. Some of the more commonly used items are shown in Table 22.5.

Table 22.5 Common DSN and Connection String Elements

Element	Description
DSN	The DSN name you have configured in the ODBC settings
UID	The user ID to use to log in to the database
PWD	The password to use for the login

For example, consider the following sample VBA statement:

```
Set db = OpenDatabase("",,"odbc;DSN=MyDSN;UID=MyUserName;PWD=MyPassword")
```

This connects to the ODBC data source using the MyDSN configuration. It also uses the user and password indicated in the parameters. Using this command, the user will not be prompted for ODBC DSN information but will be connected automatically.

> **N O T E** In this example, the db variable represents a VB variable declared as a `Database` object type. In this example, the db variable is the reference point for future actions against the database. ▪

In this example, we're using some of the data access objects to access the ODBC data source. Using this access method, you can work through the tables, fields, and information stored in the database system by using common objects and object browsing methodologies. For a simple example, consider the procedure shown in Listing 22.1.

Listing 22.1 Example of Connecting to ODBC with DAO

```
Sub DAOExample()
    'set up the variables
    Dim db As DATABASE
    Dim i As Integer

    'connect to the database
    Set db = OpenDatabase("", , "odbc;DSN=BILLING;UID=SA;PWD=;")

    'Determine how many tables there are and then print
    'the results.
    i = db.TableDefs.Count
    Debug.Print "There are " & Str$(i) & " table(s) in this database."

    'Close the connection
    db.Close
End Sub
```

The output from this routine will be a statement indicating the number of tables in the database. By using the object-oriented nature of DAO, it's easy to work quickly with the database connection once it has been established.

The final step to working with SQL is to close the connection. The specifics of how you will close it may vary between host languages, but in VB or VBA, you can simply use the `.Close` method. This closes the connection to the database and frees up the memory structures associated with the connection.

Client Configuration

ODBC drivers are installed when you install SQL Server client utilities. They are also installed or updated when you install several Microsoft products such as Office '95 and Access '95. The drivers are installed on your system, but you still nced to create the specific DSNs that 'you will be referencing when you open a connection to the database.

The ODBC Administrator is located on the Control Panel, shown in Figure 22.1.

FIGURE 22.1

The ODBC Administrator is used to manage new and existing ODBC DSNs.

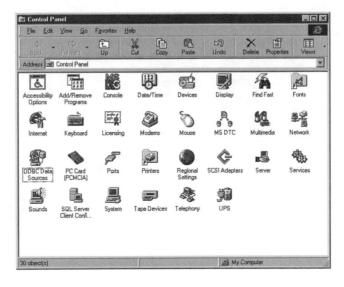

The ODBC Administrator allows you to select from the known ODBC connections so you can make any necessary changes. You can also add new DSNs to your system. Figure 22.2 shows the initial ODBC DSN listing and the different options you can access to manage the DSNs.

FIGURE 22.2

The DSNs listed are the names you specify in the ODBC connection string.

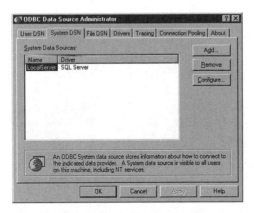

In the next section, you will see how you can work with new and existing DSNs as well as set up your system so you can take advantage of ODBC in your applications.

Working with ODBC DSNs

From the ODBC Data Sources dialog box, you have two options that relate to managing ODBC connections. The Add and Configure options let you specify the different characteristics of the DSNs you establish. Figure 22.3 shows a sample dialog of options for setting up a SQL Server connection. Note that the dialog box is the same for setting up a new connection and for making changes to an existing connection.

FIGURE 22.3

Setting the name of the data source and the SQL Server to connect to.

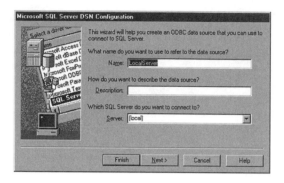

Figure 22.3 shows the first dialog displayed when setting up a data source. The key options you should always set up are as follows:

- Data Source Name
- Description
- Server

Clicking the Next button will display the next dialog as shown in Figure 22.4. This is where you have the option to authenticate by either a trusted connection or use SQL Server authentication.

FIGURE 22.4

Configuring connection authentication.

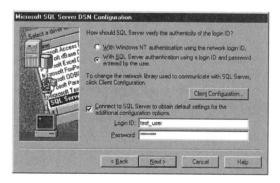

Once you are finished specifying the authentication options, clicking the Next button will display the dialog as shown in Figure 22.5. This dialog allows you to specify a default database and certain ANSI compliance options.

You should always try to establish the database name as well. Doing so will help ensure that when the connection is made, it is to the correct database and does not rely on the default database assigned to the user who is logging in.

Once you have set up the default database and any ANSI compliance options, click the Next button to display the dialog in Figure 22.6. This dialog allows you to specify any logging, character translations, and regional settings.

FIGURE 22.5

Specifying a default database and ANSI compliance.

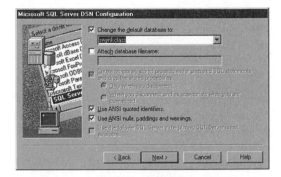

FIGURE 22.6

When you click the Finish button, you will be shown the dialog that allows you to test the connection before creating the data source or making any modifications to an existing data source.

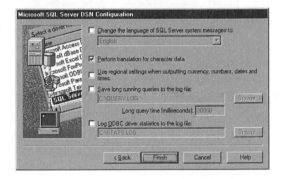

N O T E It is recommended that you test all of your connections at this point to ensure everything is running. Trying to debug an improperly configured data source during development can become very frustrating. ■

Advantages and Disadvantages of Using ODBC

Because ODBC provides abstract access to just about any popular database format available, it brings a fair amount of leverage to your development effort. A key element in the ODBC framework is the capability for your DSN to refer to any database. This allows you to develop against an Access database and implement your system in production against a SQL Server just by changing the drivers used by the DSN you have defined for the application.

The abstraction of the calls to the database engine is not without cost. The biggest downside to ODBC is that it must be able to support the capability to translate the calls. This means that additional processing overhead can slow the data access a bit. With ODBC, you can gain a significant speed advantage with a true client/server implementation. By taking the processing away from the client and into the server within SQL Server, you can eliminate much of the scrolling of information that is one of the primary slowing points for ODBC.

Consider using stored procedures as the basis for your ODBC calls when database engine processing is required. This saves processing time on both ends of the spectrum.

From Here...

You had a whirlwind tour of the different techniques and technologies that are available to you for working with, and administering, your SQL Server system and its databases. By combining these technologies with the comprehensive coverage throughout this book on the SQL language and the capabilities of SQL Server, you will be able to develop comprehensive applications for working with SQL Server.

From here, you might want to consider reviewing the following related materials:

■ Chapter 7, "Retrieving Data with Transact-SQL" reviews the syntax for the SQL language and how you use it to work with the tables in SQL Server.

■ Chapter 5, "Creating Databases and Transaction Logs," and Chapter 6, "Creating Database Tables and Using Datatypes," detail the different objects in SQL Server and how you can create and manage them. The relationships between these objects will be helpful should you need to develop your own administrative applications using SQL-DMO.

Understanding SQL Server and the Internet

Building Internet- and Intranet-Ready Solutions

Corporate database systems are built on making information widely available to qualified users. The information in these situations comes from many sources, ranging from discussion groups to proprietary systems. Probably the biggest repository of mass information is the database. If you've ever just browsed a database without specifying meaningful criteria, you know what is meant by mass information. There is often so much information as to make that information virtually useless.

By making databases available on your site, you can help users make sense of this information and, at the same time, you'll be able to provide access and presentation of the data without the need for any special software. In short, you have a new avenue to provide this access to the information that is probably already stored on your network.

Database access with the Internet Information Server (IIS) system is provided by giving you ODBC connectivity to the HTML pages that execute on the server when the user makes a request of the system. In this chapter, you'll see how to set up pages, what types of information you can provide, and how you can enhance the presentation of the information to make it as meaningful as possible to the people that request it.

> **CAUTION**
>
> Be aware that the database connector files are likely to contain and convey sensitive and sometimes very confidential information. For example, they'll contain query information that calls out column names, table names, and database sources that map to your ODBC configurations on the server.
>
> In addition, when users click a link to a database connector file, they'll be able to see where you're keeping your scripts and other programs, as it will show up in the URL that is displayed to them.
>
> It is extremely important that your programs, scripts and supporting files reside in the scripts subdirectory structure and that you provide Execute Only privileges on that directory. Be sure you do not provide Read privileges. This will open your system to the unnecessary danger of tampering because people would be able to browse and review the applications that are the core of your system.

Setting Up the Internet Database Connector

The Internet Information Server provides access to the ODBC layer with the use of the Internet Database Connector or IDC. The IDC acts as a go-between for your system, providing the interaction between what is seen in the viewer in terms of HTML, and how the information is queried at the database level. The overall access layer map is shown in Figure 23.1.

 T I P   Note that IDC technology is the older of the techniques available for accessing your databases. Make sure you also look into OLE-DB, Active Server Pages and other techniques before deciding on the technology best suited for you. With the IDC approach, the solution is likely to be extremely stable, but your options are more limited when it comes to working with the results set. This is especially true when compared with VBScript and other ASP options you have.

FIGURE 23.1

The overall access layer map.

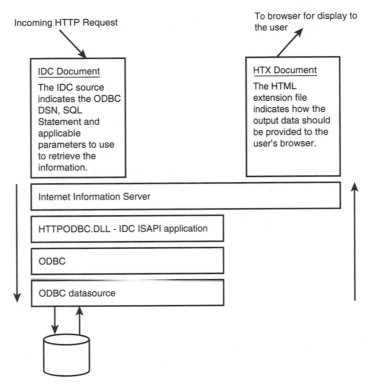

When users specify the IDC file in from the browser, they are asking the Web server to use the IDC file and its statements to query the database and return the results. The IDC is opened, but the HTX file, or HTML Extension file, is what is actually returned to the user. The HTX file, still a standard HTML file, indicates how the resulting data is displayed, what lines constitute the detail lines of information, and more.

From Figure 23.1, you can see that the engine that is doing the database work with ODBC is HTTPODBC.DLL. This DLL, included when you install the IIS system, is an Internet Server API (ISAPI) application that runs as an extension to the server software. This extension is database-aware and is able to use the two source files, the IDC and HTX files, required to give the information back to the user.

Listing 23.1 shows a sample IDC file.

Listing 23.1 A Simple IDC Source File

```
Data source: web sql
Username: sa
Template: sample.htx
SQLStatement:
+SELECT au_lname, ytd_sales from pubs.dbo.titleview
➥   where ytd_sales>5000
```

When this file is loaded by IIS, IIS examines the extension and determines what application should be used for the source file. For certain items, including the IDC extension, the server comes preinstalled knowing what to do with the source when it's requested. One of the very powerful capabilities and features of IIS is its ability to use the same Windows-based extension resolution (also referred to as Application Mapping or Registered File Types) to determine what to do with a given request. Files with a .GIF extension, for example, are known graphic images, and files with an IDC extension are database connector "applets."

The results formatting file, or HTX file, is where things can get a little tricky. As you'll see throughout this chapter, the real power and capability of your system is exposed with the HTX file. Until the information is provided to the template, it's of no use to the requester. You can have the best, most comprehensive databases around, but if the presentation of the data is not what your audience needs, the information might as well be under lock and key.

Listing 23.2 shows a simple HTX template.

Listing 23.2 HTX Source Files Provide Template Information for the Display of Results from Database Queries

```
<HTML>
<HEAD><TITLE>Authors and YTD Sales</TITLE></HEAD>
<BODY BACKGROUND="/samples/images/backgrnd.gif">
<BODY BGCOLOR="FFFFFF">
<TABLE>
<TR>
<TD><IMG SRC="/samples/images/SPACE.gif" ALIGN="top" ALT=" "></TD>
<TD><A HREF="/samples/IMAGES/db_mh.map">
➥ <IMG SRC="/SAMPLES/images/db_mh.gif" ismap
➥ BORDER=0 ALIGN="top" ALT=" "></A></TD>
</TR>
<tr>
<TD></TD>
<TD>
<hr>
<font size=2>
<CENTER>
<%if idc.sales eq ""%>
<H2>Authors with sales greater than <I>5000</I></H2>
<%else%>
<H2>Authors with sales greater than <I><%idc.sales%>
➥</I></H2>
<%endif%>
<P>
<TABLE BORDER>
<%begindetail%>
```

```
<%if CurrentRecord EQ 0 %>
<caption>Query results:</caption>
<TR>
<TH><B>Author</B></TH><TH><B>YTD Sales<BR>(in dollars)
➥</B></TH>
</TR>
<%endif%>
<TR><TD><%au_lname%></TD><TD align="right">$<%ytd_sales%>
➥</TD></TR>
<%enddetail%>
<P>
</TABLE>
</center>
<P>
<%if CurrentRecord EQ 0 %>
<I><B>Sorry, no authors had YTD sales greater than </I>
➥<%idc.sales%>.</B>
<P>
<%else%>
<HR>
<I>
The web page you see here was created by merging the results
of the SQL query with the template file SAMPLE.HTX.
<P>
The merge was done by the Microsoft Internet Database Connector and
the results were returned to this web browser by the
➥Microsoft Internet Information Server.
</I>
<%endif%>
</font>
</td>
</tr>
</table>
</BODY>
</HTML>
```

You'll probably notice several different things right away with this file. First, it's a standard HTML document. There is no strange formatting to speak of, and certainly many of the tags will be familiar if you've developed HTML before. Some of the real fun begins in the new capabilities offered by the HTX file. These new functions, above and beyond standard HTML, enable you to have the resulting Web page react to and change depending on the information that is, or is not, returned from the query. For example, in the following section of code, you'll see the introduction of conditional testing while examining for an empty set:

```
<%if idc.sales eq ""%>
   <H2>Authors with sales greater than <I>5000</I></H2>
<%else%>
   <H2>Authors with sales greater than <I><%idc.sales%></I></H2>
<%endif%>
```

There are several operators that are available when you design your pages. Throughout this chapter you'll learn more about how to use these new database-oriented features.

As mentioned earlier, the IDC source file indicates the ODBC data source that is used to access the database on your system. From the IDC file listing, you'll notice the data source item. This item indicates that the Web SQL data source will be used. Before this example will work on your system, you must have installed and configured the data source for that name using the ODBC control panel applet.

In the next couple of sections, you'll see how to set up the ODBC data sources for both SQL Server and Microsoft Access. You can use any 32-bit ODBC data source with your IIS application, and changes between setting up other data sources should be minimal. If you use the information presented here, you'll find that the IDC can work with nearly any database installation you might need to use.

Building ODBC Data Sources for SQL Server Databases

One of the most common reasons for problems with the database connector is the setup of the ODBC data source. This is true across database sources and not specific to SQL Server, so it's important to understand the details of setting up the driver for access by IIS.

You might recall that IIS is running as a service. This means that, while it's running, it's not logged in as you, the administrator, but is running in the background, logging in when needed as either the anonymous user you've set up, or as the validated user who has been authenticated by the NT security subsystem. Because you want to give this service access to a database, and because you don't know whom the service will be logging in as, you need to set up the database source a bit differently than you might be accustomed to.

Microsoft has added a new option to the ODBC configurations to support a System DSN. These special data sources give you a way to set up a globally available data source. Because users who log on might be set up to have different access to your system and resources, you need to use the system DSN to make sure they have access to the right databases, regardless of where they log in, or who they log in as. Figure 23.2 shows the ODBC setup dialog box, started from the Control Panel.

 T I P

If you find that you receive errors trying to access an ODBC data source from your Web pages, one of the first things you should make sure of is that the data source you're referencing is set up as a system data source.

If the data source is listed in the initial dialog box when you start the ODBC manager utility, it's defined as a user-based data source, not a system DSN. Remove the user-based DSN and redefine it as a system DSN, and you'll be able to see the database.

Remember, the only data sources that the Database Connector can use are system-level data sources.

FIGURE 23.2

ODBC setup for IIS requires that you select the System DSN to configure the driver.

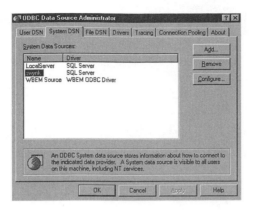

After you select System DSN, you'll be able to use essentially the same options to set up the drivers. Note, too, that you can have more than one driver set up at the system level. This allows you to set up drivers for the different applications that you'll be running on the Web. Figure 23.3 shows the Data Source Set Up dialog box.

FIGURE 23.3

Setting up a system-level ODBC driver configuration is much the same as establishing a new ODBC configuration. You'll need to indicate the driver, database, and other information required to connect to your database engine.

The Data Source Name you provide is what you'll be using in the IDC file as the data source, so be sure to make note of the database configuration names you set up.

In most cases, you'll want the configuration to be as specific as possible. If it's possible to indicate a default database or table, be sure to do so. It will take some of the variables out of your Web page design. By specifying as much information as possible, you'll help make sure the information is accessible.

Building ODBC Database Sources for Microsoft Access Databases

Microsoft Access database data sources are established the same way as they are for SQL Server. You must set up each data source as a System DSN, making it available to the IDC as it logs in to NT's security subsystem.

Of course, there will likely be changes in the SQL statement options you indicate in the IDC file. These differences relate to how Access interprets the SQL language elements. By and large, however, the statements should be nearly identical, especially in those cases where you're issuing SQL statements that are basically SELECT statements, rather than calling stored procedures, which are not supported by Access.

When you create the DSN, you'll be prompted to select the database with which ODBC should connect. Be sure to provide this information because, even though you can indicate it in code, you can make the connection to the database far more bulletproof with this option turned on. The system won't have to guess where to go to get the information.

User Rights and Security Concerns

Database access using the IDC provides a wide open query system to your database. You should avoid allowing users system administrator level access to your databases just because it provides a possible way for someone to gain unwanted administrative access to your system. Instead, consider one of two options. First, if you're allowing anonymous connections to your site, be sure that the user you have indicated as the anonymous user (usually IUSR_<machine name>) has appropriate rights to the databases that will be needed.

The way the login process works is to first validate the user using the anonymous login if it's enabled. If enabled, and that user indicated as the anonymous user does not have sufficient rights, he or she will receive an error message indicating that the user does not have rights to the object(s) requested.

If anonymous login is disabled, the IDC will use the current user's name and password to log on to the database. If this fails to gain access, the request is denied and the user is prevented from accessing the database requested.

In short, if you want anonymous users gaining access to your system, you'll need to create the user account that you want to access the information. Next, assign the user to the database and objects, allowing access to the systems needed.

The second option you have is to use NT's integrated security with SQL Server. Using this method, the currently logged-in user will be logged on to SQL Server and the same rights will be in force.

Building Dynamic Web Pages

Dynamic Web pages (those that build themselves on the fly to provide up-to-date information) will quickly become the mainstay of intranets and the Internet. With a dynamic Web page, you can always count on getting the latest and greatest information. With the IDC, you can create these dynamic Web pages and have them work against a database to retrieve the information the user needs to review.

There are three components to this type of page:

■ Initial source HTML document, often containing form fields or other options

■ The IDC file, for making and carrying out the database commands and data acquisition

■ The HTX file, for presenting the information returned

Part
V
Ch
23

While it's not the intent of this book to teach all aspects of HTML, it's important to keep in mind that the examples provided are just that—examples. You'll need to take these samples and adapt them to your organization's way of doing business on the Internet. In short, the HTML code that might be required are the field, listbox and checkbox options provided by HTML. Using these options, and the ODBC connectivity, you can create forms that present a meaningful interface for the user.

When you create a form that you'll be using to prompt the user for information, you create fields and other controls much like you do when creating an application. You'll name the fields and pass the name and its value to the IDC to be used in your database query, if you desire. In the next sections, you'll see how to go about creating these files and what makes them drive the output pages with the information from the database.

Building Initial Forms to Prompt for Values

Generally speaking, you'll start the process of working with a database by presenting the users with a form allowing them to select what information they need. As will often be the case, you have the ability to create forms that allow input to be used to form the SQL statements you'll be passing to the data source. When you create a form, there are two basic HTML tags you'll use. These are the INPUT and FORM tags. They enable you to designate actions to take and information to accept on behalf of the user. Listing 23.3 shows a simple form that prompts a search for an author name in the author's table.

On the CD

Listing 23.3 queform.htm—Simple HTML Form to Initiate a Database Query

```
<HTML>
<HEAD>
<TITLE>
Que Publishing's Very Simple Demonstration Form
</TITLE>
</HEAD>
```

continues

Listing 23.3   Continued

```
<h1>Sample Form for Database Access</h1>
<FORM METHOD="POST" ACTION="/scripts/que/QueForm1.idc">
Enter Name to Find in the Pubs Database: <INPUT NAME="au_lname">
<p>
<INPUT TYPE="SUBMIT" VALUE="Run Query">
</FORM>
</BODY>
</HTML>
```

The key elements are the POST instructions and the text box presented to the user. The FORM tag indicates what should happen when the form is executed. In this case, the form will send information to the server, hence the POST method. The ACTION tag calls out the program or procedure that is run on the server to work with the information that is sent in. In the example, the QUEFORM1.IDC is called and passed the parameters.

N O T E   The letter case is not significant when you're specifying HTML tags. INPUT is the same as indicating input and will not change the results when processed by IIS.

It's not immediately apparent what those parameters might be, but if you examine the one or more INPUT fields, you can see that they are named. The following syntax is a basic, required element when you need to pass information back to the host in a forms-based environment:

```
<INPUT NAME="<variable name>">
```

The `<variable name>` is the name you'll use to reference the value provided by the user. Much as you define a variable in Visual Basic by dimensioning it, you must define and declare the different variables and other controls that are used by your HTML. There are other properties that can be set with the INPUT NAME tag, such as VALUE, that allow you to set the initial value of the item you're declaring. For example, the following line declares a new variable, MyName, and assigns an initial value of "Wynkoop" to it.

```
<INPUT NAME="MyName" VALUE="Wynkoop">
```

For the preceding example, the intention is to create a very simple form that allows the user to type in a name, or portion of the name, that can be used to search the Authors table in the Pubs database. When the HTML is loaded as shown previously, Figure 23.4 is the result.

As you can see, the text box size is automatically determined for you as a default. There are MAXLENGTH and SIZE properties that you can place in the INPUT NAME directive if you need to increase the size of the text box. You'll also notice that if you press Enter while you're using this form, the form will automatically be submitted to the server as if you'd pressed the Submit button. Because there is only a single button on this form, the browser automatically performs the only function it can.

In this example from Listing 23.3, the browser opens a new URL on the server with the following specification:

```
http://holodeck3/scripts/que/QueForm1.idc?au_lname=<name>
```

FIGURE 23.4

Allowing the user to indicate values to pass to the database engine adds polished, functional benefits to your application.

> **Sample Form for Database Access**
>
> Enter Name to Find in the Pubs Database:
>
> Run Query

N O T E If you watch your Web browser, it might only indicate that it's loading the URL that is included up to the ? in these examples. The protocol is still passing the parameters to the host; they are simply not shown during the transfer by some browsers. ■

The *<name>* is the name you indicate in the text box prior to pressing Enter or clicking the Submit button. The next step in the process is to run the query against the database engine and see what results are returned.

Building Server Query Source Files

The query source files reside in files in your SCRIPTS area and have a filename extension of IDC by convention. When the URL is accessed, the server is going to run the indicated IDC file. As mentioned earlier in this chapter, the IDC file contains the SQL statements and directives necessary to carry out the commands as needed. In this example, Listing 23.4 shows the source for querying the database.

> **CAUTION**
>
> To reiterate the note earlier about security, be sure you place your IDC files in directories that have been set up with Execute, but not Read, privileges. This is important because if users can review your source files, they can see column names, table names, SQL login names and passwords, and so on. This is information you want to be sure is private.

On the CD

Listing 23.4   queform1.idc—The IDC File Called by QUEForm.HTM

```
Datasource: web sql
Username: sa
Template: queform1.htx
SQLStatement:
+SELECT au_lname, phone, address, city, state, zip
+ from authors
+ where au_lname like '%au_lname%%'
```

The output from this specific file is really nothing. The user will never see this file or output from it directly. This seems a bit strange, but the entire intent of the IDC is to define and perform the query against the data source indicated. After the information is retrieved, the IDC calls the Template indicated and passes in the results to be returned as a Web page.

N O T E In the example in Listing 23.4, you'll notice that the WHERE clause specifies LIKE and that there is an extra percent sign in the comparison field. This is standard SQL syntax that allows you to search for wildcard strings. You specify the part you know and the IDC will append an extra % character at the end. Because the percent sign is the wildcard for SQL Server, you'll be able to return all items that start with B, for example. ■

Some basics about this source file are important to understand to explain how it works. First, to reference a variable, you place it between percentages, as is the case with the preceding '%au_lname%' . Note that the single quotes are required as the field is a text-based type.

You can reference variables anywhere in the script. This means you can allow the user to specify even items that are seemingly hard-coded, like parameters, and then call them dynamically from the IDC file.

Also, in situations when your line length is shorter than your actual line, you can call out the item you want to work on, begin specifying the values, and continue indicating the expanding values, as long as you place the + in the first column of the file. The plus sign acts as a code continuation character for these source files.

The data source indicated in the IDC relates to the ODBC data source you establish with the ODBC Manager in the Control Panel. Remember that the data source you use with the IDC must be a system DSN. If it's not, the call to the database will fail.

The username, and optionally the password, will override any settings you might have established in ODBC, and they'll override the current username as well because it relates to the execution of the query. Other parameters that might be of interest or use in your integration of the IDC file into your installation are shown in Table 23.1.

Table 23.1 IDC Optional Parameters

Parameter	Description
RequiredParameters	By naming the parameters that must be represented on the form filled out by the user, you can make sure the user didn't just press Enter or otherwise ignore a field. Name the fields you must have information from and IIS will kick back a message if the field is left blank for any reason. When you specify the fields, do not use percent signs, but simply the name of the field. To indicate more than one field, separate each field in the list with a comma.

Parameter	Description
DefaultParameters	You can set up defaults for the fields you are expecting from the user. Name each field, followed by an equal sign and the value you want it to have. When the field is retrieved from the form, if it's a blank or non-specified field, the value you indicate will be filled in. Note that DefaultParameters are applied prior to RequiredParameters being checked, effectively making RequiredParameters unnecessary if you can indicate an acceptable default. Keep in mind that your page should indicate what the default is because the user will not see the substitution that is made in the IDC file when it's processed.
Expires	If you submit a query over and over again, you might find that you're retrieving a cached copy of the information, rather than an updated database query. This can be especially problematic when developing applications as you'll be continually testing the system, re-submitting queries, and so on. By setting the EXPIRES tag, established in seconds, to a value that represents a timeframe that should pass before the query is retried, you'll avoid this problem. In other words, consider how long will it be before the information should be considered "stale" or in need of being refreshed for viewing.
MaxRecords	If you are connected over a slower speed connection, there are few things more frustrating than receiving a huge data file, then realizing that you only needed certain bits of information. For example, you might have a need to return only the first 100 rows of a table as they will provide the most current, meaningful data to your sales effort. By limiting the MaxRecords, you can indicate this in the IDC file, limiting traffic and database interaction with the new option.

 You can call SQL Server's stored procedures from an IDC file if you want to specify it in the SQL Statement portion of the file. To do so, use the following syntax:

`EXEC MySP_Name Param1[, Param2...]`

Include the name of your stored procedure in place of MySP_Name.

In the stored procedure, be sure you're returning results sets, even if they represent only a status value indicating success or failure on the operation. Remember, as with other ODBC data sources, the stored procedure will be passed to the server and the client will await the response. If your stored procedure does not return a value to the calling routine, you might give the user the impression that you've caused the browser to become frozen.

After you've retrieved the values you want to display, you can move on to the results-set source files. These files do the work of formatting and displaying information to the user and are explained next.

Building Results Source Files

The results files are where the fun begins in working with the data that comes back from the query. The HTML extension files, with filename extensions of HTX, are referenced in the Template entry in the IDC. These files dictate how the information is presented, what the user will see, whether items returned actually represent links to other items, and so on.

Listing 23.5 shows the sample HTX file for the example you've been reviewing throughout this chapter. You can see that it has a few extra, not-yet-standard, items that make the display of information from the database possible.

On the CD

Listing 23.5   QueForm1.htx—A Sample HTX File

```html
<!-- Section 1>
<HTML>
<HEAD>
<TITLE>Authors Details</TITLE>
</HEAD>
<TABLE>
<tr>
<TD>
<hr>
<P>
<TABLE BORDER>
 <caption>Query results:</caption>
 <TR>
 <TH><B>Author</B></TH>
 <TH><B>Phone</B></TH>
 <TH><B>Address</B></TH>
 <TH><B>City</B></TH>
 <TH><B>State</B></TH>
 <TH><B>Zip</B></TH>
 </TR>

<!-- Section 2>
<%begindetail%>
 <TR>
 <TH><B><%au_lname%></B></TH>
 <TH><B><%phone%></B></TH>
 <TH><B><%address%></B></TH>
 <TH><B><%city%></B></TH>
 <TH><B><%state%></B></TH>
 <TH><B><%zip%></B></TH>
 </TR>
<%enddetail%>

<!-- Section 3>
<P>
```

```
</TABLE>
<%if CurrentRecord EQ 0%>
  <H2>Sorry, no authors match your search criteria (<%idc.au_lname%>).</H2>
<%else%>
  <H2>Authors with names like "<I><%idc.au_lname%></I>"</H2>
<%endif%>
</center>
</td>
</tr>
</table>
</BODY>
</HTML>
```

When the URL is accessed, the server is going to run the indicated IDC file. As mentioned earlier in this chapter, the IDC file contains the SQL statements and directives necessary to carry out the commands as needed. For this example, Listing 23.4 shows the source for querying the database.

N O T E   The lines starting with <!-- are comments and are not interpreted by the HTML client. ▪

When you design data-oriented pages, you'll want to make sure you take advantage of HTML's start and end tag metaphor. To put it simply, for many of the different items in HTML, when you establish a tag, for instance <HEAD>, the feature you enabled with the first instance of the keyword is in force until the reciprocal argument, </HEAD>, is encountered.

As you can see in Figure 23.5, the example file turns on the H1 heading style and then doesn't turn it off, resulting in the entire page using oversized fonts.

FIGURE 23.5

Because HTML tags are evaluated in pairs, missing the closing tag can make a style run through the balance of your HTML document.

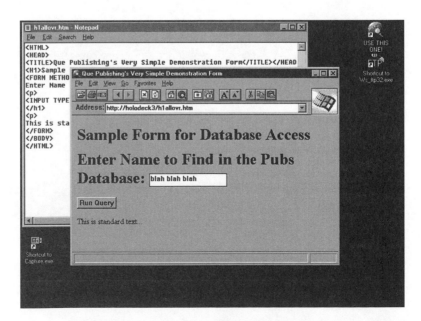

In the sample HTML in Listing 23.5, you'll notice that there are three sections called out. These sections are inserted only to make reading and explaining the HTML a bit easier. They aren't necessary for the functioning of the document.

In section one, the entire purpose is to set up the page. You'll need to establish fonts, set up background images, do any initial formatting, and so on. You'll also need to start any tables that you want to use. Because you initiate a table, add the rows to it, then turn off the table, tables represent an excellent way to present data that will include an unknown number of rows.

For example, in Figure 23.6, although two rows are shown, there could just as easily be 20. The other advantage of using tables to display your database information is that the table will size to the user's visible browser area automatically. You won't need to worry about column widths and other formatting issues.

FIGURE 23.6

If you can use tables to display data to the user, you'll be keeping with an already familiar metaphor for the presentation. Users are accustomed to table-based data represented in a columnar fashion.

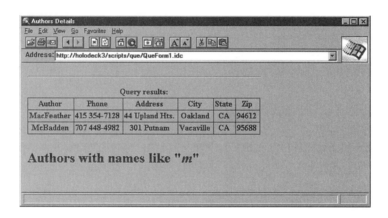

In section two you'll work with the detail lines that are returned as part of the data set. You'll notice that this section is bracketed with a <%begindetail%> and <%enddetail%> tags. Everything between these two tags will repeat once for every row returned in the data set. In the preceding example, section two consists largely of building the table to display the information returned.

```
<! Section 2>
<%begindetail%>
 <TR>
 <TH><B><%au_lname%></B></TH>
 <TH><B><%phone%></B></TH>
 <TH><B><%address%></B></TH>
 <TH><B><%city%></B></TH>
 <TH><B><%state%></B></TH>
 <TH><B><%zip%></B></TH>
 </TR>
<%enddetail%>
```

When you indicate the data to include, you refer directly to the column names that are in the table or view that is referenced by the IDC file. Place a <% before, and %> after each column name. In English, the preceding code snippet reserves a row to put new data into with the

<TR> tag, placing the information into the row with the <TH> tags, and ending the row with the closing </TR> tag.

You can do comparisons in your file as well. For example, if you wanted to check to make sure that the state was returned as AZ, you could do so in one of two ways. Obviously the preferred method would be to change your WHERE clause in the IDC to reflect the fact that you want to filter out non-Arizona states.

Alternatively, you could indicate here that you want to test. Consider the following code sample:

```
<! Section 2>
<%begindetail%>
<%if <%state%> eq "AZ"%>
     <TR>
     <TH><B><%au_lname%></B></TH>
     <TH><B><%phone%></B></TH>
     <TH><B><%address%></B></TH>
     <TH><B><%city%></B></TH>
     <TH><B><%state%></B></TH>
     <TH><B><%zip%></B></TH>
     </TR>
<%endif%>
<%enddetail%>
```

By using the If construct, you can test values and conditions in the data set. You can reference variables that come from the IDC file as well. To reference these, simply prefix the variable name with IDC. If you want to reference the incoming variable from the original HTML form, you can do so with a statement similar to the following:

```
<%if <%idc.au_lname%> eq "Wynkoop">
     <TH><B>Building series...</B></TH>
<%endif%>
```

In this case, the query would go back to the IDC and pull the value for the au_lname variable, make the comparison, and either execute or ignore the statements in the loop following the test. There are three different tests that you can perform. Each is described in Table 23.2.

N O T E You can also use <%else%> in your If...else...endif loop. ▪

Table 23.2 Comparison Operators for Use in HTX Files

Option	Description
EQ	Indicates an equivalent test. "Is item A equal to item B?"
GT	Tests for a condition where one item is greater than the other.
LT	Tests for the condition where one item is less than the other.

In addition, there are two different data set related variables. `CurrentRecord` allows you to reference the number of times the Detail section has executed. If, after the detail loop has run, you want to determine whether there are records in the data set, you can test this variable to see whether it's `0`. If it is, no information was returned and you should display a meaningful message to that effect.

```
<%if CurrentRecord EQ 0>
  <H2>Sorry, no authors match your search crit...
<%else%>
  <H2>Authors with names like "<I><%idc.au_lname%>...
<%endif%>
```

The other tag that corresponds directly to database-oriented actions is the `MaxRecords` option. `MaxRecords` relates to the `MaxRecords` IDC variable. Using this value, you can determine the total number of records that the IDC file will allow.

You use both `CurrentRecord` and `MaxRecords` in conjunction with `<%if%>` statements. They are implemented as controlling variables that help you to structure the logical flow of the HTX file. Just keep in mind that, after the processing of the detail section has completed, if `CurrentRecord` EQ 0, there are no results returned from the call.

The final section of the HTX file is used largely to close different HTML tags that were used to set up the display of information on the resulting page. Remember, HTML expects most tags in pairs, so it's a good idea to close each item properly.

```
<!-- Section 3>
<P>
</TABLE>
<%if CurrentRecord EQ 0%>
  <H2>Sorry, no authors match your search criteria (<%idc.au_lname%>).</H2>
<%else%>
  <H2>Authors with names like "<I><%idc.au_lname%></I>"</H2>
<%endif%>
</center>
</td>
</tr>
</table>
</BODY>
</HTML>
```

Notice, too, that the `CurrentRecord` variable is used to determine the message that is displayed to the user. There will be either a message indicating no matches, or one explaining what was searched for is shown. You can also see that by referencing the `<%idc.au_lname%>` variable, you can pull the user-specified value from the form.

The results of a successful search are shown in Figure 23.7.

If the search of the database tables is not fruitful, the HTX will display a different message indicating the failure of the process. Figure 23.8 shows this dialog box.

FIGURE 23.7

A successful match will show the hits on the Pubs database table, and will then show the message indicating what was searched for.

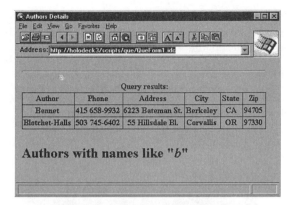

FIGURE 23.8

If matches for information are not found, you should code a branch of logic to indicate the problem to the user.

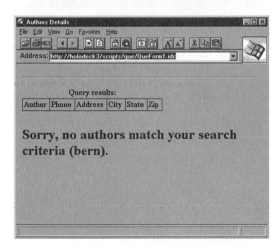

Internet Database Connector: A Summary and Example

To recap how the IDC works overall, first you will code a form or other HTML document that calls the IDC file on the server. The IDC file is located in the protected /SCRIPTS directory and contains the information necessary to open the ODBC connection and submit a query to the database engine. As the results are returned, they are merged into another document, which is the HTX or HTML extension document. This HTX file includes the information needed to work with both the detail records and the header/footer information for the page.

The result to the user is the display of the requested information in an HTML document style. Of course, the resulting document, based on the HTX file, can include further links to queries or drill-down information if needed. By using this technique, you can allow a user to select high-level values and then narrow the scope. You can still increase the detail level provided, using the information given from the user as drill-down parameters.

An excellent example of the drill-down technique is provided in Microsoft's samples, in the GuestBook application. As you query the GuestBook, you are returned high-level detail about the names found. Here's a look at the HTX file's Detail section to see what exactly is done to display the information from the database.

```
<%begindetail%>
Name: <a href="/scripts/samples/details.idc?FName=<%FirstName%>&
➥ LName=<%LastName%>"><b><%FirstName%> <%LastName%></b></a>
<p>
<%enddetail%>
```

For each name returned by the original query, the result will show the first and last names. This HTML sets up the names as links to their own details. The code indicates the A HREF tag and references the IDC that retrieves the detail information, DETAILS.IDC. As a result, when the users click this in their browser, they'll immediately be executing the IDC file and retrieving the next level of detail. Figure 23.9 shows what this initial screen of details looks like when the items are first retrieved.

FIGURE 23.9

The initial display of the GuestBook contents allows the user to select a name and drill down into the details for that name.

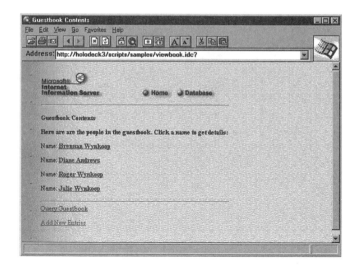

When you click a name to get the details, the IDC is called that retrieves the details from the Guests table on your system. If you take a look at the IDC, you'll see that it's quite simple, returning only a few columns of information based on the name selected from the previous query.

```
Datasource: Web SQL
Username: sa
Template: details.htx
SQLStatement:
+SELECT FirstName, LastName, Email, Homepage, Comment, WebUse
+FROM Guests
+WHERE FirstName = '%FName%' and LastName = '%LName%'
```

The final step is to show the information to the requester. The DETAILS.HTX template is called out in the IDC file, and it shows the detail information for the user as requested. The detail section simply displays the user information that has been provided. The HTX file uses the <%if%> operator and the comparison of the contents of a given field to ensure that the only information provided to the user is those fields that are non-blank.

On the CD

Listing 23.6   The Detail Section from the DETAILS.HTX File

```
<%begindetail%>
<h2>Here are details for <%FirstName%> <%LastName%>:</h2>
<p>
<b><%FirstName%> <%LastName%></b><br>
<p>

<%if Email EQ " "%>
<%else%>
Email Address: <%Email%> <br>
<%endif%>
<%if Homepage EQ " "%>
<%else%>
Homepage: <%Homepage%>
<%endif%>
<p>
Primary Web Role: <%WebUse%>
<p>
<%if Comment EQ " "%>
<%else%>
Comments: <%Comment%>
<%endif%>
<p>
<%enddetail%>
```

Providing this type of increasing detail based on a user's selection is good for all parties concerned. It's good for your system because it can provide only the information needed to determine the direction to go to for the next level of detail. In addition, it's good for the users because it can mean less content to shuffle through to get to the information they really need. Because they will be determining what information is delved into, they'll be able to control how deeply they want to go into a given item.

This technique is really great for supplying company information. You can provide overview type items at the highest level on everything from marketing materials to personnel manuals. Letting people select their research path also absolves you from the responsibility of second-guessing exactly what the user is expecting of the system.

Using SQL Server's Web Assistant Wizard

The race to bring content to your Internet or intranet site and make all different types of information available to the user base has been fast and furious. One of the recent advances is the capability of having the database engine automatically generate Web pages for you based on content in the database.

With SQL Server, you have the ability to schedule a task in the system to automatically create these HTML documents at time intervals ranging from a one-time run to many times per day. You can use this capability for a number of things, including reporting on your server's activity levels to you as an administrator.

In this section, you'll see how to set up these automatically generating pages and what the results of the process are. In these sections, you will get a sense of what it takes to use the Wizard to create updated content for you if you so desire.

Prerequisites for SQL Server

Before you can successfully use the Web Page Wizard and the processes it will create, you'll have to have set up your server to allow this type of access. Specifically, the Web Page Wizard relies on the task manager and SQLAgent service. You must have the SQLAgent service set up to automatically start upon startup of your server.

To confirm that the service is set to automatically start, open the properties sheet for your server and confirm the setting of the SQL Agent startup. See Figure 23.10.

FIGURE 23.10

Make sure the SQL Agent service is set to start automatically.

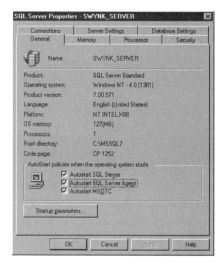

You can manually start and stop the service by using the SQL Server Service manager, the application that resides in your status bar. Double-clicking the status bar icon for SQL Server and then selecting SQLServerAgent from the Services drop down list box lets you check the current status of the service.

N O T E It's a requirement that the information you provide as it relates to the user and password is valid in SQL Server. You will also need to ensure that the account you indicate has access to the database you're reporting against. It will need to have SELECT permissions on the tables you're querying, and must have CREATE PROCEDURE permissions on the database you'll be using.

If you do not set up the SQLAgent to automatically start, the services required to generate the Web content you are setting up will not be available and the page will not be generated. ■

FIGURE 23.11

You can quickly check the status of the SQL Agent by using the SQL Server Service manager.

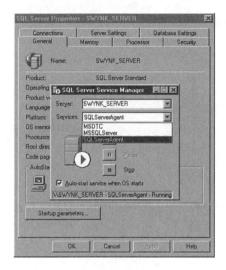

Starting the Web Assistant Wizard

The SQL Server Web Assistant Wizard is located in the Enterprise Manager under the Management Object tree. You can run the Wizard from a workstation or the server. In either case, it will generate the pages for you in a directory you'll specify later in the process.

Right-click the Web Publishing option, then select New Web Assistant Job. The result will be the initial opening screen for the Web Assistant. From here, you'll need to indicate the source and destination of your content, combined with the look and feel options available to you for the presentation of this information.

Selecting the Content for the Page When you select Next>, you'll be prompted to choose the database that you want to use for the pages you want to create. The list box will show the various databases currently available on your system. See Figure 23.12.

Select the database and then select Next. When you do, you'll have three different options presented. These are the different ways the assistant can query the database to get information from the tables in your system.

- ■ Data from tables and columns I select
- ■ Result set(s) of a stored procedure I select
- ■ Data from the Transact-SQL statement I specify

FIGURE 23.12

Select the database that you will use as the source of information for your Web pages.

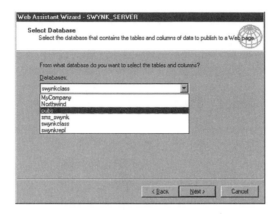

Each of these options has unique starting points, and they come together where you set up the scheduling options for the queries. The final steps, starting with the scheduling, are common to the different approaches.

The next sections explain the use of these options.

Data from Tables and Columns I Select   The first option, "Data from the tables and columns I select," allows you to use the point and click interface to indicate the tables and other items you want to include in your query that will be used to generate the page. Figure 23.13 shows an example of what the list boxes look like when you select this option.

FIGURE 23.13

The easiest interface is the "Data from tables" option because it allows you to select from the listing of objects on your server when deciding which items to provide for a report.

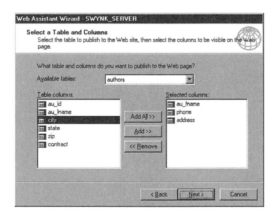

The next step is to indicate any applicable filtering options. By setting these types of options, you can limit the number of rows that are returned from the table(s) you indicated. By default, all rows will be returned, but you can select specific columns and then test the values in those columns as a means of limiting the results set.

You can also provide a WHERE clause in standard SQL form that will be used to fine-tune the results. More information on WHERE clauses is found in Chapter 7, "Retrieving Data with Trans-act-SQL." You can apply the techniques outlined there to this option.

Figure 23.14 shows an example of the filtering selections.

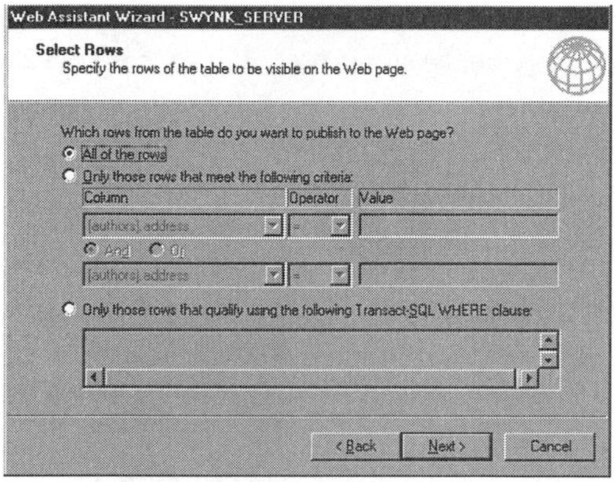

FIGURE 23.14

Use the Select Rows options to help filter the information for your Web pages.

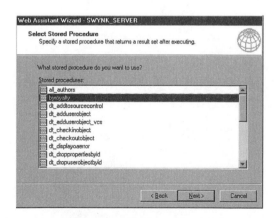

The final steps are common to the different query techniques and start with the "Scheduling Options" section later in this chapter.

Result Set(s) of a Stored Procedure I Select   The next option you have in setting up the source of information for your page is to call a stored procedure. When you select the Result set(s) option, you'll be able to select the stored procedure you want to use.

Select the stored procedure from the listing shown, pulled from the database you indicated earlier. See Figure 23.15.

FIGURE 23.15

Calling a stored procedure is a good way to share coding you've done for an application and put it to use for your Internet server.

Stored procedures are a powerful mechanism for optimizing your server and providing good database query tuning. If you have another system based on SQL Server, and you're using a stored procedure to produce the results for a printed report, you might be able to reference the same stored procedure in the dialog box and create the report in HTML, making it available at any time.

▶ For more information on stored procedures, **see** Chapter 14, "Managing Stored Procedures and Using Flow-Control Statements," **p. 355**

If there are any required parameters to your stored procedures, you'll be prompted to provide the information needed to execute the stored procedure. See Figure 23.16 for an example.

FIGURE 23.16

You'll need to provide appropriate parameters if the stored procedure you're calling requires parameters.

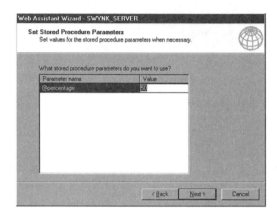

The final steps are common to the different query techniques and start with the "Scheduling Options" heading later in this chapter.

Data from the Transact-SQL Statement I Specify   If you select the Transact-SQL option, you'll be able to create any SQL statement you need to fulfill the requirements for your software.

Using this option means that you're taking all responsibility for the formation of SQL Server–specific calls. The query you enter will be passed along and executed by the server. Figure 23.17 shows an example of this option.

FIGURE 23.17

Entering the query manually can be powerful and painful all at once. If you're not sure of the syntax, be sure to use the more automated features of the Wizard for a few instances of information you want to publish. After you've completed a few, you'll begin to better understand the different issues involved in creating the queries manually.

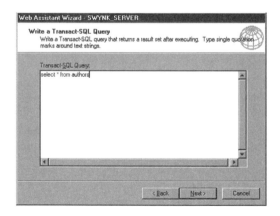

▶ For more information on creating the SQL statement, **see** Chapter 7, "Retrieving Data with Transact-SQL" and Chapter 9, "Using Functions," **p. 155**

The next step is to indicate the scheduling options you want for your Web Assistant Job. That process is covered in the next section.

Scheduling Options   The next dialog box will prompt you for the frequency at which you'd like to have the page rebuilt. Because the database is the source of information for the page, this item might take some work. This is because you'll need to talk with all the users of the application that creates the data in the database and determine how frequently it is changed.

A frequency set too low will cause additional overhead on the server as it handles the request. The impact on performance should be minimal, but if there are many, many requests for data pages such as this, it can begin to show on the access times to the server.

Your time-frame options and their associated parameters are:

- Only one time when I complete this wizard
- On Demand
- Only one time at…
- When SQL Server Data Changes
- At regularly scheduled intervals

There is a final checkbox that is available for all but the first option—it allows you to indicate that you want to create the web page after you've completed setting up the options with the wizard. This gets your initial page created right away. It will be replaced automatically if you select a scheduled interval option.

Figure 23.18 shows the options available.

FIGURE 23.18

Be sure to select a useful time interval. A too-frequent interval will force the server to rebuild the page without reason. A too-infrequent update process makes the information less useful, as it can become out-of-date for the users of the information.

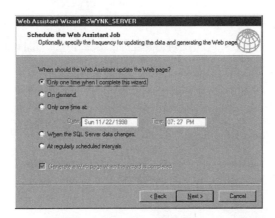

If you select the Regularly scheduled interval option, you'll be prompted for the schedule that you'd like to use. This information will be used to drive the SQLAgent processes—you may recognize the options from setting up other jobs that require scheduling on your system.

Part

V

Ch

23

The final step is to name the page that you'll be saving. This is the filename that it will be stored into, and the source of the URL that you'll give your users to access the page. See Figure 23.19.

T I P   The default directory for IIS-related content is \inetpub\wwwroot. If you're using IIS, this will place the file in the root directory of the Web site.

FIGURE 23.19

Be careful to note where you're saving the file; it's the basis of the URL that you'll be giving your users so they may access the information online.

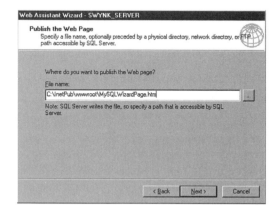

Formatting the Page

There are two different options with information about final formatting. You can have the assistant help you call out formatting, or you can use a format file that includes information on where to put the data that is returned from your server.

Selecting the format file option lets you indicate that you'll insert the results information into a template page. On the template page, you can include the special tag

```
<%insert_data_here%>
```

where you want to have SQL Server place the information. Additional options are available to formatting data that mirror those found when using IDC/HTX files.

If you let the wizard help you and select Next, you'll be prompted for the layout of the H1 (heading 1) tags, whether column headings are displayed, and so on. Figures 23.21 and 23.22 show the options that are available for these initial formatting steps. These first two steps are HTML-oriented. The remaining two steps are oriented toward the management of your data.

When you're working with data formatting, you'll have additional options that help in the presentation of the information (see Figure 23.22).

FIGURE 23.20

If you want the Web wizard to help you, select the Yes option and the character set, if necessary.

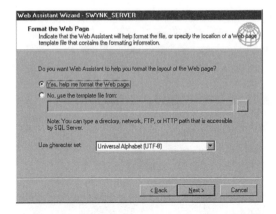

FIGURE 23.21

Provide a title and other high-level options for your page—it's a good idea to use the timestamp option.

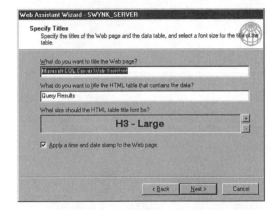

FIGURE 23.22

The key item in these options is the column headings. It's generally a good idea to include these in your output page.

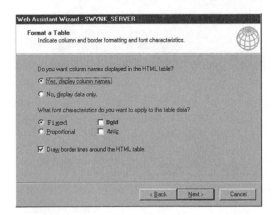

As you can see in Figures 23.23 and 23.24, you can also limit the rows returned, or have the wizard build successive pages for you when the results become larger. These are very helpful options that let you build sites that can dynamically change to meet the output requirements of the data.

FIGURE 23.23

It's almost always a good idea to place a link back to the home page of your site, or to the referring page that brought the user to the query results.

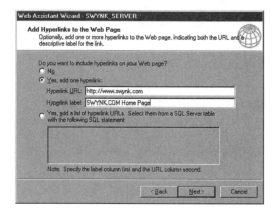

FIGURE 23.24

Two content automation options that can be key are the TOP and multi-page capabilities of the wizard.

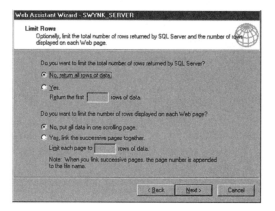

N O T E If you're using the multi-page option, be aware that if your data both expands and contracts, you can end up with extra pages on your system. This is because the data for the current run is smaller (the output requires fewer pages) than the last run.

While it may not seem significant at first, it can really present a challenge if you're using a search engine on your site. It's possible that the search engine will still see the older pages, in effect potentially showing the user old information.

If you're using this option, consider also having a set process to remove pages from the site—perhaps running that process immediately before the scheduled wizard task runs. ■

Finally, after you've set all of the different options, you'll be shown a confirmation of the options you've selected. There is an interesting option here to output the stored procedure call that will be used to create the Web page assistant job for you.

Here's an example of a simple Web assistant job's output—it's shown wrapped here. In reality it's a single line, calling the `sp_makewebtask` stored procedure.

```
EXECUTE sp_makewebtask @outputfile = N'C:\MSSQL7\HTML\WebPage1.htm',
➥ @query=N'SELECT [au_id], [au_lname], [au_fname], [phone],
➥ [address], [city], [state], [zip] FROM [authors]',
➥ @fixedfont=1, @HTMLheader=3, @webpagetitle=N'Microsoft SQL
➥ Server Web Assistant', @resultstitle=N'Query Results',
➥ @dbname=N'pubs', @whentype=1,@procname=N'pubs Web
➥ Page',@codepage=65001,@charset=N'utf-8'
```

Seeing the Results in SQL Server

It's helpful to review your SQL Server installation to understand what's happening when you implement a Wizard-generated Web page. There are a couple of things that happen when you create a page this way:

- A new job is created under Web Publishing
- A new task is created for the SQL Agent to watch over

As mentioned earlier, the `sp_makewebtask` is the stored procedure that is called to create the page with the parameters you indicate in the wizard. This statement in turn becomes the item that is scheduled as a job for the SQL Agent if you are creating a recurring job.

Note that your job is not saved under Web publishing unless it will be rerun later. That is to say, if it's a one-time run job only, it will not show up in that listing.

Seeing the Results on Your Web Site

Implementing the page(s) you create on your site is a simple matter. You need to create a link to the pages, or publish the URL to your user base. After the SQL engine creates the page, it appears just as any other HTML document. Listing 23.7 shows the sample page created by the Web Page Wizard.

On the CD

Listing 23.7 WebPage1.html—A Sample Page Created by the Wizard

```
<HTML>
<HEAD>

<META content="text/html; charset=utf-8" http-equiv=Content-Type>
<TITLE>Microsoft SQL Server Web Assistant</TITLE>
</HEAD>
<BODY>
<H3>Query Results</H3>
<HR>
<PRE><TT>Last updated: Nov 22 1998 10:44PM</TT></PRE>
<P>
<P><TABLE BORDER=1>
<TR>
```

continues

Part
V

Ch
23

Listing 23.7 Continued

```
<TH ALIGN=LEFT>au_id</TH><TH ALIGN=LEFT>au_lname</TH>
<TH ALIGN=LEFT>au_fname</TH><TH ALIGN=LEFT>phone</TH>
<TH ALIGN=LEFT>address</TH><TH ALIGN=LEFT>city</TH>
<TH ALIGN=LEFT>state</TH><TH ALIGN=LEFT>zip</TH>
<TH ALIGN=LEFT>contract</TH>
</TR><TR><TD><TT>172-32-1176</TT></TD><TD><TT>White</TT>
</TD><TD>
<TT>Johnson</TT></TD><TD><TT>408 496-7223</TT>
</TD><TD><TT>10932 Bigge Rd.</TT></TD><TD><TT>Menlo Park</TT></TD>
<TD><TT>CA</TT></TD><TD><TT>94025</TT>
</TD><TD><TT>1</TT></TD></TR>
<TR><TD><TT>213-46-8915</TT></TD><TD><TT>Green</TT></TD>
<TD><TT>Marjorie</TT></TD><TD><TT>415 986-7020</TT></TD>
<TD><TT>309 63rd St. #411</TT></TD>
<TD><TT>Oakland</TT></TD><TD><TT>CA</TT></TD>
<TD><TT>94618</TT></TD><TD><TT>1</TT></TD>
</TR>
<TR><TD><TT>238-95-7766</TT></TD><TD><TT>Carson</TT></TD>
<TD><TT>Cheryl</TT></TD><TD><TT>415 548-7723</TT></TD>
<TD><TT>589 Darwin ln.</TT></TD>
<TD><TT>Berkeley</TT></TD><TD><TT>CA</TT></TD>
<TD><TT>94705</TT></TD><TD><TT>1</TT></TD></TR>
<TR><TD><TT>267-41-2394</TT></TD><TD><TT>O'Leary</TT></TD>
<TD><TT>Michael</TT></TD><TD><TT>408 286-2428</TT></TD>
<TD><TT>22 Cleveland Av. #14</TT></TD>
<TD><TT>San Jose</TT></TD><TD><TT>CA</TT></TD>
<TD><TT>95128</TT></TD><TD><TT>1</TT></TD>
</TR>
<TR><TD><TT>274-80-9391</TT></TD><TD><TT>Straight</TT></TD>
<TD><TT>Dean</TT></TD><TD><TT>415 834-2919</TT></TD>
<TD><TT>5420 College Av.</TT></TD><TD><TT>Oakland</TT></TD>
<TD><TT>CA</TT></TD><TD><TT>94609</TT></TD>
<TD><TT>1</TT></TD>
</TR>
...


...
<TR><TD><TT>899-46-2035</TT></TD><TD><TT>Ringer</TT></TD>
<TD><TT>Anne</TT></TD><TD><TT>801 826-0752</TT></TD>
<TD><TT>67 Seventh Av.</TT></TD><TD><TT>Salt Lake City</TT></TD>
<TD><TT>UT</TT></TD><TD><TT>84152</TT></TD>
<TD><TT>1</TT></TD>
</TR>
<TR><TD><TT>998-72-3567</TT></TD><TD><TT>Ringer</TT></TD>
<TD><TT>Albert</TT></TD><TD><TT>801 826-0752</TT></TD>
<TD><TT>67 Seventh Av.</TT></TD><TD><TT>Salt Lake City</TT></TD>
<TD><TT>UT</TT></TD><TD><TT>84152</TT></TD><TD><TT>1</TT></TD>
</TR>
</TABLE>
<HR>
</BODY>
</HTML>
```

When you view the page, all your SQL table data will be placed into an HTML table. If you specify links to be added, they will be shown at the top of the page prior to the data from the site.

A great use of the Web Page Creation Wizard is to query the IIS logs that can be placed into SQL Server. For more information, see the following section to find out how this can be used to remotely monitor your site.

Logging IIS Accesses to ODBC Databases

Perhaps one of the biggest improvements you can make to your system administration abilities is to log your IIS access activity to an ODBC database. This is because you can start amassing excellent information about your site, including what information people are retrieving, how frequently they're visiting your site, and more.

As mentioned earlier in this chapter, in order to allow IIS to access your database, you'll need to set up a System DSN. After you've completed this, you can create the database, table, and user that you'll need to establish the Internet Service Manager for the Web, FTP, and Gopher services you're using.

▶ For more information about setting up the System DSN, **see** "Building ODBC Database Sources for Microsoft Access Databases," **p. 584**, and "Building ODBC Data Sources for SQL Server Databases," **p. 582**, earlier in this chapter

To set up logging to use your ODBC database, first double-click the service from the Internet Service Manager that you want to use. In the example shown in Figure 23.25, you can see the logging options for the Web Services. Note that all the different services use the same logging tab, so when you've set one up, you'll understand how to establish the remaining services.

Before you can point the services to the ODBC database, you'll need to create the database and corresponding table. Table 23.3 shows the column information for the table that will be used for the logging.

Table 23.3   Table Structure for Logging Table

Column	SQL Datatype*	Access Datatype	Size
ClientHost	Char	Text	50
UserName	Char	Text	50
LogDate	Char	Text	12
LogTime	Char	Text	21
Service	Char	Text	20
Machine	Char	Text	20

continues

Table 23.3 Continued

Column	SQL Datatype*	Access Datatype	Size
ServerIP	Char	Text	50
ProcessingTime	int	Number	Integer
BytesRecvd	Int	Number	Integer
BytesSent	Int	Number	Integer
ServiceStatus	Int	Number	Integer
Win32Status	Int	Number	Integer
Operation	Int	Number	Integer
Target	Char	Text	200
Parameters	Char	Text	200

Note: NULLs are allowed for all columns in the case of SQL Server.

You might recognize this information from the discussions about installing and setting up the server components because the table structure maps directly to the different components of the standard log file when logged to ASCII files. You set up the log table to be used by all the different services you're logging for. You'll notice the Service column will show exactly what was being done by the user and what operation the server was performing. Listing 23.8 shows the SQL Server script for creating the table.

On the CD

Listing 23.8   makelog.sql—The SQL Server Script to Create the Logging Database

```
/****** Object:  Table dbo.LogTable
➥ Script Date: 4/28/96 10:04:11 PM ******/
if exists (select * from sysobjects
➥ where id = object_id('dbo.LogTable') and
➥ sysstat & 0xf = 3)
    drop table dbo.LogTable
GO

CREATE TABLE LogTable (
    ClientHost char (50) NULL ,
    UserName char (50) NULL ,
    LogDate char (12) NULL ,
    LogTime char (21) NULL ,
    Service char (20) NULL ,
    Machine char (20) NULL ,
    ServerIP char (50) NULL ,
    ProcessingTime int NULL ,
    BytesRecvd int NULL ,
    BytesSent int NULL ,
    ServiceStatus int NULL ,
```

```
        Win32Status int NULL ,
        Operation char (200) NULL ,
        Target char (200) NULL ,
        Parameters char (200) NULL
    )
    GO
```

Now that the table exists for logging information, you can indicate where to log information for each of the services. From the Internet Service Manager, double-click the service you want to update. Select the Logging tab to work with the different logging options. See Figure 23.25.

FIGURE 23.25

The next step to begin using ODBC for logging is to select the ODBC option and indicate the login and database information.

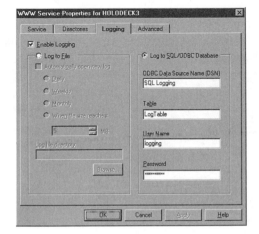

After you've selected the Log to SQL/ODBC Database radio button, you'll be able to access the different setup fields for the logging. It's a good idea to set up a different database to manage the logging. If you do, you'll be able to more easily manage the logging information separately from the other information on your system.

In the example, a specific database, table, and user have been created to use for the logging. If you create a user, be sure you set the rights to at least Insert when you establish them on the table. After you apply the changes, stop and restart the service—you'll be logging all server accesses to the database.

N O T E If a user is accessing your server by using the FILE: protocol, the accesses will not be logged. These types of URLs are accessed by the client and handled by the client. Although the server will be providing the file to fulfill the request, it will not show up in the database. This is one detriment to using the FILE: type URL. If you want to be able to log accesses, consider making all links standard HTTP: type URLs, rather than providing direct links to the files. ■

When the logging is established, you can begin querying the database real-time to determine the activity on your server. In the next sections, you'll see some ways to provide this information in an easy-to-use and meaningful manner.

Sample Queries to Use in Reviewing Logs

The log data can quickly become overwhelming unless you can wrap it in some meaningful queries. Some good information to know about your site includes the following, just as a start:

- What pages are most popular?
- What time of day are people accessing the server?
- Who is accessing the server (by IP address)?

In the sample query in Listing 23.9, you can see that the database is examined to find out exactly this information, providing summary information for hits against the server.

N O T E For the following scripts, you'll need to change the database table they reference to correctly identify your system configuration. Replace wwwlog and ftplog with the logging database you use for your system logging. ■

On the CD

Listing 23.9   www.sql—A Sample Script to Use for Server Reporting—Web Access

```
SELECT "Total hits" = count(*),"Last Access" = max(logtime)
FROM wwwlog
SELECT ""

SELECT "Hit summary" = count(*), "Date" = substring(logtime,1,8)
FROM wwwlog
GROUP BY substring(logtime,1,8)

SELECT ""

SELECT "Time of day"=substring(logtime,10,2),
➥ "Hits" = count(substring(logtime,10,2))
FROM wwwlog
group by substring(logtime,10,2)

SELECT ""

SELECT "Page" = substring(target,1,40), "Hits" =
➥ count(target)
FROM wwwlog
WHERE
    (
     charINDEX("HTM",target)>0
    )
GROUP BY target
ORDER BY "hits" desc
```

In Listing 23.10, a similar script provides good feedback on FTP accesses, showing what files users are accessing on your system. Again, it's important to understand what types of things people are finding most, and least, helpful on your site.

On the CD

Listing 23.10   ftp.sql—A Sample Script to Use for Server Reporting—FTP Access

```
select "Summary of volume by day"

select substring(logtime,1,8), sum(bytessent), sum(bytesrecvd)
from ftplog
where  bytessent > 1000
group by substring(logtime,1,8)

select ""

SELECT "Time of day"=substring(logtime,10,2), "Hits" =
➥ count(substring(logtime,10,2))
FROM ftplog
group by substring(logtime,10,2)

select ""

select "Target" = substring(target,1,40),
       sum(bytessent),
       sum(bytesrecvd),
       count(substring(target,1,40))
from ftplog
where bytessent> 1000
group by Target
order by sum(bytessent) desc
```

Keep an eye on your site and always look for things that can be removed or demoted to a less prominent presence on your site, while at the same time providing room for more new content that people are looking for on your site.

Reviewing System Logs Online

Of course, a great use of the IDC is to combine all these different activities (logging, the IDC, the Web Page Wizard and dynamic Web Page creation) to provide excellent feedback information online. Setting up the page is easy enough. You simply use the Web Page Wizard to query the database you've set up for logging. Calling it up is easy as well because it's established as a Web page.

Using this technique, you can create a Web page, similar to the one shown in Figure 23.26, that will let you review your site activity all while online.

From here, it's a matter of pruning your SELECT statement to deliver more selective information. One idea would be to change the listing to return the hits against the server by minute only, for example. Then, by using an IDC link you can offer the user the ability to drill down into a given time slice to gain more detail about an activity.

Another approach to this is to provide summary information by user with links to detailed log information for that user. The initial HTML page will show all users. The viewer can select the user to review, and click the name. The next HTML page shows the user's access times individually. By clicking a specific access time, the reviewing party can see the details about what was accessed by that user during that session.

FIGURE 23.26

Keeping the site activity only a hyperlink click away is a good way to put the database query capabilities to use at your site.

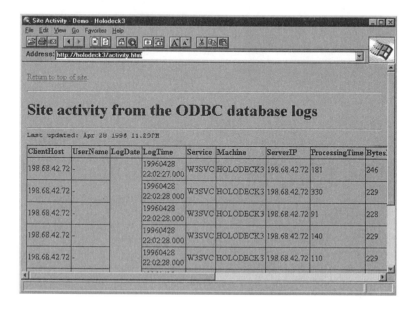

Integrating the IDC and drill-down informational research like this can really bring great leverage to you as an administrator. Remember, too, that you can place these pages into a protected subdirectory, making them available only to authorized users of your system.

Configuring IIS To Wait for SQL Server to Start

If you're using SQL Server for your logging, you might notice that, when you restart the server, the IIS service is unable to begin logging to SQL Server. You'll receive an error message if you select the World Wide Web service from the Internet Service Manager that indicates that the logging configuration is invalid.

This is because SQL Server requires more time to start than do the Internet services. Because the services start and immediately attempt access to the logging system, they are unable to get to the database because SQL Server is still starting. To avoid this, you'll need to make an entry in the system registry that tells IIS to wait for SQL Server when it starts the services.

From the Registry, select the following key:

```
HKEY_LOCAL_MACHINE\System\CurrentControlSet\Services\
➡  W3Svc\DependOnService
```

Add a new service as part of this key for each application that you need to have IIS wait on. With SQL Server, the service name is MSSQLSERVER. You'll also want to update the Gopher and FTP service keys. They reside in the same key location, but you'll need to substitute either

GOPHERSVC or MSFTPSVC for the preceding W3Svc. If the keys do not already exist, you will have to create them. The resulting keys are

```
HKEY_LOCAL_MACHINE\System\CurrentControlSet\Services\
➥  GOPHERSVC\DependOnService
```

```
HKEY_LOCAL_MACHINE\System\CurrentControlSet\Services\
➥ MSFTPSVC\DependOnService
```

For each of these, you can set the DependOnService value(s) to include the appropriate processes.

Note that if you have selected logging to SQL Server and do *not* do these steps, the logging will fail to start and you'll end up with no logging occurring for your site. It is very important to set up these keys as soon as possible after you begin using SQL Server to log your site accesses.

Additional Emerging Options

Internet development tools are evolving so quickly it's nearly impossible to keep up. This book references the Reality Check site in every chapter as a point of reference to additional resources on new technologies that were released or standardized after going to print. Be sure you check in at the Reality Check site frequently to see what's new. The URL for the site is www.swynk.com/realitycheck and it contains information on all sorts of technologies, including those briefly mentioned here.

Database access is one of the most hotly developed areas on the Internet. This is due to the obvious fact that, if you are to use your existing systems to their fullest potential, you'll almost certainly be referencing existing or new databases. This chapter has focused on the IDC and HTX combination as a good way of accessing this information. There are additional means of getting to this information, including your choice of scripting languages.

Microsoft has been pushing hard into the Active Server components and technologies. This approach moves the processing to the server for some or all the content customization, including database access, for your pages. This brings back the whole approach that has been emphasized so heavily with SQL Server—that of providing client/server applications as an efficient way to use both your server and client systems accessing.

Choosing the Right Approach

There is a lot of debate right now about the "right" approach to providing database access to users. The choices fall into two distinct areas: providing client-side access to server-based databases, and providing server-resolved access to server-based databases.

This might seem strange, but the issues really come down to how well defined and controlled your audience is. The choice is how the connection to the database will be handled. Because Microsoft is providing the software, and because they have a Web Browser, you can pretty much pick and choose between the approaches, if you can ascertain that all users of your systems will have Microsoft product.

If, on the other hand, you can't absolutely promise what browser will be used, you'll need to consider using a server-based approach. A big benefit of the IDC approach is that it's server-based and completely browser-independent. When it was first released, it was the *only* way of getting to databases, but now it's become what amounts to the lowest common denominator.

When you move to very recent browsers, like Internet Explorer 4.0 and upcoming promised versions of Netscape's product, you get some additional options, outlined next.

Active Server Pages and ADO

Most of the options that you have available are moving to using DAO-like statements in VBScript or other scripting languages. These statements are getting added functionality that lets them reference server-based objects that are handling the server-side connection to the database. For example, consider the code shown in Listing 23.11, taken from one of the sample files provided with IIS.

On the CD

Listing 23.11   ADO1.ASP—Sample VBScript for Database Access

```
<HTML>
<HEAD><TITLE>ADO Examples</TITLE><HEAD>
<BODY>
<H3>ADO Examples</H3>
<%
  Set Conn = Server.CreateObject("ADODB.Connection")
  Conn.Open "ADOSamples"
  Set RS = Conn.Execute("SELECT * FROM Orders")
%>
<P>
<TABLE BORDER=1>
<TR>
  <% For i = 0 to RS.Fields.Count - 1 %>
     <TD><B><%= RS(i).Name %></B></TD>
  <% Next %>
</TR>
<% Do While Not RS.EOF %>
  <TR>
  <% For i = 0 to RS.Fields.Count - 1 %>
    <TD VALIGN=TOP><%= RS(i) %></TD>
  <% Next %>
  </TR>
<%
  RS.MoveNext
  Loop
  RS.Close
  Conn.Close
%>
</TABLE>
</BODY>
</HTML>
```

The first thing you'll notice is the CreateObject method referenced as a server object. The ADODB object, based on the server, provides the information needed to connect to the server based on the connection information provided in the Conn.Open call. When the connection is opened, the server is ready to receive statements. You might recall from the chapters on developing with SQL Server that you initiate a recordset by setting up the SQL Statement that is used to define the recordset.

This is accomplished with the EXECUTE method, establishing the results to work on. You can then reference the results set exactly as you do with standard ADO calls in Visual Basic.

When you're working with the information in your database in this manner, it's a simple thing to populate the page and get the data formatted the way you need.

Part

V

Ch

23

From Here...

As you can see, the IDC is a very powerful extension to the IIS environment. Chances are good that, after your initial installation of IIS to provide access to static HTML content, you'll quickly find that database-driven information is even more popular with the users you are serving.

ADO furthers these capabilities, giving you object-, method- and property-level control over the information in your databases and tables.

This chapter touches on a number of different things. More information is provided about these topics in the following areas:

- See Chapter 22, "Backward Compatibility Options for Developers," for more information about building applications to work with SQL Server.
- Visit http://www.swynk.com for all the latest news in connecting your database to the Internet, ASP, ADO and other internet and BackOffice technologies.

CHAPTER 24

Creating and Using Cursors

Cursors are a way of manipulating data in a set on a row-by-row basis, instead of the typical SQL commands that operate on all the rows in the set at one time.

These cursors have an easy access method from front-end application development tools such as Visual Basic and PowerBuilder or other development platforms. Cursors provide a way of doing result-set processing inside the server without the need for a client program to manage the data sets being worked on. For example, before SQL Server 6.0, it was difficult to write a fast-performing application that had to perform multiple actions on a set of data. This was because each row in the data would need to be sent back to the front end and the client application would be responsible for initiating further activity on each row. Cursors provide a way for advanced Transact-SQL stored procedures to do all this processing without needing to return to the client.

> **CAUTION**
>
> Cursors can be terribly hard on your application in terms of performance. They are, by their very nature, much slower to execute and respond than are standard set-based operations. Make certain you've exhausted set-based operations before you look to cursors and make sure you're not only looking at the ease of use, but also the performance issues inherent in using them.

Distinguishing Between Front-End and Back-End Cursors

With SQL Server, two types of cursors are available for use in an application. These are front-end, or client, cursors and back-end, or server, cursors. They are two very distinct concepts, and it's important to be able to distinguish between them.

> **N O T E**   Microsoft refers to back-end cursors, or cursors that are created and managed by the database, as *server cursors*. To avoid any confusion from this point on, unless the text specifically refers to cursors on the client or server, it is to be assumed that any text referencing the term *cursor* is describing a cursor that's created in the database server. ■

When writing an application, you'll often find that you need to perform a given operation on a set of data. Using an UPDATE statement when it's necessary to change data values, or a DELETE statement when it's necessary to remove data values can normally perform this set-based operation. These set-based operations often provide great flexibility in an application, provided that the tasks that need to be performed can appropriately be defined by a WHERE clause.

Suppose you want to change the ZIP code for all those authors in the Pubs database who live in Menlo Park to be 94024. A simple UPDATE can be used, as Listing 24.1 shows.

Listing 24.1   24_01.SQL—Using Update to Change a ZIP Code

```
Update      AUTHORS
Set   ZIP = ''94024''
Where City = ''Menlo Park''
Go
```

On the other hand, what if you need to do different kinds of operations on a set of data? There are two possible solutions. You can perform multiple operations on exclusive sets, or you can get the whole set of data and, based on values in it, perform the required operations. This second solution is the concept of cursor-based processing.

Relying on the set-based updates and deletes can be inefficient. This is because your updates may end up hitting the same row more than once. It's possible to create a "view" of data in the database called a *cursor*.

One of the best advantages of cursor processing is that you can perform conditional logic on a particular row of data in a set independently of the other rows that might be in a set. Effectively, you're issuing commands or SQL on single-row data sets. This granularity of processing is often required in complex applications, and has many benefits.

- *Performance*. Set-based operations tend to use more server resources, compared with cursor operations.

- *Better transaction control*. When you're processing sets of data, you can control what happens to any given row independently of the others.

- *Special syntax*. WHERE CURRENT OF cursors enable positioned UPDATEs and DELETEs that apply to the row now being fetched and directly hit the table row without the need for an index.

▶ For more information on updates, **see** the section titled "The Process of Updating Rows," in Chapter 8, **p. 198**

- *Efficiency*. When you're performing a number of operations on a large data set, such as calling multiple stored procedures, it's more efficient for the database to process the data doing all actions per row rather than perform each task serially on the entire data set. This is because data is kept in memory caches.

Understanding Client Cursors

Before SQL Server 6.0, Microsoft realized that its customers needed to be able to process data and to scroll backward and forward through a result set. Customers needed this scrolling functionality to support complex applications that users needed for browsing data fetched from the database.

At the time, Microsoft couldn't incorporate the server-based cursors that some of the other vendors supported, and so chose to mimic some of their behavior in their client API to the SQL Server database, DBLibrary.

N O T E DBLibrary is a client interface that Microsoft inherited from Sybase to interact with the SQL Server database. DBLibrary is a set of commands and functions that can be executed in C to perform operations on the database. With SQL Server 6.0 and later releases, Microsoft changed its preferred interface to the database to be that of ODBC. For more discussions on interfacing with the database from client applications and programming languages, see Chapter 21. ■

To achieve this functionality, Microsoft added cursors to the data sets on the client side, which are client cursors.

These cursors work by having DBLibrary interact with the database as normal, fetching data from the tabular data stream, TDS, as quickly as the client requests. The TDS is the method of communication that DBLibrary uses to fetch data from the database. Typically, DBLibrary will discard any data that has been fetched from the database and given to the client application, relying on the client to perform any additional work. With cursors activated, DBLibrary will cache these records itself until the client cancels the cursor view on the data.

This caching has a number of limitations:

■ SQL Server has no way of controlling or minimizing the locks held on the database, and so any locks held will be held for all data pages in the cursor, not just the affected data pages. This is because SQL Server is basically unaware that anything other than a select activity is occurring on the data.

■ Client-side resources can be consumed very quickly if there are large sets of data.

■ The caching is inefficient when processing large amounts of data because all the data is being sent across the network unnecessarily.

Microsoft's client cursors were just a stopgap measure until the real work of server cursors could be completed. Server cursors provide all the same benefits of client cursors without any of the overhead or limitations. Aside from backward-compatibility issues, there are few good reasons to use client cursors in a SQL Server 7.0 application.

Server cursors generally have five states when being used, as shown in Table 24.1.

Table 24.1   The States of Existence of SQL Server Cursors

State	Explanation
DECLARE	At this point, SQL Server validates that the query that's going to be used to populate the cursor is valid. SQL Server creates a structure in shared memory that has the definition of the cursor available for compilation at the OPEN phase.
OPEN	SQL Server begins to answer the DECLARE statement by resolving the query and fetching row IDs into a temporary workspace for the use of the client, if it decides to fetch the rows that this cursor has identified.
FETCH	The data is now being returned from the cursor, and any activity that's required can be performed.

State	Explanation
CLOSE	SQL Server closes the previously opened cursor and releases any locks that it might have held as a result of opening it.
DEALLOCATE	SQL Server releases the shared memory used by the DECLARE statement, no longer permitting another process from performing an OPEN on it.

Using SQL Server Cursors

Using a cursor in SQL Server involves following the states previously described. This section explains the steps required to use a cursor effectively in your applications.

You first must declare the cursor. After a cursor has been declared, it can be opened and fetched from. During the *fetch phase* or *state* of a cursor any number of operations can be performed on the currently active row in the cursor. When you have finished working with a cursor, you need to close and deallocate it so that SQL Server does not waste resources managing it any further.

> **CAUTION**
>
> Cursors are the second most resource-intensive operation you can perform in SQL Server. They can consume large amounts of resources very quickly and also maintain a large number of locks. Make sure that you always close and deallocate cursors when you are finished with them.

Declaring a Cursor

Declaring a cursor is very similar to requesting data using a standard SELECT statement. Note that the SELECT statement used to declare a cursor can't include any of the Transact-SQL extensions such as COMPUTE, COMPUTE BY, or SELECT INTO.

The syntax for declaring a cursor is as follows:

```
DECLARE name_of_cursor [INSENSITIVE] [SCROLL] CURSOR
FOR Select_Statement
[FOR {READ ONLY ¦ UPDATE [OF Column_List]}]
```

> **N O T E** Because cursors must fetch row values into variables inside the stored procedure or command batch, you can't use the asterisk (*) in your SELECT statement. You must use named columns in the data tables that correspond one to one with the variables used in the FETCH clause. ■

The options for the Transact-SQL command DECLARE CURSOR are as follows:

- ■ name_of_cursor—The name of the cursor must comply with the standard object identifier rules of the database.

Part
V

Ch
24

■ INSENSITIVE—A cursor created with the INSENSITIVE keyword is completely unaffected by the actions of other users. SQL Server creates a separate temporary table of all the row data that matches the query and uses this to answer requests on the cursor. Insensitive cursors aren't modifiable using the WHERE CURRENT OF cursor syntax and, therefore, will impose index update hits when any updates are done.

CAUTION

Be careful when using the INSENSITIVE keyword in defining a cursor. Applications that use this keyword can run into problems of inaccurate data if the application has high transaction loads on the underlying table or tables that the cursor is being opened on. If the application being written is time-driven, however , INSENSITIVE cursors are a requirement. An example of this might be "Tell me what our balance sheet position is as of right now."

■ SCROLL—The SCROLL keyword, which is the opposite of the INSENSITIVE keyword, enables the cursor to read from committed updates and deletes made by other server processes. The SCROLL keyword is also required if the application needs to do anything other than fetch the data sequentially until the end of the result set.

■ READ ONLY—As its name implies, this option stops the cursor's data from being modifiable. Internally, this makes a big difference in how SQL Server chooses to retrieve the data and generally makes it more likely to hit a clustered index if one is available. Unless you need to modify data that the cursor is declared for, it's recommended that you use the READ ONLY clause. This will provide substantial performance gains.

■ UPDATE—This is the default option on a single table cursor like those created when you issue a select without any join conditions. A cursor declared in this fashion will enable the WHERE CURRENT OF syntax to be used.

Listing 24.2 shows a basic cursor that's being declared to fetch the data from a single table (Employee) in the Pubs database.

On the CD

Listing 24.2   24_02.SQL—Cursor Being Declared to Retrieve Information from Employee Table

```
Declare Cur_Empl Cursor
For   Select EMP_ID,    LNAME,
             JOB_ID,    PUB_ID
      From   EMPLOYEE
      Order By EMP_ID
Go
```

The Cur_Empl cursor, as shown in Listing 24.2, provides no greater application flexibility than a simple SELECT on the data. If, however, the application required absolute row positioning, as shown in Listing 24.3, it's possible to add the SCROLL keyword to the DECLARE statement that makes the cursor very different in comparison to a table SELECT.

On the CD

Listing 24.3   24_03.SQL—Scrollable Cursor Being Declared to Fetch from the Employee Table

```
Declare Cur_Empl_Scrollable SCROLL Cursor
For    Select EMP_ID,    LNAME,
               JOB_ID,    PUB_ID
       From  EMPLOYEE
       Order By EMP_ID
Go
```

Opening a Cursor

After a cursor is declared, SQL Server reserves handles for its use. To use a cursor and fetch data from it, you must open the cursor. To open a cursor, use the following syntax:

```
Open Cursor_Name
```

In the preceding examples, the code required to open the cursor would have been either

```
Open Cur_Empl
```

or

```
Open Cur_Empl_Scrollable
```

When a cursor is opened, SQL Server resolves any unknown variables with their current state. If a cursor was declared with a variable in the WHERE clause and then opened, the value used to resolve the query would be the value that the variable held at the time the cursor was opened. For example:

```
Declare     @nHighJobID integer,
            @nLowJobID  integer
Declare Cur_Empl_Where Cursor
For    Select      LNAME, FNAME
From   EMPLOYEE
Where JOB_ID Between @nLowJobID And @nHighJobID
/* note that if the cursor were to be opened now,
probably no data would be returned because the values
of @nLowJobID and @nHighJobID are NULL */
/* now we set the values of the variables */
Select      @nLowJobID = 3,
      @nHighJobID = 10
/* open the cursor now */
Open Cur_Empl_Where
...
```

N O T E You can determine how many rows were found by the cursor by evaluating @@Cursor_Rows. If the number of rows is negative, the cursor hasn't yet determined the total number of rows, as would be the case where it might still be serially fetching the rows to satisfy the cursor definition. If the number of rows is zero, there are no open cursors, or the last cursor that was open has been closed or deallocated. ■

Part
V

Ch
24

Fetching a Cursor

After a cursor is in an opened state, you can fetch data from it. Unless a cursor is declared with the SCROLL keyword, the only kind of fetching permissible is serially/sequentially through the result set.

The syntax for the FETCH statement is as follows:

```
FETCH [[NEXT ¦ PRIOR ¦ FIRST ¦ LAST ¦
       ABSOLUTE n/@nvar ¦ RELATIVE n/@nvar ]
FROM] cursor_name
[INTO @variable_name1, @variable_name2]
```

The options for the Transact-SQL command FETCH are as follows:

- NEXT—The NEXT keyword, implicit in normal fetching operations, implies that the next available row be returned.

- PRIOR—If the cursor was defined with SCROLL, this keyword will return the prior record. It's unusual for stored procedure-based applications to take advantage of this keyword unless they're responding to some kind of error condition by logically rolling back the previous row update.

- FIRST—This keyword fetches the first record of the result set found by opening the cursor.

- LAST—This keyword fetches the last record of the result set found by opening the cursor.

- ABSOLUTE n—This keyword will return the nth row in the result set. If you specify a positive number, the rows are counted from the top of the data set. If you provide a negative value for n, the number of rows will be counted from the bottom of the data set.

- RELATIVE n—This keyword will return the nth row in the result set relative to the current record that has most recently been fetched. If the number is negative, the row will be counted backward from the current row.

- FROM—This is an unnecessary keyword provided to make the code slightly more readable. It indicates that the next word will be the cursor that's being fetched from.

- INTO—The INTO keyword is provided for stored procedure use so that the data returned from the cursor can be held in temporary variables for evaluation or other use. The data types of the variables in the INTO clause must match exactly the datatypes of the returned columns of the cursor. If not, errors will be generated.

Closing a Cursor

Closing a cursor releases any resources or locks that SQL Server might have acquired while the cursor was open. To close a cursor, use the following syntax:

```
CLOSE cursor_name
```

A closed cursor is available for fetching only after it's reopened.

Deallocating a Cursor

Remember, cursors are keeping track of where you are in the database and are maintaining an active, open structure of pointers to the next and previous row information.

Deallocating a cursor completely removes any data structures that SQL Server was holding open for a given cursor. Unlike closing a cursor, after a cursor is deallocated, it no longer can be opened.

To deallocate a cursor, use the following syntax:

```
DEALLOCATE cursor_name
```

An Example of Using Cursors

In the previous sections, all the separate elements that are used to work with cursors in SQL Server were discussed. This section will show how all the elements are put together.

In Listing 24.4, you'll see an example of the use of cursors and see them in action. Refer to the comments in the script (placed between /* ... */) to get a good understanding of what the cursors are doing, but to summarize, the following steps are taken:

- Drop the procedure and recreate it if necessary. This makes sure the current procedure is the one that will be executed. Note also that, if you have SQL Enterprise Manager generate the code for a stored procedure, these statements to drop the existing stored procedure, if any, are generated automatically.

- Create a cursor to find the information you need to work with. This allocates the memory structures and sets up the cursor so you can retrieve information from it in later logic.

- Open the cursor and retrieve the first sets of information from it.

- In the loop, retrieve information from the cursor until the logic to determine books on order has been completed. Return the results to the calling application.

- End the procedure, cleaning up on the way out.

Here's a look at the code:

On the CD

> **Listing 24.4   24_04.SQL—Using Cursors to Process the Stores Table in the Pubs Database**

```
/* In this example we will be working with the stores table
of the pubs database.
To illustrate the cursors most easily, we will create a stored
procedure, that when executed:
- declares,
- opens,
- fetches, and
- processes
the data returned from a cursor. */
/* First we drop the procedure if it exists. */
```

continues

Listing 24.4   Continued

```
If exists( select object_id( 'proc_Stores' ) )
    Drop Procedure proc_Stores
Go
/* Step 0: Declare the procedure. */
Create Procedure proc_Stores
As
/* Step 1: Declare some working variables. */
Declare     @nOrderCount     integer,
    @nSQLError       integer,
    @nStorCount      tinyint,
    @sState          char(2),
    @sStorId     char(4),
    @sStorName       varchar(40),
    @sCity           varchar(20)
/* Step 2: Turn off result counting.
Turns off unnecessary "0 rows affected messages" showing on the front-end */
Set NoCount On
/* Step 3: Declare the cursor that is going to find all
the data.
This step causes SQL Server to create the required
resource structures needed to manage the cursor. */
Declare Cur_Stores Cursor
For     Select      STOR_ID,     STOR_NAME,
        CITY,            STATE
    From      STORES
    Order By      STOR_ID
/* Step 4: Open the cursor.
This step causes SQL Server to create the initial result set
and prepare the data for returning to the "Fetching process. */
Open    Cur_Stores
/* Step 5: Perform the first fetch.
Fetch data from the cursor into our variables for processing
and evaluation. */
Fetch     Cur_Stores
Into     @sStorId,       @sStorName,
    @sCity,         @sState
/* Step 6: Initialize counters. */
Select      @nStorCount = 0
/* Step 7: Fetch and Process Loop.
Process the data while the system variable @@Fetch_Status is = 0
(meaning that a row has been fetched from the cursor */
While @@Fetch_Status = 0
Begin
    /* Step 8: Increment counter */
    Select      @nStorCount = @nStorCount + 1
    /* Step 9: Do a quick operation to determine books on order */
    Select      @nOrderCount = Sum(QTY)
    From     SALES
    WHERE     STOR_ID = @sStorID
    /* Step 10: Return a result set to the front-end so that it knows
    what is happening */
    Select      "Store ID" = @sStorId,
        "Store Name" = @sStorName,
        "# Books on order" = @nOrderCount
```

```
        /* Step 11: Continue Fetching.
        If no rows are found then @@Fetch_Status will be set to a value other
        than zero, and the looping will end. */

        Fetch     Cur_Stores
        Into      @sStorId,      @sStorName,
            @sCity,             @sState
End
/* Step 12: Cleanup - Deallocate and close the cursors.
Note that for a stored procedure this is really unnecessary because the cursor
will no longer exist once the procedure finishes execution.
However, it is good practice to leave the procedure cleaned up */
Close     Cur_Stores
Deallocate Cur_Stores
/* Step 13: Send a totalling result.
Send total count of employees to front-end */
Select "Total # of Stores" = @nStorCount
/* Step 14: Turn on counting again */
Set NoCount On
/* Step 15: End Procedure */
Return 0
Go
/* Now we execute it to see the results. */
Execute proc_Stores
Go
```

The resulting output from running this listing follows:

```
Store ID Store Name                                    # Books on order
-------- ------------------------------------------- ----------------
6380     Eric the Read Books                                        8
Store ID Store Name                                    # Books on order
-------- ------------------------------------------- ----------------
7066     Barnum's                                                 125
Store ID Store Name                                    # Books on order
-------- ------------------------------------------- ----------------
7067     News & Brews                                              90
Store ID Store Name                                    # Books on order
-------- ------------------------------------------- ----------------
7131     Doc-U-Mat: Quality Laundry and Books                     130
Store ID Store Name                                    # Books on order
-------- ------------------------------------------- ----------------
7896     Fricative Bookshop                                        60
Store ID Store Name                                    # Books on order
-------- ------------------------------------------- ----------------
8042     Bookbeat                                                  80
Total # of Stores
----------------
        6
```

Part
V

Ch
24

TIP Sorting variables in large procedures alphabetically will make it much easier to find them. In addition, you can sort the variables by datatype as well, so that it is even easier to find them. This will happen automatically if you prefix variables with a datatype indicator such as: s for strings, n for numbers, and dt for date/times.

Using Nested Cursors

You can have multiple layers of cursors in a stored procedure that you use to provide flexible result-set processing. An example of this might be when you're opening a cursor, as shown earlier in the Cur_Empl example. In addition to the cursor you've already reviewed, you can add nested cursors to impose some additional conditional logic and perhaps open a second cursor to perform additional work with the data set.

Listing 24.5 shows some possibilities with nested cursors and provides an example of retrieving the employee record and then using that information to retrieve detail records for the employee.

On the CD

Listing 24.5 24_05.SQL—Using Cursors in a Nested Fashion

```
Create Procedure Maintain_Employees
As
/* First declare variables that are going to
be required in this procedure */
Declare      @dtPubDate   datetime,
             @nEmplCount  smallint,
             @nEmplID     empid,
             @nFirstHalf  smallint,
             @nRowCount   integer,
             @nSecondHalf integer,
             @nSQLError   integer,
             @nYtdSales   integer,
             @sLName      varchar(30),
             @sPubID      char(4),
             @sLastType   char(12),
             @sType       char(12)
/* Now Declare the cursors to be used
Note that because variables are used in the
where clause on the second cursor, it is not
required that the second cursor be Declared inside the first.
Take advantage of this functionality so that unnecessary
declaring of cursors does not take place (this will
save resources on the server. */
Declare Cur_Empl Cursor
For   Select EMP_ID,    LNAME,
             PUB_ID
      From   EMPLOYEE
      Order By EMP_ID
Declare Cur_Titles Cursor
For   Select  TYPE,   PUBDATE, YTD_SALES
      From    TITLES
      Where   PUB_ID = @sPubID
Order By TYPE
/* open the outer cursor and fetch the first row */
Open  Cur_Empl
Fetch Cur_Empl
Into  @nEmplID,    @sLName,
      @sPubID
```

```
/* Initialize counters */
Select      @nEmplCount = 0
While @@Fetch_Status = 0            /* only fetch while there are rows left */
Begin
      /* increment counter */
      Select @nEmplCount = @nEmplCount + 1
      /* Return a result set to the front-end so that it knows
      what is happening */
      Select      @nEmplID,   @sLName
      If @sLName < 'D'   /* Skip all the D's by using a GOTO */
            Goto Fetch_Next_Empl
      /* Now open inner cursor and count the different types
      of books for this employee's publisher */
      Open Titles
      Fetch Titles
      Into  @sType, @dtPubDate, @nYtdSales
      /* Reset totals */
      Select @nFirstHalf = 0,
            @nSecondHalf = 0,
            @sLastType = NULL
      While @@Fetch_Status = 0
      Begin
            If @sType != @sLastType AND @sLastType != NULL
            Begin
                  /* send back a total record to the front-end */
                  Select @sLastType, @nFirstHalf, @nSecondHalf
                  /* reset totals */
                  Select @nFirstHalf = 0,
                        @nSecondHalf = 0
            End
            If @dtPubDate <= '6/30/95'
                  Select @nFirstHalf = @nFirstHalf + @nYtdSales,
                        @sLastType = @sType
            Else
                  Select @nSecondHalf = @nSecondHalf + @nYtdSales,
                        @sLastType = @sType
            Fetch Titles
            Into  @sType, @dtPubDate, @nYtdSales
      End
      Fetch_Next_Empl:        /* label to skip inner loop */
      Fetch Cur_Empl
      Into  @nEmplID,   @sLName,
            @sPubID
End
/* Deallocate and close the cursors. Note that for a stored
procedure this is really unnecessary because the cursor
will no longer exist once the procedure finishes execution.
However, it is good practice to leave the procedure cleaned up */
Close Cur_Empl
Deallocate Cur_Empl
Deallocate Cur_Titles
/* Send total count of employees to front-end */
Select @nEmplCount
/* End proc */
Return 0
```

Part
V

Ch
24

T I P SQL Server treats object names case-insensitively, regardless of the sort order defined for the server. You can take advantage of this and make your code easy to read by using upper- and lowercase emphasis when possible.

However complex this example might seem, it is important to remember that using cursors is really not that difficult provided that you follow the basic steps outlined in the previous examples and throughout this chapter.

Processing Cursors from Front-End Applications

A key consideration of using cursors in an application is how they're accessible from front-end programming tools such as Visual Basic or PowerBuilder.

If the cursor returns a single set of data, which is the most common type, most front-end application languages won't be able to distinguish the data from that returned by a normal select statement. Typically, the tool will have a function for executing SELECT statements. This function is designed to work with a single set of data and, therefore, probably will work fine with stored procedures or cursors that return a single result set.

The execution of the stored procedure is followed by looping that forces the return of results to the front-end and then the fetching of the data in each result.

Most programming languages have similar functionality available and whatever programming language in which you choose to do your development should be able to support anything that SQL Server can return.

Reality Check

Cursors are, at first glance, a great feature for your applications. Indeed, cursors offer good functionality for your application should you need to provide database browsing abilities without the desire to develop this type of functionality on the client side of your application.

In real-life use, I've found that cursors bring quick payback on the development cycle, but to the detriment of the performance of the application. Though it will depend on your implementation, including the hardware on which the server is running, cursors can have a significantly negative impact on the overall throughput of your application. In almost every case, seek to use other methods than cursors whenever possible.

From Here...

In this chapter you learned about SQL Server's server-based cursors and how they can be used to provide much more processing power to your applications without the need to return to the client for help.

From here, you can use the following chapters to implement what you've learned:

- Chapter 14, "Managing Stored Procedures and Using Flow-Control Statements," explains how to start embedding cursor processing in your stored procedures.

Using the SQL Server Agent

Understanding the SQL Server Agent

In version 6.5 of SQL Server, the SQL Executive managed all the tasks on a server. The SQL Executive provided adequate support for most applications. However, it suffered from the necessity of defining multiple tasks and having no way to gracefully make them interact.

SQL Server 7.0 has made great strides in this area. The SQL Server Agent has replaced the SQL Executive with much greater functionality. Tasks have been replaced by jobs, which give a much better description of their functionality. A single job can consist of multiple steps. With this capability, SQL Server has finally included an industrial strength job-scheduling engine that allows an entire batch process to be self-contained.

Version 7.0 still includes the capability to be integrated with the Windows NT Performance Monitor. Via mechanisms called *alerts*, the SQL Server Agent provides the capability to automatically react to events that occur within SQL Server.

Not only does the SQL Server Agent give you the capability of defining multistep jobs, it also enables you to manage these from a central location. A single SQL Server can be set up as the source for all processing in the environment.

Configuring the SQL Server Agent

Start Enterprise Manager, select the server you want to configure the SQL Server Agent, expand the tree view, and highlight the SQL Server Agent as shown in Figure 25.1.

FIGURE 25.1

Using the SQL Server Agent to automate your environment.

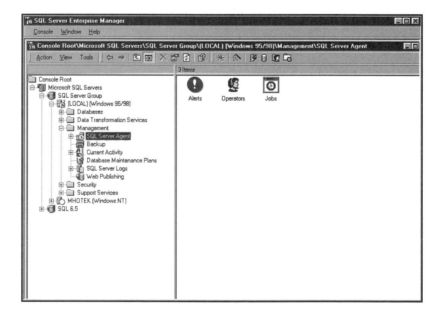

Select Action, Properties to display the dialog shown in Figure 25.2.

FIGURE 25.2

You can specify numerous items for the SQL Server Agent such as a mail profile, idle processor definition, connection information, and job history retention.

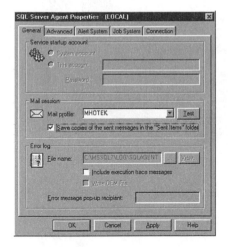

The General tab of the dialog box in Figure 25.2 allows you to specify global options for the SQL Server Agent. The first section defines the account the SQL Server Agent service will run under. The middle section allows you to specify a mail profile to be used for sending email messages. In order for the email system to work, SQL Mail must be configured on the machine.

▶ **See** Appendix A, "Mail-Enabling Your SQL Server," **p. 701**, for more information about how to set up your system for SQL Mail.

The bottom section is for defining what error log the SQL Server Agent will use. You can specify the file name and location of the error log. The check box to include execution trace messages configures the SQL Server Agent to write additional diagnostic information to the error log for use in troubleshooting. The check box to write an OEM file enables the SQL Server Agent to write to the error log in non-Unicode format, which will save space. The final edit box allows you to send a network message to a workstation when the SQL Server Agent encounters errors.

When you are finished filling in the General tab, select the Advanced tab to display the page as shown in Figure 25.3.

The first section allows you to specify if you want SQL Server and the SQL Server Agent to automatically restart if they stop unexpectedly. It is recommended that you select both of these check boxes.

The full depth of alerts will be discussed later in this chapter in the section titled "SQL Server Alerts." The important thing about this configuration option is that you can specify what server to forward all or particular events to. If you configure a central server to handle events forwarded from other servers in your environment, make sure that server does not participate in normal activities. The event forwarding and handling can consume many resources on a server. Choosing a very active server as a forwarding server can quickly bog down that server's normal processing.

Part
V

Ch

25

FIGURE 25.3

You can configure automatic restarts, forwarding of alerts, and idle conditions.

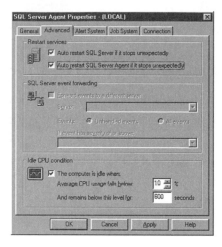

You have the ability to execute jobs during idle times on the processor. The last section is where you define what constitutes an idle processor in your environment. This will prevent jobs from consuming valuable processor time at the first instant the processor is under-utilized.

After configuring the options you want here, select the Alert System tab to display the tab page as shown in Figure 25.4.

FIGURE 25.4

When sending pager notifications, you can specify standard information.

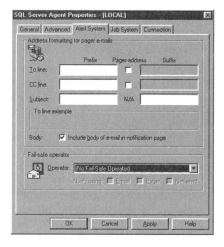

The top section of this dialog box allows you to specify message properties for email notifications as well as the inclusion of the error message text in the pager message. The bottom section of this page is for defining a fail-safe operator. For information on creating an operator see the section titled "Creating an Operator" later in this chapter. It is highly recommended that you specify a fail-safe operator. If for some reason the operators defined for an alert can not be reached, the message will be routed to the fail-safe operator.

When you have finished entering all the properties for the alert system, select the Job System tab page as shown in Figure 25.5.

FIGURE 25.5

Defining default parameters for all jobs on a server and job step security options.

Every job that is executed by the SQL Server Agent places an entry in a history log. The top section specifies limits on this log size and the maximum number of entries per job. The middle section specifies a wait interval for jobs to finish executing before shutting down the SQL Server Agent. The bottom section allows you to place limitations on jobs that use Active Scripting or CmdExec. Each of these types of jobs run at the operating system level and have full access to all resources available to the NT account the SQL Server Agent is running under.

> **CAUTION**
>
> Any user can create a job on your SQL Server and have it executed. This can pose a significant security threat to a system if not properly protected. Keep in mind that SQL Server and the SQL Server Agent must run under an account with administrator privileges. This can allow a person access to all the resources on your server with the authority of an administrator. It is highly recommended that you select the check box to allow CmdExec and Active Scripting jobs steps to be executed by only those users with system administrator permissions.

After restricting the execution of Active Scripting and CmdExec job steps, select the Connection tab as shown in Figure 25.6.

When you have specified all the properties for the SQL Server Agent, click the OK button.

Operators

The first step toward deriving the full benefit of the SQL Server Agent is to define an operator or set of operators to be notified. This allows the SQL Server Agent to send messages to an operator.

FIGURE 25.6
In the Connection tab, you can specify the type of authentication used for logins by the SQL Server Agent.

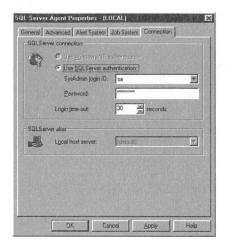

Creating an Operator

To define an operator, select Action, New, Operator to set the new operator properties as shown in Figure 25.7

FIGURE 25.7
From this dialog, you can set up multiple notification methods and the time frames the operator is on duty.

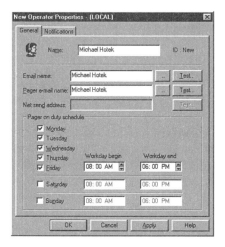

From the first tab in this dialog, you can specify numerous options. If you have set up SQL Mail as shown in Appendix A, "Mail-Enabling Your SQL Server," you will be able to configure the email name. This is a valid mailbox name to send messages. If your email system is configured with a pager add-on or you have a separate piece of software to enable paging, you will be able to configure the pager email name.

N O T E Most messaging systems like Microsoft Exchange have add-ons that enable you to communicate with a pager simply by sending a message to a designated inbox. ■

The Net Send address is the name of the computer to send a network message to. This will cause a dialog box to pop up on destination computer with the message you sent.

The bottom half of the tab allows you to specify the on duty hours for an operator. If you have enabled paging, you will want to designate what hours a particular operator will be on duty. This will prevent pages from being sent to that operator during off duty hours.

When you have finished designating the properties for the operator, select the Notifications tab as shown in Figure 25.8.

FIGURE 25.8

Alerts to notify an operator about.

In the bottom portion of this tab page, you will see information concerning the last time the operator was emailed, paged, or notified over the network. The top portion of this tab page is where you would define the alerts a particular operator will be notified for. I will discuss alerts later in the chapter in the section titled "SQL Server Alerts."

Click OK to add this operator to the SQL Server. If you now expand the SQL Server Agent item and highlight the Operators item, you will see the newly added operator, as shown in Figure 25.9.

SQL Server Jobs

The most basic capability of the SQL Server Agent is to perform periodic processing. Most SQL Server installations require the import of data from external systems or export their data to external systems. This processing is best enabled using the job scheduling capabilities of SQL Server.

Creating a Job

A job consists of one or more steps. Each of these steps, along with the schedule, is configured through the New Job Properties dialog. For the purpose of this exercise, I will take a typical

Part

V

Ch

25

import scenario. The first step of the process is run by a stored procedure that BCPs data into a set of staging tables and verifies that all the data got imported. The second step performs some manipulation and aggregation on the data using a second stored procedure. The final step is to load the data into the production tables and then truncate the staging tables. I will assume that all the stored procedures have already been created. If at any point a particular step fails, you want to branch to a cleanup process to reset the staging area. Because this process is critical to your environment, if there is a failure at any point other than loading the production tables, the job will branch to the corresponding cleanup process, which will then restart the job from the beginning.

FIGURE 25.9

Operators defined for a server.

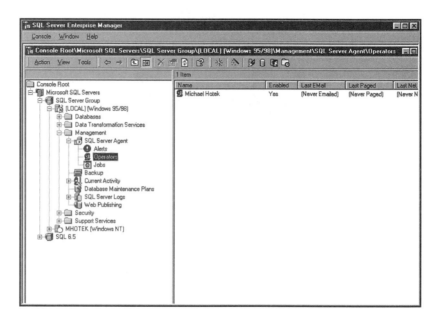

N O T E   This type of job flow would not have been possible in previous versions of SQL Server, except by using third party tools. ▪

Expand the tree under the server you want to create a job for, and highlight the SQL Server Agent.

Each job that is defined within the SQL Server Agent can belong to a category. This gives a simple way of grouping similar jobs together. The SQL Server Agent comes preconfigured with a set of categories. Select Action, All Tasks, Manage Job Categories to display the dialog as shown in Figure 25.10.

Unfortunately, many of the jobs you will create do not fall into these neat categories. To add job categories of your own, Click the Add button to display the New Job Category, dialog as shown in Figure 25.11.

FIGURE 25.10

SQL Server comes with a set of predefined job categories.

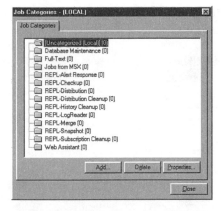

FIGURE 25.11

Adding a new job category for grouping like jobs together.

Enter a name for the new category and select OK. When you are done adding job categories, click the Close button.

When you have some categories defined, you are ready to create a job. Select Action, New Job to display the dialog as shown in Figure 25.12.

FIGURE 25.12

Defining a new job.

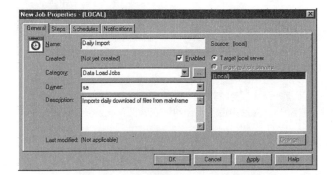

On the General tab, we will define the properties of the job. Every job must have a unique name. Be as descriptive as possible here to make it simple to tell all your jobs apart. Select a category that this job will fit into. An owner and description can be defined. The enabled check box determines whether this job will be run on the schedule defined. A disabled job will not run unless explicitly started by the owner. This gives you the ability to temporarily halt the scheduled processing without losing the job definition. The target server for this section will be local. You can also define multiple servers as a target for this job. This will be covered in detail in the section, "Establishing a Central Server for Jobs and Alerts" later in this chapter.

After defining the job properties, select the Steps tab as shown in Figure 25.13.

FIGURE 25.13

For a job to be useful, you must add one or more steps to be performed.

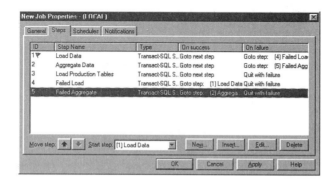

The New Job Step and Edit Job Step dialog are the same for defining a job step. To create the first step in the process, click the new button (on Figure 25.13) to display the dialog as shown in Figure 25.14.

FIGURE 25.14

Multiple job steps with success and failure dependencies can be defined. You can also define steps using multiple languages.

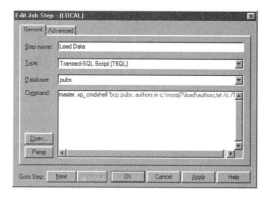

The first thing to fill in is the name, up to a maximum of 128 characters. This will help you identify steps within your jobs. The Type drop-down gives you the ability to specify what type of command will be run. For this exercise, we will be using TSQL type commands. This gives you the ability to select a database for them to run in and also the TSQL command to run.

A new addition to version 7.0 is the availability of an active script type. This allows you to create job steps using VBScript, JavaScript, or another language.

NOTE The use of an alternate language to create jobs in has not been defined as of the Beta 3 edition. This should give users the ability to write job commands using any scripting language recognized by SQL Server (such as Perl). ■

You can define a step using an operating system command such as a batch file, or various replication processes. The Open button on Figure 25.14 allows you to open a file that includes a command text (TSQL, Script, and so on). Clicking the Parse button results in syntax checking for your command text.

After filling in a name, selecting the TSQL type, selecting the pubs database, and entering a command, select the Advanced tab as shown in Figure 25.15.

FIGURE 25.15
On the Advanced tab, you can define output files, what account to run the step under, and success and failure job flow.

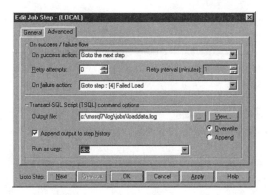

Part
V

Ch
25

The first section of the dialog gives you the ability to redirect output to a file. You designate whether any output should be appended to an existing file or if the file should be overwritten each time. Each job step maintains a history of its successful completion or failure. If you select Append Output to Step History, any results from the job step will be appended to the history. The Run as User drop-down gives you the ability to run the job step under the context of any user defined on the server. You have the ability to control the job flow in the final section. On a success or failure, you can quit the job or branch to another step defined for the job. For some jobs you might want to set a retry interval and a number of retries. This is the method we will set up for the first step in the process. The files to load into SQL Server might have been delayed from the external system due to multiple factors. Setting a retry interval gives us the ability to pick up these files as soon as they arrive. When you are finished defining the properties, click OK to have the job step added to the job.

 Because the selection for branching to another job step is only available for steps that have been defined, you should define all job steps first before going back and setting the job flow.

You should establish a directory where output from all jobs will reside and then set the output file options for every job step. This will be extremely useful when trying to debug job failures.

When the job steps have been defined, the next step is to create the schedule for the job. Select the Schedules tab as shown in Figure 25.16 from the New Job Properties dialog.

FIGURE 25.16

One other new addition to the SQL Server Agent is that you can define multiple schedules for the same job.

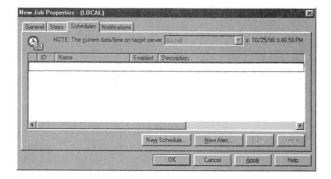

If you haven't been able to tell yet, the SQL Server Agent is greatly enhanced from the previous incarnation as the SQL Executive. Every facet of the SQL Server Agent has been greatly enhanced. The first thing you'll notice in this dialog is the capability to define multiple schedules for the same job. This greatly simplifies scheduling and creating jobs because multiple jobs do not have to be created to meet varying schedules.

N O T E I once had an implementation in SQL Server 6.5 that required various schedules. One particular task was required to be run every business day, a second time at noon on Wednesday, and then again on Friday at 8 AM. The run every business day was required to start at midnight. What complicated this even more was the fact that this process had 12 separate steps that depended on the previous steps. The SQL Executive was incapable of meeting these needs, so I had to purchase a third party scheduling system at a cost of a few thousand dollars.

Had we been doing this in SQL Server 7.0, the SQL Server Agent could have easily met my needs. ▪

Clicking the New button gives you access to the dialog as shown in Figure 25.17.

FIGURE 25.17

Define the time or event constraints under which the job will execute.

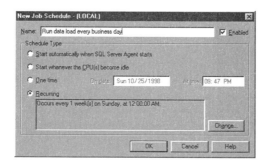

Because you can have multiple schedules for a single job, each one requires a name. Notice that there is also an enable check box. This operates at a schedule level the same way the enable box works for an entire job. You can disable a schedule without losing any of the configuration information. Two new scheduling options are now available: on start up and on idle.

On start up gives you the capability to run a job when the SQL Server Agent starts. This is usually an indication that SQL Server is restarting because both SQL Server and the SQL Server Agent are normally configured for automatic startup. This allows you to run any type of prep or cleanup jobs within your server whenever they restart.

On CPU idle gives you the capability to smooth out the processing on a SQL Server while continuing to meet your processing requirements. This is best used when you need to achieve a particular processing capacity on the machine and want to maximize response time while also running frequent jobs. This allows the jobs to kick off and run during idle times on your CPU so that they don't interfere with the normal processing being done by the users of the system. An excellent use of this option would be in a reporting application.

One time allows you to execute the job a single time at a specified date and time.

Recurring allows you to execute the job on a regular schedule. This is the scheduling option we want for your scenario. To define the periods it will recur on, click the Change button to display the dialog in Figure 25.18.

FIGURE 25.18

Define recurring schedules for the job.

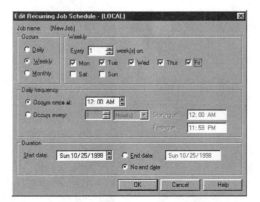

The schedule your scenario requires is every business day. Many people would be tempted to select the Daily option. This will execute the job every day of the week including weekends. Paradoxically, the weekly option is what we want. This allows you to specify the job to run on each day of the week and recur every week. This means that the job will recur on each Monday through Friday.

The next section allows you to specify the frequency of execution. We only need the job to execute once at midnight, so the option button for Occurs Once At: is selected and 12 AM is entered. You have the option to set up the schedule so that it recurs many times within each day. This can be set up to recur every so many hours or minutes, and also start at a particular time and end at a particular time.

The final section allows you to specify a duration. You can configure the job to begin on a particular date and end on a particular date, or to have no end date.

When you have defined your schedule, click the OK button and then click OK again to add the new schedule and return to the New Job Properties dialog.

The final step is to add any notifications. Select the Notifications tab as shown in Figure 25.19.

FIGURE 25.19

You can set up a variety of notification methods for a job.

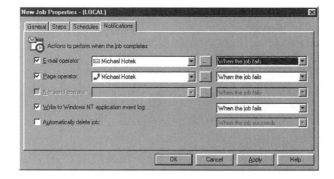

The notifications tab is dependent upon having operators defined, as was shown in the section titled "Creating an Operator" earlier in this chapter.

You can optionally email, page, or send a message across the network to a designated operator. In addition to those methods, an entry can be written into the NT event log. These notifications can be sent in three cases: every time, on success, and on failure. How critical the job is will determine which cases you will send a notification for. You also have the ability to delete the job when it completes. This is applicable for those jobs that happen only once.

This is not advisable to do simply because it is very likely that you might need to run that job again. It would be much better to simply disable the job when it has completed.

This checkbox (Delete) can be useful if you know that a job will not be performed again. This prevents the jobs from accumulating in your job list, which can make it more difficult to find the job you want quickly.

> **CAUTION**
>
> Most people will be tempted to define a notification every time a job completes. If you have a lot of jobs running on your server or in your environment, this can become very intrusive to the operator. If the operator is constantly being interrupted with notifications, it will be very difficult to complete the rest of their duties. In extreme cases, the operator will figure out a way to disable the notifications by turning off the pager, closing the email application, and so on. You will generally need to notify an operator only when a job has failed. Only in the case of mission-critical jobs should an operator be notified every time.

When you have set up the notification schedule you desire, click the OK button to create the job. If you have defined a circular reference as we have in this example, you will see the dialog in Figure 25.20 displayed. If this is what you require for the job, click the Yes button. If you have inadvertently defined circular processing, click No to go back and fix your job dependencies.

FIGURE 25.20

Verifying a circular reference.

If you now open the tree view for the SQL Server Agent and highlight the jobs item, you should see the job you have just defined as shown in Figure 25.21.

FIGURE 25.21

The jobs item will list all jobs defined on the server.

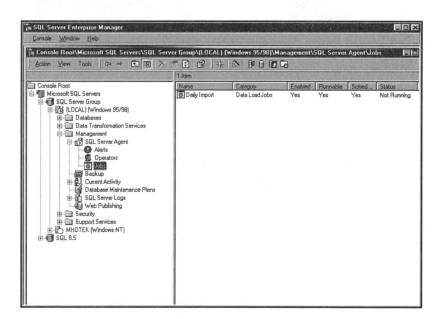

SQL Server Alerts

Alerts in SQL Server consist of several components. Most alerts you will define are based upon counters in Performance Monitor. Some additional alerts will be defined based upon internal SQL Server events that are normally based upon severity level or error message content.

▶ For a full discussion of Performance Monitor counters, **see** Chapter 21, "Optimizing Performance," **p. 539**

The SQL Server Agent has been defined with much tighter integration into the Windows NT Performance Monitor. This integration has greatly streamlined the process of creating alerts based upon Performance Monitor counters.

N O T E In previous versions of SQL Server, integrating the SQL Executive with the NT Performance Monitor was a rather convoluted process. First you would define an alert in Performance Monitor on a specific counter. When the alert was raised within Performance Monitor, a message was written into the Windows NT event log. Periodically, SQL Server checked the event log. If a match was found in the event log for an alert configured in SQL Server, the SQL Executive would raise the alert and execute any actions you had defined. ■

Defining an Alert

Alerts can be defined for two different types of events. The first way is based upon events trapped within the Windows NT Performance Monitor. The second way is based upon error messages within SQL Server.

N O T E Even though SQL Server can be run under Windows 95/98, neither of these platforms contains a Performance Monitor. As such the alerting capabilities are limited on these platforms. ■

Highlight the alerts item under SQL Server Agent and select Action, New Alert to display the dialog shown in Figure 25.22.

FIGURE 25.22

Defining a new SQL Server alert.

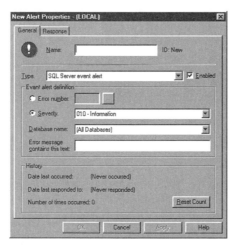

Within this tab, there are a few steps that will need to be performed. Specify a name for the alert that will help you identify it. The type drop down has two different values which lead to different configuration options.

Select SQL Server Event Alert if you want to detect internal events within SQL Server such as error severity levels or particular error messages. This will give you the option to specify either an error number or severity level. By selecting the error number button and clicking the ellipsis button, you will be presented with the dialog shown on Figure 25.23.

FIGURE 25.23
Browsing the severity level and messages of errors.

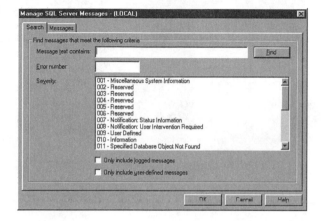

The Search tab allows you to search for error messages that match certain criteria such as severity level, error number, or message text. Selecting the 019 severity level and clicking the Find button will display the messages for that level, as shown in Figure 25.24.

FIGURE 25.24
You can search for specific error messages to match an alert level.

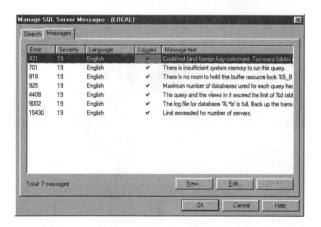

Most likely, you will want to define your own error message for the alerts that are defined. This is accomplished by clicking the New button to open the dialog shown in Figure 25.25.

When you have defined an error message, it can be used as the basis for an alert. When you are finished adding error messages, if any, click the OK button. Notice that the error number that was highlighted on the Messages tab is entered into the edit box for the Error number. Selecting the option button for a severity level allows you to specify an alert for any message of a particular severity level.

Part
V
Ch
25

FIGURE 25.25

Creating a new error message.

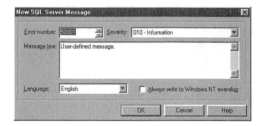

> **CAUTION**
>
> Be careful when defining an alert based upon a severity level because some severity levels can have hundreds of error messages associated with them.
>
> Some error messages accept parameters. Any error message defined for an alert is not allowed to take parameters.

The drop-down for database name allows you to restrict the alert to errors in a particular database. The final edit box allows you to restrict the errors based upon message content.

Selecting the SQL Server performance condition alert type will change the dialog as shown in Figure 25.26.

FIGURE 25.26

Defining an alert based upon a Performance Monitor counter.

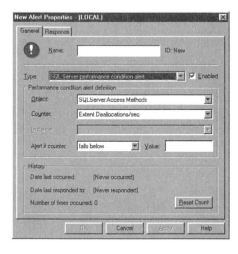

This type corresponds to the Windows NT Performance Monitor counters for SQL Server.

In this section, we will define an alert to detect any deadlocks. As has been noted in previous chapters, a deadlock is a very severe condition and should be detected and fixed in any installation. In the Object drop-down select SQLServer: Locks. In the Counter drop-down, select Number of Deadlocks. In the Instance drop-down, select Database. In the Alert if Counter drop-down, select Becomes Equal To and enter 1 in the Value edit box as shown in Figure 25.27.

FIGURE 25.27

Defining an alert to be raised every time a deadlock occurs.

Any time an alert is raised, you will want to be notified by some mechanism. This is accomplished from the response tab page as shown in Figure 25.28.

FIGURE 25.28

Specifying a notification and optional action for an alert.

The first item you will notice is a check box to run a job. In some cases, you will want to automatically execute a job whenever an alert is raised.

N O T E One of the most common alerts to define is the Percent Log Used counter. When this passes a certain threshold, a job is executed that dumps the transaction log. ■

The next check box allows you to raise an SNMP trap when an error occurs. SNMP traps are used by various network monitoring agents to gather network information at a central location.

The list box in the middle of the dialog will display all the operators you have defined for your server as outlined in the section titled, "Creating an Operator." If you need to notify an operator that is not on this list, a new operator can be added through the New Operator button. Within the operators list, you can specify the mechanism they will be notified by. This will simply send a message to the operator. If you want the error message associated with the alert to be sent as well, you can specify that below the list of operators, as well as an additional message to be sent.

The final option is, perhaps, the most important one. When an alert is raised based upon a condition, that condition can persist for an extended period of time. Failure to set an appropriate delay between notifications can quickly generate a few hundred notifications for the same error. By setting this value, the error will be raised the first time the condition occurs and a notification sent. If the condition still persists after the delay that has been specified, another notification will be sent. For most conditions a delay of 1–5 minutes should be sufficient especially for those that execute jobs to correct the condition.

When completed, click the OK button.

N O T E   In previous versions of SQL Server, when setting up an alert on a Performance Monitor counter, both the SQL Executive and Performance Monitor had to be running on the SQL Server machine. This is no longer the case. An alert will fire based upon a Performance Monitor counter even if Performance Monitor is not running. ■

Establishing a Central Server for Jobs and Alerts

So far, we have seen how to create operators, jobs, and alerts on a single SQL Server. This approach will generally suffice for most implementations. However in environments with many SQL Servers, this can become very tedious. In addition to that, many tasks and alerts that you will configure should be run on multiple machines.

To streamline administration of multiple servers, the SQL Server Agent is capable of being configured as a master server. The master server will contain all jobs and alerts for your entire environment. Target servers will connect to the master server and process scheduled jobs. Alerts are forwarded from the target server to the master to be handled.

Setting Up a Master Server

There are a small number of prerequisites that are required to set up a master server and one or more target servers.

- The master server must be running Windows NT.
- Each target server must be running the MSSQLServer and SQLAgent services under a domain account that has login privileges to the master servers.

N O T E The books online are incorrect in telling you that the master server must be running Windows NT Server. A master server can also be set up on a machine running Windows NT Workstation. However, you cannot configure a master server running under Windows 95/98.

The domain accounts that SQL Server and the SQL Server Agent are running under for a target server should be a member of the domain admins groups. This allows the target server to login to the master as the sa using integrated security. This is a security risk, but it is the easiest way to configure the target servers. ■

CAUTION

Before configuring a master server, make sure you want this to be a master server permanently. At the time of this writing, designating a server as the master was a one way ticket. The books online state that you can simply reverse this process to remove the master designation. In the process of testing, the only way to remove the master designation was to reinstall SQL Server on the master and all target servers.

When you have set up all the prerequisites, designating the master is a simple matter of following a wizard. Start Enterprise Manager, highlight the SQL Server Agent on the server you want to designate as the master, and select Actions, Multi Server Administration, Make This a Master to launch the Make MSX Wizard as shown in Figure 25.29.

FIGURE 25.29
When you click the next button, you will be prompted to designate the account for notifications.

N O T E When setting up notifications for jobs and alerts on a single server, you could specify one or more operators to notify. In a master server scenario, all notifications go to a single operator. It is suggested that you set up a centralized email account that all members of your staff have access to and forward all messages to that mailbox. Any notifications for multiserver jobs will be sent to the operator you designate here. ■

Designate the email, pager, and Net Send addresses for notification and click the Next button. The next dialog will prompt you to register any target servers that are not already registered in Enterprise Manager as shown in Figure 25.30.

FIGURE 25.30

You can register multiple servers that will act as target servers for multiserver jobs.

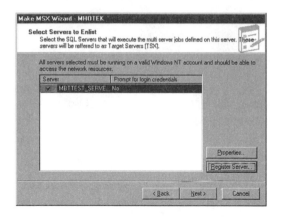

N O T E When you register any target servers, it is recommended that you select use Windows NT authentication. ▪

Clicking the Next button will enable you to enter a description for each target server. It is recommended that you do this in order to identify servers more easily. When you have finished entering the descriptions, click the Next button. This will take you to the final dialog as shown in Figure 25.31.

FIGURE 25.31

Designating the master server and creating the master operator.

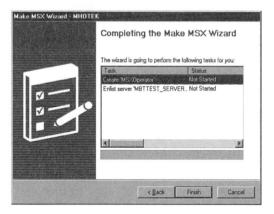

When you click the Finish button, an operator called MSXOperator will be created on the master server and all target servers. It will also enlist each of the target servers.

If everything succeeds, you will see the dialog as shown in Figure 25.32.

When you click the OK button, you will be taken back to Enterprise Manager. You will notice that the SQL Server Agent now has an MSX designation after it. This denotes a master server. The operators will also have a new entry name, MSXOperator. When you open the Jobs items, you will also now have entries for local jobs and multiserver jobs.

FIGURE 25.32

Successful creation of a
master server.

Creating a job is the same as it has been outlined. The difference at this point is that you now have the capability of designating a job for multiple servers within the job definition.

Target servers will now periodically connect to the master server and check for any jobs designated to be run. If any jobs are found, they will be downloaded to the target server and executed. When completed, a notification will be sent to the MSXOperator at the location specified for the operator.

Centralized administration has some advantages and disadvantages. The advantages are centralization, scalability, and efficiency. The disadvantages are increased network traffic, single point of failure, and heavy loading on the master server.

Reality Check

The SQL Server Agent is a relatively straightforward module. However, within this simplicity lies a very powerful interface for managing your environment.

The SQL Server Agent by itself can streamline all the periodic data loading that occurs in most production systems. This is just the tip of the iceberg. Integrating the SQL Server Agent with the performance monitor using alerts gives SQL Server the ability to notify an administrator when it is having problems. This allows the SQL Server to run in an almost hands-off mode.

Integrating SQL Mail with the SQL Server Agent gives a very powerful reporting mechanism to your SQL Server. This can be used to notify an administrator of problems, execute queries, and also administer a SQL Server in some rare cases.

The SQL Server Agent is frequently overlooked in most installations. By using the information in this book, you should be equipped to take full advantage of all the features in SQL Server to help streamline your environment.

N O T E   An excellent companion to this book is *SQL Server System Administration*, part of New Rider's Professional Series. This book contains a chapter on the SQL Server Agent that provides tips and case studies for utilizing the capabilities of the SQL Server Agent. ■

From Here...

The SQL Server Agent provides a very powerful interface for automated processing. The alerting mechanism provides an excellent mechanism for monitoring your SQL Server. Using jobs in conjunction with alerts gives you the capability of almost completely automating the administration of any SQL Server.

Part

V

Ch

25

- Chapter 19, "SQL Server Administration" details the periodic procedures that need to be run on a SQL Server. Because these are periodic, the SQL Server Agent is an excellent choice to automate those procedures.

- Chapter 21, "Optimizing Performance" details ways to keep your SQL Server running at optimal levels. It also outlines ways of monitoring the health of your server.

- Appendix A, "Mail-Enabling Your SQL Server" details the process for integrating email capabilities into SQL Server.

CHAPTER 26

Integrating Microsoft Office Applications and SQL Server

In this chapter

Microsoft Office 97 brought into being a comprehensive solution for developing applications based in the productivity tools that make up the suite. Office 97 now has Visual Basic throughout the suite, from Word to Excel to Access. In each of these environments, you have the ability to develop complete applications based on the language.

Throughout this book, you've seen how to set up and work with SQL Server, but in this chapter, the focus is on interacting with SQL Server rather than administering the server itself. Much of the access to SQL Server can be standardized into a discussion of the Data Access Objects, and there are special considerations when working from Access. By and large, the ability to work with data from a SQL Server can be a good addition to your applications. In addition, by using some client/server techniques to work with information, you can leverage the processing power of the SQL Server system in your applications.

This chapter focuses on two distinct areas. First, you'll see how to move your databases from Access to SQL Server and how to work with databases and tables that are based in SQL Server from within Access.

The second area of focus is that of developing an application in VB that can work with database tables. Each of these will be highlighted here.

Upsizing to SQL Server from Access

As of this writing, there is no Upsizing Wizard yet available for Access 97. You can check back with the Microsoft Access site, located on the Web at `http://www.microsoft.com/access/`, and generally download the utility when it becomes available. The Upsizing Wizard is currently available for Access 95, and for Access 2.

The upsizing tools help you migrate a database schema to SQL Server by moving your tables and relationships to SQL Server-based objects. The utilities will move your tables to the server by exporting them and creating the necessary indexes and other supporting objects. In addition, triggers can be created that will enforce any relational integrity rules you've implemented in Access.

What results is a system in Access that contains linked tables that reference the tables in SQL Server (see Figure 26.1 for an example).

FIGURE 26.1

When you link to tables in SQL Server, they are shown with the Link icon, but can be accessed with your standard BASIC instructions.

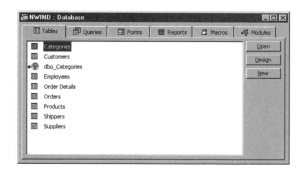

The Wizard will not create stored procedures to take the place of data manipulation you might be doing in your Access Basic code. In these cases, you'll want to work through the information in this book on stored procedures and compare it to the types of things you're doing in your BASIC code. Wherever possible, consider moving database manipulation statements and processes to stored procedures and out of your code.

In the next sections, you'll see how you can manually migrate your tables to SQL Server. You'll also see how to create the links you'll need to work with the tables as seamlessly as possible.

Using the Microsoft Access with SQL Server

Microsoft Access gives you an excellent development environment with many of the capabilities of SQL Server available for testing and implementation planning. Because Access is a smaller engine and not truly client/server, its use as a server system in a larger implementation is somewhat limited, but it still provides an unmatched development environment for database work.

 TIP This chapter is by no means a complete tutorial on the use of Microsoft Access. For detailed operation information, how-to assistance and the like, be sure to get a copy of any of several books from Que, such as *Special Edition, Using Microsoft Access 97*, Roger Jennings, ISBN 0-7897-1452-3.

This chapter is meant to provide a quick overview of what you'll need to do to work with database and table information that is shared between Access and SQL Server.

Access gives you a good user interface with which to develop the tables and relationships. There are some differences in how Access works with databases, including the physical storage aspect and slightly different terminology when discussing some items. Some examples are

- With Access, views are called queries. As with SQL Server, you can create updateable queries, select rows from a query, and create multi-table joins represented in a query.

- In SQL Server, individual columns represent specific data items within a row. Although data item groups are referenced as rows in Access, columns are referenced as fields.

- Datatypes do not use the same name, and are physically different in many cases between SQL Server and Access.

There are others, but these are the key differences that will likely help in your use of SQL Server with Access. If you have an application in Access, it's made up of up to six different elements. See Table 26.1 for a quick explanation of the different components and whether they are things you'll likely be upsizing or converting to SQL Server.

Part
V

Ch
26

Table 26.1	Basic Elements of an Access-Based System
Element	Description and Upsizeability
Tables	Same as SQL Server. This is probably the single most important item that you'll be upsizing. Tables represent the rows of information in Access that you want to convert to SQL Server.
Queries	Queries will likely need to be converted, but it will be a largely manual task to do so. This means you'll have to review the SQL behind the query and create the appropriate view on SQL Server. Remember too that you can LINK to a view on SQL Server and use it as you would a table, assuming you declare an index on the view.
Forms	Forms will not be converted to SQL Server. Remember, in the client/server model, the client system is responsible for the management of the user interface and the server has responsibility for the management and manipulation of the data.
Reports	As with forms, this item will not likely be converted. Of special note, however, is any report based on a query. In Access, you can code the query into the report. To get the best results, you'll want to review the property sheets for the report, convert the hard-coded query, and make it a view in SQL Server. In the query, reference the new view. Performance will be enhanced, the report will run the same as it did with the hard-coded query, but the result is a client/server implementation of the report.
Macros	Macros are strictly an Access item. Macros might be calling on queries, and they might be issuing some higher-level commands that are worth reviewing. As with reports, you don't want to have a macro that relies on a query you can place into SQL Server for better performance.
Modules	Modules are rarely an automatic decision to upsize. What this means is that you need to consider each and every procedure and subroutine to determine what's best upsized. With the modules, you have several options. You might be converting a subroutine to a stored procedure, a view, or a dynamic query. It will depend entirely on the processing you're doing in the database. Remember to do changes in short batches and continue testing. It's important to test changes thoroughly before moving on to the next conversion goal as you start working with the core functionality of your system.

Upsizing an application usually takes several different steps, outlined in the next sections.

Upsizing Access Applications—An Example

When you convert pieces of your application to use SQL Server, it can be helpful to do so in stages that let you test each step of the way. In these examples, you'll see how to convert portions of the Northwind Traders demonstration database. The sample database is provided with Access as a learning tool and can be installed when you set up Access on your system.

CAUTION

Moving your information to SQL Server should be done when no other users are on your system. If information is added to the Access tables during the process, it will not be reflected in the SQL Server tables. In addition, there is no easy way to re-synch the tables to gather any information that had been missed in the transition. Be sure you have exclusive use of the database if dynamic changes are typically made to the system.

Moving the Tables to SQL Server The first step is typically moving your tables and their associated data to the SQL Server system. This is done pretty simply in Access, by using the Export functionality built in to the system. To start, open the Northwind application and select the Tables tab (see Figure 26.2).

FIGURE 26.2

The Northwind system lets you work with a largely functional ordering system and includes several tables to work with.

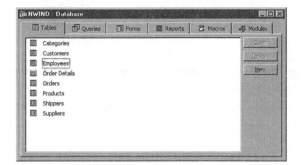

The first thing you'll do is to select a table and then right-click it. Select Save As/Export from the resulting menu. Select To an External File or Database from the dialog box that comes up. This allows you to send the information to an alternative destination, rather than copying it within the current database (see Figure 26.3).

FIGURE 26.3

You can use the Export option to make copies of data in an existing Access database. For sending information to SQL Server, however, you'll need to send it to an external database.

When you make your selection and click to continue, you'll be presented with a dialog box that asks you what type of export you want to perform. Select the type of export you want to perform, as shown in Figure 26.4.

Part
V

Ch
26

FIGURE 26.4

The option to export to SQL Server is supported as an ODBC setting. ODBC is the last selection on the Save as Type list box.

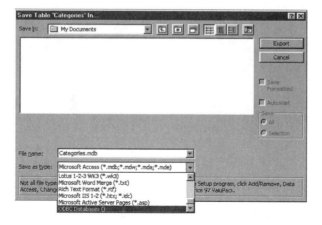

When you select ODBC, you'll be asked to specify the name of the table you'll export to. The default will be a table with the same name as the table you're exporting. For most systems, it's a good idea to accept the default name. This will save confusion when you're linking to the table later. Finally, you'll be prompted to select the ODBC data source that you'll use to connect with the database on SQL Server. In Figure 26.5, you can see that you are able to select from all installed data sources, or you can create a new data source for the conversion batch.

 TIP If you'll be using this in a production environment, you'll save trouble later if you create a new data source for the linked tables. Write down the name and use it only for this task. That way, if a user name or password changes, you can update it in one place, which will update all your links using that DSN to get to SQL Server.

FIGURE 26.5

Select the appropriate DSN that you'll use to gain access to the database and tables you need.

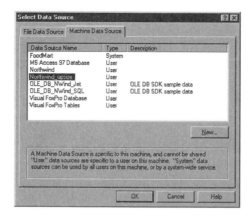

After you select the ODBC DSN to use, the export process will begin. You'll be asked to log in to the server first, allowing you one final chance to select the database you want to use. To use the option, select the Options button on the dialog box. In the example shown in Figure 26.6, the Northwind database is used for the export.

FIGURE 26.6

When you log in, you'll have the opportunity to select which database you want to export into.

During the export process, you'll see an indicator in the lower left corner of the Access workspace that will tell you the status of the process. When completed, the table will be on SQL Server, with the structure and data intact. As you can see in Figure 26.7, the table now shows up in the Enterprise Manager. You should always confirm that the table was converted without a problem. Perhaps the best way to do this is to run a simple SELECT * FROM *table* and compare the results from Access with those from SQL Server. Repeat this export process for each table, resulting in a total of eight tables exported to the server.

FIGURE 26.7

You should verify that each table has exported to the correct database before you continue with the upsizing of your application.

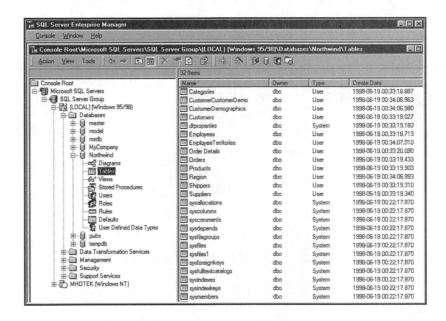

Part
V

Ch
26

At this point, there is no difference in your Access application. You've only exported the structures and data to the SQL Server system. The next step is to make your application reference SQL Server tables when it is run. Doing so requires that you first rename your existing tables, then create the links to the SQL Server-based information.

From Access, rename each table by right-clicking it and choosing the Rename option from the menu. Simply type **OLD** before the existing name and press Enter. You can use anything you would like here. The key is to keep the old table and rename it, so you can create the active links that point to the SQL Server. When you're finished, you'll have a list of tables that resembles those shown in Figure 26.8.

FIGURE 26.8

By renaming each table, you leave yourself the option of falling back to the original tables without a problem.

The last step to begin using your now-SQL Server-based tables is to link to them from Access. Right-click on the Tables form and select Link Tables... from the menu. Once again you'll be prompted for the table and type of table to link to. Select ODBC Databases () from the Files of Type list box (see Figure 26.9).

FIGURE 26.9

As with the export process, you'll be using an ODBC data source for the linked tables from SQL Server.

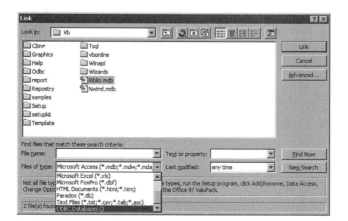

Select your ODBC data source and you'll be prompted to log in to SQL Server. Remember, if you're using a different database, select the Options button to select it prior to completing the login. As soon as you log in, Access will display the list of tables from the database. You'll notice, as shown in Figure 26.10, that each table has a DBO prefix, representing the database owner.

FIGURE 26.10

Access will automatically query SQL Server to determine what tables are available.

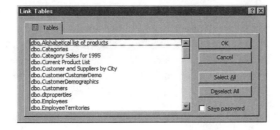

You'll also notice that any file name characters that were allowed in Access, but not in SQL Server, will be replaced to be correct for SQL Server. In the example, the Access table Order Details was updated to be named Order_Details. Click each table you want, or in this case, click Select All. Next, click the OK button to begin the linking process. After you've linked the tables, Access tables will be updated to show the new links. You'll notice a globe next to each of the SQL Server tables, indicating that it's accessed externally. Figure 26.11 shows the results of linking the tables to the Access database.

FIGURE 26.11

When added, the linked tables are shown with a different icon next to them.

Of course, you've probably noticed that the tables came in with names that aren't quite right. You need to rename the tables, removing the dbo_ prefix that's been added to them. As before, you can rename them by right-clicking them, selecting Rename and removing the prefix. The result is a series of tables with the original names, but linked to SQL Server.

At this point you should run your application and make sure it still performs as you expect. If you have any problems, check the filenames you've provided and make sure the SQL Server information you've provided is accurate relative to login names, passwords, and so on. If you have any trouble at all, do not continue in the upsizing until you've corrected the problem.

You might notice that you already have better performance on the application. It's interesting to see that even by moving the data to SQL Server, you can obtain some benefits, even without optimizing select statements, queries, and other functions.

After you're satisfied that you've successfully converted your tables to SQL Server, you can review the queries and see which ones are likely candidates for translation into a view or stored procedure in SQL Server.

Part
V

Ch
26

Reviewing the Queries, Making Views Converting your queries to SQL Server is not quite as straightforward as exporting and linking to tables, but it can certainly be faster than writing the views from scratch. The basic premise of moving the queries to SQL Server is that you'll create a view in SQL Server, then link to it just as you do a table. Because Access sees queries and tables as functional equivalents, you can make the changes to the data here without making changes to the application, and still get the benefits of a client/server implementation.

In this example, you'll convert one of the queries from the Northwind database, Order Sub-total, to a view. Then, you'll see how to reference the view and use it in your applications. Of course, the goal of this, as mentioned previously, is not to change code, but to change only the source of information.

To begin, select the Queries tab in Access. Select the Order Subtotal query and click Design. You'll be presented with the Query Designer, probably in Design mode, looking like that shown in Figure 26.12.

FIGURE 26.12

In the default design mode, you can visually design the query by dragging and dropping fields to the query. This isn't, however, the best way to work with the query for creating the associated view.

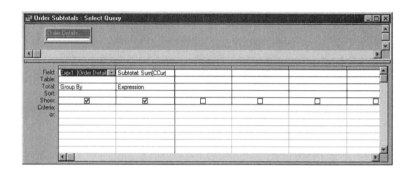

The first thing you'll want to do is change to SQL mode for the query. You can do this in one of two different ways. First, you can select View, SQL View from the menu. This will change the display to the associated SQL statements that represent it. You'll get the same result from the second approach, selecting the View drop-down list and selecting SQL View. In either case, the result is that Access will give you the SQL statements, such as those shown next.

```
SELECT DISTINCTROW [Order Details].OrderID AS Expr1,
Sum(CCur([UnitPrice]*[Quantity]*(1-[Discount])/100)*100) AS Subtotal
FROM [Order Details]
GROUP BY [Order Details].OrderID;
```

There are a couple of things you'll notice right away from this statement. First, it has refer-ences to the tables enclosed in square brackets. Because Access allows you to have spaces in your table names, brackets are used to delineate the names. These aren't allowed in the upsizing process to SQL Server, and neither are the spaces in the object names.

You might recall from the work in linking the tables to SQL Server that the names that con-tained a space were changed to include an underscore character in place of the space. In this example, the table that was changed during the linking demonstration is referenced and will have to be updated to include the underscore.

N O T E Even though you updated the name of the object reference in Access, what you really
updated was the shortcut to the table in SQL Server. The table in SQL Server still contains
the underscore, even though the reference in Access has the space in the object name. ■

You'll need to change DISTINCTROW, inserted automatically by Access, to DISTINCT. SQL Server
won't recognize the DISTINCTROW function provided by Access.

Another thing you'll notice is the use of the CCUR function, one that converts numeric values to
currency representation. This will have to be either replaced or coded around to format the
information as you'll need.

 TIP In this case, the value will be left unconverted because it's used in reports. The Access report writer will
format fields for you, saving you the need to format them before using them.

The final thing you'll need to change is the trailing semicolon on the statement. SQL Server
doesn't need this and will point it out as a syntax error on the statement.

The first step you can take in testing statements like this is to cut and paste the statement into
ISQL/W and run it. See what the results are and step through the changes you need to make
to get the right results set. In this example, the first thing that's pointed out is a syntax error, as
outlined here.

```
Msg 170, Level 15, State 1
Line 1: Incorrect syntax near '['.
```

This error is referencing the brackets around the object names. Remove the brackets and
rerun the query to find the next item that you need to consider. Of course, when you remove
the brackets, change the object name as well so it includes the underscore character. If you
don't, SQL Server won't see the table. The result is shown next.

```
SELECT DISTINCT Order_Details.OrderID AS Expr1,
Sum(CCur(UnitPrice*Quantity*(1-Discount)/100)*100) AS Subtotal
FROM Order_Details
GROUP BY Order_Details.OrderID;
```

At this point, you have two final things to update. You need to remove the reference to CCUR,
and you need to remove the final semicolon. When you do, the results set will start off like that
shown in Listing 26.1.

Part
V

Ch
26

Listing 26.1 Sample Output Listing

```
Expr1        Subtotal
----------   -------------------------
10268        440.0
10269        1863.39987182617
10250        1552.60003662109
10251        654.060005187988
10252        3597.89990234375
```

continues

Listing 26.1 Continued

```
10253    1444.79998779297
10254    556.62003326416
10255    2690.49996948262
10256    517.800003051758
10257    1119.89994049072
10258    1614.88000488281
10259    100.799999237061
10260    1504.64999389648
10261    448.0
10262    583.999996185303
10263    1873.79995727539
10264    695.625
10265    1175.99995422363
10266    346.559997558594
10267    3536.60000610352
10268    1101.19993591309
10269    642.200012207031
10270    1376.0
10271    48.0
```

By comparison, the same query run against the linked SQL Server table from within Access produces the results shown in Figure 26.13.

FIGURE 26.13

The results are the same in the newly modified SQL query that will be used for the View. The only exception is the formatting of the information.

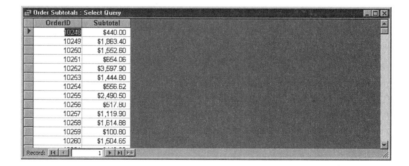

You're ready now to use this query as the basis for a view. In SQL Enterprise Manager, right-click the SQL Server Views in the Northwind database. Right-click and select New SQL Server View from the menu. This will display a dialog box that lets you provide the SQL statements that will comprise the instructions for the view. Cut and paste your SQL statement into the middle pane that has a SQL statement started for you. Change the `<View Name>` to the name you want to know the view by.

TIP

Even if you have to place an underscore in the name of the view where a space exists in Access, you should name the view as close to its original name in Access as possible. This will make debugging and tracking down table/view links easier when you're debugging your application.

In Figure 26.14, you can see an example of the view with the name updated and the code pasted in.

FIGURE 26.14

Use the tested SQL statement as the basis for your new view.

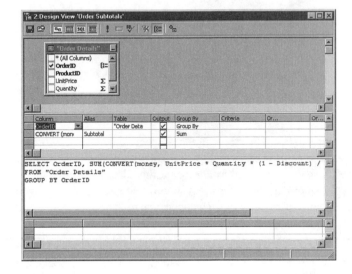

Press the Run button to run and store your new view in the database. When it runs, it will be tested for syntax validity, compiled, and stored. You won't get any results back from the query until you open it explicitly. If all goes well, the query dialog box will be cleared and you'll be able to create another view if needed.

Now you've got the view in the SQL Server system and you're able to use it in a query. You can test the view in Query Analyzer by simply issuing a SELECT * FROM Order_Subtotals. The results should match those shown earlier in the test run of the query.

Now the fun begins. What remains is linking the application to the new view and testing the application. Again, the goal is to not have to change any code in the application but only the objects that are referenced in the Access user interface.

Perhaps surprisingly, Access will allow you to link to the view just as you do a table in SQL Server. When you walk through the link process, you'll notice that the view is listed, along with the other tables that are available, automatically.

When you combine this with the fact that Access treats queries and tables the same logically in your application, you can quickly see that you'll be able to link to the view and run your application. Link the view to your Access application as you would a table (see Figure 26.15).

Views are listed right alongside available tables. Before you can rename the view to the name of the original query, you'll need to rename the query. As with the tables that were linked in earlier, rename the query with an **OLD** prefix, keeping the query around should the need arise later. When the query has been renamed, rename the newly linked view to the name of the query. In this case, it's dbo_Order_Subtotals that should be renamed to Order Subtotals.

Now is the time to test. This goes without saying, but keep in mind that queries have the potential to be a difficult testing proposition. It's a bit less obvious where in your application they're referenced. They can be called from reports, modules, and from macros. In addition, forms can reference the query. In short, be sure you fully test your application from every conceivable angle before you roll out a converted application to a production environment.

Creating Client/Server Systems with Microsoft Access

Microsoft Access is not a client/server system in and of itself. Applications that you develop with it are not inherently developed with both the client and server components of the solution. You can, however, use Access as a development tool, providing the user interface for applications. The tools it offers, such as the report writer, the query tools, and so on, give you good leverage in creating your applications. These are all helpful development tools.

When you create the application, consider first doing so in Access against a database you can test against, break, and repair. By doing so, you can use Access for what it's best for, and still use SQL Server to manage the database aspects of your work.

You've seen throughout this chapter how you can convert those items that should be server-based to SQL Server. Tables, queries, and views are objects best managed by SQL Server, and they're easily converted to SQL Server after you've designed them.

Access basically becomes a development environment, giving you tools to manage the interface that is presented to the user, and letting you work with SQL Server on the back-end.

Creating Pass-Through Queries

When you create queries in Access and submit them to SQL Server, they are first parsed for the ODBC connectivity layer, and then submitted to SQL Server as a sort of temporary stored procedure to be run. The results are returned to your application—you can work with the data from there.

What happens if you want or need more control? What if you want to call a stored procedure and use the output from it directly? That's where pass-through queries come in. In Access, you can create a pass-through query that bypasses the translation and submits exactly what you indicate to SQL Server. To set up a query for pass-through operation, first open the query by highlighting it and clicking Design. Next, select Query, SQL-Specific and finally Pass-through from the menus. When you do, you're presented with the SQL statement equivalent of the query, as shown in Figure 26.16 for the Invoices query in the Northwind database.

FIGURE 26.16

When you choose to make a query a pass-through query, Access will switch to SQL mode so you can edit the statement if needed.

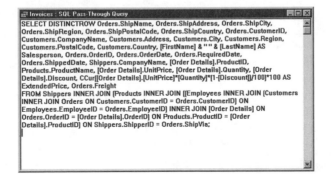

Pass-through queries let you call stored procedures, reference views, and use other features of SQL Server that might have been unavailable using the more typical query from Access. To run a stored procedure, for example, you can just use the EXECUTE command and call out the stored procedure.

For example, to call the stored procedure AccessProc from a pass-through query, you can use the statement:

```
exec accessproc
```

When you do, the stored procedure will be executed and the results will be presented from the query. It's a simple thing to incorporate this type of logic in your application by creating the queries you need, or by establishing your queries in Access Basic to be pass-through queries.

Reality Check

Access is a great tool. It provides the ability for corporate developers to create solid, database-centric applications that can be put into production. The applications can include security and can be quick and easy to use. It's a natural way to introduce and test-market an application with users in the business environment.

When completed, upsizing the application to SQL Server can make a good application even better. Performance can be improved, security can be added, and the open availability of the application's information can be expanded, providing corporate-wide access to the application if needed.

In practical application, using Access as the development and test platform works well. I've used this approach at several sites with good success. The issues that don't tend to get ironed out appropriately in test situations that rely on Access include:

- Performance issues on indexing and heavy-insert type applications—this will generally have to be revisited when you move to SQL Server because you'll have more opportunity to optimize the system. You can look to better indexes and other server-side processes to

Part
V

Ch
26

help with the performance in SQL Server, whereas these options are not available at the same level in Access. You can add indexes in Access, but they can have completely different results.

■ Fine-tuning queries, views, stored procedures—by working hard to optimize your stored procedures and other Access-migrated objects, you can significantly improve performance over the initial conversion effort. After the initial conversion and testing has been completed, re-examine your stored procedures and views. Make sure they're coded to take advantage of as many SQL Server features as possible to make them operate efficiently. Be sure to review the chapters in this book on triggers, rules, defaults, and other automated capabilities of SQL Server. Again, by shifting around functionality as much as possible, you'll be able to let the system do much of the work without specifically calling for it.

One example is that of hard-coding "trigger-type" transactions. Don't do the check from one table against another manually to determine whether a delete will be allowed. Instead, implement a rule or trigger that will enforce the relationship for you, saving you time and coding in the stored procedure.

■ Security—don't forget, when you migrate your application, you still must handle the security on the SQL Server side of the system.

After your first application is converted, you'll come up with additional items pertaining to your development style that need to be reviewed. The best thing you can do is to make a list of these items and make sure you check them on each and every system you upsize.

From Here...

In this chapter, you've seen how to move an Access-based application to SQL Server while still maintaining compatibility with the code you have based in Access. You'll do best by your application if you add the special things to your database that are possible in SQL Server. These include these items in the following closely related chapters:

■ Chapter 10, "Managing and Using Views," covers how you can further modify the queries that you upsize from Access for use in SQL Server.

■ Chapter 11, "Managing and Using Indexes and Keys," will help explain how you can optimize the storage and retrieval of the data in the tables in your system.

■ Chapter 13, "Managing and Using Rules, Constraints, and Defaults," can help point out the things you can do in SQL Server automatically without stored procedure–level coding to ensure data integrity in your system.

■ Chapter 15, "Creating and Managing Triggers," covers how you can control the way SQL Server manages the information updates to your system, preventing unwanted updates or deletions from your system, regardless of the client-side application used to make the changes.

■ A mailing list that works with Office-related development issues is available. Send an email to listserv@peach.ease.lsoft.com and include SUBSCRIBE msoffice-l *firstname, lastname* in the body of the message, including your name as indicated.

CHAPTER 27

Using Advanced Data Objects with SQL Server 7.0

In this chapter

Providing what is probably the most comprehensive database integration capabilities, the Active Data Objects, or ADO, gives you Visual Basic-like database capabilities. If you've used Visual Basic before, and have used the Data Access Objects (DAO), you're already familiar with many of the capabilities and approaches of the ADO.

N O T E This chapter refers to using ADO in Web development. Code samples work largely unchanged in Visual Basic, and the object model is the same in other development environments, but the code samples here will be in Active Server Pages (ASP).

For additional information on integration of your SQL Server and other aspects of Web development, see http://www.swynk.com/seusingsql7. ■

There is strong leverage in using ADO and fully understanding the objects, methods, and properties exposed by it. When you do understand it, you'll be able to develop database-aware applications for Visual Basic for Applications, Active Server Pages, and Visual Basic. The models are the same, the approaches are the same, and the code itself can be used between these environments with only very minor modifications.

Understanding the Core Components of the ADO

The ADO is based on an object model that exposes the collections, methods, and properties necessary to access and work with the database. This object model is available from your ASP code and works in conjunction with the OLE DB layers. The ADO is responsible for making the ODBC connections, working with OLE DB, and making your code usable and readable, all at once.

ADO, based in your ASP application, works by using the ODBC driver to connect to the SQL Server. This driver definition initiates when you create the data connection in Visual InterDev, or when you create the DSN manually using the ODBC applet from the Control Panel. Figure 27.1 illustrates the connection between the ADO in your ASP, these drivers, and the database.

FIGURE 27.1
The flow of the ADO connection to the database and data sources.

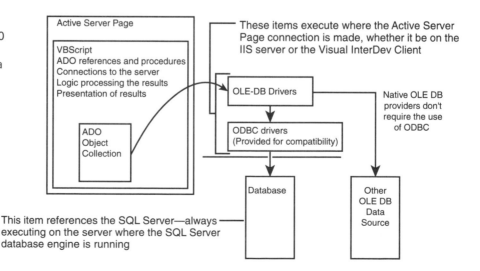

It is important to understand where calls are initiated with the flow of access to the database from your ASP application. The application is always the source of the connection to the server databases. It's important to understand that ASP applications are executed on the IIS server system, not the SQL Server. In the case of working with Visual InterDev, the abstraction from the server is even greater. When you work in InterDev, the connection to the database is made from your workstation to the SQL Server, not the IIS system to the SQL Server.

The ADO object model is broken into four functional parts, each of which you'll use in your work with SQL Server.

- The Recordset object defines the fields and properties associated with database information. You use the Recordset object heavily in working with SQL Server.

- The Command object contains the parameters and properties associated with commands you send to the server, whether to call stored procedures that you've developed, or issue commands to the server to perform administrative tasks.

- The general Properties collection for the Connection object contains information about the Connection to the server. These properties pertain to the user name, login ID, and so on, that define the connection to the SQL Server.

- The general Errors collection is where to look to find out if there were problems with a query, or problems with another access to the server. The Error collection is indispensable in writing a responsible application with the ability to react to problems that arise during its use.

- The Fields collection lets you work with the different column values that are returned. You'll be able to build pages that dynamically change based on the specific information returned by querying these properties. You'll see examples of this later in this chapter.

You use these objects in your pages to bring Web sites into the realm of Web-based applications.

How Is the ADO Integrated into Your Web Page or Application?

To begin using the ADO, you don't turn any specific option on. It doesn't require any action on your part aside from setting up the database connection that you want to use. When you create a connection, you set up the Provider Information, the variables driving how the connection is managed, which username is used, and so on.

The global.asa is typically the home of any connection you'll use across multiple pages. Because it's always available, items declared in the global.asa are available and persistent as the user navigates your site. In the next sections, you'll see how to create your global.asa file, what its uses are, and the typical options are that you'll be setting up.

Global.asa—The Foundation for Your Connection

When you create a project in InterDev, a global.asa file is automatically created for you. This file is where you put site-wide procedures that can run when specific events are initiated. For example, if you wanted a procedure to start every time any page is loaded on your site, you can use the `Session_OnStart` procedure and place the program logic in that subroutine.

Listing 27.1 shows a default global.asa file.

Listing 27.1 Global.asa Sample

```
<SCRIPT LANGUAGE="VBScript" RUNAT="Server">

'You can add special event handlers in this file that will be
'run automatically when special Active Server Pages events
'occur. To create these handlers, just create a subroutine with
'a name from the list below that corresponds to the event
'you want to use. For example, to create an event handler
'for Session_OnStart, you would put the following code into this
'file (without the comments):
'Sub Session_OnStart
'**Put your code here **
'End Sub

'EventName              Description
'Session_OnStart        Runs the first time a
➥ user runs any page in
your application
'Session_OnEnd          Runs when a user's session
➥ times out or quits
your application
'Application_OnStart    Runs once when the first page
➥ of your application
is run for the first time by any user
'Application_OnEnd      Runs once when the web server
➥ shuts down

</SCRIPT>
```

When you add a data connection to an ASP site, you'll notice that InterDev creates the connection configuration and places it in your global.asa file. The settings placed in the file give you access to the database so you can code the individual pages to do the work without the need to replicate the database connection logic. Listing 27.2 is an example of a global.asa and how it applies to a connection to a database.

Listing 27.2 Global.asa Sample (Continued)

```
<SCRIPT LANGUAGE=VBScript RUNAT=Server>
Sub Session_OnStart
    '==Visual InterDev Generated - DataConnection startspan==
    '--Project Data Connection
```

```
        Session("SWYNK_ConnectionString") =
"DSN=MyDSN;Description=MyDSN;
SERVER=MyServer;UID=MyUserID;APP=Microsoft (R)
Developer Studio;WSID=MyWS;DATABASE=MyDB"
        Session("SWYNK_ConnectionTimeout") = 15
        Session("SWYNK_CommandTimeout") = 30
        Session("SWYNK_RuntimeUserName") = "MyUserID"
        Session("SWYNK_RuntimePassword") = "MyPassword"
    '==Visual InterDev Generated - DataConnection endspan==
End Sub
</SCRIPT>
```

You'll notice that this code only sets up the variables that are used to define the connection. Later, when your page makes the connection to the database, it uses these variables to define the connection. Also, when this information is defined in InterDev, the Data View tab is available and each data connection is shown as a sub-entry under the global.asa file in the Explorer listing. See Figure 27.2 for an example.

FIGURE 27.2
InterDev shows you all connections declared in the global.asa.

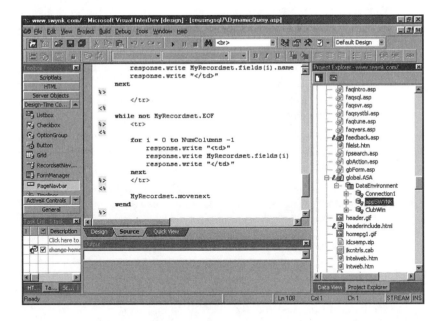

The Data View tab gives you an Explorer-based view of the database, its associated tables, stored procedures, and views. For each of these collections, you can see the objects and work with both the data represented by them and the source statements used to produce them. For example, in Figure 27.3, you see there are seven stored procedures associated with the SWYNK data source.

The capability for InterDev to connect to the database is a good initial test of the parameters you specified when you created the data source. If InterDev connects and shows you the correct information under the Data View tab, you're assured that your connection from your Web page is accurately defined.

FIGURE 27.3

Data View lets you work with database objects directly.

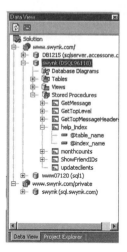

You can indicate these same values in the individual Web pages on your site as well. Your connection to the database will still work properly, but there are a few benefits that you give up in maintaining this information at the page level:

- IIS is not able to cache the page, resulting in a possible performance hit as each page has additional lines of code to process when loaded. Though the global.asa is small, the fact that it is loaded once for the user's session, and then cached in most cases, makes access to its routines and initialization code faster.

- If you change a setting, you must make sure you update all the pages that refer to that setting. By contrast, if it's in global.asa, the setting is automatically referenced any time a page is loaded.

- InterDev won't recognize page-level connections, making it harder to manage your database with InterDev. If you want to use the Data View approach to working with databases, you'll need to be sure to use the global.asa to store the base settings.

In short, unless you have a compelling reason to have the database connection information locally managed, you'll find that keeping the information in global.asa is a straightforward, easy to use tool. In general however, don't open your connections to the database at the global.asa level. Instead open them in your pages where you'll be using them. When you move the connection action to the page, you allow IIS to better manage the connection for you, taking advantage of connection pooling and other optimization techniques.

With the base connection parameters established, it's time to open and work with the connection. In the next section, you'll learn about the parameters, properties and methods available as you work with the database.

Working with the Connection

The Connection object is defined, typically at the page level, to make the working connection to the database provider. This connection is the pipe you use to send information to, and receive information from, the database. It's the overall governing object that controls the database interaction. This means that, at the highest level, you have to have a connection, and that connection is referenced in the other objects used to work with the database, (commands, Recordsets, and so on).

You set up the connection by first establishing the properties, and then using the OPEN method. The following code sample shows how you reference those variables called out in the global.asa, and how you will set up the connection and issue a SELECT statement using the Command object, explained in upcoming sections. See Listing 27.3.

Listing 27.3 Setting Up the Connection

```
Set SWYNK = Server.CreateObject("ADODB.Connection")
SWYNK.ConnectionTimeout = Session("SWYNK_ConnectionTimeout")
SWYNK.CommandTimeout = Session("SWYNK_CommandTimeout")
SWYNK.Open Session("SWYNK_ConnectionString"),
Session("SWYNK_RuntimeUserName"),
Session("SWYNK_RuntimePassword")
```

A number of things relating to managing different aspects of the connection or Recordset are happening here. Although each of these options, and others not indicated here, will be covered in the coming sections, it's important to take a quick look now before diving in.

The first statement creates Connection object and names it SWYNK. This simply allocates and initializes the Connection object and makes it ready to get to work. The reference to the ADODB object is because ADODB is the parent to all these operations—the interface to OLE DB from the ADO. When this SET statement has completed, the database connection is ready to be set up and started.

N O T E When InterDev creates a connection, it names the connection variables with a prefix that matches the DSN that they map to. Because the DSN in this example is named "SWYNK," the prefix selected is also SWYNK. ■

Next the ConnectionTimeout, CommandTimeout, ConnectionString, RuntimeUserName, and RunTimePassword are set up. Because these were set up in the global.asa file, the parameters that are passed are retrieved from the Session collection by providing the name of the variable. To review, you establish those variables in the global.asa as follows:

```
Session("SWYNK_ConnectionTimeout") = 15
```

and the values are retrieved here by reading back in the values for the property.

```
SWYNK.ConnectionTimeout = Session("SWYNK_ConnectionTimeout")
```

At this point, SWYNK.ConnectionTimeout is set to 15 and, should the value change application-wide, it is updated in this portion of the Web site as well because it's coming from the global settings. The call to the SWYNK.Open method takes these properties and opens the connection based on them.

Part
V

Ch
27

There are a number of properties to consider with your connection. Each of these is covered in the next section. Note that, because the connection is established at the outset of your work with the database and then left alone, you need to set these properties before establishing the connection.

The Properties Associated with a `Connection` Object

The properties control the interaction between the OLE DB layers and the ODBC interface in the case of an ADO Web application. With this in mind, many of these properties will look familiar compared with options in the ODBC settings. Where applicable, and where your access rights permit, the settings you indicate here will generally override those set up in ODBC.

The exception to this can come from the ODBC provider. If the driver does not allow for the override of property values, you need to investigate setting them from the ODBC level. As of this writing, this should not present a problem for most existing ODBC drivers.

The `CommandTimeOut` Property   With the default value of 30 seconds, this value is one you might need to review frequently. The uses for this property include several different areas. First, it's a way to react to overly heavy traffic on your server. If you find that people are waiting too long because of traffic, you might want to either leave this value at 30 seconds or even decrease it for small, short queries.

Second, if your queries genuinely take a bit of time to execute, consider making this value larger. There are few things more frustrating than waiting on a query for a bit of time, only to have it return as a timeout error. There are many times when you need some added time to complete a complex operation and you don't want to give up the server processing just because a connection timed out. You should still place an upper limit on this value based on average experience with the query when done manually, as this helps prevent the user from waiting for an extremely long time.

> **N O T E**   If you find that the user is waiting for a given query on a regular basis, increasing the timeout should not be your only response. Make sure you're using stored procedures whenever possible, and use views and indexed tables in every case possible. Stay away from clustered indexes, except where they are truly warranted. ■

The `ConnectionString` Property   The `ConnectionString` property lets you establish the string passed when the OLE DB provider of ODBC is initiated. If you're familiar with the Data Access Objects, or DAO, method where you indicate the ODBC parameters in a single connection string passed to ODBC, you'll understand the approach used here too.

The difference is that the OLE DB `ConnectionString` property can contain either the name of a DSN already established on the system, or the individual settings used to create the connection. With DAO, you must call out the parameters to the connection, even if they were indicated in the DSN settings you established in ODBC. The driver can tell which approach you're using, either indicating the values in the string or providing a DSN name, by inspecting the string for an equal (=) sign. If found, it's assumed that you'll provide the parameters in the string, rather than the name of the DSN to use.

In the examples of connecting to the database shown earlier with the references to the ConnectionTimeout properties as an example, the parameters were provided, in line with standard DAO use.

```
"DSN=MyDSN;Description=MyDSN;SERVER=MyServer;UID=MyUserID;
➡ APP=Microsoft (R) Developer Studio;WSID=MyWS;
➡ DATABASE=MyDB"
```

In this example, the DSN, MyDSN, could also have been called out as the `ConnectionString`.

```
Session("SWYNK_ConnectionString") = "MyDSN"
```

There's no advantage to one method over the other. The differences come in where the connection is managed. When you indicate the DSN alone, you assume that the ODBC DSN manages the connection information. This can make things very simple to administer. On the other hand, if you want to have the flexibility to update some of the parameters associated with the connection, declaring the values in the string is the right alternative for you. You'll likely be deciding on a case-by-case basis.

The `ConnectionTimeOut` Property   As with the `CommandTimeOut` property, the `ConnectionTimeOut` property lets you help the user with excessive time spent working with the server. In cases where you want to let the user get on with business, even when the server is slow in responding, you can use this value to tell the access layer to stop trying the connection and return an error. You can trap the error within your application and give the user the option to retry the connection, or work in another, perhaps non-database–intensive, portion of your application.

The default for `ConnectionTimeOut` is 15 seconds. If the connection is over the Internet, you will want to consider increasing this value to 30 or more if you're experiencing trouble connecting, especially if you've developed an application using SQL Server's integrated or mixed security options. In these cases, you not only have the traffic on the Internet to take into account, but also the traffic on the domain controller associated with the SQL Server.

The `DefaultDatabase` Property   There are three different ways that you control which database is active when you sign in to SQL Server. The first is at the user level where you designate a default database based on the user login information. The second is to indicate the default by selecting it in the ODBC configuration.

The final option you have is that of setting the database using the `DefaultDatabase` property of the connection. By setting this option, you're ensuring that the database you need is indeed the one that will become the default upon opening the connection.

There is a Database option that you can indicate as part of the connect string if you choose to use that approach rather than the named DSN approach. According to Microsoft, there are times when, if you indicate an option as both a property and a parameter to the DSN connect string, results might be "unpredictable."

If you're using the fully qualified connect string approach in the connection statement, indicate the database there, but not as a property. Conversely, if you're using the named DSN approach, be sure to use the `DefaultDatabase` property because you won't have any other option for giving this information.

Part

V

Ch

27

The Mode Property   The Mode property, like many of the other properties associated with the connection, is set before you open the connection. The Mode property is used to control the type of access you have to the underlying database, and to optimize the connection a bit.

This optimization can result from setting the mode to Read-Only, and letting the database engine know there won't be any updates. This can help in performance because the database engine often doesn't maintain the same level of detail on the connection if no updates are expected.

The following constants are in the ADO include files. You can use either the constants or the Values they represent, as shown in the following table.

Table 27.1   Mode Values

Constant	Value	Description
adModeUnknown	0	No permissions have been set. They are at their default levels (Default).
adModeRead	1	Read-only
adModeWrite	2	Write-only
adModeReadWrite	3	Read/write
AdModeShareDenyRead	4	Exclusive permissions for Read. Other users cannot open the data source in read mode.
AdModeShareDenyWrite	8	Exclusive permissions for Write. Other users cannot open the data source in Write mode.
AdModeShareExclusive	12	Exclusive permissions for Read/Write. Other users cannot open the data source in read/write mode.
AdModeShareDenyNone	16	Exclusive access altogether. Other users cannot open the data source.

Perhaps the most helpful application of these modes is when you need to ensure exclusive access to certain pieces of information. This might be the case where you're developing an accounting application for example. There are times when you need to update the system and want to make sure no other changes are going on. In those cases, you might want to use the Exclusive modes that are available.

The Provider Property   You can use the Provider property to indicate a provider other than the default, ODBC. As the OLE DB standard is implemented for additional data sources, you can indicate here if you're using one of these other sources. Note that you should not indicate a provider with this property and as a parameter to the connect string. Doing so might confuse the OLE DB system.

Methods

The connection properties control how the connection is made between your client application and the server. When established, you can execute operations impacting the connection and all operations associated with it using the methods supported by the Connection object.

The key thing to keep in mind in working with these is that they affect, or have the potential to affect, all the actions you execute against the connection. This includes Recordset operations, SELECT statements, and the transactions that you control with this object.

Disconnecting from the Database with the Close Method

Perhaps the easiest and most obvious method to use is the Close method. Close does just that—it closes the connection to the database. When you close the database connection, all Recordsets are also closed automatically. If you attempt to work with a Recordset, connection, or other object associated with the Connection object, you receive a message indicating that the connection is closed and your operation cannot be completed. When you close a connection, you also close all objects associated with it.

```
'Close the connection
MyConnection.Close
```

Although it's not necessary to close every connection because it will close automatically when the connection goes out of scope, you should always close it explicitly to release server-side resources as quickly as possible. An open connection takes a client license on the server and can use valuable memory and other resources that could be put to use elsewhere if your connection is finished with the work.

Your connection goes out of scope when you leave the page, start another application, or leave the Web site and allow your Web browser connection to time out, typically 20 minutes after you leave the site.

Sending Commands to the Engine: The Execute Method

There are many times when you need to simply execute a statement against the database, but not necessarily work with a given Recordset or other active data connection. Such might be the case when you want to see if a row exists prior to continuing a query process, or at a time when you need to update a row independently from the current Recordset.

Execute allows you to send a SQL statement directly to the database. There are several parameters to the command. These parameters let you dictate some of the commands handling of your statement and they help the database engine understand what you're doing.

```
Set MyConnectionObject = server.createobject("ADODB.Connection")
MyConnectionObject.execute command [, rowsaffected] [, options]
```

You can also use the Connection object as the basis for creating a Recordset object.

```
Set MyConnectionObject =
  ➡server.createobject("ADODB.Connection")
Set MyRecordset = MyConnectionObject.execute(command
  ➡[, rowsaffected] [, options])
```

The `ConnectionObject` is the overall connection object that you're using to access the server. You must have already opened the `Connection` before you can use the `Execute` method. An example of querying the PUBS database would be

```
Set MyConnectionObject = server.createobject("ADODB.Connection")
MyConnectionObject.execute "Update Authors
➥set au_lname = 'Wynkoop' where au_fname='Julie'"
```

This statement would return no values, but would update the Authors table, changing everyone's first name to Julie where the last name was Wynkoop.

 T I P In the command string, you'll notice the use of single quotes around the string values. When you build a string, you'll have a problem with the database engine parsing the string if you use double quotes. It takes the double quotes as the end of the string and you end up with a syntax error for the statement. By using single quotes around your string values, you avoid this problem. If you have single-quotes in your strings that you're sending the engine, you may have to use escape sequence or HTML Encoding to prevent errors from the database engine.

There are three parameters to the `Execute` method, two of which are optional.

Table 27.2 Execute Parameters

Parameter	Description
Command	The SQL statement that you need to send to the server.
RowsAffected (optional)	A variable returned from the process that contains the number of rows that were impacted by your statement. This is identical to the footer message on statements that you issue from the Query Optimizer, where the footer indicates the total number of rows impacted by your query.
Options (optional)	The options parameter lets you tell the database engine about the type of information you're sending to the server.

The options available are shown in Table 27.3.

Table 27.3 Option Settings

Option Value/Constant Name	Description
1/AdCmdText	Treat the command string as a standard SQL statement. This is the same as typing in your command in Query Optimizer and then executing it.
2/AdCmdTable	Typically used when you use the Execute statement to create a recordset, the AdCmdTable option opens the table indicated in the command string passed in and assigns the resulting rows to the Recordset you assign.

Option Value/Constant Name	Description
	The command string you pass in should only be a table name, not an SQL statement.
4/AdCmdStoredProc	Instead of creating a statement that includes the Exec portion of the statement, for example, Exec MyStoredProcedure, you can just pass in the name of the stored procedure and set the Options flag to the AdCmdStoredProc constant. The server knows to use the name you provide as the name of a stored procedure to be executed.
8/AdCmdUnknown	If you're creating a generic utility, the unknown command type option would make some sense, but, because the command processor will assume this anyway, your use of this option is limited at best. If you use this option, SQL Server submits the statement as-is and runs it. Again, this is exactly as if you type it into the Query Optimizer.

N O T E The constants called out previously are provided in the adovbs.inc file. You need to make sure you include the file in your ASP page in order to have access to the constants. ■

Using the Open Method You must open a connection before you can reference its methods or collections and begin working with your database. Although you first set the properties of the connection and then call the Open method, you cannot work with Recordsets or other dependent objects until the connection has been opened and the database is aware of your presence.

There are several options associated with the Open method, each controlling exactly how the connection is managed and how the data interaction with the database is accomplished. The overall syntax for calling the method is

```
<%
    set MyConnection = server.createobject("adodb.connection")
    MyConnection.Open ConnectionString, UserID, Password
%>
```

You'll recall from earlier in this chapter there is a ConnectionString property that you can establish outside the call to the Open method. When you do, that setting is used as the parameter to the Open method. When the ConnectionString property has been previously defined in this manner, you don't have to pass it as part of the Open method.

```
MyConnection.Open , UserID, Password
```

N O T E For additional information about the ConnectionString, UserID, and Password properties, see the sections detailing how their property values are established earlier in this chapter. See the sections starting with global.asa and continuing with detailed sections on these and the other properties that determine the connection's characteristics. ■

The UserID and Password are also optional and are automatically used from properties that you set up for the Connection object. In short, you can just call the Open method if you've set up the properties ahead of time. The most important thing is to make sure these properties are set correctly to the connection you want to establish. Make sure the DSN is named correctly and that the UserID and Password are what you want to use to get into the SQL Server.

Working with SQL Server

Now that you have the connection to the server, you can concentrate on getting the work done against the database and tables. The prerequisite of this entire section is that you have a valid connection object. You use this object in your work with the Command and Recordset objects. In addition, as you've seen, you can use the connection object to submit commands and SQL statements directly without using them as the source of a Recordset.

There are two different objects that you use to work against the server: the Command object and the Recordset object. The vast majority of your work entails the use of the Recordset object because this is the set of methods, properties, and capabilities that let you work with the columns and their respective values from the database tables.

The Command Object

The Command object is the hub of the ADO session. The Command object is used to establish the Recordset, and its used to pool your connection to the database, saving time and server-side resources as you can optimize the number of connections you must support at any given time. The optimization comes from using the same connection for multiple Recordsets. By doing so, you help optimize the server connections. At the same time, you improve the performance of your application.

The performance boost comes from not needing to sign on to the database each time you start a new Recordset. Because you're not opening a new connection, the overhead associated with connections does not have to be completed.

N O T E   In one recent application makeover, the length of time to complete an operation was taken from more than 10 minutes to fewer than 30 seconds. A fair portion of the improvement came from moving away from using a new connection for every query. The other contributing factor to improving performance was a movement to stored procedures and away from client-side SELECT statements. ▪

The Execute Method   The tendency for a new ASP developer is to place a SELECT statement in the Recordset creation statement, and forget that stored procedures and other statements can be used as the source of a Recordset. In addition, you can use the Execute method to send any other SQL statement, regardless of whether it returns rows. You can use it to create a management tool, you can use it to send administration commands to the server, and so on.

Of course, the Execute method is also the source of Recordsets, letting you use the commands you send to the server to define the contents of the Recordset. There are two ways to call the method, depending on whether there will be returned values. If you'll be populating a Recordset, you use the following syntax:

Set MyRecordset = MyCommand.Execute(*CommandText, RowsAffected, Options*)

In this manner, the Connection is used to send the SQL statement in the form of the CommandText. The SQL Statement can take nearly any form and need not necessarily be a SELECT statement. For example, if you find that your SELECT statement amounts to SELECT * from MyTable you can simply use MyTable as the CommandText. The provider layer automatically knows that you mean to use the whole table as the source for the Recordset. You can also simply specify the name of a stored procedure and it will be executed.

The provider knows whether you're passing in a stored procedure name, a table, or a SELECT statement by the value you pass for the options parameter. The following table shows the values, and their associated constants, that you use for this option.

Table 27.4 Command Type Values

Option Value/Constant Name	Description
1/AdCmdText	Treat the command string as a standard SQL statement. This is the same as typing in your command in Query Optimizer and then executing it.
2/AdCmdTable	Typically used when you use the Execute statement to create a recordset, the AdCmdTable option opens the table indicated in the command string passed in and assigns the resulting rows to the Recordset you assign. The command string you pass in should only be a table name, not an SQL statement.
4/AdCmdStoredProc	Instead of creating a statement that includes the Exec portion of the statement, for example, Exec MyStoredProcedure, you can just pass in the name of the stored procedure and set the Options flag to the AdCmdStoredProc constant. The server knows to use the name you provide as the name of a stored procedure to be executed.
8/AdCmdUnknown	If you were creating a generic utility, the unknown command type option would make some sense. Because the command processor assumes this anyway, your use of this option is limited at best. If you use this option, SQL Server submits the statement as written and runs it. Again, this is exactly as if you type it into the Query Optimizer.

Part
V

Ch

27

If you use the method to simply work with information, make changes to table structures, or complete other operations that don't create a Recordset, you call the method slightly differently.

```
command.Execute CommandText, RecordsAffected, Options
```

The difference is that you're calling just the method, and you're not expecting it to return any values except for the `RecordsAffected` if applicable. Because this is the case, there are no parentheses around the parameters. As a point of reference, there is a corollary if you're familiar with Visual Basic. When creating a `Recordset`, you use the method as a function, but, when just calling the method to do other tasks, you're using it as a subroutine.

The `ActiveConnection` Property   This property indicates which `Connection` object the `Command` is associated with. If you issue a `Command`, for example using the `Execute` method, without setting this parameter, you'll generate an error. You need to first set this property to the applicable connection.

```
Set MyCommand.ActiveConnection = MyConnection
```

If you want to change the connection associated with a `Command` object, you can set the property to `NOTHING` and then reestablish the setting as before. Note that if you have used the `Command` object as the basis for a `Recordset`, the `Recordset` is reset when you set the property to `NOTHING`.

N O T E   When you associate the `Command` with a `Connection` object, the `Connection` must already have been opened. If it's not, it will generate an error. ▨

The `CommandText` Property   As you might imagine, the `CommandText` property contains the actual string that you want to send to the Provider layer to be executed. With SQL server, this pertains to the SQL statement you want to execute. You can provide a full SQL statement, the name of a stored procedure, or the name of a table. If you provide the name of a stored procedure, you can either prefix the name with `EXEC` or set the `Option` on the `Execute` method to indicate that you're passing in a stored procedure.

The `CommandTimeout` Property   The `CommandTimeout` property can be helpful when you're developing applications over the Internet. Because you can't control the traffic, congestion, and response times over the Internet, and you don't know the loading situation at the server in many cases, you use the `CommandTimeout` property to give the user back some control over the connection.

`CommandTimeout` lets you establish, in seconds, the time the ADO object waits for a given command to complete. The default value of 30 seconds is typically sufficient, but keep in mind that several factors weigh upon this parameter.

```
MyCommand.CommandTimeout = 60
```

First, if the query you're running is particularly complex, it might be worth setting this value higher to allow the query to complete. If this is the case, you'll have to experiment not only with the query to find out an average, acceptable running time, but also to find out the times that are unacceptable and indicate a problem.

This property is a good candidate to be set up in the global.asa as it gives you the flexibility to update your entire application should you decide to change the value. You won't have to go from file to file setting the value, it will just be inherited from the global settings. In fact, if you use the Data Form Wizard capabilities of InterDev, you'll find that the CommandTimeout is set, by default, for you in the global.asa as one of the default properties and parameters. See Listing 27.2.

Listing 27.4   Global.asa Settings

```
    '==Visual InterDev Generated - DataConnection startspan==
    '--Project Data Connection
        Session("SWYNK_ConnectionString") =
➡ "DSN=MyDSN;Description=MyDSN;
➡ SERVER=MyServer;UID=MyUserID;APP=Microsoft (R)
➡ Developer Studio;WSID=MyWS;DATABASE=MyDB"
        Session("SWYNK_ConnectionTimeout") = 15
        Session("SWYNK_CommandTimeout") = 30
        Session("SWYNK_RuntimeUserName") = "MyUserID"
        Session("SWYNK_RuntimePassword") = "MyPassword"
    '==Visual InterDev Generated - DataConnection endspan==
```

You reference the setting by indicating the name as DSN-NAME _CommandTimeout, an example of which is shown next with the DSN name of SWYNK.

```
MyCommand.CommandTimeout = Session("SWYNK_CommandTimeout")
```

The Recordset Object

If there is one place in the ADO automation that things get interesting, it's the Recordset. The Recordset offers you such functionality that you can do nearly anything with the underlying database and information. You can do it dynamically, querying the Recordset for table structures, or you can work with the information in a static fashion, hard-coding your way through the application you're developing.

For an example of one of the things you can do with Recordsets in a dynamic Web page, consider Figure 27.4 and Listing 27.5. The screen prompts you for the User ID and password and an SQL statement to use. When you provide this, the statement you enter is submitted. If it's a SELECT statement that returns rows, the table structure is automatically output in terms of column names, and then the first five columns are output to the Web page. This happens dynamically, without hard-coding column names or data values.

This page is built on-the-fly with the code shown next.

Part
V

Ch
27

FIGURE 27.4

A dynamic query utility.

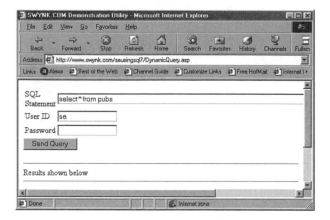

FIGURE 27.4

A dynamic query utility.

Listing 27.5 Dynamic Query Page

```asp
<%@ LANGUAGE="VBSCRIPT" %>

<HTML>
<HEAD>
<META NAME="GENERATOR" Content="Microsoft Visual InterDev 1.0">
<META HTTP-EQUIV="Content-Type" content="text/html; charset=iso-8859-1">
<TITLE>SWYNK.COM Demonstration Utility</TITLE>
</HEAD>
<BODY bgcolor=white>

<FORM Action="msgbox.asp" Method=get>
    <table>
        <tr>
            <td>
                SQL Statement
            </td>
            <td>
                <input type=TEXT name="selectstatement" size=100>
            </td>
        </tr>
        <tr>
            <td>
                User ID
            </td>
            <td>
                <input type=text name="UserID" size=15>
            </td>
        </tr>
        <tr>
            <td>
                Password
            </td>
            <td>
                <input type=password name="Password" size=15>
            </td>
        </tr>
```

```
    </table>
    <input Type=SUBMIT value="Send Query">
</form>

<hr>
Results shown below<br>
<hr>

<%
Set MyConnection = Server.CreateObject("ADODB.Connection")
Set MyCommand = Server.CreateObject("ADODB.Command")
Set MyRecordset = Server.CreateObject("ADODB.Recordset")

MyConnection.Open "SWYNK", request("userid"), request("password")
if session("connected")="T" then
    session("connected")="F"
    MyCommand.CommandText = request("selectstatement")
    response.write MyCommand.CommandText
    response.write "<br><br>"
    MyCommand.CommandType = 1
    Set MyCommand.ActiveConnection = MyConnection
    MyRecordset.Open MyCommand, , 1
    response.write "Fields returned: "
    response.write "<br>"
    for i = 0 to MyRecordset.fields.count -1
        response.write MyRecordset.fields(i).name
        response.write "<br>"
    next
    MyRecordset.movelast
    MyRecordset.movefirst
    response.write MyRecordset.RecordCount
    response.write " row(s) returned."
    If MyRecordset.fields.count > 5 then
        NumColumns=5
    else
        NumColumns = MyRecordset.fields.count
    end if
%>
    <table>
        <tr>
<%
    for i = 0 to NumColumns -1
        response.write "<td>"
        response.write MyRecordset.fields(i).name
        response.write "</td>"
    next
%>
        </tr>
<%
    while not MyRecordset.EOF
%>      <tr>
<%
        for i = 0 to NumColumns -1
            response.write "<td>"
```

continues

Listing 27.5 Continued

```
                response.write MyRecordset.fields(i)
                response.write "</td>"
        next
%>          </tr>
<%
        MyRecordset.movenext
    wend
%>
        </tr>
    </table>
<%
end if
session("connected")="T"
%>

</BODY>
</HTML>
```

There are a number of properties, collections, and methods at work here. Each of these, and the balance of those not specifically used here, are explained in this section. With the methods, collections, and properties you have available, the sky's the limit for the types of database-based applications you can build for your Web site.

The Fields Collection The Fields collection is the heart of the Recordset, providing you with the information necessary to work with the data from the underlying tables. The properties associated with each field in the collection tell you everything from the defined column size and type to the actual size of the field and its name.

To access these properties, you simply refer to the field you need and the property you want to query. As in the earlier example, shown in Listing 27.5, to retrieve the name of each field in the Recordset, you can use two of these properties: the Count property and the Name property.

```
for i = 0 to MyRecordset.fields.count -1
    response.write MyRecordset.fields(i).name
    response.write "<br>"
next
```

N O T E Because the properties are zero-based, if the Count property indicates that you have 12 fields, you need to read in fields 0 through 11 to get the 12 fields. This is why, in the example preceding, the For...Next loop runs from 0 to MyRecordset.Fields.Count –1 instead of going from 1 to the value of the Count property. ▪

The Name Property As the name implies, this property provides you with the underlying table column's name. You can use this value to show the user what columns are available in the column headings of an HTML table, for example, as shown in the ASP page example earlier in this section.

```
for i = 0 to NumColumns -1
    response.write "<td>"
    response.write MyRecordset.fields(i).name
    response.write "</td>"
next
```

Using this approach, you can build a dynamic page that uses the table's field names as the headings for the table.

The `Value` Property   The `Value` property contains the actual value for the field, whether it is text or numeric. You can use the `Type` property to determine what type of value to expect. Your application might need to respond differently to the value based on the `Type`, so be sure you know what the field type is before you use it in equations, expressions, and so on.

The `AddNew` Method   The `AddNew` method initializes the `Recordset` and prepares it for values that will be saved to the underlying database. You use AddNew in conjunction with the `Update` method. After you call AddNew, set the fields to the values that you need, and then call the `Update` method to save the value to the table. If you don't first call `AddNew`, you'll be overwriting the values of the current record, rather than creating a new record.

```
<%
    …
    MyRecordset.AddNew
    MyRecordset.Fields("Lname") = "Wynkoop"
    MyRecordset.Update
    …
%>
```

The `AddNew/Update` method combination does the same thing as issuing an `INSERT INTO` and using the `Execute` method of the `Command` object, with one exception. That exception is the fact that, after the `Update` method has been called, the `Recordset` is up to date with the new row. If you use the `INSERT INTO` command, you'll still need to Resync the database with the `Recordset`. Both approaches work, but the AddNew approach is much more consistent with the ADO approach to working with your databases and their associated tables.

If you call `AddNew`, make changes to the `Recordset`, and then call `AddNew` again before calling the `Update` method, ADO will automatically call `Update` prior to clearing the `Recordset` in anticipation of the new record. Even with this in mind, you want to make sure you explicitly call the `Update` method to ensure that all changes are saved to the database.

You can also pass a `Fields` collection to the `AddNew` method, causing multiple fields to be updated at once. When you do, ADO switches the update mode to Batch and you'll need to use `UpdateBatch` instead of `Update` to save the contents of the new records to the database.

The `Close` Method   As with the other objects in the ADO, the `Close` method closes the `Recordset` and releases all resources associated with it. You should always close a `Recordset` when you're finished working with it because it releases resources on the server as well, even in cases where those resources simply manage the concurrency in the database relative to other users.

```
MyRecordset.Close
```

Your `Recordset` will also be closed if the `Connection` object is closed.

Part

V

Ch

27

The Delete Method   You use the Delete method to remove the current row from the Recordset and the underlying database table. If you use the Delete method in conjunction with the Filter property, you can flag an entire batch of records for removal from the database.

If you delete rows while operating in batch mode, you'll have to call UpdateBatch to remove the rows from the underlying database tables. If you don't, the changes are lost and the rows are not deleted.

If you're writing an application that uses transactions, and you enclose a Delete call within the Transaction, you can abort the Delete operation by rolling back the transaction with the RollBackTrans method. Of course, if you call CommitTrans, you'll save the changes to the database, removing the rows from the database table. These are methods of the Connection object.

The MoveFirst, MoveLast, MoveNext, and MovePrevious Methods   If you're going to work with ADO, you must understand the MoveFirst, MoveLast, MoveNext, and MovePrevious methods. This is because these methods provide you with the access to the Recordset that you'll need to be able to move through the rows and elements of your data set. From the earlier example, Listing 27.5, you can see several of these in action.

Listing 27.6   Move Samples

```
MyRecordset.movelast
MyRecordset.movefirst
response.write MyRecordset.RecordCount
response.write " row(s) returned."

...
...

<%
while not MyRecordset.EOF
%>         <tr>
<%
    for i = 0 to NumColumns -1
        response.write "<td>"
        response.write MyRecordset.fields(i)
        response.write "</td>"
    next
%>
    </tr>
<%
    MyRecordset.movenext
wend
%>
```

N O T E   If you're using a static cursor for your recordset, you'll be able to refer to the RecordCount without the need to use the MoveLast method shown above. ■

You might recall from the RecordCount property that you must first call the MoveLast method to get an accurate count of rows in the Recordset. This is because Recordsets are dynamic in how they are populated and how they related to the underlying tables. Until you've retrieved all rows from the data source, the database access layer won't know how many rows are available.

The Move methods are pretty self-explanatory, each providing easy navigation methods for your Recordset.

- MoveFirst will move to the first row in the Recordset. BOF will be TRUE immediately following calls to this method.

- MoveLast moves to the last row in the Recordset. EOF will be TRUE immediately following calls to this method.

- MoveNext moves to the next row in the Recordset, relative to the current position in the Recordset. If the end of the file is reached, EOF is set to TRUE. If you do receive an EOF, you should call MoveLast to establish your positioning on the last row.

- MovePrevious will move to the previous row in the Recordset, relative to the current position. If you hit the beginning of the file, BOF will be set to TRUE. If this is the case, be sure to call MoveFirst to get to the first row in the Recordset and establish positioning there.

N O T E   When you're using the Move methods, be sure to always pay attention to the BOF and EOF properties. It's common to hit the end of the file and then try to read another row from the Recordset, resulting in an error in your application. It's simple to test the two values as you navigate the Recordset, so make sure the values are tested in your logic loops. ▪

The Open Method   Before you can start working with a Recordset, you need to first Open it, establishing the connection between your objects and the underlying database table. When you open the Recordset, you have several options that determine how the information is presented, whether it's updateable, and so on.

MyRecordset.Open *SQLStatement, ActiveConnection, CursorType, LockType, Options*

The SQL Statement is one or more SQL statements, separated by a semicolon. This statement is what is used to query the database table, or is passed to the database engine for execution or processing. Note that you need not pass a SELECT statement. Instead, you can simply indicate a table name or a stored procedure name, and set the Options flag appropriately to indicate the type of query string you're submitting. You can also reference an existing Command object here and use it as the source of your Recordset.

The ActiveConnection parameter refers to an existing Connection object by its name. If you don't specify a connection object, a new connection is created for this Recordset. Note that if you don't indicate a connection string, the new connection requires an additional server connection, possibly impacting your server licensing. It's a good idea to reference an existing Connection object for this reason.

The CursorType can be one of four values, as indicated in Table 27.5.

Part
V

Ch
27

Table 27.5 `CursorType` **Values**

Constant Name	Value	Description
AdOpenForwardOnly	0	(Default) Designed to be single-pass approach to the database table, the `adOpenForwardOnly` cursor can be faster because navigation is limited.
AdOpenKeyset	1	The key set approach is one of two different dynamic access methods. With a key set cursor, you cannot see records added by other users because a set of keys, representing the information in the table at the time you open the `Recordset`, is used for navigation, rather than dynamic reads of the information.
AdOpenDynamic	2	When you open a dynamic cursor, as the name implies, the view of the database is automatically changed whenever information in the table changes. If other users add rows, your record will reflect that when it next reads in rows from the table.
AdOpenStatic	3	If you're familiar with Visual Basic data access methods, the `Static` cursor is akin to the `Snapshot` data access method. The `Static` view is a static snapshot of the underlying tables at the time the `Recordset` is opened.

When you provide the `LockType` parameter, you have four choices, which are listed in Table 27.6. Each controls how locks are applied as you work with and change the information in the `Recordset`.

Table 27.6 `LockType` **Values**

Constant Name	Value	Description
AdLockReadOnly	1	The information you're retrieving is read-only. With this option set, you cannot make changes to the underlying tables.
AdLockPessimistic	2	The slowest and most resource-intensive option, pessimistic locking locks each row individually as needed prior to initiating changes.
AdLockOptimistic	3	Optimistic locking accepts changes to the row and then, just before the row is to be written, locks the row, saves the changes, and then releases the lock.
AdLockBatchOptimistic	4	The batch optimistic option is the same as the standard optimistic option, with the exception that it applies to the batch updates you process.

Finally, the Options parameter indicates the type of SQL statement you're passing in. This helps the provider layer know how to work with the Open statement and what type of statement needs to be passed to the provider layer.

The options available are shown in the Table 27.7.

Table 27.7 Option Values

Option Value/Constant Name	Description
1/AdCmdText	Treat the command string as a standard SQL statement. This is the same as typing your command in Query Optimizer and then executing it.
2/AdCmdTable	Typically used when you use the Execute statement to create a recordset, the AdCmdTable option opens the table indicated in the command string passed in and assigns the resulting rows to the Recordset you assign. The command string you pass in should only be a table name, not a SQL statement.
4/AdCmdStoredProc	Instead of creating a statement that includes the Exec portion of the statement, for example, Exec MyStoredProcedure, you can just pass in the name of the stored procedure and set the Options flag to the AdCmdStoredProc constant. The server knows to use the name you provide as the name of a stored procedure to be executed.
8/AdCmdUnknown	If you were creating a generic utility, the unknown command type option would make some sense. Because the command processor will assume this anyway, however, your use of this option is limited at best. If you use this option, SQL Server submits the statement as-is and runs it. Again, this is exactly as if you type it into the Query Optimizer.

The Update Method   The Update method works in conjunction with both the AddNew method and the act of updating an existing row in the Recordset. After you call the AddNew method and set the values in the fields to those that you want to save, you call the Update method to save the new record to the database.

If you're updating information in a record, you first find the record you want to change and then make the changes to the data values. When completed, calling Update will save the changes to the database, updating the underlying tables.

The ActiveConnection Property   This property indicates which Connection object the Recordset is associated with.

```
Set MyRecordset.ActiveConnection = MyConnection
```

Part
V

Ch
27

If you want to change the connection associated with a Recordset object, you can set the property to NOTHING and then reestablish the setting as preceding.

The BOF Property　If this property is set to TRUE, the Recordset is currently positioned at the Beginning of File (BOF), or first record in the Recordset. This is true, for example, just after calling the MoveFirst method.

The EOF Property　When set to TRUE, EOF indicates that the current row in the Recordset is the End of File. This is true when you've just called the MoveLast method or when you've used the MoveNext methods to work down through a file and have exhausted all rows in the Recordset.

The RecordCount Property　The RecordCount property gives you the total records known to the Recordset. Note, however, if you've not moved through the Recordset yet by using MoveLast or MoveNext, this value will be defined as the highest number of rows visited.

From Here...

In this chapter, you've seen the basics of how ADO works with your applications. You can find additional information on these topics at the following locations:

- The author's Web site, http://www.swynk.com/seusingsql7, has constantly updated code samples, FAQs, and additional examples.

- http://www.activeserverpages.com contains many how-to articles dealing with ASP, ADO, and Internet development in general.

- The Microsoft database Web site, http://www.microsoft.com/data, contains additional information on ADO, OLE-DB, and other database integration topics.

PART VI

Appendixes

Mail-Enabling Your SQL Server

In this chapter

The Components of SQL Mail

SQL Mail comprises many different components and settings that must be configured in a certain order for the mail capabilities of SQL Server to be utilized.

SQL Mail is capable of interacting with any MAPI-compliant mail system, but the authorís experience is that it only works with Microsoft Exchange. To complete this configuration, you must be logged on to the Windows NT machine with administrator privileges.

The components required are as follows and are discussed in detail in the next sections:

- Mailbox on the Exchange Server for use by SQL Server
- The Microsoft Outlook or Exchange mail client installed on the machine running SQL Server
- A profile setup for Outlook that accesses the mailbox on Exchange
- The services that SQL Server runs under configured with the proper logins
- The SQL Mail service

Setting Up the Components of SQL Mail

Before you begin to configure all of the components that you need, make sure you become good friends with your Exchange Server administrator. You will require this personís help during part of the setup process. He or she will also be providing troubleshooting help should you encounter communications problems.

Because you will also need to install the Outlook client, locate your installation CD at this point.

Setting Up the SQL Server Services

SQL Mail runs under the account in which the SQL Server service is logged on. Because this is the fact that trips up most SQL Mail configurations, we will get it out of the way before going on.

The services are configured through the Control Panel, Services applet as shown in Figure A.1.

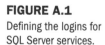

FIGURE A.1

Defining the logins for SQL Server services.

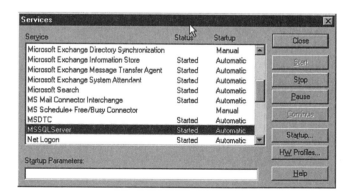

App

A

Clicking the Startup button will display the dialog in Figure A.2. This is where you define the account under which SQL Server will be logged in.

FIGURE A.2
Changing the NT logins for the SQL Server account.

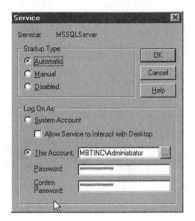

> **N O T E** Most SQL Server installations run under the System Account. In order to get SQL Mail to function, you have to specify a particular NT login. The NT login must have the Administrator privilege. ▪

After you have changed the login to a specific NT account, click the OK button. You should stop and start SQL Server to ensure that it is still functioning properly.

> **N O T E** If the SQL Agent is running, you will be prompted to close it down as well. You can shut down the SQL Agent at this point. ▪

Before continuing to the next step, you have to log out of NT and log on using the account that you specified for SQL Server to run under. When you log back on, ensure that all of the SQL Server services started properly.

Installing the Outlook Client

SQL Mail requires that you have installed the Outlook client software on the machine that is running SQL Server.

> **CAUTION**
>
> Outlook gives you the ability to configure offline folders. Do not configure the offline folders. Doing so causes all messages to accumulate in the outbox until someone manually uploads them.

When you run the Microsoft Office installation, make sure you select the Custom option. You can get a lot of extra, unneeded software on your machine very quickly. The only thing re-quired is the Outlook client. You do not need to install forms, clipart, or other items. However, it is recommended that you install the Help files. The Outlook install should require approximately 22MB. When you log in after rebooting, make sure you log in using the account SQL Server is running under.

Setting Up the Exchange Mailbox

This step must be completed by your Microsoft Exchange administrator.

Start up the Microsoft Exchange Administrator as shown in Figure A.3.

FIGURE A.3

The Microsoft Exchange Administrator is used to set up and administer an Exchange Server just like Enterprise Manager is used for SQL Server.

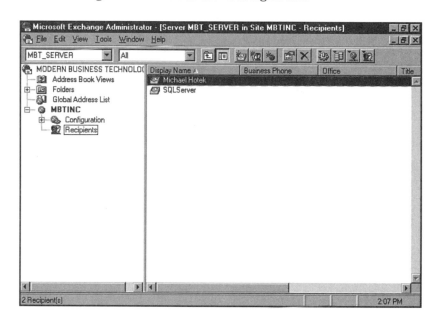

Click the New Mailbox button and fill in the mailbox name as shown in Figure A.4.

Click the primary Windows NT account button on the General tab, choose the Select an Existing Windows NT Account option button, and click OK.

Double-click the NT account that SQL Server was configured to run under in the section titled "Setting Up the SQL Server Services." See Figure A.5.

Click the OK button and set up any additional options required by your Exchange installation, then click OK. A new mailbox has now been created for use by SQL Server.

▶ For more information about installing, configuring, and administering Microsoft Exchange Server, see *Special Edition Using Microsoft Exchange Server 5.5* from Que.

FIGURE A.4

Setting up a new mailbox.

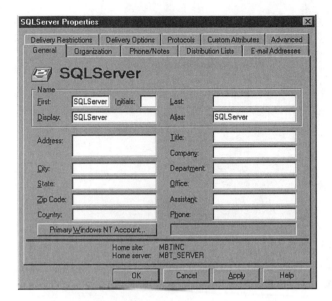

FIGURE A.5

Selecting the Windows NT account for the Exchange mailbox.

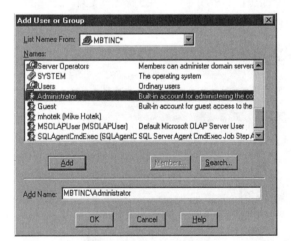

Configuring the Outlook Client

After Outlook has been installed and you have a mailbox for SQL Server, the next step is to configure the Outlook profile to use this mailbox. The profile is configured through the Mail and Fax applet in the Control Panel. Starting this applet will display the dialog as shown in Figure A.6.

FIGURE A.6

Configuring a mail and
fax profile.

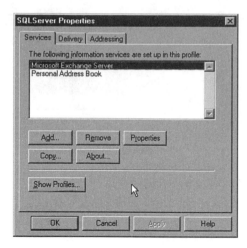

You can use the default profile that is created, but it is recommended that you create a new
profile for use by SQL Server.

To add a new profile, click the Profiles button. The dialog shown in Figure A.7 will be displayed.

FIGURE A.7

Creating a new profile.

Clicking the Add button will take you through a wizard to help set up the profile. On the first
dialog, deselect the Microsoft Mail and Internet Mail options because they are not needed. The
next dialog is where you can name the profile. Select a name such as SQLServer to aid in identification.

N O T E   This is the only place you can set the name of the profile. If you want to change the name
of the profile later, you will have to remove the old profile and add it back in using the new
name. ■

After selecting the name, you proceed to the next dialog. This is the most important dialog in the process. This is where you specify the name of the Exchange Server and the mailbox the profile will use, as shown in Figure A.8.

FIGURE A.8

Entering the name of the Exchange Server and mailbox.

After completing the rest of the steps, you will be returned to the Profiles dialog box. The last thing to do before going on to the next step is to test the profile. Select the profile you created and click the Properties button. When the Properties dialog is displayed, select Microsoft Exchange Server, and click the Properties button. The dialog shown in Figure A.9 will be displayed.

FIGURE A.9

Configuring the properties for your profile.

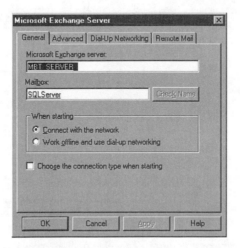

If the names of the Exchange Server and mailbox are not underlined, click the Check Name button. If you have the profile configured correctly with the proper name for the Exchange

Server and mailbox, these two entries will be underlined. If not, you will receive an error message. Before closing this dialog, make sure the Connect to Network option is selected and Choose the Connection Type When Starting is not selected. This enables Outlook to start up and connect to the Exchange Server without any user intervention.

N O T E   This is a very important test to perform. If the name of the Exchange Server or the mailbox is not correct, you will not be able to continue until this is fixed. ∎

Testing the Exchange Connection

At this point, all the prerequisites have been completed. The next step is to ensure that you can in fact send and receive mail.

Start Outlook. By default, the first time Outlook is started, it prompts you for a profile. Select the profile created in the previous section and click OK.

After Outlook has started, compose a new message and send it to the mailbox that was set up for SQL Server in the section titled, "Setting Up the Exchange Mailbox." You should receive a message in your inbox as shown in Figure A.10.

FIGURE A.10

It is important to make sure that you can send and receive mail using the profile that you configured.

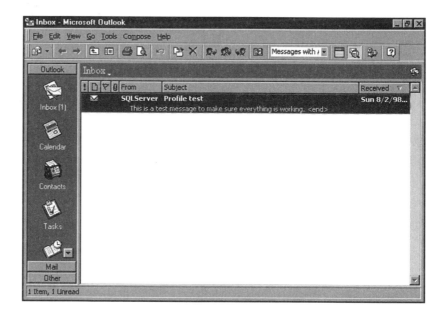

If you receive an error message or if you do not receive mail, there is a problem with your profile or Exchange configuration. Go back through the previous sections to ensure that everything is configured correctly.

Once you are done, make sure you place an Outlook shortcut in the Startup folder for the All Users profile. This ensures that Outlook automatically starts if you ever need to reboot the server.

N O T E While SQL Mail is supposed to be able to send and receive mail without the Outlook client open and running on the machine, it is the experience of the author that SQL Mail works much better when the client is running. You should leave the client minimized on the machine that is running SQL Server. ■

Configuring, Starting, and Testing SQL Mail

This is the final step in getting SQL Mail to run. Start Enterprise Manager, open the tree view for the SQL Server on which you want to set up SQL Mail, highlight the SQL Mail item, right-click and select Properties from the popup menu. You will be presented with the SQL Mail Configuration dialog as shown in Figure A.11.

FIGURE A.11
Configuring SQL Mail.

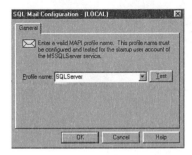

In the Profile Name box, type the name of the profile that was created in the section titled, "Configuring the Outlook Client." Select the Test button. If everything has been set up correctly, you will see the dialog box shown in Figure A.12.

FIGURE A.12
Confirming a successful setup of SQLMail.

Once you have a successful test, select the Auto-start SQL Mail When SQL Server Starts check box. This ensures that SQL Mail will always start up whenever you need to restart SQL Server. Click the OK button.

Now that SQL Mail is configured, right-click on the SQL Mail icon and select Start as shown in Figure A.13.

Once SQL Mail is started, the final thing to check on the system is to make sure SQL Server can send mail, using the extended stored procedure xp_sendmail. Start the Query Analyzer and execute the following query:

```
exec master..xp_sendmail 'SQLServer', 'This is a test.'
```

FIGURE A.13

Starting up SQL Mail.

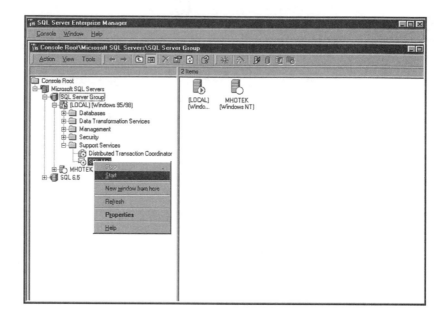

N O T E The first parameter is the name of the Exchange recipient. If you are using a different recipient name, substitute that name for SQLServer. ■

Now maximize the Outlook client. You should see the message in the inbox as shown in Figure A.14.

SQL Mail is now running and functioning perfectly.

FIGURE A.14

Successfully sending a message from SQL Server.

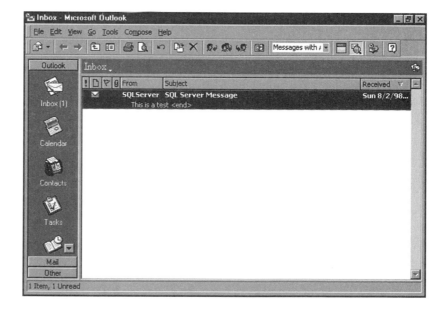

Working with SQL Mail

SQL Server has a small set of extended stored procedures for working with Exchange Server through SQL Mail. These procedures can be used to send mail and also to read and process mail as part of your SQL Server processes.

To start SQL Mail from the command line, execute the following procedure in which @user and @password are optional and specify the username and password for the mail account. If you start the mail client first, as is recommended, you do not need these parameters.

```
xp_startmail @user, @password
```

Stopping SQL Mail is simply a matter of issuing the following:

```
xp_stopmail
```

SQL Mail gives you the capability to simply send mail messages as you saw when testing the SQL Mail setup. The procedure to send mail is the following:

```
xp_sendmail @recipients,@message,@query,@attachments,
    @copy_recipients,@blind_copy_recipients,@subject,@type,
    @attach_results,@no_output,@no_header,@width,@separator,
    ➥@echo_error,@set_user,@dbuse
```

The only required parameter is @recipients, which specifies the user to send the message to. This command has a variety of interesting features as outlined in Table A.1:

Table A.1 `xp_sendmail` **Parameters**

Parameter	Description
@recipients	You can specify as many recipients for the message as you want. These can be Exchange Server mailboxes or Internet email accounts.
@message	The message that will be sent.
@query	You have the ability to specify a valid query to be executed and attached to the email. This query can reference any object except the inserted and deleted tables in triggers.
@attachments	Specifies a file to be attached to the message.
@subject	The subject of the mail message.
@attach_results	Specifies that the query should be executed and sent as an attached file.
@no_header	Allows you to suppress the column headers for a query.
@set_user	Specifies the security context the query should be run under. The default is guest. If you have not enabled the guest account for access, you must specify an account that has the authority to execute the query.
@dbuser	Specifies the database context to run the query in. This should always be specified. The default is the default database for the user.

SQL Mail has the ability to read mail messages from a designated inbox. This is accomplished by the `xp_readmail` procedure.

```
xp_readmail @msg_id,@type,@peek,@suppress_attach,@orginator,
    @subject,@message,@recipients,@cc_list,@bcc_list,
    @date_received,@unread,@attachments,@skip_bytes,
    @msg_length,@originator_address
```

Some of these parameters are outlined in Table A.2:

Table A.2   `xp_readmail` **Parameters**

Parameter	Description
`@originator`	The email address of the user sending the message.
`@subject`	The subject of the message. This is normally a query that will be executed by SQL Server.
`@message`	This is the text of the mail message. This can also be a query to execute. This variable is only capable of handling 255 characters. This can be a serious limitation and has prompted many very involved workarounds. It is best to keep messages very short.
`@recipients`	Specifies the recipients of the message.
`@skip_bytes`	The number of bytes to skip when reading the mail message. This is used to sequentially retrieve the chunks of the mail message. Fortunately, in version 7.0 a variable can be 8,000 characters. This means you can sequentially read in 255-character chunks and concatenate them in a variable. 8,000 characters should be sufficient. If you need more, you should consider moving the query being sent in the message body to a stored procedure.
`@msg_length`	Specifies the total length of the message in bytes. This is normally used with `@skip_bytes` to process long messages.

To sequentially process mail messages, execute `xp_findnextmsg`.

```
xp_findnextmsg @msg_id,@type,@unread_only
```

After you are finished processing a message, you normally want to delete that message. To do this, execute `xp_deletemail`.

```
xp_deletemail {'message_number'}
```

If you do not specify a message number, all messages in the inbox are deleted.

To this point, you might be thinking that this can be a lot of work. SQL Server has given you a very powerful procedure to sequentially process mail. The procedure that ties everything together is `sp_processmail`.

```
sp_processmail @subject,@filetype,@separator,@user,@dbuse
```

This procedure is normally used in an unattended mode. This procedure uses the four extended procedures outlined above to work with an inbox. Mail is read using xp_readmail. The incoming messages are expected to have a single valid query as the message text. This query is executed and xp_sendmail is used to return the results to the sender as an attachment. The processed message is then deleted using xp_deletemail. Finally the next message is located using xp_findnextmsg. This process continues until all messages have been processed.

By using sp_processmail, you have essentially turned SQL Server into a low-level report server!

Reality Check

SQL Mail contains a large number of components that have to work together. This can cause a large amount of frustration during the setup phase. The time spent configuring SQL Mail will save a tremendous amount of time down the road.

SQL Mail is one of the most powerful components you can run in your system. SQL Mail by itself is rather benign. When you combine SQL Mail with stored procedures, batch processing, and alerts, you stitch together a very powerful notification system that can alert you when there are problems. This frees up your time to concentrate on more important things such as the stream of new products coming from Microsoft!

From Here...

In this chapter you learned how to configure and use SQL Mail.

From here you should look at the following chapters for more information:

- Chapter 14, "Managing Stored Procedures and Using Flow-Control Statements," shows how to create stored procedures in which you can utilize SQL Mail.

- Chapter 15, "Creating and Managing Triggers," explains how to create triggers. You can add mail capabilities to certain triggers for data auditing purposes.

- Chapter 17, "Setting Up and Managing Replication," shows how to set up and administer a replicated environment.

- Chapter 18, "Using the Distributed Transaction Coordinator," explains how to set up and perform distributed transactions.

- Chapter 19, "SQL Server Administration," shows how to manage a SQL Server and perform backups and restorations.

- Chapter 25, "Using the SQL Server Agent," explains how to setup automated processing and system alerts.

Redundant Arrays of Inexpensive Disks

Redundant arrays of inexpensive disks (RAID) currently has six implementations to provide a set of physical devices that will offer better data device integrity and performance. Those levels are described in this appendix.

RAID is a technique that provides several different approaches to data protection. RAID is meant to have both performance and stability characteristics, but the emphasis is on fault-tolerance for the data first, performance second.

Fault tolerance is achieved by striping—a technique of spreading data across the media and storing information that will let the system recover from a failure. When media fails (and it always does), this check information (parity, and so on) will help the system "fix" the data automatically. It won't fix the failing media, but will correct data errors while you correct the physical storage device.

Mirroring is used to store more than one identical copy of the data. Mirrored systems have more than one physical drive, but storage capacity is equal to 1/2 of the total drive space installed.

Mirroring is accomplished when information is written to the disk—when this happens, it is actually stored to two different disks. If one should crash or experience problems, you can switch the active disk to the backup drive. Typically this happens with little or no downtime, and provides for time required to fix the primary drive without taking your systems offline.

Windows NT supports software-based RAID levels 0 and 5 for striping (without parity and with parity). Windows NT also supports RAID level 1 for disk mirroring.

In the balance of this appendix, you'll get more information about the specific implementations of RAID that are on the market (at least the most popular ones) and what the different RAID levels represent.

Level 0

RAID Level 0 is basic data striping across multiple physical devices. The *striping* refers to the fact that multiple drives are allocated for data as a group. The data is then placed across the drives evenly so that each drive has a portion of the data. Striping provides better performance than single drives because multiple I/O threads from the operating system are allocated to servicing each drive. In addition, multiple physical reads and writes can occur simultaneously on the separate physical devices.

RAID Level 0 does not provide any fault tolerance and is purely a performance enhancement.

Level 1

RAID Level 1 is device mirroring. As discussed in Chapter 19, mirroring provides an absolute duplication of the data on any given physical device on the mirror device. Mirroring can improve read performance (depending on physical implementation) if both drives are read in parallel and data is returned to the operating system in a single stream composed of the parallel reads. Mirroring generally imposes a slight performance cost when writing because two writes are done instead of one.

Mirroring is fault tolerant and an automatic and complete switch generally handles media failure over to the mirror device.

Level 2

RAID Level 2 is an error-correcting algorithm that employs striping across multiple physical devices. It is more advanced than Level 0 because it uses error correcting "parity" data that is striped across the devices, and copes with media failure on any particular device in the stripe set. The parity data, however, consumes several disks and is quite inefficient as a storage mechanism.

RAID Level 2 is generally not used because it does not offer significantly better performance benefits than the straight mirroring implementation of Level 1.

Level 3

RAID Level 3 is a different implementation of the striped, parity algorithm. It differs from Level 2 by utilizing only a single device in the stripe set for storing the parity data.

RAID Level 3 offers some performance boost to reads and writes because it's only using the single volume for parity.

Level 4

RAID Level 4 is the same as Level 3, except that it implements a larger block or segment storage size. This means that the basic unit that is being striped is large in size and generally gets better performance due to the more advanced modern physical devices that are able to read and write bigger blocks of data in a single I/O operation. RAID Level 4 stores the parity information on a separate device from the user data that is striped across multiple physical devices.

RAID Level 4 is an inefficient algorithm and is generally not used.

Level 5

RAID Level 5 is currently the most commonly implemented RAID level. It is a striped implementation that stores parity information on the same striped drives. This enables an individual device to fail and the other devices in the stripe set contain enough information to recover and keep processing. The parity information for any particular device is always stored on another device in the stripe set, ensuring that if media failure occurs on a particular device, its parity data is not affected.

App

B

RAID Level 5 uses the same large block algorithm as Level 4, and is quite efficient. Level 5 will offer performance gains to reads and writes, until media failure occurs. When media failure occurs, reads suffer because the information on the failed device must be constructed from the parity data stored on the other devices.

Understanding the SQL Server System Tables

SQL Server is built using the "practice what you preach" motto. The entire system, from the tables you create to the columns in those tables to configuration options that control SQL Server's operation, is all stored in relational tables within the system.

These tables, installed automatically when SQL Server is installed on your system, contain the information that SQL Server needs to manage and operate your system. In this appendix, you'll get a better idea about what's in each of these tables. While it's not typically necessary to manually modify these tables, it can be helpful to understand what the purpose of them is, and what you can expect each of them to contain.

For each table, the table name and a brief description of the purpose of the table is provided.

Table C.1   SQL Server System Catalog

Table Name	Description
sysaltfiles	Contains information about the databases in your system. This is where you'll find the parameters that you specified in the database and transaction log Properties dialog.
syscharsets	Contains the different character data sets and sort orders available to SQL Server. For example, on a default installation, the character sets shown in the bulleted list later in this appendix are installed on your server.
sysconfigures	Settings for your SQL Server. For example, as mentioned above, it references the character set definition from the syscharsets table in use.
syscurconfigs	Much like sysconfigures, syscurconfigs contains the values that represent the configuration of the system. sysconfigures contains the values that are the current saved values, while syscurconfigs contains the values currently in effect. If you make changes, the syscurconfigs table contains those changes until the next time you restart your server.
syscursorcolumns	Contains column information about each open cursor.
syscursorrefs	Contains a reference pointer to each open cursor and the scope of that cursor.
syscursors	Contains the handle and name of each open cursor.
syscursortables	Contains a list of the tables involved in the definition of each open cursor.
sysdatabases	As the name suggests, sysdatabases contains one row for each database in your system. You can select * from sysdatabases to see each database defined in your system, along with the different attributes that define it. This table is found in the MASTER database.

syslanguages	For each language known to SQL Server, there's a single row in this table. It is important to know that English is always available and not included in the listing.
syslockinfo	Each lock in the system is represented as a row in this table. It contains the IDs of the user requesting the lock, what type of lock it is, and what object is locked.
syslocks	When locks are issued against a table, they are represented by a row in this table. The tables build dynamically when you query, so syslocks is more of a view of the static representation of locks currently held. Remember when you view this table that the locks shown were in effect when the query was issued but may have been released in the time since the query. The type column indicates the type of lock, as shown in Table C.3.
	If any of the locks appears with 256 added to it, it indicates that the lock is blocking another user. You can query the spid to determine what processes is holding the lock.
sysmessages	Containing roughly 2,200 rows, this table contains all of the text messages that you receive when SQL server issues an alert, error message, or informational message.
sysperfinfo	Contains SQL Server performance counters.
sysprocesses	As with several other system tables, the sysprocesses table is billed dynamically when you query it. It contains information about all current processes being managed by SQL Server at the time of the query.
sysservers	sysservers defines the servers on which you can run remote stored procedures.
syslogins	There is one row in the syslogins table for each login for the system. This table also indicates the default database for a user, along with the other configuration options, including disk allocations.

App

C

Table C.2 SQL Server Database Catalog

Table Name	Description
sysallocations	Contains a row for each allocation unit consumed by a database.
syscolumns	Contains one row for each column defined in every table and view. The rows define the datatypes and behavior of each of the columns in the other tables.

continues

Table C.2   Continued

Table Name	Description
syscomments	syscomments is used to document your system. The rows in the table contain information regarding each rule, default, trigger, and constraint. They also outline the stored procedures in your system. The Text column of the table contains the SQL statement that makes up the object. If the SQL statement is too long for the column, there can be more than one row in the table. This is essentially pieced back together when needed. A given object definition can take up to 255 rows for its associated SQL statement.
sysdepends	Outlines all dependencies between stored procedures, tables, keys, and so on.
sysfilegroups	Contains the file groups that are defined for the current database.
sysfiles	Contains two rows for the current database that define how the database was created. You will get such information as name, filename, maximum size, and file growth.
sysfiles1	Contains an alternative view of the sysfiles table that contains basic information about each database file.
sysforeignkeys	Contains the foreign key constraints that are defined within the database.
sysfulltextcatalogs	Contains the information about any full text indexes that have been created.
sysindexes	Contains one row per index defined for a given database's tables. Indexes defined include both clustered and nonclustered. sysindexes has replaced the syskeys table, although syskeys is still included for legacy systems.
sysindexkeys	For each column of an index, one row is created in this table.
sysmembers	For each role a user has in a database, one row is created in this table.
sysobjects	From tables to indexes, this table contains the information that defines the objects in your system, including the object ID and type of object.
syspermissions	This table contains an entry for each object that a user has permissions to and what those permissions are.
sysprotects	Provides the security parameters for users of the system. It provides the information on what types of restrictions are applied to user IDs.

Table Name	Description
sysreferences	The sysreferences table contains information on all foreign keys in your tables.
systypes	For each datatype in your system, there is one row in this table. This includes both user-defined datatypes and those provided by the system. By default, those types shown in Table C.4 are installed on your system.
sysusers	This table, which is database specific, contains one row for each user allowed access to the database. It contains information about NT users and groups and SQL Server users and roles.

The default character sets are

App

C

- Code page 1252 (ISO Character Set)

  The default character set. Also known as the ISO 8859-1, Latin 1, or ANSI character set, code page 1252 is compatible with the ANSI characters used by the Microsoft Windows and Windows NT operating systems.

- Code page 850 (Multilingual)

  Includes all characters for most languages of European, North American, and South American countries. Use this character set when you have MS-DOS-based client applications that use extended characters.

- Code page 437 (U.S. English)

  Although the most commonly used character set in the United States, this character set includes many graphics characters not usually stored in databases. Unless you have an overriding reason to select this character set, choose code page 1252, which provides more compatibility with languages other than United States English.

- Code page 932 (Japanese)
- Code page 936 (Chinese, simplified)
- Code page 949 (Korean)
- Code page 950 (Chinese, traditional)
- Code page 1250 (Central European)
- Code page 1251 (Cyrillic)
- Code page 1253 (Greek)
- Code page 1254 (Turkish)
- Code page 1255 (Hebrew)
- Code page 1256 (Arabic)
- Code page 1257 (Baltic)

Table C.3 Type of Locks

Value	Description
2	Schema Stability
3	Schema Modification
4	Intent Share
5	Intent Share without key range
6	Intent Share with composite key range lock
7	Intent Share with exclusive index lock
8	Shared, Intent exclusive on the index
9	Shared
10	Update, changes to an exclusive lock when row is written
11	Insert intent for index row level locking
12	Intent to update, exclusive on index row level locking
13	Intent to update, exclusive lock on index row
14	Intent share, update lock on index rows
15	Exclusive lock

Table C.4 Default Datatypes

binary	bit
char	datetime
datetimn	decimal
decimaln	float
floatn	image
int	intn
money	moneyn
numeric	numericn
real	smalldatetime
smallint	smallmoney
sysname	text
timestamp	tinyint
varbinary	varchar

Using SQL Server Profiler

In this chapter

Microsoft SQL Server Profiler is a graphical utility that is used to monitor database activity. The monitoring can be done in real-time or can be done on particular users, applications, hosts, or events.

Profiler takes the place of SQLTrace, which was available in earlier versions of SQL Server. Profiler, like just about everything else in version 7.0, has taken giant steps forward. You now have the capability to set up a trace on a wide variety of events that just was not possible before. Traces can be set up on such things as deadlocks, stored procedures, index and table scans, and distributed transactions.

Starting Profiler

The name of the Profiler executable file is SQLTRACE.EXE and it is located in the SQL Server BINN directory. By default, the SQL Server 7.0 installation places a shortcut to Profiler in the SQL Server program group. This (or another) shortcut can be used to start the utility or it can be started from the command line.

Profiler, like all of the SQL Server utilities, uses the same registrations. This means that any server registered in Enterprise Manager is available to Profiler.

After Profiler has started and connected to a database, filters can be added, deleted, edited, started, stopped, and paused. In addition, several other utilities can be started from within SQL Profiler:

- Query Analyzer
- SQL Enterprise Manager
- Windows NT Performance Monitor

N O T E When starting a Query Analyzer session from within Profiler, Query Analyzer will attempt to log in with the login information used to connect Profiler to a SQL Server database. ■

Using Profiler

The Profiler interface is divided into two sections:

- Trace Activity pane
- Current Command pane

Activities that meet a trace's criteria are displayed in the Trace Activity pane. The name of the trace being displayed is shown in the title bar. Later, in the "Setting Up a Trace" section, traces are explained in more detail.

At the bottom of the Profiler window is the Current Command pane. This pane is made up of several items that display information about traces defined for the current server. Figure D.1 shows a Profiler window with a Trace Activity pane and Current Command pane visible.

FIGURE D.1

Capturing trace output to the screen.

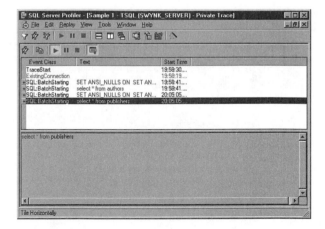

Setting Up a Trace

To create a new trace, follow these steps:

1. Either select New Trace from the File menu or click the New Trace button. The New Trace dialog box appears (see Figure D.2).

FIGURE D.2

Defining a new trace.

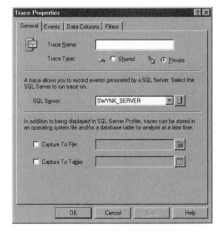

2. Enter a Trace Name, whether the trace will be public or private, the SQL Server to trace, and whether to capture the trace to a file or to a table.

> **NOTE** New in version 7.0 is the ability to save the trace output to a table in the database. Doing so creates a central repository of trace information that can be used by multiple users on different machines or locations. You can create these traces so that only you have access to them (private) or everyone who can log in to the machine can access them (public). ∎

3. Select the Events tab. This tab allows you to specify which events you want to set up a trace on, as shown in Figure D.3. You can set up a trace on a wide variety of events ranging from SQL commands to errors. A trace can be set up on inserts, updates, deletes, and selects. One of the more interesting events is the deadlock chain. This allows you to set up a filter that will capture the statements leading up to a deadlock for further analysis.

FIGURE D.3

Defining events for a trace.

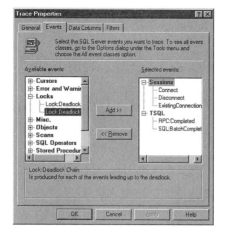

4. Select the Data Columns tab. This tab gives you the ability to specify which information about the events is captured and displayed, as shown in Figure D.4.

FIGURE D.4

Defining the information to be captured by the trace.

5. Select the Filters tab. The Filters tab allows you to specify applications and users to include or exclude. It also gives you the ability to define threshold values for certain captured events, as shown in Figure D.5.

FIGURE D.5

Creating filters for captured events.

N O T E The threshold values are some of the most powerful filtering you can use when setting up a trace. Unrestricted traces generate an overwhelming amount of data in a very short time. The threshold values allow you to specify a certain selectivity of events to capture.

In most cases, you are going to be using Profiler to track down performance bottlenecks. The simplest method to find these is to set up duration, reads, or writes. This can quickly pinpoint those queries consuming an inordinate amount of resources. ▓

6. Click the OK button to add the trace to the defined traces for the current server.

When using SQLTrace in version 6.5, this is where the functionality ceased. The Profiler dramatically extends the functionality to give you a very robust and full-featured tuning tool.

One of the most significant new features of Profiler is the ability to play back a trace, as shown in Figure D.6. As long as the output of a trace was saved to a file or table, you can open the captured information and replay everything that was captured.

FIGURE D.6

Replaying a saved trace.

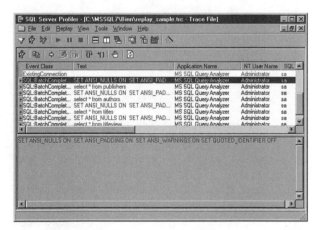

APP

D

TIP This can come in very handy when you are trying to benchmark performance or track down poor performance. You can setup a trace on a particular query or application. After the data is gathered, you can connect to a test or development server and replay all of the commands.

In addition to being able to replay a trace, some powerful execution features have been added. Checkpoints can be placed throughout the trace. This causes the trace to execute at full speed, but to stop at a specified point for evaluation. The trace can also be played back one step at a time, as shown in Figure D.7. This capability gives the developer the ability to successively work through a trace and eliminate bottlenecks as they occur and then continue on to the next problem.

FIGURE D.7

Stepping through a trace.

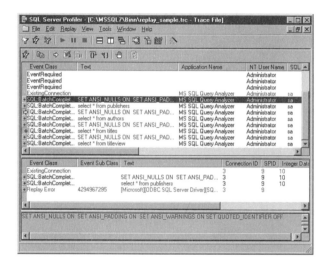

Along with the ability to set up tracing, Profiler also includes the ability to run SQL scripts directly within the Profiler application, as shown in Figure D.8.

FIGURE D.8

Running a SQL script.

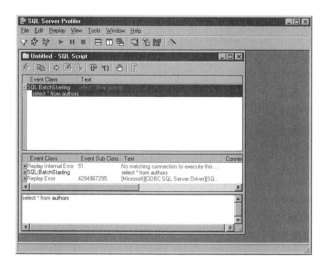

The scripts can take full advantage of the other execution features for a trace, such as step execute and checkpoints.

Profiler is a simple but powerful tool. It can be used for many purposes. Debugging applications can be simplified by using Profiler to monitor SQL statements issued from an application. Performance issues can then be addressed by recording a particular user's activity. These can then be replayed on another server for additional testing and evaluation purposes. When combining SQL scripts with captured trace output, a complete testing and scenario can be put together and tested.

One additional thing Profiler can do is check for dangerous activity on a server. You can then use this information to address any security concerns you might have.

Index

Symbols

A

Global Variables - pg 379

X

Other Related Titles

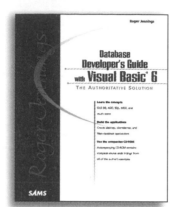

Roger Jennings Database Developer's Guide with Visual Basic 6
Roger Jennings
ISBN: 0-672-31063-5
$59.99 USA/
$84.95 CAN

What's on the Disc

The companion CD-ROM contains useful third party software, plus all the source code from the book.

Windows 95 Installation Instructions

1. Insert the CD-ROM disc into your CD-ROM drive.

2. From the Windows 95 desktop, double-click on the My Computer icon.

3. Double-click on the icon representing your CD-ROM drive.

4. Double-click on the icon titled START.EXE to run the installation program.

5. START.EXE runs the opening screen.

NOTE If Windows 95 is installed on your computer, and you have the AutoPlay feature enabled, the START.EXE program starts automatically whenever you insert the disc into your CD-ROM drive. ■

Windows NT Installation Instructions

1. Insert the CD-ROM disc into your CD-ROM drive.

2. From File Manager or Program Manager, choose Run from the File menu.

3. Type *<drive>*\START.EXE and press Enter, where *<drive>*corresponds to the drive letter of your CD-ROM. For example, if your CD-ROM is drive D:, type D:\START.EXE and press Enter.

4. START.EXE runs the opening screen.

By opening this package, you are agreeing to be bound by the following agreement:

Some of the software included with this product may be copyrighted, in which case all rights are reserved by the respective copyright holder. You are licensed to use software copyrighted by the Publisher and its licensors on a single computer. You may copy and/or modify the software as needed to facilitate your use of it on a single computer. Making copies of the software for any other purpose is a violation of the United States copyright laws.

This software is sold as is without warranty of any kind, either expressed or implied, including but not limited to the implied warranties of merchantability and fitness for a particular purpose. Neither the publisher nor its dealers or distributors assumes any liability for any alleged or actual damages arising from the use of this program. (Some states do not allow for the exclusion of implied warranties, so the exclusion may not apply to you.)